The State of
the Social Sciences

The State of the Social Sciences

Papers presented at the 25th Anniversary
of the Social Science Research Building
The University of Chicago
November 10–12, 1955

Edited by **LEONARD D. WHITE**

 THE UNIVERSITY OF CHICAGO PRESS

*The Social Science Research Building,
dedicated December 16 and 17, 1929,
was made possible by a grant
from the Laura Spelman Rockefeller Memorial Fund.*

*This volume has been published with the co-operation
of the Paul V. Harper Memorial Fund.*

Library of Congress Catalog Number: 56-9131

THE UNIVERSITY OF CHICAGO PRESS, CHICAGO 37
Cambridge University Press, London, N.W. 1, England
The University of Toronto Press, Toronto 5, Canada

The University of Chicago celebrated the twenty-fifth anniversary of the Social Science Research Building, November 10–12, 1955, with a program of round tables, conferences, and professional addresses. These events fell into three major groups, reflecting three basic orientations of the social sciences in the middle of the twentieth century: social sciences as science; social sciences and the civic arts; the social sciences and the humanities. Science, art, and values enter into the work of social scientists in varying proportions from time to time and among different groups, but all three serve to enrich and to make significant their contribution to society.

The Social Science Research Building was commemorated in 1929 at its foundation by two volumes, *The New Social Science* (Leonard D. White, editor) and *Chicago: An Experiment in Social Science Research* (T. V. Smith and Leonard D. White, editors). In those days we optimistically spoke of the future. "These papers," it was written in the Preface to *The New Social Science*, "testify abundantly to a feeling of confidence among social science researchers; confidence not so much in results achieved as in prospects." The conferences at the end of the first decade, published under the title, *Eleven Twenty-six: A Decade of Social Science Research* (Louis Wirth, editor), gave visible evidence of the ten years' production, both in the papers read by faculty members and guests and by the collected bibliography of the social sciences staff.

Optimism remained the underlying tone of this volume and of the 1939 conference. "The existence of a modern building dedicated to social science research has meant more than can be indicated by reciting the specific research results that have been achieved through its facilities," wrote Louis Wirth. Our experience at Chicago, recorded in *Eleven Twenty-six,* was described "in the confident hope that it will be a stimulus to better social science research both at the University of Chicago and elsewhere in the years that lie ahead."

Fifteen more of these years have now elapsed, marking a full quarter-century for the Social Science Research Building. Five of them were substantially lost to basic research as World War II absorbed the energies of the social science faculty in military and civilian service. During the last ten momentum has been renewed, although retarded for five years by the task of education presented by postwar GI veterans, and for five years more by financial restrictions. The record nevertheless reveals impressive research achievements.

Light is shed on these achievements by noting the present organization of the Division of the Social Sciences. Since 1929 there has been stability in the central departments, numbering eight: Anthropology, Economics, Education, Geography, History, Political Science, Psychology, and Sociology. Geography also holds membership in the Division of the Physical Sciences; Psychology in the Division of the Biological Sciences; and History in the Division of the Humanities. The interests of the social science faculty, stimulated by propinquity, were not, however, confined to these departments. New constellations of interests appeared, crossing departmental lines and resulting in a series of interdepartmental committees, some concerned primarily with research, more with graduate and professional training. In 1955 they numbered eleven: the Committee on Communication; on Far Eastern Civilization; on Home Economics; on Human Development; on Industrial Relations; on International Relations; on Nursing Education; on Planning; on Social Thought; on South Asian Studies; and on Statistics. Collectively, these committees comprised valuable centers of research and instruction, supplementing and diversifying the contributions of the older departments.

To chronicle the research enterprises of the members of the Social Sciences Division in an Introduction would be both unnecessary and tedious. On the other hand, the reader of these papers may have a proper interest in ascertaining whether the optimism of 1929 and 1939 has been reasonably justified. In partial response to this interest, and in lieu of a now unmanageable bibliography, the following paragraphs highlight some of the major contributions arranged by departments.

Anthropology.—Major work by members of this department includes the development of the concepts of "folk society" and "folk-urban continuum" by Robert Redfield, an enterprise resulting in his books, *Tepoztlan* and *Folk Culture of Yucatan,* and a related work by Sol Tax, *Penny Capitalism.* Another group of studies deals with the social structure of the American Indians, under the leadership of Fred Eggan; two works in this field are his *Social Anthropology of North American Tribes* and *Social Organization of the Western Pueblos.* The archeological work of Fay-Cooper Cole was a related line of investigation. Most recently Redfield, Milton B. Singer, and Gustave E. von Grunebaum have begun a long-time Comparative Study of Civilizations, and the department has initiated a Philippine Studies Program, with Professor Eggan in charge.

Economics.—Among the notable contributions of the economics faculty we note the pioneering work of Paul H. Douglas on the production function, an original contribution that has become known as the Cobb-Douglas Production Function; the outstanding work of Jacob Viner in the theory of international trade; and the contributions of Frank H. Knight: *Risk, Uncertainty, and Profit* and *The Ethics of Competition.* Milton Friedman made a major original contribution in his theory of the consumption function. A many-sided long-term contribution in the field of agricultural economics, domestic and overseas, is the responsibility of Theodore W. Schultz and D. Gale Johnson; two of its products are *Agriculture in an Unstable Economy* by Schultz and *Forward Prices for Agriculture* by Johnson.

Education.—Members of this department have made major applications of the basic disciplines of the social sciences, as well as philosophy, physiology, and psychiatry, to the process of education. Among the principal developments are a deeper understanding of the nature of the growth processes of the child and the interrelationships of intellectual, psychological, and emotional elements; an awareness of cultural influences in the development of intelligence, a long-term study (1945–53) directed by Professor Allison Davis; a critical re-examination of the structure and functioning of schools, a co-operative undertaking with the educational authorities of a number of midwestern states generously supported by the Kellogg Foundation and directed by Francis S. Chase; the continuing study of the optimum content of school curriculums; and the basic studies in reading, initiated by Dean Charles H. Judd and Guy Buswell and carried forward by William S. Gray.

Geography.—Three lines of inquiry have been consistently pursued by members of this department for a quarter-century: urban geography, initiated by Charles C. Colby, and pushed forward by Chauncy Harris and Harold M. Mayer; natural resources and land use, initiated by Harlan H. Barrows and carried on by Wesley Calef and Gilbert F. White; areal functional organization, concentration on the regions related to urban areas, initiated by Robert S. Platt and developed by A. K. Philbrick.

History.—Among the many writings of the members of the History Department may be cited, by way of example, Bernadotte E. Schmitt's Pulitzer prize pioneer work on the antecedents of World War I; Avery O. Craven's reconsideration of the whole Civil War period; James L. Cate's collaborative work on the history of the Air Forces in World War II; Louis Gottschalk's lifetime study of Lafayette; and Bessie L. Pierce's definitive history of Chicago, of which three volumes have now been completed. The department has given consistent attention to the historical method in its graduate instruction and its publications, of which three volumes may be cited: *Some Historians of Modern Europe* (Bernadotte E. Schmitt, editor); *The Marcus W. Jernegan Essays in American Historiography* (William T. Hutchinson, editor); and *Medieval and Historiographical Essays in Honor of James Westfall Thompson* (J. L. Cate and E. N. Anderson, editors).

Political Science.—The whole field of political science was thrown into new perspective by Charles E. Merriam, who taught a generation that politics was intimately and necessarily bound up with anthropology, economics, sociology, and psychology as well as with history, its traditional ally. Merriam is also remembered for his stirring defense of democracy in the years when it was first challenged by authoritarianism and for his contributions to the study of the city. He stimulated an impressive number of younger men: Wright in the causes of war, Lasswell in the psychology of politics, Gosnell in political statistics, White in the prestige studies and in the history of public administration. Other major lines of inquiry are those now pursued by Morgenthau in the philosophy of international relations, Strauss and Easton in political theory, Pritchett in the analysis of the predispositions of members of the Supreme Court, and Finer in comparative government.

Psychology.—Amid a wide range of research contributions by members of this department, two may be singled out for mention: psychometric measurement by L. L. Thurstone and psychotherapy and personality by Carl R. Rogers. Both of these represent long-term programs; both have changed thinking and practice in their respective fields; both men trained distinguished groups of students. Thurstone's work is represented by three major publications: *Vectors of the Mind; Multiple-Factor Analysis;* and *Primary Mental Abilities.* Rogers' contributions are illustrated in his two works, *Client-centered Therapy* and *Psychotherapy and Personality Change.*

Sociology.—Unity in diversity characterizes the research of this, as other, social science departments at the University of Chicago. A department is not an institute and does not lend itself to a single orientation of its members. The study of the structure and dynamics of the modern city has been one of the continuing interests of sociologists, notably Robert Park, Louis Wirth, W. Lloyd Warner (in his influential studies of social class and social mobility), and Philip M. Hauser (in his population studies). Another long-range focus has been the nature of racial and nationality differences, pursued by Wirth and Everett C. Hughes. A third has been the study of crime, the family, and gerontology, spearheaded by Ernest W. Burgess, notable for his invention of predictive methods for success on probation. Still another is the various types of statistical analysis of social phenomena developed and refined by William F. Ogburn and Hauser. For the most part since World War II the Sociology Department, and the division as well, have been buttressed by a number of centers, such as the Chicago Community Survey; the Population Training and Research Center; the Family Study Center; the Center for the Study of Leisure; and the National Opinion Research Center.

The divisional committees normally comprise faculty members who also hold departmental appointments and the nature of whose research is exemplified in the examples included in the previous paragraphs. If space permitted, the research enterprises of the Committee on Human Development would warrant particular attention, as well as the humanistic contributions of the Committee on Social Thought, Professor John U. Nef, chairman. The group of interdepartmental committees has made a valuable and at times a unique contribution to the division, partly research, partly instruction, partly the interpretation of the contemporary world in the light of the great historical value systems.

The Social Science Research Building looks within the campus on a pleasant quadrangle, and without on the wide world, thus typifying the dual role of the social scientists. Few, if any, of them belong exclusively to the ivory tower; most of them are occupied now with the professional tasks of their disciplines, now with the application of their special knowledge to the affairs of the world. This dualism is not new, but it was emphasized by the crises of the Great Depression and of World War II. Military and civilian appointments after Pearl Harbor drew many members of the division out of their studies to Washington, to London, and to the fighting fronts on land and sea. Consulting obligations to civil and military authorities kept many of them busy commuting from Chicago to Washington. Research and systematic study suffered inevitably, but this crisis allowed no alternative. Postwar years gave little respite except as members of the division were adamant—and the choice of the greater good in the struggle between research and its application was not always easy. Now the demand for American insight and knowledge in the application of the social sciences for reconstruction and reconversion overseas has grown beyond parallel. In response members of the division have literally crossed the seven seas.

These experiences are valuable to us as well as to our friends abroad. The social sciences in America have been limited to some degree by the boundaries of American life and American problems. To be forced to operate in a consulting capacity in a different culture—to have to bridge the gap between a less-developed or differently developed culture and our own—is a chastening and an educative affair. The social scientists of the University of Chicago have not only joined in the academic life of the University of Frankfort and the tribal ceremonies of the American Indians; they have been in the Near East, in the Philippines, in India, in the Indonesian Republic, in South America, in Burma, and in Africa. Our horizons are more definitely global, our experiences more nearly universal, our insights more fully humane.

The celebration of the twenty-fifth anniversary considered the social sciences as sciences, their function as a part of the civic arts, and their interpretive role as humanistic studies. The emphasis in the contemporary scene at the University of Chicago is on the scientific rather than the humanistic or the prudential aspects of the subject matter. The center of the stage is now held by the so-called behavioral sciences; the new constellation is anthropology, sociology, psychology, with strong links in economics and political science and with an underwriting of statistics and mathematics. It would appear probable that notable advances will be made in the next decade, or the next quarter-century, from this fruitful and powerful combination of forces. Older forms of inquiry will nevertheless persist, for wisdom and understanding come from other sources as well as mathematical analysis.

The social science faculty at the University of Chicago enter the second quarter-century in their tightly packed building with courage and confidence. They know that their role in the evolving society of the future is important, even as they refuse to overestimate their capacity to control the events of the morrow. They are dominated by no single school of thought, by no single methodology, and by no one of their sister disciplines. They are habituated to working together both within and among the several departments; they lend each other strength. They have made a notable contribution to the last quarter-century, and they are prepared to make their talents useful to the next—in scholarship, in the practical affairs of the nation and the world, and in the emerging science of society.

The division acknowledges with appreciation the co-operation of the Paul V. Harper Memorial Fund in facilitating the publication of this volume.

The Index has been prepared by Mr. Rolf Meyersohn.

LEONARD D. WHITE

January 17, 1956

Table of Contents

ADDRESS OF WELCOME, *Chauncy D. Harris* 1

SCIENCE, SOCIETY, AND THE MODES OF LAW, *Frank H. Knight* . . 9

TOWARD A GENERAL THEORY FOR THE BEHAVIORAL SCIENCES, *James G. Miller* 29

MODELS: THEIR USES AND LIMITATIONS, *Herbert A. Simon and Allen Newell* 66

IMPACT OF PSYCHOANALYTIC THINKING ON THE SOCIAL SCIENCES, *Harold D. Lasswell* 84

TOWARD A COMPARISON OF VALUE-EMPHASES IN DIFFERENT CULTURES, *Clyde K. M. Kluckhohn* 116

POLITICAL MOIETIES, *George Peter Murdock* 133

TASK STATUS AND LIKEABILITY AS A FUNCTION OF TALKING AND LISTENING IN DECISION-MAKING GROUPS, *Robert F. Bales* . . . 148

PSYCHOLOGICAL NEEDS AS A FUNCTION OF SOCIAL ENVIRONMENTS, *Murray Horwitz* 162

EMOTIONALITY AND WORK IN GROUPS, *Herbert A. Thelen* . . . 184

BIOSOCIAL THEORY IN HUMAN DEVELOPMENT, *Willard C. Olson* . 201

THE EGO AND STATUS-ANXIETY, *Allison Davis* 212

ECOLOGICAL ASPECTS OF URBAN RESEARCH, *Philip M. Hauser* . . 229

THE CULTURAL ASPECT OF URBAN RESEARCH, *Everett C. Hughes* . 255

INDUSTRIAL ORGANIZATION AND ECONOMIC PROGRESS, *George J. Stigler* 269

SOME INTERNATIONAL ASPECTS OF ECONOMIC STABILIZATION, *Jacob Viner* 283

THE STUDY OF PUBLIC OPINION, *Bernard Berelson* 299

SOME OBSERVATIONS ON THE "OLDER" AND THE "NEWER" SOCIAL SCIENCES, *David Riesman* 319

THE CHANGING TIMES, *Walter Lippmann* 340

THE SOCIAL SCIENCES TODAY, *Lawrence A. Kimpton* 348

xiv / *Contents*

THE ROLE OF GOVERNMENT IN PROMOTING ECONOMIC STABILITY,
Roy Blough 353

THE ROLE OF GOVERNMENT IN PROMOTING ECONOMIC GROWTH,
Theodore W. Schultz 372

NEW BRIDGES BETWEEN THEORY AND PRACTICE, Herbert Emmerich . 384

THE SOCIAL SCIENTIST AND THE ADMINISTRATIVE ART, Gordon R.
Clapp 393

AMERICAN DIPLOMATIC NEGOTIATION, POSTWAR, John Nuveen . . 398

THE ART OF DIPLOMATIC NEGOTIATION, Hans J. Morgenthau . . 404

SOCIAL SCIENCE AND HUMANISM, Leo Strauss 415

HUMANISM AND THE SOCIAL SCIENCES: BUT WHAT ABOUT JOHN
DE NEUSHOM? James L. Cate 426

THE HISTORIAN'S USE OF GENERALIZATION, Louis Gottschalk . . 436

GUILT BY ASSOCIATION: THE GAME OF PRESUMPTIONS, Robert E.
Cushman 451

THE DILEMMA OF SPECIALIZATION, F. A. Hayek 462

APPENDIX: PROGRAM 475

INDEX 481

Address of Welcome

On behalf of the Division of the Social Sciences of the University of Chicago I extend to each of you a hearty welcome to the Twenty-fifth Anniversary Celebration of the Social Science Research Building. In 1929, through the generosity and vision of the Laura Spelman Rockefeller Memorial, the Social Science Research Building was erected at 1126 East Fifty-ninth Street on the Midway just east of Harper Memorial Library. Here for the first time was created a modern building at a great university to be devoted wholly to research in the social sciences.

As background for this celebration I should like to recall something of the history and activity of the social sciences at the University of Chicago. I select three phases: (1) the founding in the 1890's; (2) the expansion and co-ordination in the 1920's and 1930's; and (3) the social sciences today.

Establishment in the 1890's

From its very founding the University of Chicago pioneered in the development of the social sciences.

Scholars such as John Dewey in education, J. Laurence Laughlin in economics, Hermann Eduard von Holst in history, Harry Pratt Judson in political science, Albion W. Small in sociology, and James R. Angell in psychology endowed each of the social sciences with intellectual vigor and status from the establishment of the university. As Wesley C. Mitchell once said, "In the 1890's [at its very birth] Chicago was the most stimulating school of social science in the country."

Sociology provides a good example of Chicago leadership. The old ninth edition of the *Encyclopaedia Britannica*, completed in 1889, summarized the organization and level of knowledge at the time the University of Chicago was initiated. No article on sociolo-

1

gy graced the pages of the encyclopedia. Yet President William Rainey Harper had the imagination and courage to bring Albion W. Small, then president of Colby College, to become the first American professor of sociology, to found the first department of sociology, and to establish the first scholarly American journal in the field.

Expansion and Co-ordination in the 1920's and 1930's

Three events in the period 1923–31 increased cohesion in the social sciences at the University of Chicago: (1) the establishment of the Local Community Research Committee in 1923; (2) the erection of the Social Science Research Building in 1929; and (3) the creation of the Division of the Social Sciences in 1931.

In 1923 the Laura Spelman Rockefeller Memorial under the direction of Beardsley Ruml began to provide funds for research in the urban community of Chicago. As far back as 1894, the sociologists had spoken of the city of Chicago as a great social laboratory. Early interest in the city had prepared the Chicago scholars to seize the new research opportunity with vision and vigor. A local Community Research Committee was formed under the stimulation of Ernest DeWitt Burton, president of the University, and the leadership of Albion W. Small, then dean of the Graduate School of Arts. Many pathbreaking investigations of city life were launched. In the years 1923–29 alone, forty-four books and monographs were written and published under the guidance of the Committee; many, but not all, of these were concerned with Chicago. This effort represented the greatest massing, up to that time, of the research artillery of the social sciences upon a single city. The spirit of this period in midstream is caught in the book, *Chicago: An Experiment in Social Science Research*, edited by T. V. Smith and Leonard D. White, published in 1929.

The second of the events, the erection of the Social Science Research Building, is the particular event which we are commemorating on this occasion. The addresses delivered at the dedication of the building were published in the volume, *The New Social Science*, edited by Leonard D. White, who happily is chairman of the committee for our present celebration.

Rereading the addresses of that event, one is struck with the spirit both of thankfulness for the building and of great hope for research in the social sciences, particularly for more quantitative analysis and for more co-operative work among the various disciplines.

The *Encyclopaedia of the Social Sciences,* published in 1930–34, provides a bench mark of the state of achievement in the social sciences at the time of the erection of the Social Science Research Building a quarter of a century ago.

The third of the events, the organization of the Division of the Social Sciences in 1931, grouped the social science departments together as an administrative unit under a separate dean. Beardsley Ruml, Robert Redfield, Ralph W. Tyler, and Morton Grodzins in turn have provided distinguished leadership.

Some of the great figures at the University of Chicago in this middle period of the 1920's and 1930's were Andrew C. McLaughlin and William E. Dodd in history; Charles H. Judd in education; John M. Clark, Harry A. Millis, Paul H. Douglas, Jacob Viner, Simeon Leland, and Frank H. Knight in economics; Charles E. Merriam in political science; Robert E. Park, William F. Ogburn, and Ernest W. Burgess in sociology; Harvey Carr and L. L. Thurstone in psychology; and Edward Sapir, A. R. Radcliffe-Brown, and Fay-Cooper Cole in anthropology.

The tenth anniversary of the Social Science Research Building was commemorated by a series of papers and round tables in 1939. These were published in the volume, *Eleven Twenty-six: A Decade of Social Science Research,* edited by Louis Wirth. Five round tables examined questions that persist today: "The Social Sciences, One or Many," "Quantification," "Training for Social Science Research," "Generalization in the Social Sciences," and "Social Science and Social Action." Papers were concerned mainly with urbanism, social trends, and factor analysis.

The Social Sciences Today

Appreciation of the high achievements of the past should not divert us from consideration of the lively state of social science research today. Research is cumulative; the findings of past studies provide the points of departure for new investigation. Furthermore, as society and fields of knowledge evolve, interests shift, compelling new questions arise, entirely new domains invite exploration, and some old fields decline.

The changes in the quarter-century since the dedication of the Social Science Research Building are revealed in the topics to be discussed during these sessions.

The study of public opinion may serve as an example. As Bernard Berelson points out in his paper, much that was written only twenty-five years ago in the field of public opinion is now considered archaic; it has been superseded by later work or different interests. The field has moved from broad historical, theoretical, and philo-sophical interests to technical research on specialized restricted topics subjected to detailed controlled quantitative surveys or polls. One might oversimplify by saying that the field of public opinion has moved from philosophic scholarship to scientific research. In the process the field has increased in size, lost a certain grandeur, but acquired more precision.

The University of Chicago has played an active role in the evolv-ing social sciences during the last quarter-century. No strong bias has marked this university. Many types of viewpoints and research are represented.

There is appreciation for scholars who emphasize values and philosophy such as John U. Nef or Leo Strauss, on one hand, or others who focus attention on statistics and quantitative measure-ment such as W. Allen Wallis or Philip M. Hauser, on the other.

We have room also for a different kind of contrast—that between inclination to social and governmental action as represented by Rexford G. Tugwell or to rigorous laissez faire as represented by Milton Friedman and the Chicago school of economists.

Co-operative interdisciplinary projects thrive. The University of Chicago through its flexible organization and venturesome spirit has stimulated many significant contributions along the frontiers that do not lie entirely within the province of any single discipline. One current seminar on urbanization, for example, is co-directed by Everett C. Hughes, a sociologist; Gustave E. von Grunebaum, an Islamist; and Sylvia L. Thrupp, an economic historian. It has attracted the active participation of scholars from a dozen or more different fields. The agricultural economics seminar under T. W. Schultz has similarly elicited the co-operation of many diverse specialists bringing contrasted points of view to broad social problems. Such fields as communication, human development, international relations, and race relations have been cultivated at this university mainly by such multidisciplinary groups.

On the other hand, the work of individual scholars toiling alone in the cloistered study is warmly admired. I think of W. T. Hutchinson's quiet and prolonged attention to the life of Frank O. Lowden or of Leonard D. White's detailed investigations in the history of American public administration.

A variety of scale of study also is welcome. In history Louis Gottschalk's lifelong devotion to Lafayette stands as one example of a sustained concern with a single figure. In contrast William H. McNeill attempts a wide-ranging overview of the whole sweep of Western history.

In the animated interchange among scholars the Quadrangle Club serves an important function. Since it is so much complained about, I am sure it is effective. Round-table conversations, committee meetings, chance chats by twos and threes—all are important avenues of intellectual communication among our community of scholars. The initial idea for one of my own research papers came as a result of a conversation at the Quadrangle Club with a scholar in an entirely different field.

Students as well as faculty lend distinction to a university. The University of Chicago has been blessed with generation after generation of able students, who have been stimulated by their teachers, who in turn have excited their teachers and fellow students, and who have developed into distinguished scholars themselves.

The vigor of intellectual life can be illustrated from the work of any of the departments, committees, or centers. As an example, I shall take the Department of Anthropology, the youngest of the departments.

An anthropologist today is likely to be about to leave for X or to be just returned from Y. At the moment Washburn is in Africa and Redfield in India, and Braidwood recently returned from Iraq, Romney from Mexico, Singer from India, and Howell from Africa.

Sherwood L. Washburn is attempting to understand the mode of origin of variations in primate anatomy and thus to shed light on the early evolution of man. Toward this end he is literally living with baboons and gibbons in Africa. Let me read from his letter: "I've simply been with baboons for hours and hours, three hours' continuous observation this morning for example. . . . There are whole classes of behavior which are hardly mentioned in the literature because they do not take place unless the group is happy, fed, and undisturbed. What people have described are the dramatic fights and flights but not all the daily events and the little causes of the bigger events."

The next step in human history is being investigated by F. Clark Howell, who is studying the evolution of early men during the Pleistocene period. He spent six months of last year in Africa engaged in research on the evolutionary significance and relative age of the australopithecine fossils, the earliest known members of the family which includes man. His analysis includes the environments and tools of our earliest human ancestors.

Robert J. Braidwood is engaged in a long-term study of a later stage, the earliest transition of human society from hunting and food-gathering to food production from planted crops. This great revolution took place about seven thousand years ago in western Asia around the northern fringes of the Fertile Crescent in Iraq. Last year's archeological expedition included, in addition to Braidwood and anthropologists, a geologist specializing in Pleistocene geology, a zoölogist expert in the problems of the domestication of animals, an agricultural botanist, and a specialist in the recovery of organic materials for radiocarbon dating. This diverse but well-co-ordinated team is illuminating our understanding of the origin of settled human life.

Robert M. Adams is making a comparative study of the next stage, the rise of early civilization the world around. After the independent achievement of sedentary food production in the Old and New Worlds, there emerged in a few areas the institutions we associate with civilized life: cities, monumental temples and palaces, writing, and codes of law.

Norman A. McQuown is engaged in a long-range linguistics project on what he has termed the Macro-Mayan stock of Central America. He hopes the studies will contribute not only to the basic principles of linguistic understanding but also to other aspects of culture.

Kimball Romney has just spent the last year in Mexico living in a small village making studies of the personality and social structure of the Mixtec Indians. The Mixtec peoples appear to offer a clue to the relationship of the Maya and the Aztec cultures, the two best-known and highest Indian cultures of North America. The older and little-known Mixtecs may be an unrecognized source of much of the culture both of the Mayas and of the Aztecs.

Two large-scale studies are in progress on the problems of indigenous groups confronted by modern civilization. Sol Tax is working intensively with a community of six hundred Indians fifty miles west of Cedar Rapids at Tama, Iowa. His is an action research program designed to study experimentally means of helping American Indians adjust to new ways of life.

Fred Eggan, well known for his work with American Indians, particularly the Hopi, is now engaged in a Philippine study project which is heightening our understanding of the various Philippine peoples and their relation to one another and to the Western world.

Robert Redfield, having served his apprenticeship in the study of so-called primitive peoples, has now turned his attention to the comparative study of the great civilizations. With the co-operation of Milton Singer, he has enlisted some of the world's leading authorities in comparative analyses of the civilizations of China, India, and Islam.

W. Lloyd Warner bridges the gap between Stone Age–like Australian aborigines and modern American communities. He has just completed a study of American business leaders and is currently engaged in further analyses of symbol systems in Yankee City.

This is the roll of just one department. It is an intellectually vigorous group, in which each scholar pursues individual research, yet the whole department exhibits a well-co-ordinated organized structure.

I wish there were time to tell of the work of the members of each of the other departments—economics, education, geography, history, political science, psychology, and sociology, which follow anthropology in alphabetical order, or of the committees on behavioral sciences, communication, divisional Master's, Far Eastern civilization, home economics, human development, international relations, nursing education, planning, race relations, social thought, and statistics; or of the centers—the Center for the Study of Human Evolution, the Economic Research Center, the Midwest Administration Center, the Center for Teacher Education, the Center for the Study of American Foreign Policy, the Population Research and Training Center, the Center for the Study of Leisure, the Family Study Center, the Counseling Center, and the Chicago Community Inventory; or of special foundations such as the Charles R. Walgreen Foundation or the Norman Wait Harris Foundation.

Suffice it to say on this occasion that these departments, committees, centers, and foundations are vigorous centers of faculty and student intellectual life. They justify a firm faith in a robust and significant future. At this university the social sciences promise to continue major contributions both to the national welfare and to the intellectual life of the nation.

Science, Society, and the Modes of Law[1]

To speak on so general a subject, one must put away modesty and not ask whether he has anything to say that is at once significantly true and new enough to his hearers to be interesting. Even more after Dean Harris' very appropriate words, I feel badly cast for my role on this occasion. Doubting whether I have ever done anything properly called either "science" or "research," I am hardly the one to "whoop it up" for scientific research as the method for dealing with social problems. And I could wail at the impossibility of the task of giving any view of those problems in the scope of a lecture. Far too much must be said if one is to say anything not too misleading or open to misinterpretation. About man, individual and social, practically anything one could say would be more or less true and relevant; hence opposite statements would be more or less equally so—which calls for endless explaining. Moreover, there is a serious

1. The writer would not have these paragraphs go into print without some words of disclaimer and admonition. They were prepared as a "speech," which implies other limitations as well as that of length. The paper does not purport to give a balanced discussion of any of the subjects touched upon. This applies in particular to the main theme, a critique of the use of scientific method in the study of society, which is a frankly one-sided treatment. It places the emphasis where I think it is needed—on the "limitations" of scientific prediction and control in this field of action. This in no way implies that there is no place for systematic inquiry into social phenomena, with such classification and quantification as can be validly carried out. That brings up the whole subject of methodology, which would call for a long treatise. It would have to begin with the wide differences in the meaning of "fact" and of "observation" in the main divisions of knowledge—especially the meaningful and communicable, and of intelligibility to a more or less general public in contrast with a small elite. (The latter, in the limit, may become hard to distinguish from a cult.) As briefly indicated in the paper, the reference to economics and its laws is particularly inadequate. In that field regular quantitative comparisons and the working of markets do result in at least some approximation to that "measurement" without which "knowledge is meager and unsatisfactory"—though the magnitudes cannot be used intelligently without an understanding of the way in which units are established and the conditions which enter into them. A large and important area of fact and of law which could not even be mentioned is the plurality of cultures and related political units, culminating in the notion of international law.

divergence between what is true and relevant and what is interesting or even acceptable. There are proprieties, a form of law, as well as truth, which forbid boring people or rubbing prejudices the wrong way—prejudice commonly meaning others' beliefs with which one disagrees.

Sticking to safe generalities, one fact about man is that he is a romantic and opinionated animal rather than inclined to truth-seeking or fact-facing. A rational being—indeed! he says so himself, as a compliment, hardly meant as truth. People will have answers, even to questions that make no sense; and they will "do something"— will "monkey" where they do not understand. They demand absolutes, and there is none—truth no exception. If we all started telling the truth, the whole truth, and nothing but the truth, the world would be a shambles before sundown the first day. And in morals, "Do right though the world perish" is the most monstrous of absurdities. Typical of man is one extreme or the other—to be marvelously intelligent or amazingly stupid—and well satisfied with himself in either role, and similarly with heroism and meanness. The great psychologist, P. T. Barnum, made fame and fortune on the maxim that the public loves to be swindled. I know of no "research" on the interesting question of how far that is true of all success; but we may note that Voltaire said his clearest idea of infinity came from observing the credulity and gullibility of the human race.

Whatever truth, or entertainment, such reflections may hold, you are warned not to expect too much from this lecture. It will consist of jottings, not very defensibly selected or put in order, and ending only by command of the clock, that despotic ruler of civilized life. Nor will it be very constructive; unhappily, clearing away rubbish must often precede building. Myself when young did have ambition to contribute to the growth of social science. At the end, I am more interested in having less nonsense posing as knowledge; that is, of course I am in favor of nonsense, good nonsense, and in its place, as well as poetry, romantic fiction, compliments, and jokes— modes of expression with values other than objective accuracy. The great task of education in our field is, in my view, to get people to make those distinctions—just what romantic and impatient man is loath to do. A once-popular humorist said, "It's not ignorance does the most damage; it's knowin' so derned much that ain't so." That is quite literally true in economics, I am sure—the field in which my professional life has mostly been spent.

Even in relation to the natural environment, where some realism means life or death, men constantly look for miracles and tilt at windmills. In that field a few have very recently turned to an interest in truth; and so we have natural science, tolerated because it produces marvels—it has been defined as magic which works—and others use its results without understanding them or caring to understand. If driving a car required knowledge of thermodynamics, cars would not be causing the traffic problems of today. Respecting democratic society, however, knowledge must be possessed by the masses if it is to be useful. And the other side of the contrast is as important; it is a romantic delusion that application of "scientific method" to its problems could produce similar marvels of prediction and control. That prejudice I particularly have to antagonize. To begin with, it is infinitely harder in social problems to free our terms from ambiguity, and few care to try. So we must stumble on, using language which, as the philosopher Paulhan remarked, was made by ignorant barbarians. And to another Frenchman, Talleyrand, speech seemed to have been given to men to disguise their thoughts.

What I shall attempt in this hour is to point out some features of free society and its problems which seem to me to need more attention than they get—problems that often have no solution but yet must and will be solved, for better or worse. Since the essence of society is order, legal and moral, the argument will center on law, its meanings and roles, and their changes through past time. To be stressed is the unique problem of free society—to combine freedom with order. It is soluble only through some compromise. Order, or law, is, of course, universal in nature—until man appears, with his mysterious freedom, the capacity to break law, and turn the very laws of nature to his own purposes. Finally, I shall come to the even more remarkable capacity of making law—of a different kind. As devotees of freedom, we must accept the fact that order is a necessity, freedom a comparative luxury. And as regards the legal order, it is unanimity that is imperative; if free agreement is not reached, it must be imposed, or chaos will ensue. A free society must agree on the maximum of freedom to be had with the needful minimum of order. Democracy could be defined as the socialization of the problem of law, and it is only democracy which confronts social problems, properly speaking. They must be solved by free agreement of the citizens in balancing among degrees and kinds of orderliness and in balancing stable legal order itself against more literally free association. Human nature being as it is, freedom and order reciprocally limit each other, although there is no effective freedom without order. Order is also a condition of security; the degree of freedom for each individual implies a corresponding insecurity for all others. This is the crucial conflict of values, among others which cannot be ignored. Compromise is inevitable; complete freedom would be chaos, and the limit of order would be the condition of ice. But, in fact, a perfect crystal is impossible, and perfection is a romantic illusion where values are involved; at higher levels, as in works of art, formal imperfections contribute to the value.

The long history of science itself, with what it replaced, reveals the nature of man as a romantic and superstitious animal. As all students know, the attitude toward nature, primitively and through the ages, was "animistic." Events were explained by "spirits" in things—by acts of will—and prediction and control were sought, and supposedly achieved, by performing rites and the arts of magic. Myth and ritual took the place held in our thinking by both science and history. Of course, these went with the practice of the techniques, more or less effective, by which people really lived; and, strangely, they were not allowed to interfere—too much or too often —with really effective action. But the latter procedures were routine, a matter of course (like the language spoken, which will come up later); it was myth and dramatization which were the active concerns. Nor has this attitude been outgrown, but only in part overgrown, in our day. Man is a religious animal; he now typically thinks, as the savage did not, that the religion into which he has happened to be born is "true" and all others "false." And these, be it noted, are the "beliefs" men will fight about. Montaigne observed that men assert most confidently where they have the least grounds, in fact, especially where they have none, but believe arbitrarily "by faith." Bacon neatly stated the principle: "The more absurd and incredible any divine mystery is, the greater honor we do to God in believing it."

A little attention to the history of words could be illuminating here. Most, if not all, the terms we use with an impersonally objective meaning had only the opposite import before modern times; and they still have it, with their new meaning—one source of the ambiguity we must contend with. "Truth" meant "fidelity" or "loyalty," and "false" the opposite. How can we think straight, using the same word for a true statement and a true friend, not to mention a true religion or philosophy? Our word "why" is an old ablative of the relative pronoun, meaning "by whom" or "for what"; and we use "reason" for both cause and motive, as well as a valid ground for a belief or act. Even in mechanics, the simplest and most empirically objective of sciences—the model for those who spell "science" with capitals—European man believed for two thousand years in the metaphysical physics of Aristotle, contrary to all experience. The impact theory of Descartes on the eve of the revolution was not much better, and the revolutionary Galileo was a thorough scholastic until over forty, well past the age at which most physicists make their great contributions. Strangely, it was the disclosure by the telescope of the satellites of Jupiter which overthrew medievalism in the learned public mind a lifetime after Copernicus. Everyone should know the kind of arguments used against Galileo's discovery. The head professor of philosophy in the University of Padua disposed of it thusly: There are seven openings in the human head—two eyes, two ears, two nostrils, and a mouth; these correspond with the seven planets; therefore, the number cannot be more or less. Moreover, your Medicean Stars (as Galileo called them) are invisible to the naked eye; therefore, they do not influence human affairs and so are useless; therefore, they do not exist. And it was a lucky coincidence of circumstances that Galileo was only forced to recant and put under house arrest, not burned alive as Giordano Bruno had been a few years before, for talking a little sense, by our standards.

What happens to impress me most is the history of medicine, and one might start with the words "medicine man." What people have done to themselves and others to cure disease is a tale of horror which seems even worse than war and almost as bad as religious persecution (incidentally, a near-monopoly of Christianity, distinguished as it is in history for authoritarian dogmatism and intolerance). A doctor and student of medical history was asked at what date doctors may have begun to cure more people than they killed; he replied that it might take another generation or so. Not to go into revolting details, one may think of bleeding people for practically any symptoms, which was general practice until recently in Western civilization. And nostrums and quackery are still about us, despite hesitant efforts at legal control. Still, as I have noted, we have had the recent growth of an objective attitude toward physical reality, even including the human body as physical and organic. On the side of mind and social relations, where morals and politics are involved, the rampant theorizing and disputing over the rudiments testify that the objective or critical attitude continues subordinate to other motives. In our field, interest centers largely in the discovery of effective techniques of propaganda—for each to use on all the rest, one must infer, since the results are published.

Rather the worst, to my mind—still harping on human romanticism as requiring a skeptical attitude—is that, having at very long last recognized that inert natural objects are *not* like men, beings of mind and will, moved by exhortation, persuasion, and deception, many of the best heads draw the strange conclusion that men are *like* inert objects, mechanisms responding to situations strictly in terms of cause and effect. A social scientist of distinction in his field once said to me in a matter-of-fact tone, "You know, I *think* there is no such thing as *thinking*." And much that is currently published in psychology and sociology advocates or rests upon the absurdity of behaviorism. One may ask: Is it for that that society selects the brightest *minds* and spends hard-earned money of taxpayers, or public trust funds, to give them an expensive education! Perhaps we should drop modern education and go back to ancestral lore, nursery jingles, proverbs, and the sort of reasoning used against Galileo—and under threat of hell-fire renounce progress for the beaten paths as the sum of human wisdom. If, that is, we cannot leave one absurd extreme without going whole hog for the opposite one, as bad or worse. But if men must be strictly scientific, in the sense of the natural sciences, these people are right; the way is to deny or ignore the most patent, relevant, and vital facts. After all, the myth and magic, divinations and incantations of savages were fairly harmless, while the opposite is true of natural science, if misapplied. That can easily destroy civilization, or the race itself, if men do not reach a working agreement on problems of the laws of values, which have to be treated in quite different terms. Up to a point, on both sides; for, of course, there is a place for science in the study of man, and, as I have no time to argue here, science itself is not empirical or its laws rigorous in the naïve sense that positivists, pragmatists, and scientificists assume. Its problems are finally value problems also.

It is true that we all confront, in a sense, the same practical tasks, prediction and control. But as should be self-evident, self-prediction and self-control, individual or especially collective, are categorically different matters from the relations of purposive man to inert objects. Man looks at nature from the outside, the standpoint from which alone scientific prediction is possible. He looks at himself and his society from the inside, which makes nonsense of the simple instrumental approach. I have little faith in a priori truth, or any absolutes, notably generalizations about impossibility. But I think I know that no one will ever learn to lift himself by his own bootstraps; nor, more pertinent to the social situation, will two persons be able to lift each other at the same time. Similarly, a scientist cannot by scientific method predict his own behavior in investigation. To do so, he would have to know the answers in advance, and then the questions would not be questions, or the problems problems. Further, prediction of the behavior of predicting runs into the familiar logical impasse of the infinite regress. And socially, if even two people predict each other's behavior and redirect their own accordingly, both will be falsified, or at least one must be. To the claim that social changes are scientifically predictable by a member of the society, a fair answer is the challenge to predict the stock market and make a fortune, enough times to show that it was not by chance. And it is a logical impossibility, not merely the matter of accurate observation and measurement. Nor does probability theory help much; on that it should suffice to observe that one cannot get insurance on a contingency where there is a substantial moral hazard, which practically means where any human choice is involved. (As will be noted later, there are economic laws of the market which are valid and useful for prediction and control.)

Modern physics has proved what anyone should have seen—that

the notion of absolute causality was a logical-metaphysical prejudice all along. If it were true, we could never know it. Physical causality is now conceived statistically, recognizing the fact of contingency in the world. In biology, of course, the case is more extreme. To talk sense in that realm, we must use teleological terms like function, a will or urge to life, competition and adaptation; and in the higher species we must recognize hestitation, effort and error, which distinguish them from mechanisms. Human conduct manifests still higher categories of activity, in sharper contrast with passive process—explicit desires, critical evaluation, will and choice. Man not only errs but "sins," and shows bad taste; he is the pretender, trickster, hypocrite, and liar of the known world, and equally unique for cruelty and obscenity. Absurdly, we call people brutal or beastly for deeds and traits foreign to animal nature. In short, man is subject to laws of a *pre*scriptive kind, contrasting sharply with the *de*scriptive laws which he figuratively says "govern" natural phenomena and by which he partly understands and predicts and uses natural events. These other laws he makes, in part, as well as breaks—no one can say how far or how they are made or found or, indeed, how laws are broken. At least they are chosen by decision, an activity of mind—in part by each person for himself, in part collectively, by groups, in emotional and intellectual intercommunication in cultural life, which changes and is changed through historical time.

Thus what man, the romantic, wants from social science he certainly will not get, not in a society with any freedom whatever. Prediction and control cannot be mutual; but what each naturally wants is to predict and control the rest, and wants social science to tell him how. For instrumental intelligence—and intelligence is basically instrumental—it is a real dilemma. To act intelligently in relations with others, each needs *first* to know how the others *will* act. Social life is possible for intelligent beings because of three facts. The first is law, a legal-moral-customary order sharply restricting the range of conduct to be expected; the second is collusion or preconcerting of activities involving mutuality. In free society "the law" is ideally a generalized form of preconcerting; but, of course, much of it, of which language is the type, "just grows" without raising any questions. Third, men as more truly rational, do not expect or want to live so very intelligently, in the instrumental sense; our days would be dull indeed without a large element of uncertainty and surprise. About collusion, either agreement *ad hoc* or on enduring rules, scientific method has virtually nothing to say, beyond information on what is possible; it cannot tell what should be done, as desired or as a matter of duty. If companions get separated in a crowd, neither can find the other by scientific prediction; they must agree in advance on a course of action.

A note: One-sided control—the only correct use of the word—has a place in a democracy. It applies in the relations between adults and children, and between the agents of society and criminals or defectives—cases involving individuals who are not responsible members of the community. The fields of medicine and education present special cases of power relations, needing extended consideration impossible here. Control is also meaningful for a dictator, up to a point, in contrast with the citizen of a free society. But the fact of his subjects having minds—opinion, feeling, and will—would still set the dictator's methods off sharply from those used to control inert objects. Even our relations with the higher animals are in part persuasive, even mutual, not purely mechanistic.

The great source of difficulty in interpreting man and society is that scientific laws apply but are limited by the prescriptive kind, with several subspecies, to which man is also subject. Science itself as a human and social activity works under at least two kinds of law that fall in the normative class. First are the laws of clear and valid thinking, of logic and criticism; about these I cannot say more in this lecture, or of aesthetic norms which are also operative. More to be emphasized is the scientist's subjection to moral laws. He must be honest, have intellectual integrity, be "devoted" to truth. Science has a high and austere code, bordering on the religious. Verification presupposes valid intercommunication, in which the moral factor bulks as large as the intellectual (and the aesthetic is never absent).

More or less apart from the main dichotomy, a third general type of law calls for notice—the historical. Accepted historical laws are few; but such law undoubtedly pervades both the phenomena of nature and those of man. In the natural domain, sciences like cosmology and geology find order in the temporal sequence of events—

largely exemplifying the great law of the degradation of energy—and they yield some literal prediction, of the future, by projection or extrapolation. The ordinary laboratory sciences, of course, predict only hypothetically—"if *A*, then *B*," or they go on to measure covariation. It is chiefly such laws that are directly useful to man; the process of discovery shows how to interfere in their working by acts that man "can" do, and so to "control" a course of events. For conduct these become hypothetical imperatives: "If you want result *B*, you must perform act *A*." Such laws are not wholly wanting in society; if an enactment is to be obeyed, it must carry some penalty for infraction, and the most conspicuous case is the laws of the market or of "demand and supply." But the whole matter of the instrumental view of rules-making by groups needs special consideration impossible here. Historical laws are closely dependent on the generalizing sort, but I must pass over that, too, and over the reasons why the historical laws of nature are of little use. In biology we have evolution, a historical law which does not enable prediction, still less control, though the opposite is true of the underlying general laws of heredity, adaptation, and survival. In fact, the use of strictly historical law is solely to tell us what will happen "regardless," what we cannot do; hence the given conditions of action. But the first would be true of physical laws if they held rigorously for man himself. Absolute laws of matter would be purely historical, and no one would know them; ideas of knowing and using would be nonexistent in a universe of process, devoid of meaning as well as of rights or values.

In considering history and its laws, we must remember that history also has *its* history; like science, it developed along with mind and culture. We contrast "scientific" history with the romantic, animistic, supernaturalistic myths of the ages down to yesterday, for critically authentic history is also a recent innovation. (A note: Here and at other points, some exception should be made for the Greeks; but all their advances and more were lost in the succeeding Dark Age—Gibbon's "triumph of barbarism and religion.") As to method, we learn history largely by prediction; but for the past, this is valid, since we *are* on the outside of the people and events we study. The absence of intercommunication limits the data (and, of course, there is no possibility of control), but predictions backward are not affected by people being told what they are going to do. That limitation of social science is commonly an intention of the predictor—to exhort or warn or deceive—making prediction a technique of control. History is of the essence in the study of society. All direct knowledge, by observation or report, is, of course, of the past; the future is only inferred, and the present is a mere imaginary line between the two. Further, while everything has a history and is the product of history, this is true in a quite special sense of man and human society. The late Ortega y Gasset said (paraphrasing Dilthey) that "man has no nature, what he has is . . . history." But it has been a history of seeking a nature, of progressively creating humanity, in and with cultures. Finally, the task of our society is historical—to direct intelligently the future course of history.

An honest view of that problem must face up to how little anyone knows about history, especially its causality or laws, or about how to learn from it or apply it. We recall Hegel's sad witticism that we learn from history that men do not learn from history. Here, again, a major obstacle is the romantic character of human interest. Apart from still being, in varying degree, makers or purveyors of myth—for reasons good or bad—historians naturally write mostly about what they and their readers are most interested in. That is, the deeds of the great, glorious victories, and tragic defeats in war or political struggle. Man, we must note, is a social animal, but in contrast with other social species he is also antisocial, a lawbreaker and a gangster; as spectator or participant, he likes a good fight, and a good war may redeem a bad cause. Further, it is about the spectacular that records are most available. These features of history are unfortunate for the student of social process in quest of historical law. We are more concerned with the commonplaces of past situations, activities of which the contemporaries were unaware or only passively aware. It is things like language that, because they are hardly affected by purposive action, yield the most definite laws, either scientific or historical. What students of society need from history is a descriptive portrayal of human development in the large: how beings we could call human emerged out of some animal species and gradually became civilized; and civilization's fitful advance until it produced societies more or less intelligently committed to ideals of truth, freedom, and progress.

What to my mind is most important in the long sweep of change is the recurring emergence of novelty, with the new generally not replacing the old but superimposed upon it, giving rise to ever increasing complexity. Most notably, man requires a pluralistic interpretation, as a being full of contradiction and paradox. He is a physical mechanism and an organism, subject to the laws of both these kinds, and somehow joined to them is a mental or spiritual nature with unique attributes and subject to different laws. Not much will ever be known about human beginnings, the transition from the merely animal to the human. And we must look back beyond man, at least to the appearance of consciousness and the mental faculties we find in some degree in the higher animals. Consciousness can never be "explained" in terms either of physical process or of biological utility. There is no reason of either sort why men should not live and behave exactly as we do, as unconscious mechanisms—which the behaviorist pretends to "think" we are. Consciousness is "epiphenomenal"; we only know it is there, and seems to be active, notably in the scientificist's act of denying it. Another revolutionary change was the shift from a biological to a cultural basis of continuity and development. The inheritance of behavior patterns, like other traits, and including social behavior, as "instincts," through the gene mechanism, somehow gave place in large part to transmission through imitation of the mature by the young. This process, culture or custom, could have been at first as mechanical and unconscious as the older method, a matter of psychological conditioning. If so, it presently turned into the activity of learning, joined by teaching. The new system could be biologically useful, in enabling transmission of learned behavior, thus affording more flexibility and rapid adaptation than the accidents of favorable gene mutation.

The advent of culture gives rise to historical laws in the broad human meaning—descriptive laws of culture change—without voluntary action, as in the case of language, mentioned before. Acquisition of speech was the great advance, providing a tool of thought—fantasy and emotion as well as reasoning—and the main vehicle of cultural continuity and change, of which it is now the most prominent example. Language illustrates culture's virtual independence of physical and biological conditions or laws. The people who carry a culture pattern play much the role of the soil which supports many forms of plant life indifferently. Purely historical laws of culture change are hard to isolate and do not yet amount to a great deal, outside of linguistics. But they show up with a vengeance, negatively, in limiting our ability to make changes. Language itself goes its own way; our society is helpless even to get absurd anachronisms out of English spelling—not to speak of establishing a common medium of communication between peoples, so much needed in science and scholarship and for world organization. In other fields we have in varying degree more freedom in lawmaking. But I shall come to that after touching on another revolutionary emergence.

At some time, far back in prehistory, developing *Homo* became aware of the customary law to which he had previously conformed automatically. When he realized that he was bound by laws, being human, he resented it, found it interfered with various private urges, and began his unique career as a lawbreaker; he became antisocial as well as social. When custom ceases to be mere historical process and becomes compulsory, as mores, we cross the great divide into the new age of prescriptive law, as morality. (I can only mention the development of felt desires opposed to customary requirements, and other prescriptive laws, notably of logic and of taste.) In a familiar way of putting the change, man "fell" from innocence into sin. I will not raise the great question of life, whether it was really a fall or a rise, and will be reversed in heaven. As I picture the primitive attitude, it would have been a blend of feeling the law—moral law—as in itself compulsory, like, say, wearing clothes, with viewing it as a command to be obeyed, subject to infliction of penalties. In accord with their animistic world view, primitive men thought of law as command by supernatural powers which (or who?) would punish not only the individual culprit but also the society which tolerated him in its midst—at least without retributive treatment and rites of reconciliation and purification.

Such feelings and fears, however, were not enough to prevent lawbreaking. And since man had become social, of biological necessity, and since a society must have laws in order to exist, laws which are consciously obeyed if they do not function automatically, evolution, so to speak, "had to" produce means for enforcing the most necessary rules. Thus arose religion and politics, the beginnings of church and state; and the relations between the two, especially their conflicts, with men's love and hatred for both, have been the red thread running through history ever since. The institutions have been supported by aspects of men's highly ambiguous attitudes—they love order as such as well as hate it, and, in particular, resent lawbreaking by other people, though this may also be admired. If men had in fact been rational, if they had had "common gumption," they would have seen that laws are necessary; hence those that exist must be obeyed until others, supposedly better, are proposed and accepted. But that is not "human nature." One thinks of Marx, the archromantic, who denounced religion as the opium of the people—descriptively enough, but without asking how its necessary function would be performed without it—for men cannot be ruled or kept in order by force alone. With the rise of agencies for enforcement, jural law is differentiated from that which is moral only; but that difference is one of social mechanics rather than of categories. Liberals, too, have been romantic in imagining an impossible amount of freedom to change the laws; men can never be "liberated" from custom or convention, for law must be predominantly a matter of habit, use, and wont. And it must also be in considerable part formally enforced.

We may now take a backward glance at some features of the transition which seem to be somewhat neglected. The development of mind tends to be considered too much in terms of intelligence, itself treated as a biological function; and with the biologizing of man goes the mechanizing of biology. Changes in the life of feeling need more emphasis. Nearly a century ago, Darwin made a good beginning of studying emotion in animals, but it seems to have been little followed up. Man is strikingly unique as the animal that laughs and weeps. More remarkably, people will pay others to make them laugh, and pay even more to be made to cry, if done in some proper way. Emotional changes, some of which had a physiological and even an anatomical basis, underlie our moral and aesthetic values, as well as individual desires and aversions. Somewhere and somehow occurred a remarkable inversion of the instrumental relation between "mind" and body. There must have been a time, an epoch, when the brain and nervous system were, in fact, instrumental to the life of the organism and the species. In civilized man this is reversed; the mind thinks of the body as a means to its own life of "experience." Indeed, it often seems ashamed of having a body at all; this is called the coffin of the spirit and is "mortified" for the latter's well-being, or "salvation." The mental life is less a matter of reasoning than of feelings, wishes, and value-judgments, which provide the ends of reasoning, such at it is. Hume's dictum, that the intellect is the slave of the passions, is, in general, true, though I have reservations when he adds that it has no right to any other role. That also I must pass over, and, of course, I cannot go into the confused, romantic, and paradoxical character of human passions. I would stress that neither our desires nor our higher values, which, largely opposed as they are, together define what we mean by the "useful," show any consistent relation to biological advantage, of the individual or the species. They seem about as often to be antibiological. Man is the animal who "works," virtually meaning that he has an aversion to useful activity as such; and it is most true of civilized man. He is the slave-maker, and then the builder of machines to replace the slaves—after civilization has made him soft-hearted. I puzzle especially over many of our higher values, as I would guess that on the whole idealists do more harm than the criminals. The soft heart proverbially needs the hard head; but this has little romantic or sentimental appeal.

I must hurry on, to say a little about the most important topic, the last and rather the greatest revolution in the modes of law—the coming of democracy. That was just beginning to be talked about when Hume wrote, a short two centuries ago, though a major turning point in its direction had occurred a century before, in the victory of Parliament over Stuart absolutism. Hume disliked democracy and did not live to see it; he died a few days after another high point, the adoption of our Declaration of Independence, in a war which was a prelude to the French Revolution. A still earlier turning point was the Protestant Revolt. This destroyed the unitary ecclesiastical absolutism of western Europe, but it did not destroy either authoritarianism or its supernatural foundation; both were transferred to nation-states, under autocrats ruling by the grace of God. Nor did the Age of Reason, with its political revolutions, introduce democracy, which came gradually in the nineteenth and twentieth centuries. Our own Founding Fathers feared it—the famous Declaration was written by and for slaveowners. Just so, none of the protagonists in the terrible "religious" wars following the "Reformation" wanted even toleration, not to mention the general liberation which finally resulted. History, like nature, moves in mysterious ways its wonders to perform. None of the thirteen states adopting our Constitution in 1787 had universal *male* suffrage; and no one then thought of free secular, non-dogmatic education, even for literacy, as a requirement for citizenship in a free state, or as a human right.

It is hard to realize the historical suddenness and vast sweep of the change, in a few generations, from the medieval system—the most extreme totalitarianism known, at least in the Western world before Hitler and Stalin—to our libertarian and equalitarian democracy of today. The accepted human values were largely inverted—an *Umwertung aller Werte,* in the Nietzschean phrase. Culturally and spiritually, the basic fact was the freeing of the mind, from dogma, for the progressive pursuit of truth and well-being, material and ideal. Everyone should know Professor Bury's two books—at least the earlier chapters—*History of Freedom of Thought* and *The Idea of Progress.* I mention them, as I cannot go into detail. The two great drives back of the whole movement (not the immediate motivation of the heretical religious revolts) were the development of science and the economic interest in trade and production, both of which seem to be naturally individualistic. Modern science is unique in looking toward applications—as preached by Bacon and inaugurated as a movement by his younger contemporary, Galileo. The role of the "Renaissance," reviving classical pagan learning, was important but is, I think, commonly exaggerated.

For our purpose here, the central fact is the revolution in the conception of law. From its historical beginnings through the ages, the law had been sacred, hence in theory eternal and immutable—and so was, of necessity, the authority for its interpretation and enforcement, that is, the uneasy partnership of autocratic church and autocratic state, both divinely ordained and sanctioned. (Note previous reference to reservations for Greece and Rome.) The essence of democracy is the freedom of the people to change the laws at will, by equal participation, and to have them enforced by agents held responsible in the same way. In norms of conduct, a new age began when men first thought that their laws could be wrong, contrary to a "higher" law. For this we unfortunately still use the words "moral" and "ethical," giving them, as usual, a radically new additional meaning. The coming of freedom to change, of course, ended the sanctity of law. The idea of improvement had been impossible before, since the laws, jural or moral in the original sense, contained the whole meaning of right and wrong. Verbally, the right means the regular. At this point, man took or underwent his second great "fall," in the sense of the first; as he had then fallen from the innocence of insouciance into responsibility for obeying laws, he now took on the far more onerous responsibility for determining the content of the law itself.

There was, indeed, a transitional stage when "positive" law was distinguished in theory from "natural law," opening the way to some change in the former—but never very much, and only by the sacred authority. I can only mention the curious history of the ambiguous concept of "nature"—standing for fact versus norm, or used in contrast with the supernatural or the artificial. In culture, it is hard to separate the natural and the artificial, and only in that sense does natural law or natural right have meaning. Life has its scientific laws, as part of nature; but conformity with any sort of standards is unnatural, against nature. Men have the rights recognized in the legal and moral order in which they live. My right to life means only that no one has a right to kill me, unless he has that right—mayhap the duty. I feel some impatience with the solemn cant that passes for inspired wisdom on the most vital questions. The notion of men being born free or equal is one example, and another is that loving people tells how they ought to be treated, which is commonly not as they wish to be. And what "you" would like, with no conditions stated, would as typically lead to misguidance. The phrase "natural-law" is current today—used to cloak dogmatic pronouncements on what ought to be law or ought to be done. If free society endures, this will be outgrown, as legal thinking is struggling free from the conception of law as a command. When people "command themselves," individually or collectively, a different word is called for.

Advisedly I say "individually or" collectively. It is essential to free society that, even when law is made by free agreement as far as possible, its scope still be minimized, leaving each person to "command himself." Limits to freedom must be set only by general agreement—not the fiat of whoever can contrive to carry an election —to meet the need for common restraints or for group action to realize group values. But there's the rub! With the progress of liberal civilization, individuals pursuing their wants and needs or ideals run more and more into conflict; and more and more do human needs become social, requiring a consensus in action. Basic like-mindedness is requisite for discussion itself—the method of democracy, and Lord Bryce's familiar definition. Conflict is not only, or even mainly, because of "sin." The minimum requirements for harmony expand, making agreement hard, and threatening resort to force. Agreement must come in part through compulsory legal action, while the basic consensus is the task of education. Hence above all, the schools must be kept free and not allowed to be used for indoctrinating the young with dogma.

The broad crucial task of free society is to reach agreement by discussion on the kind of civilization it is to create for the future; hence it must agree on the meaning of progress. The living adult generation legislate for their children, and also beyond them for the unborn. For that task, attitudes toward persons are not in point; even for infants already born, freedom has no meaning and equality means all equal to zero, or to digits in a census of units biologically defined. Discussion of legal change must run in terms of general values or ideals. The politics of democracy cannot be a contest between individuals or interest groups in getting what they want at the cost of others. Right must be defined in relation to obligations as well as to possibilities. One of our worst verbal confusions is using the same term, "value," for both subjective desires and ideals which, in seeking agreement, must be recognized as objectively valid, hence as "cognitive." Social problems arise out of conflicts at either of the two levels; but they can be discussed only as differences in critical-intellectual judgment of norms. Mere assertion of opposed claims cannot tend toward agreement, but must intensify conflict.

In a realistic view, the problem of legislation is hardly one of means to ends, or of efficiency—and not at all in the sense of scientific technology. A useful analogy is the making of rules in games or sports. The individual interest will be in winning, but the general interest is the ideal of a good game. I once heard of a business efficiency expert who suggested for the improvement of football first to put all the men on the same side. Sportsmanship, incidentally, looms very large in the ethic of free society and has been very important in the history of democracy; but little is said about it in either connection, by moral philosophers and preachers or by historians.

Society in its rules-making must of course give a high place to efficiency, which also is largely ignored in idealistic and religious ethics. I digress to say explicitly that in referring to anachronisms in religious teachings on morals I do not condemn religion. People should of course have any religion they choose, provided they allow others that right, do not indulge in "offensive" practices, and keep it out of politics; this last was, of course, the clear intention of Jesus and the Apostles. But I would make one remark on the obvious: Surely all who have bowels of feeling share Henry Wallace's view that babies everywhere should have their bottle of milk at feeding time. And that may well be a condition of peace in the world. It will not come about if the number of babies exceeds the number of bottles of milk per feeding period; and the contribution of church ethics to that situation is more babies and fewer bottles of milk.

Efficiency as a social problem is the province of economics. The history of the free-enterprise economy has shown its capacity to promote efficiency, up to any reasonable expectations, but there are other values to be considered. The system is widely criticized, damned as "capitalism" by agitators for radical change. Undoubtedly there are evils, some more or less remediable by intelligent political action. A primary criticism relates to unjust distribution. There are many formulas for justice in that sense; they conflict among themselves, and no one could ever be fully realized or pushed very far without unduly neglecting others. And compulsory redistribution infringes on freedom; but conflicting definitions of that are also in dispute. The citizen must learn critically to compare and balance among possible alternatives, first knowing what these are. The economic order is also condemned for the aesthetic and cultural values it fosters. It is blamed for a civilization denounced as ugly, crass or trivial, as well as for enslaving the working masses, not giving them real freedom or the good life.

I only mention these things, without passing judgment, at the end of an overlong discourse, in order to suggest the kind of problems we face, in one important area, in trying to realize the revolutionary ideal of a society combining freedom with order. The problem involves "laws" of all the values of the familiar triad—Truth, Beauty, and the Good—in their broadest meaning, everything that enters into a high civilization and the good life for man. We tend to include it all in a vague concept of social justice—again a complex new meaning for an old term. Its historical meaning, as the word shows, was accord with law, which was assumed to be known. That made good conduct a matter of will, of conformity and obedience, to law, established authority, and "conscience." In consequence of our second "fall," however, the issues in conduct are as much intellectual and aesthetic as moral. No longer is good will the whole story; rather, the view of modern man is expressed in the proverb: "The road to hell is paved with good intentions."

As a final word, I stress again two main difficulties or dangers. The first is in the survival of traditions which do not fit the facts and problems of our free society. Traditions, even freed from sanctity as they must be, are still hard and slow to change. Intelligent action demands, first of all, that men accept that method, eschew wishful thinking, face the problems and try to understand them. Our older maxims of sentimental, personal-relations morality were formulated in and for a society with "static" ideals. Whatever their adequacy in the original setting, they have little to say about the main problems of a society dedicated to progress in truth, freedom, and well-being. The second menace I have dwelt on at still greater length. It is "scientificism," another fatal oversimplification—the insistence on attacking problems of social change entirely by methods adapted to the understanding and use of the natural environment. They are irrelevant to the more crucial problem of democratic society, which is agreement on cultural norms. These must supply—not goals, for goals are always provisional, to be redefined as they are progressively realized—but must point the *direction* of change, that we may have progress and not stagnation or retrogression.

Toward a General Theory for the Behavioral Sciences*

I dare say that I have worked off my fundamental formula on
you that the chief end of man is to frame general propositions
and that no general proposition is worth a damn.—OLIVER WEN-
DELL HOLMES, JR.

About 1949 a group of scientists at the University of Chicago, some
of whom have now moved to the University of Michigan, began to
consider whether a sufficient body of facts exists to justify developing an empirically testable general theory of behavior. To refer to
the biological and social fields involved, we coined the term "behavioral sciences." We adopted this phrase, first, because its neutral
character made it acceptable to both social and biological scientists
and, second, because we foresaw a possibility of someday seeking
to obtain financial support from persons who might confound social
science with socialism.

In 1946 Senator Fulbright of Arkansas in a Senate debate on
establishing the National Science Foundation indicated that such
misapprehension exists when he said: "There may be some misconception with regard to a study of social sciences being confused
with what we commonly think of as politics, socialism, or some form
of social philosophy. It certainly was not in the minds of the authors
of the [Foundation] bill to promote any particular social philosophy
of that kind. But a study of certain human relationships and certain
scientific bases would have nothing to do with socialism or any subjects of that kind."[1] Comments of certain other senators during the
Seventy-ninth Congress showed that some of them actually labored
under such confusion. And in the vote on including the social sci-

* Acknowledgment is made to the courtesy of the American Psychological Association and the editor of the *American Psychologist* for permission to republish
this article, which appeared in the September, 1955, issue of that journal.

1. *Congressional Record* (79th Cong., 2d sess.), p. 8041.

ences explicitly in the Foundation, most of the liberals in both parties voted "aye" while the conservatives voted "nay."

That the misapprehension was not completely dispelled six years later was indicated in the report of the House committee to investigate foundations, of which Representative Cox was chairman: "Many of our citizens confuse the terms 'social,' as applied to the discipline of the social sciences, with the term 'socialism.' And since the social sciences may be defined as the study of man's relationship to man, the problem of every man considering himself an expert in the field is ever present. . . . But these and other subjects within the orbit of the social sciences are proper subjects for objective study and analysis under conditions of control which give promise of revealing scientific facts."[2]

The Planning

Long before we had need to solicit financial support, however, our behavioral science group in Chicago began regular planning meetings. We decided to concentrate for a time upon constructing theory, first attempting to agree upon creating a set of interrelated assumptions and theorems capable of being tested by individuals using the empirical techniques of various disciplines. We aimed toward the ultimate goal of a theory embracing all aspects of behavior, but short of that we hoped to structure our research strategy to make possible a salvage of confirmable microtheories about specific areas of behavior.

In the late spring of 1952 a "theory group" began meeting intensively. At first each professor in turn sketched his background and interests and gave his notions on how to approach the building of a general behavior theory. It soon became clear that we would need to have much patience if we were eventually to develop a common language. It became apparent, also, that certain persons found such group activity unprofitable or uncongenial, either because of well-developed patterns of solitary work, or because of ego involvement with a single point of view and fixed commitment to it, or for other reasons. Such individuals dropped out; new ones were included. Because of the need for the group to maintain its integrity over a relatively long period, we have added members only infre-

2. House of Representatives (82d Cong., 2d sess.), H.R. No. 2514, pp. 9–10.

quently. The participant disciplines have been history, anthropology, economics, political science, sociology, social psychology, psychology, psychiatry, medicine, physiology, and mathematical biology. From time to time we have also met with representatives from other areas, such as physics and philosophy. A number of persons have contributed to the work, but the author alone is responsible for distortions present in this effort to give his personal interpretation of the present state of our group thinking. In all probability, each other participant would view our work somewhat differently.

As soon as we had arrived at a degree of primitive agreement, some of us began empirical tests of theorems evolved by the group. Also we searched the literature for elements to add to our theory and for studies to test our theorems.

We have assumed from the start that any adequate theory of behavior would represent in large part a selection from among viewpoints—some even from opposing schools—which have already been stated succinctly and capably. Our quest was *not* for originality with a capital *O*.

We chose certain working assumptions, not because we were certain they were more valid than alternatives chosen by other theorists, but in order to get on with the task. First, we agreed to accept as confirmation of theorems only *objective* phenomena available to public inspection by more than one observer, excluding private experience. Second, we tried when possible to state hypotheses *quantitatively*, so that they might be precisely testable and could subsequently be corrected. Third, we attempted to make statements capable of being disproved as well as proved, by *crucial experiments*. Finally, as will be explained below, in so far as possible we employed dimensions of the natural sciences related to the centimeter-gram-second system.

General Behavior Systems Theory

Of the various possible integrations of the relevant data, we have found most profit in what we call *general behavior systems theory*. Systems are bounded regions in space-time, involving energy interchange among their parts, which are associated in functional relationships and with their environments. General systems theory is a series of related definitions, assumptions, and postulates about all levels of systems from atomic particles through atoms, molecules, crystals, viruses, cells, organs, individuals, small groups, societies, planets, solar systems, and galaxies. General behavior systems theory is a subcategory of such theory, dealing with living systems, extending roughly from viruses through societies. Perhaps the most significant fact about living things is that they are open systems, with important inputs and outputs. Laws which apply to them differ from those applying to relatively closed systems.

All behavior can be conceived of as energy exchange within an open system or from one such system to another. Any exchange of energy across a boundary results in some alteration or distortion of the energy form. Those specific functions of systems which we can stipulate and whose magnitude we can measure in a relative scale, we will call "variables" if they are within the system and "parameters" if they are in its environment. Each system except the largest of all—the universe—has its environment. The system and its environment together constitute a suprasystem. Each system except the smallest has subsystems, which are any components of an organism that can affect a variable.

Inputs and outputs may be either coded or uncoded. Coding is a linkage within subsystems whereby process A_1 is coupled with process A_2 so that either will elicit the other in the future. Coding involves conditioning, learning, or pairing of two processes in a system and the memory or retention of this union over a period of time. Any action is uncoded unless—like speech or gesture—it has some added significance as a result of such a bond. It then conveys information.

All living systems tend to maintain steady states of many variables, by negative feedback mechanisms which distribute information to subsystems to keep them in orderly balance. Not only are subsystems ordinarily kept in equilibrium, but systems are also usually in balance with their environments, which have outputs into systems and inputs from them. This prevents variations in the environment from destroying systems, either by collapse or by explosion. There is a range of stability for any parameter or variable in any system. It is that range within which the rate of correction is minimal or zero and beyond which correction does occur. Inputs (or loads), either coded or uncoded, which, by lack or excess, force the variables beyond the range of stability constitute stresses and produce strains within the system. These strains may or may not be capable of being reduced, depending upon the equilibratory resources of the system.

The foregoing general statement can be translated into terminology of several behavioral sciences. In individual psychology, for instance, the system has generally been known as the organism; the input, as the stimulus; and the output, as the response. Uncoded inputs, we have recognized, can result in strains or disequilibria within the organism which are known as primary or somagenic drives. Coded inputs result in secondary, learned, acquired, or psychogenic drives. Reduction of strains is called "drive satisfaction." When inputs or loads create strains great enough to call into play complex subsystems to restore equilibrium, we sometimes refer to such processes as "defense mechanisms." When these mechanisms fail, severe disruption of the steady state of the organism, known as mental or physical illness, or ultimately death, occurs. The total of the strains within the individual resulting from his genetic input and variations in the input from his environment is often referred to as his values. The relative urgency of reducing these individual strains determines his hierarchy of values.

Specific Aspects of the Theory

System

Our definition of "system" is very general and at first sight might appear to apply to almost everything in the world. And, of course, the function of general theory is to be inclusive. However, it may be helpful to indicate what is not a system. The dark-colored half of the Pied Piper was not a system. The opposing lines of two football teams in scrimmage, independent of their backs, would not ordinarily be considered together as a system. If the Headless Horseman of Washington Irving had not been fictional, he could not have held his head in his arm and yet behave like an intact system. All the blondes in the United States are themselves not a system unless they are organized by some sort of communication, like the Red-headed League of A. Conan Doyle. In simple, naïve, commonsense terms, then, a real system is all of a thing. Even though it is possible to construct a conceptual system which includes grandpa's mustache, Chinese *hokku* poetry, and the Brooklyn Bridge, this would not correspond to a real system of general systems theory, because these things are not surrounded by a single boundary, are not continuous in space-time, and do not have recognizable functional interrelationships.

Some may wonder whether "system" is identical with "Gestalt." Are there laws of the whole which do not apply to specific parts? We hold that both the parts, or subsystems, and the whole behave according to similar laws. However, the fact that subsystems are equilibrated together by system-wide organizing processes (even though these mechanisms can be explained by the behavior of component parts) means that there are characteristics of the whole which do not apply to any part. This is true of systems at every level.

Boundary

Boundaries of systems are not always clear cut and round like the rind of a watermelon. Sometimes they have intricate geometrical design, more like the surface of a branching coral, but even more complex than that. A naval task force maneuvering blind at sea can be a system, even though its boundary is complicated and in continual flux. It is a system organized by communications which require at least a small filament of contiguous space-time of ether, to transmit radio, radar, or other signals. When a typhoon hits the "Caine" and her sister destroyers, wiping out radio and radar contact, then the flotilla is no longer a system, because usual functional interrelationships are impossible. Communications make feasible complex organizations of systems, like the American Psychological Association or the United Nations. A given individual or behaving subsystem can, of course, be part of several systems at the same time, equilibrating at least partially with all of them. To deal with this fact, the concept of "role" has been developed in social psychology.

Subsystems

How could one disprove our contention that every system except the smallest has subsystems? The answer is that if one found a homogeneous distribution of energy in any system, so that no boundary between its subsystems was discoverable, then that system would have no subsystems. How does one locate a boundary, i.e., a region where energy or information exchange is significantly less than inside or outside the system? One decides upon the order of magnitude of difference in rate of exchange of information or energy which one will accept as indication of a boundary. Let us call this amount d. This differs according to the level of system with which one intends to deal. Then, having decided on this, one can empirically locate the boundary as that region where there is d less interchange of energy and information than either outside or inside. In general, d is progressively less from larger systems to smaller so that ordinarily it is great for societies, less for individuals, and much less for cells.

We know a great deal about the input-output relations of the peripheral sensory and motor subsystems, but it is extremely difficult with present methods to determine these relations for processes in the human central subsystems. Electronic technicians know that if there is only one subsystem between two test electrodes which contact the input and the output respectively, 100 per cent of the variance will be in that subsystem; if, however, there are two subsystems, and there is no way to put a test electrode between those systems, all the variance may be in Subsystem A; all of it may be in Subsystem B; or the variance may be accounted for by an infinite set of possible combinations of the relationships between the two. Extremely complex mathematics is required to study the input-output alterations of multiple systems whose components cannot be isolated. For this reason precise study of central subsystems of the individual—often said to be the main variables of his "personality" —presents a difficult or impossible scientific problem by present methods.

Coding

In living organisms the important process of coding, which makes it possible for energy exchange also to be information exchange, is accomplished by at least three means, which are perhaps basically the same but which for convenience can be classified as (a) instinct; (b) imprinting; and (c) conditioning or learning. The first is irreversible; the second may be; and the last is reversible. Instinct is a "wiring in" of the relationship before birth, either in the endocrine or in the nervous system. Imprinting is "wired in" before birth or hatching and stamped in by "social releasers" during early hours after birth or hatching. Conditioning or learning is usually acquired after birth, and it may be lost.

As the link between energy theory and information theory, the process of coding is of prime importance. While both the biological and the social sciences share a dual concern with energy transfer and information transfer, the predominant emphasis of the biological sciences is energy transfer, whereas that of the social sciences is information transfer. The social sciences deal chiefly with verbal or symbolic behavior. Information theory abets the union of the natural and the social sciences, but is probably more likely to be useful to the latter. General behavior systems theory incorporates most aspects of modern information theory, but it is more encompassing, for it deals with the transmission of both information and energy, and with the relationships between information and energy transfer.

Ancient philosophers, including Aristotle and Plato, were concerned with the metaphysical question of the relation of form to matter. Plato thought matter to be the feminine aspect of the universe, a "receptacle" capable of accepting any form. To him form was the masculine aspect of life, which, when united with matter, produced the real or concrete object. So reproduction could be explained, being a special case of the more general notion that any object—as we would say, any "system"—was the union of form and matter. The form could be in the head of the sculptor, and he could put it into the rough matter of Carrara marble in order to fashion a bust. This form could also have been wrought in brass, iron, or other substances. Conversely, some other form, like a table or chair, could have been imposed on the marble. Together, form and matter were thought to define the object.

These conceptualizations were sheerly metaphysical until recent years, when certain empirical and quantitative discoveries have made possible a more precise linkage between these notions, bringing them closer to science.

First came the work in the late nineteenth century, which developed the second law of thermodynamics, the law of entropy. Energy (E) and entropy (S) were seen to have a specific relationship. Then in the early twentieth century, Einstein produced his theory of relativity which included the basic equation:

$$E = m c^2 \, ,$$

energy equals mass times the square of the speed of light.

Within the last ten years, Wiener and Shannon have written equations which connect the notion of entropy with the notion of information. The basic equation is:

$$S = -H \, .$$

That is, entropy equals the negative of information (H).

What does this all mean? It has many implications, but a simple illustration might be as follows:

If an electric impulse of random character, like a lightning stroke, were to be sent over a wire and fed into a speaker, you would hear noise. A similar current passing into a television set would show "snow" on the screen. So the ultimate result of entropy, randomly distributed energy, produces noise when conveyed over a communication system to a speaker. On the other hand, if a modulated current, including only selected frequencies, is conveyed over such a circuit, you will hear a tone; on a television screen you will see organized form. That is, as energy distribution becomes less random, "noise" (which in information theory is the negative of information) tends to disappear, and information tends to increase.

Anyone who has listened on a many-party, old-fashioned country telephone line knows that the higher the noise level the less the information that can get across. As noise is decreased in communication systems, more and more of the message can be conveyed.

Let us now observe the following combination of the above equations:

$$E = m c^2$$
$$S = -H \, .$$

This demonstrates that there is a highly complex, but nevertheless understood, and to a degree quantifiable relationship between mass (matter or energy) and information. It is not pure coincidence that the word "form" appears as a syllable in the word "information." We find, therefore, that dimensions of energy transmission and information transmission, in some ways like the matter and form of the ancient Greeks, are in recent years for the first time quantitatively relatable.

This suggests a basic role for information theory in general science. Information, which can be measured quantitatively in bits or similar units, can convey qualitative or formal structural aspects of any system. It can describe the non-random relationships in which energy is organized. Information and energy coexist as companionate aspects of every system. Perhaps this fact may lead to better understanding of the special case of the system known as the brain and the messages or information conveyed or stored in it.

As mentioned before, we are attempting to employ only dimensions and units related to the centimeter-gram-second system in quantifying all aspects of behavior, coded and uncoded. Perhaps it would be better to coin a word to represent our precise meaning and say that we employ "*u*-units." Under this term we include: First, measures that can actually be made in centimeters, grams, and seconds, like the size of a system, its weight, or the length of its existence. In addition, we include complex dimensions of the natural sciences, whose relationships to centimeters, grams, and seconds have been demonstrated, like the temperature dimensions scaled in degrees above absolute zero. Furthermore, because we believe that equations can be written which indicate the systematic relationships between units of information and the units of energy measured by the CGS system, we include units of information like bits in our *u*-units.

We recognize the arbitrary nature of all coding. Almost any configuration of energy can in some language or other represent or symbolize almost anything else. However, once these code linkages are developed as traces in the brain or in the programming of an electronic computer, they are then processed according to principles of energy transformation which can ultimately be measured in the derivatives of CGS units of the natural sciences. It is of these various sorts of units we speak when we employ the phrase *u*-units.

We envisage a far-off scientific utopia in which we can reduce to comparable dimensions the Oedipus complex, repression, submissiveness, physiological traces, acculturation, the pH of blood, and every other factor related to behavior. At present the social sciences wrestle with a congeries of completely unconnected terms and dimensions. It is true that factor analysis has made efforts to improve this situation. Factor analysis attempts to plot the domain of a number of dimensions whose relationships previously were unknown. When this is done, you still may not know the relationships between one domain and another, but you could presumably pyramid a whole series of factor analyses until ultimately a common dimensionality of behavior emerged, relating all the terminologies of the behavioral sciences. However, it may be more rapid and effective simply to translate these terms into the dimensions of the natural sciences. This may be true, first, because scientists have had a good deal of experience with these particular modes of measurement. Second, because use of such dimensions permits quantitative comparisons between the actions of non-living systems and the behavior of living ones. And, third, because no one is particularly ego involved with these dimensions. This is not true of most terminological systems and scaling techniques in the social sciences that often are emotionally toned for representatives of various schools or viewpoints.

Even though many of the problems of such a translation to CGS units have not yet been worked through, a few examples can be given of how some behavioral traits can be measured in such units. A phlegmatic person can, of course, be recognized by his usual rate of motion in space; so can a hyperkinetic or manic patient. The trait of "initiative" may be viewed as originating motion in space, and "passivity" as waiting to be moved. When one individual directs more initiative toward a second person than the latter does toward the former, the first is "dominant" and the second "submissive."

These and many other behavioral traits, however, are frequently evidenced in words and gestures. On first thought, such symbolic behavior might seem unamenable to description in u-units. What sorts of equilibrations in what subsystems can explain the intricate, subtle intonations, speech, and acts of a civilized man?

Let us assume that memories of past experiences are stored in the brain as traces, whose nature we do not exactly understand but which we may call "information analogues." These analogues are combined in the nervous system, perhaps in much the same way as electronic computers handle information. When this process is complete, a specific behavioral output is elicited, but this is a resultant act of a more complex process than a simple reduction of strain in a subsystem. Of course the molecular activities which transfer information analogues in the brain at cellular and subcellular levels follow the natural laws of systems just as do electronic calculating machines. Therefore decision-making and other "higher mental processes" ultimately are explainable in terms of general behavior systems theory.

Equifinality

The concept of *equifinality* advanced by Bertalanffy explains purposive behavior in animals and men more effectively than vitalistic assumptions, and also more consistently with our general theoretical framework.[3] Teleological notions of goal striving are not necessary if we accept this principle. It operates only in open systems which circumvent the effects of the second thermodynamics law of entropy, since materials necessary to create and maintain a certain organization may be selected from the input and surplus products or wastes be rejected in the output. For example, consider a chemical system made up of two solutions, silver nitrate and hydrochloric acid, which when combined precipitate silver chloride. If an indefinitely large input of both substances is available and output is possible for this system, then the rate of precipitation will become constant at a specific equilibrium level. Moreover, this rate will not depend on the amounts of silver nitrate and hydrochloric acid present at the beginning of the experiment. There could be either a dram or 100 gallons of each. Rather, it depends on the solubility characteristics of the components (H^+, Cl^-, Ag^+, and NO_3^-). This reaction, then, looks as if it always strives teleologically toward the same goal—that is a specific rate of precipitation—no matter whether the system at first was poor or rich in silver nitrate or hydrochloric acid. Actually, however, it is clear that this "equifinal" result is determined by the nature of the constituents of the system.

We contend that this is true of all behaving systems. Whether an infant be three months premature and weigh two pounds or be born of a diabetic mother and so weigh fifteen pounds, he will ordinarily be of normal weight a few months later. The small one will grow more rapidly than an average baby and the big one less rapidly.

3. L. von Bertalanffy, "The Theory of Open Physics and Biology," *Science,* CXI (1950), 23–28.

This may appear like vitalistic teleology, but it can be explained simply by stating that the constituents of human subsystems determine what their equilibrium levels shall be. Many of these together, in turn, fix the size of the child.

So the "goals" which "impel" the rat to run the maze, the woman to marry, and the candidate to file for public office can be interpreted as internal strains which elicit efforts to achieve inputs of energy and information that will reduce the strains toward an equilibrium point. And no matter whether he is nurtured at court to become Pharaoh or cast away in the bulrushes, a man will search until he finds an environment with inputs capable of diminishing the particular drives within him—strains established by his genetic inputs as modified by later inputs of energy and information, by learning or acculturation.

Formal Identities

Implied throughout the above discussion is the principle that similar aspects of systems follow similar laws. Examples are propositions, to be considered in detail later, such as the statement that the growth of all systems in time is comparable within certain ranges. Or that transmissions across all boundaries involve step functions. Or that spatial spread of state throughout all systems follows comparable laws. Our attempt is to see how much of all behavior we can explain by a series of such formal identities, recognizing of course the differences or disanalogies which exist between one behaving system and another.

We must remain continuously alert to the danger of neglecting these differences, a danger which arises from the fact that a chief goal of any general theory is to recognize, describe, and measure pervasive similarities, formal identities, or analogies.

The analogy has often suffered vilification from scientists and philosophers. Still, if it is carefully employed, it is scientifically useful. Perhaps the phrase "formal identity" is more acceptable, but that term is essentially equivalent to some senses of "analogy." As clear a definition of "analogy" as any is that of John Stuart Mill, who used it as an adjective in the phrase "analogical reasoning," whose sense he formulated as follows: "Two things resemble each other in one or more respects: a certain proposition is true of the one, therefore it is true of the other. . . . Every resemblance which can be shown to exist affords ground for expecting an indefinite number of other resemblances."[4] Currently there are several ways the term "analogy" is used. One is as a statement of the subjective experience of an observer that two or more phenomena appear similar to him or arouse in him similar feelings. This is a statement about his private experience, and as such it is irrelevant for operational science. To some persons it is a purely literary term like "metaphor" or "simile," which is frequently modified by the slighting adverb "mere" and which is of artistic value to the writers of poetry and prose, but not to scientists. Another usage is a logical one, referring to a form of inference whereby it is argued that, if two or more things are similar in some respects, they will probably be similar in others, though not necessarily all others. It is apparent that there is no general agreement about the word among different disciplines. "Analogy," for example, means one thing specific to logicians and something quite different but equally specific to biologists.

Any general scientific use of the word should indicate that analogies or formal identities are the bases of all inductions which underlie scientific laws. The perception of similarity among phenomena must precede their classification. Then one can generalize, predicting that if some members of a class of phenomena are observed to operate in a certain way, so will the other members of that population, even though they have not been observed. So recognition of analogy or formal identity underlies all generalization and all science.

In modern electromechanical analogue computers one can find a good example of the scientific use of quantitative analogies or formal identities. An analogue computer[5] employs differing amounts of some physical quantity to match similarly differing amounts of some measurement. For example, in the differential analyzer designed by Vannevar Bush and finished at the Massachusetts Institute of Technology in 1942, a small wheel presses on a large disk, which is supported on a vertical axle running through a block. This block can be moved back and forth in a horizontal direction by turning a long

4. J. S. Mill, *A System of Logic* (New York: Harper & Bros., 1874), pp. 393–94.

5. E. C. Berkeley, *Giant Brains, or Machines That Think* (New York: John Wiley & Sons, 1949).

screw. In the operation of the analogue computer, one turn of the screw represents a certain amount of one variable in a differential equation. One turn of the vertical axle represents a certain amount of another variable. And the resultant turn of the small wheel riding on the disk represents, turn by turn, a third unknown variable in the equation. For example, if the screw represents the speed at which a train travels and the disk measures the time, then the small wheel might measure the distance traveled. Such a mechanism can successfully solve differential equations, even though the motions of the various parts have only analogous relationships to the variables involved. Indeed, this analogous operation represents one of the most successful—if not the most successful—ways now known to solve many differential equations. Such an analogue is similar to a physical model, and operations carried out on such a model can accurately quantify aspects of some comparable phenomenon of the real world.

Throughout this article the word "system" used without modifiers refers to "real" systems which exist in the veridical world of space-time co-ordinates. They should therefore be distinguished from formal or "conceptual" systems, which are mathematical or logical in character. The latter can, but do not always, describe such real systems. A formal identity between two conceptual systems is an "isomorphy." A formal identity between two real systems is a "homology"—a common biological concept. (A special case of homology is a formal identity between an inanimate and an animate system, like Lillie's iron-wire homology of neural conduction or Ashby's homeostat.)[6] And, finally, the term "model" may well be reserved for a formal identity between a conceptual system and a real system, although it is sometimes used also for homologies like Lillie's.

Generalization, or the use of analogy in the social sciences, has often bogged down in semantic difficulties. This had led to unnecessary disagreements between generalists and those concerned primarily with the special case. For example, Freud was impressed with the similarities between a number of related types of experiences which he included under his conception "sexuality." He recognized the similarity between physiological sexual gratification, on the one hand, sensual satisfaction from art, music, and other sensory

6. W. R. Ashby, *Design for a Brain* (New York: John Wiley & Sons, 1952).

experiences, and feelings of love and affection. In stressing these similarities in order to make a generalization, he at times neglected the differences between them, although he undoubtedly recognized them and would have acknowledged them immediately if they had been pointed out. There are theorists like Freud, concerned with making broad generalizations among dissimilar phenomena, in every discipline.

On the other hand, in every field we find persons who are concerned with a specific case, whether it be a clinical study of a specific individual or a complete analysis of all the characteristics of the culture of a single tribe on a Pacific island. They tend to emphasize the differences between the phenomenon they study and other phenomena. However, if similarities between their special case and other such cases were called to their attention, they would be willing to recognize them.

In mathematics the relation between similarity and disparity, between formal identity and individual difference, between analogy and disanalogy, can be easily made clear. The similarity is described by a general function, like $ax + by = cz$. The differences are indicated by constants written into the same equation or mathematical sentence, like $3x + 7y = 6.4z$, which is different from $7x + 8.5y = 17z$.

In prose, which is the usual language of the social sciences, conveyance of such ideas is more difficult. It is ordinarily inconvenient —though possible—to construct a sentence which has as its combined subject both a similarity and a difference, both preceding the main verb. Not accustomed to such cumbersome linguistic usage, we commonly make a straight assertion of either the similarity or the difference, which results in a false bifurcation we do not intend, and we neglect the opposite consideration which we would readily admit to be true. We often proceed to the logical and emotional fallacy of committing ourselves to the importance of one and neglecting the other, and so arise many of the schoolistic battles in the social sciences.

Between any two phenomena there is an analogy, and between any two phenomena there is also a disanalogy. We hope to develop a theory in which both are recognized, the analogies by general functions and the disanalogies by constants.

Table 1 illustrates the general paradigm of how we intend to proceed. The first vertical column under "Propositions" represents one formal identity, the growth function, which within certain ranges is an exponential curve. This may be observed at all levels of behaving systems—cell, organ, individual, group, and society—and perhaps in some aspects of non-living systems like electronic circuits. The next column represents the formal identity of boundary functions, which, as will be explained later, appear to be step functions. The third column represents a diffusion proposition concern-

TABLE 1

GENERAL PARADIGM OF BEHAVIOR THEORY PROPOSITIONS

SYSTEM LEVEL	UNIT	PROPOSITIONS		
		Growth Function	Boundary Function	Diffusion Function
Cell	μ			
Organ	mm.			
Individual	cm.			
Group	m.			
Society	km.			
Electronic Circuit	From μ to km.			

ing spread of states in space. So we might go on for many propositions which are true of all systems.

On the other hand, the constants differ for each level. Growth for the cell is most conveniently measured in micra; for the organ in millimeters; for the individual in centimeters; for the group in meters; and for the society in kilometers. Similar spatial constants would at each level apply to diffusion rates, etc.

There are also other constants for different types of systems according to the materials of which they are constituted, their densities, and many other factors. There is, then, a systematic "horizontal" relationship among constants of the systems described in Table 1 which represents the disanalogy between levels, just as there is a systematic "vertical" relationship within columns, representing the analogies. The ultimate problem of predicting behavior is to learn what are the quantitative characteristics of the general laws, on the one hand, and the individual differences, on the other, using both in a specific prediction. Such is the basic strategy of the program for empirical testing of general behavior systems theory.

This is a specific method. It does not deal in vague, poetic, or metaphorical similarities between systems which are not operationally demonstrable, like "growth" in size and "growth" in tactfulness. Nor does it simply identify comparable processes in different systems, as, for example, storage of information in electronic memories; traces in the nervous system; secretarial minutes of committees; and libraries of a nation. But this method does make predictions of behavior by transferring a set of assumptions, definitions, and theorems from one class of behaving systems to another, at the same time making allowance for the distinctive specific characteristics of the systems being considered. This does not differ from the classical method of the natural sciences, from the method of Newton and many others. Newton made a real contribution in developing his laws so that they explained at once the fall of an apple from a tree, the flowing of the tides, and the revolution of the earth, even though these are vastly dissimilar phenomena. Yet such generalization can be effective only when these analogies or formal identities are recognized, even though no proper scientist may blind himself to the fact that there are also always disanalogies.

A Critique of Analogy

What have been the common sources of dissatisfaction with analogy in science?

We have already referred to a frequent basis for such discontent —the confusion of poetical or metaphorical analogy with comparisons which are useful scientifically. Suppose that one says, "He has a heart of gold." Suppose one adds, "Gold is heavy." Syllogistic logic then concludes, "Therefore his heart is heavy." But this makes no operational sense. Science cannot be made from logical operations upon metaphors.

Another cause for dissatisfaction with analogy, already mentioned, is the tendency of those who generalize through analogies to neglect the obvious disanalogies. An example of this is Spiru C.

Haret's book *Mécanique sociale,* which appeared in 1910 and in which the author based a theory of sociology on the attraction of people to each other precisely according to the inverse square law of gravitation.[7] It is possible that unself-critical recognition of similarities is appropriate in the initial stages of scholarly inquiry, but no scientific task can be completed until the degree of comparability is precisely determined, as well as the degree and forms of the dissimilarities. It is an interesting idea, relevant to some aspects of general behavior systems theory, that the development of societies historically has been in some ways similar to biological evolution. But a vast amount of effort has been wasted in the last seventy-five years by theorists who have compared the two without being precisely clear about the facts of both biological evolution and social process and also without being accurate concerning the details of how they are similar and how they differ.

Much of the criticism of analogy in behavioral science has been directed particularly at formal models like the ones we expect to incorporate into general behavior systems theory. One such argument is that models simply describe what was already known and do not reveal anything new. Certainly this is not true of all models, as, for instance, those concerning the learning process, which have led to the discovery of many new facts. This criticism is apt only when applied to poor models. It has been clearly shown that models are useful in natural science if they are properly employed. There is no a priori reason why this should not also be true in the behavioral sciences.

One often hears the comment that formal models are useful only to a limited degree in the social sciences because many of the data of those areas are not quantifiable. It may appear that such behavioral phenomena as foreign relations and politics or cultural customs and content of language are difficult to measure. But important aspects of such behavior can at least be rank ordered. If cardinal numbers cannot be used, ordinal numbers can, and this has been the first entrance into measurement of other young, complex sciences.

There is truth in the critique that the value of formal models is sometimes sharply restricted because inappropriate parameters are chosen, and consequently the relevant variables in the situation be-

7. S. C. Haret, *Mécanique sociale* (Paris: Gauthier-Villars, 1910).

ing analyzed are not made apparent. This may happen if model-builders are not intimately acquainted with social or behavioral phenomena. This criticism applies to poor models and not to all models. If appropriate parameters are chosen, the model can be progressively modified to approximate more and more closely to the real system. If model-builders are sufficiently informed about the phenomena that they select the proper dimensions, they can throw much light on the nature of the process they are studying.

It is sometimes said that, because of the many variables, it is more difficult to use formal models in the behavioral than in other sciences. But models have been used to study complex, multivariant problems in the physical and biological sciences. Continually techniques are being developed to deal with such problems, including the giant electronic computers which can handle a previously unthinkable order of magnitude of variables. Precise application of a model, also, may reveal certain variables to be irrelevant which we otherwise might have considered. This can simplify the problem.

Another criticism is that models are always in error, never being precisely correct. It is hard to say how correct a model must be to be scientifically useful. The answer is that there is probably no correct model, but the goal is to find one which will explain the largest number of known facts. As further empirical data are collected and more thinking goes on, models usually are rejected and more satisfactory ones substituted. The purpose of the scientific process is to improve the goodness of fit of the model to the empirical data, that is, its predictive power. Ordinarily this is a long process of making successively better approximations. Actually models can describe complex phenomena like the social structure of a community more economically, precisely, and fully than most verbal descriptions. In addition, they can suggest new variables or relationships to investigate. From models explicit predictions can be made, whereas in the past social scientists have typically made very loose predictions if they have made them at all. Furthermore, it is possible to calculate the error of the outcome of a prediction, which has not been a common social science method.

Another criticism often made of the use of models is that, if you find several sorts of behavior which can be described by the same model, you have shown nothing necessarily valuable. It may be simple coincidence if you discover that the rate at which a snowball forms on rolling downhill, the rate at which a new political party picks up members, and the rate at which an audience enters a theater are similar quantitative functions. So what? The answer to this is of basic significance for general behavior systems theory. If the comparable functions are for processes which by other criteria have similar status in different systems, and if the general or "vertical" functions (cf. Table 1) in specific systems have "horizontal" constants identical to or of known relationship to constants determined for other general functions for that system, the observations have importance and are much more than coincidence.

It is sometimes said that in the social sciences, with the exception of economics and psychology, no formal models have been developed which can be helpfully applied to social phenomena. This is not a criticism of models, as has been implied. When relevant basic assumptions are made and proper variables are selected, there is no reason why all social phenomena cannot be profitably analyzed by formal models.

Some have found fault in formal models because assumptions must be made before a model can be built. Merely adding assumptions, they contend, does not advance behavioral science. One can reply that this does not differ from the scientific method of the physical sciences. Assumptions are tested by each step of application of any model. As experiment after experiment is performed which checks the model, assumptions get more and more support, or else the assumptions or other aspects of the model are altered to include new parameters or variables, in order to predict the phenomena more accurately. This is more productive than a traditional procedure in social science, which has been to build assumption upon assumption in a complex theoretical structure, without being certain that they refer to important facts and without constantly testing them.

It is said that formal models in the behavioral sciences suffer by being caricatures of human beings, seeming to have nothing about them like the warm reality of human life. So models of the learning process seem to have little in common with the way children pick up facts in school. The only reply to this is that you cannot judge a model in terms of such appearances, but rather by its effectiveness in explaining and predicting. To the physicist, the granitic Rock of Gibraltar, for instance, is just a mass of seething subatomic particles.

To some thoughtful persons it appears that indicating similarities between either formal models or real systems, on the one hand, and man's behavior, on the other, can never fathom the complexities and richness of human experience. Others recognize that we ordinarily lose ability to observe objectively as the subject matter becomes more and more like ourselves. Freud realized the scientific need to allow for this effect, which in the psychoanalytic relationship he labeled "countertransference." Few antivivisectionists strive to prevent cruelty to bread molds and amoebae, but many are concerned for the welfare of cats and dogs. An earthquake on a Mediterranean isle will disturb us more than the disappearance of a moon of Jupiter, even though the latter phenomenon is much vaster. The question is whether our ego involvement with ourselves, other humans, and organisms like us does not prevent us from recognizing otherwise obvious similarities between us and other behaving or acting systems in the universe.

One final criticism can be made of naïve formal models which do not distinguish between energy transmission and information transmission or uncoded and coded behavior. This is a critique of poor models and not of all models. It is usually unproductive to compare a physical model not involving information transfer—like the oscillations of a pendulum—with a behavioral phenomenon which involves information transfer and highly symbolic components—like the swings of business cycles. Formal identities between various sorts of systems are valuable only if they make this distinction. Persons eager to advance rapidly our understanding of behavior at times manifest their impatience by hurriedly taking a model from physics or biology and applying it to human behavior. This commonly leads to unjustifiable oversimplification, particularly because information transfer is a much more significant aspect of group and social behavior than it is of physical action or biological function.

Electronic Models

Since we are concerned with quantitative formal identities among various kinds of systems, it is natural that we should be interested not only in formal models of behavior but also in homologies with electronic systems. It may someday be possible to develop a comparative psychology or sociology dealing not with animals but with electronic models. These are in some ways less adequate than animals, in that they do not have some characteristics of life inherent in protoplasm. But they are better in other ways. Greater precision is possible in quantifying their actions. Also one can manipulate their parts and alter any of their circuits quantitatively by electronic "surgery," without danger of destroying them.

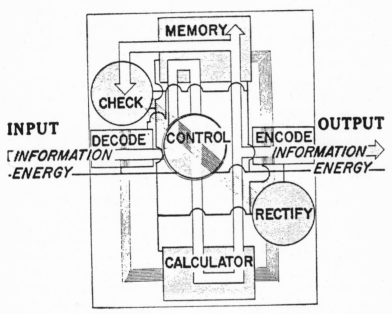

Fig. 1.—Diagram of a typical electronic computer

The modern giant electronic computers are open systems with significantly large magnitudes of inputs and outputs. Consequently, their action is in many interesting ways like living behavior. Figure 1 depicts the chief subsystems typical of such a computer. It has two sorts of input: input of energy (the line voltage which operates the machine) and input of information (a teletype tape which conveys the coded problem into the decoding subsystem of the machine). Coded data and instructions are decoded and fed electronically through the control to the memory. The control then, as directed, takes the appropriate information electronically out of the memory and puts it into an electronic calculator which manipulates voltages or other analogues of numbers, adding or subtracting (or carrying out more complex mathematical operations, all of which are derivatives of addition or subtraction). The subtotals, and finally the totals, are returned to the memory, the ultimate answers then being coded in the encoder subsystem for information output on a teletype tape or by a typewriter.

Some of these electronic devices contain internal monitoring or checking circuits, not unlike human proprioceptor or pain pathways, which transmit a "squeal signal" whenever anything goes wrong in any of the subsystems. In fact, some electronics systems can perform automatic repairing functions, replacing units or rectifying circuits when the "squeal'" indicates they are worn out or operating improperly.

In individual animals and human beings these same processes occur. There is sensory input at the boundary of the system as well as energy input, like intake of food, sunlight, water, and so forth. You also find the decoder (whatever the subsystem be that interprets speech and gesture); the memory; the internal communication system; the internal motor system; the association areas; the executive, decision-maker, or "calculator" which determines the outcome; and the output, either coded or uncoded. There are also pain or proprioception "checking" circuits, and repair or rectification mechanisms. At the level of the small group, you again find these functions —the secretary's written minutes representing one sort of memory; the chairman representing the control; and so on. Similarly in a society there are intelligence services providing information from outside; import agencies bringing in material supplies; an executive in control; an army and diplomats to provide output; and internal communication and transport services. A first step in comparing these various sorts of systems is to recognize their comparable functions. But to obtain greatest profit from the comparison, we must press further and state propositions about them which are quantifiable and testable.

Propositions

Several dozen specific theorems or propositions, each empirically testable at the levels of cell, organ, individual, small group, and society—often for both energy and information exchange—have been derived by us or related by us to our general theoretical framework. In some cases it is clear that electronic systems can be built to which they would also apply. The testing of these propositions would involve empirical research to discover exactly under what conditions and within what ranges they do or do not apply, and what are the related variables which, when altered, change the character of the general function. Only a few of these propositions can be mentioned here.

Proposition 1. The rate of growth of a system in a medium which has an essentially unrestricted amount of energy available for input is—within certain ranges—exponential. How this proposition can be tested at various levels is suggested in Table 2. The formal identities mentioned in this table are assumed to exist because of a general characteristic of all behaving systems or perhaps of all systems. An exponential growth curve appears in any expansion process in a system in which further subsystems are constantly being produced which are capable of expanding themselves or dividing into or producing other subsystems. If the newly produced subsystems could not also expand or reproduce, the total function would more likely be linear than exponential. Information transfer will probably increase exponentially in growing systems for one (or a combination) of several reasons: either (*a*) there are more units, multiplying exponentially, to transmit information; or (*b*) there are more combinations of interaction possible; or (*c*) if information transmission · facilitates drive reduction or equilibration among the subsystems, there is exponentially more of this sort of interaction to occur. Of course a whole program of research is required to discover which, if any, of these alternatives is correct.

There are probably several shapes of exponential growth curves, differing in different classes of systems. It is also apparent that the constants involved in growth functions will differ from level to level of systems. (Cells, as we have said, grow in micra and societies in kilometers.) The growing period of cells is measured in hours and of societies in decades. Furthermore, there are species differences: hamsters grow faster than dogs. All these other considerations must be weighed in making a prediction about growth of a system.

The original proposition states that an essentially unrestricted input of energy is required if the growth curve is to be exponential. This is a limiting condition which must be stated, because, of course, malnourished ova, children, or societies do not grow at the

TABLE 2

PROPOSITION 1: THE GROWTH PROPOSITION

System	Energy Transfer	Information Transfer
Cell........	Measure the rate of growth of a yeast cell or amoeba under the microscope	None thought of
Organ......	Measure by repeated X-ray the rate of growth of a bone or other organ in the embryo	Measure by electrodes implanted in the brain of an embryo the rate of increase of impulse transmission with maturation
Individual..	Measure the volumes of embryos of different ages and plot the volumes against the ages	A broad extension of the above to the whole nervous system, together with measurement of the rate of increase of hormonal secretion, will indicate the general magnitude of increase of total information transmission in the individual
Group......	Measure the rate at which a crowd gathers around the goal posts to tear them down after a big football game (or around the President when he appears unexpectedly on a county courthouse lawn; or around a sudden street fist fight)	Measure in words per minute the rate at which a group of eight strangers in a European railway train compartment begin to interact
Society.....	Collect or analyze population growth figures to test the validity of Malthus' law	This is extremely difficult to measure because the experimental method cannot be used, and societies do not develop *de novo*, but from fragments of former civilizations. The historical method is difficult to use here because of the great differences of communication methods in different eras. Perhaps the rate of increase of message transmission across a boundary, after the end of a civil war or of the partition of a country, could be measured

same rate as those with plenty of food. Furthermore, there appear in most living systems to be mechanisms that slow growth after a period, so that this proposition obviously applies only within certain ranges. The nature of these limiting mechanisms is an intriguing question for study.

We have discussed this first proposition at a length which we cannot devote to the others. It is apparent that, while there is a rationale behind the proposition, it might be disproved at any or all levels. If it is valid, it can be valid for various reasons. The explanations may even be different at various levels, or for energy and information transmissions. But we believe it most likely that an unavoidable characteristic of all systems in space-time accounts for the formal identity we have pointed out. Only an extensive set of integrated empirical studies can reveal the facts about even this single proposition.

Let us turn, more briefly, to other propositions, any one of which raises similar complex issues and implies a major research program for its confirmation or disproof.

Proposition 2. Greater energy is required for a transmission across a boundary than for a transmission in the suprasystem immediately outside a boundary or in the system immediately inside it. Step functions, whose importance for behavior is outlined by Ashby, are characteristic of transmission across boundaries.[8] Neurophysiological and psychophysical threshold phenomena commonly appear to be functions of this type. At the level of the cell, more pressure is necessary to rupture the membrane than to move mechanically in the tissue fluids outside or the cytoplasm inside. More pressure is necessary to rupture a spleen or liver than to move through the space outside the capsule of such an organ, or inside it. As we have noted, there is much work concerning thresholds for the individual. Special output of effort is necessary to join a group like a fraternity or country club, as well as to pass through customs and immigration across a border into the society of a new country. This extra physical effort or symbolic activity at boundaries can easily be measured to test this proposition.

Proposition 3. Spread of energy or information throughout systems is quantitatively comparable. After a transmission crosses a boundary into a system, it ordinarily diffuses. Rapoport has written moderately complex probability equations describing the spread of excitation in a "random net," originally conceived as a net of inter-

8. *Op. cit.*

connected neurons.[9] Later the same type of equation was found applicable to the spread of epidemics and to the spread of information or rumors in a group or society.

Proposition 4. There is always a constant systematic distortion— or, better, alteration—between input of energy or information into a system and output from that system. Manuals issued by the manufacturers indicate the input-output "distortion characteristics" of vacuum tubes. The distortion can be determined for any electronic system, like an amplifier. A comparable alteration occurs when glucose enters a cell and lactic acid comes out. Sound frequencies pass through the cochlea of the ear and come out in volleys on the eighth nerve. A Rorschach card is an identical stimulus for many patients, but the characteristic distortions of each one result in different responses from each patient. Communication between one person and another inevitably results in distortion because these individuals are not coded identically, and for other reasons. This is often illustrated in the old parlor game when one person whispers a story to his neighbor on his right, and he to his neighbor on the right, and so on around a circle. When it gets back to the originator, it is nearly always greatly altered. Likewise distortion may occur in the passage of information from one group to another, say, when a report of the Bureau of Labor Statistics is interpreted first by the CIO and then by the NAM. Distortion also appears in the crossing of such massive barriers between cultures as the Iron Curtain.

Such alterations may be explained by another, interrelated, proposition:

Proposition 5. The distortion of a system is the sum of the effects of processes which subtract from the input to reduce strains in subsystems or add to the output to reduce such strains. Though ultimately all our propositions should presumably interdigitate to form the organized conceptual structure of general behavior systems theory, at present their precise interrelationships usually are not clear. Propositions 4 and 5 are exceptions, however, for the latter suggests a measurable explanation for the process mentioned in the former. Such alteration or distortion can be explained by the fact

9. A. Rapoport, *Some Mathematical Models of the Spread of Information through a Population* (Behavioral Sciences Publication, No. 1 [Chicago, 1953]), pp. 19–23.

that every system takes out of its input essentials for the maintenance of its own equilibrium, rejecting all substances that do not contribute to that steady state. This alters the output. Particular systems distort some categories of input more than they do others, because of their specific equilibratory needs. In human beings we find certain alterations in sense organs; others in perceptual areas; others in association areas; others in motor areas; and so on. The difference between the energy input which we call a "stimulus" and the output which we term a "response" is the sum of all these changes.

Proposition 6. When variables in a system return to equilibrium after stress, the rate of return and the strength of the restorative forces are stronger than a linear function of the amount of displacement from the equilibrium point. To test this statement, one could set up a number of experimental conditions in which the equilibrium range of a variable in a behaving system could be determined. Stimuli could then be applied to this system to disturb it a specified amount away from this point of equilibrium. The rate at which it returned to equilibrium and the strength of the forces restoring it could be measured and compared with similar measurements when there were greater or lesser degrees of disturbance from equilibrium. The characteristics of the curves for different sorts of behaving systems could then be compared quantitatively.

For example, the rate of motion and the amount of energy expended by an amoeba moving out of cold or hot fluids into fluids of comfortable temperature might be measured. Or similar studies might be made of amoebae moving out of acid or alkaline fluids to those of optimal pH.

At the level of the human individual, the rate of return to a position of balance and the amount of energy expended in return to it, after various amounts of displacement, could be measured. Similarly, the "firepower" of the defense employed by a player in a simplified chess game to re-establish the equilibrium of his pieces after it had been disturbed by losses of various categories of men could be measured. This would permit quantification of forces restoring equilibrium in a problem-solving situation.

At the level of social phenomena the strength of various degrees of disturbing influences on group activity could be calculated and measures made of the rate of return to equilibrium and strength of restorative forces employed by the group to establish balance. In various experimental balloting situations in small groups, votes could be used as quantitative indices of the strength of these equilibrating forces.

Disanalogies among various species of systems as to methods of returning to equilibrium depend upon the subsystems or mechanisms of defense available to them for maintaining their study states. Amoebae can swim out of an overly acid medium, but sessile forms cannot. The prisoner sings for the wings of a bird that would be able to fly the coop he is locked in. A man recognizes the threat

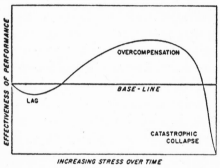

FIG. 2.—Representative curve of effectiveness of performance as stress is increased over a period of time.

in an approaching tornado and takes cover, but a child may not have learned about such storms and so may be killed. However, the existence of such disanalogies does not make the general proposition less applicable.

Proposition 7. Living systems respond to continuously increasing stress first by a lag in response, then by an overcompensatory response, and finally by catastrophic collapse of the system. Selye investigated the effects of varying degrees of many physiological stresses on the organism.[10] He has employed such stresses as extreme variation in temperature and intravenous injections of glucose and typhoid toxoid into animals. The charts of his data, of which Figure 2 is representative, show for each stress an initial dip in the curve in the direction of the final collapse, which is the alarm re-

10. H. Selye, *The Physiology and Pathology of Exposure to Stress: A Treatise Based on the Concepts of the General-Adaptation Syndrome and the Diseases of Adaptation* (Montreal: Acta, 1950).

action. It is followed by a rise of the curve above the level normally maintained by the organism, which constitutes a sort of overcompensation or overdefensiveness. As the stress is increased, more and more defenses are called into play, until finally no additional ones are available, and the system collapses suddenly into death.

We have collected data which suggest that coded or symbolic stresses like those in battle may well elicit response curves similar to those of Selye. While extreme stress always worsens performance, moderate stress can improve it above ordinary levels. One of the tests which shows such improvement is the crossing out of *C*'s randomly distributed in a field of *O*'s. However, the same stress increases microtrembling of the fingers, the same fingers used in crossing out *C*'s. It is thus clear that, while finger muscle performance worsens, compensatory defense mechanisms come into play, so that the total operation of crossing out *C*'s improves. This is an illustration of how certain subsystems may develop strain under stress but the whole system compensates for it.

All this conforms with Ashby's notion of a multistable or ultrastable system.[11] An analogy to such a system is an army cot made up of a number of wire links. Pressure on the central link will at first be compensated for by the central link alone; but, as pressure increases, the ring of immediately contiguous links will be called into play; then the next ring; and so on. In the end the cot can support 1,000 pounds on wires, none of which alone could carry 80 pounds without breaking.

Proposition 8. Systems which survive employ the least expensive defenses against stress first and increasingly more expensive ones later. In individual psychology we speak of the physiological or somatic drives, the needs for water, air, vitamins, proteins, and the like, and the psychogenic drives which are concerned essentially with the social environment, coded inputs. Either lack or excess of rate of input of either of these two sorts constitutes a stress, and the system must respond readily to defend itself against such stress if it is to maintain equilibrium. This equilibrium is not static, as when a ball rolled up an incline returns to its original position in a trough at the bottom, but is rather the dynamic interaction of forces in flux

11. *Op. cit.*

to maintain a steady state in a rapidly changing environment, like a salmon struggling up the Columbia River to spawn.

If a continuously increasing amount of acid is injected into a dog's veins, a number of mechanisms will be brought into play to defend or protect the steady pH of the blood from this stress. The first which appears to reach its maximal effectiveness will probably be overbreathing, which produces generalized alkalosis to compensate for the acidosis. Excretion of a more acid urine than usual and the "chloride shift" from blood plasma to red cells are other mechanisms which can aid in counteracting the stress and which probably will achieve their maximal effects later than overbreathing does. It is possible that those organisms which can survive longest under such stress are those which first mobilize the protective mechanisms that employ the most easily replaceable inputs (e.g., oxygen) and only under more extreme conditions use the mechanisms involving inputs not so easily replaceable from their environment. At any rate, this hypothesis can be experimentally tested.

A person's defense mechanisms to protect against coded, psychodynamic stresses are comparable to the physiological mechanisms and may ordinarily be mobilized in order of their expensiveness. For example, if a man is unable to solve a problem or achieve a goal, he may lower his level of aspiration and say, "Well, I'll try something simpler." This is relatively inexpensive. The next thing he may do is rationalize his behavior, saying, "I could have done it if I had had more time." This is a little more expensive, since it places him in a tactically difficult position. Someone might say, "All right, take all the time you need," and he would then be shown to be unable to do it. Repression, a yet more expensive defense, might be his next way of handling the stress if he is forced to continue working toward his goal. His "attention might turn to other things," but that would leave the unresolved strain within him, which some have said can cause psychosomatic symptoms—a serious consequence. Finally, to avoid the frustration of the unsolved problem constantly obtruding on him, he may deny the reality of his total input, and a psychotic state may result which can cut him off from close human contact and in other ways be extremely expensive to him.

Proposition 9. Systems which survive perform at an optimum efficiency for maximum power output, which is always less than maximum efficiency. This is a principle suggested by Odum and Pinkerton.[12] They apply it to living and non-living systems at several levels—weights on a pulley (Atwood's machine); water wheels which run grindstones; electric batteries which charge other batteries; metabolism; animal food capture; photosynthesis; a plant community; and a civilization. This principle applies to all systems the notion of efficiency from physics or economics, and the concepts of survival from evolutionary theory. It questions the traditional view that the most efficient system survives and suggests that this is true only if, on occasion, it can also put out maximum power. It also broadens natural selection theory to apply to all systems under stress in a changing suprasystem, from cells, organs, and individuals through groups like clubs and corporations to societies which, like Rome, can fall. Unless in a battle an animal can, by an "emergency reaction" like that described by Cannon, transfer blood flow temporarily from the gut to the extremities, he will fight less well, and blood in a cut will clot less effectively. This is directly related to survival. Also, if the cooks in an army under attack, as in the Battle of the Bulge, are not permitted to leave their stoves and pick up guns to aid in a maximum effort, the army may not survive. Throughout all these examples runs a single principle.

Proposition 10. When a system's negative feedback discontinues, its steady state vanishes, and at the same time its boundary disappears and the system terminates. At this moment it becomes part of a larger system which is its environment and at the same time divides into several subsystems. This hypothesis mentions two independent variables which can be measured separately. One is the degree of negative feedback or the steadiness of the equilibrium in the system; the other is the permeability of the boundary. If too much water enters a red cell, it will swell up and eventually rupture. It can be demonstrated physiologically that the osmotic equilibrium within the cells disappears at about the same time that the cell membrane ruptures. Separate molecules of the cells then become small systems in the much larger system of the circulating blood. A similar sequence occurs in physiological death. It may also occur in the breakdown of psychological defense mechanisms. Certainly a

12. H. T. Odum and R. C. Pinkerton, "Time's Speed Regulator," *American Scientist*, XLIII (1955), 331–43.

comparable process is seen when a committee dealing with a practical problem cannot agree. It finally dissolves, the members dispersing while the next larger organizational unit, which set up the committee, takes over the responsibility for settling the issue.

Proposition 11. The dimensionality of the output of a system is always less than the dimensionality of the input. This principle is derived by Platt from electronic amplifier theory.[13] Amplifiers are systems which increase the volume of a specific output, but along with amplification there is always selection or discrimination. For example, a high-fidelity phonograph amplifies only certain vibrations of the needle in the groove. It does not amplify the motion of the pickup arm, the light in the room, the temperature of the room, the pressure of the air, the line-voltage input, or many other variables in the input to the amplifier from its environment. Consequently, the dimensionality of its output involves fewer variables than its input. This is true of sense organs. It is also probably true of any individual, group, or society which makes decisions among options and follows one rather than another, for selection and amplification always go hand in hand.

Proposition 12. Decentralization of the maintenance of variables in equilibrium is always more expensive of energy than centralization, although it can increase utility (i.e., the rate of strain reduction). This is an example of the group of propositions that combines economic concepts with other behavioral notions.

Proposition 13. As decentralization increases, subsystems increasingly act without the benefit of information existing elsewhere in the system.

Proposition 14. The more subsystems there are in efficient systems, the more variables they can maintain in equilibrium, but there are also proportionately more subsystems whose destruction will result in collapse of the system.

Proposition 15. The equilibratory range of a system for a specific variable increases proportionately to the amount of storage of the input in the case of a lack strain along that variable, or spillage of the input in the case of an excess strain.

Proposition 16. When reduction of several strains is not possible simultaneously, the order in which they are reduced in systems

13. John R. Platt, personal communication.

which survive is from strongest to weakest, if the effort required for their reduction is identical.

Proposition 17. There is a range of optimal rates for development of coding. If it develops too rapidly, the system cannot properly equilibrate to the probable variations in input; if it develops too slowly, the system cannot profit adequately from past inputs. In other words, since the environment varies somewhat, two events may not always be associated tomorrow as they were yesterday. One-trial learning would lead to the rigid and maladaptive expectation that they would be. On the other hand, a system that never learns from past experience cannot adapt so well as one that does. The optimum learning rate for adaptive systems that survive is somewhere between these two.

Proposition 18. Up to a maximum, the more energy in a system devoted to information processing (as opposed to metabolic and motor activity), the more likely the system is to survive. In general, evolution appears to have resulted in the more complex species having more and more of their total cells devoted to information collection and processing (e.g., larger and larger nervous systems). No one has yet demonstrated a species which failed to survive because too much of its total mass was neural tissue.

Proposition 19. When one living species (the predator) feeds on another (the prey) in a given suprasystem and both species continue to survive, an oscillation of numbers of predators and prey occurs around an equilibrium point. This is the cat-and-rat farm situation, or the ecological problem of foxes and rabbits. As the foxes increase in number, they eat more rabbits. As the rabbits decrease in number, there is less food for the foxes, and so fewer of them survive. Then rabbits rapidly become more numerous. When cells or organs or individuals of other species compete for food, or oxygen, related phenomena are observed, of which this is a special case.

These, then, are a few illustrative propositions. Some may be correct; others may be wholly wrong; still others may require modification. To test all of them at all levels would be a vast empirical program. We intend to embark on it piecemeal, realizing that the waters are murky and full of shoals and that our vision is limited.

We shall try it, though, because of the alluring distant shore of an integrated behavior theory.

The Role of Subjectivity

All this discussion has dealt with publicly observable evidence. Some readers will have wondered about the place of subjective experience in all this. This traditional enigma is too important to avoid entirely—we cannot in day-to-day life deny our subjectivity. Since operational science yields no relevant facts, we can only state a belief about this issue—a belief that the most satisfactory solution seems to be Whitehead's. He contended that there is a subjective pole to all phenomena occurring in each subsystem and system.[14] In complex living systems we recognize this as experience. Its character in simple systems is unimaginable to us—less comprehensible than the "blooming, buzzing confusion" of James. In order to have experience continuous over a period of time, all the equilibratory mechanisms which add up to what we call the behavior of the individual, the group, or the society are essential. The concept of responsibility in the law—for example, in the law of torts which concerns damage of one's boundary or limitation of one's input or output, or the law of contracts and civil rights which guarantees coded inputs and outputs—depends on the morality that we may not destroy the equilibrium of other systems which we suspect are experiencing as we do. Social systems remain organized because they are capable of handling larger numbers of stresses and maintaining the experience of all their members more adequately than any individual can. It may be that ultimately, through having explained behavior scientifically, we can understand the processes which enable each of us to maintain his experiencing subjectivity. And, by application of our findings to living and non-living systems at various levels, we may be able to improve the external human and non-human conditions which provide satisfaction in experience. This ultimately is what makes the behavioral sciences important.

This article is an affirmative statement of a general position. Very many aspects of so vast a problem obviously cannot be considered in such short space, so in many ways it is incomplete. An effort is made to embrace core subject matter from several biological and

14. A. N. Whitehead, *Adventures of Ideas* (New York: Macmillan Co., 1933).

social sciences, including such notions as natural selection, efficiency, homeostasis, and other powerful concepts which appear to have cross-disciplinary implications. Obviously, no approach to a general theory of behavior at present could encompass even a small percentage of the phenomena which must be considered. The negative criticisms of this view could consume as much if not more space than this positive presentation. As we have observed earlier, models and theories are never perfect but simply approach the limit of correct explanation, and another theory that explains more than this will probably appear soon and should properly supplement this one. At the moment we have only a sketchy map which perhaps shows the route to a first approximation of a general behavior theory. Only a program of empirical testing such as we are now undertaking can demonstrate how much value, if any, it may have.

HERBERT A. SIMON[1] and ALLEN NEWELL

Models: Their Uses and Limitations

In contemporary usage the term "model" is, I think, simply a synonym for "theory." I am to speak, then, on "Theories: Their Uses and Limitations." This is a topic I can handle very briefly: the uses of theories are obvious, and their only limitations are that they are often bad theories.

However, the persons who arranged this meeting did *not* presumably intend that "model" should mean simply "theory." I suspect— but it is only a suspicion—that by "model" they meant "mathematical theory," and they intended to exhibit in this arena another instalment of the prolonged guerrilla warfare between mathematics and language.

With respect to these hostilities, I have two comments. First, I stand with J. Willard Gibbs: "Mathematics *is* a language"—and, to my ear, the most dulcet of languages. Second, I do not believe that the form in which we clothe our thoughts is a matter of indifference —or even of taste, as my last comment may seem to imply. It may be true that words without thoughts never to heaven go; but the converse is equally true: wordless thoughts, too, are earthbound. The matter has been put very well by Roget, the author of the *Thesaurus*. In the Introduction to his work he has this (as well as many other wise and even profound things) to say:

> The use of language is not confined to its being the medium through which we communicate our ideas to one another; it fulfills a no less important function as an *instrument of thought;* not being merely its vehicle, but giving it wings for flight. Metaphysicians are agreed that scarcely any of our intellectual operations could be carried on to any considerable extent, without the agency of words. None but those who are conversant with the philosophy of mental phenomena can be aware of the immense

1. Since most of the notions discussed here are by-products of my collaboration over the past several years with Allen Newell, I have asked him to permit me to present this paper as a joint product—which it is. For infelicities of form and manner, and for downright errors, I alone am responsible.

influence that is exercised by language in promoting the development of our ideas, in fixing them in the mind, and in detaining them for steady contemplation. Into every process of reasoning language enters as an essential element. Words are the instruments by which we form all our abstractions, by which we fashion and embody our ideas, and by which we are enabled to glide along a series of premises and conclusions with a rapidity so great as to leave in the memory no trace of the successive steps of the process; and we remain unconscious how much we owe to this potent auxiliary of the reasoning faculty.

If we interpret the term "word" literally, then Roget is probably wrong. But if he means that the form of our thought exercises a great control over the course of that thought, he is almost certainly correct.

To select a suitable language with which to wing our thoughts, we must understand what languages there are, and we must be able to compare them. In this paper I should like to discuss three main kinds of scientific languages or theories: the mathematical, the verbal, and the analogical. It will appear from our analysis that these three kinds of theory are really indistinguishable in their important *logical* characteristics; hence, that the choice among them must be based on certain *psychological* criteria. And since analogies, employed as theories, are somewhat less well understood than either verbal or mathematical theories, I shall devote the last part of the paper to two important current uses of analogies.

Before we can plunge into the comparison, however, we will need a clearer understanding of the nature of theory, and of these three types of theory in particular. The next two sections will be devoted to these preliminaries.

Models and the Modeled

It will be convenient for our purposes to define a theory simply as a set of statements or sentences. (They may, of course, be mathematical statements, or equations, instead of verbal statements.) It is important to observe that this definition refers to the form in which the propositions are clothed, that is, the actual explicit statements set forth. Thus, we distinguish the theory, so defined, from its *content*, to be defined next.

By the *content* (or logical content) of a theory I shall mean the totality of the empirical assertions that the theory makes, *explicitly or implicitly*, about the real world phenomena to which it refers.

That is, the content of a theory is comprised of all the assertions about the world, whether true or not, that are explicitly stated by the theory or that can logically be inferred from the statements of the theory.

Consider now some body of phenomena, and imagine that there is a theory whose content tells the truth, the whole truth, and nothing but the truth about these phenomena. By this I mean that any statement that is true of the phenomena is stated in or derivable from the theory and that any factual statement contained in or derivable from the theory is true of the phenomena. Then we may define the *content of the body of phenomena* as identical with the total content of this particular theory.

The particular theory I have just mentioned is, of course, non-existent for any actual body of phenomena. The theories that actually occur do not have the same content as the phenomena to which they refer. They do not tell the truth—or at least they do not tell the whole truth and nothing but the truth.

The most conspicuous inadequacy of theories is that they do not tell the whole truth; they have a very much smaller content than the phenomena. Borrowing a term from statistics, we may call these errors of omission "Type I errors." But I think it can be shown that almost all theories also err in the other direction—they say things that are not so, as well as failing to say things that are so. Their errors of commission we may call "Type II errors." To the extent that theories commit errors of Type II—asserting some things besides the truth—they have, of course, a larger total content than the phenomena.[2]

The notion of content that I have introduced relates to the *logical* properties of a theory—to the facts that can be extracted from it by applying the laws of logic. Of at least equal importance to the scientist is its *psychological* or available content—the empirical propositions that the scientist is in fact able to derive from it. One theory can have exactly the same logical content as another but be

2. The ideas discussed in this section have been developed in a somewhat different manner by W. Ross Ashby in his book, *An Introduction to Cybernetics*, in which he discusses the relations among theories and between theories and phenomena by use of the concepts of isomorphism and homomorphism. We are indebted to Dr. Ashby for making his work available to us in preliminary mimeographed form. The printed edition of his book is to appear shortly.

infinitely more valuable than the other if it is stated in such a way as to be easily manipulated, so that its logical content is actually (psychologically) available to the inquirer.

For example, one theory (a trivial one, but one that will illustrate the point) tells me that the number of years from the birth of Christ to the Hegira is DCXXII; and from the birth of Christ to the present, MCMLV. A second theory tells me that the former interval is 622 years; the latter interval, 1,955 years. From the second theory, I deduce readily that it is 1,333 years from the Hegira to the present; from the first theory I also deduce, but much less readily, that the interval from the Hegira to the present is MCCCXXXIII years.

The distinction between the logical and the psychological content of a theory helps us to understand Roget's assertion that language gives thought its wings. Man is not an omniscient logician; he is an information-processing system—and a very limited one, at that. The logical content of a theory is of use to him only to the extent that he can make that content explicit by manipulation of the theory as stated. All mathematics (and verbal logic, to the extent it is rigorous) is one grand tautology. The surprise that is occasioned by the Pythagorean theorem derives from the psychological properties of mathematics—from the new information obtained by processing the explicit statements of the mathematical theory—not from its logic.

Three Kinds of Theories

In the preceding section I have introduced the notion of the content of a theory and the important distinction between logical and psychological content (i.e., between what is inferrable "in principle" and what we can actually succeed in inferring). I have pointed out that theories can and do make errors of omission (Type I errors) and errors of commission (Type II errors). I should now like to characterize several types of theories in the light of these distinctions. I shall use as an example certain phenomena that are of central importance in economics: national income, investment, saving, consumption, and similar variables that occur in "macroeconomics." I will distinguish three kinds of theories:

1. *Verbal theories.*—An example of a statement in such a theory is: "Consumption increases linearly with income, but less than proportionately."

2. *Mathematical theories.*—The approximately corresponding statement in the mathematical theory is: "$C = a + bY; a > 0; 0 < b < 1$."

3. *Analogies.*—The idea that the flows of goods and money in an economy are somehow analogical to liquid flows is an old one. There now exists a hydraulic mechanism, the Moniac, designed in England and available in this country through Professor Abba Lerner of Roosevelt College, one part of which is so arranged that, when the level of the colored water in one tube is made to rise, the level in a second tube rises (*ceteris paribus*), but less than proportionately. I cannot "state" this theory here, since its statement is not in words but in water. All I can give is a verbal (or mathematical) theory of the Moniac, which is, in turn, a hydraulic theory of the economy.

The three types of theory I have just illustrated by an economic example could have been equally well illustrated by psychological or sociological examples. Corresponding to Guthrie's verbal learning theory we have Estes' mathematical counterpart, and a number of robots have been constructed by Shannon, Grey Walter, and others incorporating Pavlovian conditioning and associational learning.[3] Homans (*The Human Group*) has constructed a verbal theory of group behavior which I have mathematized. As far as I know, no electromechanical analogue has been constructed, but it would be extremely simple to make one if the task struck anyone's fancy.

Verbal, mathematical, and analogical theories represent, I think, the main kinds of theories there are, but it is of interest to consider a few special cases to see where these fit into the classification.

Geometrical theories appear at first glance to be mathematical theories. Thus, we can represent income and consumption as the abscissa and ordinate, respectively, of a graph, and represent the postulated relation by a straight line with a positive slope of less than 45 degrees cutting the ordinate above the origin. However, if we look at the matter a little more closely, we see that this geometrical theory is really a mechanical analogue of a mathematical theory, for we do not usually employ geometry in a rigorous axiomatic way but instead draw diagrams—which are, of course, actual

3. See Robert R. Bush and Frederick Mosteller, *Stochastic Models for Learning* (New York: John Wiley & Sons, 1955), and W. Grey Walter, *The Living Brain* (New York: W. W. Norton & Co., 1953).

physical objects in a space that we hope is approximately Euclidean. (For the benefit of non-economists, I should observe that most so-called "non-mathematical" economists are, in fact, mathematical economists who prefer arithmetical and geometrical analogues to algebra, calculus, and set theory. There are few verbal economists in the strict sense.)

Computing machines that have been programed to represent a particular theory constitute a slightly more complicated case.[4] In a so-called analogue computer there is generally a one-one correspondence between the circuits of the computer, on the one hand, and the equations of a mathematical theory of the phenomena, on the other. In the special case of a simulator there is a direct correspondence between the analogue and the phenomena. In addition to the Moniac, mentioned above, which can be considered a hydraulic simulator, Strotz and others have used electrical analogues to represent the theory of macroeconomics.[5]

In the case of the digital computer—of which most modern general-purpose electronic computers are examples—there is no direct correspondence between the computer circuits and particular features of the phenomena. First, a mathematical theory of the phenomena is constructed, and then the computer is programed to carry out the arithmetic computations called for in the mathematical theory. Thus, the computer is an analogue for the arithmetic process. *This is not, however, the only way of employing digital computing machines as theories*—an important point to which I shall return later.

Verbal and Mathematical Theories

We are now in a position to compare verbal and mathematical theories with respect both to their content and to the availability of that content to the theorist. At the very outset we are confronted with a paradox. It is usually argued that mathematics has certain logical advantages against which must be weighed its psychological disadvantages. A closer examination of the case shows that the truth is almost the exact opposite of this. In the arguments ordinarily

4. To program a computing machine is to instruct it as to what it is to do in sufficient detail (and in an appropriate language) so that it can execute its tasks.

5. See Arnold Tustin, *The Mechanism of Economic Systems* (Cambridge, Mass.: Harvard University Press, 1953).

used to compare the relative virtues of mathematics and words as languages, we find that the advantage claimed for mathematics is, in fact, largely psychological, while the advantage claimed for words is largely logical.

The mathematician is aware how difficult it is to squeeze more than an infinitesimal part of the logical content out of verbal theories, because of the awkwardness in their manipulation. On the other hand, the verbal theorist (assuming he knows enough mathematics to understand the issues) finds that the logical content of most mathematical theories is quite small compared with the logical content of verbal theories. I do not say that this is the only issue between the mathematician and the non-mathematician, but it is certainly one issue that is often stated explicitly.

Now, I am not a neutral in this particular dispute. I believe that the psychological advantage claimed by mathematics is real and vitally important and that the logical advantage claimed for words is often illusory. With respect to the psychological difference—the importance of ease of manipulation—my example of Roman and Arabic numerals will provide, perhaps, some food for thought.

The logical difference—the relative logical content of verbal and mathematical theories—requires additional comment. It can be verified, I think, by the examination of almost any verbal theorizing that makes claims of rigor that only a very small part of the logical content of the theory is or can be employed in the reasoning at any one time. It is almost impossible to handle more than two or three simultaneous relations in verbal logic. Hence verbal reasoning (i.e., manipulation of theories stated in verbal terms) is replete either with logical gaps, or with *ceteris paribus* assumptions, or with both. For this reason the potential advantage derivable from the rich logical content of verbal theories is almost entirely lost by their intractability. The incompatibility of the theory with the information-processing skills of the scientist makes most of this logical content inaccessible to him.

Let me illustrate. Suppose we wish to theorize about the lynx and rabbit population in Canada. Lynxes eat rabbits; hence, if the lynx population is very large relative to the rabbit population, the latter will presumably decrease. On the other hand, if the rabbit population is too small, the lynxes will have a hard time finding a square meal and will also decrease in number. Now I should like a verbal theorist to predict for me the outcome of this competition. Will the lynx population become extinct, will the rabbit population become extinct, or both? Or will both species increase in number? And, if a large number of squirrels is introduced (which lynxes also like to eat), will the rabbit population increase or decrease?

There is a perfectly good mathematical theory, due principally to Volterra and Lotka (*Elements of Physical Biology*), that answers all these questions in a definite manner. (Roughly, the answer is that under reasonable assumptions there will be cyclical fluctuations in both lynx and rabbit populations; neither will become extinct; and under most assumptions the introduction of squirrels will decrease the rabbit population.) This theory has also been fitted to the data and has been found to hold reasonably well.

Now, of course, the illustration I have used is biological and has nothing to do with social phenomena. But Lewis F. Richardson has produced a mathematical theory of armaments races that is closely analogous to the lynx-rabbit theory. And he has been able to show the conditions under which an armaments race is consistent with peace and the conditions under which it leads to war. Moreover, the theory has been tested, to a certain extent, against data.

Other examples can be supplied;[6] but I do not wish to appear more partisan than I feel. The construction of good theory is such an arduous task at best that it is foolish to tie our hands behind our backs by limiting the range of tools that we utilize.

Of all three types of tools—words, mathematics, and analogies—analogies are perhaps the least frequently used and certainly the most poorly understood. Instead of continuing a discussion of the more familiar verbal and mathematical theories, I should like to turn my attention to the problems and possibilities of making fruitful use of analogy in social science theory.

6. I invite comparison of my mathematical "Homans model" ("A Formal Theory of Interaction in Social Groups," *American Sociological Review*, April, 1952) with the verbal theorizing by Henry W. Riecken and George C. Homans on the same subject in the *Handbook of Social Psychology*, ed. Gardner Lindzey, Vol. II, chap. xxii. A similar comparison may be made between the model that Harold Guetzkow and I have constructed of Festinger's theories of social influence ("A Model of Short- and Long-Run Mechanisms Involved in Pressures toward Uniformity in Groups," *Psychological Review*, January, 1955), and the verbal theory of Festinger himself ("Interpersonal Communication in Small Groups," *Journal of Abnormal and Social Psychology*, January, 1951).

Analogy as Theory

Analogies are the object of considerable distrust. An important reason for this distrust is that there have been some prominent examples in the not-too-distant past of their gross misuse—for example, Spencer's analogy between society and an organism and his uncritical social Darwinism.

I believe that the usual reason given for distrusting analogies (as contrasted with other theories) refers to logical content: analogies cannot be depended on to tell "nothing but the truth," while theories, it is alleged, can. That is to say, theories may be lacking in content, and hence be guilty of making Type I errors; analogies, on the other hand, have a great deal of content that has no correspondence with the phenomena—their serious errors are of Type II.

It is undoubtedly true—and Spencer's theory is only one of many examples that could be cited—that analogies are particularly susceptible to Type II errors. *But I believe it can be shown that verbal and mathematical theories are also susceptible to such errors.* The exaggerated use of the concept of instinct, for example, that characterized one period in the history of psychology can be traced simply to difficulties in handling the nature-nurture distinction in a verbal theory. The tendency of Freudian theory to proliferate mental entities—the id, the ego, the superego—probably has something to do with the preference of our language for nouns over verbs.

Why should theories of all kinds make irrelevant statements—possess properties not shared by the situations they model? The reason is clearest in the case of electromechanical analogues. To operate at all, they have to obey electromechanical laws—they have to be made of something—and at a sufficiently microscopic level these laws will not mirror anything in the reality being pictured. If such analogies serve at all as theories of the phenomena, it is only at a sufficiently high level of aggregation.

A little reflection shows that the same is true of verbal and mathematical theories, but in a more subtle way. These theories must be fitted to a particular computing device—the human brain—and at a sufficiently microscopic level a theory will more closely mirror the neurological and psychological properties of that information-processing system than it will anything to be found in the outside world.

This was observed a long time ago by nominalistic philosophers, who noted that Aristotle's *Prior Analytics* bore a suspicious resemblance to Greek syntax. The same observation is the foundation of Kant's synthetic a priori and of modern phenomenology.

At this point you may wish to object. The theory, you will say, does not consist of the individual letters or words. It is the *meaning* of the statement or equation that contains the theory, not the mounds of ink or the neural circuits that are its physical embodiment.

Even if we were to change our definition of "theory" to agree, the same could then be said of the analogy. It would then not be the water and glass tubes of the Moniac that constituted the theory but rather the relations among variables that these exhibit. If propositions and equations live in the Platonic heaven of ideas, why cannot their earthly representatives be constructed of glass and water as well as of paper and ink?

The truth seems to be that we are accustomed to words and equations as analogies; consequently, we do not often mistake the paper and ink, or even the grammatical structure, for the meanings that are supposed to model the phenomena. Few of us are any longer convinced by the ontological argument—one of the classical Type II errors of verbal theory. Gradually over the centuries we have acquired the sophistication in handling words and equations that is essential to avoid errors of this kind.

We are not so accustomed to non-verbal analogies and particularly to electromechanical ones; hence, we do sometimes mistake the irrelevant properties of the analogy for parts of the theoretical model. But if analogies are intrinsically useful devices as vehicles of theory, this difficulty is certainly one we can learn to overcome.

In specific terms, the argument amounts to this: The content of the theory embodied in the Moniac is identical with the content of the theory embodied in the corresponding set of Keynesian equations or the corresponding set of verbal statements. All three are simplified aggregated theories of the economy, having virtually the same *logical* content. If we have a preference for one of these theories over the others, it must rest not on logical grounds but on information-processing considerations—the relative ease with which the theory can in fact be manipulated in order to extract from it the implicit logical content.

The relative power of words, equations, and computers to convey, psychologically, their logical content has to be determined case by case; and the answer, even in specific applications, may well depend on the time at which it is asked. For the ease with which a mathematical system or an electromechanical analogue can be manipulated will depend heavily upon the current state of the mathematical and computer arts, respectively. (For the last two thousand years no comparable progress has been made in the verbal art.)

I should like to devote the final portion of this paper to a discussion of the probable fruitfulness, as matters stand in the year 1955, of two analogical theories that have recently received considerable attention. These analogies present fresh and novel problems of methodology that should illuminate our general analysis. My first example will be the "natural" analogy—the organism analogy—that has been advanced by the proponents of general systems theory. My second example will be the digital computing machine as an analogy for human thought processes.

General Systems Theory: The Organism as Analogue

The premise that underlies the advocacy of "general systems theory" or "general behavioral systems theory" is that each of the classes of things designated a *system* is an analogy, in significant respects, of each of the other classes.[7] So an organism may be regarded as an analogue to a cell or to an organization, or vice versa. Our question is whether these analogies are likely to be useful, and whether some of the fallacies of earlier theorizing of this kind (e.g., Spencer) can be avoided.

First, let us specify the conditions of the problem. We suppose that there exists a theory, at some stage of development, for each of the classes of things we call "systems." There is a theory of cells, a theory of organisms, a theory of species (meaning by this term an organism and its descendants), a theory of groups, a theory of

7. James G. Miller, "Toward a General Theory for the Behavioral Sciences," *American Psychologist,* September, 1955.

organizations, and a theory of societies. Each of these theories may include verbal, mathematical, and even electromechanical components. Each theory has a definable logical content.

A general systems theory is feasible to the extent that these several theories, as they develop, have common content. This is obvious enough. If there are no statements about cells that are not true also (with appropriate changes in correspondences) of organizations, then a general theory that embraces both classes of systems is simply not feasible. Miller, in his paper at this session, mentions a number of propositions that apply, or might apply, to all classes of systems. As he points out, whether they do in fact apply is a question that has to be answered by empirical research.

But if a general systems theory were feasible, would it be useful? I think this is simply a question of economy of learning, specifically, a question of transfer of training. The relevant questions are these: (1) How easy or difficult is it to set up a correspondence between the elements of, say, an organism and the elements of an organization? How does the effort required compare with the conjectured common content of the two systems? (2) Has one or more of these bodies of theory evolved so much beyond the others that it would prove a cheap mode of discovery to borrow from the former in order to add to the latter?

On the whole, I suppose I am rather skeptical with respect to the first question and a bit more sanguine with respect to the second. This reaction probably reflects little more than my own habits of thought and my desire to appear a man of Aristotelian moderation. However that may be, I remain unconvinced that the common content of the several systems theories is sufficiently great to justify the investment of much effort in the construction of an elaborate formal structure.

Beyond my general doubts, my skepticism has a very specific basis. One of the analogies that general systems theory proposes to encompass is the human organism. The human organism contains as one of its parts the central nervous system, which appears to be a completely general computer capable of constructing any finite proof—hence of imitating any other computing program; hence of serving as analogue for *any* conceivable theory. (Technically, such a general-purpose computer is known as a Turing machine.)

The same thing may be said in another way. Because of the flexibility of the central nervous system, the human organism can in principle be programed to produce almost any physiologically possible output for almost any stimulus input. It seems unlikely that with this potential flexibility of behavior the analogy of this organism with a cell or even with an organism lacking such a central nervous system can have much content.

Having expressed these doubts as to how far the formal development of a general systems theory can be carried, I do not want to discourage the curiosity of the biologist who wishes to learn about social systems or the social scientist who wishes to study biology. It is probably useful for a scientist who wants to contribute to the theory of one of these systems to familiarize himself with the theories of the others. However incomplete, the analogy certainly has sufficient content to be of great heuristic value. I think I can cite a number of examples where this heuristic value has already been exploited in useful ways:

1. The lynx-rabbit cycle, already discussed, is a case in point. This biological theory was a major stimulus to Richardson's *Generalized Foreign Politics,* a theory of international competition; and it influenced also, directly or indirectly, Rashevsky's theories of social imitation and my own model of the Homans system.

2. W. Ross Ashby's theory of the central nervous system, set forth in his important book, *Design for a Brain,* might be regarded as a form of "neural Darwinism." Dr. Ashby has accomplished a transfer of the principle of natural selection from the theory of species to the theory of cerebral learning.

3. There is a broad class of frequency distributions, often encountered in biological and social data, that are highly skewed and may be regarded as the logarithmic counterparts of the normal, binomial, Poisson, and exponential distributions. The so-called Pareto income distribution is one instance; Fisher's log series distribution, which fits many biological "contagious" phenomena, is another; a third is the log-normal distribution; a fourth is a distribution, applicable for example to city sizes, that I have christened the "Yule distribution" in honor of the statistician who first provided it with a theory. The kinds of probability mechanisms that will generate distributions of these types and the reasons for their frequent occurrence in biology

and sociology are beginning to be pretty well understood and will broaden the base of analogy among these phenomena.[8]

4. A final example is provided by information theory, first developed to handle certain problems of coding messages for electrical transmission, which has recently found exciting applications in genetics—specifically in contributing toward an understanding of how genes transmit the characteristics of the organism.

You will note that all the examples I have cited are at a relatively concrete level. They have not involved the construction of a common theory so much as an imaginative use of analogy to suggest special theories. It is perhaps also worth observing that what is transferred in these examples is largely the mathematical frameworks of the theories and only to a slight extent the more special content. I do not believe that there is between Miller and me any difference in principle on this point; there is, perhaps, a difference in strategy and tactics—a difference in the importance we attach to the construction of a formal general systems theory.

The Electronic Digital Computer as Analogue

As my final illustration of the relation of analogues to theories, I should like to talk about the fantastic modern toys that have been called "giant brains." Two supposedly fatal objections have been raised against regarding these systems as "brains." The first is that the anatomical structure of the central nervous system is demonstrably quite unlike the wiring diagram of a digital computer. The second is that the computers allegedly cannot do any "thinking" beyond simple arithmetic and that, like clerks and schoolboys, they must be instructed in detail what arithmetic to do.

The first objection is misdirected, and the second is not correct. The first objection rests on the common misconception about the nature of analogies that we have already discussed at length. Although the circuitry of a modern computer is clearly a very poor analogue to the anatomy of the brain, it does not follow at all that this disqualifies the functioning of a programed computer from serving as an analogue to the processes of human thought.[9]

8. See "On a Class of Skew Distribution Functions," *Biometrika*, December, 1955.

9. See John von Neumann, "The General and Logical Theory of Automata," in Lloyd A. Jeffress (ed.), *Cerebral Mechanisms in Behavior* (New York: John Wiley & Sons, 1951).

The usefulness, if there is one, in employing a digital computer as a theory of human thought processes rests not on any supposed similarities of gross anatomy but on the fact that the computer is a Turing machine. It is a general-purpose device that, subject to limits on its speed and memory, can be programed to imitate the behavior of *any* other system—and, in particular, to imitate human thought. (Lest this statement depress my listeners, let me observe again that a human being is a Turing machine too. In fact, we can assert with considerable conviction that there is nothing a digital computer can do that a human being, given time, patience, and plenty of paper, cannot do also.)

Whether the computer will in fact prove a useful tool for the study of thought depends on whether it is powerful enough for the task within the limits established by time, memory size, and the complexities of programing it. The question, to put it briefly, is whether a computer can learn to play a reasonably good game of chess or to become a geometer at, say, the level of a high-school sophomore; and whether it can acquire and execute these skills using, at least qualitatively, the same tricks and devices that humans use.[10]

The proposal to program a computer to play a game is not new. As a matter of fact, several reasonably powerful checkers-playing programs have already been constructed for digital computers. But in previous attempts of this kind the objective has been to get the machine to play a good game and not to simulate human problem-solving processes. Hence, the rational man of game theory and statistical decision theory (an entirely mythical being) has been taken as the model, instead of the problem-solving organism known to psychologists.[11]

10. For an extensive discussion of the problem of programing a computer to learn chess see Allen Newell, "The Chess Machine: An Example of Dealing with a Complex Task by Adaptation," *Proceedings of the 1955 Western Joint Computer Conference*, pp. 101–8. A remarkable analysis of the problems discussed in these concluding pages will be found in Edwin G. Boring, "Mind and Mechanism," *American Journal of Psychology*, April, 1946.

11. The important differences between these two creatures are discussed in "A Behavioral Model of Rational Choice," *Quarterly Journal of Economics*, February, 1955; and "Rational Behavior and the Difficulty of the Environment," *Psychological Review*, January, 1956. For an example of a game theoretical approach to the chess machine see C. E. Shannon, "Programming a Computer To Play Chess," *Philosophical Magazine*, March, 1950.

I will not be tempted into a prediction as to how long it will be before we know how to teach these things to a computer. Nor do I wish to enter into the technical problems that are involved. This much I can say with confidence on the basis of some participation in such an undertaking. One cannot think seriously about the problem of programing a computer to learn and to solve problems without gaining very great insights into the ways in which humans learn and solve problems. Regardless of whether this analogy between machine and man can in fact be realized "in the metal," its heuristic value can hardly be exaggerated.

But apart from the heuristic value, what is the particular virtue of the computer analogy? Why not work directly toward a mathematical (or verbal) theory of human problem-solving processes without troubling about electronic computers? If we were sure that the construction of such a mathematical theory were within our powers, the question would have no answer. But it is at least possible, and perhaps even plausible, that we are dealing here with systems of such complexity that we have a greater chance of building a theory by way of the computer program than by a direct attempt at mathematical formulation. Let me indicate why I think this is so.

Remember, the proposal is not to program a computer to play chess but to program it to *learn* to play chess. It can be shown that to program something to learn means to program it to alter and modify its own program and to construct for itself new subprograms.[12] This means that, as the learning process progresses, the activity of the computer will be more and more self-programed activity. The scientist will be no more aware of the details of the program inside the computer than he is aware of the details of his own thought processes.

Suppose that we could achieve the goal of programing a computer to learn to play chess. How would we use the computer as a theory?[13] First, we would experiment with various modifications of the learning program to see how closely we could simulate in detail

12. Self-programing of digital computers has already been achieved at simple and elementary levels and is now a standard part of programing technology.

13. For a penetrating discussion of the use of a computer as theory see Walter Pitts, "Comments on Session on Learning Machines," *Proceedings of the 1955 Western Joint Computer Conference*, pp. 108–10.

the observable phenomena of human problem-solving. The program that achieved this simulation would provide, at a suitable level of aggregation, a theory explaining these observable phenomena and would without doubt suggest a number of crucial experiments.

Second, human beings have great difficulty in introspecting—and particularly in introspecting reliably and comprehensively. The computer, however complex its over-all program, could be programed to report, in accurate detail, a description of any part of its own computing processes in which we might be interested. Because of this, and because of our exact knowledge of the physical structure of the computer, we could find out directly a great deal more about what was going on in the computer than we are likely ever to find out directly, by introspective techniques at least, about what is going on in the human mind.

Third, it might prove easier to construct a mathematical theory of human problem-solving after we have constructed a mathematical theory of machine problem-solving. Ordinarily, we use a computer when we are confronted with a mathematical theory whose equations are too complicated to be solved explicitly. Then we program the computer as an analogue to the mathematical theory— which is, in turn, an analogue to the phenomena. The present proposal involves a quite different use of the digital computer in theory construction. If a computer were used to simulate human problem-solving activities, the analogy between computer program and the phenomena would be direct. Mathematical theory, as it first enters the picture, enters as a theory of the computer program and hence only indirectly as a theory of the phenomena.

Conclusion: Science as Analogy

The basic postulate underlying this discussion has been that, contrary to general belief, there is no fundamental, "in principle" difference between theories and analogies. All theories are analogies, and all analogies are theories. Two theories are not equivalent for the scientist simply because they have the same logical content. The choice between theories depends critically on the ease with which their logical content can be extracted by the manipulations of information-processing systems operating upon them and the ease with which errors of omission and commission can be detected and avoided. This is the real core of the debate about the relative virtues of mathematical symbols and words as materials of theory.

We must not suppose, simply because verbal and mathematical theories have been with us a long time, that methodology is a static matter—an unchanging substratum for the changing substance of science. Methodology requires a re-examination today, both because of the novel substantive problems that the behavioral sciences face and because of the novel devices that are now available to help us solve these problems.

A theory of man that takes account of his characteristics as an information-processing system is just beginning to emerge. Already, the theory suggests a system exhibiting a degree of complexity with which the sciences—and certainly the behavioral sciences—have not hitherto dealt. Modern electronic computers have been, and continue to be, an important influence, by way of analogy, on the emergence of this theory. If the argument advanced here is correct, these same computing devices may provide us with the materials for a methodology powerful enough to cope with the complexity of the theory as it emerges.

Impact of Psychoanalytic Thinking
on the Social Sciences

The topic is a challenge to use all the tools available to the social sciences including the innovations for which psychoanalysis is mainly responsible. From one viewpoint the problem is one of diffusion and restriction and especially of restriction by partial incorporation of psychoanalytic ideas and methods. The record is of absorbing interest in a day of interdisciplinary awareness, since the spread of psychoanalytic thinking is an instance of receptivity to original and controversial developments from beyond the conventional boundaries of the social sciences.

Several factors initially dampened the impact of psychoanalysis. The center of origin was an academic faculty not of philosophy or law but of medicine; psychoanalysis was connected by a tenuous thread with even the faculty of medicine. Freud's association with the University of Vienna weakened as his preoccupation with psychoanalysis grew.

American scholars in the social sciences were not oriented toward the University of Vienna. Although Vienna was one of the world's distinguished universities, its influence in the United States was appreciably less than the major universities of Germany, Great Britain, or France. In philosophy the orientation was overwhelmingly toward Germany. In political science the leading professors in public law, political philosophy, comparative government, and politics usually turned toward Germany or Great Britain. Our economists had most in common with England, after the triumph of the historical school in Germany. They did, however, keep in touch with the marginalists of Austria. In sociology there was the famous cleavage between the French influence of Giddings at Columbia and the German emphasis of Albion W. Small at Chicago. Even though the story would differ in detail if one were to add history, anthropology, or social

84

geography, it is unmistakably clear that Vienna was not strategically located for the diffusion of intellectual innovations to the United States.

It would, however, be a mistake to assume that there were no important factors making for the reception of Freud in America. We know that the United States is where psychoanalysis received its fullest opportunity to influence the social sciences. I suspect that the marginal position of the United States in relation to European centers was significant in this connection. Scholars from subcenters are often better informed about the topography of the intellectual life of their time than the intellectuals who are at the greater nuclear craters. Intellectuals from smaller or less conspicuous countries usually follow more attentively the output of the principal university centers. In part this is a result of relatively fewer academic posts and less specialization at the subcenters. The peripheral intellectuals feel obligated to keep up with developments at the dominant centers, while the man in the thick of things is likely to take it for granted that his contribution is less in knowing the whole intellectual map than in cultivating a specialized area within it. I suspect that G. Stanley Hall was one of the best-informed men in the world about the intellectual currents touching upon psychology. Freud's visit to Clark University in 1909 was an outcome of Hall's perception of the intellectual contours of the Western world.

It would be a mistake to overlook the sheer abundance of the resources at the disposal of social scientists in the United States in recent years. In the United States the expansion of the social sciences fostered the growth of separate departments and the union of departments into social science faculties. The social sciences succeeded in escaping from the faculty of law, on the one hand, and the faculty of philosophy, on the other. The Continental structure kept economics, political science, and kindred disciplines in the status of ancillary professorships in the faculty of law; and psychology was tied in unhappy marriage to philosophy. In the new, independent, and relatively opulent setting in America the cultivation of novelties was feasible; and psychoanalysis was an innovation, however faddist in some hands, that came to provoke and fertilize the growth of the behavioral sciences.

Since academic men were themselves reared in American culture, they were implicated in the several factors congenial to the reception of psychoanalysis. The prevailing note of individualism heightened the tensions to be found within the "self-system" of Americans. From the withering or blasting-away of the European inheritance sprang new academic disciplines—disciplines, to be sure, with roots and parallels elsewhere, yet requiring the American environment to germinate and flower. The interplay of personality and culture (social psychology) became a major locus of intellectual growth, as the names of William James, John Dewey, George Herbert Mead, Charles Horton Cooley, and Thorstein Veblen suggest.

More specifically important for the spread of psychoanalysis than individualism was the sexual tension of American life. There were sexual tensions from the Puritan tradition. There were sexual tensions in the South connected with restraints imposed upon the white male by the decline of slavery and a reduced supply of Negro concubines. There were sexual tensions in the West as the process of settlement introduced housewives and schoolmarms into the wide-open spaces where men were men and women had been distant fantasies or immediate bargains. And there were the tensions of urbanization and the uprooting of country boys and girls or peasants from the ties of primary neighborhood. The father-centered home proved to be vulnerable to the ideology of equality and the fact of advancing economic opportunity for women. And in the 1920's—the high tide of psychoanalytic receptivity—the United States was in the throes of a sexual revolution, colorful in its way though pale when contrasted with social upheaval in eastern Europe.

It was in the twenties, in fact, when many elements favorable to the reception of psychoanalysis came to a peak. By that time champions of psychoanalysis, or tolerant or even hopeful critics, were in influential positions. William A. White was the superintendent of St. Elizabeth's Hospital in Washington, where he encouraged the work of a staff having analytically oriented psychiatrists. Some private foundations were willing to take a flyer on behalf of social science in the hope of building up a body of knowledge for the eventual guidance of policy in the United States. No doubt they were inspired in part by the hope of deflecting the lightning of proletarian revolt from these shores. Great programs of child development were encouraged to knot together all kinds of specialists

and every promising approach. (We do homage in this connection
to Beardsley Ruml and L. K. Frank, among others.) The social
sciences (especially political science and sociology) were in a state
of acute dissatisfaction with themselves. Their abler thinkers were
hospitable to any hypothesis or method that seemed to offer some
hope of improving their somewhat humble status. In the twenties
we witnessed a great outburst of interdisciplinary enthusiasm and
the launching of co-operative enterprises like the Social Science
Research Council and such centers as the Division of the Social
Sciences at the University of Chicago.

Most of us are acquainted with the more prominent disseminators
of psychoanalytic thinking among social scientists in this country.
Alfred L. Kroeber was one of the first of the anthropologists to give
serious consideration to Freud's work (and was honored by the
famous misspelling of his name in one of the professor's books).
Bronislaw Malinowski's rhetorical gift was a potent spark. We cannot overlook the infectious quality of Edward Sapir's speculations
on the theme of culture and personality, coupled with his serious
concern for creating a band of co-workers knowing psychoanalysis
from the inside. Among sociologists, William F. Ogburn gave the
weight of his name to the cultivators of the field. In political science
the channel of diffusion was the permissive environment created by
Charles E. Merriam. The development would have been far slower
than it was had it not received respected support inside the psychiatric profession. The principal figure was William A. White, who
influenced public health, education, and related areas. The most
creative mind was Harry Stack Sullivan (though one must not pass
over James A. Plant or Anton Boisen and some of the tireless protagonists of Freud who were squarely in the center of orthodox
psychoanalysis [such as it was in the twenties]).

I have suggested that the openness of the behavioral disciplines
to outside influence was connected with the low self-appraisal then
prevailing among many members of these professions. Economics
is clearly a test case. If our interpretation is correct, departments of
economics should be comparatively unreceptive to what psychoanalysis had to offer. And I think it would be agreed that this is so.
The economists were relatively satisfied with themselves and continued to improve their methods of constructing theoretical models

and processing data. The economists are a test case for another proposition about the diffusion of psychoanalytic influence. I suppose that psychoanalysis had the best chance of spreading where the problem concerned, not the social aggregate, but particular persons, or small groups of decision-makers. As a rule, the most distinguished university departments of economics have devoted themselves to studying large aggregates. It is in schools of business that we find relatively deeper penetration by psychoanalytic conceptions (often reverbalized to reduce resistance, as with Elton Mayo). Schools of business concern themselves with the management problems that arise in smaller segments of the economic process. The impact of personality factors is more obvious in these situations than in the whole economic aggregate.

Challenging ideas make their contribution to the intellectual life by mobilizing the energies of those who reject and oppose as well as those who accept and adopt. The result is the sharpening of issues and the scaling-down of exaggeration by the consideration of opposites. Hence the impact of psychoanalysis can be summarized in two ways: the ideas and methods directly taken from Freud and the emphases developed in the attempt to disprove or improve psychoanalysis.

The assertion that ideas have in some sense contributed to their opposites is not to be understood as a transempirical proposition of the Hegelian type. What is meant is that the appearance of an opposing point of view is partly conditioned by the fact that an initial statement was made. In the present discussion I am principally engaged in sketching trends that have manifested themselves to date or that I anticipate in the immediate future. To some extent I offer explanations of the factors that account for a trend. But this is not the principal aim of this paper, which is more concerned with the "historical" and "developmental" line than with putting forward a body of hypotheses stemming from a "science of science." The scope of the latter enterprise is beyond the present intention.

Since for the most part I describe trends as passing through a phase of acceptance and moving toward counteremphasis, it may be assumed that I am offering a general theory of how scientific ideas are diffused (and restricted); in particular, that I purport to have discerned an "iron law" governing the order in which peaks of acceptance and rejection occur. Such is not my intention. I do not affirm a general tendency for peaks of acceptance to come before a peak of rejection. The mode of presentation is adopted solely because of the fact that a great many parallel sequences relating to psychoanalysis have attracted my notice. I am putting these forward quite tentatively in the hope that our discussion of the impact of psychoanalysis on the social sciences will stimulate systematic research upon the subject.

A further word should probably be said about the hypothetical sequences. Psychoanalysis has itself been changing through the years. And it is to be understood that the various sequences are intended to refer to the broad line of these internal transformations as well as to the changes that have been facilitated outside the "orthodox" corps who kept in close association with Freud until the time of his death. I shall suggest that Freud's new observational standpoint ("free association" interlarded with "interpretations") brought about a continual shift in the axis of psychoanalytic theory. I shall suggest that these shifts have been occurring within the "hard core" of organizational orthodoxy (notably with the advent of the "ego psychology" developed by Anna Freud and others). But the point is also made that these changes have not been fully articulated into the theory of the more orthodox schools, even though there is evidence of important shifts in therapeutic practice. I shall suggest that the implications of the inner transformations of psychoanalysis are often more clearly seen in the positions taken by "defectors" from the "core" than by those who remained organizationally faithful. And among anthropologists, sociologists, and social psychologists these implications have begun to be drawn because the specialists in question possess a context that is the very one toward which psychoanalytically trained physicians and psychologists have been moving. In turn the social scientists have received an ultramicroscope from Freud's original work that adds unprecedented depth to the observational tools available for the study of human interactions. I shall propose the idea that psychoanalysis has been moving social science toward the discovery of a whole new subdivision of inquiry which has gone by default to official medicine and that psychoanalysis has likewise been moving traditional medicine—and especially psychiatry—toward the discovery of a neglected context.

In a word, a major impact of psychoanalysis has been toward the disclosure of the field of sociopsychosomatic disorder. This is by no means the only impact, however, as we shall show.

Persistence of Childhood Predispositions; Modifiability of the Adult

Psychoanalysis was able to document the maxim about the child as father to the man in a manner that carried challenge and conviction to a large number of social scientists. It is true that the persisting effect of early character formation upon subsequent conduct was no novelty in the folklore or the scientific knowledge of western European civilization. But the cases described in rich detail by the psychoanalysts created a wealth of material whose impact produced an assessment of the significance of childhood experience. In particular, it became apparent that repetitive compulsions were vastly more important than had been understood. Today it is commonplace to note the strength of demands to reinstate early situations. We see this in the choice of sexual partners, for instance, when a whole series of partners may be selected with similar characteristics, some of which can be related to the early fixation of ambivalent demands for dependence and domination. In politics, especially, we are more aware than previously of the dynamics of persons who are so intent upon obtaining an emotional response from the social environment that they manage to transform the dullest occasion into an opportunity for notoriety. We also understand why some individuals go to such lengths to maintain hostile relations to authority.

The sheer abundance of documentation has, I think, led to some weakening of the original emphasis. For one thing, we know of rather remarkable "maturations" in the behavior of adults. Sheldon and Eleanor Glueck, for example, called attention to offenders sentenced for serious offenses who have suddenly and permanently changed their mode of life. In one sense it is commonplace to see the fires of youth subside to the ashes of middle age. Confronted by instances of this kind, the rejoinder can be that the balance of forces set up in childhood are working themselves out. It is reasonable to suggest that hostilities may be strong enough to goad a youth or young adult to overcome obstacles in the path of success, after

which he "settles down." But this answer is not an altogether satisfactory one, especially when existing methods render it difficult to
differentiate the case reports (or the measured traits) of those who
change from those who do not.

By this time there are enough instances of the modification of
adult conduct to suggest that the persisting influence of childhood
structures has been taken too literally. The complex equilibrium of
a personality system may provide more opportunity than was formerly recognized for creating intervention during adult years. In a
sense this has been obvious all along, for the therapy of adults has
often borne fruit. The challenge is to improve these strategic inter-
ventions at later cross-sections of individual career lines.

Plasticity of Original Nature; Persistence
of Original Nature

The emphasis laid by Freud on the formative significance of
early experience was a challenge to many prevailing ideas about the
immutability of inborn nature. If the relationship with the nipple,
or the modes of toilet training, and the like, are so crucial for fixing
the pattern by which subsequent deprivations and indulgence are
met, the effective impact of physiological determinants on behavior
was evidently reduced.

I think that a number of circumstances have contributed to a
renewal of emphasis upon the persisting effect of original predisposition upon subsequent development. The multiplication of case
reports creates some confusion, since instances multiply of individuals exposed to remarkably similar environments who respond differently, or respond similarly to different environments. In trying
to account for therapeutic failures (or successes, for that matter),
the scrutiny of both environmental and predispositional factors was
pushed farther and farther back toward (or within) the womb or
made the function of vaguely characterized configurative contexts.
It became credible to bring into the picture once more the patterns
presumed to be imbedded in the constitution of the body and to
suggest that capacities to withstand stress as well as to perceive
stimulus bands in the environment depend to a greater extent than
generally admitted upon specific determiners transmitted from one
generation to the next. It cannot be said that these interpretations

have made much headway among social scientists generally. But in some branches of psychology they are gaining, especially in connection with specific aptitude studies. (Some of the work using L. L. Thurstone's technique is pointing toward small persisting clusters.)

In many branches of psychiatry the older stress upon the potency of the genetic constitution has remained unimpaired through the years (Kallman, for example). But whatever shifts there have been toward a revival of the "persistence" school owe less to the positive results obtained by the geneticists than to the disillusionment of what may be called "frustrated environmentalists."

The Impact of the Unconscious; the Strength of the Conscious

Before Freud's work the dimensions of the unconscious were relatively schematic, meager, and innocuous. We must go back to Plato to discover explicit and forceful anticipations of psychoanalysis. The impact of Freud's conception of the unconscious was prodigious and has permeated our way of looking at people and societies. New stock figures in social myth have been created by the study of unconscious factors, such as the offender whose sense of guilt drives him to punishment by commiting a readily apprehended offense; the martyr who unconsciously goads society into annihilating him; the overprotective mother who is masking deep hostility against her child. These ideas broke with lightning illumination and suddenness upon our culture.

The success of the conception of the unconscious was so overwhelming that the main question began to be how public order is attainable when the basic nature of man is hag-ridden with lust and animus. Obviously, Freud had put a terrifically high estimate upon the potential strength of conscious processes. The entire socializing experience of the child is a long exercise in acquiring an ego-system strong enough to stand the stampeding impetus of primitive drives or the upsetting impact of exceedingly indulgent or deprivational surroundings. A great many individuals and groups succeed in making the grade. As the author of the report on the psychiatric state of America's armed forces during the war (William Menninger) remarked, it is worth emphasizing the point that 90 per cent of the forces came through without becoming clinical problems.

Psychosomatic Processes; Socio-
psychosomatic Processes

Psychoanalysis came to the notice of psychologists, anthropologists, and other behavioral scientists as a systematic conception of the psychosomatic process in individuals. The principal emphasis appeared to be upon the prodigious importance of basic physiological drive for the fate of man. The accent was upon the new dimensions of man's inner life disclosed by the disciplined use of free-association methods. The fabulous riches of fantasy and dream were earnestly recorded and seriously reported, and every science was stimulated by the new categories developed by Freud for classifying and explaining interactions among symbols and between soma and symbol.

From the beginning, of course, Freud's picture of the developing personality emphasized the extraordinary depth and endurance of the impact of the social context into which the infant is born and with which he interacts. But the focus was upon diagnosis and therapy and the winning of acceptance on the part of medical colleagues. At the center of Freud's interest were "intraorganic" events, the psychosomatic processes occurring within the somatic envelope. This was the traditional context used by the physicians to describe symptoms of disorder and the course of a pathological process. It is true that the sequence of events internal to the organism was understood to be affected by influence from outside the boundaries set by the skin. But these influences were conceived as extraneous to the process itself. This traditional conception is undergoing a profound redefinition.

In accord with established frames of reference Freud counterposed to the original nature of man with its imperious physical drives the restraining influence of human association. At the same time psychoanalysis supplied an observational procedure whose result has been to show the intricate, subtle, and multitudinous ties that bind the whole personality of one person with others. Random movements, slips of the tongue, and body posture were ascribed new significance when they were utilized as clues for predicting the direction and intensity of human acts or for exposing the sequence of interaction within organisms and among organisms. Specialists in anthropology, in particular, seized upon the new emphasis and upon the new methods; and ensuing years have made it plain that the intensive observational procedures invented by Freud constitute major innovations in the study of man in society. The clues perceived by the psychoanalytically oriented observer turned out to be expressions of "covert" culture (a term Clyde Kluckhohn brought into general use). The intensive standpoint of the analyst (which permits the use of free association) is a potent instrument of research for the study of the refined structure of the culture-personality manifold.

The initial influence of psychoanalysis upon the data of anthropology was chiefly in the study of child-rearing practices. Hypotheses inspired by Freud—no matter how manhandled—concentrated the attention of field workers upon the socialization sequence, leading to minute explorations of adult-child and child-child relationships. Concurrently the effort to link personality systems with situational challenges led to the formation of working conceptions of "national character" or "basic personality type," patterns believed to be brought into existence by the sequence of indulgence and deprivation constituting cultural, subcultural, and class environments (e.g., Ruth Benedict, Margaret Mead, Abram Kardiner).

The merging of interest, skill, and data among anthropologists and physicians is bringing about the recognition, however belated, of the interactionist context of pathological processes. This implies that only part of the relevant context has been studied in the past. It is no longer useful to conceive of the locus of pathological process as restricted by the cutaneous boundaries of an actor in the social process. To be sure, there are situations confronting the physician in which no one is in doubt about the incapacitation of the organism. This is true when the patient is disoriented in time and space or where there are skeletal fractures or organ breakdowns. Even in these cases, however, the "symptoms" are parts of a larger pathological whole. The larger whole may be the "personality system" of the sufferer in the sense that internal contradictions have created an "accident-prone" individual or weakened the functioning of the gastroenteral or the circulatory system. Even this cannot be regarded as a satisfactory characterization of the "pathic" process, since the locus of a "personality system" is usually conceived as a single actor, a "personality trait" being understood as a term of reference to the persisting patterns displayed in behavior. When the entire pathic sequence is taken into consideration, the interpersonal context reappears at the focus of the observer's attention. The environing provocation is as much involved as the events regarded as internal to the actor who is the locus of the specific events we call "symptoms." The destructive acts of the parent of the child who suffers from certain symptoms is also part of the pathic process, as is the spouse or the foreman or the boss in relation to many of the symptoms shown by the marriage partner, the employee, or the subordinate.

Clearly, it is more precise to speak of "sociopsychosomatic" difficulties than of psychosomatic troubles alone, since the prefix points to the relevant context.

Communication versus Non-communication in Therapy; the Comparison of Joint Therapies

The therapeutic impact of Freud was initially made by stressing the use of communication devices. The psychoanalyst relied upon language as the chief instrument of accomplishing curative results; and he was guided by the interpretation that he gave to the words, gestures, and postures of his patients. If anything is clear about a communication, it is that it is one of the most difficult though most distinctive skills of man.

A great many circumstances have created a medical profession rather adversely disposed to the protracted use of communication as a therapeutic agent. Trained in the routine of medical schools, physicians were initially at a loss for convenient methods of recording the mass of verbiage and the welter of gesture to which they were exposed by analytic patients. When psychoanalysis came into prominence, the easily available means of obtaining efficient sound recordings were inefficient and expensive. (As recently as 1930, when the Social Science Research Building was opened, it was necessary to use rather clumsy equipment to obtain continuous-interview recordings. We used two dictaphone machines and kept an assistant on the job to change the rolls. Magnetized wire gave better results, though it was too expensive to store.) To this day the motion-picture machine has not been turned into a suitable observational aid.

Of more importance was the fact that methods were undeveloped for condensing the content of communication in manageable summaries for comparative purposes. It was necessary at that time to attack the problem directly and to invent or adapt the technique that came to be called "content analysis." The crucial innovation was not the rather obvious idea of counting the frequencies of key words, gestures, or assertions. The challenging question was the categories. Which categories would serve as operational indexes for the conceptions of psychoanalysis? The theory was itself far from constituting a well-systematized whole. It had not been laid out by Freud or anyone else in the form of defined and undefined terms and with key definitions and hypotheses. It was necessary to set about formulating, or instigating others to formulate, the entire theoretical system.

Another technical limitation was the statistical procedures then available for dealing economically with problems of flow. In the study of the analyst-patient relation the important questions relate to sequences of events: If pattern p^1 is observed in the first interview, and the interviewer adopts policy i^1, what is the probability that pattern p^2 rather than p^3 will emerge in interview two? The question may be varied in reference to each time section of the interview or for any subseries thereof. Eventually it is relevant to relate the events in the interview to current, antecedent, and subsequent events (co-, pre-, and post-interview).

If rigorously formulated, the concepts of psychoanalytic theory call for the use of operational indexes in reference to the therapist-patient relationship. In this setting Freud made his principal innovation by combining free-associative activity with interpretations by the analyst. So important is the method that the whole theoretical superstructure of Freud may some day be modified beyond recognition by the cumulative results obtained by making use of it. This is the sense in which I believe that psychoanalysis carries within itself "the seeds of its own correction." Whenever the observational standpoint is shifted, it is necessary to choose another set of operational indexes for the conceptual terms in which the theory is couched. The shift may be relatively slight, as when free-association periods are combined with narco- or hypnoanalysis. Or the shift may be substantial, as when the concepts originally referring to the words and gestures of articulate adults are used to describe prelanguage children.

It would be a mistake to imply that whatever deficiencies were current in medical education were peculiar to the physician's preference for "hard data" of the kind that could be hammered, cut, split, or seen through a lens. Even such pioneers as the early logical positivists were seeking to "reduce" events of reference (symbols) to other events (the "physicalistic" bias).

The desire to get rid of the complexities of communication in therapy was fortified by the remarkable results often obtained by non-symbolic methods. Sensational results came with the use of drugs and of brain surgery. Why there is a ready market for non-communication therapies is evident. From the administrative point of view it is cheaper to operate or to narcotize than to analyze. The pressure of potential patients combines with shortage of manpower to bring about an unparalleled vogue for such therapies.

At the same time, however, we may reserve judgment on the relative efficacy of non-communication methods. There have been past cycles of emphasis followed by somewhat remorseful de-emphasis. Often quick results obtainable by shock therapies have worn away. If the effect was originally induced by impairing the patient's organic structure, his latter state became worse than before. The history of psychiatry fluctuates as though physicians became irritated from time to time by the recalcitrance of their patients and took after them with knives, gases, and hypodermics, eventually to go back to work at the arduous task of communication after a collection of human wreckage had convincingly testified to the non-rational element in the original psychic seizure on the part of physicians.

If anything, professional students of political and social processes have been unduly indifferent to the challenge of non-communication methods of getting results of importance. Nevertheless, practical applications have been widely instituted. In Japan, for example, workers in munition factories during the war and soldiers at the front were given regular stimulants in order to increase their psychic happiness and to enable them to work longer and to take bigger risks. For a generation it has been increasingly common for police to use drugs in obtaining confessions. (All this brings closer to reality the specter that I once christened "Machiavelli M.D.")

Nor have the constructive potentialities of non-communication methods been adequately investigated. Is it feasible to speed up the rate of rote learning and of other forms of learning by the systematic use of drugs? Is the problem to bring about passivity on the part of the learner without erasing his propensity to recall and apply on waking? Will our schoolrooms one day represent sanitariums in which hours of routine transmission are handled by nurses and teachers jointly?

We are beginning, I think, to witness more deliberate attempts to bring the use of communication and non-communication therapies into more balanced relationship to each other. Instead of stressing the traditional gulf between the two, the trend emerging in some quarters is to compare patterns of joint therapy with each other. As in the study of "psyche" and "soma," the original separations represent first approximations. All acts involve both communication and non-communication, since they include "symbols" (interpretations by the communicator and the target) and "signs" (the signs are the physical components).

The Curative Pair; the Curative Group

Classical analysis put the accent on the interplay between a physician and one patient at a time. The therapeutic pair was always an abstraction, and physicians have become increasingly aware of the participation of others in the curative enterprise. This is most apparent and controllable in the social environment constituting a hospital, where persons who figure recurrently in the life of a patient include, besides the physician, at least the nurse, the attendants, and other patients. A leading idea was essential to ignite and guide research talent to the study of the hospital community. This germinal idea did emerge.

Clearly a severely ill patient is unable (or unwilling) to perform according to the minimum norms of the society by whom he is regarded as ill. A "recovery" (or a "social recovery") can be described as the outcome of a sequence of stages in which the patient is willing and able to perform in more and more approximate accordance to acceptable conventions of the society. Possibly, therefore, the process could be expedited if the hospital environment were composed of groups with varying levels of approximation to these final requirements. Attendants even more than nurses appear to represent the non-patient world. Hence a strategical move might be in the management of patient-attendant groups. This conception led to such bold experimentation as that introduced by Harry Stack Sullivan in the treatment of schizophrenics at the Sheppard and Enoch Pratt Hospital at Towson, Maryland. Experiments of the kind inaugurated by Sullivan were made and have since been made with other groups. The degree of success has led to a reappraisal of some ancient practices, such as the granting of permission to peasant families in certain Belgian villages to take psychotics into their homes. The drastic experiments of Aichhorn in Vienna with "wayward youth" opened vistas of what might be done by special and supportive environments. Group therapy in all its varied manifestations is part of the flood of readjustive ventures from which much is to be learned. (In the light of contemporary theory and observation the impact of Alcoholics Anonymous, for instance, is comprehensible.)

The Noncommittal Therapist; Value Disclosure

The classical model of the psychoanalyst portrayed the therapist as uninvolved in the value confusions and conflicts of the patient. The noncommittal role was assumed by Freud as a conscious therapeutic strategy. I suspect that it was more than that. It expressed an ideal of human dignity that motivated much of his work and set limits upon his choice of method.[1]

That the noncommittal role was a deliberate strategy is beyond reasonable dispute. The rule of free association is unqualifiedly permissive. The therapist grants an exemption to the patient that frees him from the standards of conventional speech. It is not easy for the patient to take advantage of the new freedom. Hence the analyst must conduct himself in such a manner as to reward free disclosure and to refrain from the imposition of penalties for disclosure. The rewards (indulgences) of the patient by the analyst may include outright expressions of approval for the courage shown in allowing points of particular difficulty to be made articulate. It would consti-

1. The details of Freud's life (notably in the account provided by Ernest Jones) depict Freud's defenses against dependency drives. Part of the defense was an intense demand to dominate others, especially in the intimate circle. This in turn was held in check by the use of the enlightenment provided by skilled insight and through the influence of such an ideal as respect for the basic freedom of human beings to choose for themselves. Freud was also influenced by a conception of moral responsibility (rectitude), of the obligation of everyone to take a serious attitude toward the problems of life. This implies a helpful role toward others who were struggling for a satisfactory image of the "self" in relation to "others."

tute an inhibiting deprivation of the patient were the therapist to voice his resentment at the way his role is depicted in reported dreams and associations. No one, I suppose, would seriously contend that a physician should add his "right" or "wrong" to every evaluative statement of the patient.

That the analyst must be able to exercise great control of the self in order to live up to the noncommittal role is evident. The tensions connected with the countertransference were among the first technical problems to confront the practitioners of psychoanalysis. Ferenczi was among the first to suggest that the hammering that the self-system of the analyst had to undergo in ordinary practice was so severe that reanalysis at intervals is a sound precaution.

It is also probable that even orthodox psychiatrists fall short of the ideal of noncommitment. (I am not, of course, referring to the simulation of exasperation or other attitudes for the sake of accomplishing a therapeutic result.) I am now dealing with a topic about which we have very little satisfactory information. We can leave to one side the physicians who have become so involved with their patients that the whole analytic process has gone on the rocks, and confine the inquiry to more subtle issues. My impression is that an investigation of the impact of "orthodox" psychoanalysts upon patients would indicate a considerable degree of "personal" impact upon the patient. Whatever the conscious intention, many of the evaluative attitudes of the subject impact upon the patient, whatever the conscious intention of the psychiatrist may be. In addition, the non-psychotic patient is able to make direct observations upon the analyst that are ordinarily outside the scope of the analyst's direct observation of the patient, such as taste in interior decoration, choice of office location, and choice of secretary. There are indications that psychoanalysts retain marks of their class origin in dealing with patients who come from the same or other classes. There are indications that Jewish, Catholic, or Protestant backgrounds leave significant residues in the patterning of conduct and that these are not abolished by a training analysis plus a period of control. And there are indications that national cultures impress themselves so deeply during childhood and youth that analytic training does not eradicate them completely or place them wholly under conscious control.

Has there been a trend toward deviation from a noncommittal role in the direction of more complete disclosure of values (as urged by Erich Fromm and David Riesman, for instance)? Among schools that deviate from "orthodox" organizations, it is almost beyond dispute that the trend is toward self-disclosure by the analyst. In many cases this is viewed as a reversion to the practice of indoctrination against which Freud was originally seeking to protect the patient. Freud was well informed of the use of "confessional" techniques for the sake of maintaining the authority of a religious or political ideology. He was quite prepared to say that personal disorganization was often mitigated, rectified, or avoided as a result of confessionals. But as a clinician he was concerned with the cases that failed to respond to such didactic treatment. It seems to me that the problem of self-disclosure by the therapist is reposing itself at a more scientific level as a result of the subtle methods of observation introduced by psychoanalysis itself. To what extent does the betrayal of evaluative judgments through unconsciously expressive acts of the therapist advance or endanger the therapeutic process? Is the seeming contradiction easily turned into an accusation by hypocrisy at a deep level where it contributes to an apparent "recovery" that depends chiefly upon simulating the deeper norms of the analyst? Does the transitory nature of a significant number of cases depend upon a recurring drive to get revenge on the analyst who insists upon maintaining a one-sided supremacy that precludes full sharing of values?

These questions are amenable to research, since varying degrees of self-disclosure can be investigated. For instance, the national, religious, and class preferences of the analyst may be frankly expressed by different methods at various stages of an analytic sequence.

Disease Entities; Competing Conceptions of the "Pathic Process"

When psychoanalysis first appeared, it did not challenge the prevailing notions about a neatly definable set of pathological entities. However, the latent ambiguities in the norms of "health" and "disease" were gradually brought into prominence by the psychoanalyst's emphasis upon the unconscious and the crucial role of anxiety. Visible marks of anxiety did not pose serious issues. But what of seeming absence of anxiety when found coupled with non-conformist conduct? Many psychiatrists have been strongly inclined to classify all deviations from the "cultural norm" as unhealthy, especially when the deviate is exposed to the risk of social reprisals. But this runs counter to some cherished ideals of our civilization where there is supposed to be room for the man of courage and conviction who refuses to be intimidated by the interpretations of values that are put forward by his immediate contemporaries. On the whole, the presence of psychopathological elements has been emphasized among the non-conformists. So far as I know there has been less emphasis upon the "pathic" element among conformists; and the idea that strict conformity to majority conceptions may indicate more pathology than some degree of deviation is not generally entertained or considered.

Although physicians are not yet reconciled to the fact, the emerging situation is a far cry from the day when value assumptions could be ignored and every clinical entity was expected to be understood in the same way by everybody. As we see in the conflicting testimony of psychiatrists before the courts—and in more private consultations —the conceptions of "psychopathic character," or of "sexual deviation," for instance, vary considerably depending upon the value postulates of the specialist. It seems to me that the most significant point is that it is coming to be recognized that competent and well-intentioned people may disagree in their conceptions of "health" or "disease" and that, far from constituting a scandal, this pattern is characteristic of a multiformed civilization.

The probability is that specialists will become accustomed to think in terms of postulated values and draw the consequences for their definitions of the pathic process (the sociopsychosomatic process). In the role of scientist it is not necessary for the specialist to commit himself finally to any system of defining or specifying values. He may postulate any system and set ahead with translating it into descriptive variables to be used in research.

In the role of therapist, however, the relationship of the specialist to values is quite different. As a rational physician he cannot close his eyes to the value consequences of his therapeutic goals for the patient or for those who are likely to be adversely affected. At every stage of treatment the physician is weighing value consequences for the patient, for persons likely to be affected by the patient, and for the future career of the doctor himself. It is essential to weigh the cost of more therapy against the probable degree of "improvement" by the patient; and this depends not only upon the criteria by which "improvement" is assessed but upon estimates of the nature of the stress likely to occur in the environment to which the patient will probably be exposed during the years following the termination of the treatment.

In deciding how far to carry a course of treatment, the physician may set before himself the ideal of a "shockproof" person who is capable of achieving a postulated degree of capability to share affection, respect, and other values with other members of any imaginable civilization, culture, class, or personality system. If engineers were to adopt such a standard, they would build every house as though it were to withstand the strongest possible wind or the most shattering earthquake; and everyone recognizes that the costs of construction and repair on such a scale would be prohibitive. The same objection holds to the "shockproof" conception. Anything short of this, however, places a heavier burden of responsibility upon the therapist for the degree of conscious and unconscious influence that he exerts upon the patient. When the potential course of treatment is shortened, the patient has less opportunity to confront all the issues that might be raised by the therapist on a longer process.

We may interpret what is happening in this sphere as another exemplification of the heightened "value consciousness" characteristic of our epoch of world revolutionary crisis. It would be inadequate to attribute all this to the effect of the discovery of the unconscious. But the intensive methods of study invented by Freud have contributed to the sharpening of value awareness among physicians, psychologists, and social scientists generally. The process has been accelerated by the migration of psychoanalysis from Freud's Vienna (plus Berlin and Budapest) to America. Differences were brought vividly to the attention of many European analysts who became aware of the contrasting perspectives relating to the structure of authority in the home (and, indeed, throughout industry, government, and other institutions) to be found in Europe and America. It is not to be forgotten that European Jews in general and American Jews in particular found in psychoanalysis a mode of expression that was less relevant to Jews in America, where the demand for internalization (subjectivization) is less intense (owing to a relatively permissive environment). It is significant that many of the "deviates" from the orthodox organizations of psychoanalysis sought to make use of tools of thought influenced by the social sciences, notably from social anthropology (Karen Horney, Erich Fromm, for example). At the same time the methods and findings of psychoanalysis (though modified) were adding a depth dimension to the conceptions of personality and culture current among the scientists of behavior.[2]

"Criminal" Entities; Competing Conceptions of the "Correctional Process"

Psychoanalysis has had an impact on our conception of "crime" that is much like the effect I have been describing on "disease entities." The idea that "crimes" are clear-cut categories is deeply ingrained in the ideology of legal institutions and in traditional theories of jurisprudence and criminology. Yet psychoanalysis initiated a series of far-reaching complications whose end is not yet.

The emphasis put by psychoanalysis upon the strength of unconscious factors had a disquieting effect upon the legal process. First of all, the appropriateness of some established criteria for establishing criminal responsibility was cast in doubt, such as "knowledge of the difference between right and wrong." It has also been tension-producing for a judge to be made cognizant of the depth of the unconscious gratification obtained by judges, jurymen, and the community at large from the prosecution and punishment of offenders. If the new knowledge were taken seriously, it might raise awkward questions about who had the depth of impartiality (non-involvement) to make it possible to live up to the "fair trial" requirement of legal prescriptions on behalf of "due process of law." (One merit of American "realists" among students of jurisprudence was that they were cognizant from an early time of the new dimensions that were being added to our understanding of the judicial process by psychoanalysis [notably Judge Jerome Frank].)

2. The relatively rapid expansion and partial incorporation of psychoanalysis has been accompanied by the "toning-down" of radical challenges to the local culture in which physicians practice. It is a plausible hypothesis—though not established—that in its germinal stage the psyhoanalytic movement appealed to many brilliant and often unconventional personalities. To the extent that "deviational" ideas tend to be accepted by deviational personalities, the movement would be expected to recruit at first from more "deviates" than it attracts recently. As the selection of analysts becomes more representative of society, competing psychoanalytic doctrines reflect the prevailing distribution of values and value interpretations.

Our traditional conceptions of "criminal law" are full of confusion and contradiction when they are examined in the perspective of any comprehensive theory of the sociopersonal process. And psychoanalysis, by bringing a great many anachronisms into the open, shattered the plausibility of the older entities and is substituting a clarified, if competitive, understanding of what is involved. I shall not carry this analysis far at the present time, chiefly because one of my colleagues and I have begun to deal with these matters at some length elsewhere (I refer to my lately deceased and much-lamented colleague George H. Dession and the symposium on *Law and Psychiatry* published under the auspices of the American Psychopathological Association).

A brief word about the confusion. Acts are often called "criminal" that are, in fact, attended by no public stigma. The "severity of sanction" imposed upon the violator of a community prescription is also an inadequate test, since many "civil" proceedings involve such severe sanctions as expropriation or dissolution. My prediction (and recommendation) is that we single out as constituting a "corrective" problem those offenders whose violations of community prescription are traceable to intense unconscious motivation. Offenders who constitute corrective problems are not amenable to influence by the system of rewards and penalties that get results from most of the community. The offenders who "take a chance" and lose a calculated risk are quite likely to think twice before taking such a chance again. The persons who are corrective problems are driven by deep unconscious motives to repeat their offensive. And they include many persons who are not today regarded as offenders but who should be so regarded, such as the "accident-prone." In dealing with offenders who require correction, one objective of policy is to render them "educable" by the ordinary range of rewards and penalties. If the methods available to the community at a given time are too ineffective to accomplish this result, it will be necessary to limit the future contact of the offender with society.

The value issues raised by such a conception are numerous and, as in the case of the "pathic" process, leave room for competent and well-intentioned individuals to differ with one another. Of great importance for the future of research is the quest for knowledge concerning how to identify those who are educable by the ordinary range of rewards and penalties and those who require "corrective treatment"; and "who" responds to "which" mode of treatment (sanction).

Only a few pioneers have tackled the fields of "sanction law" (such as E. W. Burgess on parole systems). We know little of who takes the initiative under various circumstances to demand severe deprivations on behalf of the community as a matter of legislative prescription; who invokes the "code" under various fact circumstances; who applies the code with varying degrees of severity under specified conditions.

Biological Impluses; Theories of the Social Values of Adults

We have been looking at the consequences of psychoanalysis for the relationship between social scientists and the norms of disease and offense. One way to sum up the changed impact of psychoanalysis is to say that it is gradually showing the advantages to be obtained in some matters by reversing the original approach. Instead of beginning with innate biological impulses, it now appears that the fruitful method is to start with categories to describe the social values of the adults in all systems of culture (and components thereof).

Psychoanalysis first came into the picture with convincing demonstrations of the potency of biological impulses in man. But evidence kept piling up of the minute and continuous modification of original predispositions through interactions with the environment and especially with the values of the adults in the environment—including, of course, their evaluation of children and the endless specific practices used in interpreting the value significance of children. The unconsciously hostile mother may be typical of certain cultures and social classes; and the ambivalence that she has toward the infant may express itself in discernible patterns of deprivation and indulgence, whether we are speaking of feeding, cuddling, or other activities. If the mother feels that she is losing her health and her husband's love as a result of the child and that her economic security and social position are at stake, this will probably influence the values that she gives or withholds from the child. A sickly infant may arouse guilt feelings; and such low estimations of the self in terms of rectitude may influence the satisfactoriness of her ministrations to the child. Should the mother imagine that she is clumsy and ignorant in dealing with her family responsibilities, these low self-evaluations in terms of skill and basic enlightenment may add complications. If the infant represents an opportunity to domineer over another human being, the power overtones of this unconscious demand may mold the gratifications accessible to the child.

With growing knowledge of the permeative significance of the sociopsychosomatic context it has become increasingly obvious that a systematic theory of the adult social values of a culture will overcome the limitations of the original psychoanalytic emphasis.

Toward Sociopsychoanalysis

As a means of making clear some implications of what has been said, I shall refer to certain explorations of my own. It is to be understood from the outset that these fragmentary notes are intended to specify the roads along which future research can profitably go rather than to report a final body of results. In several fields inspired by psychoanalysis—whether acknowledged or not—the trend toward procedures of the kind to be discussed has been unmistakable (in counseling, for instance). Some of the psychiatric schools that have branched off from the mother matrix of orthodoxy have also taken more or less drastic steps in the same direction (Harry Stack Sullivan, for example). Within the orthodox camp it is quite apparent that the emphasis upon the social context increased rapidly after the "ego revolution" of Anna Freud and others. Although the professional journals maintain much the same range of preoccupations as in earlier years (laying the accent upon "mechanisms"), the newer orientation is visible in "orthodox" literature on child analysis.

For the development of the potentials now present in joint therapies (free association, interpretation, re-education) a more systematic approach is desirable. The elements of such an approach would include: (1) the use by the therapist of a systematic set of categories about the sociopersonal context in order to guide his thinking about the phenomena with which he is concerned (and enough training in the handling of these categories to provide operational definitions related to the local, regional, and transregional situation in which the scientist or the therapist operates); (2) the comparative investigation of the therapeutic results obtainable with subjects of certain predispositional characteristics (including the symptoms of a difficulty) by guiding the course of therapy in a manner designed to provide insight and orientation in the sociopersonal context; and (3) the explicit choice of the goal values of therapy and the prediction of the future conduct of patients under probable environmental conditions (followed by the appraisal of the accuracy of prediction and the social cost of the original therapy and of the subsequent conduct of the patient).

My explorations have been conducted for the most part with individuals displaying rather light neurotic symptoms or suffering from somatic troubles with a large functional component (a "psychosomatic difficulty"). My conception of the sociopersonal process may be overbriefly summarized by saying that it is conceived as an endless chain of interaction in which valued consummations are being consciously and unconsciously sought by the use of available values as bases in order to influence the outcomes of interaction and that the specific interpretations of a valued event and the strategic methods employed are institutional practices of a society (or private patterns unstandardized in any society). Hence any act is more precisely described as part of an "inter-act" and typically involves various degrees of mutual indulgence or deprivation according to cultural or private patterns. The occurrence of a response is sought to be explained by hypotheses stimulated by the postulate of maximization, according to which the response is selected—given capability—which is expected to maximize value indulgences and to minimize value deprivations. A short list of value categories is employed that has been chosen on the basis of its convenience in making comparisons across cultures and within a culture. The categories are defined "functionally," of course; that is, they are defined in ways that make it possible to decide whether an institution or an interaction for which a name is "conventionally" (locally) given conforms to one or another category as defined by the scientific observer for comparative purposes.

In the conduct of interviews the psychoanalytic rule of free association is agreed to by the subject, who is given entire latitude at the start to adapt himself to the situation with minimum guidance. The material is as usual employed by the interviewer as a basis of inference about the nature of the predispositions of the subject and the probable course of future developments.

A variation is presently introduced by the interviewer when he selects a set of value orientations to be probed in more detail. It is explained that part of the task of self-observation is to become aware of the values sought in relation to other human beings and that, for example, there appears to be a great deal of concern about being slighted or gaining signs of *respect* from others. It is pertinent, therefore, to review in the interview the history of the respect that one has given or received and the degree to which such relationships have figured in plans or in fantasies and dreams. The subject is encouraged to ramble as he sees fit, but his attention is guided back to the consideration of respect by asking for associations to certain figures who occur in dreams and other productions. The current orientation toward the interviewer is gone into in this perspective, as is, also, the attitude toward other contemporaries. In this way the proclivities to give or withhold positive respect (admiration) and negative respect (as in ridicule) are gone into. Value demands and expectations are gradually clarified.

Without waiting for an exhaustive rundown on the respect history, we introduce another set of relationships, like *affectation*. The attempts of the subject to describe himself in reference to siblings and other age and sex mates as among the loved or not-loved, the congenial or the uncongenial, bring a great deal of material into the open.

When the productions in this realm begin to thin out or to become repetitious, the interviewer introduces another value which has already figured prominently in the subject's behavior in the situation, such as the making of appraisals in terms of "good" and "bad" or "guilt" and "righteousness" (the *rectitude* value). American civilization relies to a distinctive degree upon the giving or withholding of positive or negative appraisals of this kind. The inner evaluations of the "self by the self" typically include a liberal supply of these judgments, as do the inner or the communicated assessments of "others" by the self.

Since the subject's psychosomatic difficulties are often at the focus of attention, it is often convenient to begin with the well-being value and to review the past state of health, disease, defect, and care. Disproportionate emphases may rather speedily become apparent, such as the recurrence of symptoms when a problem-solving situation begins to get tough. If a sociopersonal context has been built up by the time well-being is considered in some detail, it may be feasible to aid the subject to recognize the degree to which illness has been exploited in obtaining physical comfort (also a "well-being" value according to our scheme of classification), affection, respect, or other values. Rectitude, for instance, may be involved if the illness is allegedly "borne with pious resignation for the Will of God."

In a society that attaches importance to *wealth* the efforts made by subjects to gain perspective on their economic history are usually illuminating to all concerned. The evaluation of saving, investment, and levels of consumption, as well as of risk, uncertainty, and profit, is in point. Since wealth is so important as a base value for obtaining respect, well-being, and other values, the side associations that spring from economic topics are especially rich in clues to the structure of the self-system.

Our society is inclined to overlay *skill* (and taste, which we treat together) with considerations of other values. As a result, the account of the growth of skill and of aesthetic judgment often brings the self into new focus for the subject. Associations are especially useful when the individual deals with the circumstances in which he became greatly attached to the arts of selling, or the study of rocks, or the driving of fast cars, or the paintings of El Greco.

We speak of the *enlightenment* value as a matter of access to the current stock of information and informed prediction about social policy. The significance of enlightenment is often overlooked by those who take our culture for granted; but it becomes more apparent to the participant when he undertakes to review the extent to which he has had access to "inside information" at the disposal of the leaders of groups and organizations to which he is affiliated. Formative experiences are often connected with exclusions from information, with the resulting, though unrecognized, conception of the self as dumb and uninformed and as a tool of the well informed. It is likewise important to disclose the role of access to an understanding of the larger context of affairs. The first intelligible visions of nature or of social relationships may be "critical experiences" in personality development.

A self-survey in reference to *power* typically brings out a flood of new insights. This is more than a problem of reviewing the success or failure of the nation-states, political parties, or pressure groups with which one has been affiliated and whose identifying terms have been incorporated at various times in the "identification system" ("identity" system) of the self. In a deeper sense, power is involved in all relationships in which severe deprivations are at stake. In many of the situations previously referred to it appears on re-examination that the demand by a person to impose himself upon others, or to become dependent upon one in such a position, creates the central core around which the personality system is organized. Frequently these demands are not directed in adult life toward the institutions conventionally known as governmental or political. The attempt by the individual to map the extent of his involvement with power in the family, the business, and every sphere of human relations frequently becomes one of the most clarifying experiences in the interview sequence.

The interviewer makes no attempt during the early stages of a "sociopsychoanalysis" to give strict definitions to the subject or to insist upon any particular set of terms for the eight categories of value made use of for theoretical purposes. Subjects gradually begin to employ the words in much the same sense that the interviewer does. At a later stage the semantic situation is brought to the notice of the participant, who is explicitly freed from any demand to adhere to one set of labels. But the importance of the use of intellectual tools capable of designating the sociopersonal context is made explicit.

As the interviewer listens to the productions of the subject, he pays attention not only to the emerging image of the self-system and the intensities with which the conscious system of values, identities, and expectations is supported or opposed by the unconscious components of the personality. He examines the "mechanisms" upon which the person relies in coping with conflicting parts of the entire personality. There are degrees of reliance upon internalization and externalization and upon repression, resistance, suppression, or rejection; upon images, moods, and conversions; and upon condensation (and the like). In general, the strategy of the interview series is to enable the subject to achieve the minimum level of effective insight and understanding that provides a moderate degree of protection against future crises. And the interviewer regards it as desirable to render these objectives quite explicit (to himself) and, as mentioned above, emphasizes the importance of conducting systematic research in which strategies are studied as fully as possible. It remains to be seen at which point the methods outlined here will establish connection with therapies designed to aid psychotics or defectives. If some of the more severe disorders depend upon the limited capability on the part of the somatic components of a system to withstand stress, therapy will presumably consist in restoring capability to behave satisfactorily under moderate stress. Therapy of the type we have been describing may increase the skill with which the individual is able to function by keeping his stress exposure within the limits of the capability of his personality system.

Ideological versus Material Factors; Comparisons of Values and Practices

The significance of psychoanalysis for the sociopsychosomatic context is but one aspect of the impact of Freud's work on the emerging image of the social process. At first, psychoanalysis was hailed as a formidable reinforcement of the influence of ideological as distinct from material components in human affairs. Hence the Marxist intellectuals and politicians were disposed to take a hostile position toward psychoanalysis save to the extent that it could be used to discredit "decadent" capitalism with its "petty bourgeois subjectivism."

And the adverse judgments by Marxists were justifiable in the sense that psychoanalysis has contributed to the growth of a more adequate frame of reference for the analysis of the social process than the Marxist system was able to provide. But the result has not been to sharpen the historic dichotomy between ideological and material categories but rather to reformulate the issue in terms that cut across them. We have seen the same process at work in moving from psychosomatic to sociopsychosomatic frames of reference and from "impulses" to social values established in interaction. The significant question about social process is not "material" versus "ideological" but "how much" impact one set of combined factors has upon another set. The operational definitions of "values" and "institutional practices" typically include details that once upon a time, if they were considered at all, would have been squeezed into the older mold.

Part of the early impact of Freud was to re-emphasize the importance of personality in the social process, thereby modifying the simple timing conceptions of the kind that had so often misled Marxist prophets of imminent revolution. Some of their errors sprang directly from the intellectual inadequacy of the Marxist system to cope with the differentiations introduced in a more intricate scientific and technical society than had been anticipated in the mid-nineteenth century.

It has made sense to recognize the significance of the "attention frame" ("social perception") at two phases in every interaction sequence. An act initiated by A would have different effects on B than on C if B and C perceived it differently. More satisfactory categories for describing and comparing ideological patterns led to the elaboration of such distinctions as the "system of identifications" ("reference symbols"), "systems of expectation," or "systems of demand." "Ideology" was generalized to include "utopias" as well as the established "doctrine," "formula," or "folklore" ("miranda"). A great many scholars figured in this extensive redefinition of the sociopolitical process (I mention Karl Mannheim, in particular). The result has been an intellectual weakening of rigid Marxist theory, not by polemical assault, but by subsumption under more comprehensive conceptions. The intellectual liquidation of dogmatic Marxism has been going forward to a degree that is only beginning to be understood; and outside the Soviet bloc it has every prospect of further development.

Toward a Configurative Frame of Reference; Employing Multiple Standpoints of Observation

From the beginning, psychoanalysis introduced a frame of reference whose full significance became visible much later. Freud was thinking in terms of the orthodox desire to explain and influence the nature and course of pathic processes. He wanted to build a body of verified propositions about the etiology of sundry disturbances and in this way to lay a solid foundation for further therapeutic advances. Gradually the scope of Freud's work expanded until he became fully aware of the fact that he was making fundamental discoveries about the biological, psychological, and social life of man.

And this brought with it the recognition that more complex tools were being used than seemed at first to be the case.

The therapist is always oriented toward the future, since he must guide his intervention in the life of the patient according to an estimate of contingent outcome. The overriding goal value is relatively clear: to improve the health of the patient. It is well known to every policy-maker who influences or estimates the future that systematic knowledge is always insufficient for his purposes. Hence he becomes accustomed to employ whatever information is at hand that will provide a basis of inference about the future. Some of this stock of available intelligence is systematic knowledge of past trends (e.g., the incidence of illness in psychosomatic types and the gross result of past therapies). Some of it is scientific knowledge (e.g., the impact of adrenalin on cardiac function or of occupation on the incidence of heart difficulties). Some of the available information is unsystematic, yet it helps in imagining and assessing a "developmental construct" of the sequence of future events. It is evident on analysis that the maker of therapeutic policy cannot wisely close his eyes to all these contributions. For instance, he cannot extrapolate trends or scientific interrelationships and remain blind to less systematic information that may provide a credible ground of inference about the order of developments. With a clearer image of order, the pertinence of scientific knowledge can be better appraised. The therapist goes further. He may invent courses of action designed to increase the likelihood that desired outcomes will, in fact, occur.

The foregoing points are in no sense uniquely related to psychoanalysis, but another point is, namely, the place of insight and understanding in the total context. The patient is modifiable by the act of being exposed to information about his own conduct in past situations. Furthermore, the physician is modifiable in the same way. (We may speak of "insight" in reference to the individual's own past; of "understanding" in relation to others.) The great and creative insistence by Freud on the efficacy of insight carries with it a challenging and dynamic implication for the future of man in society. It puts into a special category the data obtained by scientific procedures and the generalizations on hand at any given cross-section in time, when they relate to human interactions. These results of scientific effort enable predictions to be made of the future. This they have in common with scientific information about events other than human interactions. But knowledge of interaction may produce insight and in this way modify future events in ways that result in changing the scientifically established relationships themselves. It is not that scientific laws are unverified; it is simply that they are always to be taken as historical summaries of event relations, and the assessment of the likelihood that they will obtain in the future is a special problem.

Psychoanalysis has enabled social scientists to achieve a sounder grasp of their role in the social process. It differs in at least one important respect from the specialist on physical events. We do not expect the stars to step out of their courses when the astronomer announces to the world how they have moved in the past. When we tell human beings about the stars, we expect them to try to control physical events not by altering the past "regularities" of nature but by operating within this framework. By contrast, when we tell human beings about their interactions, we entertain the possibility that the relations confirmed by past observation may be altered as a result of the reporting of this intelligence.

The configurative conception of the place of the social scientist in society is not yet widely understood. Already, however, we are engaged in reconstructing our institutions of enlightenment. Our specialized agencies of self-survey are expanding in reference to every value-institution process in society. The story is the same whether we consider the reporting and analysis of economic, demographic, military, or other trends and conditions. We are moving toward a situation in which our knowledge of trends and scientifically verified relationships will be kept up to the never resting moment of choice.

Not the least significant implication is the renewal of emphasis upon the maxim "Know thyself." Machines are available to take over the repetitive choices that need to be made in industrial and other operations, leaving more time and talent free for discretionary choices.

Viewing the picture as a whole, I think we are justified in saying that psychoanalysis has accelerated the pace of self-discovery among human beings and notably among those who are self-selected specialists upon the explanation of man's pursuit of values through institutions utilizing all the resources at his disposal.

CLYDE K. M. KLUCKHOHN

Toward a Comparison of Value-Emphases in Different Cultures[1]

There are a number of recently published and thoughtful discussions[2] of the comparative method in anthropology which I have read with great profit. But I shall limit myself to one aspect of this vast subject: How can we compare with minimal ethnocentrism the more general or thematic value-tones or value-emphases that constitute the structure-points of whole systems of cultural values? I take this topic because I am convinced that, if the essence of culture consists in patterned selectivity, this selectivity can be parsimoniously described and understood only if we are able to isolate and compare the key values that give different cultures each a distinctive quality.

Let me start with a restatement of some familiar premises. The facts of situation, biology, and psychology will take us far toward an understanding of cultural universals but are not of themselves

1. This is a contribution from the Comparative Study of Values in Five Cultures Project of the Laboratory of Social Relations, Harvard University. I am indebted to numerous colleagues on that project for advice and help, both empirical and theoretical. I also express my gratitude to Warren Seulowitz for his careful criticism and checking of this paper. Finally, I profited from the discussions, both those of Professors Herskovits and Singer and those from the floor, at the session at which this paper was read. However, because of the preliminary nature of this communication, I have not attempted all the revisions and expansions which full account of these criticisms and suggestions would require. Indeed, my changes in the body of the paper are minimal. I have put in the Addenda some of my notes for further work.

2. E. H. Ackerknecht, "On the Comparative Method in Anthropology," in R. F. Spencer (ed.), *Method and Perspective in Anthropology* (Minneapolis: University of Minnesota Press, 1954), pp. 117–25; J. W. M. Whiting, "The Cross-cultural Method," in G. Lindzey (ed.), *Handbook of Social Psychology* (Cambridge, Mass.: Addison-Wesley Press, 1954), pp. 523–32; Fred Eggan, "Social Anthropology and the Method of Controlled Comparison," *American Anthropologist*, LVI (1954), 743–64; Oscar Lewis, "Comparisons in Cultural Anthropology," in W. Thomas (ed.), *Yearbook of Anthropology—1955* (Baltimore: Lord Baltimore Press, 1955), pp. 259–92.

sufficient to explain the diversities of human cultures. Culture is a way or style of doing things. Vomiting is a biological process. The division of labor and the giving and obeying of orders are social processes. But the inceptive and terminative cues that initiate and close such sequences are partly cultural, and the precise form of the processes is definitely styled by culture. Since our subject today is the cross-cultural comparative method, we shall be concerned with culturally patterned, qualitative emphases and not with the comparison of peoples or societies as such.

The immediate intellectual background of this paper may appear heterogeneous but actually has a single connecting thread: that of systematic analysis that departs from bipolar categories. My attention was first attracted to this kind of thinking when I studied some of Wittgenstein's work on logic, particularly his discussion of "atomic sentences."[3] Since then I have gained some familiarity with information theory and with the success attained by McCulloch and other neurologists in dealing with neural events by all-or-none categories. Psychological studies of "traits" and "attitudes" have sometimes utilized dichotomous scales. Most directly, my approach follows that of certain linguists.

Some linguists[4] in their elegant analyses of one aspect of culture have found it extremely useful to set up a series of distinctive contrasts or oppositions, usually binary, which serve to identify each separate phoneme. A "lump" or "bundle" of such "distinctive features" defines a phoneme. In its simplest form the process is like a specialized and sophisticated version of the "twenty questions game." Thus one may ask, "Is the phoneme vocalic? Yes or no." "Is the phoneme strident? Yes or no." In Russian eleven such questions will identify each phoneme uniquely. In the French phonemic system[5] the indispensable binary oppositions are the following: vowel-consonant, nasal-oral, saturated-diluted, grave-acute, tense-lax, and

3. Sentences so completely simple in nature that one cannot usefully discuss their contents but can only assert their existence or nonexistence.

4. See especially R. Jakobson, C. Fant, and M. Halle, *Preliminaries to Speech Analysis* (Massachusetts Institute of Technology, Acoustics Laboratory, Technical Report, No. 13 [2d ed.; Cambridge, Mass.: 1952]).

5. Cf. R. Jakobson and J. Lotz, "Notes on the French Phonemic Pattern," *Word*, V, No. 2 (August, 1949), 151–58.

continuous-intercepted. While the particular principles or distinctive features and their combinations vary from one phonemic system to another, there are some (e.g., vowel-consonant) found in all languages, and a total list of the oppositions utilized in known languages would certainly not exceed forty.[6]

There seem to me to be grounds, both theoretical and empirical, for suspecting that a similar approach might yield good results in the realm of value culture. There is a certain orderliness in nature, and language and values both are a part of the same general category of nature, namely, culture. Dichotomies are very slippery, to be sure, and the use of them often produces a false simplification of the phenomena. Yet they are not merely convenient. The fact that human beings have two eyes, two hands, two feet; the alternation of night and day; the existence of two sexes and other circumstances make it almost inevitable that people tend strongly to think and feel in terms of "either . . . or" and "yes and no." In every culture there are many paired opposites: "love and hate," "friends and enemies," and the like. Hence, however false to the complexity of the natural world this anthropocentric two-valued logic may be, it remains true that human behavior often takes place on this binary basis,[7] and this propensity introduces some regularities useful for scientific analysis. No multivalued logic has thus far been very successful except at the level of formal mathematical notation.

Empirically, it seems to be true that human nature and the human situation are such that there are certain fundamental questions of value upon which all cultures have felt compelled to take a position, explicit or implicit. As in the case of language, the foci are largely supplied by the limits and potentialities given by the physical world, human biology, and social requirements. With language, the properties of sound waves, the anatomy and physiology of the speech organs, and social (communicative) needs constrain

6. Jakobson, Fant, and Halle (*op. cit.*) tentatively isolate only fifteen, three of which are prosodic.

7. Joan Rayfield, "Duality Run Wild," *Explorations*, No. 5 (1955), pp. 54–67, maintains this is more true in the Western tradition. This may be the case, but one can instance many dualities in non-literate cultures. Certainly early historic religions are full of dualities: Yang and Yin (comprising such opposites as heaven and earth, sun and moon, fire and cold, active and passive, strength and weakness, male and female); God and the Devil; the Zoroastrian antithesis of Truth and Lie; myths of the conflict between Order and Chaos or Light and Darkness.

the range of variation between sound systems and make all phonologies comparable. And linguists now recognize that not all sound change is "blind." Both phonemic systems and sound change exhibit regularities that cut across the specific diversities traceable to historical accident. With values, such facts as dependence upon the external environment, birth and death, and social relatedness make value "choices" in these areas inescapable. Nor here again is the range of loci for selection or indeed of possible selections at each "locus" unconstrained. Just as all phonemic systems include nasals, stops, and sibilants of a limited variety of types, so all value systems place their weightings on the desirable relations to nature, other individuals, and self within a describable set of alternatives.

The entities of value-culture cannot be expected to have the all-or-none character of a simple physical event like a phone found in language-culture. Rather, they will have the character of weightings or emphases that are, on the whole, dominant in a culture. Even here there are parallels. A language or a phonemic system is, after all, a high order abstraction. Concretely, each person's speech is an idiodialect, and even this varies through time and between situations. Similarly, some individuals or groups may accept the variant rather than the dominant cultural values. They may reject some or many of the core values. To those values, whether dominant or variant, that they do accept each individual gives an interpretation and a coloring that is more or less private. It nevertheless remains meaningful to abstract common elements both in language and in values.

In working out a first sketch of suggested "distinctive features" of cross-cultural core value-emphases, I shall not hesitate to draw upon the broadest categories of human experience as revealed in history, philosophy, psychology, and the arts. In my opinion, most recent anthropology has been too timid about resorting to general experience. There is assuredly a need for severely technical description and analysis. But there is equally a necessity in some contexts for breadth and sweep. The resultant first approximations can later be subjected to precise and refined scrutiny. Likewise, I shall not hesitate to employ ordinary language. I am much less than satisfied with the terms I shall suggest. I feel that their denotations are fairly adequate, but the connotations evoked by English words (or

those of any other single language) introduce elements of equivo-
cation. Nevertheless, as a first step, I think this alternative is preferable to the proposal of neologisms.

Some Cultural Value-Emphases[8] and Their Clusters

CLUSTER 1: MAN AND NATURE.—These emphases are, in the first
instance, existential rather than evaluative, but, as Northrop and
others have argued, basic values are always tied to and dependent
upon a culture's conception of the ultimate nature of things. All
fundamental views of nature have implications for the total value
system.

1a. *Determinate-Indeterminate.*—This contrast hinges upon the
priority given to orderliness (lawfulness) in the universe as opposed
to chance or caprice or any factor or factors that make prediction
or control impossible *in principle.* A "mechanistic" emphasis does
not necessarily make human effort, including ritual effort, irrelevant.
On the contrary, as the cases of Navaho, Zuni, and many other
non-literate cultures show, this conception may heighten the amount
and detail of ritual behavior, both negative and positive. The Epicurean and Buddhist instances show in other ways how this contrast
is not that between theism and atheism. Nor is this exclusively the
polarity between "fatalism" or "predetermination" versus "free will"
or "accident." Rather, the essential contrast is between a state of
affairs conceived as operating in consistent and lawful fashion and
one where an indeterminism (of whatever sort) reigns. The former
case may eventuate in the outlook of Western science as stated by
Karl Pearson or in the attempt to control events by supernatural
techniques or in "fatalistic" acceptance. The latter, however, may
also have a "fatalistic" toning in a different sense: resignation to
"taking things as they come" without rhyme or reason. The indeterminate emphasis may also take the form of extreme voluntarism
(either human or divine), since nothing is held to be completely
determined or determinable. The outcome in the case of both alternatives will depend upon how this emphasis is juxtaposed with
other cultural emphases. Nevertheless, I believe this particular
binary opposition to be of absolutely crucial significance.

8. The reference is always to the "dominant," not the "variant," modalities in
the culture: the emphases preferred in feeling and idea as well as expressed be-
haviorally to at least a considerable extent.

1*b. Unitary-Pluralistic.*—Is the world, including human life, thought of as a single manifold or as segmented into two or more spheres in which different principles prevail? At first glance this contrast might appear to be a special case of the first. Certainly it would seem logically probable that the unitary emphasis would be likely to be found where the mechanistic emphasis dominates. But there are innumerable instances of "mechanistic" cultures exhibiting the familiar dualisms of "sacred and profane," "mind and body," not merely as categories in a larger whole but as altogether separate realms governed by distinct "laws" and with one construed as more permanent and superior to the other. Conversely, the classical Greeks who believed in ineluctable laws had a profoundly unitary conception of life.

1*c. "Evil"-"Good."*—Cultures ordinarily attribute to inanimate nature, to supernatural beings, and to human nature properties that are positively or negatively toned. Nature is threatening or beneficent; the supernaturals may or may not be effectively propitiated; human nature is basically good or evil. To be sure, the judgments often—or perhaps usually—come in somewhat mixed or qualified form, but I suspect that one polarity or the other usually stands out.[9] Emphasis upon "good" does not mean in the least that the problem of evil is ignored. Thus the Zunis show considerable fear of the evil intentions of individuals and groups outside the intimate household; they likewise are concerned with disaster from events of nature. Yet the Zunis still conceive the cosmos as fundamentally a good place. All things are in the final analysis benevolent functioning parts of a universal, timeless order. The dead join a legion of beneficent beings who stand ready to help those living at Zuni. The Navaho, on the other hand, who exhibit no more fear of witches and natural events than do the Zuni, nevertheless conceive the order of

9. Florence Kluckhohn in her theory of value-orientations (*Social Forces,* XXVIII [1950], 276–93) distinguishes three positions: evil, neither good nor bad (or mixed), good. There is no doubt that in some ways the trichotomy here as elsewhere (past, present, and future; lineal, collateral, and individualistic; subjugated to nature, in nature, and over nature) corresponds better to empirical reality. Trichotomies also, however, do not exhaust the empirical actualities, and I believe there are certain methodological advantages in at least trying out the binary scheme. Nevertheless, the present paper has benefited greatly from various writings by F. Kluckhohn on value-orientations. See especially the book by F. Kluckhohn, F. Strodtbeck, and J. Roberts, *A Study of Value Orientations* (Evanston, Ill.: Row, Peterson & Co., 1955).

the universe as "evil" in the sense that it is dominantly harsh and implacable. The dead are neither happy nor beneficent.

Dominance of the "evil" aspect in men or gods or both commonly leads to "the tragic sense of life," but this may also result from a belief in man's being at the mercy of the caprices of impersonal nature. Whether cultures take what Florence Kluckhohn calls the subjugated-to-nature, the in-nature, or the over-nature position depends upon how the mechanistic-indeterminate, good-evil, and active-acceptant value emphases are combined. Other combinations lead to dominance of optimistic, pessimistic, or resigned attitudes as dominant.

CLUSTER 2: MAN AND MAN.—These emphases tone the relationship of persons to their fellows and their notions of themselves and their own goals. They also affect the human relationship to nature in so far as exploitation of resources and dominance over or submission to nature are concerned.

2a. Individual-Group.—Is the individual or some collectivity (family, clan, local group, clique, occupational group, or tribe or nation) given priority? Is the individual a means to the ends of some collectivity or vice versa?

2b. Self-Other.—This refers to the relative emphasis placed upon egoism and altruism. The "other" consists in other individuals rather than in various solidary collectivities. For example, loyalty and devotion—at some expense to the interests of the self—are enjoined toward wife, children, and other relatives as persons rather than as a family entity. Or the emphasis may be directed primarily toward friends or occupational or ritual associates or to a god or gods. In any case the needs of the self are placed as high or low in reference to the needs of others (*as individual personalities*).

2c. Autonomy-Dependence.—This contrast is closely related to the foregoing but is not coextensive with either. It is similar to Riesman's "inner-directed"–"other-directed" polarity. A culture, like that of the Soviet elite, may give clear primacy to group goals and yet insist sharply on the autonomous responsibility of the individual. Traditional Russian culture, on the other hand, also favored group goals but encouraged the dependence of the individual upon the group. Dominant American culture at present makes a fetish of "individualism," though one can think of few complex cultures where individuals are in fact so sensitive to the pressures of the ephemeral standards of the peer group. "Dominant" Americans are typically "individualistic" but rarely autonomous. Similarly, cultures like Kwakiutl or Plains Indian which support flagrant egoism demand at the same time dependence upon the group. Modern French culture would fall in the self-autonomy category, but medieval Christian culture (Fromm) accentuated altruism and personal autonomy simultaneously. Perhaps this latter is the position of all "genuine" cultures (in Sapir's sense).

All human beings have experienced dependence as infants and children. This is one of the universal "cues" from which value selection and elaboration take off. Cultures vary in the extent to which this dependence in different forms is extended into adult life or taken as the basis for reaction-formations.

2d. Active-Acceptant.—This opposition is intimately tied to the determinate-indeterminate and autonomy-dependence pairs but is, again, not coextensive. Autonomy may take the active form of self-assertion or the passive form of withdrawal. The Epicureans postulated the existence of gods but believed that they too were bound by universal laws with the working-out of which the gods themselves were powerless to interfere. The Epicurean therefore accepted his lot with serene pessimism. The Buddhist also conceives of an order of things lawfully determined but intervenes very actively if only in a somewhat mechanical—and often withdrawing—way. The dichotomy is thus not strictly that between activity and acceptancy. The Spanish-Americans of New Mexico, to give another example, are acceptant but active in a "being" sort of way. They take Florence Kluckhohn's "subjugated-to-nature" position yet nevertheless are far from completely "passive."

2e. Discipline-Fulfilment.—Roughly, this is the "Apollonian-Dionysian" contrast. The issue is between safety and adventure, between control and expansion, between "adjustment" to the culture and internal harmony. Cultures stressing the "evil" in nature are likely to give emphasis to discipline, yet some of these cultures do emphasize either the self-realizing or the orgiastic dimensions.

2f. "Physical"-"Mental."—Are sensual or sensuous activities and reactions given a higher place in the hierarchy than the intellectualized? This is approximately Sheldon's "cerebrotonic" category versus his "somatotonic" and "viscerotonic" combined. This pair, once more, cuts across other pairs. Thus "discipline" may be predominantly motor or otherwise "physical" or may, on the other hand, be mainly artistic and intellectual.

2g. Tense-Relaxed.—Aspects of culture other than sounds exhibit these pervasive qualities which refer to the whole style of life and the general tone of all, or most, activities. One might anticipate that cultures with value-emphasis upon autonomy and discipline are more likely to be "tense," but this tendency, if it exists, is by no means an exceptionless uniformity (cf. Table 1). Nor does "relaxed" deny the presence of anxiety or even fairly frequent paranoid-like suspicion. The test is the degree to which tension of any kind is pervasive or is more than balanced by sense of humor and calm easy-goingness. This opposition could be called "intense-bland."

2h. Now-Then.—Cultures vary widely and importantly in their conceptions of time as an unbroken continuum or as segmented by a moving present or as homogeneous and instantaneous. But from the angle of values the most significant accent would appear to be that upon the here-and-now as opposed to either past or future.[10] The case of emphasis upon this life as contrasted with the hereafter is merely a special case of the now-then opposition.

CLUSTER 3: BOTH NATURE AND MAN.—There are certain value-emphases where existential and evaluative assumptions are clearly linked. They also apply both to the nature of the external world and specifically to that of man.

3a. Quality-Quantity.[11]—This contrast will reflect the degree of measurement or other standardization other than purely qualitative found in the culture. It will also be manifest in the extent to which the culture indicates that the natural world and human experience can be atomized. Conceptions of space and time will be largely influenced by the prevalence or absence of concepts of quantity beyond ordinal and cardinal numeration.

3b. Unique-General.—According to Northrop, this is the basic opposition between oriental cultures and those of the West, between the "undifferentiated aesthetic continuum" and "the method of logical postulation." Cultures emphasizing the individual event in all of its uniqueness are not, however, likely to be quantitative.

10. See n. 9 above.   11. See n. 15 below.

Experience is too much a sequence of events that may not properly be dismembered. Abstractions are either avoided or treated with great suspicion. The concrete and the literal are what count. Cultures, on the other hand, that favor the general are more interested in similarities than in differences. One sensitive index of this contrast is the tendency toward stereotyping present in the culture. In sum: discreteness and particularity contrasted with abstraction and universalism.

Discussion.—Let me repeat: this is a system of priorities, not a set of all-or-none categories. Each member of a pair will have some representation in every culture if only in variant value-emphases held by individuals or subgroups in the larger society. In some idea and behavior systems the secondary emphasis will be more prominent than in others. While in far the greater number of cases cultures take a pretty definite position one way or the other, there are instances where it would be plainly false to ascribe a definite "choice." Thus the Spanish-Americans regard the evil-good pair not so much as "mixed" as "uncertain." Potentialities for human afterlife and for a divine order in the universe are religiously defined as "good." Though this variety of Catholicism does not take a fully Augustinian position on the evil in human nature, elements of this view are also present. But the decisive fact is that as regards the outcome of any particular set of events Spanish-American culture does not stress either evil or good or some blend of the two. It simply says, in effect, "We do not know." In such cases we shall follow the practice of linguists and call this a "zero-feature."

There are two other binary oppositions that are at a different conceptual level from the foregoing which they cut across. It makes a difference whether or not the dominant value-emphases are conscious in the sense of being frequently and easily verbalized. The explicit emphases become subject to rational consideration and criticism and are probably therefore more labile. The implicit emphases are taken for granted, almost as unchangeable conditions imposed by nature. The whole of the explicit culture is analogous to what the linguists call "langue" as contrasted with "parole" or to cultural phenotype versus cultural genotype. All of the assumptions and categories that are unconsciously begged in the implicit culture make up the cultural genotype. Most of the core value-emphases in most cultures are—at any rate for the majority of the culture-carriers —genotypic in nature.

It would also appear to make a difference whether or not the core value-emphases take on a positive or a negative character. It is an induction from ordinary experience that the proportion of specific prescriptions (the "do's" and "don'ts" of every culture) may be weighted more or less heavily in one direction or the other. It seems probable that the value-emphases are "felt" primarily as avoidances or as seekings.

Trial Application to Five Cultures[12]

Let us now examine the profiles one gets if one compares the profiles for the five southwestern cultures studied by the Harvard Values Project. They seem to me to come out as follows:

Mormon: determinate, unitary, good, group, other, dependence, active, discipline, "physical," tense, then, quantity, general.

Homesteader: indeterminate, pluralistic, evil, individual, self, autonomy, active, fulfilment,[13] "physical," relaxed,[13] then, quantity, general.

Spanish-Americans: indeterminate, unitary, zero-feature, individual,[14] other, dependence, acceptant, fulfilment, "mental," relaxed, now, quality, unique.

Zuni: determinate, unitary, good, group, self, dependence, active, discipline, "mental," relaxed, now, quality, unique.

Navaho: determinate, pluralistic, evil, individual, self, dependence, active, fulfilment, "physical," tense, now, quality, unique.

Some of these assignments are admittedly arguable. The weight of the evidence, however, strikes me as reasonably clear in most instances. The average disagreement between my own original independent ratings and those of the "experts" is just over one category per culture. In some of these cases the cultures in question have changed radically during the past generation. In making my ratings, I tended to weight the older values as expressed, for example, in

12. In making these assignments, I have read the published and unpublished writings of our "experts" on each culture in the Values Study Project. I have also compared my own tentative "ratings" with several of the "experts" available for oral consultation. The "reliability" of our independent judgments was extremely high. In a very few particulars I have ventured to disagree with my expert colleagues on the grounds of written material and my own personal experience with these cultures over a period of more than thirty years.

13. There is a strong variant here: tense-disciplined. These could be called, following the linguistic analogy, "allo-values."

14. The dominance of individual-other is quite recent.

myths, while some of my colleagues laid greater stress upon present attitudes and behavior. I think also that the profiles make sense in terms of more general information. Each total profile is completely distinct, but Mormon and Homesteader appear as variants of Protestant American culture, while the Spanish-American, which is

TABLE 1

	Indeterminate (2 cases)	Pluralistic (2 cases)	Good (2 cases)	Group (2 cases)	Other (2 cases)	Dependence (4 cases)	Acceptant (1 case)	Fulfilment (3 cases)	Mental (2 cases)	Relaxed (3 cases)	Then (2 cases)	Quantity (2 cases)	General (2 cases)
Determinate (3 cases)	....	1	2	2	1	3	0	1	1	1	1	1	1
Unitary (3 cases)	2	....	2	2	2	3	1	1	2	2	1	1	1
Evil (2 cases)	1	2	....	0	0	1	0	2	0	1	1	1	1
Individual (3 cases)	2	2	0	....	1	2	1	3	1	2	1	1	1
Self (3 cases)	1	2	1	1	....	2	0	1	1	2	1	1	1
Autonomy (1 case)	1	1	0	0	0	....	0	1	0	1	1	1	1
Active (4 cases)	1	2	2	2	1	3	....	2	1	2	2	2	2
Discipline (2 cases)	0	0	2	2	1	2	0	....	1	1	1	1	1
Physical (3 cases)	1	2	1	1	1	2	0	2	....	1	2	2	2
Tense (2 cases)	0	1	1	1	1	2	0	1	0	....	1	1	1
Now (3 cases)	1	1	1	1	1	3	1	2	2	2	....	0	0
Quality (3 cases)	1	1	1	1	1	3	1	2	2	2	0	....	0
Unique (3 cases)	1	1	1	1	1	3	1	2	2	2	0	0	....

a fusion of Catholic European and Indian, stands somewhere between the Protestant and the Indian groups. Of the two Indian cultures, Zuni emerges as closer to Spanish-American, which is, again, expectable on historical grounds.

Table 1 (which was prepared after all assignments were final) shows ranges and combinations. "Quality" and "unique" give identical distributions, which suggests that they really represent only a single value-emphasis.[15] "Now" also gives an identical distribution,.

15. They might well be collapsed under unique-general as being the more inclusive category.

but it appears more doubtful that this is yet another instance of a single category. "Physical" and "tense" are fairly similar. "Evil" and "autonomy" bring out distinctions very sharply, but this may reflect the fact that only two cases and one case, respectively, are involved.

A central problem in value theory is: What combinations are likely—or possible? Definitive results on this point could make possible a kind of "scaling" or a statement of the really fundamental value-emphases from which others could be derived. Hence, in spite of the fact that in a number of instances only a single opposition is involved, I have analyzed, following Bloch,[16] into relative distributions. Taking the value-emphases on the left-hand column of Table 1 as P and the horizontal column as Q, I distinguish as "complementary" those cases where the ranges of P and Q are mutually exclusive, as "coincident" those where they are the same, as "incorporating" the instances where the range of P is wholly included within the range of Q but not conversely, and as "overlapping" the cases where a part of the range of P is a part but not all of the range of Q.

1. *Complementary*
   a) All of the original pairs (by definition)
   b) determinate-acceptant, evil-group (good-individual), evil-other, evil-acceptant, evil-mental, self-acceptant, autonomy-good, autonomy-group, autonomy-other, autonomy-acceptant, autonomy-mental, discipline-indeterminate, discipline-pluralistic, discipline-acceptant, physical-acceptant, tense-indeterminate, tense-acceptant, tense-mental, now-quantity (then-quality), now-general (then-unique), quality-general (quantity-unique)
2. *Coincident*
   evil-pluralistic, evil-fulfilment, individual-fulfilment, discipline-good, discipline-group
3. *Incorporating*
   determinate-dependent, unitary-dependent, evil-fulfilment, autonomy-indeterminate, autonomy-pluralistic, autonomy-fulfilment, autonomy-relaxed, autonomy-then, autonomy-quantity, autonomy-gen-

16. "Contrast," *Language*, XXIX (1953), 59–61. My attempts to combine this technique with some of those used by Harris on "discourse analysis" (*Language*, XXVIII [1952], 1–30, 474–94) have thus far proved unsatisfactory—even to myself. I still feel that some combination of these two approaches may prove extremely fruitful toward supplying a system for objective analysis of core value elements in cultures. In my adaptation of Bloch to cross-cultural analysis it may be objected that his technique is designed to investigate distributions and environments *within* single languages. I do not see why in principle it is not applicable comparatively. This may be methodologically wrong. If so, I wait to be shown wherein.

eral, discipline-dependent, tense-dependent, now-dependent, qual-
ity-dependent, unique-dependent
4. *Overlapping*
   All remaining cases

These results strike me as suggestive in a number of particulars,
but I cannot pursue the analysis further at this time. I do feel that
the investigation of the environments of all known value-emphases
should be carried much further because only in this way, I believe,
can we determine empirically what are the genuine contrasts between these basic elements in value-culture.

Final Remarks

No one could be more conscious than the writer that the foregoing
constitutes at best a point of departure rather than a point of
arrival. I would insist only that schemas of this general order need
to be worked on theoretically and tried out empirically if cross-
cultural comparison is to become parsimonious, comprehensive, and
fruitful. As is well known, Talcott Parsons[17] has developed another
set of dichotomies as the core of a rather complex theory. His pattern variables include:

> affectivity:affective neutrality
> self-orientation:collectivity-orientation
> universalism:particularism
> ascription:achievement
> specificity:diffuseness

It is evident that his schematization and the one proposed in the
present paper cut across each other. But he takes the actor and the
social system as his central concepts, whereas I take the "qualities"
or emphases in cultural values. Both types of analysis are legitimate
and, I suspect, necessary if we are to attain conceptual equivalence
across cultural boundaries.

Addenda

1. How did I arrive at the categories used in this analysis? By a series of
successive approximations. I examined somewhat similar lists such as those
appearing in Charles Morris' *Paths of Life* and *The Open Self*. I dipped into
the philosophical and anthropological literature in contexts I thought to be
relevant. By eliminating distinctions that appeared to be purely verbal or
special instances of a wider category, I constructed a set of categories which

17. *The Social System* (Glencoe, Ill.: Free Press, 1951).

I then tried out on data. This led to further deletions but also to some additions. I stopped revising at the point where most judgments came fairly comfortably and where little or nothing pertaining to core values (as stated either by participants or analysts) appeared to be left out.

The discussion at Chicago and subsequent talks with colleagues to whom the paper was circulated have generated the following pairs as suggested additions:

> skepticism-credulity
> "tough"-"tender"
> lineal-individual *or* group
> sober-humorous
> youth centered–age centered

Some (but not all) of these—or their equivalents—I worked with during preliminary stages. On the basis of this experience and also on logical grounds, I suspect that these positions are derivable from combinations of the categories I have used. But full empirical testing is crucial, and there is not sufficient time for this before publication. In any case I should hesitate to seem to "freeze" the list at this early point, for I know that much investigation by many workers will be required before even a "semifinal" set of categories can be taken very seriously.

I might add that of the present provisional list the "physical"-"mental" has given most trouble to my colleagues and myself. This, I think, is not due solely to the unsatisfactory terminology. The contrast itself needs better analysis. As it stands, it is equivocal, for it can mean, on the one hand, motor-visceral vs. cortical; on the other hand, sensuous vs. aesthetic-intellectual. Yet we all know how much sensuousness is involved in immediate aesthetic experience.

2. Professor Herskovits, who so kindly reported the results of trial applications by himself and his colleagues and students to cultures in Africa and Australia, said that in each case these additional raters found some categories on which their intuitive judgments were fairly immediate and decisive but others where they found it impossible to answer in yes-or-no terms. It seems likely that fuller and more precise "instructions to coders" would resolve some of these uncertainties. There is, however, another theoretical possibility that needs consideration. Perhaps in some—indeed in very many—instances the only proper answer is "both-and." The genuine distinctiveness of each culture may rest on those emphases that are unequivocally present—as juxtaposed with some but not others of the possible "both-ands." The special case of one set of value-emphases for males and another for females likewise requires further consideration. It may be that sexually dichotomous profiles will always need to be worked out as routine procedure. On the other hand, it may be that the single one holding for the culturally dominant sex might well stand as representative of the core-value emphases in that culture.

3. Some discussants suggested a rating scale for the intensity of each value-emphasis. This suggestion has merit, for experience is unanimous that even where one can unhesitatingly plump for the same emphasis in

two or more different cultures one is aware that this emphasis is more intense, decisive, or pervasive in one or more of these cultures than in others. However, attempts with members of the Values Study group to make such ratings were disappointing. The high reliability on all-or-none characterizations waned to about 60 per cent when ratings were given. This might be corrected were criteria spelled out fully and with great care.

4. With the suggestion of Professor Charles Morris that it would be better to regard these pairs not as dichotomies but rather as bipolar dimensions I have much sympathy. Surely the two-feature pairs are not so constituted that one empirically excludes the other in the culture, even though, in a formal sense, the relationship is in some cases that of contraries. Sufficient materials analyzed in terms of the complementary and other distributions may eventually show that in fact there are both "contradictories" (one negates the other) and "contraries" (one excludes the other).

5. Warren Seulowitz has analyzed the distribution of the pairs, proceeding from the value-emphases opposed to those used as the starting points in Table 1. We present below his main findings and hope that commentators and critics will give us the benefit of their interpretations of the logical implications—which are not altogether clear to us at present!

Working with the data presented in Table 1, it is possible to find the relative distributions of the converse pairs of value-emphases. It is worth noting that less than half of these converse pairs fall in the complementary, coincident, or incorporating categories. We will exclude those which are overlapping as this is a residual category and contains all remaining pairs. Further, in terms of relative distribution, it can be said that (1) where the pairs of value-emphases are incorporating, the converse pairs are not complementary; or where the pairs of value-emphases are complementary, the converse pairs are not incorporating; (2) where the pairs of value-emphases are coincident, the converse pairs are not complementary; or where the pairs of value-emphases are complementary, the converse pairs are not coincident.

There are four instances in which the value-emphases and their converse pairs are both in complementary distribution:

evil-group	(good-individual)
now-quantity	(then-quality)
now-general	(then-unique)
quality-general	(quantity-unique)

This tends to confirm the suggestion that "quality," "unique," and "now" are probably intimately related to a single value-emphasis.

There is but one instance where a pair of emphases is coincident both as stated above and in the converse. The associated emphases "individual-fulfilment" and the converse "group-discipline" occur here, whereas "discipline-good" is coincident and the converse, "fulfilment-evil," is incorporating. These cases suggest a possible relationship among "group," "discipline," and "good."

Finally, in the incorporating category there are five pairs which are also incorporating in the converse:

autonomy-relaxed	(dependent-tense)
autonomy-fulfilment	(dependent-discipline)
autonomy-then	(dependent-now)
autonomy-quantity	(dependent-quality)
autonomy-general	(dependent-unique)

This seems to indicate that the value-emphases of "autonomy" or "dependence" are being incorporated in the distribution of the other emphases. It is worth nothing that "quality," "unique," and "now" appear in similar distributions.

Of the thirteen original complementary pairs defined above, the following do not occur in any of the converse contexts but rather in the overlapping category:

> determinate-indeterminate
> unitary-pluralistic
> self-other
> active-acceptant
> physical-mental

Perhaps this indicates a complexity which requires further distinctions or different conceptualizations. It is quite possible that the above pairs are not as "genuine" as the eight others and hence require redefinition.

WARREN SEULOWITZ

Political Moieties

The comparative study of social structure, as conducted by anthropologists and sociologists, has numerous objectives. One of these is certainly that of shedding new light on the institutions of our own society, either by viewing these in cross-cultural perspective or by applying to their study the methods tested and found useful in the investigation of societies with simpler cultures. It is doubtless no accident that the two discussants on this program are distinguished by especially noteworthy contributions along these lines. Talcott Parsons (1949) has cast new illumination on the structure and functioning of the family in modern American society by applying the methods of kinship analysis worked out by generations of anthropologists among simpler peoples. Lloyd Warner (1941 and elsewhere) has adapted to the study of contemporary American communities the techniques of ethnographic structural analysis and has revealed the existence of a complex but largely covert organization into social classes which had eluded other methods of investigation.

My purpose today is to follow the lead of Parsons and Warner in the application of anthropological perspectives to the understanding of our own social institutions. I shall not, however, concern myself with the family, or kinship, or social class structure but rather with political organization.

Admittedly certain special difficulties stand in the way of viewing the political systems of the modern era from a cross-cultural orientation. For one thing, at least half of the simpler societies known to us lack any governmental structure transcending the level of the local community, and their political institutions are consequently in no way comparable with our own. In the second place, most of the remaining primitive societies are ruled by authoritarian paramount chiefs or kings, and the same is true of nearly all the early civilized peoples of whom we possess historical records. They

133

may be compared with profit to reveal certain parallels in the early development of states in different parts of the world, as has been done by Steward (1955), or to shed light on the fundamental structure of modern authoritarian states like those of Soviet Russia and China, as has been done most effectively by Wittfogel (1956).

But where can we go for instructive parallels to our modern democratic and representative political institutions? Surely our houses of Congress or of Parliament are important elements of our own social structure; our presidents, prime ministers, and constitutional monarchs occupy social statuses with highly significant functions; our mechanisms of popular election are no less worthy of analysis than rules of hereditary succession; our political parties and machines and our administrative bureaucracy are structures which impinge vitally upon all of us; and our international alliances, conventions, and organizations like the World Court and United Nations are as truly a part of our regulative system as are the rules of formal hospitality, blood vengeance, and market peace among nonliterate peoples.

To date, the comparative study of democratic political structures has been left largely in the hands of the political scientists. They have repeatedly and exhaustively examined the institutions of the ancient Greeks, the early Romans, and the Germanic peoples, with occasional references to the Slavic *mir* and house community, for insights into the structure and functioning of political democracy. All these peoples, however, are Europeans, linked closely to ourselves by historical and cultural ties. All reflect, in essence, a single tradition. Comparisons among them, consequently, are still culturebound, yielding knowledge only of the several variants of a single historical phenomenon. Is it not possible to break out of this circle? Cannot we find, in the rich resources of ethnography, at least a few strictly comparable situations whereby we can achieve a measure of cross-cultural perspective?

My paper is an attempt to actualize this possibility on a limited scale. I shall deal only with the subject of political moieties. Before approaching it, however, I must clarify, for the non-anthropologists in the audience, what is meant by the term "moiety." In its broadest sense, a moiety is any dual or dichotomous division of a society into two opposing or contrasting subgroups. The term is most commonly applied by anthropologists to what I shall call "social moieties." These are dual unilinear kin groups, characterized by either patrilineal or matrilineal descent. In a society with social moieties, every individual belongs to one of two such groups—that of his father, where descent is patrilineal, and that of his mother, under matrilineal descent. The two groups usually, but not universally, bear distinctive names, such as Eagle and Raven among certain American Indian tribes of the Northwest Coast, and they commonly assume reciprocal ceremonial obligations. Their most typical function, however, is the regulation of marriage. A member of one moiety is permitted to marry only a member of the opposite moiety; any sexual union within the same moiety is forbidden as incestuous, no matter how remote the actual kinship ties may be. This is what anthropologists mean when they speak in technical terms of moiety "exogamy."

Exogamous social moieties occur in somewhere between 10 and 15 per cent of all known societies, and they have figured prominently in the theoretical literature of anthropology on the interpretation of social structure. They appear more commonly in matrilineal than in patrilineal societies, despite the greater frequency of patrilineal descent, but the reasons for this lie beyond the scope of the present paper, as indeed does all the very substantial body of knowledge which we now possess about the origin and functions of social moieties.

Anthropologists have also devoted considerable attention to a second type of dichotomous division which is at least equally widespread and which I shall distinguish under the term "local moieties." Where these occur, a village, band, or district is divided into two opposing components which are often physically separated (e.g., in houses on either side of a central street or plaza). Occasionally, social moieties are thus localized and play a secondary role as local moieties, but more commonly the two divisions have nothing to do with the regulation of marriage and seem to fulfil functions of quite a different kind.

The possible sociological function of local moieties has challenged my interest for several years. In *Social Structure* (1949, p. 90) I called attention to the frequency with which communities are divided into two opposing factions and cited such cases as the

Tartharol and Teivaliol divisions of the Toda in India, the rivalrous districts of Faea and Ravenga in the Polynesian island of Tikopia, the local moiety cleavages of the Go tribes of eastern Brazil, and the striking dual alignment which Miner found in the French-Canadian parish of St. Denis, based ostensibly on political party affiliations. I noted how frequently such divisions oppose one another in games and how often their reciprocal relations are marked by rivalry, boasting, and covert forms of aggression, and I advanced the tentative hypothesis that such a dual organization "may provide a sort of safety valve whereby aggression generated by in-group disciplines may be drained off internally in socially regulated and harmless ways instead of being translated into out-group hostility and warfare."

Subsequent ethnographic reading has brought to my attention a third type of moiety organization, in which an entire political system is structured on a dichotomous basis, and it is of such "political moieties" that I wish especially to speak. I shall not be concerned with cases where local moieties have assumed political functions, of which the Eastern Pueblo Indians present an excellent example. Here each village has a dual ceremonial organization, the so-called two-kiva system, and the political affairs of the community are run alternately, for six months of each year, by the priests of each kiva organization (see Hawley, 1937). Nor will I do more than allude to cases where authoritarian states are organized in political moieties. In the Inca empire, for example, the communities (*ayllu*) of each province were usually grouped into two moieties (*saya*), called "upper" and "lower," respectively, whose representatives were seated in opposition on ceremonial occasions. Rowe (1946, pp. 255 ff.), who summarizes the scanty available information, notes specifically that these Inca moieties "were also rivals in war and religion." Evans-Pritchard (1948), who has described the political organization of the Shilluk tribe of the Anglo-Egyptian Sudan, notes that the two provinces into which the Shilluk kingdom is divided have no administrative functions but are exceedingly rivalrous and play opposing roles in the election and ceremonial installation of a new king.

I should like to dwell at greater length on two fairly complex political systems which are structured on a moiety basis and are found in societies whose institutions are essentially democratic. Since both lie outside the European cultural tradition, they can conceivably serve as a basis for cross-cultural comparison with the political structures of the modern Western world. Our first case concerns the confederations of the Indians of the southeastern United States, of which the most familiar is the famous Creek Confederacy, which bound together the Alabama, Creek, Hitchiti, and Koasati tribes and at a later date admitted the remnants of the Yuchi and Natchez. Since the political structure of the confederation was modeled upon the social structure of the local community, we must first examine the latter.

In the larger tribes of the Southeast the local unit was the so-called town, which might in fact be either a single stockaded settlement, a central village with outlying hamlets, or a neighborhood of scattered homesteads. In any case it was a community of neighbors who maintained face-to-face social relationships with one another and whose unity was symbolized by a centrally located ceremonial center and plaza. The inhabitants of a town were divided into lineages belonging to a number of different exogamous matri-sibs. The women of each lineage with their husbands and children were normally brought together, through matrilocal residence, in a particular section or ward, forming a matri-clan. A man usually married a woman of the same community and merely moved from his mother's to his wife's clan section of the town. The members of each localized matri-lineage seem to have been organized under a chief who was entitled to a particular seat in the plaza on ceremonial occasions and at political assemblies.

The lineages (and sibs) of a town were regularly distributed between two matrilineal social moieties, which were exogamous in some tribes but apparently not in others. One of these divisions was called the White moiety. The other, for the sake of convenience, may be termed the Red moiety, though various other names were more commonly applied to it. The civil officials of the town were regularly chosen from the White moiety; its military leaders, from the Red moiety. The chief of the ranking White lineage was usually ex officio the hereditary headman of the town. His primary function was supervision of the plaza, of the meeting house and the ceremonies conducted there, and of the public granary and the communal labor which filled it. The second-ranking civil official, a speaker or ceremonial leader, normally came from another White lineage, and the town's war chief was selected from one of the lineages of the Red moiety. Lesser civil officials and military lieutenants were likewise chosen from the appropriate moieties. The town also had a council composed of lineage heads and other prominent members of the White moiety who held assigned seats in the plaza. The war chief, his lieutenants, and the organization of warriors belonging to the Red moiety were responsible not only for military matters but also for the execution of the decisions of the council and for the punishment of civil offenders. The above description is severely streamlined for brevity's sake, since appreciable differences existed not only between tribes but also between towns of the same tribe.

The political integration of towns into tribes and confederations seems to have been accomplished by a relatively simple extension of these local institutions to a national or international level. The tribe or confederation was treated as a sort of supertown within which the component towns held positions comparable to those of the clans or localized lineages within the community, since lineages were grouped into social moieties on the local level. Moreover, these political moieties were regularly called White and Red, and peace functions were assigned to the former and war functions to the latter.

The civil head of a confederacy was sometimes the hereditary headman of the leading White town, sometimes an executive elected by the White town chiefs from among their own number. He enjoyed great prestige and was borne in a litter on ceremonial occasions, so that Europeans usually looked upon him as a king. His actual authority, however, was slight, and he was thus more nearly comparable to a modern constitutional monarch. The separate towns remained essentially autonomous except that they refrained from fighting one another and often combined in waging war against outsiders. Some tribal confederacies had a military commander-in-chief from a Red town, like the Great Red War Chief of the Cherokee, but the Creek Confederacy had no national military organization. In addition to its "king" or Great White Peace Chief, each federation had other officials, whose functions were primarily ceremonial, and a national council which met annually or oftener at the plaza of one of the member towns. These meetings, at which common problems were discussed and common policies agreed upon, were regularly associated with elaborate feasts and ceremonies.

Despite the similarity of names, a source of considerable confusion in the literature, the political moieties had functions quite distinct from those of the matrilineal social moieties. They did not regulate marriage, for most unions occurred within the same town, nor were they based on unilinear descent, for each component town included members of both matri-moieties. They seem to have served primarily as a mechanism for channeling aggression in socially harmless ways. Within each confederation the people of any town regarded the inhabitants of the other towns of the same political moiety as firm and dependable friends but looked with deep distrust and thinly veiled hostility on the citizens of the towns belonging to the opposite moiety. Sources of friction tended to be suppressed within the in-group and displaced toward the out-group moiety.

The mechanism by which this was exressed was the game of lacrosse—not the form borrowed by modern American colleges from the Algonkian tribes of the Great Lakes region, in which the ball is caught, carried, and thrown with a single hooked and netted stick, but the Southeastern version, in which each player carried two shorter sticks, one in either hand. When played for sport within a town, the sides were determined as a rule by the matri-moiety affiliations of the players. As a political instrument, however, it was always played between teams representing a White and a Red town of the same confederacy. In its emotional and ceremonial connotations it was looked upon as warfare, for which in actual fact it was a substitute.

Whenever antagonisms between two towns of opposite political moieties mounted to a high pitch, one would challenge the other to a lacrosse game. Envoys from both sides met to arrange a time and place for the contest and to agree on the number of players to a side, the location of the goals, the ground rules, and so forth. The game itself was played in dead earnest as though it were mortal combat. Spectators from both towns cheered on their respective teams, and at the conclusion of the match usually engaged in a free-for-all fight. The aggressions of the winners were drained off by victory and its celebration, and those of the losers had at least found vigorous expression at no more serious cost than a few cracked heads and could still be expressed in a challenge to a return match the following year.

Swanton (1922, 1925), upon whose work our knowledge of the Southeast chiefly rests, found great difficulty in determining which Creek towns belonged to the White and which to the Red political moiety, since his sources for different periods gave contradictory information. Haas (1940), in her linguistic work among the Creek, accidentally came across a fact, subsequently confirmed by Spoehr (1941), which provided not only an answer to Swanton's problem but also the capstone to our knowledge of the functioning of the Creek political system.

What Haas discovered and Spoehr substantiated was that any town which lost four successive lacrosse matches to a particular opponent was compelled to shift its political moiety affiliation. Thus a White town which lost four straight games to a Red opponent became a Red town. It had no choice, for it was deserted by all its former friends, who now regarded it as an "enemy," and would have been completely isolated if it had not accepted its old enemies as new friends. One can scarcely conceive of a device more admirably suited to preserving the unity of the entire body politic by preventing intertown rivalries from degenerating into permanent feuds. The political system of the Southeast was one in which unity was achieved through division, and peace through regulated conflict. It differed fundamentally in kind from other political systems of native North America; for example, that of the Aztec, which was based on conquest and military force; that of the Natchez, which was unified by a powerful religious ideology compelling loyalty to a divine king; and that of the Iroquois, which rested on an elaborate network of interlocking kin relationships.

Our second case is that of the sedentary Berber peoples of North Africa, whose political institutions have been worked out in detail by Montagne (1930) through both field study and comparative research. The Berbers have achieved political integration on three levels which must be sharply distinguished. The first level is that of the local community, which may consist either of a single compact village or of a cluster of smaller hamlets. Socially, a community is composed of a number of patri-lineages, sometimes but not always exogamous. Only rarely are these lineages related to one another, for the system is not typically a segmentary one. Each is localized in a clan-barrio, either a separate hamlet or a ward or "quarter" in a larger settlement. Government at the local level is vested in a democratic assembly (*jemaa*) composed of all the adult males of the community. The assembly has a presiding officer, but he is not a headman and exercises no executive functions. All decisions are reached by unanimous consent after general discussion. The heads of lineages and of extended families naturally exert more influence than other men and are often assigned special seats, but even the youngest arms-bearing man is privileged to attend and express his opinions.

The lineages of a community are frequently aligned in two opposing factions or local moieties (*sof*), whose relations are rivalrous and in some of the oasis towns positively hostile. In the Libyan oasis of Gadames, for example, Chavanne (1879) reports that the members of the two local moieties live in separate walled quarters of the town and never meet except at the market or in other neutral territory, where their encounters are often marked by bloody fighting. In the Egyptian oasis of Siwa, according to Cline (1936), their quarters are separated by a street rather than a wall, the inhabitants of each small outlying hamlet are affiliated with one or the other of the two moieties of the town, and overt hostilities were formerly common.

A number of adjacent communities form a district, representing the second level of political integration. Authority at this level is vested in a council composed of representatives of each of the lineages in the component communities. Though usually called by the same name (*jemaa*), the council has a more oligarchical character than the democratic local assembly, for its members are usually the older, wealthier, and more influential men. Each year the council elects one of its own members as president (*moqaddem*), usually selecting him from the various communities in rotation. He presides at meetings of the council, executes the decisions of this body with the help of appointed assistants, and, if influential, may be called upon to arbitrate private disputes; but his authority is severely limited, and he is jealously watched lest he usurp autocratic powers. The council reserves for itself all legislative, administrative, diplomatic, judicial, and fiscal functions.

When a district becomes involved in a war, the council appoints a military leader (*amghar*) with absolute authority for the duration of the emergency. From time to time such leaders, if strong and successful, have refused to relinquish their authority with the termination of the war, have usurped personal power and suppressed democratic institutions, and have even established small conquest states. This is, however, exceptional, for where the Berbers have achieved a higher level of political integration they have usually done so through quite a different mechanism.

An aggregation of districts forms a tribe, a group characterized by a common name, a contiguous territory, a distinct dialect and subculture, and occasionally, though not typically, a fiction of common descent. We might expect that the tribe would be politically organized, on the model of the district, under a representative council. Actually this does not occur, except temporarily and under highly exceptional circumstances such as the threat of alien conquest and subjugation, and even then the impromptu tribal council which assembles to deal with the emergency is more likely to be modeled on the local popular assembly than on the representative body which governs a district. Under normal conditions the Berber tribe is not a political unit.

Integration transcending the level of the district is achieved through an alternative principle—that of the political moiety or a dual system of alliances. This reflects the prevailing condition of constant warfare, raiding, and feuding. Each local group must be on guard at all times against a surprise attack. Hence every town and most villages are protected by a high encircling wall and by constantly manned watchtowers, and every hamlet by at least a dense surrounding hedge of almost impenetrable thorny shrubs. In addition, each community or district usually possesses a fortified granary at some central location, where each family stores its valuables and surplus food in special locked chambers. When danger threatens, the people drive their flocks into the courtyard of the granary and defend its high battlemented walls against attack.

In a further attempt to protect itself against hostile neighbors, each district enters into a series of defensive alliances with other and relatively adjacent tribes, until the districts of a region are linked into two opposing sets of alliances or political moieties called *lef*. Montagne (1930), in mapping the *lef* among the Kabyle of coastal Algeria, the Riffians of northern Morocco, and the Shluh of southern Morocco, discovered that in every instance they presented a checkerboard pattern, with each district bordered by some of the same and some of the opposite moiety. The agreements between the districts of a *lef* provide for reciprocal grazing rights during periods of seasonal transhumance and above all for mutual assistance in defensive war. These bonds of alliance are cemented by traditional forms of hospitality and by great annual feasts to which the members invite one another.

Warfare is confined almost exclusively to districts of opposite *lef*. When one Shluh district is attacked by another, it dispatches messengers to fire gunshot signals at the border of each friendly district, and shortly the forces of the *lef* allies pour in from every quarter to overwhelm the aggressor. Coon (1931) describes how the Riffians cope with an act of aggression involving several districts. All the districts of the victimized *lef* send representatives to an *ad hoc* council, which assesses a heavy fine against each aggressor district. If this is not paid, the forces of the entire *lef* assemble and attack the recalcitrant districts one at a time. As each is defeated, its fine is collected and divided among the victors, and the vanquished are compelled to join in attacking the next district, sharing in the division of its fine. Understandably enough, submission usually occurs well in advance of the conquest of the last offending district.

Since *lef* are primarily defensive rather than offensive alliances, they serve as a powerful force for peace in a region where warfare is endemic. There is evidence that this moiety system has been the prevailing type of political organization among the Berbers for more than two millenniums and that they have reverted to it whenever possible in preference to the only alternative they have ever known —that of total despotic power under an authoritarian state.

It may be of interest to note, parenthetically, that the republic of the ancient Carthaginians, which has aroused the curiosity of political scientists from Aristotle to the present day, was clearly modeled on the Berber system of government. Carthage, founded as a colony of Tyre about 814 B.C., originally had a monarchy of characteristically Phoenician type, but around 450 B.C. it underwent a revolution and instituted a republic with a popular assembly, a senate composed of representatives of the ruling mercantile families, and two annually elected presidents (see Gsell, 1918–20). For more than two thousand years the Carthaginian political system has remained an enigma to scholars, who have thought to compare it with the democratic institutions of ancient Greece and early Rome but not with those of the neighboring Berbers, which are identical at almost every point. Here is not the place to marshall the evidence that it was the Carthaginians who borrowed from the Berbers rather than vice versa. But it may not be amiss to observe that it is one of the fascinations of anthropology that field work done in the twentieth century A.D. is capable of shedding direct, and not merely indirect, light on important historical events which occurred in the fifth century B.C.

If we now view the political systems of modern western Europe and the United States from the cross-cultural perspective provided by those of the Southeastern Indians and the North African Berbers, certain general similarities become quickly apparent. The Creek Confederacy, which bound a number of different peoples together in a loose but co-operative peace union under a monarch with great prestige but little authority, bears at least some resemblance to the modern British Commonwealth, and the republics of the Berbers and of ancient Carthage, with their bicameral legislatures and their elective presidents, reveal unmistakable likenesses to our own American system of government, including even the principle of representation which has commonly been regarded as a unique invention of western Europe. Methodologically, however, such general parallels seem to me less instructive than specific similarities which suggest common basic functions. Hence I want to focus particular attention on the role of political moieties in all three groups of societies.

The Red and White moieties of the Creek Indians seem to have served a function very much like that of political parties in modern democratic states where a two-party system prevails, as in the

United States and most of the nations of the British Commonwealth. Like the Creek, we tend to displace the aggressions arising in our public life to the opposite political moiety, and like them we have a technique for draining these off periodically in formalized and relatively innocuous channels—not, to be sure, in lacrosse games but in another type of sporting event which we call elections. Having blown off steam and even, perhaps, effected some minor realignment in the forces of the opposing moieties, we, like the Creek, settle back to the ordinary business of life. Possessing such a safety valve, neither we nor they are ordinarily compelled to suffer the gradual accumulation of suppressed grievances and pent-up resentments until they burst their bonds in destructive revolution—the only recourse in states lacking such formalized channels of expression. That the moiety principle—or what John C. Calhoun, speaking of the American political system, called the principle of "the concurrent majority"—possesses certain inherent advantages over that of multiple factions is strongly suggested by the greater internal stability of those modern states with a two-party system than of those where political pressures operate through shifting blocs. In countries like France, Germany, Italy, and certain Latin-American states it is notorious that elections do not produce a lessening of political tensions and that aggressions, perhaps because they are diffused rather than focused, tend to be directed against the democratic political order itself and to find expression in experimentation with various types of authoritarian regimes.

The Berbers, with only local and temporary interruptions, have apparently preserved their democratic forms of government for well over two thousand years—a vastly greater span of time than any European democracy has endured. Throughout this period they have faced essentially the same fundamental political problem as that which faces the modern Western world, namely, that of defending their native democratic institutions from the dual threat of the rise of personal despotic power from within the society and of the imposition of authoritarian absolutism through conquest or subversion from without. That they have succeeded as well as they have for as long as they have should not only give heart to modern lovers of democracy but should also suggest that perhaps one reason for their success may reside in the inherent efficacy of an organization into political moieties.

It is to be noted as specially significant that the Berbers extended the moiety principle from the national to the international level. The modern European nations, of course, have done precisely the same thing, except that in this realm we are accustomed to speak of the moiety principle as the principle of "the balance of power." What essential difference can one note, as a matter of fact, between the *lef* alliances of the Berbers and the dual alignments of great powers which have characterized all modern history: Triple Alliance versus the Triple Entente, the Axis powers versus the Allied powers, the "iron-curtain countries" versus "the free world." Political scientists have convinced most people that the balance-of-power principle is dangerous, inherently unstable, and ephemeral. In this they may well have done us a disservice, for the Berbers seem to demonstrate that a balance-of-power situation can endure for millenniums. They also show that, though an international moiety organization by no means prevents war entirely, it certainly limits and inhibits it and, at the very minimum, makes possible the preservation of democratic political institutions over an unparalleled span of time.

Their confidence in the balance-of-power principle having been undermined, many well-intentioned people have been led to grasp at the most insubstantial of alternatives, such as limitation of armaments treaties, non-aggression pacts, and those (in my opinion) gigantic hoaxes: the League of Nations, which could not prevent a world war, and the United Nations, which could not even forestall small wars in Korea and Indochina. From the comparative evidence it would seem to me at least arguable that our country and the democratic principles upon which it rests would be safer if we frankly accepted the balance of power as an arrangement demonstrated by history and ethnography to be inherently workable and, recognizing its equally proved defects, devoted our efforts to correcting these, instead of deluding ourselves with mirages constructed of well-meaning words and pen strokes. Perhaps, with time and experience, we might even become as civilized as the Creek Indians and replace war with an athletic sport—if not lacrosse, then conceivably Olympic games or a Davis Cup match.

REFERENCES

CHAVANNE, J. *Die Sahara*. Wien. 1879.

CLINE, W. "Notes on the People of Siwah and El Garah in the Libyan Desert," *General Series in Anthropology*, IV, 1–64. 1936.

COON, C. S. "Tribes of the Rif," *Harvard African Studies*, IX, 1–417. 1931.

EVANS-PRITCHARD, E. E. *The Divine Kingship of the Shilluk of the Nilotic Sudan*. Cambridge. 1948.

GSELL, S. *Histoire ancienne de l'Afrique du Nord*, Vols. II–IV. Paris. 1918–20.

HAAS, M. R. "Creek Inter-town Relations," *American Anthropologist*, N.S., XLII, 479–89. 1940.

HAWLEY, F. M. "Pueblo Social Organization as a Lead to Pueblo History," *American Anthropologist*, N.S., XXXIX, 504–22. 1937.

MONTAGNE, R. *Les Berbères et le Makhzen dans le sud du Maroc*. Paris. 1930.

MURDOCK, G. P. *Social Structure*. New York. 1949.

PARSONS, T. "The Social Structure of the Family," in R. N. ANSHEN (ed.), *The Family: Its Function and Destiny*, pp. 173–201. New York. 1949.

ROWE, J. H. "Inca Culture at the Time of the Spanish Conquest," in J. STEWARD (ed.), *Handbook of South American Indians* ("Bulletin of the Bureau of American Ethnology," Vol. CXLIII), II, 183–330. Washington, D.C. 1946.

SPOEHR, A. "Creek Inter-town Relations," *American Anthropologist*, N.S., XLIII, 132–33. 1941.

STEWARD, J. H., ADAMS, R. M., COLLIER, D., PALERM, A., WITTFOGEL, K. A., and BEALS, R. L., "Irrigation Civilizations: A Comparative Study," *Pan American Union, Social Science Monographs*, I, 1–78. 1955.

SWANTON, J. R. "Early History of the Creek Indians and Their Neighbors," *Bulletins of the Bureau of American Ethnology*, LXXIII, 207–86. 1922.

———. "Social Organization and Social Usages of the Indians of the Creek Confederacy," *Annual Reports of the Bureau of American Ethnology*, XLII, 23–472. 1925.

WARNER, W. L., and LUNT, P. S. *The Social Life of a Modern Community*. New Haven. 1941.

WITTFOGEL, K. A. *Hydraulic Society*. New Haven. 1956.

ROBERT F. BALES*

Task Status and Likeability as a Function of Talking and Listening in Decision-making Groups

One of the most interesting problems in small-group research is the relationship between the network of affective relations, such as liking and disliking, among members, and the network of relations that grows out of the performance of functions required by the more technical tasks of the group. The problem as to how these two networks fit together in the small group is an analogue of the problem of informal versus formal structures in larger organizations. A very similar problem is encountered again in the study of full-scale societies, as the relation between the "primary-group" structures such as family and peer group relations as compared to the "secondary-group" structures such as occupational and market relations.

A very general belief, and one which I have held in various forms, is that there is some kind of almost inevitable contrary or interfering relation between the strength and elaboration of the technical division of labor and the strength and elaboration of the network of solidary affective ties within a given group. That is, as one network is increased in strength and elaboration, the other is likely to suffer interference. As an illustration, consider the fact that there is hardly any more familiar theme in sociology than the contrast between the technologically primitive societies, with their generally strong and elaborate kinship system, and the technologically elaborate societies, with their relatively weak and simplified kinship systems. The belief in this contrariety between technical and social demands appears in many versions.

This paper is concerned with small experimental decision-making groups. But the problem on which attention is centered has close analogues in other types of groups and, indeed, I believe, in every

* Although I am responsible for this draft of the paper, the ideas and the work with the data are the product of close collaboration with Arthur S. Couch and Philip E. Slater on a research project under the Laboratory of Social Relations at Harvard.

148

social system of whatever size and scope. This does not imply that the empirical relations between the affective network and the network formed by the division of labor will be the same in every type of group or social system. But it does imply that a better understanding of the relation for one type of group may result in conceptual distinctions that may be helpful in the study of other types of groups. I hope to illustrate this point with a short review of some findings of small-group researchers and with some new data that, I think, clarify some issues.

Review of the Literature

A recent study by Wispé provides an excellent example of what might be called the "hypothesis of contrariety."[1] Wispé refers to "Riesman's recent provocative analysis of the character structure of the American middle class."[2] Riesman, he says, "contends that in the shift from 'inner-' to 'other-directedness' the individual has become not only an overconformist but at the same time a lonely member of a lonely crowd. Whereas the inner-directed individual internalized adult authorities, the other-directed person is completely dependent upon peer-group sanctions and is thus in the dilemma of seeking rewards and approbation from the very individuals with whom he is forced to compete. This paradoxical situation has led Riesman to suggest that increase in achievement in the group is made at the expense of peer-group affection."

Wispé's study is concerned with a set of ratings and choices made of each other by a group of insurance salesmen in an insurance organization. After a factor analysis of his data Wispe interprets his results as congruent with Riesman's hypothesis. He finds a "paradoxical situation: the hard-driving agent, who may be a valuable asset on one's debit, is not the person to invite home for a relaxing evening, while the person with compassionate qualities, who makes a pleasant house guest, is not the person to select if you have to make your daily quota of sales. This conflict of expectancies reveals the agents' dilemma. As insurance salesmen these men would like to be successful, and as human beings they would like to be accepted. Yet, according to the analysis, the traits which make for success as

1. Lauren G. Wispé, "A Sociometric Analysis of Conflicting Role-Expectations," *American Journal of Sociology*, LXI (1955), 134–37.

2. D. Riesman, R. Denney, and N. Glazer, *The Lonely Crowd* (New Haven, Conn.: Yale University Press, 1950).

an insurance salesman *preclude* acceptance as a friend." (Italics mine.)

A closer look, however, suggests that Wispé has misinterpreted his data. His factor analysis indicates that the two factors to which he is referring, "aggressive salesmanship" and "sociability and sympathy," are not opposites which *preclude* each other but are rather approximately *orthogonal* to each other. That is, the traits to which the factors refer are found going together as often as not going together. They are uncorrelated; at least they are not linearly correlated.

Wispé actually found three orthogonal factors, which he describes as follows:

Factor A, *insurance intelligence,* has high loadings on items 4 and 7, which pertain to "help with an insurance problem" and "technical insurance information," respectively. This factor seems to describe the kind of person to whom the men turn for technical insurance information.

Factor B, *sociability and sympathy,* has loadings on item 3, "choices for a house guest," and item 6, "the most sympathetic man in the district."

Factor C, *aggressive salesmanship,* has high loadings on items 1, 2, and 5. Item 1 refers to "choices for an assistant for a day on the debit"; item 2 refers to "someone to present a new sales plan"; and item 5 is the selection of the "most aggressive man in the district." This factor seems to be the stereotyped aggressive salesman.

These three factors bear a very strong resemblance to the findings of a number of other factor analytic studies in which members of small groups rate and choose each other on a wide variety of descriptive criteria, or are assessed by observers. Carter[3] indicates the generality of the factors in reviewing a series of factor analytic studies, such as those by Couch and himself,[4] Sakoda,[5] Wherry,[6] and Clark.[7] Carter describes the factors as follows:

3. Launor F. Carter, "Recording and Evaluating the Performance of Individuals as Members of Small Groups," *Personnel Psychology,* VII (1954), 477–84.

4. Arthur S. Couch and Launor F. Carter, "A Factorial Study of the Rated Behavior of Group Members." (Paper read at Eastern Psychological Association, March, 1952.)

5. J. M. Sakoda, "Factor Analysis of OSS Situational Tests," *Journal of Abnormal and Social Psychology,* XLVII (1952), 843–52.

6. R. J. Wherry, *Factor Analysis of Officer Qualification Form QCL-2B* (Columbus: Ohio State University Research Foundation, 1950).

7. R. A. Clark, "Analyzing the Group Structure of Combat Rifle Squads," *American Psychologist,* VIII (1953), 333.

Factor I. *Individual prominence and achievement*—behaviors of the individual related to his efforts to stand out from others and individually achieve various personal goals. [This seems similar to Wispé's "aggressive salesmanship."]

Factor II. *Aiding attainment by the group*—behaviors of the individual related to his efforts to assist the group in achieving goals toward which the group is oriented. [This is similar to Wispé's "insurance intelligence."]

Factor III. *Sociability*—behaviors of the individual related to his efforts to establish and maintain cordial and socially satisfying relations with other group members. [This is similar to Wispé's "sociability and sympathy."]

These factors seem to represent underlying dimensions in the evaluations persons make of each other, whether as observers or as fellow group members. It may be that the best way of looking at these factors is not as personality traits but as frameworks in which personality traits of others are responded to by the perceiver.

But the important thing to note is that these three factors, which I shall call "activity," "task ability," and "likeability," are, in the studies mentioned, including Wispé's, not mutually exclusive, so that a high standing on one precludes or interferes with a high standing on the other, but, rather, they are in general uncorrelated.

Now this in itself may be regarded as anomalous. Indeed, when I first set out to examine data from my own experimental groups, I made the working assumption that there might be some such thing as a "simply organized group," that is, one in which the rank order of members on activity, task ability, and likeability would coincide, and that these groups would in some sense or other be the most successful or best satisfied.[8] It turned out that for the groups examined there was some positive correlation between the three, especially activity and task ability, but the top man in activity, in particular, was unaccountably low on the average as to likeability.

This problem has been explored at some length with my colleagues Slater, Couch, and others.[9] Some of us were loath to believe,

8. Robert F. Bales, "The Equilibrium Problem in Small Groups," chap. iv in Talcott Parsons, Robert F. Bales, and Edward A. Shils (eds.), *Working Papers in the Theory of Action* (Glencoe, Ill.: Free Press, 1953).

9. Robert F. Bales and Philip E. Slater, "Role Differentiation in Small Decision-making Groups," chap. v in Talcott Parsons *et al.* (eds.), *Family, Socialization, and Interaction Process* (Glencoe, Ill.: Free Press, 1955). Cf. Edgar F. Borgatta, Robert F. Bales, and Arthur S. Couch, "Some Findings Relevant to the Great Man Theory of Leadership," *American Sociological Review*, XIX (1954), 755–59.

as I hypothesized, that there was something about arriving in a top status position, owing to technical contribution to the task problems of the group, that tended to "lose friends and alienate people."

One hypothesis which might lead one to expect this result is an expectation based on the psychoanalytic finding of the ubiquity of transference. One might be led to expect a tendency to transfer whatever negative attitudes there may be toward authority to any person who begins to achieve prominence or high status.

Another line of thinking which suggests a similar result is the hypothesis that, in a decision-making group, the person who takes the lead in finding some solution to the problem will generally threaten some values held dear by some members of the group and may collect by displacement the negative affect generated by the general value conflict, as well as that due to the disturbance he directly provokes.

Still another line of thinking suggests that, in groups of the sort we were studying, it is very difficult to make a substantial contribution to the task without talking a great deal, and overtalking may be resented by other members as a threat to their own status and a frustration of their own desire to talk. Results of other experimenters provided some findings that are congruent with this line of thought. Let us look for a moment at some of these results.

Leavitt and Mueller[10] explored the effect of one-way communication in a restricted communication situation where the receiver of the information is given no opportunity to "feed back" acknowledgments, questions, or negative reactions to the sender. They find that an initial reaction of hostility toward the sender tends to appear.

Thibaut and Coules[11] find that receivers who are permitted to communicate back to a person who has sent them an act of hostility show more post-experimental friendliness to the sender than those not permitted to communicate.

A peripheral position in a restricted network in some ways approximates the position of a receiver with no opportunity for feed-

10. H. J. Leavitt and R. A. H. Mueller, "Some Effects of Feedback on Communication," *Human Relations*, IV (1951), 401–10.

11. J. W. Thibaut and J. Coules, "The Role of Communication in the Reduction of Interpersonal Hostility," *Journal of Abnormal and Social Psychology*, XLVII (1952), 770–77.

back. Leavitt,[12] in an experiment where members are allowed to communicate only in written form through set channels on a task of assembling information, finds that members in peripheral positions are less well satisfied with their jobs than those in central positions.

Apparently one-way communication or restriction on amount of communication prevents not only expressive catharsis but also the opportunity for building new understandings and norms by which the members can manage their further social relationships and their process of communication. From this basic impairment other problems may then develop.

These results suggested to us that the relatively low average shown by top participators on the receipt of liking might be due to the presence of some men in the total population of top men who overtalk, in the sense that they do not allow an appropriate amount of feedback of objections, qualifications, questions, and counter-suggestions to occur. Our method of observation allowed us to examine the amount of interaction a given man received in relation to the amount he initiated. We thus arrived at the hypothesis that the ratio of interaction received to that initiated might help distinguish beween those top interactors who were proportionately well liked and those who were not.

The Sample and Design

The sample which provided data for the investigation consisted of sixty sessions of five-man experimental groups. The subjects were a hundred and fifty Harvard Freshmen who were recruited by a letter sent to a random sample of the entering class, briefly describing the experiment as concerned with group problem-solving and decision-making. Volunteers were offered six dollars for about six hours' work, including the taking of several personality tests and participation in two group meetings, one fall term and one spring term. Each subject is thus represented twice in the data, having participated in two different groups.

The task of each session was the discussion of a human relations

12. H. J. Leavitt, "Some Effects of Certain Communication Patterns on Group Performance," *Journal of Abnormal and Social Psychology*, XLVI (1951), 38–50.

case, a five-page presentation of facts about a problem facing an administrator in his organization. Members were given copies of the case separately, to read ahead of time, and were told that, although each was given accurate information, we intended to leave them uncertain as to whether they each had exactly the same range of facts. The cases were collected after they had been read by the members individually, to prevent direct comparison of typed copies, although members were allowed to take notes. The task defined for each session was to assemble the information, to discuss why the people involved were behaving as they did, and to decide what should be recommended as action for the solution to the problem presented. The groups were asked to time themselves to forty minutes and to dictate the group solution for the sound record in the final one or two minutes of the meeting.

After the task session the subjects were asked to make a series of ratings and choices of each other and to respond to a number of evaluative items on a questionnaire designed to tap various aspects of their satisfaction with the meeting.

Among the rating questions were the following:

1. Who contributed the best ideas for solving the problem (i.e., showed the best understanding and grasp of the problem, the keenest insight, the most reasoning ability)? Please rank the members in order. Include yourself.

2. Regardless of how valuable you felt he was to the group, how well do you like each of the other members of the group? Please rate each of the other members on a scale of 0, 1, 2, 3, 4, 5, 6, 7, where "0" is equivalent to saying: "I feel completely neutral toward him," and "7" is equivalent to saying: "I like him extremely well."

3. To what extent do you find qualities in other members of the group which you personally dislike or which seem to irritate you? Please rate each of the other members on a scale of 0, 1, 2, 3, 4, 5, 6, 7, where "0" is equivalent to saying: "There is nothing I dislike about him," and "7" is equivalent to saying: "I dislike everything about him."

It will be noted that the first question lies in the area of task ability; the next two have to do with likeability, asked both positively and negatively. The factor of activity or amount of participation was measured directly through the observation of the interaction using the method described in my book, *Interaction Process Analysis*.[13] We have found that there is a very high correlation,

13. Robert F. Bales, *Interaction Process Analysis: A Method for the Study of Small Groups* (Cambridge, Mass.: Addison Wesley Press, 1950).

about .90, between subjects' judgments as to amount of interaction of each other and the scores obtained by our own observations using this method. It is also of interest in the present connection that, when we ask subjects to rate each other on "who was most aggressive, tried hardest to lead, was most assertive," the result is very highly correlated with gross activity.

We thus believe that we have fair representative measures for our situation of the three factors that have turned up in so many other studies: activity, task ability, and likeability. In addition to the factors measured as described, observers also rated each subject directly, using as guides the three trait names.

It has been mentioned that each subject participated twice, in two different groups. For the first meeting in the fall, subjects were randomly assembled into thirty five-man groups. These will be called the "R" groups, to stand for "Random Assembly." On the basis of this meeting subjects were individually assessed on the three factors mentioned above, using both their own and observers' ratings.

For the second meeting in the spring, subjects were carefully assembled according to a design, using the assessments from the fall term. These groups will be called the "C" groups, to stand for "Composed Assembly."

The composition plan was an attempt to vary experimentally the way in which the traits of high activity, task ability, and likeability were distributed among members. We wanted to compare groups where one man was present who had been assessed as high on all three factors with groups where a high value on each factor was represented by three separate persons. The design for composition used all subjects, attempting to utilize the talents of each and to counterbalance what we felt were liabilities of given members with complementary high qualities of others, in such a way as to obtain, on the average, higher satisfaction for the subjects than was obtained by random assembly.

The composition was based on a typology obtained from the factor assessments. Types were defined as follows:

1. The *"great man"*: High on all three factors, activity, task ability, and likeability. (Called GM.)
2. The *"task specialist"*: High on activity and task ability, somewhat lower on likeability. (Called T Men.)

3. The *"social specialist"*: High on likeability, somewhat lower on activity and task ability. (Called S Men.)

4. The *"deviant"*: High on activity, low on task ability and likeability. (Called D Men.)

5. The *"residual member"*: Characterized by their rate of activity, grading from medium to low, with task ability and likeability also grading from medium to low. (Called R Men.)

The design divided the total number of thirty groups into batches of six groups. Twenty-four of the groups were used in a two-by-two design for analysis of variance. In this two-by-two design, half of the groups were provided with a person assessed as a Great Man. The other half were provided with what we hoped would be a complementary combination of a Task Specialist and a Social Specialist. Along the cross-cutting dimension of the design, half the groups were provided with a person assessed as a Deviant; the other half were spared this trouble. There were thus six groups in each of four types.

All twenty-four of these groups were composed according to an additional principle: namely, that the assessed activity rates of all members within each group should grade down as evenly as possible, from the leadership structure through the range of Residual Members. This was most difficult, of course, in those groups containing a Deviant, since these were persons who by definition had high activity rates. For these groups, however, we reserved the most active of the Great Men and the Task Specialists and tried in each case to match the Deviant with one other man of one of these two types who had a higher rate or one almost as high.

For the remaining six groups out of the thirty, we adopted a principle of homogeneity for composition, putting persons of each type together in the same group. I shall not comment on these groups further, but I mention them because they are included in the data now to be reported.

Results

The problem of this paper is to attempt to get some additional insight into the relation between activity, task ability, and liking. In general, as has been indicated, these appear in many studies as orthogonal factors, uncorrelated with each other over the total population assessed. It is important to recognize, however, that the relationship discovered is always relative to the population assessed. Thus it is possible that subparts of the population, or a different population, may show the variables related in a way other than the original population. It is the possibility that subparts of our population may show different relationships of these variables that we now explore. In other words, the factor analytic results of other

TABLE 1

AVERAGE RATINGS RECEIVED ON LIKING, DISLIKING, AND IDEAS, BY MEN OF EACH BASIC INITIATING RANK (B.I.R.), ACCORDING TO THEIR FEEDBACK RATIO (PARTICIPATION RECEIVED TO PARTICIPATION INITIATED, R/I), AND BY TYPE OF GROUP ASSEMBLY (RA = RANDOM ASSEMBLY; CA = COMPOSED ASSEMBLY)

B.I.R.	Low R/I		Medium R/I		High R/I		Total All Types
	Assembly						
	RA	CA	RA	CA	RA	CA	
Mean* Like Ratings Received							
1	13.6	11.9	17.6	15.4	16.3	16.4	91.2
2	14.9	15.1	17.2	18.3	14.6	16.0	96.1
3	15.5	14.8	13.4	18.4	15.5	15.2	92.8
4	13.7	16.4	14.3	15.6	14.0	14.3	88.3
5	12.3	15.6	13.4	9.5	11.1	13.3	75.2
Mean Dislike Ratings Received							
1	8.6	9.3	5.5	7.6	6.9	7.8	45.7
2	7.8	6.2	4.0	5.7	5.9	6.2	35.8
3	5.3	8.0	6.6	5.5	4.3	6.7	36.4
4	5.3	5.6	7.0	6.0	4.9	8.0	36.8
5	3.8	5.4	3.4	8.5	6.0	7.4	34.5
Mean Idea Ratings† Received							
1	11.1	12.5	14.4	12.9	13.3	12.0	76.2
2	12.2	11.0	12.2	12.3	11.6	11.2	70.5
3	11.1	9.9	10.2	11.4	9.9	11.0	63.5
4	7.7	9.3	8.6	9.1	8.6	7.9	51.2
5	5.4	7.2	6.6	5.3	6.9	7.0	38.4

* Each entry, with the exception of the totals, is the mean for ten persons.
† Actually the question required ranking. For more direct comparison with the other entries, summed rankings have been subtracted from a constant, 20, to make a high number correspond with a high rank.

studies are taken as a criterion of important variables to explore. We then explore the relations of the variables within subparts of our total population.

We first make a basic division of the population according to the rank of each person within his own group on the gross amount of

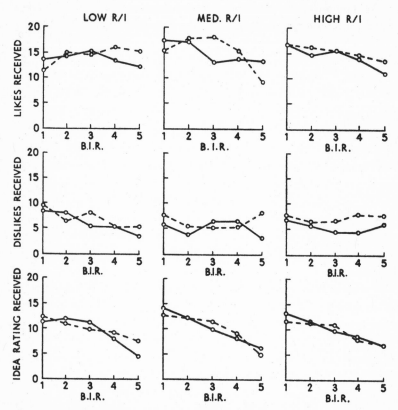

Fig. 1.—Average ratings received on Liking, Disliking, and Ideas, by men of each Basic Initiating Rank (B.I.R.), according to their Feedback Ratio (Participation Received to Participation Initiated, R/I). Solid lines=Randomly Assembled groups; Dashed line = Composed groups.

participation he initiated, that is, his Basic Initiating Rank. Five ranks are thus recognized, since the groups were five-man groups.

The second division of the population is made within each rank. All the men of each rank are divided into three subpopulations according to their own ratio of amount of participation received from others to the amount of participation they initiate. This ratio is known as the *R/I*, or Feedback Ratio. Within each rank, then, there are three subpopulations of ten men each, Low, Medium, and High on the Feedback Ratio.

Table 1 shows the average values of ratings or ranking received for each of the subpopulations of ten men, on Liking, Disliking, and Ideas. The ratings or rankings were given to each man by his fellow four group members in answer to the questions detailed earlier.

Discussion

The first point deserving comment, perhaps, is the pattern of Liking received as related to Basic Initiating Rank. The total population shows a tendency toward a curvilinear correlation in which the top-ranking man on activity is lower on Liking received, on the average, than the second or third man. This result replicates previous findings of our own that set the problem for the present study.[14] However, as one examines the three subpopulations according to the Feedback Ratio, it is clear that there is no *consistent* correlation, either linear or curvilinear. This heterogeneity among the subpopulations is apparently consistent with the factor analytic studies mentioned, which find sociability and activity to be generally orthogonal.

With regard to the Idea rating received and Basic Initiating Rank, it is equally plain that there is a rather consistent linear correlation over nearly all subpopulations. This finding thus differs from other studies which find these two variables to be generally orthogonal. We attribute the correlation in our groups at least partly to the fact that we are dealing in this study with data from first meetings entirely. Previous data on groups running over four sessions indicate that this correlation tends to fall over time, especially in groups where the initial consensus as to who has the best ideas is low.[15] The correlation between Ideas and Liking also tends to fall. In short, the three factors tend to separate out as independent more clearly in later meetings than in the first.

But the point of real interest in the present context is the marked difference in the relations of Liking received to Basic Initiating

14. Bales, "The Equilibrium Problem in Small Groups," *op. cit.*

15. Philip E. Slater, "Role Differentiation in Small Groups," *American Sociological Review*, XX (1955), 300–310.

Rank when the Feedback Ratio is taken into account. Table 1 indicates that among the third of the population with a Low Feedback Ratio, the correlation between Liking received and Basic Initiating Rank is zero, or, for the C groups, perhaps even negative. The Medium third on the Feedback Ratio, especially for the C groups, indicates a curvilinear correlation. Liking received is positively associated with Basic Initiating Rank from the lower ranks up to about rank 3. The correlation then disappears or turns negative for ranks 2 and 1. Finally, for the third with a High Feedback Ratio the correlation appears to be positive and approximately linear.

To sum it up briefly: In the groups in this total sample there is no *linear* correlation between Liking received and Basic Initiating Rank, providing one makes no breakdown into subpopulations. But for about one-third of the population there *is* a positive and linear correlation between how much a man talks and how well he is liked. This is the third, who, in their interaction, receive more in proportion to the amount they initiate, that is, who have a High Feedback Ratio. The falling-off of Liking received among the top ranks in the averages for the total population is attributable especially to the other extreme third of the population, who talk proportionately most above the amount they receive. It is for this third that the "hypothesis of contrariety," mentioned earlier, tends to hold.

The data obtained by asking about Dislikes present essentially the same picture. The Dislike curves, though obtained by a separate question, are close to the mirror image of the Like curves. It is of some importance to be able to say, however, that the highest participators among the third of the population with the lowest Feedback Ratio not only are less well Liked but are more Disliked than their less active colleagues in the same subpopulation. In this third of the population, the more the person talks, the more he is Disliked. But in the opposite third of the population, those who have a High Feedback Ratio, there is no relation between how much a man talks and how much he is Disliked.

In general, the correlation between Idea rankings received and Basic Initiating Rank is positive and linear, as indicated above. However, there is some indication that among the Randomly Assembled groups the highest participators in the third of the population with the Low Feedback Ratio tend to suffer on Idea rankings received, as they do on Liking received, although the effect is not nearly so marked. This effect seems to disappear in the Composed groups.

It can be inferred, by reference back to the design, that the method of composition was such as probably to introduce a greater congruence between the rank order of members on activity and their rank order on task ability within the Composed groups than in the Randomly Assembled groups. It may be that a composition plan such as the one adopted can do something useful in reducing the dissatisfaction of group members (other than the Deviant) by reducing the discrepancy between how much a person talks and how valuable his ideas are felt to be.

Questionnaire responses of members after the session indicated that the mean satisfaction with the quality of task performance was significantly higher in the Composed groups than in the Randomly Assembled groups. There was no significant difference, however, on the mean satisfaction with the quality of interpersonal consideration shown in the interaction. It appears that Deviant members still constituted a thorn in the flesh but no longer interfered so drastically with the solution of task problems in the more specific sense.

Within the design on the Composed groups, those we provided with a Deviant showed some significant and near-significant differences in *interaction* from those with no Deviant. They showed more disagreement, more tension, less tension release, less solidarity, and less asking for opinion. However, the post-meeting *questionnaires on satisfaction* did not show significant differences between the cells in the design. It may be that the interaction measures are more sensitive, particularly in that they are less subject to a kind of "falsification" for defensive purposes. In our detailed analysis of factors in the satisfaction questionnaire (a major piece of analysis only alluded to here) we found two factors that appear to be just that. Some groups which show definite evidence of difficulty, disagreement, tension, and antagonism in the interaction tend to deny especially vehemently items in the post-meeting questionnaire that express rejection of the task and rejection of the group.

Psychological Needs as a Function
of Social Environments*

Most of us would agree that theoretical and empirical work on psychological motivation falls short of what has been achieved in the study of physiological motivation. Investigations of physiological needs typically begin with questions about what conditions in the internal environment will produce the need, what need-reducing behavior is then activated, what new conditions are necessary for need reduction. Questions such as these seem scarcely to have been considered in relation to psychological needs, despite the frequent appearance of need terminology in psychological discussion. Indeed, much of the work on such psychological needs as aggression, achievement, security, affiliation, etc., appears to be less concerned with properties of needs than with properties of *valences*, i.e., attractions or aversions. Reinforcement theory, for example, uses the concept of drive mainly in relation to the learning of preferred responses, focusing thereby on problems of the acquisition of valence. Role theory, as another representative approach, inquires into the effects of normative processes on response preferences, thus emphasizing questions concerning the induction of valence.

The distinction between valence and need has been systematically elaborated by Lewin.[1] It is clear from his exposition that one can treat a great variety of problems in terms of valences—those, namely, which involve consideration of the strength and direction of

* This paper grows out of a research program supported in large part by the Group Psychology Branch, Office of Naval Research. The writer is indebted to Dr. Alfred C. Raphelson for opportunity to discuss the theoretical issues raised in this paper.

1. Kurt Lewin, "The Conceptual Representation and Measurement of Psychological Forces," *Contributions to Psychological Theory*, I, No. 4 (1938), 1–247; cf. his *Field Theory in Social Science* (New York: Harper & Bros., 1951), chap. i.

162

response tendencies or, in his terminology, forces toward locomotion. In contrast to such forces, needs refer to tension or energy systems within the organism. Need concepts appear to be necessary to handle questions concerning the conditions under which already established valences become operative and inoperative, or, more generally, as I shall try to show, questions of energy arousal, management, and reduction.

This paper proposes a method for conceptualizing the need aspects of psychological motivation. I would like to show that, just as physiological needs can be related to characteristics of the internal, organic environment, so can at least some psychological needs be related to characteristics of the individual's external, behavioral environment. If this proposal seems somewhat surprising, I would suggest this may be due to the ubiquitous assumption that "stable" attributes of the person cannot be based on "unstable" properties of the psychological environment.[2] On this assumption psychological needs are extra-situational, and there would be little point to examining seriously the possibility that energy systems within the person can be generated by characteristics of the person's situation.

In the sections to follow, I wish to consider five types of problems which I suggest can be handled only by treating psychological motivation in terms of need concepts as distinguished from valence concepts. These problems—in relation to which the proposed formulation of psychological needs will be examined—are as follows: the environmental conditions which determine whether potentially attractive responses become actually relevant to behavior; the conditions under which they become irrelevant; problems having to do with range or depth of conflict within the person; problems having to do with veridicality of responses to a given need; problems having to do with the effects of needs on what aspects of experience will be learned or forgotten.

Ability to deal with these problems is necessary, I believe, if we are to attain a more adequate social psychology of personality. Research in social psychology has extended clinical notions about the effects of needs in shaping the behavioral environment. These re-

2. M. Horwitz, *Group Standards and the Management of Hostility* (ONR Technical Report [Urbana: Bureau of Educational Research, University of Illinois, 1955]).

searches can be classified, according to Lewin's formula,[3] under the relationship, $E = F \ (P)$, that is, the behavioral environment as a function of properties of the person. The proposal that psychological needs can in turn be derived from the behavioral environment moves us to the converse of this relationship: $P = F \ (E)$, the person as a function of properties of the environment. And in exploring this general relationship, as I shall suggest below, small-group research enjoys a particularly strategic role.

A General Approach for Deriving Needs from Environmental Conditions

Our primary concern is with the social determinants of psychological needs. The generality of the present thesis may be indicated, however, by considering need-arousal in relation to physically determined aspects of the behavioral environment. Hilgard, in company with other functionalist theorists of perception, has suggested that perceiving has its own distinctive goals, even when it operates in the service of some other specific goal.[4] He suggests that these goals are to keep the perceived environment stable and to achieve definiteness in what we perceive. He conjectures that these perceptual goals arise out of general needs for the conditions of our world to support our efforts to satisfy specific needs. The existence of two classes of needs is suggested. One class is particularistic, which sets the immediate task of the organism in any given problem-solving situation. The second class, which may be designated as meta-needs, and which may operate concurrently with the first, applies over different problem-solving situations to insure that the general conditions necessary for goal-striving are met. On the level of lower animals, the operation of such meta-needs is supported by Nissen's evidence for a generalized drive in primates to know about the environment[5] and by Harlow's animals who learn how to learn—who are motivated, that is, not only to solve immediate problems, but

3. *Field Theory in Social Science,* chap. x.

4. E. R. Hilgard, "The Role of Learning in Perception," in R. R. Blake and G. V. Ramsey (eds.) *Perception: An Approach to Personality* (New York: Ronald Press, 1951), chap. iv.

5. H. W. Nissen, "The Nature of the Drive as an Innate Determinant of Behavioral Organization," in *Nebraska Symposium on Motivation* (Lincoln: University of Nebraska Press, 1954), pp. 281–321.

by the meta-task of learning how to solve problems generally in environments of the type in which they are situated.[6]

To use a cybernetic analogy, the problem-solving person may be conceived of as a machine which can simultaneously carry out two functions. One is to solve the specific problem entered into the machine. The second is to inspect the conditions affecting performance on the problem, taking present performance as a sample of general performance on problems of this class. If the present problem is solved, this terminates the goal-seeking sequence and registers to confirm the adequacy of the machine's functioning on the general class of problems. Failure to solve the problem, however, registers as a signal of inadequacy in the machine or deficiency in the behavioral environment (i.e., in the action possibilities given by the information fed in). We might now suppose that the machine is constructed so that it tends not only to strive toward completing the unsolved problem but to generate a new and more urgent meta-task, namely, to rectify its own or its environmental deficiencies. Such a conception would say, in more psychological language, that the machine would be capable of operating under conditions both of task involvement and of ego involvement. For, in addition to attainment or non-attainment of specific goals, it could register success or failure in relation to the pervasive conditions which are required for adequate functioning. The thesis I wish to explore is that, just as deficiencies or required states within the organism can produce physiological needs, so deficiencies in requirednesses of the behavioral environment can produce psychological needs. Psychological needs may be generated in the course of work on some specific task as tendencies to restore, maintain, or enhance the adequacy of the person or the fitness of the environment in relation to the class of tasks of which the specific task is representative. In particular, I would like to examine need-generating circumstances which may arise out of social environments.

The Arousal of Psychological Needs

Let us consider need aggression or hostility as an example of a psychological need. I would like to show how this may be treated

6. H. F. Harlow, "Motivation as a Factor in the Acquisition of New Responses," in *Current Theory and Research in Motivation: A Symposium* (Lincoln: University of Nebraska Press, 1953), pp. 24–49.

as a meta-need generated by deficiencies in the generalized conditions for goal-striving in a social environment.

As organizational theorists point out, one of the characteristics of any co-ordinated social enterprise is that conflicts may occur among the desires of various members about the course of their joint activity. To resolve such conflicts, organizations frequently develop rules according to which the desire of each member is assigned some legitimate weight. Each member's weighted desire can then be reckoned up to arrive at a decision which will be binding for the group. The weight assigned to any member's desire may be viewed as that member's legitimate power in the group. It represents a fundamental condition affecting the member's ability to satisfy particular needs, since a reduction in power reduces the probability of his being able to act so as to satisfy any specific need which may arise in this social system. The experiments we set up attempted to test the hypothesis that phenomenal hostility corresponds to a meta-need, whose strength varies directly with the degree of reduction of the person's expected power within a given social environment.[7]

Each of a group of students was set the immediate task of learning how to make a series of objects under the instruction of a class-room teacher. The experiments were designed so conflicts would arise between the desires of students and teacher over whether or not instruction on each object should be repeated. The legitimate power of students and of the teacher over the course which the group should take was specified in advance. Based upon this legitimacy system, the legitimate decision strongly favored the teacher's desire in one condition, weakly opposed his desire in the second, and strongly opposed his desire in the third.[8] In all three treatments, irrespective of the legitimate decision, the teacher followed his own desire, thereby blocking the student's desired activity. And, as the effect of these manipulations, students reported that the teacher neither reduced their expected power nor increased his own in treatment 1, reduced theirs and increased his own slightly in treat-

7. F. J. Lee, M. Horwitz, and M. Goldman, *Power over Decision-making and the Response to Frustration in Group Members* (ONR Technical Report [Urbana: Bureau of Educational Research, University of Illinois, 1954]). Cf. also M. Horwitz, M. Goldman, and F. J. Lee, *A Further Study of the Effects of Power Reduction on Arousal of Hostility* (ONR Technical Report [Urbana: Bureau of Educational Research, University of Illinois, 1954]).

8. Horwitz and Goldman, *op. cit.*

ment 2, or reduced theirs and increased his own greatly in treatment 3.

The immediate task of the student was to learn certain skills, but a background condition for work on the immediate task was that he would be operating in a social environment in which he could expect a given amount of power. If the environment proved deficient in this respect, according to our hypothesis, the student should develop a meta-need to correct the environment in the direction of restoring his power to its expected level. Since social power represents a fundamental condition for need satisfaction in social situations, reduction of one's power should be phenomenally experienced as an "attack" on one's ability to function effectively; restoring one's own power should imply reducing the teacher's usurped power and, by the same token, should be experienced as "counterattacking." The evidence was clear cut that phenomenal hostility, as expressed in verbal "counterattacking," increased as a direct function of the degree of reduction of the person's expected power. Pre- and post-ratings of personal characteristics of the teacher, for example, showed no reliable shift toward unfavorable ratings in the zero-reduction condition but became increasingly unfavorable going from the conditions of weak to strong power reduction.

The present formulation, it might be pointed out, is capable of predicting theoretically the recent, empirically derived amendment to the Frustration-Aggression Hypothesis, namely, that frustration elicits aggression under the condition that the frustrating act is perceived as "arbitrary."[9] For if the power-reducing agent acts on his own desire in violation of the legitimacy system, it is unlikely that he will be seen as acting according to external requirements. Rather he should be perceived as acting "wilfully" to satisfy his own desires, rejecting the "rules of the game." We predicted, and found, that the degree of perceived "arbitrariness" of the teacher indeed varied with the perceived degree of his reduction of others' legitimate power or (what is equivalent here) the degree to which he illegitimately augmented his own power.

9. N. Pastore, "The Role of Arbitrariness in the Frustration-Aggression Hypothesis," *Journal of Abnormal Social Psychology*, XLVII (1952), 728–31. Cf. A. R. Cohen, "Social Norms, Arbitrariness of Frustration, and Status of the Agent of Frustration in the Frustration-Aggression Hypothesis," *Journal of Abnormal Social Psychology*, LI (1955), 222–26.

We co-ordinate phenomenal hostility, then, to a meta-need for restoration of own expected power or, closer perhaps to intuitive notions concerning hostility, to a need for reduction of another's illegitimately augmented power. I have no way of knowing whether all cases of what might be classified as phenomenal hostility can be understood in these terms, but I would argue, in view of the fundamental role played by power expectations in social environments, that this formulation should cover a large range of instances of hostility arousal.

The proposed treatment of hostility as a meta-need is conceptually similar to the treatment of hunger, for example, as a physiologically based need. It specifies the deficiency conditions under which the need will be aroused and, by implication, the properties of the general class of activities which can reduce the need, and the conditions of environmental restoration under which the need will be reduced. Dealing with valences of activities, reinforcement or role theory can tell us, for example, why the person will prefer to cast knives or barbed innuendoes once a hostile need is aroused. But they give no analytic account of the conditions which imply arousal of the hostile need and therefore cannot state when a potentially preferred response becomes actually relevant to behavior. Nor can they tell us—as will be discussed below—what it is about such different activities as knife-throwing or aspersion-casting which makes them both included in the general class of activities which are capable of reducing hostile needs.

Our discussion of the conditions underlying the arousal of hostility might profitably be closed by considering the present view in relation to the Frustration-Aggression Hypothesis. The formulation presented here is in line with clinically derived observations, such as Levy's,[10] that aggression tends to be generated under conditions of threat rather than simple goal-blocking. Subjects in all treatments in our experiment experienced goal-blocking in relation to their own desires; but hostility arose in relation to "threat" to their ability to pursue goals in general rather than to blocking of any particular goal. Moreover, the Frustration-Aggression Hypothesis appears to require the notion of a relatively specific, unlearned "anger" state,

10. D. M. Levy, "The Hostile Act," *Psychological Review*, XLVIII (1941), 356–61.

based on an assumed biological drive within the organism which can be reduced by aggressive activity.[11] The view proposed here does not require us to assume such a physiologically unlocated aggressive drive but treats hostility instead as a meta-need produced by specifiable deficiencies in the behavioral environment. Finally, as we have pointed out above, the present view can predict, as the Frustration-Aggression Hypothesis cannot, the association between arousal of aggression and the perception of arbitrariness in the frustrating agent.

The Reduction of Psychological Needs

The statement of the conditions under which both organic and psychological needs arise implies the conditions under which these needs will be reduced. If tensions arise within the person, whether from deficiency states in the organism or the environment, the general class of activities which will have satisfaction value are those which rectify the organic or environmental deficiencies.

It should follow, if phenomenal hostility corresponds to a need system for power restoration, that hostility should be reduced to the degree that power is restored. The experiment designed to test this hypothesis followed the previous one in developing high initial hostility in students toward a power-reducing teacher.[12] Three treatments were designed to allow different degrees of power restoration varying from zero, partial, to full restoration. In all treatments students planned a course of action to recover their power. In the zero restoration treatment, hostility was measured before the teacher could have had opportunity to change. In the partial restoration treatment, the teacher changed as a result of supposed intervention by a third party with whom students now "shared" their power. In the full restoration treatment, the teacher changed in direct response to student action. As predicted, hostility was highest where power restoration did not occur, intermediate where power was partially restored, and least where it was fully restored.

This study indicates that by the use of need concepts questions

11. J. Dollard, L. W. Doob, N. E. Miller, O. H. Mowrer, and R. R. Sears, *Frustration and Aggression* (New Haven, Conn.: Yale University Press, 1939).

12. M. Horwitz, M. Goldman, and F. J. Lee, *Effects of Two Methods of Changing a Frustrating Agent on Reduction of Hostility* (ONR Technical Report [Urbana: Bureau of Educational Research, University of Illinois, 1954]).

are opened for investigation which involve matters of satisfaction *value* (i.e., need reduction) as distinct from matters of *valence* (i.e., attractions or aversions). If we can state the deficiency conditions which arouse the need, then it is possible to investigate such questions as whether particular activities and conditions tending toward correction of the deficiency will have more or less value for reducing the need. It becomes possible, too, to ask whether seemingly disparate activities like knife-throwing or aspersion-casting are or are not functionally equivalent for need reduction. More generally, it enables systematic examination of the problem: Given a need, what are the different sorts of activities which will have value or "substitute" value? The difference in conceptual consequences of need versus valence concepts is rather neatly brought out by the fact that need satisfaction leads to termination of an activity or to irrelevance of a potentially valent activity. By contrast, need satisfaction tends to augment the valence (or habit strength) of an activity and thus to make preference for it more difficult to extinguish.

Range of Conflict as a Dimension Related to Needs

We consider next how the use of need concepts and the proposed derivation of needs from environmental conditions aids in the attack on problems of psychological conflict.

The theory of conflict as elaborated by Lewin[13] and Miller[14] can be viewed as dealing primarily with effects of conflicts between valences, that is, between approach or avoidance tendencies. The theory seems adequate for handling the various consequences of conflict which can be derived from the direction and magnitude of competing action tendencies. However, there are other aspects of conflict behavior, particularly as related to decision-making, as we have tried to show elsewhere,[15] which appear to call for analysis in terms of the need systems underlying the conflicting action tendencies.

13. *Field Theory in Social Science*, chap. x.

14. N. E. Miller, "Experimental Studies of Conflict," in J. McV. Hunt (ed.), *Personality and the Behavior Disorders* (New York: Ronald Press, 1944), I, 431–65.

15. M. Horwitz and F. J. Lee, "Effects of Decision-making by Group Members on Recall of Finished and Unfinished Tasks," *Journal of Abnormal Social Psychology*, XLIX (1954), 201–10.

In the present section, I wish to show how need formulations open for additional consideration problems of the *range* or depth of inner conflicts, problems which are central to clinical practice and personality theory. Let me indicate what I mean by the dimension, "range of conflict," and some of the phenomena which appear to make this notion necessary. Consider the situation of a person who is conflicted about his hostile impulses. If hostile needs operate like organically derived ones, they should tend to activate a number of functions within the person aimed at reducing the hostile tension. If I may be allowed a rough listing of the types of functions thus activated, tendencies will be established to *locomote* toward the consummatory aggressive activity, in humans to *communicate* relevant aggressive content, to *think* about aggression and the outcomes of aggression, to *perceive* such activity possibilities and outcomes. Now it is possible that forces may exist which oppose each or all of the various functions energized by the hostile need, so that the tendency of the need to activate the given function must be inhibited. Inhibition implies that the organism is committing energy to blocking off the operation of the need, and, as such inhibitory energy systems increase in scope, we can talk of the conflicted person having increasing range or depth of conflict. In the case of zero range of conflict the individual will inhibit neither action, communication, thinking, nor perception. He may, as in the situation of catharsis, inhibit a single function—action—but neither communication nor any other function. Suppression would imply inhibition of two functions—action and communication—but none of the others. Repression would imply inhibition of three functions—action, communication, and thinking. Denial would extend the range of inhibition to perception as well.

We are saying then that it is possible to analyze conflicts as these operate in innerpersonal regions of the individual; that is, in relation to needs, as distinct from basing our analysis on competition between valent activities alone. The conception of inhibitory energy systems, to which we are led by this analysis, appears to correspond to what are more commonly referred to as defenses. Inhibitory systems or defenses may serve to "resolve" conflicts based on competing action tendencies, and they may therefore free the person for some one course of action. But the present formulation implies that such defensive resolutions differ from non-defensive ones in that they continue to leave some need unreduced and, in addition, are achieved at the cost of mobilizing energy for inhibition. As they increase in range, we should expect, according to Lewin's view of the dynamics of regression, a general deterioration in the person's performance.[16]

In the experiment testing this hypothesis, we again produced hostility toward a power-reductive teacher.[17] Four separate treatments were then designed which could be ordered as follows: "active need-meeting," which involved no inhibition of action, communication, or thinking; "catharsis," which involved inhibition of action alone; "suppression," involving inhibition of communication and action; and "repression," involving inhibition of thinking, communication, and action.

In order to oppose or encourage subjects' assumed tendencies to initiate aggressive action or communication, we varied environmental restraints or opportunities for the exercise of these tendencies. To oppose subjects' hostile thoughts about the teacher, we adapted the method used by Asch,[18] in which he succeeded in influencing subjects to distort the evidence given by their own senses in judging physical reality by furnishing fictitious information about a contradictory group consensus. Thus, although subjects in the "repression" condition initially reported disliking the teacher, they were given the information that everybody else in the group liked him. In line with Asch's results, subjects exhibited a general tendency to shift their private expression concerning feelings about the instructor in the direction of the reported norm.

The four treatments, involving increasing inhibition of the effects of the original hostile tension, produced progressively deteriorating performance on the three measures used in the experiment. These measures tapped such basic abilities of the person as retention of

16. *Field Theory in Social Science*, chap. v.

17. M. Goldman, M. Horwitz, and F. J. Lee, *Alternative Classroom Standards Concerning Management of Hostility and Effects on Student Learning* (ONR Technical Report [Urbana: Bureau of Educational Research, University of Illinois, 1954]).

18. S. E. Asch, "Effects of Group Pressure upon the Modification and Distortion of Judgments," in G. E. Swanson, T. M. Newcomb, and E. L. Hartley (eds.), *Readings in Social Psychology* (New York: Henry Holt & Co., 1952), pp. 2–11.

learned material, ability to focus attention as revealed by the digit backward test, and ability to overcome an inappropriate problem-solving set as tapped by an Einstellung test. I do not believe that problems of the type represented by this study can be formulated in valence terms. The study indicates that, by dealing with needs, rather than directions and magnitudes of opposing activity tendencies alone, one can meaningfully inquire into environmental effects on the defensive organization of the person or, more generally, into problems of the range or depth of personal conflict.

Veridicality of Responses as a Dimension Related to Needs

There is no necessary correspondence between the valence or attractiveness of an activity and its value for need reduction. Although the organism could not survive if the discrepancies between the two became too great, it seems clear that valences can be learned or induced which have little or no value for need reduction. Similarly, not all activities which have satisfaction value become valent. The existence of such discrepancies makes it possible to speak of the veridicality of responses vis-à-vis needs.

Consideration of the veridicality of psychological processes has been largely confined to the area of perception—as in questions of the veridicality of color experience to given wave lengths or the veridicality of size perception to the objective diameters of coins. To speak of veridicality requires the existence of some objective reference for "reality"—in the cases cited this being the physical environment. In the area of motivation, physiological processes of the organism have been used as the objective reference for determining veridicality of organically related responses, e.g., Young's[19] studies of appetites or valences which lack nutritive value, or compulsive eating in the face of objective satiation of hunger.

Where psychological motivation is concerned, however, the tendency to deal with valences rather than with needs has led to neglect of problems of motivational veridicality. Thus we lack any systematic method for answering such questions as whether or not behaviors related to psychological needs are "healthy" or "appropriate." And indeed our treatment of psychological motives—as

19. P. T. Young, "The Role of Hedonic Processes in Motivation," in *Nebraska Symposium on Motivation* (Lincoln: University of Nebraska Press, 1955), pp. 193–238.

opposed to organic drives—seems to lead us to a somewhat extreme position of situational relativity, with meaningful scientific and practical questions being obscured under the slogan *De gustibus non disputandum est.*

The position taken here is that objective reference for the veridicality of responses related to psychological needs can be found in characteristics of the behavioral environment. Hostility, or the psychological need for power restoration, can be objectively grounded as we have seen in specifiable environmental deficiencies. We can therefore assert of any given activity that it is or is not veridical with respect to this need. In the "repression" treatment, mentioned above, subjects who made favorable evaluations of the power-reducing teacher can be said to have been engaging in non-veridical or "distorted" activity. For in so far as the power-reductive stimulus situation impinged on them, these subjects would be expected to have generated hostile needs, whether or not they were aware of these. On the assumption that such needs tend to seek attitudinal expression, it would follow that non-veridicality of attitudes requires the mobilization of inhibitory energy to oppose the operation of the need. In the study I wish to mention next,[20] we asked whether performance would deteriorate, as it did in the "repression" treatment, if non-veridical attitudes were induced in relation to a "liking" need tension instead of to hostility.

Conditions were experimentally set up which were designed to produce liking toward a teacher who acted consistently with students' power expectations. To manipulate veridicality of attitudes, norms favorable to the teacher were reported in one treatment, while unfavorable norms were reported in a second treatment. Again we found that non-veridical attitudes produced by the unfavorable norms resulted in deterioration of performance on both of the measures used: retention of learned material and digit span. An interesting feature of this experiment is that a few individuals disliked the objectively likeable teacher despite their exposure to favorable norms. Evidently personal factors, carried into the experimental situation by these subjects, rendered them hostile, inde-

20. M. Horwitz, M. Goldman, G. M. Della Piana, and F. J. Lee, *Veridicality of Attitudes toward Authority and Effects on Retention of Learning* (ONR Technical Report [Urbana: Bureau of Educational Research, University of Illinois, 1955]).

pendently of the objective situation. Is their attitude then veridical, since it probably reflects enduring personal dispositions? The position taken here would say "No." If the objective situation should produce a liking tension, whatever is distortive of this—whether group pressures or personality dispositions—should result in deteriorated performance. These expectations were significantly confirmed even for this class of subjects who might be said to be behaving consistently with their personal feelings, although inconsistently with environmental requirements.

Similar results were obtained in a subsequent experiment in which we employed a 2 × 2 design,[21] comparing the effects of objective instigation of liking by a power-enhancing teacher and objective instigation of hostility by a power-reducing teacher under conditions of induced veridical and non-veridical attitudes. Interestingly enough, whether the teacher objectively instigated liking or disliking per se made no difference in rate of student learning. For both conditions, however, rate of learning slowed markedly where non-veridical attitudes were induced.

We have been concerned thus far with phenomenal hostility and liking which arise as meta-needs while the person is pursuing some more immediate goal in his social environment. Having mentioned liking needs, I should like in closing this section on veridicality to allude briefly to Maslow's criticism of the tendency to regard needs as arising exclusively from deficiency states.[22] While we have treated hostility as arising from a deficiency state of the environment, liking does not appear to lend itself to this sort of treatment. Our own insufficiently tested assumption is that where another's behavior accords with or augments the subject's expectations of power, a meta-need may be generated to maintain or extend this state of affairs. We may note that in principle, at least, it appears possible in these conceptual terms to relate what Maslow terms "growth motivation," as distinct from "deficiency motivation," to characteristics of the social environment.

21. M. Horwitz and M. Goldman, *Veridicality of Attitudes toward Authority and Effects on Rates of Learning and Psychological Satiation* (ONR Technical Report [Urbana: Bureau of Educational Research, University of Illinois]). (In preparation.)

22. A. Maslow, "Deficiency Motivation and Growth Motivation," in *Nebraska Symposium on Motivation* (Lincoln: University of Nebraska Press, 1955), pp. 1–30.

Differential Learning and Needs

The distinction between valence and need suggests some rather interesting consequences for the motivational dynamics of learning and forgetting. Reinforcement theory asserts that responses acquire valence or increased probability of evocation when they have had the effect of reducing some need or drive. And it would be surprising indeed if this relationship, or one like it, did not exist. For otherwise, in confronting various activity possibilities, the individual could not profit from experience in selecting the one which is most probably satisfying or need reductive. However, although reinforcement theory can tell us which among a number of responses the individual will tend to prefer (if he has experienced at least one of the number), it does not enable us to determine in any systematic way whether a possible response belongs to the general class which can serve for need reduction. Thus it gives no indication as to whether a particular response is potentially learnable under a given need condition, nor what features of experience will be differentially learned under different need conditions.

Pertinent data on differential learning are given by studies of the Zeigarnik effect and its vicissitudes.[23] Under some motivational conditions subjects tend to recall more interrupted than completed tasks, while the reverse can be obtained under other conditions.[24] Recall of interrupted tasks has been interpreted as a kind of functional memory, which is maintained by motivational energy while the task is psychologically in process, but from which energy is withdrawn when the problem is solved or when resumption is perceived as no longer possible. Recall of interruptions is usually found only for "trivial" tasks, that is, tasks which the subject defines as having no significance for him beyond the immediate problem-solving situation. Under these conditions differential memory favoring interruptions is short range, decaying rapidly after the person leaves the situation. Reversal of the Zeigarnik effect, the tendency to recall completions or successes, is typically obtained using "ego-

23. Lewin, *Field Theory in Social Science*, chap. i.

24. S. Rosenzweig, "Need-persistive and Ego-defensive Reactions to Frustration as Demonstrated by an Experiment on Repression," *Psychological Review*, XLVIII (1941), 347–49; cf. also C. W. Eriksen, "Psychological Defenses and 'Ego Strength' in the Recall of Completed and Incompleted Tasks," *Journal of Abnormal Social Psychology*, XLIX (1954), 45–58.

involving" tasks, or, in our terminology, tasks based on meta-needs which by definition extend beyond any particular situation. And although this point has not been tested, one would expect to find longer-range memory operating under such meta-need conditions.

If successful performance of a task is tension-reducing, the tendency to recall successes would seem to be a paradoxical result on the assumption that memory is sustained by unreduced motivational energy. However, the tendency to recall successes can be handled in a unified conceptual scheme with the tendency to recall interruptions by means of the distinction between immediate and meta-needs. Success on any immediate task can be said to reduce some immediate motivational system and therefore to remove the short-range basis for motivated recall of the task. But if a meta-need has been generated, memory for what has been successful can continue to be relevant to—and continue to be sustained by—the still unreduced meta-need. This conception may be clarified by noting that the distinction between short- and long-range memory can be related to the previously considered cybernetic analogy for immediate and meta-tasks. Short-range memory corresponds to information which is stored within the machine only for the duration of a given problem, as in the case of retention of previous steps in a multiplication sequence; long-range memory corresponds to information stored over different ones of a variety of sequences. In these terms one may ask, for example, on what motivational basis does the rat's problem-solving for food in a maze get converted into learning, that is, into memory of the maze beyond what is required for solving the immediate problem? A possible direction for answering this question is to look for the operation of unreduced meta-needs. Finding food reduces the immediate hunger need, but memory of the maze may be sustained by general needs to know how to satisfy specific ones in environments of the given type, as suggested by Nissen[25] and Festinger,[26] or even needs to learn how to learn, as suggested by Harlow.[27]

The foregoing discussion, it should be noted, is not meant to im-

25. *Op. cit.*

26. L. Festinger, "Motivations Leading to Social Behavior," in *Nebraska Symposium on Motivation* (Lincoln: University of Nebraska Press, 1954), pp. 191–219.

27. *Op. cit.*

ply that meta-needs necessarily lead to increased recall of successes. The effects of meta-needs on memory would be expected to vary with the conditions of their arousal and the modes of their management. We have suggested, as distinct from the preceding example of a need "to know one's environment," that some meta-needs may be aroused mainly under conditions of "ego-threat," in which the individual receives information that there is a high probability that he is suffering from some personal or environmental deficiency. If the person mobilizes a defensive system against the operation of this threat-induced meta-need, he may attempt to minimize the evidence of probable failure by recalling a predominance of successes. On the other hand, in the absence of defensive reactions, the meta-need may lead to increased recall of failures. For, by rectifying his failures, the individual could restore the need-producing deficiency state, and recall of failures would then become instrumental to need reduction.

I would like to describe one experiment bearing on differential recall in relation to psychological needs which illustrates at the same time how meta-needs can be engendered by other than power characteristics of social environments.[28] Social environments, more frequently than physical ones, have the character of being able to move the person toward or away from goals or avoidances even though the person is himself inactive. Not only may the inactive person find himself in desirable or undesirable states by virtue of locomotions by a group of which he is a member but, upon being confronted with a decision, he may find himself carried beyond the choice point before he has made up his mind. Lewin points out that the act of decision-making occupies an extremely important place in the psychological economy of the functioning organism.[29] If a person is subject to two conflicting activity-tendencies, indecision implies that both tendencies are still striving for control of the person's behavior. Making a decision, on the other hand, implies resolution of this type of conflict by a reduction in the potency of one of the two competing activity tendencies. Thus, if the social environment is such that the person is obliged to act while still in a

28. Horwitz and Lee, *op. cit.*

29. K. Lewin, "Group Decision and Social Change," in G. E. Swanson, T. M. Newcomb, and E. H. Hartley (eds.), *Readings in Social Psychology* (New York: Henry Holt & Co., 1952), pp. 459–73.

state of indecision, he should remain conflicted about the particular activity in which he does engage, and the effectiveness of the activity should be impaired.

Environments which induce locomotion while the person is indecisive should signify to the individual that the background conditions for effective action are deficient. He should therefore generate a new psychological need in the situation which may be defined as reducible by the class of activities which can restore his ability to be decisive. And if such restorative activity is impossible for him, one should expect him to defend against this need, that is, to mobilize some form of inhibitory energy.

Our experimental results show that for tasks on which persons are decisive—where they are able to make decisions about one of two paths toward a goal—they tend to recall more failures than successes. Their behavior is thus in accord with other Zeigarnik findings. On the other hand, where they find themselves indecisive, they recall more successes than failures. Presumably meta-needs are established for restoring decisiveness; subjects are unable to take action on this psychological need; and the recall of successes is in service of the resulting defensive or inhibitory tension system. It should follow from this—although we have not tested this derivation —that, whereas the decay of short-range, Zeigarnik memory of failures is extremely rapid, the extinction of defensive memory of successes should be relatively slow.

We should expect, in addition—and are currently attempting to test this hypothesis—that if meta-needs are developed under nondefensive conditions the person should show better (long-range) recall of failures as opposed to successes. The person should be nondefensive where he believes that he can act on his meta-needs either to alter the characteristics of the deficient environment or to alter his own abilities in relation to these environmental characteristics. Under these conditions, learning about failures or about the source of the difficulties he confronts should be more functional than learning about successes.

To conclude this section, we may point out again the dearth of information concerning the ways by which psychological needs affect the types of learning the individual will acquire from the manifold aspects of his experience. We have described in **extremely** sketchy form how one might approach this problem from the stand-point of environmentally generated meta-needs. And we have indicated that consequences are to be expected which differ from those which might be predicted from reinforcement theory—the latter again being viewed as restricted in the main to problems of valence rather than of needs.

The Role of Small-Group Research in Identifying Psychological Needs

How would one set about the problem of identifying the various possible environmentally produced meta-need systems? Unfortunately, psychology is afflicted with a great diversity of lists of proposed psychological needs. Such lists as those developed by Murray[30] and McDougall[31] appear to be based on the unsystematic predilections of the individuals developing them and lack any attempt to specify the conditions which arouse, sustain, or reduce the alleged needs. From the viewpoint outlined here, I would suggest that the phenotypical character of these need descriptions is a result of linking them to implicit and therefore unexamined assumptions about the character of the person's psychological environment.

It is here, I would suggest, that small-group research can make a distinctive contribution to our understanding of personality theory. In order to specify the nature of organic needs, it is necessary to investigate the internal physiological environment which underlies such needs. Similarly, to specify the nature of psychological needs, it would seem to be necessary to observe and experiment with the need-generating properties of the external behavioral environment. In the absence of any general opportunity to experiment with real-life institutional or societal environments, small-group methodology provides the vehicle par excellence for examination of effects of varying the characteristics of social environments. By means of such systematic alteration of social environments, small-group experimentation should enable us to examine in detail the arousal and reduction conditions of psychological needs, particularly those having social reference. If this were done, it should not be surprising if we

30. H. A. Murray *et al., Explorations in Personality* (New York: Oxford University Press, 1938).

31. W. McDougall, *The Energies of Men* (New York: Charles Scribner's Sons, 1933).

found that our present phenotypical lists would be conceptually modified in much the same manner, for example, as is implied by the present proposal that the notion of need aggression be replaced by that of a need system generated by environmental conditions of power reduction.

Besides need arousal and reduction, we have indicated that social environments can directly influence the character of personal defenses which one mobilizes in the management of psychological needs. We have shown, thus, how environmental forces can induce defensive systems which resemble repression and suppression. In principle, at least, it should be possible to vary institutional arrangements to determine whether other defense mechanisms (e.g., denial) can be similarly induced or changed.

In discussing the problem of motivational veridicality, we have suggested, at least by implication, a limitation in any thoroughgoing phenomenological account of behavior. Recent work in social psychology has taught us that a variety of attitudes and judgments can be relatively easily changed by normative manipulations. Such attitudes may have little relation to the person's actually operative need systems. Thus, for example, a morale campaign may use normative devices to develop favorable attitudes toward a company but may leave unchanged the environmental conditions objectively producing hostility (and may therefore be self-defeating as far as productivity is concerned). If attitudes and judgments do not always faithfully represent objectively instigated needs, how then is one to ascertain the needs actually operating in a given social environment? Here, again, I would propose that our knowledge can be effectively advanced by experimental manipulation of environmental conditions in order to determine the types of psychological needs to be expected in particular social situations.

Finally, we indicated in a rough way some of the phenomena of learning which appear to be opened for investigation by a systematic need analysis. What can we expect the individual to learn given the potential complexity of his experience? Under what conditions will the student, for example, carry away information about his successes versus his failures, develop a passive orientation to what has been rewarding in the past versus an active orientation to what must be known for solving future problems, and acquire learnings about coping with the teacher as against the knowledge which is communicated by the teacher? Again, both with respect to understanding the processes involved and with respect to the social management of the psychological needs affecting learning, it would seem necessary to consider effects produced by variations in social environments.

I do not wish to minimize the difficulty of systematic environmental study of the determinants of psychological needs. This conception suggests the necessity of a similar structural and dynamic investigation of psychological environments as has been pursued in the study of internal organic environments, with the objective of being able to talk as meaningfully of requirednesses of the psychological environment as one does of requirednesses of the organism.[32]

Despite the obvious difficulties attendant on this conception of the strategy of formulating research problems in this area, there is evidence as to its feasibility. Although I have only cited studies drawn from our own program of research, there is an accumulating body of investigations in the small-group field which support the view that psychological needs can be defined in terms of social environmental characteristics. As a more or less random example, I might cite Deutsch's study in which persons are set to work on specific learning tasks but in the course of which environmental requirednesses come to define new self-oriented versus affiliative needs.[33]

32. A further complication is that physiological and psychological factors will quite likely be found to interact in the production of some psychological needs. For example, it is possible that psychological oversatiation on repetitive tasks (A. Karsten, "Psychische Sättigung," *Psychologische Forschung*, X [1927], 142–254) results somehow from the summation of refractory phases of nervous processes when these are not centrally controlled, e.g., by cognitive goal-setting. The organism could then be supposed to generate a physiological "need for setting goals" for any repetitive response which is mainly elicited by continual external stimulation. But effective goal-setting for some types of repetitive activities can be shown to depend on normative characteristics of the person's social situation (M. Horwitz, R. V. Exline, M. Goldman, and F. J. Lee, *Motivational Effects of Alternative Decision-making Processes in Groups* [ONR Technical Report (Urbana: Bureau of Educational Research, University of Illinois, 1953)]). If the environment is deficient in these characteristics, the "need for setting goals" would be aroused by the joint action of physiological and psychological factors.

33. M. Deutsch, "Experimental Study of Effects of Cooperation and Competition upon Group Process," *Human Relations*, II (1949), 199–231.

In summary, we have suggested that psychological motivation has tended to be approached largely on the conceptual level of valences as distinct from needs. A mode of conceptualization was suggested whereby one could conceive of psychological needs as based upon deficiency states, among others, in the social environment. Implications of this conceptual treatment include the possibility of dealing systematically with the conditions underlying arousal and reduction of needs, of dealing with problems involving range of inner personal conflict, with problems of motivational veridicality, and with problems concerning the varieties of content which the person can be expected to learn under given need conditions. Finally, we considered the ability of small-group research to investigate experimental variations in social environments and the special role it thereby acquires in the investigation of problems of this type—problems which appear central to the development of a full-fledged social psychology of personality.

Emotionality and Work in Groups

This paper summarizes a series of investigations conducted since 1951 in the Human Dynamics Laboratory of the University of Chicago. The research has been supported chiefly by the Group Psychology Branch of the Office of Naval Research. Its results are given in two monographs; one, on methods[1] and the other,[2] to appear shortly, giving detailed findings and theoretical implications.

The Nature of the Theoretical Problem

Any study of human behavior must assume, implicitly or explicitly, some basic dynamism. It may be equilibrium displacement and return, conflict between personal needs and social demands, id versus ego, or some other. Whatever dynamism is proposed as fundamental to human behaving should also, we would suppose, be operative in group situations. Conversely, any terms found to have fundamental explanatory usefulness for the complexities of group events should also illuminate the larger human enterprise. Underlying the more specific theories of group operation is the more general theory of human behavior; and this more general theory provides the broad context for the theory of groups.

We should like to begin by presenting a series of propositions about human behavior in general. These propositions have been generated over the years by the reflection of our group theories against prevailing thought in learning theory, therapy, social problem-solving, and evolution.

1. Man is always trying to live beyond his means. Life is a se-

1. Herbert A. Thelen, Dorothy Stock, *et al.*, *Methods for Studying Work and Emotionality in Group Operation* (Chicago: Human Dynamics Laboratory, University of Chicago, 1954). Pp. 208.

2. Stock and Thelen, *Emotional Dynamics and Group Culture*, to appear as Research Monograph No. 2, National Training Laboratories, 1201 Sixteenth Street, N.W., Washington 6, D.C.

quence of reactions to stress: Man is continually meeting situations with which he cannot quite cope.

2. In stress situations, energy is mobilized and a state of tension is produced.[3]

3. The state of tension tends to be disturbing, and man seeks to reduce the tension.

4. He has direct impulses to take action, and there appear to be a limited number of kinds of impulses (or drive-actualizations). Bion proposed four major internal purposes or needs of groups and

3. Proposition I conceives that behavior is purposive. If purpose be assigned to man as actor, then there is required further the concept of something acted on, e.g., environment. From this distinction of "inner"-"outer" flows also the possibility of the self-concept as distinguished from the object- or other-concept; and also the acceptance of a priori realities apart from man. A rigid phenomenological view is thus inadequate; as is also a strictly interactionist view *if* the interacting entities are alleged to be similar in kind.

We see the group-as-a-whole as a system surrounded by an environment and containing individual subsystems. "Personality" is the term for the unique patterning of drives or predispositions of an individual subsystem; and "tension" is the term for the tonus or state of mobilization of drive-pattern. The group-as-a-whole is a "social system" which exerts control over interpersonal and person-environment (or, more precisely, Dewey's internal-objective) interactions. This control is exerted through the group "culture," consisting of agreements, perceptual biases, values, threats (etc.), which are imputed or ascribed by the individuals to the "group" (as superego) for the sake of maintaining order to the extent required for individual need-meeting and accomplishment of convening purposes.

These public or task purposes are achieved through attack on problems to be "solved," that is, through taking action to change particular conditions perceived as lying "outside" the group. To bring about these changes, the group must define and accept two kinds of reality demands: (a) demands for a particular character of action dictated by the "logic" of the problem and directed against the conditions to be changed and (b) demands for reorganization of the culture so that the necessary participant roles can be developed and the needed human resources mobilized. This latter problem is complicated by the existence of many internal-objective relationships (such as loyalty to one's ethnic, class, family, or institutional groups) which are to be maintained while changing the particular internal-objective relationships whose unsatisfactoriness led to identification of the problem and purposes. These "hidden" or "process" problems are products of the group as a system—they come from the social interrelations within the group and not from the internal individual subsystems per se.

In our view, the demands of the "hidden" problems, like the demands of the task problems, result in stresses lying outside the individual subsystem. The group may or may not have public awareness of a particular stress, and different members may respond in different ways and have different thresholds of sensitivity to a particular stress. But the "underlying condition," capable of mobilizing each person's tensions at a given time, is comprehended as a hypothesized stress.

societies to which impulses contributed, and he labeled these fight, flight, dependency, and pairing.[4] We have since found that the same categories can be used to describe tendencies within the personalities of individuals.[5]

5. Impulses may be translated directly into action. This may reduce the tension and render a person temporarily incapable of further reaction to the initiating stress. If the stress has objective basis in "real" danger, then the person remains in danger, and the behavior is non-adaptive. If the stress is projected from the subjective domain (such as a threat to the self-concept), then the emotional discharge may be a prelude to reflection; and the behavior, while not itself adaptive, may make adaptive sequelae possible.

6. Direct *acting-out* of impulses has varying consequences, depending on the nature of the impulse. Pairing increases adequacy to cope, without reducing objective dangers. Dependency neither increases nor decreases adequacy nor removes the danger; its effectiveness depends upon whether the sought protection is forthcoming. Fight, if successful, destroys the danger, but it also tears up the lawn and makes enemies out of middle-class persons. Flight gets one out of danger without development of adequacy or removal of stress from the situation. From a long-range point of view all these kinds of acting-out are for the most part non-adaptive because little or nothing is learned from the acting-out experience.

7. Impulses may be temporarily thwarted or blocked, and the emergent feelings or other behaviors diagnosed. The nature of the stress is made known by the behaviors it tends to engender. Instead of acting-out, there is *inquiry* or "reality-seeking." Behavior is mediated by thought processes in which previous experience is brought to bear, and alternatives formulated, selected, and evaluated in action.

4. W. R. Bion, "Experiences in Groups I–VII," a series of seven articles in *Human Relations*, I (1948), 314–20, to IV (1951), 221–28.

5. Our confidence in the generalizability of these concepts has been increased through perception of an evolutionary basis for the four kinds of impulses. This is discernible in Weston La Barre, *The Human Animal* (Chicago: University of Chicago Press, 1954). Fight and flight impulses are as ancient as the nervous system and predate the present species of man. Dependency and pairing impulses probably developed much later as part of the psychic equipment for maintenance and reinforcement of familial and societal (or communal) relationships.

8. All human events contain a blend of acting-out and inquiry modes. There is acting-out in the sense of spontaneous, involuntary expression of impulse; there is inquiry in the sense of developing awareness of factors in the situation and in the sense that something is learned from experience. Bion's concepts of work and emotionality are essentially concepts of inquiry and acting-out, respectively, referred to the group culture or the group-as-a-whole.[6]

9. We note that man is capable of using both acting-out and inquiry to meet the stresses of trying to live beyond his means, and we anticipate that "successful" adaptation (i.e., in both short- and long-range terms) in each situation requires a particular blending of elements of acting-out and inquiry modes.

10. The major theoretical question with respect to human behavior in general is: What conditions tend to predispose men toward modes of acting-out or inquiry, and what is involved dynamically in producing and maintaining an adaptive blend of the two modes?

In our research we are concerned with this question primarily as applied to the behaviors of groups of people rather than of single ("isolated") individuals or communities. We have further stipulated that we shall use (initially, at least) the terms suggested by Bion and that our method of investigation is to be experimental and observational.

Conceptual Approach to the Group

Discernible in most approaches to groups is a central notion of part-whole relationships. Thus, the "group" may be taken as the "whole" and the individuals as the "parts." The group-as-a-whole may be seen as a single social instrument fabricated from individual-resource-parts. One may conceive a dynamically maintained "culture" or modus vivendi as the whole, and microscopic interpersonal events as the parts. Or the whole might be thought of as patterned distributions along such sociological dimensions as influence and prestige, with the parts becoming the reactions of individuals to their perceived locations along these dimensions. Again, a theo-

6. Bion suggests that some amount of work is always present but that emotionality may or may not be present. Bion is dealing with the culture of a group rather than with the behaviors of an individual; with molar rather than with microscopic episodes. Individual affect is expressed even though the culture of the group may be work-oriented.

rized pattern of group needs or purposes (at some level of awareness) might be seen as the whole, and patterns of individual needs as the parts. The "culture" approach would see the parts as the sub-cultures "carried" into the group by one or more individuals, and the whole as the miniature society built from these subcultures through conflict and conflict-resolution.

In general, our predilections have been toward an interactive or dynamic approach. Behavior is not literally a *response;* it is an *event* which arises out of a complex system of part-whole relationships. By "personality" we mean the tendencies for the individual to be involved in certain kinds, or qualities, of events. Psychologically, at least, the "individual" is the locus or center of strains within the total system. The relief of strain within one part of the system tends to cause strains in other parts; and this communication or transmission of strain is mutually influenced by properties of the system as a whole. The most significant property of the group as a whole—according to Bion—is its "basic assumption" of group purpose or need; and about this basic assumption the group organizes its expectations, standards, and roles (i.e., its culture). Research-wise, then, we are concerned with the group-relevant tendencies of individuals, the way these tendencies produce a matrix of forces in the group, the dynamics through which the "basic assumptions" emerge from the forces and shift from time to time, and the characteristics of the control system developed to implement the basic assumptions. And, substantively, we are especially interested in these matters as they relate to the central theoretical problem of dealing with simul-taneous capacities and tendencies toward "acting-out" and "inquiry" with each change of the stresses internal to and imposed on the system.

These concerns developed gradually through the process of doing research. At first we thought of them as assumptions which predis-posed us to identify and give operational definition to Bion's cate-gories; and these were to be the objects of study. It seems clear to us now that, if we think of Bion's categories as interaction variables, then the "assumptions" are actually broad propositions of relation-ships among the variables. These may be arranged as a series of propositions in a developmental sequence; and these propositions may, during experiment, serve almost interchangeably as hypotheses or assumptions. Under these conditions, Bion's variables become both categories for the organization of primary data and propositions about the dynamics of interaction.

In brief, and in summary, our system of propositions may be presented as follows:

1. Each person has the capability for meeting stress by "acting-out" and by "inquiry." The capabilities are different, however, from person to person.

2. Which particular capabilities or tendencies will be actualized in the behavior of a particular person depends in part upon the situation in which he finds himself. There is, however, enough consistency in his behavior from situation to situation that he is recognizable as the same personality.

3. Persons come together in the expectancy of mutual benefit in coping with objective problems and meeting their personal needs.

4. When persons get together, tensions are mobilized[7] and interaction results. Out of the interaction emerges the characteristics of "groupness," including a social order and structure.

5. The social order exerts control over the interactions among individuals and gives the interactions a discernible pattern and sequence; this, in turn, can be comprehended as necessitated by the group-as-a-whole.

6. This pattern and sequence change in character from time to time, thus creating the appearance of different units or phases of interaction. The organizing principle for interpretation of each phase is that the group culture has shifted distinctively to a different configuration of "basic assumptions."

7. The culture-units differ in the quality of their blend of "acting-out" and "inquiry" and hence in the nature of their contribution to the group's adaptation to the "inner" and "outer" stresses which were present initially and which are created as they live together.

8. The intensity of stress developed in each situation during tension release depends upon the extent to which the mode of tension release is "acting-out." "Acting-out" tends in itself to be non-adaptive, but it builds stress; "inquiry" tends to be adaptive, but it reduces tension with the minimum development of stress. The prob-

7. Consider, for example, the fact that rather clear sociometric differentiations are made during the first few minutes of a meeting with strangers.

lem of the group-as-a-whole is to maintain the "appropriate" blend, balance, or oscillation between these two modes of behavior.

9. As the group continues to meet, individuals adapt to the group, and they adapt the group (culture and basic assumptions) to the individuals. Thus changes occur in the modal tendencies of the units of interaction. The amount of change depends primarily on the extent to which inquiry is the dominant mode, for inquiry is associated with learning; the amount of "group growth" is primarily determined by the amount of energy flowing into inquiry components of adaptive process.[8]

10. In general, the potentialities for amount and adaptiveness of cultural development, and the range of "problems" (stresses) with which it can deal, are limited ultimately by the "composition" of the group. The extent to which and the rate with which the group actualizes these potentialities depend upon its "leadership" (i.e., its development of means for controlling and selecting and actualizing needed contributions). In view of the basic theoretical problem, optimum leadership would strike a balance between the encouragement and support of direct expressions of affect (so that the existence of stresses could be known) along with diagnosis and bringing into awareness (through problem redefinition) of the factors giving rise to the stresses to which the group was reacting.

Research Findings

From the total range of researches, to be reported in a forthcoming monograph,[9] I wish to select and comment on those which are most directly relevant to the propositions listed above. I shall endeavor to clarify some of the propositions by showing "what they

8. These statements hold best when inquiry is thought of as a conscious process, for then change would certainly be accompanied by learning and adaptation. The statements are more tentative in cases where there seems to be change but little or no learning. One group, for example, developed a culture in which there was considerable freedom to "fight" but no freedom to "work"—the amount of conscious inquiry was practically zero. The group fought for fifteen meetings and apparently never resolved any of its problems. At the same time, however, there were changes in the way it fought and in its perception that it was fighting—e.g., the unspontaneous planning and dogged engagement in "social" activities whose purpose seemed to be denial of their hostilities. A precise statement would probably be that the amount of *adaptive* change is related to the amount of inquiry but that non-adaptive changes can occur without inquiry.

9. Stock and Thelen, *op. cit.*

mean" in the instances of our investigations, and I shall further attempt to define some of the intervening variables in terms of which the propositions have been investigated.

These intervening variables were first suggested at the conceptual level by Bion in the articles cited in footnote 4 above. Our research has added considerable meaning to these concepts and has led us to modify them in many specific ways. I shall not attempt to trace the course of the increasingly closer "successive approximations" that occurred during the research but merely indicate where we now stand with respect to the terms.

The Nature of "Acting-Out": Flight

Acting-out is the direct expression of impulse, unmediated by conscious thought processes or conscious goal-seeking. The impulses are the actualizations of drives which exist at deep and unaware levels in personality. In our studies of individual change, these drives are not affected appreciably by three weeks of intensive interpersonal interaction in a "training group," but the behaviors by which the drives are expressed do tend to change.

Bion suggested that the group culture can be organized around these drives and that these drives serve the purpose of maintaining the group as an organism. The purpose is not at a conscious goal-seeking level and may be unknown to or even denied by the group. Since the drives are essential to group survival, it would be expected that they would dominate the culture during the time they were in force—that they would become, in effect, basic assumptions of the group *raison d'être*.

Bion identified fight, flight, pairing, and dependency as basic assumptions within the modality of "emotionality" (as differentiated from "work"), and he defined "emotionality" in terms equivalent to our broader category of "acting-out."

Let us give substance to these categories by illustrating some of their meanings in our researches. I shall use the category of flight as summarized by Dr. Dorothy Stock for our monograph.[10]

The group is seen as operating on the basic assumption of flight during phases in which it appears to act as if it wishes to avoid stress by running away. As an individual tendency, it is evident

10. *Ibid.*, chap. xxiii.

when the individual acts as if he were trying to distance himself from group experience by withdrawing or expressing irrelevancy.

Glidewell[11] and Gradolph[12] studied groups so composed that there were strong individual predispositions for flight. Glidewell selected from fifty groups those whose members gave most flight responses on a diagnostic sentence-completion test developed in the laboratory for this purpose; and Gradolph composed a group of six people whose dominant tendencies as measured by the same test were toward flight. In both studies the groups were assigned certain problems to solve, and both groups had no designated leader. Compared with other groups, both groups showed the same kinds of symptoms, and these were consistent with the core concept of flight: efforts to dismiss the problem quickly, a narrow range of ideas, and constricted expression of affect. The group deliberately composed of strongly flight individuals showed an astonishing array of behaviors for avoiding the problem: misunderstand instruction, fail to believe the researcher, squelch individual expressions of feeling about the problem, pick the easiest solution, take the least possible amount of responsibility for acting on their decision, and the like.

Lieberman, studying individuals, found that "flight" members tended to reject "pairing" members of the group—presumably because they were threatened by the invitation pairing members give for emotional involvement.[13] They tended toward the end of the sessions to choose each other as "spokesmen" for the group—a banding-together which seems especially significant in view of the fact that within the culture of their groups "flight" is stereotyped as a "bad"-member characteristic.

Lieberman's flight members saw themselves as making irrelevant comments and as not being work oriented, which was an accurate perception. But, more than others, they also characterized the total group in these same terms. Interestingly enough, they also saw

11. John C. Glidewell, "Group Emotionality and Productivity" (unpublished Ph.D. dissertation, Department of Psychology, University of Chicago, 1953); see also Stock and Thelen, *op. cit.*, chap. xiii.

12. A summary of the experiment is contained in Stock and Thelen, *op. cit.*, chap. xiv.

13. Lieberman's Ph.D. dissertation, Psychology Department, University of Chicago, is in process. A summary of the work appears in Stock and Thelen, chaps. v, viii, and xv.

themselves and the group as being warm and friendly; this is not a flight characteristic per se but is suggested as a reassurance reaction of flight-oriented people in a group which sees flight as "bad."

With respect to changes occurring during training, flight members were alike in showing no change along the dependency-counter-dependency dimension, which suggests a lack of emotional involvement to the point of unconcern over the extent of their own autonomy and power to influence the situation in order better to meet their own personal needs.

Kinds of Predispositions for "Acting-Out"

We have attempted to illustrate some of the behavioral meanings of flight, both as an individual tendency and as a group basic assumption. The subjects involved above were people carefully selected as having strong predispositions for flight.

In our earlier studies we rather naïvely felt that there should be a close correspondence between the tendencies projected in a sentence-completion test and the affect expressed by the person during group discussion. Actually there is a positive relationship, but its magnitude differs among persons and also among situations. A series of predicative case studies has led us to break down this predisposition into three more specific types: (a) predisposition to express the emotion affectively in the group; (b) predisposition to become active at times when the basic assumption is dominant in the group culture—quite apart from expression of the same emotion one's self; and (c) tendency to become "concerned" with expressions of the emotion as cues which mobilize disturbing feelings or anxieties within one's self. Stock has demonstrated that precision of prediction of individual behavior is greatly increased by making distinctions among these three kinds of predispositions.[14]

Bion uses the term "valency" to refer to the capacity of individuals to "combine with others to establish or maintain a given basic assumption in the group culture." In Ben-Zeev's study of co-participation, he found that "pairing" co-participants tend to select each other sociometrically, whereas co-participants in "fight" tend not to select each other sociometrically—thus suggesting that "combining"

14. Stock and Thelen, *op. cit.*, chap. xix.

can represent (at least) either co-operation or conflict.[15] It seems clear to us that co-participation—if that be the evidence of combination—may have bases in all three of the kinds of predispositions with respect to any particular emotionality category.

Phases in the Life of Groups

The notion that groups vary in the mood or content of their discussion arises from common observation. But the problem of knowing just where to draw the line between any two phases is by no means easy to solve. If, however, different phases represent different basic assumptions or needs in group life, then one would expect that these phases would be achieved through different ways of using the resources of the members. In other words, the participants during one phase would be a subgroup different from the participant subgroup during the next phase.

Ben-Zeev tested this notion by using it as the basis for identifying units of group interaction.[16] He has demonstrated that from knowledge of the code number of each participant in a sequence it is possible to divide the sequence into "natural units" and that these units so identified agree remarkably well with units determined from full knowledge of what the discussants said, what affect they expressed, and what was diagnosed to be the purpose of the group at each moment. These natural units were found by Ben-Zeev to differ in the thematic content and in the most frequently expressed emotionality (which he took to be also the basic assumption).

Co-participants during a particular phase, such as a "fight" unit, do not necessarily all express fight. They may be people who have one of the other two types of predispositions indicated above. Thus they may be rendered anxious in a fight situation and attempt to change its climate to work, pairing, or some other basic assumption. We have come to see that the concept of a fight phase in group life means that during this phase the overt participators act as if the basic assumption is fight; but they react to this condition each in his own way. In other words, those who meet fight with fight may ex-

15. Saul Ben-Zeev, in Stock and Thelen, *op. cit.*, chap. ix.

16. Saul Ben-Zeev, "The Construction and Validation of a Method for Unitizing Sequences of Group Interaction" (unpublished Ph.D. dissertation, Department of Education, University of Chicago, 1955).

press fight; those who meet fight by running away may be silent or may express flight; those who seek protection when they sense hostility may attempt to get the leader to intervene (dependency); and those who dislike hostility but are still able to cope with it may attempt to build rapport in the group through pairing or may attempt to bring fight under control through work. In any case, however, the post-meeting reaction sheets show that most members do tend to perceive the unit as fight-oriented, and fight is the most frequent expression, although it may have a plurality rather than a majority.

The Adaptive Balance

We have proposed that the composition of the group determines ultimately the extent of its growth toward an adaptive culture and that leadership probably determines the extent and rate of realization of its composition-determined potentiality. In the case of a leaderless group, composition would determine both ceiling and rate; in the case of a group with a designated leader or trainer, his authority imposed "from without" can be used to inhibit or encourage particular sorts of reactions—but the capability of the group for these reactions is determined by the composition.

Accordingly, we should expect to be able to study the adaptive balance (between "acting-out" and "inquiry" or, in Bion's terms, between work and emotionality) as a consequence of composition and as a cause of growth and increased productivity. We should also expect that groups in which the designated trainer was fully aware of, and not threatened by, the full range of emotional-work cultures should develop further in a given time than one in which the trainer was made anxious by some kinds of emotional expression.

A number of case studies of growth have been undertaken. I shall discuss two which were most carefully and comparatively done by Hill and Stock.[17] The compositions of the two groups were compared by factor analysis of self-perceptual Q-sorts thrown by the members. The Q-sort items were keyed to the various emotionalities and work. In one group of sixteen there was a common factor shared by all but two members, and this factor represented an expectation for work and for friendliness without intimacy. Additional factors, occurring along with this in different subgroups of four members,

17. Stock and Thelen, *op. cit.*, chap. xxii.

were tendencies toward intimate pairing and toward fight. A third subgroup of two had the common factor plus a tendency to withdraw. The second training group of eighteen had no common factor. There were three subgroups, and two of them were in direct opposition. One subgroup of six aspired to be leaders; the other would not accept leadership from aspirants and had some confusion over whether they would accept leadership from the designated leader. The trainer himself belonged to this subgroup. The third subgroup, also of six, was immobilized by conflict over leadership.

We would expect the first group to develop a common culture rapidly, the second group to have extreme difficulty in this regard. We would further suppose that the first group would develop, in general, a culture conducive to growth and productivity, whereas the second group's culture would be oriented around the problem of suppressing conflict simply so it could survive. Finally, we would expect the trainer of the first group to be helpful and the trainer of the second group to be useless.

Productivity and growth are difficult to measure, but in gross terms there is no question. At the end of thirteen meetings, Group 1 was characterized by listening to each other, expressing a wide range of affect, planning and carrying out activities. Group 2 was still fighting with high affect, was split in three, and had no clear agreement on what they were fighting over. Group 1 had solved the process problems centering around a rather sick assistant trainer —and it was not easy. Group 2 had set up one chairman after another—the trainer was one of these—and had rejected each one in turn.

When the units or phases during the thirteen meetings were plotted, we found that Group 1 remained at the same level of affective expression throughout but that the level of work had gone up markedly, whereas group 2 had not developed to a higher level of work and showed immense swings in the amount of affect expressed.

Further, Group 1 showed four clear-cut phases in which there is a discernible trend toward integration of personal feelings in support of work, whereas Group 2 showed no clear-cut phases or trends.

The researchers, who carried on daily interviews with the trainers, found the trainer in Group 1 to be constantly trying to describe the emotional life of the group, and he engaged in effective interpretations to the group of "where we are now." The trainer in Group 2 was unaware of much of the fight over dependency, constantly sought to suppress feeling by assigning tidy but trivial exercises, and, on one occasion, played a trick—which went sour—on the group. Thus the differences in trainers operated in the same direction as the differences in composition; but we regard composition as the more determining factor because the problems with which the groups dealt—regardless of the second trainer's efforts to shift direction—were predictable from the composition of the group.

Some findings from other experiments add additional suggestions about the adaptive balance. Thus Gradolph composed a group of people whose predispositions were all predominantly toward pairing and work; they were efficient and sound in their solution of the assigned problem and contrasted most markedly with the flight group mentioned above. A group composed half of flight and half of pairing-work people was less effective than the all-flight group; this finding tends to support the notion that dichotomously opposed subgroups—probably almost regardless of what they are opposed about—will have low productivity. Glidewell found that work-fight groups which tended to integrate emotion and work were more productive than eleven other combinations.

In general, we suggest that an adaptive balance will be achieved when there is (a) some conflict, openly expressed; (b) recognition and acceptance of the fact of conflict; and (c) inquiry into the basis of the conflict and externalization of the conflict in the form of conditions to be changed or problems to be solved. It is our belief that the most effective composition for a training group, at least, is one in which there are spokesmen for and against fight, pairing, dependency, and, possibly, flight.

Carrying the same reasoning to the intra-individual level, Mathis found that positive indicators for change during training were predispositions toward fight and pairing, plus acceptance of internal conflict, and that negative indicators were predispositions toward dependency and flight, plus tendencies to become immobilized under stress.[18] Other studies suggest that, of these, the most confident

18. Andrew Mathis, "Development and Validation of Trainability Index for Laboratory Training Groups" (unpublished Ph.D. dissertation, Department of Education, University of Chicago, 1955).

indicator is the acceptance of internal conflict; but it is possible that the other indicators would be as important if one could deal more precisely with the specific subjective meanings of the emotionalities.

I have attempted elsewhere to test the concept of the adaptive balance by applying it to the problems of teaching, training, and leadership in general.[19]

Composition, Dynamics, and Bion's Categories

It seems clear, on the basis of our studies, that no simple predictions can be made on the basis simply of predispositions toward or expression of the basic categories of fight, flight, dependency, and pairing, with regard either to individuals or to groups. We have demonstrated to our own satisfaction that the core ideas of dynamisms designated by these terms are extremely useful and that they refer to basic drives, either of the individual or of groups during a period of time. I may say that this is just the way Bion used them: as molar concepts descriptive of states of being in his therapy groups.

I have pointed out that for individual predictions we must distinguish among at least three relationships to these terms: tendency to express the emotion; tendency to participate in situations in which the emotion is expressed; and tendency to be concerned over expressions of the emotion. Direct predictions for individuals can be made on the basis of the broad concept alone only when we select one of those rare (probably not more than one in twenty) individuals for whom one of the emotionalities dominates all the others. In general, we must consider not only the amount of the emotionality but how it fits into a pattern with the other emotionalities and how, in a variety of situations, the emotions are controlled.

The same things can be said of the emotionalities with respect to groups. The most direct and gross results are achieved by composing groups homogeneously with respect to some dominant emotionality. But, in other cases, the extent of communality, the existence of conflict, and the constrictedness or integrativeness of the control system are at least as important. These points seem to be well demonstrated

19. H. A. Thelen, *Dynamics of Groups at Work* (Chicago: University of Chicago Press, 1954), chaps. ii, v, and xi, respectively.

in the case of individuals by Stock[20] and in the case of groups by Glidewell.

I wish to close with Hill's experiment,[21] which may point the way to a major simplification in our analysis of the dynamics of groups. We retain the notion that individuals somehow "combine," but we reject both sociometric choice and identity of emotion-work patterns as the basis of combination. Hill instead used perceptual communality: the individuals tend to perceive situations in the same way. They may or may not have any special kinship feeling for each other—the correlations here are low but positive. They may or may not have very similar patterns of emotionality as revealed by our sentence-completion test. But what they do have in common is a factor-analyzed theme or concern, such as those mentioned above in the discussion of group growth.

Now this theme is arrived at by studying the items on the Q-sort that the members choose as most characteristic of themselves (as group members). And each of these items *is* keyed to a particular one of Bion's emotionalities. But the theme integrates the selected specific aspects of the emotionalities underlying the commonly chosen specific items into a more complex and precise purpose than can be obtained just from the emotionalities alone. In Hill's study the number of subgroups thus identified was limited: there were five. In effect, the major dynamic of the group was successfully conceived to be the resolution of inter-subgroup conflict. Instead of regarding the group as a matrix of eighteen members, each with his unique pattern, it could be viewed as an interactive system composed of five basic types, which would be in conflict, alignment, or out-of-field under specifiable conditions.

Such an approach seems to me to make proper use of Bion's basic ideas of emotionality; it pays due respect to the way in which these basic categories integrate into unique patterns; and it opens the

20. Dorothy Stock, "The Relationship between the Sociometric Structure of the Group and Certain Personality Characteristics of the Individual" (unpublished Ph.D. dissertation, Department of Psychology, University of Chicago, 1952).

21. William F. Hill, "The Influence of Subgroups on Participation in Human Relations Training Groups" (unpublished Ph.D. dissertation, Committee on Human Development, University of Chicago, 1955).

door to consideration of subgroup formation and structure of the total group.

Further research will be required to discover whether it is reasonable in general to expect such a limited number of "types."

Finally, it seems to me that the adaptive balance is basically a model against which to compare, evaluate, and inquire into group phenomena. Groups, in general, appear to try to achieve it. And it points the direction for two major kinds of research to go on from here: first, research on the dynamics by which one culture gives way and another takes over—and here we must pay a great deal more attention to the non-participants who turn out to be participators in the next unit—and, second, research aimed at conceptualizing and determining the pattern of stresses in any given problematic situation, so that we can sharpen prediction by knowing far more precisely than we now do the nature of the situation to which we are trying to predict.

WILLARD C. OLSON

Biosocial Theory in Human Development

The persistent problem in the social sciences in the interpretation of the findings of research, and in progress toward system and theory, is how to take into account the circular problem involved in the nature of the organism and in the nurturing environment. In lower forms we sometimes see such specificity in behavior that it seems to be almost solely attributable to the characteristics of the species. In man we see such possibilities for lability that the social scientist may develop theories within the framework of institutions, groups, and experience. Theories of culture and personality at times seem to assume a standardized human animal which becomes what he is primarily through experience. The student of growth and development sees differences among people as a part of the essence of the equation of man in society and sees these differences not only as a static element but also as a highly dynamic factor determining both the experiences that will be selected and the reactions of those about him to the differences present.

In contemporary concepts of development the contributions of heredity and environment are agreed to be indeterminate, and the important task is to study the process of interaction and, for a given individual, to improve the environment.

Thus, while the maturation process describes the potential capacities of the individual, experience determines the expression of that potential in development. Environment supplies the conditions for growth, and development is the end product of the interaction. Biological determinism has tended to place a strait jacket on planning for improvement through other than genetic means. The social approach also has at times excluded the additional processes which are at hand and the refinements which may be introduced by working with difference in a dynamic fashion. Much of the evidence

201

which exists requires order and relationship and justifies an excursion into biosocial theory in a scrutiny of social science as science.

The Role of Theory

As the base for a science broadens and strengthens, a need commonly appears for some ordering of the observations and relationships. There is a new interest currently in theory in problems of culture, personality, and development. It is relatively simple to cut out narrow segments or specialized points of view for a theoretical system. It becomes difficult when one wishes to secure a general behavior theory or general development theory. If one can build a set of concepts connected by definitions to observed behavior, progress will have been made toward laws, and these in turn might be related to more general theory from which other laws might be deduced as verification of those already existing or others yet to be tested. In fields closely related to the totality of human development learning theory, field theory, and psychoanalytic theory are probably receiving the greatest theoretical and experimental attention at this time. While some of these theoretical frameworks have prominently in them the idea of time and individual difference as important factors, they seem, on the whole, to ascribe a minor role to the differences that come about through differential rates of maturation. To the person immersed in the human development approach, this seems to be a serious omission, since he finds greater powers of prediction when individual differences are taken into account.

A Model of Individual Differences in Development

Is it possible to enunciate a biosocial theory consistent with other theories, embracing a wider range of data and giving greater powers of prediction, or at least supplying a useful elaboration of other theories?

The fundamental equation for such a theory is:

$$\text{Maturation} \times \text{Nurture} = \text{Development}.$$

Development embraces personality and achievement as well as physical changes. Maturation includes the genetic factors. Nurture includes experience, formal and informal, and may vary for a particular type from zero to a maximum. At zero nurture (deprivation) development fails. For example, life and physical growth cease in the absence of food, and there is illiteracy when opportunity for reading experience is not provided. At constant nurture development still varies with maturational rate.

A graphic schematic model (Fig. 1) representing the product of the equation can be constructed from findings of longitudinal studies of

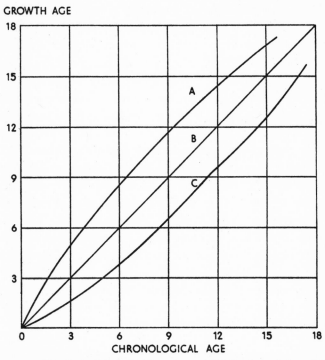

Fɪɢ. 1.–Model of rapid (Child A), average (Child B), and slow (Child C) growth according to the equation, Maturation × Nurture = Development.

growth and development where the substrate of the organism has been sampled and described by a composite value called the organismic age. In operation this has consisted often of weight age, height age, mental age, reading age, grip age, carpal age, and dental age. The chart is constructed by showing chronological age along the X-axis and average growth age or organismic age along the Y-axis. The model shows the growth of one highly developed child (A), one below average development (C), and one who is just average (B).

We can then set up a series of concepts involving known facts surrounding the model. These are of varying degrees of generalization, and each should be preceded by the qualification "other things being equal." The model is based on the assumption that the growth represented by the curves represents a composite according to the equation—maturation times nurture equals development. Viewed alone, it appears as a relatively static model with much stability and continuity. Injected into a social field, however, the children represented become dynamic in the sense of relationship to other individuals and to meeting the requirements of each situation.

What general theory can be built about the model in the illustration?

Principles in Human Development

Concepts that will stand the test of universality, of experiment, and of prediction are hard to come by in a field governed by multiple causation. When stated, such concepts are apt to be suspect in the sense that other postulates may account for the phenomenon in part. There is always something of an indeterminant character when variable individuals experience variable nurture.

The following postulate comes close to having generality: "For all achievements which increase with chronological age, the rapidly growing child will yield the achievement earlier, and the slowly growing child will achieve the status later, than the average child of a given age."

From such a postulate one can predict in advance the individual differences that will exist, the factors that must be observed in an adequate experimental design, and the constant errors which must be allowed for or adjusted. We can predict in advance the results of many types of experiment. With such a postulate a person can predict, as an average trend at least, most of the types of data that can be secured in a classroom group or even in bacteriological, chemical, and physiological experiments. The basic evidence needed for the predictions is a fairly accurate account of age change.

For example, knowing that emotional outbursts decrease in number and severity with age, we can predict that a child showing such outbursts will have many characteristics of the slowly growing child.

Some of the objective findings on associations with the model furnish a basis for more general theory.

Associations with the Model

Here are some operational associations and deductions from the model. It should be noted that the effects are not only in the model as constructed but also in the matrix of all the associated factors that go into the loading of the model. The differences shown have important associations with socioeconomic status, social acceptability, responsibility, levels of interests, reaction to frustration, age of accomplishment of developmental tasks, and many valued traits of character and personality. The differences also run in families and are remarkably resistant to planned change although reflecting changes in design over the years.

More specifically, A as contrasted to C will be higher in social age, will be advanced in interests, and will be superior in social status in the group. C, contrasted to A, will have more behavior problems whether checked by self, teacher, parent, or associates. Child A as contrasted to Child C will be characterized by more active seeking behavior in general, including motivation for achievement. His appetite and interest in food will be greater, although calories per unit of body weight will be less in accord with the age trend.

The associates of A will be more like A than they are like C, and, similarly, the associates of C will be more like C than they will be like A. The rationalization of the association may be in terms of social status, interest, values, levels of development, or comparable skills of achieving or performing.

Some examples of the significance of the associations for other systematic approaches can be illustrated.

The Model and Psychoanalytic Theory

Psychoanalytic theory emphasizes the fundamental maturational significance of the aspects of human life concerned with ingestion-excretion-reproduction and the ramifications of these in interaction with the environment. Psychologically, development comes to be represented by the id, the ego, and the superego. Within the developmental cycle dominance of a phase is often identified such as the prenatal, neonatal, oral (first year), anal (one to three years), phallic (three to five years), latency period (five years to pre-puberty), prepuberty and adolescence, and adult. Adult character has been described in terms of the trauma of a period or the domi-nance of one aspect over the others.

Observations by the writer suggest that additional insights are added and some mistakes corrected when the theory of the model is added. Thus children such as C of the model will remain later in each of the above phases, and problems of conflict, coercion, and repression will be more prominent. The significance of clinically and hospitally selected children for general theory requires correction for the downward selection of the sample in such populations. With such adjustments the conflicting evidence on the significance of early childhood experience and child-rearing practice might, by allowance for the theory of the model, make more systematic sense. The theory of the model, of course, allows for both cultural and biological factors, effects, and interrelationships.

The Model and Frustration-Aggression Theory

In classic frustration-aggression theory one has two opposing courses, one of which is restraining. Operationally, frustration occurs when there is interruption in progress toward a goal. The conse-quences may be aggression, regression, physical strain, and tension. In reference to the model we can make some predictions in accord with the theory. The theory demands that the effects be related to the strength of the tendency, the extent of the thwarting, the fre-quency of frustrated responses, and the competing tendencies re-sulting from anticipation of punishment. Biosocial theory demands that Child C have greater frustratability, a greater past frequency of frustration, will be frustrated by less difficult environmental fac-tors, and will have more competing tendencies for avoidance. This appears to be in accord with the facts when C is contrasted with B or A.

The Model and Theories of Intelligence

The conflict in emphasis between those psychologists who see in individual differences a large element of human biology and those social psychologists who see the differences among people or groups of people as primarily determined by the culture is most dramatically illustrated in the attempt to produce so-called culture-fair tests. In such work the experiences attributable to a particular social class position have been studied in a meticulous manner, and tests that differentiate social class experiences have been excluded. After this work is done, it is of interest to note that large individual differences still remain in the children of all social class positions, that these individual differences far transcend the average differences between social class groups, and that the reapplication of so-called culture-fair tests, as contrasted to the contaminated tests, still produce differences in the same direction.

The model allows for the fact that intelligence must be nurtured, that under constant supply of nurture A will be contrasted to C primarily by maturational factors, and that with varying degrees of deprivation in the nurtural supply (with constant maturation) the end product in development will vary. More commonly the end product will be determined by the complexities of variable maturation multiplied by variable nurture.

Reconciliation of Explanatory Theories

It appears clear that mistakes or at least a constricted view will be held when there is a focus on a single, self-contained system. For example, a psychoanalyst recounts an incident in a progressive elementary school in which there were a number of cases of reading retardation. He reports the lack of progress made by conventional remedial reading methods (traditional learning theory) with the employment of objective diagnostic measures, instrumentation, and practice. He calls this approach a mistake, since psychoanalytically his diagnosis was that the children were suffering from severe repression of the scotophillic (looking at feces) tendencies. Work with the parents revealed that such repression had been common in the socialization of the children.

The theory and observations associated with the model inject an additional dimension of explanation which assists in understanding the conflicting diagnoses—both based on correct observations.

We have only to note that the retarded readers under discussion regularly tend toward C in developmental characteristics. They will indeed have learned less well (less learning potential in terms of growth age as contrasted with chronological age). They will also have persisted in the anal phase longer (delayed over-all growth) and will thus have created more anxiety in parents (conflict of expectation and readiness) and will have been subjected to more repressions.

The three rival explanatory systems would have these differences which might be tested experimentally and directly.

1. Traditional learning theory: Test—teach—test. Follow up after an interval.
2. Psychoanalytic theory: Test—treat—test. Follow up after an interval.
3. Biosocial theory (holistic): Test—ordinary experience and time lapse —test. Follow up after an interval.

The writer would predict that No. 3 will be as effective as Nos. 1 and 2 in terms of measured results in reading in the absence of deprivation. If properly done, he would concede that it is probable that additional comfort and serenity for parents, teachers, and children might be expected by some of the elements of Nos. 1 and 2. To establish this, measuring devices in addition to achievement would be necessary.

Individual Predictions versus Explanatory Principles

The model and associated theory may be criticized, since the relationships referred to are often small. One should recall, however, that explanatory principles are commonly based on small differences. It could not be otherwise in a world of multiple causation.

The student of total growth regularly finds small coefficients of correlation between all measured structures and functions. These give important support to the idea that there are underlying factors in development which express themselves in various ways. Some investigators have disparaged the significance of these relationships for a theory of development in education, since they are not of a size as to be very helpful in individual predictions where the goal is to predict the status of a person in a group. Before one disparages these small coefficients in a theory of development as a basis for an explanatory system, he should ponder the large differences produced at the extremes even with small coefficients. It is often at the extremes, including the gifted, the mentally retarded, the delinquent, and the disturbed, where theoretical insights are sought and practical programs constructed.

The schematic model may be criticized properly as oversimplifying many very complex problems in genetics and nurture. The science of organized complexities may be better brought out by the graphs of growth for individual children. This has been done and is being done in the hope that there may also emerge "laws of the case" as well as laws of populations.

The geneticists are moving from a single-gene theory to a polygene theory, where multifactorial genes combine to produce a continuous change among individuals in an attribute rather than the discontinuity that might be indicated by a single gene approach. As we go into a molar type of study of the child, we are concerned with such ideas as design, pattern, shape, form, configuration, or morphology. When such ideas are applied to a child, they seem to have reality in terms of his behavior. His pattern or shape thus has some significance for his behavior in addition to the actual amount or substance of things present. Thus, there is special significance in having a child with a very highly developed intellect but with less adequate general growth support. Such children have been described as "a high-powered motor in a light chassis." Similarly, a child characterized from birth by apathy and lack of strength reflects this in the totality of his behavior in play and even in retardation in a subject such as reading, where he may have a high intellect which should, from average predictions, produce outstanding achievement. His apathy and weakness are parts of a patterning of significance in understanding his behavior and achievement. The significance does not depend on a pronounced statistical correlation for children in general between strength as measured by a dynamometer and ability to read. The attempt to analyze the substrate of development, as in the model, by sampling commonly reveals important trends for both the individual and for a population sample.

Concepts of Biosocial Theory in Human Development

An extensive set of concepts has been prepared by a seminar in human development and by a conference on human relations and human development. For the most part they are related to findings growing out of longitudinal, multidisciplinary studies of the growth of children and of work in closely associated areas. Some are primarily biological in frame of reference, and others are primarily cultural.

The following samples have been selected for significance to biosocial theory, as a basis for discussion, for further experimentation, and for the building of theory.

1. The growth process itself creates needs to be satisfied through the environment.
2. Children growing at varying rates in some degree "demand" and create differential expectancies and treatment from those about them.
3. There is a familial resemblance in all measurements of growth, achievement, and behavior in children.
4. Longitudinal growth patterns for the members of the same family in school achievement will bear a substantial resemblance, the resemblance being the greatest in those areas in which similarity of experience is greatest and will diminish for those areas in which the incorporation of experience is more incidental or accidental.
5. The "environment" involved in the total environment–person situation is an environment which the individual himself has helped to create.
6. Culture is a part of human biology (ecology), since the culture built in the growing child tends to persist through succeeding generations.
7. The similarity in educational achievement in members of a family under different teachers will be greater than the similarities produced between non-related children under the same teachers.
8. A positive statistical correlation is commonly found between socioeconomic status or social class and any aspect of growth which is measured.
9. Given two children, equally well grown, the one reared under optimal conditions in early years in the family will be more productive than the one reared with less affection and security and more frustration.
10. When intelligence tests are corrected for cultural effects that contaminate them when the criteria of novelty or universality of experience have not been met, large individual differences (larger than the cultural bias) still remain which require explanation.
11. The similarities and differences in the behavior and achievement of children in school will be more related to measured aspects of growth than to ascertainable characteristics of early child-rearing practices in the home.
12. In general, slowly growing (lower growth potential) children will have early histories of child-rearing practices characterized by greater conflict and more emotional episodes than will rapidly growing children.
13. Dominance of general growth over specific experience and learning in school is illustrated by the observation that children who are retained in a grade and who repeat do not gain more than those who proceed with their group and that the practice of retention must be evaluated more largely in personal and social outcomes than in achievement in school subjects.
14. When the social structure of the classroom is viewed sociometrically as a group of biological units, it is observed that the more matured units stream toward the center or nucleus and the less mature remain on the periphery.

15. The immediate family and social class culture will be determinative of occupational choice in a substantial degree—the quality of performance within the occupational class will strongly reflect biological attributes.

16. A rapid grower will accomplish his developmental tasks earlier than a slow grower.

17. Personality is an emergent from a circular interaction between the individual and the culture in which productive variations become incorporated in the culture and these in turn modify the individual.

18. Children who are deprived (physically, socially, and emotionally) evidence the deprivation in classroom behavior characterized by apathy, absence of smiling behavior, and infrequency of talking.

19. The concepts of "modal" personality and of individual variations both have a legitimate place in the anthropological approach to the study of culture.

20. Repression and neurosis in any culture are most likely to develop around those areas of experience which—for cultural or biological reasons—are highly valued by the individual and which are tabooed or culturally kept secret (in which interpersonal communication is prohibited or restricted).

21. Behavior problems may profitably be viewed as a conflict between environmental demands and the ability of the child to meet them.

22. A fluctuating balance is maintained in normal health between cultural requirements and individual needs.

23. Emotional disturbance will be manifested in symptoms related to the developmental aspect most characteristic of the level at which the trauma occurred.

24. In projective techniques immature (in terms of measured growth) children yield immature products.

25. Just as the physiological organism constantly moves to maintain a dynamic homeostatic balance, so the affective individual is constantly motivated in the direction of a "deprivation-indulgence" balance. The latter process, more immediately and deeply influenced by environmental vagaries than the former, tends to be less stable and more subject to pathology.

26. Because of the interrelated character of growth, both deprivation and replacement of nurture produce both specific and non-specific effects. Thus disturbed emotionality is accompanied by slower growth rates; feeding and physical therapy (breathing and postural) result in improvement in a function such as reading, and counseling and psychotherapy irradiate to achievement and relationships.

27. When a group of children suffering qualitative or quantitative nutritional deprivation are placed on a more adequate diet, responsiveness is to be expected not only in physical growth, such as height and weight, but also in school achievement and in affective states.

28. The principle of parsimony, and logic of research design, demands that factors in human biology which may account for a result must be allowed for experimentally or statistically before ascribing a social or emotional explanation.

ALLISON DAVIS*

The Ego and Status-Anxiety

This paper attempts to envisage the manner in which the anxiety and hostility aroused by status are reduced and controlled in the normal personality. In my use of the concept of ego-identity as a factor in the resolution of status-hostility, I am greatly indebted to Professor Robert D. Hess.

Research on social structure and on personality indicates that all status-relationships arouse mutual hostility between individuals of different status-levels. This hostility, it is assumed, is a defensive response against anxiety, which is the fear of attack or derogation by the other member, or members, of the status-relationship.

The concept of status, as used here, refers to the position of an individual, or of a group, in a socially defined system of rank. A specific status or rank is "socially defined" by society in two ways. First, the status, whether of parent, child, or a particular social class, is defined by a *culture;* that is, by group-expectations and concepts of the proper thoughts, feelings, and acts for persons in such a status. Second, a status is defined by *group-sanctions,* either of acceptance and approval of those who act and feel in accord with the culture of their status, or of rejection and derogation of those who act in ways not included in the culture of their status.

The systems of status referred to in this paper, namely, those of parent and child, male and female, and the broad ranking systems of social classes and ethnic groups, all seek to regulate the individual's degree of access to biological or social goals. The person in any status, therefore, has a stake to be defended or attained. Every form

* For my general interest in the problems of ego-identity, I am indebted, of course, to the works of Erik Erikson, notably *Childhood and Society* (New York: W. W. Norton & Co., 1951).

212

of status, moreover, involves both psychosocial gains and deprivations for each party to the status-relationship.[1]

In the parent-child relationship, for instance, each party at times
suffers derogation by the other. The child experiences threats, criticism, and physical punishment. These are "external" attacks upon
the child's ego. They generate anxiety, which in this case is the fearful anticipation of derogation and attack. The anxiety creates hostility toward the cause of the anxiety, the parents.

This hostility, as in all status-relationships, may take one of three
courses. It may be expressed, within limits, as chronic aggression
toward the parents. This course only increases the child's guilt feelings and anxiety. Or the child's hostility may be repressed, or
"dammed up" to use Freud's phrase, and do its destructive work in
the creation of irrational anxiety. Or the child's hostility may be
transformed, or at least reduced to a tolerable level, through identification with, and reconciliation to,[2] his age-status. The child identifies with the child-group and child-status, as a means both of gaining substitutive gratifications and of controlling and reducing his
anxiety and hostility. Within his age-status, within his identity as a
"child," he may, as Professor Hess has pointed out, also find culturally approved means of developing his initiative and competence.
Accepting the ego-identity of his status, he may work within it to
make himself less vulnerable to attacks upon his ego both from
inside himself and from the outside world.

The hostility is never completely resolved, however. For the
privileges and deprivations, both of parent and of child, chronically
arouse hostility and stimulate the anticipation of counterhostility by
the other party to the status-relationship. This counterhostility moves
either "up" or "down" in the status-system. We have seen how the
child's is aroused. To the parent, himself, the evidences of his child's
hostility imply that the parent is not fulfilling the cultural expectations of a "good" parent. The child's hostility is a threat to the
parent's self-esteem, therefore, and arouses the parent's anxiety and
stimulates his counterhostility toward the child.

1. Cf. John Dollard, *Caste and Class in a Southern Town* (New Haven,
Conn.: Yale University Press, 1937).

2. A. R. Radcliffe-Brown, "The Nature of a Science of Society" (unpublished manuscript, Department of Anthropology, University of Chicago, 1937).

At the same time a protective anxiety-reducing process develops in the parent-child relationship. It includes not only the process called "identification." *The total process by which the child's anxiety and hostility are reduced involves a reconciliation both on the side of the child and on that of the parent.* The culturally "good" child and "good" parent have made a temporary peace between them such that the anxiety and hostility of each, which are chronically aroused by the system of status, are reduced. To use Erikson's language, this reconciliation consists in accepting the cultural identity of one's age-status, with its losses as well as its gains. After a long battle and much renunciation, the child accepts, or is reconciled to, the rights and duties and ego-ideals of a "child" as his best *available* way of life. The parent is reconciled to his responsibilities also. He learns the cultural identity of a "parent," which permits him authority but requires that he accept also the restrictions and the impulse-renunciations of parenthood. When he can do this, and still accept the cultural injunction to train the child and teach him self-control and responsibility, the parent has embraced the cultural identity of a "parent," which is one side of the social control that makes "peace"—or something, shall we say, different at least from open warfare—between the parent and the child.[3]

A second kind of ranked status which the child must learn to accept is the status-identity of a boy or of a girl. The derogation of feminine status and the early intimidation of the girl are general in European and oriental cultures. It seems clear, also, that in early life, girls in the United States are more severely trained than boys and more systematically intimidated with respect to nearly all the basic psychological drives. Anyone who thinks realistically about the status of women in America will recognize that women are placed at a great status-disadvantage in the economic and political systems and that within the family, itself, the division of labor, privileges,

3. The status-system of parent and offspring is subjected to violent attack by the adolescent, whose old identity-as-a-child is now rejected by his age-group and himself. His anxiety and hostility over parental derogation and control can no longer be reduced by the status-gains of safety and dependence which a child's identity afforded him. Erikson has made us aware that a new integration of psychosocial identity is the prime work of adolescence, and he has attributed this fact not only to the greatly increased power of the sexual drive but also to the greater complexity of the demands (and implied threats) from the social environment.

and authority strikingly favors the man—the opinions of European observers notwithstanding.

In fact, the differential status of men and women is a system of rank which, unlike that of parent and child, persists throughout the life of the individual. This lifelong inferiority of the female's status, in spite of her equal, or possibly greater, intellectual capacity, is of course a cultural attack upon the ego of females. Like human beings of any group and every age-level, women respond to this cultural intimidation with anxiety, and then with hostility and guilt. This hostility is directed toward males and also toward the mother who puts into effect the restrictions demanded by the male-dominated society.

We know very little about the psychology of women. Freud, himself, no doubt greatly underestimated the effects of their status upon the personality of women. One could understand why, owing both to his own personality and also to his Germanic culture, he would be less conscious of the cultural subordination of women. Psychologists, male or female, are blinded in their studies of the personality of women by an ethnocentrism which prevents our seeing clearly the powerful status-system to which the woman has to reconcile herself.

This reconciliation really means, of course, reconciliation to men, to the father, to the brother, to the husband, to the son. It takes place through the girl's learning to identify with the feminine culture and status. This identity includes the culturally approved but non-dominant behavior of tenderness and mothering and personal service to children and husband, as well as the cultural symbolization of the family's class-status, and also a certain amount of sabotage tolerated by the system.

In the normal female personality, the woman has identified with, and committed herself emotionally to, the female status. In this process of status-identification, most of her hostility toward men is resolved, but never all of it. She is reconciled to the feminine status, however, first by its opportunities for positive achievement in the roles of wife and of mother, and, second, by the feelings of acceptance, ease, and intimacy which she gets from her own status-group, that of women.

This reconciliation of the conflicting desires of parent and child and of male and female, through the commitment of each to that socially defined identity which brings him cultural acceptance, may serve as a prototype, it seems to me, of the reconciliation made by the individual, as he grows beyond the age of five or six, with other types of status-derogation, hostility, and anxiety.

The broadest systems of social ranking, namely, social classes and ethnic groups,[4] also stimulate reciprocal fear and hostility between members of different groups. The realistic anxiety generated by social class and ethnic status is the learned anticipation of social punishment. The anxiety is built upon fear, humiliation, and other painful affect which are in turn responses to social derogation, ridicule, or the threat of attack.

For most subordinate groups, low social status carries the realistic threat of starvation, eviction, physical attack, and even death. In the book by Dr. and Mrs. Burleigh B. Gardner, and Mrs. Davis and myself, dealing with the deep South, we have shown through interviews with landlords and tenants the function of whippings, shootings, and killings of tenants in the maintenance of the position of landlords on the plantation.[5] In Freiberg, Moravia, Freud's own father knew the threat of annihilation when he was struck by a Christian who shouted at him, "Jew, get off the pavement."[6]

Since he was primarily interested in the neuroses, Freud neglected or underestimated the anxiety aroused by objective social dangers, such as derogation, ridicule, and attack, in the process of normal socialization. He was not particularly interested in *social* threats against the ego. He thought of anxiety as a fear of *inner* dangers; either the ego's fear of the sexual impulses or the ego's fear of the punitive (but also inconsistently delinquent) conscience. Thus he inferred two sources of neurotic anxiety: the one, the ego's fear of the dammed-up, repressed (but not controlled) impulses—a fear intensified by the guilt aroused by a lashing neurotic conscience; the other, an "objectless, indefinite" fear, mounting to panic, which was really the return of one's old feeling of utter helplessness in the

4. My training in the study of the social stratification of American communities began with Professor Lloyd Warner, when he initiated the "Yankee City" and "Deep South" studies, and I wish to express my continuing gratitude to him and to Dr. and Mrs. Burleigh Gardner.

5. Allison Davis, Burleigh B. Gardner, and Mary R. Gardner, *Deep South* (Chicago: University of Chicago Press, 1941).

6. Sigmund Freud, *The Basic Writings* (New York: Modern Library, 1938), p. 260.

face of some overwhelming, traumatic, and forgotten danger in early life.

What, then, is "true anxiety," as distinguished from "neurotic anxiety"? Freud's answer is that true anxiety is "anxiety in regard to a known danger." By "known danger" he nearly always means the *inner* danger which the ego perceives in the sexual and aggressive impulses. But if the patient learns to recognize *within himself* this *excessive* and irrational fear of his own sexual feelings, then the inner danger of the impulses becomes a "real danger" and the fear is then a "true anxiety." Freud writes: "The neurotic danger must first be sought, therefore; analysis has taught us that it is an instinctual danger. By bringing *into consciousness* this danger of which the ego is [has been] unaware, we obliterate the distinction between true and neurotic anxiety and are able to treat the latter as we would the former."[7]

At times the clarity of this distinction between neurotic anxiety as fear of a danger in the *unconscious* (the fear of an unknown danger) and realistic anxiety (*Realangst*) as fear of a *consciously* identified danger is obscured. For instance, Freud writes that castration anxiety is "a real anxiety, a reality fear, fear of a danger, actually threatening or *believed to do so*."[8] Thus even a fantasy is a "true danger," since it is a *conscious* experience.

Freud, as the writer has suggested on earlier occasions,[9] was never able fully to bring the anxiety aroused by social dangers into his psychological system.[10] Status-anxiety, unless carried to the point

7. Sigmund Freud, *The Problem of Anxiety*, trans. Henry Alden Bunker, M.D. (New York: W. W. Norton & Co., 1936), pp. 112–17.

8. *Ibid.*, p. 37. (Italics mine.)

9. Allison Davis, "Socialization and Adolescent Personality," in the *Forty-third Yearbook of the National Society for the Study of Education*, Part I, pp. 198–216. Cf. also Allison Davis, *Social-Class Influences upon Learning* (Alexander Inglis Memorial Lecture, Harvard University [Cambridge, Mass.: Harvard University Press, 1948]), pp. 22–37.

10. I am grateful to Professor William E. Henry of the Committee on Human Development for having called my attention to a letter of Freud's in which he surmises that traumatic war neuroses are "a question of a conflict between two ego ideals, the customary one and the one the war has compelled the person to build. The latter is concerned with relations to new objects (superior officers and comrades) and so is equivalent to the cathexis of an object; it might be called a choice of an object not consonant with the (previous) ego. . . . There is thus a struggle within the ego instead of between ego and libido, but fundamentally that comes to the same thing" (Ernest Jones, M.D.,

where it is disproportionate to the actual social danger, is adaptive because it warns of real dangers. Similarly, the anxiety of the upward-mobile person, in his contacts with persons of a higher social class, is realistic and adaptive, when that anxiety warns him against behavior which is disapproved by the higher class of which he wishes to become a member.

The Life and Work of Sigmund Freud, Vol. II [New York: Basic Books, Inc., 1955], p. 252). In referring to Freud's "Preface" to *Psycho-analysis and the War Neuroses,* I find the clear-cut statement, "The conflict is between the soldier's old peaceful ego and his new warlike one, and it becomes acute as soon as the peace-ego realizes what danger it runs of losing its life, owing to the rashness of its newly formed, parasitic double." And, "In traumatic and war neuroses the human ego is defending itself from a danger which threatens it from without or which is embodied in a shape assumed by the ego itself" (Sigmund Freud, *Collected Papers,* ed. James Strachey [London: Hogarth Press], V, 83–87). A social danger is recognized, but the anxiety and defense are neurotic. Freud did not develop this idea in any detail, but both this and other passages in his writings make it clear that he recognized the threat of social subordination to the ego. Indeed, Freud includes this concept, as he does nearly all others in the field of dynamic psychology; he did not *develop* the concept of social threats to the ego, because he did not consider them so important as the "instinctual" threats. In one passage in *The Problem of Anxiety,* it is true, he seems to place the "external danger" first in the hierarchy of threats to the ego. But then he turns again to his belief that the threat from the impulses is the greater, since the ego, as he says elsewhere, *feels* more threatened by the sexual feelings. "A real danger is one which threatens from some external object, neurotic danger from an instinctual demand. In so far as this instinctual demand is a piece of reality, neurotic anxiety as well may be considered as founded on reality. We have understood that the seemingly intimate relation between anxiety and neurosis derives from the fact that the ego protects itself against an external reality danger, but that in consequence of an imperfection of the psychic apparatus this defensive activity eventuates in neurosis. We have become convinced also that instinctual demands often become an (internal) danger only because of the fact that their gratification would bring about an external danger—because, therefore, this internal danger represents an external one.

"On the other hand, the external (reality) danger must have undergone internalization if it is to become significant for the ego; its relation to a situation of helplessness which has been lived through must be recognized. An instinctive recognition of dangers threatening from without does not seem to have been among Nature's gifts to man, save to a very moderate degree" (*The Problem of Anxiety,* pp. 115–16).

In the view of psychoanalysts, generally, the threats which the ego regards as most dangerous are the demands of the "impulses" for free expression (that is, the onslaught of sexual and aggressive drives upon the ego). The ego resists these attacks through the building and maintaining of "defense-mechanisms." According to psychoanalysis, the individual is unaware of the defenses he uses against threats from the id; that is to say, the defense-mechanisms are an area of the ego (Freud said they also are an area of the id) which is unconscious. If the *inner* dangers against which the ego unconsciously erects de-

On the other hand, status-anxiety is irrational and neurotic when (a) the anxiety is more intense and the behavior more self-depreciatory than the actual danger of social derogation or attack would cause in most people, or (b) when the anxiety is chiefly generated by an irrational personality factor, of which the status-anxiety is simply one expression. The latter type of neurotic, unrealistic status-anxiety is found in many upward-striving persons who are extremely fearful of attack and derogation and therefore are compulsively driven to achieve more and more prestige and, they hope, safety. The former kind of irrational anxiety is found in the clown-type and in the unnecessarily subservient type, whose excessive fear leads them to subordinate themselves beyond the point of actual social requirement.

Some idea of the anxiety raised by status-subordination may be gained from Freud's analysis of several of his own dreams. Upon one

---

fenses are the so-called impulses, what are the outer dangers? What are the cultural sources of attacks upon the ego? Freud emphasized the goal and the power of early cultural sanctions (toilet-training, the incest-taboo, control of aggression) within the family. He was not equally attentive, however, to the other powerful systems of social restriction and control upon the individual in Western society, such as the systems of social class control. Freud underestimated the psychological effect of the restrictions wielded against ethnic groups, such as the humiliation he himself met and felt keenly in his social position as a Jew in Vienna. It is true that in his *Autobiography*, and also in the analysis of his own dreams in *The Interpretation of Dreams*, he touched upon his experiences as a Jew. He did not subject the feelings of humiliation which he and many of his patients underwent as members of a stigmatized group, however, to the same degree of analysis which he used upon the child-parent, husband-wife, and sibling relationships. Perhaps many—though, as his analysis of his own dreams shows, by no means all—of his own defenses and his own resistances were too strong in this area to be brought into consciousness and to yield to objective study.

Anna Freud recognizes "external" attacks upon the ego but holds that the individual only fears an external object or event because it symbolizes (or stimulates) his own inner dangers, his own rage or sexual desire, which he fears may be too powerful for him to control (Anna Freud, *The Ego and the Mechanisms of Defence*, trans. Cecil Baines [London: Hogarth Press, 1937], pp. 96, 109, 190–91). Fenichel has pointed out that such a view of defense against external dangers is suitable for the study of neurosis, since, by definition, "the neurotic conflict takes place between (internal) *drives*, that is, the id and the ego" (Otto Fenichel, M.D., *The Psychoanalytic Theory of Neurosis* [New York: W. W. Norton & Co., 1945], pp. 129–30). For the study of normal personalities in society, however, this theory of external threats to the ego from the social world is incomplete. The theory always leads back to the sexual and aggressive drives, and their attendant affects, as the only ultimately real dangers as viewed by the ego.

occasion he dreamed that he denied his relationship to his ethnic group by assuming a different social identity. In another case he dreamed that he attributed the social barriers raised against particular Jews, not to social subordination, but to purely individual faults: one had committed a crime, another was stupid, etc. This dream was his way of claiming, therefore, "There are no ethnic barriers. There are only barriers against criminals and incompetent people. I am law-abiding and competent. Therefore I shall be accepted." This might be called the universal middle-class-ethnic fallacy. Freud, the realist, laughed at it in his interpretation of the dream.

Freud also interprets one of his own social class dreams. He dreamed that his father appeared as Dr. Meynert, the famous psychiatrist, under whom Freud had studied. This part of the dream, Freud says, is a disguised expression of his resentment against his father's low estate. "If fully expanded," he wrote, "the dream would read as follows, 'Of course if I belonged to the *second* generation, if I were the son of a professor or a privy councillor, I should have progressed more rapidly.'"

Concerning each of these dreams, Freud concludes, however, that the ultimate defense was not against the status-threat to the ego but against an early childhood attack, within the family, upon his ego.

I feel, however, that the development of Freud's own identity as a Jew, in nineteenth-century Vienna, supports our view that status-anxiety is a powerful threat to the ego and that the ego learns deep, and largely unconscious, methods of reducing this anxiety. The rest of this paper will deal briefly with (1) the adolescent Freud's resolution of the problem of his ethnic identity and with (2) an American adolescent boy's formation of identity with a higher social class than that of his parents.

Freud's father owned a small handicraft weaving mill in Freiberg, Moravia. When the industrial revolution came to Moravia, the weavers "began to hold the Jewish textile merchants responsible for their plight."[11] Freud's father fled with his family to Vienna on a train. The circumstances of this flight probably had much to do with Freud's later fear of trains.

---

11. Helen Walker Puner, *Freud: His Life and His Mind* (New York: Howell, Soskin & Co., 1947), pp. 24–25, 29–35. Cf. Jones, *op. cit.*

Nineteenth-century Vienna, during the time of Freud's youth and early manhood, was a strongly anti-Semitic city. In her life of Freud, Helen W. Puner writes that Jews "were looked upon as aliens; they were snubbed and humiliated. . . . The Jews of Vienna were a group set aside and rejected by the other ninety per cent of the population." Freud's father lived first in a ghetto that was "not quite a slum" and later moved to an apartment in "another dreary Jewish quarter one-step removed from a slum," Puner writes.[12]

Freud, himself, refers to the anti-Semitic feelings and attacks directed against him by his schoolmates in Vienna. In his self-analysis, reported in *The Interpretation of Dreams*, Freud writes that in reading of the Punic War, his sympathies were not with beleaguered Rome but with Hannibal, whom he describes as "the Semitic commander." To quote Freud: "Moreover, when I finally came to realize the consequences of belonging to an alien race, and was forced by the anti-Semitic feeling among my class-mates to take a definite stand, the figure of the Semitic commander [Hannibal] assumed still greater proportions in my imagination. Hannibal and Rome symbolized, in my youthful eyes, the struggle between the tenacity of the Jews and the organization of the Catholic Church. The significance for our emotional life which the anti-Semitic movement has since assumed helped fix the thoughts and impressions of those earlier days."[13]

Freud's "own personal hero throughout the years of his adolescence was," as Puner writes, "Hannibal, the great Carthaginian leader who sprang from a Semitic background, and who swore undying hatred of Rome and almost succeeded in destroying it."[14] In his earlier childhood, Freud also played with wooden soldiers representing Napoleon's generals. His favorite was one he labeled

---

12. In addition to his subordinated status as a Jew, Freud lived in poverty during both his childhood and his days as a medical student and young physician. His family was no higher than lower-middle class within the Jewish class system. Jones, in his recent biography of Freud, discounts Freud's claim that one of his ancestors was a famous rabbi. By his severe sacrifices to become a physician, Freud actually began the process of upward mobility *within* the social class system of the Viennese Jews, which included many wealthy persons, the majority of all lawyers in Vienna, and a large percentage of the physicians.

13. Freud, *The Basic Writings*, p. 260.

14. Puner, *op. cit.*, p. 45.

"Masséna (as a Jew Menasse)" under the incorrect impression that Masséna was a Jew. Freud's great interests in generals and in war, during his adolescence, certainly was related to his hostility toward anti-Semites; this hostility was probably an effort to defend his sense of worth, of self-esteem, against the derogation he met from the anti-Semites.

As is well known, we are not left in the dark by Freud concerning his youthful indignation and hostility against those Jews who accepted anti-Semitic attacks without making a counterattack. For he has written, in a passage immediately following that on Hannibal, quoted above, that he looked down upon his own father for his subservience to anti-Semites.

> I might have been ten or twelve years old when my father began to take me with him on his walks, and in his conversation to reveal his views on the things of this world. Thus it was that he once told me the following incident, in order to show me that I had been born into happier times than he: "When I was a young man, I was walking one Saturday along the street in the village where you were born; I was well-dressed, with a new fur cap on my head. Up comes a Christian, who knocks my cap into the mud, and shouts, 'Jew, get off the pavement!' "—"And what did you do?"—"I went into the street and picked up the cap," he calmly replied. That did not seem heroic on the part of the big, strong man who was leading me, a little fellow, by the hand. I contrasted this situation, which did not please me, with another, more in harmony with my sentiments—the scene in which Hannibal's father, Hamilcar Barcas, made his son swear before the household altar to take vengeance on the Romans. Ever since then Hannibal has had a place in my phantasies.[15]

Puner comments on this passage, "Nor did he [Freud] fail to resent the fact that his father's birth, and consequently his own, laid him open to such attacks."[16] Freud's father, who during Freud's childhood had once said that the little Sigmund "would never amount to anything,"[17] must have seemed to the adolescent Freud little better than a coward and a failure.[18]

15. Freud, *The Basic Writings*, p. 260.

16. Puner, *op. cit.*, p. 47.

17. Freud, *The Basic Writings*, p. 274.

18. On class grounds, it is to be noticed also that Freud's father was a failure, always unable to support his family after Freud's childhood, whereas Freud himself proved his father's thoughtless prophecy concerning the boy—that he "would never amount to anything"—to be untrue, by becoming a physician and one of the most famous men of his day. As Puner concludes, "And in a sense, all this achievement constituted a hitting back—represented a re-

We know something about Freud's working-out of his hostility toward anti-Semites. The resolution of this hostility began when he first decided to be a statesman, rather than a general, that is, to fight within the law and by the law, rather than by violence. Thus Freud learned in late adolescence to be against the attacking mob. Also, he learned from the Jewish scholarly tradition to regard intellectual superiority as the only real power. In the end, he identified with this tradition, and he added to this training a fierce personal exaltation of the power of the mind in comprehending (but not in overcoming) the violence and anarchy of the world. He enthroned "the spirit of individuation and reason," as Erikson has written, and his "crowning value" was "the primacy of the intellect."[19] From the beginning, he had led his classes in the Gymnasium. As Erikson would say, he had developed "a dominant faculty"—intellect—and this faculty, of which he was superbly confident, led him to the development and acceptance of his identity as a Jew through the transformation of his hostility and desire for revenge into a desire for intellectual superiority and also for enlightenment.

Erikson has pointed out that there is a strong pressure by the Jewish middle-class family, in defense against the dominant group's criticism, to make their son "a nice little boy, in spite of his being Jewish." This is a defense against the charges of aggressiveness, foreignness, etc. But Freud was never "a nice little Jewish boy." One cannot fully agree, however, with Puner, who writes: "He became, as he was subjected to anti-Semitism in school, as scornful of the turncoats who sought to appease their oppressors by becoming indistinguishable from them, as he was of the oppressors, themselves. . . . Independence and pride . . . held him firmly away from the path of assimilation—attractive as that path might appear."[20] For, as Jones points out, he never liked Vienna, where Jews were shunted

---

venge on the man who was never able to earn enough money to support his family in comfort. But in a profounder sense, the boy—and indeed, the man—never really revolted from his father's authority at all, for if he had really not cared for his father's good opinion, he would never have been driven by the necessity to vindicate himself in his eyes" (Puner, *op. cit.*, p. 47). The second sentence in this quotation may be taken perhaps with a grain of salt, since Freud lived in a Jewish society in Vienna where there was tremendous striving for upward social mobility.

19. Erikson, *op. cit.*, p. 241.   20. Puner, *op. cit.*, p. 39.

into ghettos, and he always desired to live in England, where the ethnic and social class barriers against Jews are minimal. Perhaps here we see the typical problem of group-identity which remains to some degree unsolved in so-called ethnic and minority groups. How far may one identify with the "aggressor" without losing his sense of autonomy and self-esteem?

Defenses of the ego against the anxiety and hostility arising from *class*-inferiority are illustrated in the case of Mac, whose family is one of several which we have observed and interviewed over a period of from two to nine years. Mac's father is a machinist of Irish-Scotch ancestry, his mother has a high-school education, and his parents have the habits and values of lower-middle-class people. They have moved into a neighborhood, however, where there are some professional families of upper-middle-class status.

At the age of seven, Mac told his mother that he had visited the son of one of these professional families, that of a lawyer. He said the lawyer's family had a maid, that they had separate bedrooms for each of their children, that they owned a large car, and that they were "rich." His mother warned Mac that the lawyer's family was snobbish and ordered him not to visit their sons. "They feel," she said, "that they are better than you are and that they own this block." Whenever Mac visited the boys in the other family, his mother immediately sent his brother to call him home. Sometimes he went to play ball with the lawyer's boys, but his father always followed to order him home.

Throughout the middle years of childhood, Mac proved very "sensitive" in his relationships with these boys. He was quick to feel slighted, he refused invitations from them, and he had several bitter fist fights with the lawyer's boys over what he called their "insults." Between ten and thirteen, he no longer fought the boys in the lawyer's family, but his hostility was expressed by avoidance of them and by rejection of their invitations.

During adolescence, however, Mac's behavior toward the lawyer's sons began to change. Gradually he became a regular visitor to their home. For a time, he would not look at television in their home (his family had none), but after a year he visited regularly to see television shows. He also began to sit in the lawyer's dining room at dinner, although he would not accept the repeated invitations to have dinner with them. He began to go to the boys' rooms and watch them dress for parties to which he was not invited. Their clothes were more expensive than his and of a different style. They would joke with him about the style of his clothes, and, shamefacedly, he would laugh with them. He sat in their living room a great many evenings when their upper-middle-class clique of boys was present, and he absorbed a great deal of social punishment and condescension from them.

It was evident, however, that his open hostility of the middle years was somehow being transformed into a tentative identification with the lawyer's sons and their way of life. He worked and saved money to buy the kind of clothes they wore. Now at seventeen, he is being invited to their clique's parties, and he accepts the invitations. He no longer expresses any hostility to this group, and he has become a good friend of the lawyer's sons. Moreover, he has changed his original plan of stopping his formal education after high school. He now is preparing himself to enter college, as the lawyer's sons will. He has the intellectual ability and the competent work-habits to succeed in college.

The early interviews with this boy reveal his hostility, avoidance, and anxiety with respect to persons of higher social status. During the last two years, his behavior indicates his final identification with these very persons. These reactions may be regarded as successive forms of his ego's defense of itself. To gain the time to build a new sense of identity in accord with the higher status to which he is relating himself, his ego has had constantly to create new defenses for his self-esteem. He must win the approval of this group, for the individual's sense of identity—of knowing what he is sexually and socially, what he belongs to, and what he can do—is confirmed only through his acceptance and approval by the specific group with which he identifies.

In the slow process of learning new social relationships and new concepts of himself, the upward-striving individual, like Mac, has to defend himself repeatedly from derogation and stigmatization by society and from his resultant anxiety and hostility. It is only through such anxiety-reducing and hostility-reducing mechanisms, furthermore, that the individual of any status learns to face the reality of his status. When he can face this reality, he no longer has to depend upon defenses for his injured self-esteem. For, in his status-identity, he achieves the necessary feelings of social adequacy; he gains the confidence and initiative necessary to compete within the society available to him. And he also gains a group, with which he experiences the highest social rewards, the feelings of each, of identity, of social "naturalness" and intimacy.

Social status is one of the most difficult aspects of reality to accept. It is especially difficult for Americans to accept, owing to our having been taught that every man has the duty and the opportunity to improve his status. (In fact, however, not more than 15 per cent of Americans actually improve their class-status in their lifetimes, and at least 80 per cent of these are lower-middle-class persons who rise only one subclass.)

In the end, every man, even the socially mobile one, must accept the realities of *some* social status. Otherwise, he will play an escapist, neurotic game with a force which cannot be dreamed away or reasoned away. And he will have a weak sense of identity, a deep doubt as to who he is. This does not mean that realists cannot also "rise in the world." The people who *succeed* at upward mobility are realists concerning status. Those who fail either could not solve the problem of identity-formation in a different social class culture, or could not control their hostilities toward persons superordinated to them. The boy in our case study has identified successfully with a higher status-group, and he has learned sufficient control of his hostility so that he can be compliant with people of higher status.

He also has identified with the *culture* of a higher social class. He has sought to take this new culture into himself because he admires it and considers it superior to the culture of his own parents. This process of incorporating the values and behavior of the superior, envied, and admired higher status-group is the basic psychological process in upward social mobility and in acculturation. The process may begin with the individual's defensive "identification with the aggressor," but it does not end there. For it results in the learning of a new culture within which he can exercise his initiative and special competencies more effectively.

Identification with the culture of a higher social group, that is, the belief that their culture is more intelligent and more refined, helps to reduce the striving individual's fear of, and hostility toward, that group. But it is only when the upward-striving individual *attains* the *status*, itself, and *participates* in it, that his hostility and anxiety are effectively reduced and his sense of new ego-identity confirmed by his new status-group.

But even in this new higher status, he always will find that there are individuals or groups of *still higher* status. So, he always must learn to reconcile his desires, cravings, and drives to those of individuals who have greater social prestige and authority than he has; that is, he must learn, if he wishes to reduce his anxiety and hostility toward these superordinate individuals to a tolerable level.

When one considers that socialization in the United States consists of learning the culture and sanctions of a succession of ranked statuses—in childhood, in the school, in the armed services, in industry, in parenthood, in old age—our society and its culture do not appear nearly so "discontinuous" as Benedict and others have thought them to be. Through each of these status-relationships, whether of father to son, mother to daughter, older brother to younger brother, teacher to pupil, peer-group leader to follower, officer to enlisted man, or employer to worker, there runs a cultural and psychological continuity. It results, in part, from the status-structure of our society and of all other Western societies. This continuity is the basically similar sociopsychological processes involved in the various types of status-relationships.

With respect to both stable authority-relationships, and also to movement upward from one status to another, our society permits —in fact, it can operate efficiently only if it encourages—some degree of *change* in authority- and status-relationships. *That is, our status-systems of age, class, and ethnic groups provide cultural controls not only for maintaining these status-groups but also for recruiting individuals from one age, class, or ethnic group into a higher status.*

Our society has continuity, therefore, both in the sense of (a) *stability* (*the status-structures*) *and also of* (b) *socially controlled change through time* (*movement through various age-statuses, and individual recruitment from one class to another*).

It seems true that the parent-child relationship is the prototype from which all other structural (but changing-through-time) relationships of *authority* are learned. And the sibling-relationships and age-group constitute the basic psychosocial situations in which *competition* and social aggression are learned and from which they are displaced to the social class and ethnic competitiveness necessary for social mobility. In this area of social stability and mobility, the oedipal feelings and the sibling-rivalry drives are most directly related to later status-changes and reconciliations. The relative ease or difficulty of an individual's relationships to persons in authority —as well as to his peers—in any status-system are probably greatly influenced by the degree to which he has solved his oedipal and his sibling-rivalrous feelings in childhood and adolescence. If he has achieved a reconciliation (in which some hostility always remains) to the parent of the same sex, and if his feelings of desire for the parent of the opposite sex have been, as Freud has said, "settled and forgotten"[21] (not merely repressed), and if he has at length, after normal sibling-rivalry, become reconciled to his brothers and sisters, he seems likely to advance to other good status-relationships both with authority-figures and with his social equals.

As he advances through the long series of status-relationships in his life, such a person achieves this reconciliation, this reduction of his fear and hostility toward the other members of the status-relationships, by his continued positive identification with his "superiors," and also by his acceptance of the controls, ego-ideals, and identity of his own status-group. Within each status-identity, he may both exercise the ego-functions of relative self-direction, initiative, and competence and also enjoy approval by, and social intimacy with, a group of his own.

In each successive status he has to learn to act efficiently, to exercise initiative, to achieve, but within the cultural limits set by the society for that status. To put it differently, the ego of every normal individual achieves a certain relative autonomy, but, if the anxiety and hostility connected with this degree of autonomy are to be kept within normal limits, the individual must reconcile himself emotionally to the *objective social sanctions* of age-status, sex-status, and the other basic types of social status.

21. *The Interpretation of Dreams,* in Freud, *The Basic Writings,* p. 518.

Ecological Aspects of Urban Research

The sociologist's interest in the study of the city has resulted not only in the development of "urban sociology" as a major subfield of the discipline but also in a considerable contribution to the general fund of sociological knowledge. In terms of the sociological literature the city may be described as a cultural, social-psychological, and ecological phenomenon. That is, the city has been studied by the sociologist by means of each of these approaches, which, although they share a common sociological frame of reference, have distinct points of view and their own methods. The "ecological aspects of urban research"—the title assigned to this paper by the Committee on the Twenty-fifth Anniversary Celebration—may be interpreted, then, as applying to one subarea of sociological research on the city.

The "ecological aspects of urban research," however, may also be interpreted as encompassing more than that type of research which is regarded as "ecological" within the framework of sociology. Ecological study is by no means enjoyed as a monopoly by sociologists. Ecology was a neologism in a natural science context less than a century ago.[1] Studies labeled "ecological" were restricted to "plant ecology" in the nineteenth century. They were extended to include "animal ecology" in the first part of this century and, then, to include "human ecology" only in the last three or four decades. Moreover, the term "human ecology" has been used in disciplines other than sociology, especially in biology and in geography.

Moreover, if the substantive character of investigations rather than the labels by which they are identified be considered, then human ecological researches including urban researches embrace an even wider range of studies. For example, during the nineteenth century, although the label "ecology" was not used to describe them,

1. Ernst Haeckel, *History of Creation* (1868).

229

important elements of the work of the "human geographers" and others on "environmentalism" and of the social surveys may be regarded as ecological in character. Furthermore, the development of demography and the improvement of census and vital registration data which led to increasing bodies of factual and analytical materials also gave rise to a literature which, with contemporary hindsight, can at least in part be termed "ecological."[2]

The "ecological aspects of urban research," then, may be treated either in a narrow sense to encompass ecological studies conducted within the framework of sociology or in a broad sense to include urban studies of an ecological character without regard to their label or discipline of origin. Although the broader meaning is recognized, this paper is concerned, largely by reason of the limitations of the writer, with the narrower connotation of ecology. That is, although some reference will be made to non-sociological writers, it is the primary purpose of this paper to deal with the ecological aspects of urban research conducted within the framework of sociology. Moreover, it should be noted that, although demography is sometimes regarded as a subfield of ecology, little reference will be made here to population studies because the demographic literature is largely a separate body of knowledge and generally does not appear in an ecological framework.

The sociologist, as a sociologist, is interested in human ecology rather than ecology in general. Although a number of writers dealt with problems which were later regarded as "ecological" in character,[3] the sociologists' interest in human ecology, with special reference to the study of the city, received its first major systematic

2. E.g., Johann H. von Thünen, *Der isolierte Staat, in Beziehung auf Landwirtshaft und Nationalökonomie* (1826); Friedrich Ratzel, *Anthropogeography* (1882); Friedrich Engels, *Conditions of the Working Class in England* (1845); Henry Mayhew, *London Labour and the London Poor* (London, 1861–62); Charles Booth, *Survey of the Life and Labour of the People in London* (1891–1903); Adna F. Weber, *The Growth of Cities in the Nineteenth Century: A Study in Statistics* ("Columbia University Studies in History, Economics and Public Law" [New York, 1899]); J. Bertillon, *Élements de démographie* (Paris, 1895); P. G. Vidal de La Blache, *Principes de le géographie humaine* (Paris, 1922); A. Lotka, *Elements of Physical Biology* (Baltimore: Williams & Wilkins, 1925).

3. E.g., C. H. Cooley, "Theory of Transportation," in *Sociological Theory and Social Research*, ed. R. C. Angell (New York, 1930), pp. 75–83; Charles J. Galpin, *The Social Anatomy of an Agricultural Community* (University of Wisconsin Agricultural Experiment Station Research Bull. 34 [Madison, 1915]).

statement in the volume edited by Park and Burgess, *The City*, published in 1925.[4] The combined impact of at least four of the chapters in that volume provided both the framework and the stimulation for the series of basic studies, many of them at the University of Chicago, which contributed the major part of the literature on "human ecology" for at least the next two decades and constituted, also, an important part of the corpus of urban and general sociology.

Three of these papers had been previously published. The first was Park's germinal paper, "The City: Suggestions for the Investigation of Human Behavior in the Urban Environment," which originally had been published in 1915; the second was Burgess' classic statement on "The Growth of the City: An Introduction to a Research Project," which first appeared in 1923; the third was the first effort by a sociologist formally to define "human ecology"—the paper by R. D. McKenzie on "The Ecological Approach to the Study of the Human Community." The fourth of these basic documents was the chapters by Louis Wirth, "A Bibliography of the Urban Community," which not only summarized the relevant literature of the time but also provided an outline for the study of the city which after the passage of three decades has still to be supplanted. Park, who wrote the Preface to *The City*, was aware of the fundamental character of these four contributions. He wrote: "These three papers, with the classified bibliography by Louis·Wirth, represent whatever is novel in the point of view and the methods of study of the urban community, to which this volume is intended as an introduction."[5]

In the same year, 1925, the American Sociological Society organized its main sessions at its annual meeting around the subject "The City." Selected papers from the proceedings of this meeting were published in 1926 as the volume, *The Urban Community*,[6] under the editorship of the secretary of the association, Ernest W. Burgess. This book contained a section entitled "The Ecology of the City," which comprised five papers by as many different authors.[7]

Following the appearance of *The City* and *The Urban Community* there emerged a clear-cut and persistent interest among sociolo-

4. Chicago: University of Chicago Press.
5. *Ibid.*, p. viii.   6. Chicago: University of Chicago Press.
7. R. D. McKenzie, N. S. B. Gras, Walter G. Reckless, Shelby M. Harrison, and Harvey W. Zorbaugh. In addition, the book contained an Introduction by Park, "The Urban Community as a Special Pattern and a Moral Order."

gists both in urban sociology and in human ecology. In the three decades which have ensued a considerable ecological literature has been published by sociologists, most of it pertaining to the city.

The Development of Ecological Research

Writing in 1934, less than a decade after the publication of *The City*, McKenzie noted that "research of a distinctly ecological character is limited and fragmentary."[8] In characterizing the research which had been done "pertaining most directly to the ecology of the community," he distinguished two types: (1) "studies of the spatial phenomena within the urban areas" and (2) "studies pertaining to the determinations of the natural—as opposed to the political—boundaries of the local communal organism."[9]

The series of sociological studies of the spatial distribution of various types of phenomenon in the 1920's and 1930's, while undoubtedly stimulated by Park, took the specific form they did as a result, on the one hand, of the prevalent conception of human ecology as "a study of the spatial and temporal relations of human beings as affected by the selective, distributive and accommodative forces of the environment";[10] and, on the other hand, by the new vistas of research opportunity opened by Burgess' presentation of his conception of the growth and structure of the city.[11]

By 1940, only six years after McKenzie's brief summary of the status of the ecological literature, Quinn in his "Topical Summary of Current Literature on Human Ecology"[12] listed some 347 titles under five headings: (*a*) "The Nature of Human Ecology," (*b*) "Ecological Organization and Dominance," (*c*) "Interpretations of Spatial Distributions," (*d*) "Migration and Mobility," and (*e*) "Succession." The time span covered by the bibliography was 1925 to

8. R. D. McKenzie, "Demography, Human Geography, and Human Ecology," in *The Fields and Methods of Sociology*, ed. L. L. Bernard (New York: Long & Smith, 1934), p. 59.

9. *Ibid.*, p. 60.

10. R. D. McKenzie, "The Ecological Approach," in *The City*, ed. R. E. Park, E. W. Burgess, and R. D. McKenzie (Chicago: University of Chicago Press, 1925), p. 63. This was the first formal definition of human ecology by a sociologist. McKenzie, in setting forth this definition, prefaced his statement with the phrase "in the absence of any precedent let us tentatively define human ecology as. . . ."

11. Park, Burgess, and McKenzie, *op. cit.*, pp. 47 ff.

12. James A. Quinn, "Topical Summary of Current Literature on Human Ecology," *American Journal of Sociology*, XLVI (September, 1940), 191–226.

1939 with only occasional references to basic prior publications. The list, largely centered on the writings of sociologists, was not regarded by Quinn as complete.

Wirth, writing in the same year, 1940, describes both the earlier ecological research and the more "recent." In respect to the earlier, he indicated that "through the studies of Park, Burgess, McKenzie, and others the physical structure and the ecological processes of concentration, dispersion, segregation and succession of men, institutions, and cultural characteristics as between the various natural areas and communities that make up the physical framework of the urban world have been revealed through indices which are quite precise, quantitative, and adaptable to comparison as between cities." Wirth also stated that the "dominance of the city over its hinterland has been revealed."[13] In indicating the changing nature of ecological research, Wirth said: "In recent years . . . we have shifted our emphasis from the minute analysis of the local communities within the city to the larger sections and zones in the metropolitan region. The concept of the metropolitan region has been sufficiently well established in part through our labors here, so that many of the baffling problems arising out of the growth of the city and its interrelations with the hinterland have become amenable to analysis and treatment."[14]

Urban studies[15] made up an important part of the literature of human ecology described by Wirth in 1940 as "what amounts to a new discipline within the social sciences."[16] The studies often were contributions to general sociology as well, for, while the spatial and distributive aspects of the phenomena studied often received major emphasis, the investigations were "not confined to the purely ecological aspects of the situation." They also included data "bearing on social behavior."[17]

The studies concerned with "natural areas" involved consideration of local areas such as neighborhoods and local communities and the "regional community" which subsumed the "metropolitan community." The initial researches on the regional community were de-

13. Louis Wirth (ed.), *Eleven Twenty-six: A Decade of Social Science Research* (Chicago: University of Chicago Press, 1940), pp. 56–57.

14. *Ibid.*, p. 57.

15. Quinn, *op. cit.*, and also his *Human Ecology* (New York: Prentice-Hall, Inc., 1950).

16. *Op cit.*, p. 56.   17. McKenzie, in Bernard, *op. cit.*, p. 60.

scribed by McKenzie as having been confined for the most part "to attempts to define its area and to give statistical expression to its economic and human resources."[18]

These studies had a far-flung effect on other disciplines and especially on political science. Merriam and Wirth both tell how the urban studies conducted under the aegis of the Local Community Research Committee, the precursor of the present Social Science Research Committee, at the University of Chicago, was "caught up" in the Urbanism Committee of the National Resources Board[19] and played some part in the development of the research program of the Board. Much of the interest in state and local as well as national planning, in problems of metropolitan government, and in regional studies is attributable to the influence of ecological research on natural areas.

In less than another decade the picture of the rapid development of human ecology presented in 1940 seemed to be greatly altered. In an evaluation of the status of community research, Hollingshead, in 1948, included also a critique of human ecology. He stated: "Ecology has been in an ambivalent position for almost a decade. Alihan's criticism fortuitously coincided rather closely with McKenzie's death and Park's retirement from active writing. Although little in the way of theory has been developed in the past decade, the idea persists that there is a legitimate place for human ecology in the social sciences."[20]

In describing the important developments in human ecology, Hollingshead pointed to the criticisms and tests by such writers as Davie, Alihan, Heller, Hatt, and Firey of the work of the "classical ecologists," Park, Burgess, and McKenzie. He concluded that, despite "the efforts of Quinn, Hollingshead, Firey, Gettys, Hawley, and others to re-examine and restate the position of the ecologists, it appears that they have not extricated themselves from the equivocal problem which the classical writers set for them, namely, that the

18. *Ibid.*, p. 60. For listing of specific studies of this type see Quinn, "Topical Summary . . . ," *op. cit.*, pp. 196 ff.

19. Charles E. Merriam, "Urbanism," in Wirth (ed.), *op. cit.*, p. 30; Wirth (ed.), *op. cit.*, p. 57. At least two publications of the National Resources Board were directly traceable to this relationship: *Our Cities, Their Role in the National Economy* (Washington, D.C.: Government Printing Office, 1937), and *Urban Government* (Washington, D.C.: Government Printing Office, 1939).

20. A. B. Hollingshead, "Community Research: Development and Present Condition," *American Sociological Review*, XIII (April, 1948), 140 ff.

physical structure of the community is a response to the operation of non-cultural determinants operating in a physical and cultural milieu."[21]

Firey in his discussion of the Hollingshead paper characterized the preceding decade's research as having "emphasized the untenable character of this dichotomy"—that is, the distinction as posed by Park of the "biotic" and "moral" orders.[22] Hawley, in discussing the same paper, saw progress being made in ecology in the increased attention being paid to the community as an object of study: "Ever since sociologists turned from a preoccupation with concepts to seek an empirical basis for their theories the community has come increasingly into the focus of their attention."[23] He described the significance of studies of spatial patterns as lying in the interpretation of such patterns as community structure and stressed the importance of ecologists devoting "their efforts to the study of community structure."[24] He insisted that the special task of the human ecologist . . . [was] the analysis, description and explanation of community structure."[25]

Hawley somewhat impatiently dismissed the question of whether community structure is "cultural" or "non-cultural" in his statement: "All of these objections and the distinctions they have given rise to impress me as merely a play upon words."[26]

Only seven years have elapsed since the Hollingshead review of human ecology and the discussion which it engendered and the assignment of this paper for purposes of this anniversary meeting. However, at least two reviews of what has since transpired in ecological research on the city have already been written. Both, as yet unpublished, were written by Albert J. Reiss, the first as "A Working Memorandum" prepared for a Committee of the Social Science Research Council;[27] the second is entitled "The Sociology of Urban Life." In the former, Reiss is primarily concerned with the study of community as a social system and deals with research in human

21. *Ibid.*, p. 141. See also for further bibliography.

22. Walter Firey, "Discussion," *American Sociological Review*, XIII (April, 1948), 152 ff.

23. Amos H. Hawley, "Discussion," *American Sociological Review*, XIII (April, 1948), 153 ff.

24. *Ibid.*, p. 154.   25. *Ibid.*, p. 155.   26. *Ibid.*, p. 156.

27. "A Review and Evaluation of Research on Community" (1954). (Mimeographed.)

ecology within the context of that interest. In the latter, he reviews research in the sociology of urban life, or urban sociology, between 1945 and 1955 and considers research on human ecology as one of the three fields of urban sociology, the other two of which are social organization and social psychology.

Although Reiss did not set out to produce an annotated bibliography of all ecological research conducted during the decade 1945–55, he did consider what may be regarded as the more important studies. He appropriately characterized recent ecological research as concerned more with "the study of ecological organization" and "structure"[28] than with the study of "ecological aggregates" or "process."

In elaboration of Reiss's observation it may be noted that the more recent studies differ markedly from earlier investigations in being unconcerned, or only incidentally concerned, with spatial patterns of discrete data and their correlates and that they are preoccupied, rather, with more basic analytical considerations of the functional interrelations of the elements which make up the urban community and society—with the interpretation of spatial patterns as indications of structure and organization.

The more important ecological studies relating to urban communities which have been published during the past decade may be classified under several headings.[29]

First, there are the studies which have been concerned with the delineation of the functional urban unit, the "metropolitan community," and the ancillary problem of metropolitan influence or dominance. These include such basic contributions as those of Bogue,[30] the Duncans,[31] Isard and Kavesh, [32] Ogburn,[33] Stewart,[34] and Vance

28. Albert J. Reiss, Jr., "The Sociology of Urban Life" (unpublished manuscript).

29. This discussion utilizes but is not restricted to Reiss's listing and treatment of studies.

30. Donald J. Bogue, *The Structure of the Metropolitan Community* (Ann Arbor: University of Michigan, 1950).

31. Otis Dudley Duncan, "Gradients of Urban Influence on the Rural Population" (unpublished paper read at a meeting of the Midwest Sociological Society, Des Moines, Iowa, April, 1955).

32. Walter Isard and Robert Kavesh, "Economic Structural Interrelations of Metropolitan Regions," *American Journal of Sociology*, LX (September, 1954), 152–62.

33. W. F. Ogburn, "Inventions of Local Transportation and the Patterns of Cities," *Social Forces*, XXIV (May, 1946), 373–79.

34. John Q. Stewart, "Empirical Mathematical Rules concerning the Dis-

and Demerath.[35] They include also the studies of the Washington statistical agencies concerned with the delineation of standard metropolitan areas and economic areas, the results of which are manifest in Bureau of the Census and other publications.[36] These studies, it may be noted, are significant not only for their substantive contributions but also for their methodological innovations which lay a groundwork for further investigations.

Second, there are the studies focusing on the internal composition of the metropolitan community—its structural and functional differentiation. These include the studies of Bell,[37] the Duncans,[38] Firey,[39] Form,[40] Harris,[41] Ikle,[42] Kish,[43] Kitagawa and Bogue,[44] and Shevky and Williams.[45] Some of these studies in a sense represent the continuation of interest in the determination of "natural areas." But they differ from earlier investigations not only in their relative methodological sophistication but also in their greater concern with the total metropolitan complex and the greater awareness of the interaction of ecological, cultural, and social psychological factors.

tribution and Equilibrium of Population," *Geographical Review*, XXXVII (July, 1947), 461–85.

35. R. B. Vance and N. J. Demerath, *The Urban South* (Chapel Hill: University of North Carolina Press, 1954).

36. E.g., U.S. Bureau of the Census, *United States Census of Population: 1950*, Vol. I: *Number of Inhabitants*, pp. xxvii, xxxiii, and xxxvi; Donald J. Bogue, *State Economic Areas* (U.S. Bureau of the Census [Washington, D.C.: Government Printing Office, 1951]).

37. Eshref Shevky and Wendell Bell, *Social Area Analysis* (1955).

38. Otis Dudley Duncan and Beverly Duncan, "Residential Distribution and Occupational Stratification," *American Journal of Sociology*, LX (March, 1955), 493–503.

39. Walter Firey, *Land Use in Central Boston* (Cambridge, Mass.: Harvard University Press, 1947).

40. W. H. Form, Joel Smith, Gregory P. Stone, and James Cowhig, "The Compatibility of Alternative Approaches to the Delimitation of Urban Subareas," *American Sociological Review*, XIX (August, 1954), 434–40.

41. C. D. Harris, "Suburbs," *American Journal of Sociology*, XLIX (July, 1943), 1–13.

42. Fred C. Ikle, "The Effect of War Destruction upon the Ecology of Cities," *Social Forces*, XXIX (May, 1951), 383–91.

43. Leslie Kish, "Differentiation in Metropolitan Areas," *American Sociological Review*, XIX (August, 1954), 388–98.

44. Evelyn M. Kitagawa and Donald J. Bogue, *Suburbanization of Manufacturing Activity within Standard Metropolitan Areas* (Oxford, Ohio: Scripps Foundation for Research in Population Problems and Population Research and Training Center, April, 1955).

45. Eshref Shevky and Marilyn Williams, *The Social Areas of Los Angeles* (Berkeley: University of California Press, 1949).

Special categories of these studies are those relating to "decentralization" and "suburbanization," on the one hand, and the reconsideration of the "urban-rural" continuum, on the other. Examples of the former type of studies include those by Bogue,[46] Thompson,[47] and the forthcoming study by Hawley on metropolitan area growth since 1900;[48] examples of the latter are the work of Blizzard,[49] Duncan,[50] Martin,[51] and the forthcoming Census monograph of Duncan and Reiss.[52]

A third type of study may be described as that concerned with specific temporal and mobility aspects of urban structure and function. These include the studies by Breese,[53] Caplow,[54] the Chicago Community Inventory Reports,[55] the Duncans,[56] Freedman,[57] Schnore,[58] and Sullenger.[59]

46. Donald J. Bogue, *Population Growth in Standard Metropolitan Areas, 1900–1950* (Housing and Home Finance Agency [Washington, D.C.: Government Printing Office, 1953]).

47. Warren S. Thompson, *The Growth of Metropolitan Districts in the United States: 1900–1940* (Bureau of the Census [Washington, D.C.: Government Printing Office, 1947]).

48. Amos Hawley, volume to be published by the Free Press, Glencoe, Ill.

49. Samuel W. Blizzard, "Research on the Rural-Urban Fringe," *Sociology and Social Research*, XXXVIII (1954), 143–49.

50. Otis Dudley Duncan, "Community Size and the Rural-Urban Continuum" (unpublished paper to appear in revision of Hatt and Reiss [eds.], *Reader in Urban Sociology* [Glencoe, Ill.: Free Press]).

51. Walter T. Martin, *The Rural-Urban Fringe: A Study of Adjustment to Residence Location* (Eugene: University of Oregon Press, 1953).

52. Otis Dudley Duncan and Albert J. Reiss, Jr., *Social Characteristics of Urban and Rural Communities, 1950* (New York: John Wiley & Sons, 1956).

53. Gerald Breese, *The Daytime Population of the Central Business District of Chicago* (Chicago: University of Chicago Press, 1949).

54. Theodore Caplow, "Incidence and Direction of Residential Mobility in a Minneapolis Sample," *Social Forces*, XXVII (May, 1949), 413–17.

55. "Series of Urban Analysis Reports" (hectographed):

   No. 1. Otis Dudley Duncan, "Centralization of Retail Trade in Chicago, 1935: A Pilot Study in Cost-Utility Analysis," November, 1951.

[Footnote 55 continued on following page]

56. Beverly Duncan, "Factors in Work-Residence Separation: Wage and Salary Workers, Chicago, 1951," *American Sociological Review*, XXI (February, 1956), 48–56, and "Intra-urban Population Movement" (unpublished paper to appear in revision of Hatt and Reiss, *Reader in Urban Sociology* [Glencoe, Ill.: Free Press]).

57. Ronald Freedman, *Recent Migration to Chicago* (Chicago: University of Chicago Press, 1949).

58. Leo Schnore, "The Separation of Home and Work: A Problem for Human Ecology," *Social Forces*, XXXII (May, 1954), 336–43.

59. T. Earl Sullenger, "The Social Significance of Mobility: An Omaha Study," *American Journal of Sociology*, LV (May, 1950), 559–64.

These researches have included examination into patterns of movement between work-place and place of residence as having a particularly significant effect on the structure and function of the urban community.

Although most of what we know as ecological research on urban communities has been conducted in the United States, interest in

[Footnote 55 continued from page 238]

No. 2. Beverly Davis, "Centralization of Industry, Chicago, 1947," November, 1951.

No. 3. Otis Dudley Duncan, "Cost-Utility Framework for Measurement of Locational Patterns: Definition and Illustrative Applications," January, 1952.

No. 4. Beverly Davis, "Spatial Distribution of Occupational Groups: Chicago, 1940," February, 1952.

No. 5. Beverly Davis and Otis Dudley Duncan, "Spatial Patterns of Labor Force Industry Groups in Chicago, by Place of Work, 1947, and Place of Residence, 1940," May, 1952.

No. 6. Beverly Davis and Otis Dudley Duncan, "Inter-industry Linkage: Chicago, 1947," February, 1952.

No. 7. Sanford M. Dornbusch and Elijah L. White, "Segregation of Churches, Chicago, 1950: The Cost-Utility Approach Applied to the Spatial Patterns of Social Institutions," February, 1952.

No. 8. Elijah L. White and Sanford M. Dornbusch, "Centralization of Churches, Chicago, 1950: The Cost-Utility Approach Applied to the Spatial Patterns of Social Institutions," March, 1952.

No. 9. Beverly Davis and Otis Dudley Duncan, "Residential Rental Value as a Factor in the Ecological Organization of the City," July, 1952.

No. 10. Sanford M. Dornbusch, "A Typology of Suburban Communities: Chicago Metropolitan District, 1940," May, 1952.

No. 11. Sanford M. Dornbusch and Elijah L. White, "Commutation Movement and Urbanism," September, 1952.

No. 12. Sanford M. Dornbusch, "Manufacturing Cities in the United States: 1940," May, 1952.

No. 13. Otis Dudley Duncan and Beverly Davis, "Inter-industry Variations in Work-Residence Relationships of the Chicago Labor Force," October, 1952.

No. 14. Otis Dudley Duncan and Beverly Davis, "Contributions to the Theory of Segregation Indexes," February, 1953.

No. 15. Otis Dudley Duncan and Beverly Davis, "A New Type of 'Matter-Most' Map," March, 1953.

No. 16. Otis Dudley Duncan and Beverly Davis, "Measures of Population Distribution in an Urban Area," April, 1953.

No. 17. Beverly Davis, "Degree of Work-Residence Separation for Wage and Salary Workers: Chicago, 1950–51," April, 1953.

No. 18. Edna Raphael, "Calculation of Population Potential for an Urban Area," May, 1953.

No. 19. Donnell M. Pappenfort, "Industrial Control in the Metropolitan Community: A Study in Metropolitan Dominance," May, 1953.

No. 20. Otis Dudley Duncan and Beverly Davis, "Ecological Aspects of the Labor Force in the Chicago Metropolitan Area," May, 1953.

such research has spread to other countries. The work of Dickinson, of the University of London, for example, *City, Region and Regionalism,*[60] was subtitled "A Geographical Contribution to Human Ecology." This work, which refers copiously to the ecological literature in the United States, presents excellent comparative data for European cities as well as for regionalism.

European studies in urban sociology have increasingly included ecological studies patterned after those in the United States. The availability of such studies to American students is being greatly facilitated by *Current Sociology,* which has published a bibliography of urban sociology in France and will have one for urban sociology in England and the Scandinavian countries by December of this year.[61] Among the urban ecological studies of European cities which should be mentioned is that by P. Chombart de Lauwe on Paris,[62] De Wolff on Amsterdam,[63] and Talamanca on Rome.[64] As an additional note on ecological study of cities outside of the United States, mention should be made of the work by Hauser and Redick on Rangoon[65] and the comparative studies by Bogue.[66]

The continued flow of such ecological studies indicates that the possible loss in popularity of ecological studies in the period prior to Hollingshead's consideration of the field in 1948 has been definitely offset by developments since that date. The continued manifestation of interest in ecological research at several centers, including the University of Michigan, the University of Chicago, the University of North Carolina, Michigan State University, and the University of California, Los Angeles, as well as among the individual students

60. Robert E. Dickinson, *City, Region and Regionalism* (New York: Oxford University Press, 1947).

61. P. Chombart de Lauwe and L. Couvreur, "La Sociologie urbaine en France," *Current Sociology,* Vol. IV, No. 1. (Paris: UNESCO, 1955.) See also issue to come on English and Scandinavian urban sociology.

62. *Ibid.*; see Item 171, p. 34.

63. J. Meerdink and Pietor de Wolff, "Intelligence in Amsterdam in Connection with Data of a Demographic and Sociological Nature" (World Population Conference, Rome, 1954). (To be published by UN.)

64. Di Mario Figa-Talamanca, "Forme di gravitazione della popolazione sul territorio," *Proceedings of the International Statistical Institute, Rome, 1953.*

65. P. M. Hauser and Richard Redick (work in progress on analysis of demographic social and economic data by wards in Rangoon).

66. A comparative study of population structure of major cities of the world; experimental research being done under a grant from Population Council, Inc.

mentioned, indicates that ecological research may be expected to undergo continued development for some time to come.

Data

The development of ecological research in urban areas has necessarily been dependent on the availability of basic data for the analysis of the urban community and its components. As better data have become available, the volume and significance of ecological studies have both been affected.

The most important single body of data for the ecological analysis of the urban community has undoubtedly been the publications of the Bureau of the Census. Especially useful have been the statistics for small areas within the urban complex—for census tracts and city blocks within large cities and by townships outside large cities; and the statistics tabulated by specially designated areas designed to approximate the real urban entity as distinguished from the administrative and political units of which it is constituted.

The census-tract idea was originated by Dr. Walter Laidlow in New York City in 1906 in an effort to obtain statistics for meaningful analysis of changes within the city. For the 1910 Census, the Bureau of the Census established census tracts in eight cities, although New York City was the only one that then made use of the census-tract statistics. By 1950 there were sixty-nine tracted areas containing a total of over 12,000 census tracts. Forty-six of the areas were tracted for outlying adjacent territory in addition to the central city.[67] Moreover, in 1950, as in 1940, the Bureau of the Census bore the major expense of tabulating and publishing the census-tract statistics, in contrast with its earlier practice of making such data available at the expense of the local community.

In addition to the census-tract statistics, the inclusion of the Housing Census along with the Decennial Census of Population, beginning in 1940, resulted in the tabulation of housing statistics for individual city blocks as well as for census tracts.[68]

Simultaneously with the development of the census tract and

67. U.S. Bureau of the Census, *Census Tract Manual* (3d ed.; Washington, D.C., 1947); also *U.S. Census of Population: 1950*, Vol. I: *Number of Inhabitants* (Washington, D.C.: Government Printing Office, 1952), pp. xxxvi ff.

68. U.S. Bureau of the Census, *United States Census of Housing: 1950*, Vol. V: *Block Statistics;* also see Vol. I, Part I, *General Characteristics*, pp. xii–xiii.

block statistics, efforts were made by the Bureau of the Census in co-operation with interested parties, including sociologists and ecologists, to delineate urban areas which better approximated the metropolitan complex than did the administrative and political units. The publication of statistics for "metropolitan districts" served this purpose to 1940.[69] For the 1950 Census, however, the Bureau of the Census used two new areal concepts which provide ecologists with greatly improved data. These were the "urbanized area" and the "standard metropolitan area." The former makes possible the tabulation of statistics of the "urban fringe" which, in addition to the central cities, make up the urbanized areas. The standard metropolitan areas were designed to provide statistics for "integrated social and economic" areas and comprise one or more counties (except in New England) which include and are oriented to one or more central cities.[70]

The delineation of the urban fringe, together with that of unincorporated places of 2,500 or more for the 1950 Census, also made possible the redefinition of urban and rural areas.[71] In consequence, the statistics for 1950 and for subsequent censuses will make possible the analysis of more precise and meaningful urban and rural populations, respectively.

In addition to these innovations, the Bureau of the Census also introduced for the 1950 Census the use of "state economic areas" which include a hundred and fifty metropolitan aggregations of populations.[72] These new areas should permit broader ecological studies of "systems" of urban areas in relation to non-metropolitan areas of a type not feasible before.

On the substantive side the Census data have also improved in many respects. Particularly worthy of mention perhaps is the availability of new statistics relating to education, the labor force, internal migration, and housing beginning with 1940, and data on family

69. Thompson, *op. cit.*, pp. 1–3.

70. U.S. Bureau of the Census, *United States Census of Population: 1950,* Vol. I: *Number of Inhabitants,* p. xxxiii.

71. U.S. Bureau of the Census, *ibid.*, pp. xv ff.

72. Donald J. Bogue, *State Economic Areas,* pp. 1–6; see also "Economic Areas as a Tool for Research and Planning," *American Sociological Review,* XV (June, 1950), 409–16.

income, marital status, and married couples in 1950.[73] Although the Census data have, in the past two decades, improved considerably, there is, of course, room for further improvement. Some directions for such improvement were recently indicated by Duncan.[74]

The continually improved small area and metropolitan area data produced by the Bureau of the Census, together with special local compilations of the census and related statistics[75] and the utilization of various bodies of social and economic data from other sources, have greatly enriched ecological research opportunities of both a substantive and a methodological character.

Method

In respect to methods of research, recent ecological studies have shown relative sophistication in comparison with earlier studies. In part, this reflects the methodological developments in statistics and in sociology, in general, but in part it also results from changing conceptions of human ecology and ecological problems and developments in ecology itself.

The earliest of the ecological studies in sociology employed relatively simple techniques of research. In keeping with McKenzie's first definition of the field as "a study of the spatial and temporal relations of human beings," early techniques consisted of little else than the plotting on a map of spatial patterns of various phenomena. Hawley's observation on this activity was apposite: "It is sometimes difficult to understand why this kind of work should be called anything other than geography, except possibly—out of deference to

73. U.S. Bureau of the Census, *United States Census of Population: 1950,* Vol. III: *Census Tract Statistics;* see also P. M. Hauser, "Research Possibilities in the 1940 Census," *American Sociological Review,* VI (August, 1941), 470.

74. Otis Dudley Duncan, "Research on Metropolitan Population: Evaluation of Data" (unpublished paper presented at annual meeting, American Sociological Society, September, 1955).

75. E.g., Louis Wirth and Margaret Furez, *Local Community Fact Book, 1938* (Chicago: Chicago Recreation Commission, 1938); Louis Wirth and Eleanor Bernert, *Local Community Fact Book of Chicago* (Chicago: University of Chicago Press, 1949); Philip M. Hauser and Evelyn M. Kitagawa, *Local Community Fact Book for Chicago, 1950* (Chicago: Chicago Community Inventory, University of Chicago, 1953); Albert J. Reiss, Jr., Jay W. Artis, and Albert L. Rhodes, *Population Handbook: Nashville* (Nashville: Institute of Research and Training in the Social Sciences, Vanderbilt University, 1955); Howard Whipple Green, *Population Characteristics by Census Tracts, Cleveland, Ohio, 1930* (Cleveland: Plain Dealer, 1931).

the geographers—because of the inferior cartographic skill which is often exhibited."[76]

In addition, the data graphically portrayed on maps were sometimes subjected to correlation analysis and other forms of statistical analysis sometimes of dubious character.[77]

Maps showing spatial patterns were then "analyzed" by investigators in relation to correlative data and in terms of the prevalent battery of ecological concepts. Prominent among the concepts used as tools of research were those embodied in Burgess' "zonal hypothesis," "natural area," "gradient," and such "processes" as "invasion," "succession," "segregation," "concentration," and "centralization." Other concepts also were used, many of them drawn from biology, which were more often employed in general discussions than in empirical research. These included such terms as "community and society," "niche," "web of life," "dominance," "symbiosis," "sustenance relationships," and "competition," the latter usually in an all-pervasive and biological context.

In the ecological studies of the past decade a number of techniques appeared which, although drawn from other fields, were new to ecological research by sociologists and were adapted to such research. These methods included the utilization and development by Duncan of a method of measuring the relationship of two or more distributions ordered in space, with varying modes of ordering.[78] This technique, extensions of the use of the Lorenz curve and the Gini index, has provided ecologists with objective ways of measuring "centralization," "localization," and "concentration." Moreover, Duncan has clarified much of the confusion in the literature in respect to segregation indexes[79] and, although basic theoretical prob-

76. Amos Hawley, "Ecology and Human Ecology," *Social Forces*, XXIII (May, 1944), 401.

77. E.g., see Frank A. Ross, "Ecology and the Statistical Method," *American Journal of Sociology*, XXXVIII (January, 1933), 507–22; Frederick F. Stephan, "Sampling Errors and Interpretations of Social Data Ordered in Time and Space," *Proceedings of the American Statistical Society*, Vol. XXIX (March, 1934), Supplement; W. S. Robinson, "Ecological Correlations and the Behavior of Individuals," *American Sociological Review*, XV (June, 1950), 351–56.

78. Otis Dudley Duncan and Beverly Davis Duncan, *The Chicago Urban Analysis Project: A Summary Report* (Chicago: Chicago Community Inventory, University of Chicago, 1953).

79. Otis Dudley Duncan and Beverly Duncan, "A Methodological Analysis of Segregation Indexes," *American Sociological Review*, XX (April, 1955), 210–17.

lems remain with respect to the meaning and measurement of segregation, provided a basis for a more rational choice of index in terms of its theoretical and empirical implications. The increased use of this method should have a marked salutary effect on ecological studies not only in providing more rigorous ways of ordering and describing data but also in making available an important tool for testing ecological hypotheses.[80]

Great potential value in furthering ecological research is also to be found in the use of other techniques employed in ecological studies. These include: the use of factorial design by Keyfitz to analyze the influence of distance from the city on family size;[81] the use of techniques of multivariate analysis by Bogue to evaluate factors in metropolitan growth and suburbanization;[82] the technique, by Bogue, for the delineation of "metropolitan communities" and the study of "dominance";[83] the development by Kitagawa[84] of a method for allocating into components the difference between two rates—a method that can be used in conjunction with Duncan's extension of Lorenz curve analysis;[85] the use of the "input-output" model by Isard and Kavesh to study structural interrelations of metropolitan regions;[86] and the mathematical approaches of the type employed by Stewart and by Zipf.[87]

Finally, it should be noted that advances have also been made in cartographic as well as statistical techniques. Centrographic in-

80. Duncan and Davis, *The Chicago Urban Analysis Project: A Summary Report.*

81. Nathan Keyfitz, "Differential Fertility in Ontario: An Application of Factorial Design to a Demographic Problem," *Population Studies,* VI (November, 1952), 123–24.

82. Donald J. Bogue and Dorothy L. Harris, *Comparative Population and Urban Research via Multiple Regression and Covariance Analysis* (Oxford, Ohio: Scripps Foundation for Research in Population Problems and Population Research and Training Center, 1954).

83. Bogue, *The Structure of the Metropolitan Community.*

84. Evelyn Kitagawa, "Components of a Difference between Two Rates," *Journal of American Statistical Association,* L (December, 1955), 1168–94.

85. Duncan and Duncan, "Contributions to the Theory of Segregation Indexes."

86. Isard and Kavesh, *op. cit.*

87. John Q. Stewart, "Suggested Principles of 'Social Physics,' " *Science,* CVI (August, 1947), 179–80; George K. Zipf, *Human Behavior and the Principle of Least Effort* (Cambridge, Mass.: Addison-Wesley, 1949).

dexes,[88] "matter most" maps,[89] and "isopleth" mappings[90] represent great improvements over earlier map work in ecology for dealing with spatial distributions.

Theory

There is a tendency among students of ecology, including sociologists, to begin their considerations on a highly abstract level and in a most comprehensive manner which often transcends the boundaries of their academic disciplines of origin. A number of ecologists posit the existence of a separate discipline or science of ecology which cuts across the conventionally recognized sciences. Thus, Taylor, a zoölogist, states that ecology is the study of "all relations of all organisms to all their environment."[91] Bews, a botanist, describes ecology as a synthesis of sciences concerned with man and his environment that "unifies all the human sciences and enables each one to find its proper place in a generalized study of man."[92] Wells and his collaborators conceived of ecology as "an extension of economics to the whole of life."[93] Hawley conceives of ecology as "the study of both the form and the development of organization in populations of living things."[94] The writers in ecology tend to begin their studies with the broad framework of the adaptation of living organisms to environment, with one or another way, in fact, of stating Darwin's interest in the "web of life," a metaphor which sociologists Park and Hawley both recognized as a core idea in ecological research.[95]

88. Calvin Schmid, "The Ecological Method in Social Research," in *Scientific Social Surveys and Research*, ed. Pauline V. Young (New York: Prentice-Hall Inc., 1942), p. 402.

89. Duncan and Davis, "A New Type of 'Matter Most' Map."

90. Calvin F. Schmid and E. H. MacCannell, "Basic Problems, Techniques, and Theory of Isopleth Mapping," *Journal of American Statistical Association*, L (March, 1955), 220–39.

91. W. P. Taylor, "What Is Ecology and What Good Is It," *Ecology*, July, 1936, p. 335.

92. J. W. Bews, *Human Ecology* (London: Oxford University Press, 1935), p. 14.

93. H. G. Wells, Julian Huxley, and G. P. Wells, *The Science of Life* (New York, 1934), pp. 968 ff.

94. A. H. Hawley, *Human Ecology* (New York: Ronald Press Co., 1950), p. 66.

95. R. E. Park, "Human Ecology," *American Journal of Sociology*, XLII (July, 1936), 1; Hawley, *Human Ecology*, pp. 5 and 33.

In a sense, the sociologists' interest in human ecology began with the borrowing of a framework of theory from biology concerning the relationship of organism to environment. Curiously enough, the sociologist in borrowing from biology the concept of "struggle for existence" as a key to the process of adaptation to environment utilized a notion which Darwin himself admits he borrowed from Malthus,[96] who if he was a scientist at all was a social scientist. From the beginning, interest in ecology, however, was not an interest in individuals but, rather, in populations of living things. "Communal adaptation constitutes the distinctive subject matter of ecology," says Hawley.[97] "That the community is the essential adaptive mechanism may be taken as the distinctive hypothesis of ecology."

The source for the utilization in sociology of ecological theory borrowed from the biologist is undoubtedly to be found in the work of Park, in whom a number of diverse interests converged and achieved expression.[98] Yet Park's early work of an ecological character was essentially "a-theoretical," to use the adjective employed by Shils in describing early urban sociology in America.[99] In his early writings Park placed the ecological into the forefront of sociological consciousness as a field of exploration, but he did not provide anything resembling a theory of, or for, human ecology. None of the materials in the 1925 publication of *The City*, in which Park's earlier article was reprinted, provided or attempted to provide comprehensive theory for human ecology. Two of the papers, however, those by McKenzie and Wirth, as noted above, did set up frames for ecological and urban research; and Burgess' paper on "The Growth of the City" did provide the zonal hypothesis which certainly may be regarded as a contribution to ecological theory and the direction of empirical research.

With the publication of *The Urban Community* in 1926, Park, in his presidential address to the American Sociological Society in 1925, provided more grist for the mill of ecological theory in his

96. Charles Darwin, *Origin of the Species* (1859).

97. Hawley, *Human Ecology*, p. 31.

98. For collection of Park's writings in this field see R. E. Park, *Human Communities* (Glencoe, Ill.: Free Press, 1952).

99. Edward Shils, *The Present State of American Sociology* (Glencoe, Ill.: Free Press, 1948), p. 9.

paper on "The Urban Community as a Spatial Pattern and a Moral Order" and set the stage for the subsequent criticism of the "classical ecological school" in his differentiation of the "ecological" from the "social."[100] In this same volume McKenzie has a further elaboration of a framework for ecological investigation but nothing that can be called "ecological theory."

Although Park and other early authors published a number of papers on ecological and urban research variously incorporating ecological concepts from biology, the only materials which could be designated as providing general theory for human ecology in sociology prior to the 1930's were probably those in Park and Burgess' *Introduction to the Science of Sociology*.[101] This volume in its discussion of the processes of social interaction and especially of competition came closer, perhaps, than any other publication to providing a general theoretical frame for the incorporation of ecology into sociology.

During the 1930's several works appeared which contributed to the utilization and development of ecological theory in sociology. Park's article in 1934, "Human Ecology," not only was his most systematic statement on ecology but it also embodied a theoretical formulation with heuristic implications in its clear-cut distinction between "a symbiotic society based on competition and a cultural society based on communication and consensus."[102] In pairing his adaptation of biological theory with sociological theory, Park posed a form of dualism, in part through faulty statement, that set the stage for the criticism which was to follow.

The most important development with theoretical implication during the thirties was undoubtedly the appearance of Alihan's criticism of Park and of "the discipline of human ecology." In *Social Ecology*, published in 1938,[103] Alihan's criticism, while essentially couched in philosophical terms rather than in a framework which would further research, contributed to the sharpening of ecological thinking and to the emergence of more rigorous statement.

100. R. E. Park, "The Urban Community as a Spatial Pattern and a Moral Order," in *The Urban Community*, ed. E. W. Burgess (Chicago: University of Chicago Press, 1926), pp. 4 ff.

101. Pp. 504 ff.

102. Park, "Human Ecology," *op. cit.*, p. 13.

103. New York: Columbia University Press, 1938.

In general, it may be said the thirties produced more in the way of schematic presentations of the scope of human ecology, such as those of McKenzie,[104] Hollingshead,[105] and Quinn,[106] than of ecological theory.

An important restatement of the field of ecological investigation which attempted to deal with the criticisms of human ecology and lacunae in ecological theory and research appeared in Hawley's article on "Ecology and Human Ecology" in 1944.[107] In this article as well as in its subsequent elaboration in his book, Hawley has provided sociology with the most systematic and comprehensive statement of ecology and with at least a foundation for the development of ecological theory.[108] Hawley's subtitle to his book is "A Theory of Community Structure." It is in some respects appropriate. But it may, perhaps, more appropriately be termed a prolegomena to ecological theory in sociology for two reasons. First, it, like practically all semblances of ecological theory in sociology, is in large measure borrowed from biology. Second, it is global rather than middle range and operational in character. It is, nonetheless, the most solid basis which has yet appeared in the sociological literature for further empirical research and for further development of theory.

Hawley's great stress on the community as the unit of ecological investigation has special implications for research on the city as a communal unit. The community is described by Hawley as "the pattern of symbiotic and commensalistic relations that develops in the population . . . in the nature of a collective response to the habitat; it constitutes the adjustment of organism to environment."[109] In focusing on the community, it may be noted, Hawley has taken

104. R. D. McKenzie, "Human Ecology," *Encyclopaedia of the Social Sciences* (New York, 1931), V, 314–15; *Readings in Human Ecology* (Ann Arbor: Wahr, 1934).

105. A. B. Hollingshead, "Human Ecology," in *An Outline of the Principles of Sociology,* ed. R. E. Park (New York: Barnes & Noble, 1934), pp. 63–168.

106. James A. Quinn, "Ecological vs. Social Interaction," *Sociology and Social Research,* XVIII (July–August, 1934), 565–70.

107. *Loc. cit.*

108. It is also recognized as a contribution to general ecology (see Edward S. Deevey, Jr., "Recent Textbooks of Human Ecology," *Ecology,* XXXII [April, 1951], 348).

109. *Human Ecology,* p. 67.

the same position as his predecessors Park[110] and McKenzie,[111] a position also explicitly stated by Wirth.[112]

Human ecology is regarded by Hawley, also in keeping with the earlier writings of Park,[113] McKenzie,[114] and Wirth,[115] as a field of interest which parallels plant ecology and animal ecology and "represents a special application of the general viewpoint to a particular class of living things." Just as plant and animal ecology are concerned with the study of the form and development of plant and animal communities respectively, so human ecology is "the study of the form and development of the community in human population."[116]

It should be noted, also, that Hawley has pointed to a pathway for the better integration of ecological and demographic interests in his treatment of "population balance,"[117] and has suggested various roads for possible further development of ecological theory in his treatise.[118]

Ecological theory with special reference to the city is beginning to assume respectable proportions. Such theory includes several hypotheses in respect to urban structure and growth,[119] incorporates a framework for the study of urban dynamics in the conceptualization of processes of urban development and change,[120] and embodies a set of at least tentative propositions in respect to the factors involved in the spatial and temporal patterns in the urban complex of population, of forms of behavior and thought, and of social institutions.[121]

We have developed some theory in human ecology in respect to

110. "Human Ecology," *op. cit.*, p. 13.

111. "The Ecological Approach," *op. cit.*, pp. 63 ff.

112. "Human Ecology," *op. cit.*, p. 484.

113. "Human Ecology," *op. cit.*, p. 4.

114. "The Ecological Approach," *op. cit.*, p. 63.

115. "Human Ecology," *op. cit.*, p. 483.

116. Hawley, *Human Ecology*, p. 68.

117. *Ibid.*, pp. 149–74.

118. *Ibid.*, especially in Parts III and IV.

119. E.g., see Quinn, *Human Ecology*, chap. xii and Part IV.

120. E.g., *ibid.*, Part III.

121. *Ibid.*, Part IV.

the city. Much of ecological theory is still that which has been taken over from biology, however; and much remains to be done both in the development of distinctly sociological ecological theory and in the integration of biological with sociological theory.

Prospective Ecological Research

The improved nature of the data available for urban ecological research, on the one hand, and the utilization of more sophisticated methods, on the other, may produce major developments in ecological research in the coming decade. There are a number of avenues reasonably well marked for further development. Among these avenues for the next steps in research there may be noted the following: (1) studies utilizing the improved data and methods testing the present fund of hypotheses in respect to metropolitan structure, function, and growth; (2) further studies of the structure and function of the metropolitan complex; (3) comparative studies in urban ecology; (4) studies of "systems" of metropolitan areas—studies which deal with the metropolitan area as an element in larger "ecological systems"; and (5) integrated studies which in a sociological holistic sense attack urban phenomena through the conjoint use of the three basic frameworks of sociology—ecological, culturalogical, and the social-psychological.

In respect to the first of these types of studies, the testing of the present fund of ecological hypotheses, a pathway has been indicated in a recent unpublished paper by Bogue.[122] Ten hypotheses are explicitly formulated which result from "findings of single studies that deal with single cities or with a small sample of cities for a short period of time . . . [which] refer only to the metropolitan areas of the United States." Replications of available studies and an extension of the universe studied are much to be desired.

In respect to the conduct of new studies of the structure and function of the metropolitan complex, the road ahead has also been reasonably well mapped. Bogue, in the editing of the materials developed in a Seminar in Population, Urbanism, and Ecology at this University, has published a little volume, *Needed Urban and Metro-*

122. Donald J. Bogue, "Some Hypotheses of Metropolitan Structure and Growth" (unpublished paper).

politan Research.[123] This document, in addition to presenting abstracts of a series of discussions by leaders in various aspects of urban activities indicating the knowledge needed for their specific purposes, contains some 115 topics for urban research—many of them of an ecological character.

Studies in comparative urban ecology would, of course, be related to the studies suggested in (1) above but, in addition, would undoubtedly contribute to the development of new hypotheses and greatly broaden the fund of ecological knowledge. Some research of this character is now under way at the Population Research and Training Center at the University of Chicago,[124] and a Center proposal is available for a much broader program of research, to be spearheaded by Duncan, which has yet to be financed.

Studies of metropolitan areas as elements in regional, national, and even larger systems have barely begun, and most of the work of this character has been done by students other than sociologists. A highly suggestive paper is available by Vining[125] which provides a basis for work in this area, together with a commentary on his paper by a distinguished economist, Hoover, who has contributed much to some aspects of human ecology.[126] The recent work by Vance and Demerath constitutes an important advance.[127] In merging the traditional approach to regionalism as exemplified in Odum with the ecological approach in urban studies, a highly significant development is in the making. It should be noted that the availability of statistics by "state economic areas" in the Census may facilitate this type of investigation.

Finally, it is becoming increasingly apparent that much may be gained by team researches on the city, by sociologists utilizing the

123. Published jointly by Scripps Foundation for Research in Population Problems, Miami University, and Population Research and Training Center, University of Chicago (Oxford, Ohio, 1953).

124. E.g., Bogue is making comparative studies of selected European and United States cities.

125. Rutledge Vining, "A Description of Certain Spatial Aspects of an Economic System," *Economic Development and Cultural Change,* III (January, 1955), 147–95.

126. Edgar M. Hoover, "The Concept of a System of Cities: A Comment on Rutledge Vining's Paper," *Economic Development and Cultural Change,* III (January, 1955), 196–98.

127. *Op. cit.*

cultural and social-psychological, as well as the ecological approach. This is a point made recently by one of the founders of ecological interest in sociology, Ernest W. Burgess.[128] Studies of this type may, among other things, clarify the interrelationships of ecological, cultural, and psychological factors so as completely to dissipate whatever vestiges of dualism may still exist in Park's distinction between the symbiotic and the social orders.

Concluding Observations

A number of interests and developments, some of them stemming from the nineteenth century, found expression in the work of Park and his collaborators to make explicit an interest in human ecology as a subfield of sociology.

In the chronology of human ecology in sociology it may be stated that the 1920's were the decade in which human ecology emerged as a subfield of interest in sociology; the thirties, the decade in which the range of ecological interest was delineated; the forties, the decade in which better data and better research techniques were developed and the foundation laid for ecological theory. In the fifties, and in the x decades to come, we may hope to see augmented and improved ecological research on urban communities and the emergence of important elements of theory in ecology as a subfield of sociology.

Urban ecological research has contributed much to a better understanding of the metropolitan complex. Moreover, it may be noted, because of the interest in social engineering manifest in other portions of this anniversary celebration, ecological research on the urban community has not only enriched the fund of social science knowledge but also has made an important contribution to social engineering in providing a factual basis for dealing with many urban problems.

In the two previous published reports on developments in the social sciences of this University, as well as at this Twenty-fifth Anniversary Celebration, research in urban sociology including ecological research, has been a prominent part of the record. The continued interest of such research at this University seems assured. A number of

128. "The Ecology and Social Psychology of the City," in *Needed Urban and Metropolitan Research*, ed. D. J. Bogue, pp. 80–84.

the members of the sociology faculty, and especially those in the Population Research and Training Center, which includes the Chicago Community Inventory, have made such investigations a central research interest.[129]

There is every indication that interest in ecological research on the urban community will continue to be an important and significant subfield of sociology whatever may be the broader development of general ecology. The availability of bodies of data for research, effective techniques, at least a foundation of theory, and a corps of students eager to deal with the ecological problems they perceive, in combination, point to an accelerated pace of development in human ecology in the period that lies ahead.

129. Sociology faculty and staff members involved are Donald J. Bogue, Otis Dudley Duncan, Beverly Duncan, Philip M. Hauser, and Evelyn Kitagawa.

The Cultural Aspect of Urban Research

The social scientists of this university cut their teeth on the problems of city life in the 1890's. About thirty years later, Albion W. Small, as Leonard White has told some of us, called them together and proposed a joint offensive on the city of Chicago. The city, it seems, is always with us; it appears to be creeping closer. It is, therefore, appropriate that Philip Hauser, in his exhaustive bibliography of publications about cities, should have mentioned a great many written about Chicago and by people who worked or now work here. Many of the works he mentions concern other facets than the ecological. I will not list them again, nor will I try to give an exhaustive bibliography comparable to his. One reference to his paper I cannot refrain from making. If anyone is spoiling for a fight, I will gladly enter it to support the distinction between the moral aspect of society (the moral order) and the survival aspect (the ecological) and to deny that Robert E. Park's work on cities was atheoretical. It only seemed so to people who were used to drinking their theory in straight philosophical draughts, unmixed with the empirical juices of life. But, before the argument starts, let me recommend that you read the last of the three volumes of Park's papers, happily just now published with the title *Society*.

The burst of academic interest in cities and in this one in particular was but the culmination of a movement, both academic and popular, that had been under way for a long time. Chicago was a new city, built on flat ground by men adventurous in speculation and in building. Only a few Indian trails and a sickly river warped the expanding grid of streets. No high hill, no rugged rock, no mighty sacred oak offered resistance to the surveyors and the builders. Our greatest historic event was a fire, fit symbol of a city where tearing-down to make way for the newer and bigger (hence better) was and is as important as building itself. Sometimes the grid gets ahead of

255

the houses, and the tearing-down ahead of the building. An upstart university, founded by people *parvenu*—just in—from the East, with money made by other upstarts from the East, as a matter of course undertook an upstart program, with a faculty pirated from the East. Men with state-of-Maine accents studied the upstart city, the city where flat terrain and the absence of sacred precincts allowed city growth and city rot to approximate as closely as one can imagine the form of concentric circles. Ernest Burgess, the youngster of the team, drew the circles on a map. He practiced a bit first on Columbus, Ohio, which is as flat as Chicago, but has a nastier river and did not grow quite fast enough or quite big enough to make the perfect case.

What happened here was a break-through, both of certain tendencies of city growth and of certain movements and interests of the public and of the academic world.

The academic people of Europe and America had been speculating a good deal on the difference between great states and great cities (not always saying which they meant), on the one hand, and the smaller, more conservative, more homogeneous, and more self-contained communities in which most human beings had lived throughout most of the history of the race. Most of those who wrote about the evolution of society (before, along with, and in the wake of biological Darwinism) spoke their pieces on this distinction. One such man was Ferdinand Tönnies; his distinction between society, in which men voluntarily and consciously join forces to gain finite ends, and community, into which men are born and in which they stay because of loyalty and the impossibility of even conceiving that they can leave, is also a distinction between modern, industrial socialism (to which Tönnies would have had us aspire) and a primitive communism of kin, which he and others supposed to have been the early state of man.[1] When, in Tönnies' last years, a movement called national-socialism smote down the Weimar Republic, its leaders shouted as moral pronouncements some of the speculative propositions made by Tönnies and others concerning city and simpler societies: cities destroy racial and moral purity; they elevate reason and trade above sentiment and loyalty. Hitler shouted against the city with the voice of an Amos, but, as he shouted, he led

1. R. Heberle, "Ferdinand Tönnies' Contributions to the Sociology of Political Parties," *American Journal of Sociology*, LXI (November, 1955), 213–20.

the very urban mob to a feast of bread, circuses, and blood. I join the speculations of Tönnies' kind on the distinction of city society from folk-community with the ranting of an urban demagogue who idealized the country, not to suggest any necessary connection between them, but to document interest in the problem, and the tendency to cast not only philosophical speculation about society but also sermons, political talk, and journalistic stereotyping in the terms of the dialectic between city and something conceived as its opposite.

It was not only in the perverted political philosophy of the Nazis that the themes of academic thought concerning city and country joined with political movements. Folklore also became a link between both the emerging social sciences and the humanities, on the one hand, and certain political movements. The same ethnologist who went abroad to study the simpler cultures and the smaller and not yet literate societies could find corners of his own country where old tales were told, old songs sung, old traditions and superstitions preserved. The student of literature, music, and art, seeking the origins of the themes which turn up in works of art produced in and distributed from the cities, got to the back country and talked to the old folks. There he met, at least in spirit, the ethnologist, and they both studied a bit of the "living past." One folklorist and ethnologist, who had published things on Australian myths and legends as well as on the folklore of France, invaded the territory of political science and sociology with a treatise on nationalities;[2] he notes in it that the many peoples who sought national self-determination in Europe before and during the first World War used folklore as proof that they were true historical peoples, entitled to political autonomy. The evidence, as a rule, stressed not the urban but the rural and folkish past. Folklore and vernacular apparently are preserved in the country, in the remote places, and with them the virtues and soul of a people. These things cities, full of strangers and the temptation to betray one's past, apparently tend to destroy. If the city man takes them up again, it is as symbols of a past for which he believes he ought nostalgically to yearn. It is not without relevance to the history of social research in America that our cities, in the early days of empirical social study, were full of people from the very areas in which folk-

2. Arnold van Gennep, *Traité comparatif des nationalités* (Paris, 1922).

lore was being mustered in support of the claim to be politically free of alien domination. It was in American cities as well as in European that Lithuanian, Polish, Czech, Rumanian, and Yiddish legends were gathered, watered, and manured by self-conscious national gardeners. It was this joining of circumstance that may account for the fact that the American sociologist, almost by definition a student of cities, is so much more kin than is the English sociologist to the anthropologist; for the anthropologist has been almost by definition a student of whatever lies at the other end of the scale from the urban. The English sociologist has been not only a city man but usually a city planner and social politician.

Into American study of cities there came also the influence of the surveys of the great growing cities of England and of this country; studies which were directed at describing and altering the conditions of life in the great slums, where there was a poverty of a new kind, different from feudal and preindustrial rural and town poverty. These surveys, although they used statistics of a simple sort and gave the matter on which much of the earlier work of statisticians was based, were not polls of opinion (for which the term "survey" is now used) but descriptions of the life, habits, and institutions of the slum, more like an ethnologist's description of a folk community than like a "sample survey."[3] They were a sort of scientific counterpart of the novels of Dickens and Zola, sprinkled with tables on wages, household expenditures, housing, health, drinking, and crime. In the British surveys the pawnbroker's shop, the gambling club, and the gin-shop appear as the villain; in the American ones, the ethnic colony is always in the center of the stage, although not presented as a villain. The villains are the exploiting landlord, the corrupt politician, the saloonkeeper, and, sometimes, the labor agent. In both cases, the eye of the investigator was upon the slum and the poor, not on the city as a whole. And, in the main, he paid only lip service to the grander statements concerning the city-country or city-folk distinction.

But the theme was not forgotten. Maine, Bagehot, Tarde, Le Play, Spencer, and their precursors were introduced into the discourse of American social scientists who talked of and studied cities. Park, a

3. D. Caradog-Jones, *Social Surveys* ("Hutchinson's University Library," No. 28 [London, (1950)]).

man of philosophical as well as of journalistic bent, was steeped in this literature. In one of his latest papers he wrote:

Modern society is an urban and secular society. Earlier societies were organized on the pattern of the family and the kinship group. Present society grew up about the market place. The great cities which have reared their towers about these market places have been the melting pots of races and cultures, and the centers of intellectual life. But great cities, where men live together in relations that are symbiotic rather than social, have not yet, it seems, developed a tradition, a body of mores, or a moral solidarity sufficient to insure either the perpetuation of existing social institutions, or the orderly succession of those economic, political and cultural changes which embody the aspirations of this modern world.[4]

The general issue presented in that rather typical paragraph is by no means a dead one. Robert Redfield has devoted his career to study and reformulation of it. In *Tepoztlán* (Chicago, 1930) he studied a folk village; in *Chan Kom* (Washington, D.C., 1934), a village in relation to changes coming from the town; in *The Folk Culture of Yucatan* (Chicago, 1941), a series of communities on what he thought of as a folk-urban continuum. The emphasis, in those monographs, was put upon the impact of city and town upon individuals, culture and social organization in its more direct and immediate aspects. In his much more recent *Primitive World and Its Transformations* (1953) and *The Little Community* (1955) he treats of the problem more broadly and in deeper historical perspective and to some extent explicitly as a single historical event on the grand scale rather than as repeated and repeatable process. This perspective is explicit in the first paragraph of *The Primitive World:* "After the rise of cities men became something different from what they had been before. . . . History is here conceived of as a single career, that of the human race." In these works one will find a critical review of the classic formulations of the city versus not-city distinction.

Redfield and his co-worker, Milton Singer, are now turning from study of the "little traditions" developed within and carried by little communities to that of the "great traditions" which, under certain circumstances, build upon and integrate the small, giving them great dimensions and longer perspectives, and turning conceptions of what

4. R. E. Park, "Modern Society," in *Society* (Glencoe, Ill.: Free Press, 1955), p. 341. This was read at the Fiftieth Anniversary of the University in 1941.

is right and wrong from particular to general and universal abstract principles, transcending the local world.[5]

Redfield's work is, more than any other that I know, a continuation and a further development of the urban versus primitive, folk, or rural distinctions made by so many of the precursors of modern social science. The work on great and little traditions goes beyond previous work in that it is based on modern ethnological, sociological, archeological, and historical research rather than on the contrived stereotypes of at least some of the early work. There are, however, certain difficulties involved in carrying their work (Redfield's and Singer's) further. One of them is methodological. Redfield's *The Little Community* bears the subtitle "Viewpoints for the Study of a Human Whole." It is much easier, in practice, to study a little community as a whole than to study a great civilization, with its immense cities and its great systems of technique, thought, institutions, and arts, as a whole. He deals with the problem in a thoughtful chapter on "Wholes and Parts" but resigns himself (or perhaps there is not in his conclusion that regret which would warrant the word "resign") to saying that "the study of human wholes lies today in a borderland between science and art" (p. 163). The prolegomena of Redfield and Singer to the study of the great civilizations and the great traditions seem almost completely to abandon the study of huge communities and societies, as something existing on the ground, and having, as it were, a body in space. This is a fundamental change in method from Redfield's own studies of villages and folk societies. I do not say that the shift may not be necessary if they are to achieve their aim; I only contend that it is a shift. Nor do I suggest that anyone else has any very good set of devices for studying cities as wholes in the same way that anthropologists

5. R. Redfield and M. Singer, "The Cultural Role of Cities," *Publications in Economic Development and Cultural Change* (University of Chicago), III (October, 1954), 53–73. See also Redfield, "The Social Organization of Tradition," one of a set of lectures entitled "Peasant Society and Culture: An Anthropological Approach to Civilization," delivered at Swarthmore College, 1955, and now in preparation for publication. In it occurs this passage: "The great tradition is cultivated in schools or temples; the little tradition works itself out and keeps itself going in the lives of the unlettered in their village communities. The tradition of the philosopher, theologian, and literary man is a tradition consciously cultivated and handed down; that of the little people is for the most part taken for granted and not submitted to much scrutiny or considered refinement and improvement."

have done in very small communities and sociologists in somewhat larger ones. The point, however, is important; for it is not precisely the same thing to study some men and some things in cities as it is to study the city as a whole.

A second comment on this very interesting and promising work is that, like most dichotomous schemes, a lot of the boxes in a possible set of contingencies tables are left empty, although there are undoubtedly cases to put into them. There is, in Redfield's work, almost nothing about that very important part of human society—the city man who participates but superficially in the great, or high, tradition and who, in company with the masses of his fellows, makes the vulgar or popular culture. They mention such people, but I have the impression that they do not mean to include them very seriously in their scheme of studies.[6] These are the people and the cultural products to which our colleagues, Riesman, Benny, Denney, Meyersohn, and others are attending in their Center for the Study of Leisure.

I want, however, to make clear the direction of the wind I am stirring up. The Redfield and Singer enterprise is moving in a direction in which we need to go; I only wish to say that to get full benefit of it will require ingenious, brilliant, and, although I hate the thought, massive attacks upon the problems of method which are involved.

Perhaps I have now earned license to bring up one or two of my own pet problems. One of them has to do with the interaction between the little traditions and the great. Another is that of the image of the ideal man in various religions and cultures. In a seminar on cities which Professors Sylvia Thrupp and Gustave von Grunebaum initiated and in which I have joined them for the fun of it, it has

6. Mr. Milton Singer has, since I wrote this paper, reported some of his last year's work in India to the Seminar on Comparative Study of Cities. He did, in fact, find that urban popular culture supplied the links between the great tradition contained in the ancient Sanskrit writings and carried by learned Brahmin scholars, on the one hand, and the little traditions. Ritual storytelling in the vernaculars, interspersed with secular and even comic matter, and movie shorts on traditional tales and religious themes are among the forms of popular art in modern Indian cities. One is reminded of the morality plays of the Middle Ages in England, in which Noah and his wife became comic relief and the symbols of henpecked husband and the scolding wife.

I am happy to have been a little wrong as to the present trend of their project as well as to have been a little right in my counsel.

come out that the ideal Moslem is a city man, who moves from bazaar to mosque and back again, from trade to disputation and prayer, whether at home or in a strange city. Yet Islam has become the religion of some very isolated folk—who tend to make Islamic tradition smaller.[7] Julien tells us that rustic Berbers consider the men of the cities less devotedly and fanatically religious than themselves. The city Moslems of North Africa, for their part, regard the rustic Berbers as but crude and impure followers of the finely and curiously worked patterns of thought and practice of the true faith—a faith whose nuances can be expressed truly only in the tongue of the Prophet. The case recalls the relations between rustic fundamentalist sects, say, the snake-handlers of the South, and the learned seminaries of the great universities; or the strain between the rustic thaumaturge or fanatical unlettered ascetic, whom the Roman Church has sometimes canonized, and the very learned masters and aesthetes of the cult who must do the canonizing. In Christianity, during its first centuries an urban movement but scarcely one of intellectual or sophisticated people, the case is not always clear. An Augustine—who was a sophisticated man—writes of the City of God, but many of the sects and orders sought the Kingdom in rural settings and idealized supposedly rural kinds of piety. One may doubt whether any of the great religions has consistently held to either an urban or a rural image of the ideal man or has avoided some conflict between divergent images. In Catholic Christendom, the religious orders appear to act as a connecting tissue; sometimes they bring to the cities, and even to Rome, the naïve enthusiasms and visions of the provinces and the country; again they carry back the idea of the great universal church to nationalistic and regionally minded branches and to particularistic movements, often anti-urban. The problem is not merely that of an opposition of great and little traditions but of the forms of interaction between them and the organs of that interaction or dialectic. One thinks of Chaucer's pilgrims exchanging corrupted Greek tragedies, folk tales, and bawdy yarns of the towns as they ride to Canterbury; of wandering monk and preacher; of merchant and peasant on the way to Mecca. In these cases, however, the great and the little are fruit of the same tree,

7. C. A. Julien, *Afrique du Nord en marche: Nationalismes Musulmans et souveraineté française* (2d ed.; Paris, 1952).

although the rural-urban differences are, or were, in many respects much greater than, say, in our own part of the world. For among us the rural-urban differences in most matters of belief, knowledge, attitude, and sentiment appear measurably slight; I do mean *measurably slight,* for they appear to be of such order that it takes a bit of statistical manipulation to determine whether they exist. Samuel Stouffer has recently found some measure of difference in tolerance of certain unpopular political opinions and actions between rural and urban people in a national sample; it was still there after eliminating the influence of region, education, and certain other factors.[8] But it can scarcely be said that rural people in this country tend to produce little traditions which are either integrated with or opposed to the great systems of thought and value of our civilization as a whole or of the urban part of it; city and country are cut of the same cloth. But the parts of the world where the rural-urban contrast is great are still large, and a large proportion of the world's population is still in them. The question is still current. The Far East, most of the Middle East (leaving out, I suppose, Israel), Moslem Africa, and Black Africa certainly are regions where the difference between city and country is so great as to be one apparently of kind rather than merely of slight or moderate statistical measures on scales of common values. Students of cities ought to be and are at work in these parts of the world. A spate of work on African cities is being produced by anthropologists turned sociologists, by economists and colonial officials turned anthropologists, and by historians turned students of the current. (Even economists seldom remain pure in Africa.) The historian turned student of current matters appears somewhat the mode in Moslem Africa. It may be that the reason is that the very recent transformation of centuries-old urban layouts and institutions puts the historian's traditional objects in juxtaposition with the changes which are in the day's news. Thus Le Tourneau, who has written a history of Fez,[9] going back centuries, is in demand for meetings of administrators and scholars who want to

8. Samuel Stouffer, *Communism, Conformity and Civil Liberties* (New York: Doubleday & Co., 1955).

9. Roger Le Tourneau, *Fès avant le protectorat* (Casablanca, 1949); "Social Change in the Muslim Cities of North Africa," *American Journal of Sociology,* LX (May, 1955), 527–35.

know what is up in the cities of Algiers and the Magreb. In this case the transformation of the cities, although undoubtedly set in motion by forces from the outside and especially by European political and economic intervention, is swept on by huge immigration of poverty-stricken, uprooted people from the countryside. These rustics live on the outskirts of the growing and great cities of Africa in oil-can and shanty towns. The links between town and country appear in this case to be precisely these half-rustic, more or less unwilling, city dwellers who have one foot in the country and the other in the back yard of the cities. They are certainly neither carriers of a great tradition nor creators of folk tradition.

In Black Africa the studies of cities all point to an extreme lack of cultural links between the most urban and the most rural people. The East African studies I have read,[10] and the work of Balandier on French Equatorial Africa, picture aggregations in which the more urban people are so far removed by residential segregation, culture and language, and income and standard of living that the rural people who come to town as well as the people still in the country have no effective contact with them. The models of urban life are not accessible to the people of the country in any great degree. The city is as alien to the country as it is possible to imagine. Singer and Redfield have taken such cases into account in some measure in their memorandum on the culture roles of cities. It is a point that wants a great deal of closer study. One has to ask, then, not merely what the organs are of interaction between great traditions and the little ones where the basic cultural differences between city and country are small or moderate and within the same basic civilization; he has also to ask what happens when people are drawn to the precincts of cities that are alien in origin and style of life and where the cultural and economic gaps are so great that the organs of

10. *East Africa Royal Commission (1953–1955) Report* (London: H.M. Stationery Office, 1955), Part IV: "Conditions for Urban Development."

C. Sofer and R. Sofer, *Jinja.* This monograph, soon to be published in London, reports a survey of the rapidly growing town at the head of the Nile where a great power project has been built.

G. Balandier, *Sociologie des Brazzavilles noires* (Paris, 1955); *Sociologie actuelle de l'Afrique noire* (Paris, 1955).

Social Implications of Technological Change and Urbanization in Africa South of the Sahara (Prepared under the Auspices of UNESCO by the International African Institute [London, 1955]).

effective diffusion in one or both directions are lacking. As I read of the cities of East and Central Africa, and even of South Africa, I get the impression that perhaps this is what Rome was like when her outlying precincts were full of barbarians who did not know what the plumbing, the theater, the spoons, and the temples were for. But my heart goes out, I must say, to the barbarians rather than the Romans. The barbarians were, after all, the ancestors of a good many of us. It will be interesting, and a crucial part of the study of cities, to see how the status gap between native rural people and foreign urban people will be filled and what ladders will be built by which people may climb from the disorderly life of the half-rural, half-urban, poverty-stricken shanty towns to a more urban and prosperous way of life.

In the meantime, it is clear that what is happening in some of these places is not the mutual fructifying of the rural and urban but an opposition between the two. A portent of integration, however, may be seen in the nativistic movements which adapt symbols and ideas from the great traditions (Christianity, Islam) to the stirring-up of new half-religious, half-political movements on a grander scale than any one tribe or primitive community. These are described in Sundkler's *Bantu Prophets* and in several papers and chapters of George Balandier's work.[11] These so-called native or separatist churches are considered bastard mixtures of Christianity with native beliefs, symbols, and practices; certainly their leaders do not have benefit of the laying-on of hands by European or other authorized clergy. Still, it may be possible that this is part of the way in which the great traditions of the past have spread to new parts of the world and have taken root among hitherto tribal or rural peoples. This is certainly not the first time that missionaries have given weapons into the hands of cultural "children" only to have them twisted and turned upon their teachers and masters.

But let us return briefly to the problem of the city man, as ideal, as stereotype, and as reality in our own world. We have long since passed the stage at which it is easy to tell rural from urban people in our part of the world. The margins are too slight. Yet the image of an urban man who is different from the rural is still with us.

11. Bengt G. M. Sundkler, *Bantu Prophets in South Africa* (London, 1948); Balandier, *op. cit.*, Part III, chap. ii: "Le Messionisme Ba-kongo."

Wohl, writing of the middle and later nineteenth century, finds in fiction (the Horatio Alger, Jr., series) and in other writings the myth that it is the virtuous country boy who succeeds in a big way in the city and that it is precisely because of certain rural qualities that he does succeed.[12] A certain ambivalence is revealed by the fact that it is in the city that success lives and that the successful boy does not go back to the country. Yet the notion is there that it is the country that breeds virtue. William E. Henry, in his studies of personality, has canvassed the literature on the concept of the normal man, the good man, in a certain sense, and finds in even the scientific literature (of psychology) a sort of built-in notion of simplicity, stability, perhaps even of not being too awfully and disturbingly bright; the whole is somehow associated with a simpler, quieter life than that of the city, or at least than that of the stereotype of the city. Rural life and rural people are simple and good; city people are complex, not so good, and perhaps even a little perverse and immoral. It remains to determine what personality types and what modes of personal conduct actually exist in our society, to what kinds of experience and environment they are related and how; and, finally, what the associations of these things with actual living in the cities are.

This has led us to the threshold of the problem of deviation, of the extent to which and of the manner in which city and other communities breed and/or tolerate behavior not considered close to the proper norms. This is a problem on which I am sure that the talk has generally been bigger than our knowledge. The late Nicholas Spykman, translator and interpreter of the great urban sociologist and philosopher, Georg Simmel, wrote: "The metropolite is an individualist, a relativist, and a formalist in all aspects of moral life. The city inhabitant is a dweller in a pluralistic social universe. He participates in a great many social circles, and is thus subject to a great many different sets of social standards."[13]

"Deviation" is a term of relativity; it also is a term of evaluation

12. R. Richard Wohl, "The Myth of the Country Boy as an Aspect of American Urban Tradition" (unpublished manuscript).

13. "A Social Philosophy of the City," in *The Urban Community,* ed. E. W. Burgess (Chicago: University of Chicago Press, 1926).

and judgment when applied to human conduct. There are many dimensions in which people may deviate from either statistical modes or moral norms—in belief, in action, in combinations of beliefs and actions, alone or in company, occasionally or habitually. We, in fact, need a fresh start in study of social deviation, which ought to be almost the central problem of social science; by the time we get a real anatomy of conforming and deviating, it is likely that our conception of the conduct of both city men, as individuals and groups, and of rural people, also as individuals and groups, will be much more complicated than pictured in any of the prevailing images of either city or country man. We may well start by taking a lead from W. I. Thomas, who insisted that there cannot, in effect, be any effective description of behavior without definition of situations. We will have to study both city and country as the loci of social situations before we will get far with the complex problem of studying the differences between city men and other men and the whole related problem of deviation.

I fear I have rather abused the title and function given me. I have certainly neglected some of the most important aspects of research concerning cities. A great many historians, for instance, are taking particular cities or groups of cities as their fields of study. France seems especially to abound in such historians. Their papers made up a considerable part of a program of the French Sociological Society devoted to the relation of city and country not long ago.[14] The thing that has impressed me about these historical monographs on cities is that, no matter what the period or the cultural setting, the problems of the historian and those of the sociologist or anthropologist or other students of contemporary social institutions seem to converge. The problems seem not to be those of determining who did what but of determining the whole of which available evidence reports and reveals a part. I find this especially so in the work of Le Tourneau on Fez, in Philippe Wolff's work on medieval Toulouse, in Asa Briggs's study of Birmingham since 1865, of Bridenbaugh's study of American Colonial cities, of Sylvia Thrupp's various works on medieval cities, and very markedly in the work of the late sociologist-

14. G. Friedmann (ed.), *Villes et campagnes: Civilisation urbaine et civilisation rurale en France* (Paris, 1953).

economist-historian Robert K. Lamb.[15] In the recent studies in Kansas City in which some of us have been engaged, the historian of the group has turned out to be one of the most important members, even though we are dealing mainly with things which are happening now. His particular value comes from the fact that he helps us solve the difficult problem of seeing the community as an entity; his memorandums and comments enable us to see that the particular institutions and events in which the individuals in a number of samples participate are parts of a continuing whole whose present is more a function of the past than we may believe. So the proposition I made about the historians who study cities works both ways. They, who cannot go back and check their samples by new observations and interviews, have nevertheless to meet the problem of building out the whole as of a given moment. It is a problem on which students of contemporary going concerns and processes have something to say to the historian; yet, for all our building out our conceptions of a whole, or universe, we are a bit prone to regard the whole thing as static and as held together by some mechanical force, some social glue. The happy circumstance of having a historian who studies with us and digs up the fairly recent, but nevertheless purely documentary, past creates an optimal situation for learning from each other.

If I have not mentioned more often and by name studies made by people who belong to the other social science fraternities—economists, planners, educators, psychologists, political scientists—it is because it would have been a bit forced to do so. I am so accustomed to work with people of the various disciplines that it hardly occurs to me to make note of the fact. Furthermore, we live in an epoch when any social scientist who would avoid studying cities would have to be a very determined and ingenious escapist indeed.

15. Philippe Wolff, *Commerce et marchands de Toulouse* (*vers 1350—vers 1450*) (Paris, 1954); Asa Briggs, *History of Birmingham*, Vol. II: *Borough and City, 1865–1938* (London and New York, 1952); Carl Bridenbaugh, *Cities in the Wilderness: The First Century of Urban Life in America, 1625–1742* (New York, 1938), and *Cities in Revolt: Urban Life in America, 1743–1776* (New York, 1955); Sylvia Thrupp, *The Merchant Class of Medieval London* (Chicago, 1948).

Industrial Organization and Economic Progress

The greatest economic question of the age is contained in my title: Is economic progress better achieved through a system of private enterprise or through a system of state enterprise? This question insists upon being debated continuously by all free men, and on a planet-wide scale it is being debated by events. I shall regretfully keep my distance from it. I am poorly informed on the vast modern socialistic experiments, and even my best-informed colleagues, I believe, must speak with careful vagueness of the institutional conditions for rapid long-term economic progress. But it is only reasonable that some great questions should be skirted today: we are here to celebrate an early birthday of the Social Science Research Building, not to raze it.

Instead, I shall deal chiefly with a smaller, but in America and many other nations a more immediate, question: Is it monopoly, or is it competition, that brings more rapid economic progress?

I

To Adam Smith, and to his disciples for a century thereafter, competition denoted the regime of the bold, resourceful, and independent enterpreneur, whose equally endowed rivals disciplined him to diligence and stimulated him to innovation. The monopolist, acting usually through the chartered trading corporation, was a sheltered and unenterprising entrepreneur, inventive only of new methods of suppressing competition, exploiting consumers, and wheedling governmental favors. Smith believed that the legal monopoly was all that protected these lazy giants from "the superior vigilance and attention of private adventurers" and that in the long run the monopoly served only to support "the negligence, profusion, and malversation" of companys' employees.[1] The virtues of competition, in this period

1. *The Wealth of Nations* (Modern Library ed.), pp. 712–13.

269

of the classical economics, were equally great in securing efficiency in the conduct of economic affairs and in hastening the introduction of new techniques and products.

Beginning in the 1870's, the concept of competition—in company with most general economic concepts—began to undergo progressive analytical refinement. Where it had once embraced almost all forms of private enterprise except literal monopoly, competition now began to be given a more precise, and more restrictive, signification. Some of the restrictions imposed upon it—like the requirement that the economic unit have negligible influence on prices—were dictated by the inner logic of economic theory. Others, and especially the progressive tendency toward the model of a stationary economy, were dictated by the need for manageable but rigorously defined concepts. Gradually the concept of *perfect* competition emerged and grew in precision and popularity, until in the 1920's it reached its definitive statement in Frank Knight's *Risk, Uncertainty and Profit*.

It was now essentially a concept of the stationary economy: competition could not be unique in its workings if men did not know the consequences of their actions, and they could not know these if unpredictable change—which means most kinds of change—were present. In Knight's famous list of the conditions of perfect competition, therefore, two of the conditions served to specify stationary conditions—fixed flows of resources and consumer demands and fixed methods of organization and techniques.[2]

Only one major economist opposed this progressive refinement of the concept of competition—Alfred Marshall. He wished to retain for competition its traditional claim as the great engine of progress, and this desire was reinforced by a less comprehensible desire to avoid concepts which would frighten or puzzle tired businessmen readers. So he virtually abandoned any precise concept of competition and made "free enterprise" the great engine of efficiency and progress. It was a sound instinct, it now seems in retrospect, that made Marshall keep in the forefront the problem of economic progress. But it was unwise to abandon a concept of competition and substitute another ambiguous phrase, freedom of enterprise. On Marshall's own view, monopolies were often highly efficient in per-

2. Frank H. Knight, *Risk, Uncertainty and Profit* (New York, 1933), pp. 76 ff. (namely, Nos. 2 and 9).

forming routine tasks but usually inefficient in innovation, so a concept of competition was not irrelevant to economic progress.[3]

Be that as it may, in the main tradition of economic thinking, competition now became associated with, and virtually equated to, efficiency in the allocation of resources in a stationary economy. And soon after this development reached its pinnacle, and the divorce of the theory of competition from the theory of growth was almost complete, there began a revival of interest by economists in economic growth.

History had invited heresy, and a distinguished iconoclast of our profession, Joseph Schumpeter, accepted the invitation. Monopoly, and not competition, he said, was the organ of progress, and—since rapid progress for a generation could far outweigh inefficiency at a given time—monopoly was the preferable institutional form of capitalism.

The basic argument was not complex: The fundamental accomplishment of a private enterprise system (capitalism), Schumpeter emphasized, was a high rate of growth—through its incentives and adaptability to changes in technologies, resources, and demands. Aggregate output of the American economy has been doubling every generation and doubling per capita every two generations; this is the true measure of its magnificent performance. Concede that monopoly reduces output as compared to the stationary competitive optimum by (say) 10 per cent at any time. What matters this if—largely because of the very fact of monopoly—output will surely be 100 per cent greater in 1980?

Each institution of capitalism must therefore be appraised not only or especially with reference to its efficiency under stationary

3. He observed in a famous address on competition: "It has always been recognized that large firms have a great advantage over their smaller rivals in their power of making expensive experiments; and in some of the modern 'scientific' industries they use part of their resources in hiring specialists to make experiments for them in the technical applications of science. But on the whole observation seems to show, what might have been expected *a priori*, that these advantages count for little in the long run in comparison with the superior inventive force of a multitude of small undertakers. There are but few exceptions to the rule, that large private firms, though far superior to public departments, are yet, in proportion to their size, no less inferior to private businesses of a moderate size in that energy and resource, that restlessness and inventive power, which lead to the striking out of new paths" (*Memorials of Alfred Marshall*, ed. A. C. Pigou [London, 1925], pp. 279–80).

conditions but also relative to its contribution to secular growth. So viewed, monopoly practices have been the catalysts rather than the inhibitors of the development of capitalistic economies. The monopolies have provided the promise of protected rewards necessary to encourage bold ventures, and yet the widespread process of innovation has spared us from permanent monopolistic levies as new monopolies arise to undermine the old.[4]

The crux of this argument is that monopolies provide rewards to successful innovators but that competition does not. In Schumpeter's words:

> But perfectly free entry into a *new* field may make it impossible to enter it at all. The introduction of new methods of production and new commodities is hardly conceivable with perfect—and perfectly prompt—competition from the start. And this means that the bulk of what we call economic progress is incompatible with it. As a matter of fact, perfect competition is and always has been temporarily suspended whenever anything new is being introduced—automatically or by measures devised for that purpose—even in otherwise perfectly competitive conditions.[5]

A crucial step in Schumpeter's argument makes a rare explicit appearance in this passage: every departure from perfect competition in a stationary economy is called monopoly, and that is why it is so easy to show that monopoly is necessary to progress.

If we are to escape from such vacuous terminological circularity, it is necessary to contrive a definition of competition for the changing economy. It is by no means obvious how such a definition should be formed; there is no long-run equilibrium under conditions of growth, and we have not yet devised normal patterns of development for industries, technologies, and the like, from which we can derive a corresponding concept. Yet any extension of the concept of competition to changing conditions is better than none, and to get on with the argument I propose that competition be defined as follows:

> An industry is competitive if, once it is established, it meets two conditions: (i) no individual (and independently acting) firm can appreciably influence prices in the long run; (ii) there is no contrived barrier which

4. Joseph Schumpeter, *Capitalism, Socialism and Democracy* (New York, 1942), esp. chaps. vii and viii.

5. *Ibid.*, pp. 104–5.

prevents the entrepreneur from operating in the industry and at the output he wishes.

An industry becomes established once its prospective costs and demands have been ascertained with a fair degree of confidence.[6]

On such a definition of competition, it is improper to characterize any industry as monopolistic simply because—in the absence of collusive agreement!—only one firm will be in existence the first day of the industry's life. Clarence Birdseye developed the first commercially practicable method of quick-freezing food in 1924. In the decade of the thirties the market for frozen foods was slowly searched out, and by the outbreak of World War II the attractiveness of the industry's long-run prospects was established. We should call this industry a monopoly only if, once this stage was reached, General Foods was able to keep a dominant share of the industry's output. And in general this will occur only when the first firm or firms can impose conventional barriers to entry by new firms—patents, control over natural resources, etc.

This definition invites re-examination of a variety of economic thoughts. The competitive entrepreneur who in the stationary economy had only the task of allocating resources now has also the task of predicting—and possibly shaping—the future conditions of supply and demand. The provision of information becomes in certain types of markets a major task for the entrepreneur, and for disregard of this fact the traditional economic criticisms of advertising have not been sharply focused. But we put such problems aside and ask again: Is monopoly necessary to innovation? The answer is no longer self-evident.

In a changing economy, profits may be obtained by keeping ahead of the parade, and these profits are consistent with competition if they are not supported by monopolistic conditions. Profits arising in periods of disequilibrium are, in the absence of monopolistic conditions, the rewards for (and negative profits the punishments for a lack of) imagination, skill, tenacity, and luck, and it seems no violation of the spirit of competitive theory to treat them as the develop-

6. This definition differs from that conventionally given for competition in the stationary economy in two respects. First, the high demand and supply elasticities need obtain only in the long run. This change is desirable on both scientific and policy grounds. Second, the assumption of perfect competition—the correspondence between expectations and realizations—is abandoned.

mental counterpart of the larger wages of more able men under stationary conditions.[7]

There can be rewards—and great ones—to the successful competitive innovator. For example, the mail-order business was an innovation that had a vast effect upon retailing in rural and small urban communities in the United States. The innovators, I suppose, were Aaron Montgomery Ward, who opened the first general merchandise establishment in 1872, and Richard Sears, who entered the industry fourteen years later. Sears soon lifted his company to a dominant position by his magnificent merchandising talents, and he obtained a modest fortune, and his partner Rosenwald an immodest one.[8] At no time were there any conventional monopolistic practices, and at all times there were rivals within the industry and other industries making near-perfect substitutes (e.g., department stores, local merchants), so the price-fixing power of the large companies was very small.

On the other hand, almost every highly successful patent provides an illustration of monopoly after the industry has become established in our sense—incandescent lamps or television picture tubes or numerous chemicals might be cited. It is not self-evident that the same or a larger amount of energy and resources would have gone into the development of such fields had there been only a short initial period of monopolistic control.

Thus we may conclude that our definition of competition does not predetermine its effect, as compared with monopoly, upon the rate of economic progress.

II

Let us search now for the probable relationship between competitive and monopolistic organization and economic progress.

In new industries the rate of growth and of technical advance is

7. Even under the ordinary "stationary economy" analysis it is probably undesirable, although not wrong, to say that profits are zero under competition. There may be large "profits" simply from superior ability of the entrepreneur. Economists usually call these "rents of ability" and exclude them from profits. These same economists, however, usually take the figure at the end of the accountant's income statement as profits: never to my knowledge has an economist made an attempt to revalue *upward* the wage income of a well-to-do entrepreneur.

8. See B. Emmet and J. E. Jeuck, *Catalogues and Counters* (Chicago, 1950).

usually very high. It is also highly variable; in Burns's classic study the average of the overlapping decade rates of growth (a device to eliminate cyclical effects) and the standard deviation of these rates had a rank correlation of .54 in forty-nine manufacturing industries, and it rose to .73 if we eliminate the four industries (or rather, commodities) with the lowest average rates of growth.[9] When the rate of growth is highly variable, however, there are large risks for the entrepreneur in the industry, for there is much uncertainty as to the optimum price, investment, and other decisions.

Schumpeter looks on these risks as obstacles which the entrepreneur will surmount only if he can get some protection from competition. Abramovitz, on the other hand, has cogently argued that these risks are a major obstacle, not to entry, but to collusion among the firms in the industry, for they darkly obscure the policy which would maximize monopoly profits. Abramovitz accordingly expects that competition will be relatively active in the early period of an industry's history.[10]

The broad facts seem much in Abramovitz' favor: there is no evidence of any unwillingness of entrepreneurs to undertake the risks associated with new industries or old industries revolutionized by new processes. There are numerous industries, to be sure, which for a considerable time had only one or two firms, such as aluminum, nylon, movie cameras, rayon, electrical business machines, zipper fasteners, safety razors, etc. But in almost every case, patents and other contrived restrictions on entry were available and actively exploited. When the new industry did not have such barriers, there was an eager host of new firms—even in the face of the greatest uncertainties. One may cite automobiles, frozen foods, various electrical appliances and equipment, petroleum refining, incandescent lamps, radio, aircraft, and (it is said) uranium-mining.

In older, established industries, the presumption that competition favors rapid progress is even stronger. The restriction of output by

9. Calculated from *Production Trends in the United States since 1870*, Tables 7 and 9. I have eliminated largely duplicating series, e.g., I have included zinc and excluded zinc consumption. I also excluded vessels, whose enormous standard deviation is dominated by World War I. The four industries with low average rates of growth but large standard deviations are jute, cane sugar, roofing slate, and locomotives.

10. "Monopolistic Selling in a Changing Economy," *Quarterly Journal of Economics*, LII (1938), 191.

quotas, the introduction of common sales agencies, and the other paraphernalia of cartels seem ill suited to encourage progress and, in fact, often arise as defensive measures against more progressive industries. In industries like agricultural processing industries and anthracite-mining, it is highly improbable that continued monopolization or increased monopolization would hasten any desirable changes.

I have sought to pass from such general reflections to concrete and objective empirical tests of the relationship between industrial structure and economic growth, but with only modest success. Still, in an area where prejudice and wisdom are distinguishable chiefly by the parentage of thoughts, even a meager beginning may have some interest.

Since it is easy and unconvincing to pick individual industries whose histories are favorable or unfavorable to a given hypothesis, as we have seen, a broader statistical survey seems essential. We take as our measure of technological progress the change over a fairly long period of time (from 1899 to 1937) in labor requirements per unit of output (the reciprocal of the more familiar output per unit of labor). This measure has very serious weaknesses,[11] but it is the only one which is available for numerous industries. In Table 1 we give the change in labor requirements per unit of output in the forty-two manufacturing industries for which this information is available.[12]

We take as our measure of monopoly the level of concentration in these industries, that is, the percentage of the output of each industry produced by the four largest firms. Complete data are available or can be estimated for a year (1935) near the end of the period.[13] Concentration data are less comprehensive and less reliable for the earlier period, but we may make tolerable estimates for twenty-nine

11. John Kendrick's studies would suggest, however, that the output per unit of labor and the output per unit of labor-plus-capital move together fairly closely (see *Government in Economic Life: Thirty-fifth Annual Report of the National Bureau of Economic Research*, p. 46).

12. S. Fabricant, *Employment in Manufacturing* (National Bureau of Economic Research, 1942).

13. *The Structure of the American Economy* (National Resources Committee, 1939).

TABLE 1

SELECTED DATA FOR MANUFACTURING INDUSTRIES

Industry	Concentration Ratio, 1935	Percentage Change in Labor Requirements, 1899–1937	Percentage Change in Output, 1899–1937
Meat packing (M)	55.6	12	66
Flour (C)	29.4	−10	−8
Rice (C)	38.6	−34	416
Canned foods (MC)	22.7	−65	792
Beet sugar	68.8	−73	1,690
Cane sugar (M)	69.6	−30	86
Malted liquors (MC)	11.8	−26	60
Distilled liquors (M)	51.2	−39	315
Cigars (C)	38.5	−44	0
Chewing tobacco, snuff (M)	63.5	−63	−6
Cotton goods (C)	8.4	−30	101
Woolen goods (MC)	24.2	−22	60
Silk and rayon goods	15.2	−71	512
Knit goods (C)	5.3	−54	506
Carpets	51.1	−29	52
Leather goods	22.7	−40	61
Shoes (C)	26.0	−19	87
Gloves (C)	14.4	−25	29
Rubber shoes (M)	81.8	−20	59
Paper and pulp (MC)	18.7	−55	518
Publishing	20.3	−70	494
Petroleum refining (MC)	38.2	−66	1,920
Glass (MC)	44.9	−77	553
Paints	32.3	−33	391
Explosives (M)	82.0	−67	267
Salt (M)	60.3	−47	82
Wood distillation	53.5	−21	259
Cottonseed products	32.9	− 8	63
Fertilizers (MC)	25.9	−48	248
Railroad cars (M)	71.7	39	−22
Blast furnaces (M)	66.0	−78	171
Zinc	64.0	−45	318
Coke-over products	48.8	−75	380
Carriages (C)	45.8	−33	−95
Tanning materials	33.9	−56	292
Steel works (M)	49.3	−36	313
Ships (M)	44.8	61	−17
Industrial chemicals	76.8	−70	2,500
Copper (M)	90*	−66	272
Lead (M)	90*	−68	51
Locomotives (M)	90*	26	−79
Automobiles	69.4	−88	180,000

* Arbitrary.

of the industries as of a date near 1904.[14] The earlier estimates are for a variable number of firms, so we summarize the data qualitatively. The letter *M* denotes an industry in which concentration was high both at the beginning of the century and in 1935; the letters *MC* denote a large decrease in concentration over the period; and the letter *C* denotes a low level of concentration at the beginning and the end of the period.

We may summarize the decline in labor requirements in the three groups of industries as shown in Table 2. On this reckoning, much the largest decline in labor requirements was in industries in which concentration fell substantially during the period.[15] The investigation suggests that it is the competition of new rivals within an in-

TABLE 2

DECLINE IN LABOR REQUIREMENTS IN THREE INDUSTRIES

INDUSTRY TYPE	No. OF INDUSTRIES	AVERAGE PERCENTAGE CHANGE	
		In Labor Requirements (with Standard Error)	In Output
High concentration (*M*)	14	−19.7 (±15.84)	+111
Declining concentration (*MC*)	7	−51.3 (±7.87)	+593
Low concentration (*C*)	8	−31.1 (±4.90)	+127

dustry, not the competition of new industries, that is associated with rapid technological progress, and it hints that industries with lower concentration had higher rates of technological progress.[16]

This slight study cannot be stretched into a strong refutation of the hypothesis that monopoly favors rapid progress. Fortunately, more precise and more comprehensive tests can be devised and executed, and in the course of reasonable time we may hope to reach stronger conclusions—and in the process learn more of both monopoly and economic progress. For the time we may conclude that there

14. G. W. Nutter, *The Extent of Enterprise Monopoly in the United States* (Chicago, 1951), Tables 37 and 39.

15. Only the difference between the means of the past two classes is statistically significant.

16. For the entire forty-two industries the correlation between the 1935 concentration ratio and the fall in labor requirements was .134, and it was .178 if rate of output of the industry is held constant.

is no prima facie contradiction of the classical view of the positive relationship between competition and progress or, indeed, as much support for the contrary view as the devil usually provides for clever heresy.

III

But there is another school of thought which says: Granted that competition served the cause of progress until recent times, the sources of progress are now changing so that this will no longer be true. Specifically, increasing intimacy of the relationship between scientific knowledge and technology and the growing complexity of scientific knowledge mean that henceforth a firm must have a research program, a research laboratory, a highly trained staff, and the capacity to wait patiently for commercial results—and these are not within the means of small firms. Statistics like ours, which end in 1937, or even in 1950, are better reserved for men who look backward.

This argument is an uncomfortable one with which to deal. The very essence of scholarly irresponsibility is the assertion that the past is irrelevant to the future, but it is a sign of genius to detect the major economic developments at an early stage in their development. And at least superficially the rise of the industrial laboratory, in which science now works for industry, is in an early stage of development. In 1950 there were still only 2,795 companies with laboratories, employing 71,000 professional employees, according to the National Research Council directory—and almost 40,000 of these employees had been added since 1938.

Broadly viewed, however, the rise of the industrial research laboratory is a simple continuation of a century-old trend in industrial organization. The growth of knowledge and technique in every field —in accounting or selling or foreign marketing or research in new products and techniques—leads to the specialization of certain people, and thus certain organization units, in performing the tasks to which they give rise. The jack-of-all-trades entrepreneur gradually turns more and more of these tasks over to hired specialists, and himself becomes more and more a specialist in the pure function of entrepreneurship.

This sort of development obviously affects the optimum size of firm and—still speaking broadly—has served to increase the average size of firm greatly in manufacturing, finance, and utilities but relatively little in most lines of trade and service. Still, the increase apparently has not outstripped the growth of economic activity in our economy, for the individual firm in these areas most affected has, on average, fallen in size relative to the market in the United States in this century.

Industrial research is in fact another force which is apparently making for larger firm sizes. In 1940 there was a substantial correlation between average firm size and the percentage of an industry's labor force composed of engineers.[17] In 1951 a dominant share of the expenditures on research was made by large companies— roughly 67 per cent of the total was spent by 222 companies with 5,000 or more employees.[18] Of course some half of the research was paid for by the federal government, and departments of defense will deal exclusively with big companies up to the full limit of congressional tolerance. Moreover, the concentration of industrial research is in part an organizational and statistical illusion, for only in the larger companies will there be the full specialization of research and the segregation of research expenditures necessary for inclusion in studies such as that just referred to. I suspect that, if comparable studies were made of separately budgeted expenditures on, or specialized personnel in, labor relations or controlling inventory or paying taxes, a similar or greater concentration would be found. Yet, even with these qualifications, it is probable that research activity is much more highly concentrated than productive activity.

There are two very powerful reasons, however, for believing that the growth of scientific research in industry will not revolutionize the firm structure of industries. The first reason is simply that it has not done so in the last two centuries. The growth of scientific knowledge and its application to industrial life are in no sense new devel-

17. This analysis was made of twenty-four two-digit industry classes in manufacturing and mining—admittedly the classes are too broad, but data (from the Population Census and Statistics of Income) were not available at a more detailed level. The coefficient was .510, where firm size was measured by average total assets.

18. *Scientific Research and Development in American Industry* (Bureau of Labor Statistics Bull. 1148), p. 60. The Bureau of Labor Statistics estimated that companies making 85 per cent of research expenditures were included, but the estimate seems improbably high.

opments, and any forces they contain which make for large firms should be of the same type, although quite possibly somewhat larger (or smaller) in magnitude, than in the last two centuries. Yet in the past three-quarters of a century—the only period in which we have any quantitative notions on the firm-size structure of industries—there have been no revolutions in this structure, except the one associated with the merger movement of 1896–1904.

The second reason is that, with the growth of research, new firms will emerge to provide specialized facilities for small firms. It is only to be expected that, when a new kind of research develops, at first it will be conducted chiefly as an ancillary activity by existing firms. Thus, according to the directory of research laboratories of the National Research Council, there were about forty companies with research laboratories engaged in research on television in 1950, and, of these, thirty-three, or about 82 per cent, were manufacturing companies—many of which were willing to rent out the services of their research laboratories. In the older petroleum refining industry, on the other hand, there were about sixty companies engaged extensively in research (plus many more which did some research in the field), and, of these, thirty-one, or 52 per cent, were commercial laboratories working for hire. We may expect the rapid expansion of the specialized research laboratory, selling its services generally. These specialized laboratories need not be in the least inferior to "captive" laboratories. Indeed, if one may argue from a field like legal research, where the best lawyers are generally in independent practice and not corporation counsel because even the largest companies do not require continuously the best legal talent, one may expect that the commercial research laboratories will not have inferior professional staffs. If the performing of research, like the hauling of goods over steel rails, is most efficiently performed upon a vast scale, then vast firms will appear to undertake this work.

The problem of industrial research seems to me to be misinterpreted when it is stated primarily in terms of the application of scientific knowledge to industrial ends. A small fraction of the population has always had clever and subtle ideas, some of which were quite unfamiliar (and sometimes incomprehensible) to men of affairs. The basic task of the forward-looking entrepreneur has been to select from this large array of possibilities the few ideas that were worth putting into commercial practice. In making this hard choice, the entrepreneur has faced the problem of understanding the ideas and translating them into workable technologies. But he has also had to decide which ideas the market wants and how to devise a technology that is economical, not merely feasible—one, in other words, that pays proper attention to prices.

The crucial task of industrial research, on this reading, has not been to produce new ideas; imaginative man has turned out many of these in all but the worst ages of scientific thought. Rather, it has been to read the future demands and future costs of products and processes which have never existed. And this task cannot even now be turned over to a scientist or engineer in his professional capacity, for in his professional capacity the scientist or engineer is quite incompetent to make such estimates. (The fact that among the nation's 900,000 scientists and engineers there are some men with great entrepreneurial ability is of course no contradiction of my statement.)

One may say that we confront now merely a new stage in specialization. The entrepreneur no longer builds his own little plant, or takes home the receipts each night and hides them under his pillow, or oils the more expensive machinery on arriving at work in the morning. And now, perhaps, he is leaving more of the details of devising products and processes to another class of employees, but this does not change the fundamental nature of the economic system.

The public, which in this area certainly includes the members of the technological professions, is prone to believe that the residual task of the entrepreneur is simple—that it is hard and wonderful to find a new machine or fiber but elementary and pedestrian to arrange for its production and sale. On a broad view of economic history this is either an irrelevant or a mistaken view; only a few social organizations permit and even fewer incite the economy to continued progress. But here I find myself about to preach a sermon on the importance of social organization to a group of social scientists, and surely the glories of virtue should not be extolled to a group made up only of saints.

Some International Aspects of
Economic Stabilization

To keep my task within manageable proportions, this paper is limited to *some* international aspects only of the problems of economic stabilization. Two omissions, in particular, are important and should be noted. First, except for a brief comment on international buffer stocks, I do not deal with possibilities of and proposals for managed economic stabilization on a global, or near-global, basis, but confine myself to the international aspects of *national* stabilization programs. Second, I do not attempt to carry my analysis at any point to the stage where it could justifiably be claimed for it that it provides an adequate basis for a specific national policy decision, and I confine myself fairly strictly to technical economic analysis, without undertaking to adjudicate between conflicting objectives or to deliver final verdicts on the political or administrative feasibility of particular proposals. Further to limit my task, I abbreviate my analysis wherever I feel that it is routine and not highly controversial, and I provide detailed argument only when I am aware that my conclusions, or my methods of reaching them, go counter to widely accepted doctrine.

My major emphasis will be on the compatibilities and incompatibilities as between different stabilization objectives, bearing in mind always that one economist's "stability" may be another one's "rigidity" and that, similarly, one economist's "instability" may be another one's "flexibility." The stabilities whose compatibility with each other I will consider are, for countries in general: national price-level stability in terms of some index number; employment stabilization in terms of the maintenance of a high-level ratio of employed to those wishing employment; balance-of-payments stabilization in terms of the avoidance of undesired major deficits or surpluses on current income and capital account combined; and exchange-rate stability in terms of an index of the average value in foreign currencies of the national currency. I will also consider, as a special case, with reference to buffer-stock proposals, the desire of undeveloped or "colonial" countries for cyclical and secular stability in their commodity terms of trade with the outside world.

Unless clear indication is given to the contrary, there will be assumed throughout: free market competitive economies; flexible prices for particular commodities and factors; and the absence of important direct controls. It is also assumed throughout that relative expansion within a national economy of the production of a particular commodity will in the absence of innovations in technology take place under conditions of relatively increasing marginal costs of production. I believe this last to be a substantially realistic assumption. But, whether it is or not, a departure from it would complicate my analysis and require reconsideration of some of my conclusions.

Let us assume first that all or most trading countries successfully maintain stability of their national price levels in terms of comprehensive national index numbers. It is familiar, and I believe correct, doctrine that this would be incompatible with assured maintenance, as under an international gold standard, of stable or approximately stable exchange rates throughout either a theoretical or a historical long run. As far as I know, this has been disputed only by exponents of an unqualified purchasing-power-parity theory of the foreign exchanges, and by them only on the basis of abstraction from or disregard of the probability that through time reciprocal demands would shift, owing to disparate changes in wants and in conditions of production, and that such shifts would in the long run at least require compensatory shifts either in national price levels, however computed, or in exchange rates.

Stability of national price levels and of exchange rates may be compatible, however, for short runs of fairly long duration. What would be required to make this possible is, first, that the shifts in reciprocal demands be of moderate proportions and not continuously in the same direction and that there be available a substantial stock, widely distributed, of internationally liquid assets, including as such firm international lines of credit as well as gold to take care of temporary balance-of-payments disequilibriums. Balance-of-payments deficits and surpluses would occur, but they would grow cumulatively to unmanageable or intolerable proportions only if they maintained a chronic constancy of direction. Stable national price levels plus stable exchanges would be consistent with stable employment in all the countries, provided factor prices were flexible and there were substantial interindustry mobility of the factors of production.

The simultaneous possibility of stability for periods of some duration here posited for national price levels, exchange rates, and employment levels thus requires flexibility in other sectors, notably in relative prices within national price structures, in factor prices, in allocation of resources by the market, and in international gold and credit flows, and depends on the shifts in reciprocal demands not being sufficiently marked or continuous in duration to exceed the capacity of these flexibilities to compensate for them. The same reasoning would apply to a model identical in all respects except that all national price levels, instead of being maintained at stable levels, moved up or down simultaneously and proportionately.

These models are fundamentally unrealistic on at least two counts: first, the assumption that all, or many, countries maintain parallelism in the movement—or absence of movement—of their price levels and, second, that there prevails considerable flexibility, downward as well as upward, of factor prices. Many of the problems of international equilibrium which trouble economists and statesmen today arise in large part out of national divergences in price-level movements, and there would be general agreement that few if any industrialized countries today would enforce or even permit a substantial degree of wage deflation in preference to inflation as a means of maintaining stable employment. I move on, therefore, to some radically different models.

First, let us assume that your country successfully maintains price-level stability but that there prevails generally in the outside world an inflationary trend and that there is not under way a persistent shift against your country in reciprocal demands as a result of an unfavorable shift in wants or a favorable shift in costs. (The reasoning would not change significantly if your country also was inflating but at a slower rate than the rest of the world as a whole.)

To prevent the average value of its currency in terms of foreign currencies from rising, your country would have to accept an indefinite accumulation of gold, or lend abroad at an annual rate sufficient to offset surpluses in its annual balances of payments on current trade account, or progressively lower its import duties and other import barriers sufficiently to prevent continuing export surpluses, or adopt some combination of these procedures. Otherwise, it must allow the average exchange value of its currency to rise until equilibrium is restored in its balance of payments.

So far I have assumed that your country is determined to maintain a stable national price level, whatever other instabilities that may involve. I will now assume that the problem is one of avoiding balance-of-payments deficits when your country's price level is rising absolutely and relatively to the world price level. If the relative rise of your country's price level is the result of a relative shift in its favor of reciprocal demands, then, given appropriate strength of the various factors, it will be possible for it to maintain that rise while maintaining a stable exchange value for its currency and an even balance of payments. A country in this situation has the choice between surrendering price-level stability, surrendering balance-of-payments equilibrium, or surrendering exchange stability. In other words, it has a choice between inflation, or balance-of-payments surpluses, or exchange appreciation, with two stabilities available to it at the cost of one instability. Whichever procedure it follows, its commodity terms of trade will improve. If, on the other hand, the relative rise in your country's price level is due to internal monetary causes, a balance-of-payments deficit can be avoided by allowing your country's currency to depreciate in exchange value (or by progressively raising import tariffs). An "ideal" index of commodity terms of trade would, under these circumstances, show only moderate and temporary fluctuations and would have no trend.

Analogous reasoning would apply where it is the price levels of the external world which are remaining stable while your country's price level is falling. (a) If the relative fall in your country's price level is the result of an internal monetary deflation, with reciprocal demands remaining unchanged, your country will have either an appreciating foreign exchange value for its currency or a balance-of-payments surplus and an indefinite accumulation of gold and claims on other countries, which will have either to be sterilized or to be used in making investments abroad. There will be no trend in your country's terms of trade. (*b*) If the relative fall in your country's price level is the result of, or is associated with, a corresponding adverse relative shift in reciprocal demands, exchange stability and balance-of-payments equilibrium will be maintained; but the commodity terms of trade will move against it, and indexes of national real income and of factor prices will move downward. If factor prices do not have adequate downward flexibility, there will also be chronic unemployment.

The cases of relative shifts in reciprocal demands are of special importance for countries whose national economies are heavily dependent on the export receipts of a few staple commodities which are liable to have pronounced secular adverse relative shifts in prices on world markets and, if they are primary commodities, are also liable to have pronounced cyclical shifts in prices in the same direction as the world cycle but with greater amplitude of fluctuations. Both of these types of shifts in relative prices could occur even in a world of stabilized national price levels, although the amplitudes of cyclical shifts would then in all probability be much smaller than in recent decades or than in the nineteenth century.

It is often proposed to deal with this problem by means of international buffer stocks. It is not appropriate to enter here into an examination of all the administrative difficulties, real or supposed, major or minor, including the difficulties of obtaining international agreement, of distinguishing between cyclical fluctuations and secular trends in the prices of the buffer-stock commodities and of allocating to the participant countries the costs of financing, of storage, and of spoilage of the commodities held by the agency. In an inflationary world I do not see just what would be the appropriate criteria for purchase of commodities to initiate and maintain a buffer stock intended to stabilize price levels both secularly and cyclically. Perhaps the proper procedure in such circumstances would be to have the agency sell commodities short at a boom stage of a cycle as its first activity.

In most sympathetic studies of buffer-stock schemes it is argued or assumed that they could successfully be used as an instrument not only of stabilization of the prices of the commodities held in the stock but also of general price levels. Since, however, the commodities dealt with will necessarily not be a genuinely random sample of all commodities, the buffer-stock package is practically certain to have a cyclical and secular pattern of price behavior which, in the absence of a buffer stock, would diverge significantly from the pattern of fluctuation of a general price index. I see no reason why the existence of a buffer stock should change appreciably the secular relation of the prices of buffer-stock commodities to prices in general, except as the buffer stock may by indefinite accumulation or decumulation impose an artificial trend on the prices of the constituent commodities relative to prices in general. It seems to me, therefore, possible, in theory at least, that a "successful" buffer-stock scheme may operate to destabilize the rest of the price structure of the world and even to destabilize the world price level as a whole. I can perhaps make my point most simply by assuming that there exists a successful program of world price-level stabilization. To superimpose on this a buffer-stock stabilization scheme would make it more difficult rather than easier to maintain stabilization of the general price level. The two schemes would be compatible with each other only at the cost of introducing into the price structure abnormal synchronization of price behavior as between buffer-stock and non-buffer-stock commodities.

For countries which are heavy exporters of staple primary commodities, the instability of prices is a phenomenon of essentially external origin. For such countries a successful international buffer-stock scheme could make an important contribution to *cyclical* stabilization of national price levels, of national real and money incomes, and of commodity terms of trade and factoral terms of trade, single and double. Except by imposing an artificial relative price structure on the rest of the world, I do not see how a buffer-stock scheme could contribute to secular price-level stabilization even for the "colonial" countries.

"Colonial" countries are much concerned, and rightly so, with the trends in their terms of trade with the outside world. It needs to be recognized, however, that an adverse shift in the commodity terms of trade of a country will not involve an impairment of that country's economic position if it is causally associated with an offsetting decline in the "real" costs of production of that country's staple export commodities. In such circumstances there is no deterioration in that country's "double factoral" terms of trade, and, more important, there is no deterioration in its "single factoral" terms of trade or in the value of the imports it gets in return for the export of the product of one unit of "effort." Deterioration in the commodity terms of trade of a country reflects "economic welfare" deterioration only if the adverse trend of the commodity terms of trade arises out of an adverse trend in relative preferences of buyers for commodities, out of a rise in the "real" costs of production of its import commodities, out of a fall in the "real" costs of production of other countries' products which are close competitors abroad of this country's exports, or out of monopolistic or monopsonistic exploitation by foreign sellers or buyers.

In the preceding discussion, exchange-rate flexibility has been repeatedly postulated as offering a means of escape from national price-level instability, from balance-of-payments disequilibrium, or from unemployment or overemployment. This treatment of exchange-rate flexibility has been based on the common assumptions that an exchange rate is a market price having common characteristics with other market prices and that in free-market competitive economies which enjoy good monetary management changes in relative market prices in general perform socially useful stabilizing functions: they operate to adjust output to demand and consumption to output, to allocate resources to industries according to marginal factor productivities, to reward factors in conformity with their marginal contributions to national income, and so forth. It is, I believe, almost wholly reasoning by analogy of this kind, and almost not at all on the basis of specific examination, a priori or empirical, of the exchange market, which produces the analytical underpinning for the large, growing, and impressive literature which finds in exchange-rate flexibility either a major remedy for all or most undesired instabilities, intranational and international, or at the least a powerful instrument for moderating them.

Reasoning by analogy alone is always dangerous, however, and should always be regarded with suspicion. The currently fashionable treatment of exchange flexibility as something approaching a cure-all seems to me to be conspicuously a case in point. It is always conceivable that there may be something peculiar about a commodity and/or its market which makes the behavior of its price, or the effects of that behavior, also peculiar in some crucial respect. I believe this to be the case, to give concrete examples, for the short-term interest rate and the market for short-term loan funds and for the price of gold when it is used as a monetary standard. I believe it is the case also for the exchange rate and *its* market.

One peculiarity of the exchange market is that it is adapted to—invites—speculative activity beyond any other market except the race track and its equivalents. The commodities which the exchange market deals in, foreign currencies, are, beyond any other commodity, homogeneous, standardized, durable. They have zero storage costs, and financial carrying costs which have zero as their floor and, as their ceiling, the excess of (*a*) what could be earned by the funds employed in exchange speculation in the money market of that country, of the two relevant countries, which has the higher interest rates over (*b*) what is actually earned with these funds. Perhaps it would be more accurate to say that the ceiling of financial carrying costs is the excess of what could be earned in any other use by the funds employed in exchange speculation over what they actually earn in interest when so employed. In any case, the financial carrying costs are peculiarly low, and, when exchange rates are free to fluctuate, the swings in rates are always large enough to provide the successful speculator with an ample reward for his trouble and risk.

It is widely, and perhaps authoritatively, held that speculation tends to stabilize the price of the commodity which is the subject of speculation and that this means that the price of a commodity which is subject to active speculation will on the whole, other things equal, be more stable, relative to prices in general, and in any case be freer from abnormal or undesirable fluctuations, than one which affords no or fortuitously restricted opportunities for the speculator. If this were true, the fact that exchange rates lend themselves peculiarly to speculation would be an argument for, rather than one against, flexibility of exchange rates. The theory of speculation puzzles me. In any case, this is not a proper occasion, nor do I have the qualifications, to explore its mysteries. I will, therefore, concede, for present purposes, that, if the only relevant peculiarity which distinguished exchange rates from other prices were their special amenableness to the attentions of speculators, this would strengthen, instead of weaken, the case for flexibility of exchange rates.

Exchange rates, as compared to other prices, have, however, another peculiarity. An exchange rate is the price in terms of each other of units of two national currencies. A fiat national currency is a commodity which is produced by a single producer, or a single money-creating system. It is a commodity which, for its producer, has zero real cost, and therefore has no external or objective limitations to its output. It is produced, or can be produced, without cost, in whatever quantities its producers decide upon. There are therefore no ceiling and no floor, imposed by external and independent cost factors, to its price in terms of another national currency, and no floor to its price in terms of the prices of other commodities. It similarly has no price ceiling or price floor derived from any direct utility as a consumers' good or any indirect utility as an ingredient, a technical coefficient, in the production of producers' or consumers' goods.

Foreign exchange may be a "commodity" and an exchange rate may be a "price," but for the reasons given the "commodity" is unlike all other commodities, and the "price" is unlike all other prices. The peculiarities of the commodity and of the price could very well be relevant to a discussion of the probable mode of operation of the price if left free to respond to market forces. The peculiarities seem to me to be obvious ones and have seemed to me to be so since longer than the memory of man runs. They cannot possibly have escaped—they surely have not been allowed to escape—the notice of the enthusiastic advocates of exchange-rate flexibility. Diligent search, however, has failed to reveal any express recognition of them in the published writings of these advocates. It is surely clear that standard theory of speculation cannot be applied in routine fashion to a commodity whose supply and whose demand have no upward or downward limitations arising out of cost limitations on output or out of want limitations on "marketability."

It has been objected against the argument presented here that the distinction I draw between speculation in commodities and speculation in currencies on the basis that currencies have neither value ceiling nor value floor is an invalid one, since speculation in commodities also involves speculation in the relevant currency. It is

true, of course, that buying commodities when inflation is anticipated or selling them when deflation is anticipated is really speculating on the internal purchasing power of a currency. But is there
not a great deal of commodity speculation which is not governed
by any particular anticipations as to the general price level but is
based on expectations as to the relative price trend of the particular
commodity as compared to the trend of the general price level?
Even when commodity speculation *is* equivalent to currency speculation, moreover, it is speculation as to the value of one currency in
terms of commodities in general and not speculation in the value of
one currency in terms of another currency, so that even here there
is an important and relevant difference between commodity-market
speculation and exchange-market speculation.

It cannot be inferred from the peculiarities of the exchange rate
that I have been insisting upon that there is no influence of the
change in price of a national currency in the exchange market or in
commodity markets on the output of that currency, but such influence is exercised only via the policy of the monetary authorities and
can take very peculiar forms. Under frequent circumstances, if not
generally where there is not a monetary "policy" specifically aimed
at preventing this from occurring, a fall in the price of a national
currency tends to put pressure on the producer of the currency to
increase its output, to speed up the printing presses, or to make
larger entries in the books which in the monetary field represent, in
relation to the stock of money, what farms and factories represent
in relation to stocks of other commodities.

In the technical literature on speculation, it seems always to be
assumed that the speculator is guessing or forecasting what future
outputs or the future price will be of the commodity he is speculating on but never—at least substantially and in the long or longish
run—that the speculator is determining what the future output or
the future price is to be. So in the modern argument for flexibility
of the exchanges it seems to be generally assumed that the relations
between national price levels determine what exchange rates shall
be, with implicit denial that the levels of exchange rates determine
what the relations between national price levels shall be. The exchange rates, in this theory, are always dependent variables, never
independent variables.

Let us suppose that a "bear" drive by speculators on the exchange value of the currency of a particular country, arising spontaneously and without objective justification, lowers significantly the exchange-market quotations for that currency. Other things equal, import and export prices and the prices of import-competing commodities will rise in that country. There will be a demand for increased bank credit in consequence on the part of businessmen, and for increased wages on the part of labor, and it will be "good business," as far as atomistic calculations go, to yield to these demands. The government's expenditures also will rise, because of higher unit monetary costs; and, unless its revenue system is fully equipped with built-in stabilizers, it will incur a budgetary deficit. This deficit in the usual course of events it will finance by issuing more government money or by borrowing from the banks. An internal inflation will thus be generated. This will tend to generate a balance-of-payments deficit, which in turn will press on the exchange rate and give a profitable outcome to the original "bear" operations of the speculators, which will provide a stimulus to them to proceed further in the same direction, and so on indefinitely.

In this picture exchange rates act on relative national price levels as well as being acted upon by them, and speculators "make" future exchange rates as well as forecasting them and thus cause their forecasts to be correct. It is not a grossly unrealistic picture. It has had numerous substantial exemplifications in the past. It seems to fit reasonably closely the Chilean and Brazilian patterns today. Were it not for the operation of one automatic or "natural" factor and two "artificial" or policy factors, it would be a widespread phenomenon whenever a firm international gold standard was not operating.

The automatic or "natural" factor consists of the intellectually trivial but practically very important fact that the operations and activities of any country which tend to be exchange-depreciating for it *ipso facto* tend to be exchange-appreciating for other countries. In the exchange market the "bear" speculator is equally a "bull" speculator, depending on which of the relevant currencies you prefer to look at. The speculator selects for his "bearish" attentions, of course, the currency which he believes to be weak or already under pressure, but whether or not he is aware of it, and counting on it, his selection adds to the weakness and the pressure in a direction which will tend to make his forecast come true. But he will not succeed if an even more powerful "bear" raid is going on against the other relevant currency.

The "policy" factors which work against "bear" speculation are national concern that inflation, or at least relative inflation as compared to other countries, shall not occur and national concern that the national currency shall not depreciate in the exchange market. The former concern seems often to be absent or weak and, if present, to be wholly or largely derivative from the second. For many countries the concern that the national currency shall not depreciate in the exchange market, that is, that it shall not have downward exchange flexibility, seems to be the only factor of any strength which puts a brake on inflation.

To return to my first case, of the general prevalence of successful national price-level stabilization programs. In such a world, speculation in the exchange market could not of itself be a significant factor in determining the trend of exchange rates, and the distinction I have made between how speculation works in the ordinary commodity market and how it can work in the foreign-exchange market would not be valid. The exchange speculator would, by hypothesis, be powerless to make his forecasts true by influencing the national price levels in the direction of his forecasts. In such a world, however, the scope for fluctuations in exchange rates and therefore the role, for good or bad, of exchange flexibility would be limited. There might in such a case be a trend in reciprocal demands which would, in time, cause more or less serious balance of payments and other difficulties under stable exchanges. I am skeptical, however, as to the possibility of anyone, whether official or private speculator, forecasting such a trend with justified assurance, and I doubt that in such a case a flexibility of the exchanges which was limited to *ad hoc* adjustments after the trend had fairly clearly manifested itself would by this limitation surrender any stabilizing effect of much consequence.

For a country, however, which successfully stabilizes its price level in what is predominantly an unstabilized world, exchange flexibility becomes important and urgent if serious balance-of-payments disequilibrium, accompanied by boom, or by major unemployment, and by major distortions of the price structure, are to be avoided.

Even in such a case, however, I am, as yet, unprepared to support a fully "floating" exchange rate, if by that is meant a rate which is left free from official interference either overt or in the form of official decisions and actions which influence the exchange rate and which are themselves a response to the behavior of the exchange rate. The decision as to whether an exchange rate is actually a floating rate should not be made to depend on whether or not government acts upon it with intent to change it or to keep it from changing. This would make the criterion not what the government does but why it does it. This is often something no outsider can know, and sometimes perhaps something no one can know, even when there are formal affirmations of, or disclaimers of, intent.

Canada and Peru are now being cited as instances of floating exchanges and usually as instances of the satisfactory operation of floating exchanges. I know nothing of the Peruvian case, but that does not prevent me from being highly skeptical that it is a genuine instance of an exchange rate whose behavior in Period 1 does not lead to official action which will influence the exchange rate of Period 2. In Canada there has been disclaimer of any official intention to influence the trend of the United States dollar–Canadian dollar exchange rate. There is in Canada, however, an official Exchange Fund Account which operates in the exchange market with declared intent of smoothing out fluctuations in the exchange market without influencing underlying trends. Also, by its decisions as to whether debt-refunding operations shall be carried out in the domestic or in the American market, and by its shifts from an easier money to a tighter money monetary policy, and vice versa, the Canadian government exerts influence on the exchange market. In the case of exchange stabilization funds intended to "smooth out fluctuations," as in the case of American Federal Reserve activities to maintain an "orderly market" in government securities, the only way in which anyone, whether insider or outsider, can tell whether the operations actually influenced the trend over a period of time is to see, *ex post*, whether the holdings by the relevant fund, of foreign exchange, or of government securities, have changed over the period in question. With respect to Canadian debt-funding operations and monetary policy activities which influence the exchanges, one cannot be confident that they have not also been influenced by the behavior of the exchange rate, given the unobtainability and perhaps the nonexistence of knowledge of the precise monetary and other objectives of Canadian officialdom. But, even if the Canadian dollar has been a completely floating currency over the past few years, I can see no important lesson to be drawn from it so far, given the relevant circumstances of the period, except that in some circumstances the adoption of a floating currency does not lead to disaster—or does not lead to it quickly.

A major motivation of the strong advocacy of flexible exchanges is the belief that such flexibility, by relieving countries of balance-of-payments disequilibrium, removes or weakens the inducements to resort to direct controls. I have agreed above that under certain hypothetical circumstances flexibility of exchanges will contribute to balance-of-payments equilibrium. I readily agree also that under some circumstances, probably frequently approximated in modern times, an adjustment of the exchanges is a necessary condition of removal of both balance-of-payments pressure and direct controls. The one thing which seriously bothers me about national commitment to flexibility of the exchange is that, in many countries, it would remove the only restraint of any strength against marked inflation, namely, the widespread official and public dislike of exchange depreciation. No country, as far as I know, has as yet adopted highly flexible exchanges in order to get rid of direct controls. Historically, it seems to have been the dislike of chronic depreciation of the exchange value of their currencies which has been the most frequent and most powerful motive which has led countries to adopt direct exchange and foreign-trade controls. It has not been flexibility of the exchanges which has been, so far, the important substitute for direct controls, but rather the adoption of indirect monetary and fiscal controls to prevent relative inflation and of these internal controls and flexible tariff policy to restore balance-of-payments equilibrium.

I will conclude with some brief and negativistic comments on two types of fashionable theorizing which have been applied to explanation of the mode of operation of flexible exchange rates. I have, within the limits of my paper, found no occasion for resort to multiplier analysis. The models I have used embrace, either explicitly or implicitly, assumptions as to the behavior of national supplies of money and as to the effect of such behavior on national money income, as well as other assumptions as to market-price flexibilities, which leave no scope, except in the shortest of short runs, for the multiplier to operate in the manner attributed to it in standard multiplier theory. My assumptions are not fully realistic, but I think they are nearer to being so than the standard assumptions of multiplier theory in any situation in which substantially increased quantities of input items are not obtainable by entrepreneurs except at higher prices.

I also make no use of currently standard foreign-exchange theory which operates with partial-equilibrium national import demand and export supply curves and elasticities, treated as independent of each other, and with national demands for and supplies of foreign exchange, derived from the former. In these models, national money incomes, import demand curves, and export supply curves are treated as invariant in terms of national currencies regardless of what happens to the exchange rates, as are also prices of home commodities in home-currency terms. Analysis of this sort is used by some to show the effectiveness of exchange-rate flexibility as a balance-of-payments equilibrating device and by others to show the possibility that there may be no exchange rate which will result in stable equilibrium.

The disregard of interdependencies which this type of analysis involves has always made it a meaningless type of analysis for me, logically in all cases, practically for all countries which cannot reasonably be treated as having stocks of internationally liquid assets approaching infinity and economic entanglements with foreign countries approaching zero. There may be a way to bring such analysis into touch with reality by postulating the direction of change in its findings as elements of hitherto disregarded interdependence are introduced into the models. It seems simpler and safer to me to begin the analysis with the recognition of all the obviously important interdependencies.

It has been thrown up against me that I have myself in the past engaged in international trade analysis in terms of "elasticities." The procedure I here object to, and have upon other occasions objected to, is so prevalent, and the temptation to resort to it because of the aid it lends to the production of easy answers to otherwise difficult questions is so overpowering, that I may well be tainted with the general corruption. While this may reflect on me, however, I do not see that it reflects on my argument. I would like it to be clear, however, that it is not at all to the use of "elasticity" concepts in international trade theory that I object but only to the use of partial-equilibrium elasticities of the Marshallian demand-for-tea type.

Let me, in conclusion, state my position in a somewhat different way. Given competitive free markets and the absence of chronically disequilibrating patterns of expectations, it seems to me axiomatic in the light of general price theory that there will always be some exchange rate which in the circumstances of the period will be a balance-of-payments equilibrating one. If I have earlier seemed to argue to the contrary, I think it will be found upon examination that I was introducing into my analysis, via the naughty speculator, the assumed prevalence in the prevailing circumstances of disequilibrating anticipations as to the future. I would defend the realism and relevance of such an assumption for much of our recent history.

The Study of Public Opinion*

This occasion has two themes. One is provided by the Twenty-fifth Anniversary of the Social Science Research Building at the University of Chicago and the other by the heading under which this session is listed in the program: "Social Science as Science." These themes are particularly appropriate for a discussion of the study of public opinion.

The Nature of the Field—1930 and 1955

Before inquiring into the history of the field, I must pause to define. Years ago I learned in these halls that, before one discussed a topic, it was sometimes desirable to define it. I hope I may be excused if I define "public opinion" quickly, mainly because my use of the term will, I think, be clear as I go on. For my purpose here, let me take each term separately and point not only to its substance but also to the resultant technical development. By "public" I mean to refer to the magnitude involved—that is, to non-private, non-individualized feelings and responses of large numbers of people. This characteristic of public opinion necessitates the use of sample surveys. By "opinion" I mean to include not only the usual sense of opinion on topical, ephemeral, and typically political issues but also attitudes, sentiments, values, information, and related actions. To get at them properly necessitates the use not only of questionnaires and interviews but also of projective and scaling devices.

Now for the anniversary theme: What has happened to the study of public opinion in the last twenty-five years? The shortest answer is, "A lot." A longer answer will require the remainder of this paper simply to outline.

Think back twenty or twenty-five years. This backward glance is

* It should go without saying that this paper presents the personal view of the author and not the official view of The Ford Foundation or its Behavioral Sciences Program.

nicely facilitated by the convenient publication in those years of the *Encyclopedia of the Social Sciences* (the volume containing the article on public opinion appeared in 1933) and of the first edition of the Smith-Lasswell-Casey bibliography (1935) and by the establishment of the Roper-*Fortune* and Gallup-AIPO polls (1935) and of the *Public Opinion Quarterly* (1937). The peculiarly modern study of public opinion began in those years, and it is probably not too much to say that the period around 1935 represents a watershed in the development of the field. How different the study of public opinion is now from then!

Start with the *Encyclopedia of the Social Sciences*. The central article on public opinion was written by Wilhelm Bauer, a German scholar whose first major book on the *öffentliche Meinung* was written in 1914. His article would sound strange to a contemporary student of public opinion—if he were to read it, which he most likely would not, since it is so out of harmony with current interests. Even in the early 1930's, incidentally, Bauer was able to identify the trend: "Suspected by the systematic historian . . . it [the term 'public opinion'] has been taken over as a rule by the journalists and social psychologists and in the process frequently stripped of many of its historical associations." To the present-day student, Bauer's definition of public opinion includes both too much and not enough: "Public opinion . . . is a deeply pervasive organic force, intimately bound up with the ideological and emotional interplay of the social groupings in which since the earliest times gregarious individuals have come together; it articulates and formulates not only the deliberative judgments of the rational elements within the collectivity but the evanescent common will, which somehow integrates and momentarily crystallizes the sporadic sentiments and loyalties of the masses of the population." Of his two types of public opinion—the static ("traditional custom") and the dynamic (topical, based on the mass media, "rational")—only the latter is now considered as within the field, the former being the preserve of the historian and the cultural anthropologist. In the tradition of good European scholarship, the body of Bauer's article deals with the state of public opinion through much of Western history—an emphasis by itself enough to make it seem prehistoric to today's specialists. He starts with the ancient kingdom in Egypt; works through the older Sumerian civilizations, the Israelites, Greece and Rome, the Reformation, seventeenth-century England, and the French Revolution; and ends right up to date with the threat of radio to the newspaper. The article is characterized by phrases that would not now be found in the pages of the *Public Opinion Quarterly*—phrases like "organic force," "common will," "driving emotional forces latent in the anonymous masses," "collective mind of the community." The bibliography lists works by Tarde (1910), Dicey (1914), MacDougall (1920), Tönnies (1922), Lippmann (1922), Martin (1924), and Lowell (1926)—not a poller among them!

But polling was represented in the *Encyclopedia of the Social Sciences,* though under its earlier name (straw polls), in an article written by one of the first pollers (Claude Robinson). In this brief exposition of—even then!—the uses and abuses of the polls, perhaps the most noteworthy statement is Robinson's conclusion on what has become to some the most burning question in this field, namely, the accuracy of the polls: "Comparison of straw and official pluralities in the past shows varying degrees of correspondence, the most common differences ranging from six to 12 votes for every hundred in the total cast. For the most part, these differences are attributable to faulty sampling technique and they will probably decrease materially as sponsors become more skilled in managing such canvasses." Whether the halving of this error in twenty-five years would be considered a "material decrease," I leave to the experts to debate—as well as the prior question of whether the error has been halved!

Finally, the *Encyclopedia of the Social Sciences* contained an article on "Attitudes, Social" (by L. L. Bernard) that also would sound archaic today. Social attitudes are there classified according to "the collective relationships which standardize and stereotype attitudes through interconditioning (urban, rural, sectarian, racial, nationalistic, political, occupational, etc.); the objective or aim of the behaving person (humanitarian, exploiting, protective, etc.); the valuation placed upon the objective or the technique utilized (approving, discouraging, etc.); the object calling forth the attitudinal response (attitudes toward money, radicals, sex, etc.); and the time reference of the attitude (traditional, progressive, temporary, permanent, etc.)." "Public opinion is the highest form of collective attitudes . . . [Bernard writes]. In the collective adjustment situation it is public opinion which serves to criticize and reorganize, or sometimes to rationalize and justify, the existing collective attitudes."

So it was then. What is the general situation today? In the last twenty or twenty-five years the field of public opinion study has grown tremendously—perhaps as much as any field in the social sciences. Since 1937 it has had its own professional journal and since 1947 its own professional association. The first edition of the Smith-Lasswell-Casey bibliography contained 4,500 items from the beginning to 1934; the second edition contained 3000 items for the nine years from 1934 to 1943. The compilers of 1943 starred 150 "outstanding titles"; 60 per cent of them had appeared since mid-1934. The establishment in 1936 of the Roper and Gallup surveys was followed by the establishment of numerous polling organizations in this country, in almost all the developed countries (probably all but the U.S.S.R.), and in some of the underdeveloped countries as well. The first compilation of public opinion poll results, for the period 1935–46, runs to about 1,200 pages and includes about 12,000 items from sixteen countries covering over five hundred topics ranging, alphabetically, from "Absenteeism (Labor)" to "Worry." The latest two *Readers* on public opinion, published in 1953 and 1954, together include 130 selections (with practically no overlap) of which 102 appeared after 1940 and another 18 after 1930. According to them, then, the intellectual content of the field consists over 90 per cent of what was done in the period we are reviewing.

Nor is the expansion visible only within the field as narrowly defined. The recent publication of another *Handbook of Social Psychology* testifies to the contribution of public opinion studies to the wider field in which it falls. In the 1935 *Handbook*, one chapter out of twenty-three was devoted to "Attitudes." In the 1954 *Handbook* seven chapters out of thirty are devoted to subjects directly involved with public opinion studies—three methodological ("Attitude Measurement," "The Interview," "Content Analysis") and four substantive ("Prejudice and Ethnic Relations," "Mass Phenomena," "Effects of the Mass Media of Communications," and "The Psychology of Voting: An Analysis of Political Behavior")—and another chapter on "Public Opinion" itself was commissioned but never delivered.

Furthermore, the growth of this field can be illustrated by the fact that within a recent period of three years it received the distinction of being given full-scale criticism by distinguished critics from the three academic disciplines most directly concerned, appropriately distributed by content. The one by the psychologist, McNemar, is devoted to method; the one by the sociologist, Blumer, to concepts and theory; and the one by the political scientist, Rogers, to implications for policy. In fact, the field is apparently so important that Blumer—presumably finding it still viable seven years after his first effort!—returned to it only a few months ago in his presidential address to the Society for the Study of Social Problems.

Finally, though the field is much less developed in Britain than here, it has appropriately remained for a British scholar to crown it —or rather, to be exact, one part of it—with a classical title: psephology! In sum, the field has been extremely active and energetic in the last twenty to twenty-five years. It has not been without its moments of crisis and trial, but on the whole it has had at least its share of the Lasswellian values of income, safety, and deference.

Perhaps the 1930–55 comparison can best be summed up by a list of ten important titles that appear prominently in representative bibliographies of each of the two periods:

1930	1955
Tocqueville, *Democracy in America*, 1835	Lasswell and Blumenstock, *World Revolutionary Propaganda*, 1939
Thompson, *Public Opinion and Lord Beaconsfield*, 1886	Gosnell, *Grass Roots Politics*, 1942
Bryce, *The American Commonwealth*, 1899	Newcomb, *Personality and Social Change*, 1943
Lowell, *Public Opinion and Popular Government*, 1913	Cantril *et al.*, *Gauging Public Opinion*, 1944
Dicey, *Lectures on the Relation of Law and Public Opinion in England in the Nineteenth Century*, 1914	Lazarsfeld *et al.*, *The People's Choice*, 1945, and *Voting*, 1954
Lippmann, *Public Opinion*, 1922	Mosteller *et al.*, *The Pre-election Polls of 1948*, 1948
Tönnies, *Kritik der öffentliche Meinung*, 1922	Stouffer *et al.*, *The American Soldier*, 1949
Angell, *The Public Mind*, 1926	Adorno *et al.*, *The Authoritarian Personality*, 1950
Dewey, *The Public and Its Problems*, 1927	Cantril and Strunk, *Public Opinion, 1935–46*, 1951
Bauer, *Die öffentliche Meinung in der Weltgeschichte*, 1930	Hovland *et al.*, *Communication and Persuasion*, 1953

Now a number of observations emerge—or rather, spring!—from these lists (leaving aside the obvious point that the two groups of volumes do not always talk about the same thing). First, the titles prominent in the 1930 era were written over the period of a century; those of the 1955 era are concentrated in a decade and a half. Second, only three of the earlier authors are American; all the later authors are Americans. Third, only a few of the earlier works are written by academic people; all the later ones are. Fourth, the earlier works are all written by individuals; eight of the later works have double or usually multiple authorship by research teams. Fifth, each of the earlier titles is a broad "theoretical" treatise on the whole field or a big piece of it; none of the later titles is really that—they are field studies of particular and limited topics or a compilation of findings from such studies. Sixth, none of the earlier works could be called a technical treatise, nor are technical innovations introduced in any of them; of the later works, at least three are mainly technical contributions, and all the others could claim to make a technical contribution along with their substantive work. Seventh, none of the earlier works presents quantitative data to support its generalizations, though all make quantitative statements; all the later works are based on quantitative data. Eighth, only one or two of the earlier writers are specialists in this field, even at the time of writing; only one or two of the later authors are not. And, finally, ninth, most of the earlier writers are interested in public opinion only as part of some larger concern with a historical period or the social order or political democracy; all the later authors are concerned with public opinion per se.

Put together, these differences spell a revolutionary change in the field of public opinion studies: the field has become technical and quantitative, atheoretical, segmentalized, and particularized, specialized and institutionalized, "modernized" and "group-ized"—in short, as a characteristic behavioral science, Americanized. Twenty-five years ago and earlier, prominent writers, as part of their general concern with the nature and functioning of society, learnedly studied public opinion not "for itself" but in broad historical, theoretical, and philosophical terms and wrote treatises. Today, teams of technicians do research projects on specific subjects and report findings.

Twenty years ago the study of public opinion was part of scholarship; today it is part of science.

The Development of a Scientific Field

Here we pick up the second theme of this occasion—"Social Science as Science." For what has happened to the field of public opinion has happened to other fields within the social sciences—and over roughly the same period of time. Just as this field has been one of expansion, if not always development, and of change, if not always progress, so have other fields—for example, just to mention other topics on this program, studies of small groups, culture and personality, mathematical models, organization and administration. Accordingly, if we address ourselves to the question, "How has this change come about?" in the field of public opinion, we may hit upon certain characteristics of the development of other scientific fields as well.

I would like to try, in the most tentative way, to note certain phases that can be identified in the development of a science and then apply each of them to this particular field. These ways of developing may sometimes become a more or less orderly sequence of steps or stages, though that is by no means necessary. A particular science or field does not *have* to go through every phase, much less in sequence. I present these observations, I confess, with some trepidation. I recently put into print some observations on the state of the political theory of democracy, particularly in its relationship to empirical research, and I have not yet recovered from that bit of foolhardiness. I am not a political theorist, much less a historian of science. I set down these ideas as a call for help, not as a call to disciplinary arms.

There seem to me to be at least seven distinguishable phases in the natural history of a science. I shall use illustrations only from the social sciences, though I think this scheme is also applicable to medicine and possibly to the physical sciences as well.

First, consider the existence, the emergence, or the recognition of new problems.

It seems reasonably obvious that basic changes in society create or highlight problems that call for solution and hence invite study. The industrial revolution, for example, produced problems of capital formation, industrialism, international trade, and urbanism that directly stimulated economic thought as well as some early social surveys. The growth of British imperialism and colonialism was not without its effect upon the development of anthropology. The need to deal intellectually with practical political problems stimulated the political thought of such democratic philosophers and theorists as Hobbes, Locke, Burke, Bentham, and Mill in Britain and Jefferson, Hamilton, and Paine in America and characterized the distinctive definition given by Jacques Necker in France to *l'opinion publique* with a view to its effect upon governmental credit.

The emergence of a mass society—increased population, popular education, faster transportation, easier communication—together with the growth of democratic forms of government brought the problem of public opinion to the attention of responsive and responsible scholars. The first titles on our pre-1930 list illustrate this source of interest: Tocqueville and Bryce on American opinion in the nineteenth century, Thompson and Dicey on British opinion in the same century. The first stimulation of public opinion studies, then, came from the heightened existence and the heightened recognition of the phenomenon itself. Public opinion mattered and hence needed to be examined. As for the "revival" of the early thirties, all that needs to be said, I suppose, is that the crises of the Great Depression and the subsequent growth of big government increased sharply the people's interest in, concern with, and knowledge about public affairs and, accordingly, heightened the leaders' interest in, concern with, and knowledge about public opinion. Contributory factors were technological in origin—the invention and spread of radio, a medium that had to find and identify its audience, and, notably, the invention and spread of the Hollerith machine.

Second, there is a period of "grand" theoretical speculation about the subject.

Early in the development of a science there is room for "big new ideas," and they are usually produced. The new field is so new that observations come easy, and for some writers they culminate in the construction of a whole theoretical system, encompassing the entire subject or a large piece of it. Often such theories have a monistic character to them; sometimes they are more differentiated. Examples in the social sciences might include Marx and Adam Smith in what is now economics, Locke and Mill in what is now political science, Tylor and Morgan in what is now anthropology, Comte and Spencer in what is now sociology, Freud and James in what is now psychology.

In the field of public opinion a number of early writers would qualify—Bryce, Lippmann, Lowell, Tönnies, Bauer. Not all of them self-consciously set out to develop a theory of public opinion, but, whether they did or not, they were perceived as having done so or as having made the attempt. In any case, they opened up the field. They identified problems, they proposed concepts for use in analysis, they made empirical observations or at least references, and they helped to make the field respectable for intellectual inquiry. Whether their theories appear to a contemporary student to be "right" seems less important than these other contributions.

Third, there is the intensified collection of empirical data.

When the pioneers open up a new field of inquiry, they plow a lot of ground for lesser men to work. New ideas and concepts lead to newer ones, visible problems light up other problems, and the wheels begin to grind. Sometimes they do so in an eclectic way, sometimes in a doctrinaire. The motive may be to prove a theory right (e.g., the followers of Freud) or wrong (e.g., the opponents of Spencer's evolutionary theory) or both (e.g., the Marxians and anti-Marxians). But, whatever the motives, data begin to pile up—some good, some bad—and to gain attention. Sometimes they are collected directly for the purpose of testing theoretical formulations. More often, especially in the early stages, they are collected for other purposes but put to scientific use because nothing better is available (e.g., the use of market data by economists or census data by sociologists). This period is either the dawn of a new scientific era (if the data add up and you like what is happening) or the twilight of raw empiricism (if the data merely pile up and you do not).

In the field of public opinion, certain writers in the late twenties and early thirties can now be seen to exemplify this stage—and particularly at this university. Lasswell analyzed newspapers and leaflets for his *Propaganda Techniques in the World War*, Gosnell used election returns in his voting studies, Waples combined library and field data in his *People and Print*, Kornhauser began to relate opinion data to class position. Much earlier, Lowell had to build much of his analysis upon referendum statistics. As late as the early 1930's, in the section of *Recent Social Trends* that attempted to describe "attitudes and interests," the author had to rely not upon polled opinions but upon the content of newspapers and magazines as "reflective" of opinion. Now, thanks to years of polling, the author of such a section could rely directly upon poll data themselves. For example, a casual thumbing of the Cantril-Strunk compilation would tell him whether the distribution of information about birth control should be made legal (70 per cent "Yes" in 1936); how many Americans were eating less food in 1943 than in 1942 (21 per cent); how many people were worrying more than usual about their future (49 per cent in July, 1940); how many people thought that trial juries, in cases not involving murder, should be permitted to return a verdict by a three-fourths majority (57 per cent in 1936); and numerous other social and political facts. Indeed, there are those who believe that our society is now able, if it will, to collect systematically a wide variety of subjective and behavioral data by means of the sample survey—data on attitudes, values, patterns of morality, modes of child-rearing, religious observances, family practices, sex behavior, leisure-time activities, morale, "happiness." They believe that at present some data of this sort are being collected but only on a haphazard, fortuitous, and ephemeral basis and that it seems negligent not to take the long view and plan for the regular collection of such data for the study of cultural, social, and political trends. In time, I suppose, this would make for a new "new history."

Fourth, associated with collection of data is attention to method.

Sometimes the inadequacy of existing factual data, when applied to problems for which they were not directly intended, leads to concern with methodological matters; sometimes the development of methods leads to collection of data (as in the public opinion field). In either case technical work goes forward on both collection and analysis. To a large extent this means measurement and quantification. Now, as no audience at the University of Chicago needs to be told, arguments over methodological questions have often been, and still are, as bitter as those over substantive problems. I cannot refrain from mentioning once more the famous inscription on the side of the building we commemorate: "If you cannot measure, your knowledge is meager and unsatisfactory." I have always liked Professor Viner's comment: "Well, it's true, all right—but if you can measure, your knowledge is still meager and unsatisfactory!" The social sciences have been marked by disputes over method as much as by disputes over substance: the Menger-Schmoller *Methodenstreit* in economics, the clinical-experimental arguments in psychology, the concern with observational procedures in anthropology, the use of quantification and statistics everywhere.

It is here that the field of public opinion sticks out like—to all concerned, I am sure—a sore thumb. For if there was one factor that influenced the shift from 1930 to 1955 more than any other, it was surely the "invention" and development of a method—the sample survey. True, there were "surveys" and "polls" before, but the public opinion studies of 1936 and after were something else again. The methods developed in connection with them—in sampling, in interviewing, in questionnaire construction, in scaling, in survey analysis—quickly dominated the field and gave it the characteristic flavor it now has. To a sizable—and to some, a frightening—extent, the substance has often been defined by the technique. Not only were the newer methods used in every one of the prominent titles of the 1955 era mentioned above, but an entire methodological literature has developed: Hyman on interviewing, Payne and Kornhauser and Likert and Gallup on questionnaire construction, Lazarsfeld on survey analysis, Stouffer on design, Stephan and Hansen and Hauser and Hurwicz on sampling. Thurstone and Guttman and Lazarsfeld on measurement, and so on. A recent bibliography on interviewing listed fifteen items on interviewing in law, thirty in social casework, thirty-two in personnel administration, fifty-seven in the rest of social science, and ninety-three in opinion and attitude research. Opponents of this methodological development may fulminate against it; the one thing they cannot do is ignore it.

Incidentally, the sample survey was historically important in contributing to the resolution of the controversy of the 1920's between the "behaviorists" and the "subjectivists," as it affected this field.[1] The former typically argued that subjective states could not be handled scientifically because they were not observable, and the latter argued that without subjective states behavior was partial and

---

1. If this turns out to be a good idea, William McPhee wants credit for calling it to my attention.

empty. The sample interview made subjective data objectively reportable, observable, recordable, measurable, and analyzable. In other words—to return to our definition—before the 1930's the study of public opinion was characterized by two difficulties: it could not be accurately determined in the large numbers of people involved (witness the efforts of Bryce and Lowell) and it dealt with "unknown" and "unknowable" internal states. The sample interview survey provided a joint solution to both problems: (1) it solved the problem of the magnitude of public opinion phenomena, through the sample, and (2) it solved the problem of the internalization of public opinion phenomena, through the interview.

Fifth, the field becomes recognized institutionally.

At some point in its development a field of inquiry is accepted by major institutions of the society—by industry, by government, by the intellectual world, and by the universities. The universities are mentioned last because they are the final institutions to confer intellectual respectability and also because they are often the last by whom the new is tried. It should always be instructive for academic people to recall the number of intellectual innovations of first-class importance that did not and in many cases could not have come from the universities—Darwin, Freud, Mill, Ricardo, Macaulay. Anthropological societies existed for years before Oxford established a Chair—you will recall Cornford's principle, derived from English academic practice, that nothing should be tried for the first time! Now such academic recognition gives an intellectual interest struggling to become a discipline some confidence, some continuity, and some status. It would be mistaken, however, to forget that at the same time it tends to "freeze" and monopolize, to develop vested interests, and to narrow scope.

Perhaps the best way to indicate the institutional status of the opinion field today is to note the tacit understanding within the professional organization, the American Association for Public Opinion Research, that academic and commercial representatives should alternate in the presidency—an understanding based, I think, on the recognition that what is shared is a common interest not in ideas but in technique. Universities have made important contributions to the current state of the field, of course—after all, just to note landmarks in the vicinity, it was in 1928 that Thurstone said that "attitudes can be measured." But the basic instrument of the sample survey was not really developed by or in the universities but in the first instance by economic enterprise (newspapers, magazines, radio, industry, political parties) and in the second instance by government. The Gallup and Roper polls did much to start the modern ball rolling, and greatly to their credit too. The Lazarsfeld Office of Radio Research and later Bureau of Applied Social Research was in but not really of the university. Early sampling and interviewing contributions came from government, from the Census Bureau and the Department of Agriculture (Likert). (And while I am at it, I am pleased to acknowledge the key initiative taken by the Rockefeller Foundation—the Humanities Division!—in developing the field of mass communication about 1940.) The recent contributions on scaling were at least begun in the War Department. All in all, it is, I think, not unfair to say that the academic student has taken from the field of public opinion as well as put into it.

Little by little, however, the field became accepted, or partially so, in academic institutions—though there is by no means a hearty welcome even today. The *Public Opinion Quarterly* and the Office of Public Opinion Research were housed at Princeton. At Columbia the Lazarsfeld Bureau was allowed to move uptown, on university ground. Likert's group was given a home though not a budget at Michigan. The National Opinion Research Center came to Chicago. Courses in public opinion began to dot the curriculums of sociology and psychology departments. The first "big" textbook was, of course, produced by a university man. In a few graduate schools numerous students became trained in the field, some even in its techniques, and went to good jobs in commerce and government as well as in academic life.

With all this, however, the field of public opinion has a somewhat uneasy home in the university today. Some of the academic specialists are fearful lest they be tagged as pollers or identified with market research, and they are correspondingly careful to dissociate themselves even if it takes a jargon to do so. The recent expansion of the field generated enough vitality to produce some envy on the part of academic associates, and there was probably no one outside the field—some inside, too!—who did not hail with glee the apparent failure of the polls in 1948—including, incidentally, representatives of economics, demography, and other fields whose developing skill was something less than perfect on particular occasions! Intellectuals inside and outside the academic community who distrust or dislike public opinion in general or on some specific issue seem to take pleasure in attaching the onus to studies of public opinion—as though the questioner should necessarily be blamed for the answers he gets. The American who did most in the early 1920's to popularize this field is deeply concerned in his latest book with the powerful and, to him, wrongful effect of public opinion upon democratic government, an effect to which studies of the phenomenon allegedly contribute. Somehow the field has not achieved academic respect-ability, and I suspect that this is not entirely due simply to the weight of its intellectual contribution. And, perhaps partly because of this situation, academic leaders in the field tend to "leave" it—Lasswell for policy, Cantril for perception, Stouffer for role theory and technique, Lazarsfeld for mathematics and research training.

Sixth, the field influences and is influenced by its intellectual neighbors.

As a scientific field gathers speed in its development, it gains from its contact with some fields but not others, and the tightening and loosening of ties with other disciplines help to shape it. The appli-cation of concepts, ideas, and methods from one field to another has often stimulated development, but it has retarded or diverted it as well. For example, the Darwinian theory had an important impact upon anthropology and sociology for a time, but in the end (that is, now) social Darwinism has become antiquated. In the social sciences today, we can note the recent application of psychoanalytic ideas to anthropology and other social sciences or the current application of mathematics to all manner of subjects, from learning theory to organizational analysis, just to mention two more topics in the present symposium.

The field of public opinion once more is characterized by an important shift over this period—from the traditional disciplines of history and political science and social philosophy to the newer disciplines that some people have come to call the "behavioral sciences." The Advisory Committee for the 1935 bibliography in this field was composed mainly of political scientists; the Advisory Committee for 1953 *Reader* consisted mainly of sociologists. The earlier academic contributions came from political scientists like Gosnell, Lasswell, Odegard, Herring; the later contributions were more likely to come from psychologists like Newcomb, Cantril, and Hovland; or from sociologists like Lazarsfeld and Stouffer; or, an academic generation later, from a combined psychologist-sociologist like Hyman. I suppose that a historian of thought could name a number of complicated reasons for the movement of a specialty away from one discipline and toward another; in the present case, it seems relatively clear and simple to me, namely, the dominance of method. Political scientists were not trained in the techniques of social research, and, when the techniques became so important, the proprietors of the method took over intellectual ownership of the subject matter too. And in some important respects, they changed it. For example, the earlier concern with the effects of public opinion upon the formation of public policy (e.g., Dicey) fell off as compared to concern with the formation of public opinion itself. Here, again, this situation can be applauded or deplored, often depending upon which academic chair you occupy.

The vitality of the expanding field even reached back into the parent discipline, political science, and helped to stimulate the growth of a "new" interest—not in "public opinion" but in "political behavior"—and the banding together of an *avant-garde* group who sought to take the gospel of empirical, behavioral studies of political matters to their document-oriented brethren. This development is not identical with opinion studies—in fact, its champions are careful not to get too closely identified with the field, since the market researchers and the sociologists appear to have taken it over!—but it is certainly parallel in time and contiguous in space. Some of the leaders of the movement have even interviewed respondents, run IBM cards, and figured percentages! One of them, a political scientist in good standing, is here today as my discussant—the author of *The American People and Foreign Policy,* in which, according to the jacket, "he analyzes the sources and validity of our traditional attitudes, the fluctuation of our national moods, and the complex interplay between mass opinion and the articulate proposals of our policy-makers"; and also in which, according to the Index, he devotes 59 of 244 pages to "polling data." Another member of this group is the author of *The Governmental Process,* with the subtitle

"Political Interests and Public Opinion." Another has recently published *A Primer of Statistics for Political Scientists*, and still another a book called *The Western Public—1952 and Beyond* based entirely on the secondary analysis of survey data. All four of these authors have been members of the SSRC Committee on Political Behavior in the past few years; and all of them, as it happens, received their doctorate degrees from the Political Science Department of the University whose honored guests we are today.

Within this broad movement, other interfield influences, refinements, elaborations, and applications are apparent as well. Stouffer likes to say that the field had four grandparents—psychoanalytic theory, learning theory, cultural theory, and role theory. Lasswell, a political scientist by training, helped to introduce Freudian notions into public opinion research, and *The Authoritarian Personality* built them in. Blumer periodically warned the field that it was overlooking Mead (George Herbert), and Mead (Margaret) tried occasionally to add a cross-cultural depth. Warner and Henry brought class and the projective test simultaneously to bear. Inkeles seeks to combine survey method with the theory of social stratification. The MIT group combines the Lasswellian and Lazarsfeldian traditions in their studies of international communications, with something added. Some members of the *avant avant-garde* look to mathematical information theory or to psycholinguistics to stimulate and hopefully to fructify the next stage. As for applications to new subjects, the field has branched out via its major instrument, the sample survey, in a number of directions as the skills and the confidence of the specialists increased. In recent programs of the professional associations, papers were given on public opinion in connection with mental health, physical health, religion, law, population, medical training, civil liberties, and trade-union politics. In fact, public opinion studies have spread out so far that it is hard for the academic mind always to find or retain a neat and clean definition of when something is "public opinion" and when it is not.

Seventh, and finally, the field constructs a body of interrelated propositions that are empirically verified.

As a result of the accumulation of factual data, the refinement of methods, and the influence of related fields, the grand theories with monistic explanations are broken down into smaller pieces, and each is attacked independently. Like most other transitions, this is an especially critical stage in the development of a science. Since the grand theories are so much more dramatic and impressive than the small, seemingly piecemeal studies, the latter suffer by comparison. Too much is usually expected for the new methods—and, unfortunately, sometimes claimed—and performance does not equal promise. It is easy to give up at this point and return to broad, speculative deliberation without taking the trouble of differentiating and verifying. But, if seen through, this stage can lead to the goal. That, I take it, is the goal of precision, generality, explanatory and predictive power—what is usually meant by a scientific theory. In the social sciences, economics probably has more of it than the other disciplines; psychology and anthropology have it in parts of their disciplines but not in others; and sociology and political science have perhaps less still. Such theory is not easy to construct in any scientific field—and the task is particularly difficult in respect to human behavior. It should be no cause for wonder that the behavioral sciences have not gone farther in such a short time.

In spite, or maybe because, of the great amount of data assembled in public opinion studies in the last two decades, there is not much theory to show. But there is something which, if not theory, is at least the raw material for it. We know a good deal about the relationship of opinions on political issues to demographic characteristics like age, sex, occupation, religion, income, and "class"— enough to know that the typical generalizations of journalists and even of some scholars need qualification if not correction. We know quite a bit about who listens to or reads what, and we know something about what difference it makes. We know something about the limitations on opinion change, and we even know something about the way it comes about. A recent volume summarizing the findings of only one segment of the field was able to list 209 findings or generalizations for which there was some evidence. How to reduce those, and others too, into an economic "theoretical" statement, no one seems to know; but at least some people are concerned with trying. In short, no one has reason to be completely satisfied with the state of the field, but there are parts of the behavioral and even the social sciences that in my judgment are worse off.

Conclusion

I have tried to state what seem to me the major differences in the study of public opinion between 1930 and 1955 and to describe how the field got to where it now is. But where is it? And, more importantly, where is it going? I wish I knew. I do not, but perhaps I may be forgiven a few brief speculations on the matter.

What is required to give vitality to a scientific field? And where does the study of public opinion stand with reference to such requirements? At least five things are needed, it seems to me. First, the workers in the field must have *intelligence*. While no studies have been done on the matter, I at least am willing to assume that people specializing in the study of public opinion have about as much intelligence as people in the social sciences in general—and, furthermore, I am willing to settle for that. It may not be enough, but it is all we have a right to expect. Second, the workers in the field must have some *experience with, knowledge of, and even wisdom about the subject matter*. They should be immersed in it; they should make it a full-time concern; they should be fascinated by it. Here I am afraid the field falls somewhat short. Because of the usual way of applying the technique, too great a distance is tolerated between the subject and the researcher. When someone like David Riesman goes into the field to talk to people himself, the results are dramatic. Reliance on the technique has also promoted too high a degree of what might be called "intellectual mobility"; too many people think they have a technical key that will unlock any substantive door, and they go down the hall trying one after the other instead of going into one room and exploring it thoroughly. Third, the worker in the field must have *ideas*, or related sets of concepts. It is difficult to estimate where the opinion field stands with reference to this requirement. My own guess is that it has some but not enough. The field is often criticized for being too empirical and insufficiently "conceptual" or "theoretical" or in some other way "frameworked." But I do not take this criticism as seriously as do others. I do feel that the field does not know well enough how to formulate its problems, and I have a prejudice as to what to do about it which I will come to in a moment. Fourth, the worker in the field needs *data*. If there is one thing the opinion field has in large measure, it is data—not always the right data when they are good and not always good data when they are right—but there are certainly a lot of them. The trouble is that no one knows quite what to do with them. I would guess that the Cantril-Strunk volume is consulted only when someone is looking for poll results on a particular topic for a particular period; and, while a number of knowledgeable people talk about the tremendous potential for scientific purposes contained in the countless survey data now stored on IBM cards, there have been more disappointing attempts to exploit such materials than successful ones. The fragmentary and chance character of the data is partly responsible for this—but only partly. Fifth, the worker in the field needs *methods*. Despite the usual controversy, the public opinion field is relatively well off, to my mind. In fact, it might be said that it is too well off, in the sense that method has become so dominant that it seems in many cases to have taken over the content as well. The field cannot get along without its methods, but it has a serious problem in learning how to get along with them. Everyone acknowledges that public opinion was not invented in 1935, but some people forget that the *study* of public opinion was not invented then either.

Where do we go from here? What would we like the speaker at the fiftieth anniversary of the founding of the Social Science Research Building to say about the study of public opinion? The progress in many parts of the field over the past quarter-century does not *have* to continue; other fields have fallen back, and it is not at all inconceivable that that could happen to this field as well. Perhaps we can take a cue from our own analysis.

The watershed of twenty to twenty-five years ago brought many good things with it but some bad things too. The key term, I think, is "discontinuity." To my mind—and, for brevity's sake, I put the matter in broad terms—the field now suffers from three discontinuities. First, there is the discontinuity with the intellectual past. The new studies have driven out the old—too fully, too quickly. There is a good deal in what the earlier writers said and the way they went about saying it, and the study of public opinion today is poorer for the absence of such macrocosmic considerations. (Incidentally, there is here another fascinating illustration of the notion—prevalent even in the physical sciences, I understand—that European scholars supply the basic theoretical ideas and American scholars the technical apparatus and know-how. Certainly some of the major theorists in the social sciences in the modern period have been European, and it is difficult for America to match them—Freud, Pareto, Durkheim, Weber, Simmel.) In the public opinion field, here may be an instance of what happens when research crowds out reflection.

The second discontinuity is that between disciplines. Historians and political theorists and social philosophers have more to offer to the student of public opinion than they have been willing or prepared in recent years to say or he to hear. In return, modern developments have produced ideas that would be useful in the analysis of historical and theoretical problems involving public opinion, as has recently been pointed out, for example, by such writers as Paul Lazarsfeld and Hans Speier (note, incidentally, both transplanted Europeans). When my colleagues and I tried in a recent book to put our empirical results alongside some "big" considerations of political theory, we were criticized at a meeting of the professional organization for engaging in "high thinking"—not that we could do it, but as though it were bad in itself!

Finally, there is the familiar discontinuity between precision and importance. In some parts of the behavioral sciences now, including this field, there seems to be an inverse correlation between the importance of the problem and the technical proficiency with which it is, or can be, attacked. If this is indeed true, it will not be an easy matter to solve, but it seems to me critical to try. Too often, I fear, people in the public opinion field have forgotten that the word "significance" has more than a statistical meaning.

Let us return to our twin themes. Over the past quarter-century much has happened to the study of public opinion—and a great deal of it has also happened to other parts of social science as science. Not all of it appears now to have been fully desirable, but why should that be expected? The social and behavioral sciences are, to my mind, a leading intellectual invention of this century; and there will be, and should be, many more quarter-century reviews before they will fully have been put to, and hopefully have met, the test of providing a solid scientific understanding of human behavior.

Some Observations on the "Older" and the "Newer" Social Sciences

A few years ago I attended a conference at Northwestern University (sponsored by Carnegie) which concerned itself with reviewing the problems and prospects of interdisciplinary undergraduate courses and programs in the social sciences. Attention was focused less on integrated departments such as the Social Relations group at Harvard than on specific courses. As these were presented by representatives from a number of different institutions, it became apparent that there were very few courses which, like several of our College courses here, attempt to bring together people and materials from the two main clusters engaged in such teaching. One cluster, which I shall for brevity call the "newer" social sciences, includes sociology, anthropology, and social psychology; the other includes economics, history, political science. (Occasionally a geographer may wander into either camp.) Those that I call the newer group can, of course, when in search of ancestors, trace themselves back to some eminent Greek; but they are newer in the sense of late entry into European departments of law, philosophy, or economics; and they frequently exhibit the behavior of newcomers in their anxious concern for their independence, professional standing, and intellectual opacity. At the Northwestern conference, and on many similar occasions, the differences among themselves that these newer disciplines take so seriously were reported to provide an engrossing agenda, so that members of these courses could feel, from the toil and trouble and terminology they were in, that they were indeed being interdisciplinary and that when they did succeed in integrating, more than seriatim, anthropological, sociological, and social-psychological materials, their intellectual and pedagogic missions would be accomplished. Ordinarily, however, the achievements re-

319

ported from many different places at the Northwestern conference were less spectacular. The courses were taught by a staff drawn from two or three departments, which often saw the joint course as an opportunity for recruiting majors or graduate students into their specialty, while at the same time making efforts, more or less valiant or successful, to adopt a joint terminology—at worst a sort of pidgin English, with, for instance, psychologists learning to say "culture" or "social structure" from time to time; at best ascetic adoption of terms derived from some overarching scheme like that of Talcott Parsons.

At the conference there was a somewhat smaller representation from courses which sought to bring together the older rather than the newer social sciences—courses taught by historians, economists, and political scientists. (I will not speak here of the American Civilization programs which ordinarily bring in literature and sometimes philosophy.) The base of such courses was often at a boundary already crossed, such as government control of business taught jointly by economists and political scientists, or American constitutional developments, taught jointly by political scientists and historians. But the attempt to move beyond these junctures put participants up against the high tariffs created by the achievements of economic analysis—achievements so justly imposing that economists see no need to accept colleagueship from people with less than full literacy in them. To be sure, there are breeds of economists, such as industrial relations people (labor economists) or some so-called institutionalists, who might be viewed as sociologists with a specialized clientele, and it is often such economists who get into interdisciplinary courses. But theoretical economists are a craft, not an industrial union, and if they do get involved with such courses, they tend to insist that no halfway measures or outsider's approach will do in handling price theory, welfare functions, and like matters.

Members of other disciplines sometimes retaliate by borrowing from the business world the accusation that the economist is "merely" a theorist, an occupant of an armchair. Certain breeds of economist, however, escape the accusation by virtue of their subject matter: to be able to understand a payroll is the academic equivalent of having met one. (I might add that the clinical psychologist often also escapes the accusation directed against his fellow psychologists, for it is perfectly all right to sit in an armchair if someone else lies on a couch, since the person lying on the couch is his "field work.") In fact, a clinical approach, whether to the problems of a patient or of the auto industry, is often accepted by all parties as a way of resolving interdisciplinary difficulties. The world is messy and makes sport of definitions. Dealing, for instance, with the role of whim or sexual symbolism in automobile design, the economist has no advantage over the historian; his readings in Leontief will hardly help him here. Likewise, the experimental psychologist—who plays for the newer disciplines much the same role that the economist does for the older ones—cannot immediately bring Hullian or Hebbian theory to bear on a particular delinquent's case history.

Yet any approach in terms exclusively of the situations presented by what we choose to call "real life," no matter how stimulating pedagogically, will almost inevitably mislead the student as to the "real life" of the disciplines themselves—a life built, of course, on virtuosity of concepts, on abstractions and models. (I might add that, as long as our high-school teaching of general mathematics is as slack as it is, mathematically trained psychologists and economists will remain fairly indigestible for integrated programs, unless they are willing to check their graphs and slide rules at the entrance.)

Such difficulties, although barely touched upon at the conference, were recognized as serious ones. Nevertheless, I gained the impression that a certain complacency hovered over many instances of both types of program. Each group felt that the boundaries of its task were set by the neighboring tribes within its own group—not by those in the other group. Further steps toward integration at the really significant boundaries *between* programs never came into question, so that it seems not unfair to say that achievement of a modest integration on a lower level militates against a more significant integration at a higher one. One might, in fact, pursuing the same line of thought, raise certain questions on this Twenty-fifth Anniversary as to whether the communication promoted by the grouping of the social sciences at Chicago might not also have raised certain largely unseen barriers against transcending that grouping, both vis-à-vis the natural sciences, particularly biology, and vis-à-vis the humanities.

The barrier against the natural sciences does not, to my mind, present a serious problem for the future. As the fear of racism among civilized people diminishes, social scientists will once again be willing to consider genetic and constitutional explanations along with environmental ones. Work in psychophysiology holds great promise, whether in the style of Witkin or Lacy. The development of many geographers into human ecologists forms another linkage, as does much terrain-oriented work in planning. And beyond such concrete linkages, social scientists have, as many observers have noted, been perhaps too ready to look to the natural sciences for their model of what a science is like, incidentally often misinterpreting what they saw, with models of discourse and forms of presentation flowing downhill from the pacesetters.

But the barrier against the humanities does present a problem for future gatherings of this sort, in spite of the fact that the program of this celebration shows how philosophical and humanistic are the preoccupations of many influential members of this Division, not even counting its former dean, Robert Redfield, who has spoken so eloquently on this theme. Just because the boundaries of social science are so amorphous, there is every temptation to define them by exclusion—by stressing the "science" rather than the "social." Exclusion, moreover, has added attractions for an interdisciplinary group that wants to find an out-group to intensify its own threatened solidarity: what more natural, for example, than for a team of anthropologists, sociologists, and economists to seek unity by snarls one day at humanists, another day at humanitarians? Such processes were once important for more than morale; even as late as the time of the Social Science Building's erection, it was still necessary for social science to free itself from Victorian moralism and literary eclecticism. Today, however, the new generation of students seeking departmental and divisional identities takes repeated loyalty oaths to Science less because there is any real danger of their being "subverted" by a Robert Lynd or even a Robert Redfield, but rather because the students' own anxieties allow them to be stampeded into a crusade against even a barely palpable reminder of abandoned sensitivities. While it was undeniably creative to erect a Social Science Research Building in 1929, it is conceivable that in a decade or so from now one might want to consider other voices, other rooms, other buildings, as the basis of new groupings. To do so would maintain that grand tradition of flexibility that has been one of the characteristic opportunities and discomforts of Chicago.

Do these considerations and experiences imply that all steps toward integration are inevitably self-defeating, leading to the replacement of one scholarly nationalism by another, even if a larger and more inclusive one? Some such dialectic of advance and retreat is undoubtedly present. But perspective requires taking account of two other things which are also present. One is recognition that the more productive of the new groupings may and often should become new specialties in a continuous process of fission and reunion. We have not had nearly enough of these. Take, for instance, the situation of the anthropologists who have almost always had to be one-man interdisciplinary teams because hardly anyone would join them in the taxing and sometimes terrifying work in the field. When a Karl Llewellyn studies Cheyenne law (with Hoebel) or an Erik H. Erikson the child-training and personality of the Sioux or the Yurok (with Whiting or Kroeber), the results are often profoundly stimulating; so they might be if a macroeconomist accompanied an Evans-Pritchard or a Herskovits to an African tribe. The kaleidoscope of possible combinations is, I suspect, a good deal richer than we ordinarily think.

The other consideration is the uneven distribution of attempts at integration or new groupings in the American academic procession. So far as my eye reaches, this work proceeds at only two points of the American collegiate spectrum—at the very top, at the more vigorous *avant-garde* places, and at the very bottom, at the colleges which cannot afford the full line of departments and thus resort to having a social studies or social science group that may harbor a political scientist who doubles in economics and a sociologist who teaches psychology, group dynamics, cultural anthropology, and western European history. Sometimes I think I would feel easier in my mind if these latter places never encountered the "general education" movement, for interdisciplinary courses as taught in underprivileged places are often an *avant-garde* excuse for intellectual laxity and somnolence. Just as I hate to see social studies taught in most high schools, where they are not likely to be taught either with rigor or with intellectual honesty, so I would prefer in many a college or junior college to see some discipline, any discipline, substituted for the very best program of general education. And many small denominational colleges, or social science adjuncts to technical and business colleges, find an interdisciplinary social science course to be a money-saver. Yet communications in America are such that innovations are quickly disseminated, and perhaps there is a touch of snobbery in my attitude to the "backward countries" of American education. Certainly I would have to admit that in some impoverished schools the adoption of the model set at a leading institution has enabled them to overtake and surpass some of the middle range of colleges still largely wedded to departmentalism.

In this middle range many institutions are themselves in search of an identity; they seek to be isomorphic with the leading universities, offering as many departments and courses as the latter. They often feel too insecure to experiment—a number of the state universities fall into this category, while, of course, a number of others are among the pioneers. (But the model they follow is, as usually happens in such cases, a bit out of date; and only now, for instance, twenty or more years after Columbia and Chicago began to experiment with general education, are some of them looking into it.) The energies of many of the more unconventionally minded in such institutions are, therefore, presently harnessed to the crossing of departmental lines; and to warn them too aggressively at this point that, when they have crossed one river, there will be still other and wider ones would often simply deliver them and their students into the hands of the entrenched old guard and home guard at their respective colleges. In this perspective a conference like the one at Northwestern at least encourages the more curious and eager minds at the less curious and eager places and thus makes for more openness and vitality in the spectrum as a whole. The disillusionment with interdisciplinary work and teaching which at times assails those of us who have tried to meet the other fellow's payroll too often—those of us who have felt that the resistances only pile up the higher the more one sweeps the near boundaries away—this should not blind us to the ferment the attempt has created, the vocations it has cemented among students, and the actual achievements, more modest than originally hoped but now at many places a going concern, with still unexplored potentialities.

What I am going to say now may seem paradoxical in view of the foregoing. I have the impression that it would be easier to achieve desired integrations among the history-government-economics group, on the one hand, and the anthropology-sociology-psychology group, on the other, if each group started to work and to plan courses with members of the other rather than with their own nearer colleagues. Or perhaps this should not be stated as a substitution but as an addition. At any rate, if, let us say, anthropologists and historians work together on problems of Soviet bureaucracy, or economists and psychologists on the analysis of consumer behavior— and both of these are recent instances of productive learning situations—then it may turn out not only that boundaries are crossed which are more than accidental by-products of academic timing but also that the problems within the older and the newer areas will themselves assume a juster perspective.

However, such collaboration is not easy, for there are temperamental and intellectual differences between the adherents of the several disciplines. In order to suggest some of the dilemmas created when one "type" tries to work with the materials and personnel of another, I shall use the ideal-typical historian and his fellow in anthropology for illustration. Each has, first of all, an image of the other. The historian sees the social scientist, in general, as an uncultivated person, without knowledge of, let alone reverence for, the past. His vulgarity appears in his putting himself forward in what he writes—his often self-conscious effort to declare his own values, his own biases. In contrast to this, the historian tends to minimize the role of his own self, of his own projectivity if not his selectivity, so that even a Collingwood, no *echt*-historian, is gingerly in handling a personal anecdote. (A nice example turned up the other day when a historian was talking to a seminar largely composed of sociologists. He told us how he had happened to study Latin-American cities and then apologized for the surely not tasteless revelation.) Moreover, the historian sees the anthropologist (and his allies among the *novi homines* of behavioral science) as able by grandiose or sexy talk to capture students and foundations, leaving historians to hold hands with professors of Greek; by the same token, anthropologists have the ear of governments, always flying to Washington or Micronesia, or advising market researchers—promoters rather than scholars. Yet there is ambivalence in this disdain. These new men must have something. They talk a lot about methods —so much so that one of their number was recently heard to exclaim: "Oh, dear, why can't we just go out and *do* ethnography the way we used to." They know a lot of jargon which is villainous enough but impenetrable; they know about Rorschach tests, interviewing, and even sampling.

What happens then to the historian who is venturesome enough, and attracted enough, to try to cross the boundary? He will tend to assume that, since he has the older and higher academic status, the anthropologists he comes among will welcome him with open arms, that they will be grateful for his discovering them. But the anthropologists are quite as proud as historians and perhaps more polemical. In the past at least, they have often been men and women of high social status who have felt more at home with the chiefs of a preliterate tribe than with commoners in their own country. Until people started revisiting Tepotzlán and points east, the anthropologist was as securely in command of "his" adopted culture as any historian who had taken for his moated terrain the history of Macedonia in the first century B.C. or the intellectual life of Milwaukee between the Mexican and the Civil wars. Moreover, as already indicated, the peer group of the anthropologist, for the most part, is confined to the newer social sciences; unless he is archeologically inclined, or of unusually humanistic bent, he will not know or care enough about what historians think of him to be grateful for an exception.

But the historian's troubles have only begun at this point. The anthropologists he has heard of, the popularized ones, are, he assumes, also the ones whom their colleagues hold in high esteem; then he discovers, to his dismay, that the tight in-groups of anthropology often share the prejudices he is fleeing, only more so. I have seen it happen a number of times that historians attracted by the work of Margaret Mead or Ruth Benedict or Weston La Barre or Lloyd Warner are told by other anthropologists with whom they have on that account made contact that these anthropologists are not to be trusted (much as a historian might say harsher things about Max Weber or Pirenne than many sociologists might anticipate). Who, then, is a sound ethnographer? At this point the historian may find himself plunged into a disquisition on the differences between British social anthropology and American cultural anthropology—or any one of a hundred such topics in the repertory of any discipline. As his bewilderment grows, he will be told in effect: Why don't you go back where you came from—go back at least until you are willing to spend two or three years learning these fine points of the trade.

In this reception of the newcomer, a more general phenomenon is at work, which we can observe in many situations of group contact. The American who travels in Europe is, of course, more sympathetic to Europeans and less ethnocentric than the American who stays home; but abroad he is taken as *the* American and is belabored by his hosts for all the sins, real and alleged, of his countrymen, sins of which he has often been highly critical at home. Likewise, I have seen southern students at northern colleges put on the defensive because they were unwilling to disown, on any and all occasions, southern race attitudes, though these students would not be where they were if they wholly shared those attitudes. Lacking perspective, people are apt to take the nearest person in their own field of vision as the scapegoat for the very group he has left—a group that will ordinarily never hear of the blows he suffers on their behalf; it is as if his physical presence serves to remind people of all they dislike or criticize in the group he pro tempore is held to represent. Thus, in my own experience with students and teachers in the humanities I encounter a great many attacks on their image of the inhumane behavioral scientists—attacks I would escape if I stayed home within disciplinary confines (I feel, of course, no happier if I am exempted from the attacks and asked to join an alliance against my social science colleagues). Any person with experience in sectarian religious or political life has had similar encounters with members of sects close to his own but not identical.

Experiencing such a reception, the historian may be tempted to go home again, but he may have misgivings about it. For he probably shares the conviction of most intellectuals and many academic people—the conviction most of us seem to need to keep going—that what we are doing is a bit or more than a bit heretical. The historian has thought accordingly that he was very bold indeed to have truck with the illiterates who study preliterates; he has conjured up visions of being read out of his own trade union, of having burned his bridges. Actually, of course, the other historians are neither that interested nor that venomous nor that united, but, having this image, the wanderer will feel at times that he is a man without a country. A sad plight, indeed—especially for a historian.

If we turn now to the other side of the boundary, we see that the anthropologist also has his picture of the historian. He may see him as overbookish, a donnish person in a Gothic tower. If he is not in the humanistic wing of anthropology—a strong wing, as Kroeber's work shows, even while he criticizes it—he may associate historians with all the snobbish people who claim culture as their word and their world. The behavioral scientist may not write as well as the historian or read as much. Perhaps he may also feel that the historian is more secure in his method; his informants are dead, and he is not in the position of pursuing them with the Alice-in-Wonderland croquet mallet of the interview. And, until recently, he might also feel that historians are in control of the big and important powers, while he is confined to the inconsequential and disappearing outlanders— much as sociologists until recently could not touch economics, which belonged to the economists, and could not touch government and military affairs, which belonged to the political scientists, but had to find their clientele among criminals, children, old people, ethnics, factory workers, and other relatively powerless folk whom no one else had laid claim to.

What happens, then, when the anthropologist leaves his peer group to try to work with historians? As a student of culture and subculture, he is more likely than the historian to have "cased" the others' "joint" before venturing into it, and so he is apt to be in for fewer surprises. Moreover, there has been a renewed tendency in anthropology itself to seek historical reconstructions as well as synchronic cross-sections wherever the conditions of field work permit; some anthropologists have even revived a moderate and chastened form of evolutionism, and many are preoccupied with historically focused studies of culture change and acculturation. A certain happy eclecticism or omnivorousness survives in anthropology from the days of one-man expeditions. Despite this, anthropologists may still encounter severe conflicts when they venture among the historians. The historian is often a person whose job it is to destroy the other fellow's generalization. To recur to a noted instance, historians in the past half-century have written a whole library which takes exception to Max Weber's essay on the Protestant ethic with such comments as, "however in Florence in 1204, such and such," or "in Flanders in 1627 the Catholics were heavily engaged in the most rationalized segments of the wool trade." Your true historian will boggle at such a lay term as the Renaissance, pushing its origins ever back into what used to be called the Dark Ages, so that one sometimes gathers from reading history that nothing ever changes, since it always has a precursor. This is very hard going for those anthropologists or other behavioral scientists who seek generalizations (to be sure, not all anthropologists define science as generalization, being satisfied with descriptive ethnography).

More conflict-laden is a second possibility, namely, that the anthropologist will want to share with the historian his access to the big powers as well as to keep his monopoly of the small ones. When the Columbia University Research on Contemporary Cultures started, under anthropological leadership, to study, not Palau or the Tiv or the Hopi, but France, China, and the Soviet Union, and when the Russian Research Center started under Clyde Kluckhohn's direction, many historians and their allies among the older disciplines were bitterly resentful. They seized upon Gorer's swaddling theory with fierce and, I think, disproportionate indignation. At the Conference on Totalitarianism held at the Academy of Arts and Sciences in 1953, some able scholars could not contain their fury when social-psychological or configurational interpretations were offered for Soviet behavior. Many anthropologists, too, have been told to go back where they came from.

But possibility of return tends to be cut off, in part by ambivalence among the anthropologists themselves toward the forays some of them are making into affairs of state and states. Indeed, the shining simplicity of the earlier forms of ethical relativism has been a casualty of this development. (As many observers have pointed out, it was all very well to seek neutrality toward the exotic behavior of the vanishing Dobuans or Nanda—but not toward the racist behavior of the Nazis or the suppression of cultural pluralism and the extirpation of whole peoples in the Soviet Union.) Big-power problems brought big-power ethical dilemmas, and the anthropologist who is now "de-briefed" in the CIA or the State Department after a visit to the Laplanders or an Indonesian village feels he is losing the footloose innocence that allowed American field workers to remain (compared with British ones) quite "un-royal" until the second World War.

Before that time, anthropologists could feel they shared the common culture of having been in the field, of having had to face alone, or virtually so, often unnerving problems of grappling with a strange tongue, strange ways, and a strange social structure (problems movingly portrayed in Elenore Smith Bowen's *Return to Laughter*). It may well be that they did not always fully appreciate how various this *rite de passage* was, at least outside the American Indian groups; on the surface, the problems of field work bore similar labels, and each returned traveler could talk about "his" tribe in seemingly understandable terms, creating a greater impression of the uniformity of anthropological encounters than was warranted (or blaming themselves as individuals for any lacunae in their account). Once, however, people began to do "field work" in literate communities, or in semiliterate ones like "Plainville, U.S.A.," let alone working in New York City with foreign-born informants, the illusion of a common anthropological culture created by a common experience broke down.

In danger of being lost under these changed conditions is the traditional anthropological conviction that we can learn as much from a small power that has no navy, no archives, and only an embryonic elite as from big ones that make and consume headlines and psychological warfare. Indeed, cultural relativism has included among its non-relativistic assumptions the passionate belief that each power, irrespective of size or ability to threaten or be exploited, counts one: an international democracy of one culture, one vote. While, as I have said, anthropologists are often criticized—with some justice, I think, but without mercy—for "ignoring history," it has been an achievement of their profession to ignore merely contemporary rankings either of territories or of problems. The consequence is that anthropologists at work, usually under government subsidy, at the interdisciplinary frontier of Soviet and other big-power studies of national culture and character can be hurt not only by the attacks they meet from the already entrenched but by the fact that they have internalized many values which make them vulnerable in terms of their own discipline.

Indeed, anthropological work on culture contact helps us to see some of the consequences of such confrontation. Where a minority group seeks acceptance at the hands of a powerful majority, it opens up its own ethical system to strain but does not abandon it. Strictures by the majority may then reverberate with a double potency, since they are received in terms of the newly accepted majority values plus the still encapsulated minority ones. Thus, where native peoples on shouldering the white man's burden found themselves not treated as fully white, there has often been observed a nativist reaction—a reaction analogous to the "third-generation" reaction of American ethnic groups noted some years ago by the historian Marcus Hansen. The old values which are then returned to are altered by the very process of self-conscious return; thus, they are espoused with a chauvinism whose techniques and tenets are often taken over, as we know, from the majority. I believe we can detect something like a nativist or third-generation reaction in anthropology, as well as in a number of the other newer disciplines which have suffered frustration in attempts at integration. As I remarked at the Human Development Symposium last winter, commenting on a paper by Clyde Kluckhohn, there has been a movement in anthropology away from the culture-and-personality school, a renewed preoccupation with special methodologies, an almost pathetic eagerness to show that anthropologists of either sex are as tough-minded, hardheaded scientists as any critic from another discipline could ask.

If one traces descent from Franz Boas, one might speak quite literally of a third-generation reaction. Many of Boas' students broke away from this grand old-country patriarch—though it was hard to find areas in which he had not issued verdicts. But their students, in turn, are often the ones who have become pious toward the ancestral memories. (I recall a student of Ruth Benedict's telling me a year or so ago how much he regretted having been encouraged by her to experiment with psychological tests; if only he had been trained by a straight-and-narrow ethnographer, he felt he would have had a clearer, less conflict-ridden self-image. Back to the fold, and no more hyphenated anthropology for him.)

Similar things have happened even where the disciplines seeking integration have all been of the newer breeds, as in the Harvard Department of Social Relations or Chicago's Committee on Human Development. In both cases, while the pioneering professors continue to wander at will, the students now coming along sometimes seek refuge in a disciplinary third-generation identity at the first signs of non-acceptance of newly invented or marginal identities, and these experimental departments oscillate between Balkanization and over-serious straining for an imperial unity (signalized by a metaphoric coat of arms with definitions rampant). Such, I would suppose, is the ambiguous fate of all but the most utopian culture-contact situations.

What has just been said must be seen in the perspective of Harvard or Chicago and not in that of places which have been less ambitious. For the very fact that students worry about their departmental identity may be taken as a sign that they feel under some pressure to be interdisciplinary. Their position can hardly help including awareness of work in fields other than their own. At most universities it is my impression that people in one field think that people in other fields cannot possibly be interested in their concerns, whereas at Chicago people in one of the social sciences only wonder whether people in the other fields can perhaps fully understand them. At the student level this shows up in the relatively free wandering about among courses—and this is something our Social Science Building does encourage; both faculty and students wander into many lectures and lecture series outside their departments, and there are many serious, interdisciplinary conversations which go on, despite all barriers.

Much of what I know about these matters I have learned from my colleague Everett Hughes, a profound student of culture contact and of the professions. He is inclined from observing these encounters to believe that the departments which happen to exist in a university should be retained as protective shells, in each of which interdisciplinary effort goes on as individuals seek out collaborators and stimulators elsewhere. He argues, in effect, for something rather Burkean: that, once people have been initiated into a disciplinary tribe, they can then be free to wander with the passport that initiation gives them. His goal, if I understand him, is a series of covert coalitions, easily made, easily broken, rather than overt constitutions and convenants openly arrived at and dismayingly breached.[1] He sees a license to specialize in any one field as a license to encourage a curiosity which takes little account of fields. By keeping open lines of renewal from and even retreat into the original field, he would hope to minimize "nativist" reactions.

All that is said here is in one perspective, I suppose, one more testimonial to the power of nationalism, the power which, in the era of unqualified belief in progress and enlightenment, was thought to be passé. The movement toward social science integration has been restricted, in Harold Lasswell's famous phrase, by partial incorporation. For in the major centers it is now a rare person who will not count himself interdisciplinary in some degree (as isolationists today claim to be internationalist); thus even an economist is often willing to accept the notion of unconscious motivation or the role of culture in influencing economic process and interpretations. Either because we think we are interdisciplinary, or because we have proved to our satisfaction or dissatisfaction that we cannot be, we tend to accept the given boundaries and balances of power.

However, there is one discipline where, it seems to me, the fight still rages—a kind of Fronde—and that is in political science. Political science, which once stood *in loco parentis* to many other sciences, now finds its subject matter, the state as a subject to be studied in isolation, withering away. As power relations are discovered to exist in corporations and voluntary associations, as the state spreads its mantle over countless activities, the once firm boundaries of clientele between political science and the newer social sciences break down, and the once-lordly field is invaded by new men, nurtured within it, called students of political behavior. These men take their topic from the parent body but their methods from psychology and sociology. Often they join forces with members of other disciplines, without

1. Jules Henry has written me that, while this pattern of unideological roving is fine for faculty members, it may not be possible for students to broaden their scope when the formal institutions appear by their ground rules to make it difficult. As interdisciplinary programs lose among undergraduates the market appeal of novelty, Professor Henry feels that the students need overt faculty and institutional support against their own timidities. This makes sense to me.

asking whether the latter have read Althusius or Aristotle. Political theorists of course have never had a monopoly of topic, sharing jurisdiction with philosophers, classicists, jurists, and historians. But now important behaviorists appear to have the Foundations with them and the temper of the times; and the theorists, including the constitutionalists, though they may control departments, feel they fight a losing, if a gentlemanly, battle.

One of the ironies in this development is that it is the success of political theory in the last few generations that has been, in this respect, its undoing. It succeeded in indoctrinating politicians and the political public with its more or less rationalist outlook and vocabulary: we all of us became political theorists in the sense of talking easily about interest groups, about power, and about constitutional and legal matters that once were recondite. Courses in civics and citizenship, newspaper reports and columnists, statesmen and elder statesmen—all made us disciples, if crude and undifferentiated ones, of the masters of Anglo-American political thought. Then came the profound shock of discovering political irrationality—of finding that the mass movements of totalitarianism did not seem to fit the nineteenth century's vocabulary. People looked around for a vocabulary less colored by its very applicability to a particular epoch and its institutions, and they felt that the language of the newer social sciences was unemotional and uncommitted and could therefore somehow grapple with the puzzle presented by men who voted against reason, against interest. All language is loaded, but the loadings of sociological or psychological terms were unfamiliar—as were the events themselves. The late Professor Merriam, and those whom he stimulated and influenced—and I speak as one who read his work with excitement when I was beginning in the thirties to reflect on such matters—sought to become aware of what was going on by throwing over much apparatus that appeared to block understanding by its very translucency.

Today, however, the problem is that the contributions couched in the older vocabularies will be underestimated—and, along with them, the rule and role of reason in human affairs. In some quarters it is the widely current vocabularies of the psychoanalytic and anthropological schools which threaten understanding. We cannot think creatively without metaphors, but any metaphor is in danger of becoming a categorical imperative.

On the surface at least, economists are much less involved with these matters. Their island of rationality is big enough to provide a market for them all, whether econometricians or Manchesterians. More seriously, I think one could contend that an economy is a more theoretical construct than a state: though both are abstractions, an economy is so plainly a model to start with that it cannot wither away. And, as I have just implied, economists are in a strategic spot, as watchdogs of full employment and, if full employment should fail, as rescue teams; meanwhile, full employment allows economists to be less political, more theoretical, and, I think, more interesting.

In fact, full employment has helped the newer social sciences to make their large-scale entry, not only by somewhat reducing the political saliency of economics and political science, but also by a general inflation of the "tertiary" trades, arts, and professions (along with an as yet undisturbed expansion of the market for such "secondary" industries as auto manufacturing, including Ford). So far, this entry of the newer social scientists (like that of Negroes and southern whites in Detroit) has occurred without displacing the older intellectual skills—whatever displacement has occurred is relative—though there is perhaps some displacement of the older Anglo-Saxon groups that were once in fairly solid control in academia. It is possible that historians are becoming the genteel poor of the universities, though the field of American history appears to be the bluestockings' blue chip—in part, alas, a cold-war phenomenon. Geography is growing; it has, save in such sports as Ellsworth Huntington, low-pressure theoretical claims, and that air of concreteness, that thingmanship, which so many Americans find attractive; moreover, by adding people to places, and theories to compilations, it is far from running out of territory. Psychologists, too, old and new, experimental, general, special, and clinical, would seem to have an unsaturated market, proto-medical on the one side, proto-sociological on the other.

Let me interject at this point that, in making these observations, I am being, of course, tentative and impressionistic. Moreover, I do not imply that, because a field may not have a big-power future, people should get out of it. In the first place, every field harbors within it greater differences than those which divide it, on the average, from neighboring fields, and, while people would like to be able to say that there is only one kind of political science or only one kind of sociology or economics, this will never be so. (In fact, one of the intellectual difficulties of economics and political science, as often practiced, is their assumption that the economy serves only one purpose or that government does, as against the more anthropological assumption that there are many purposes, and cross-purposes, that need to be discovered.) In the second place, while on one level it is interesting, and possibly useful, to know something about present and future trends, for individuals to allow their vocations and curiosities to be governed by such trends would be a surrender of initiative. The exciting revival of classical studies at some institutions would never have happened if scholars had individually believed what they collectively "knew," namely, that the classics were doomed. Since we do have a full-employment society, we can afford, indeed require, many activities which might appear wasteful to a cosmic planner of the intellectual division of labor. (On this point, I am in sympathy with Michael Polanyi's concept of the well-informed but self-directing scholar.)

But prosperity, and the particular prosperity of the more social social sciences, has had another consequence for the relations among the disciplines. It has made college training and graduate study available to many people who would in an earlier day not have been able to enter the professions—people often attracted to academic life (strange as it may sound to some of us) by the presently high starting salaries, high in comparison with what their parents are used to and their own earlier level of aspiration. Rather than entering academic life at a sacrifice, because they are curious about some phase of man's behavior or because of a call to teach, they regard it as a handy avenue for mobility. This, of course, is as true in the natural as in the social sciences. Dr. Austin Brues, of Argonne National Laboratory, speaking as president of the Association for Cancer Research last spring, mentioned applicants for academic positions who asked what the working hours are; and he went on to describe some of the ways in which soft money for cancer combined with hard careerists to create an almost hysterical pressure for results. All this is familiar enough to us, though rarely so observantly faced. But at least the young man who has gone into cancer research does not have to explain to himself or to his parents what it is that he is doing, while those who go into sociology want that label to become as clear cut and to possess as available a public rhetoric of motives as medicine or accountancy or law. New labels like "human development" or "social relations" or even perhaps "economic history" may not only be hard to market realistically but hard to interpret unambiguously. A recent study of graduate students (done at the University of Illinois by Howard S. Becker and James Carper) shows that philosophy students suffer analogous identity problems—just what is it that we *do?*—while physiologists and mechanical engineers are relatively immune. It seems to me that a good deal of the drive to professionalize each of the social sciences, to assign it an unambiguous jurisdiction, and to follow the dubious (and in some schools now abandoned) lead of the medical schools in asking for an early commitment—that this drive is one of the concomitants of the rise of these sciences to the point where they offer worldly success.

At this point the newer social sciences may endanger themselves by overselling their practical accomplishments, even as cancer research might do. The overselling is, in part, a humane response to evident societal needs, but it is also, in part, the effort of mobile men to justify their line of goods. It becomes increasingly difficult—I can speak for myself here—not to get involved in a series of institutional and personal commitments in which the success of each research project is necessary not in its own intrinsic terms but as part of an institutional strategy of inter- and intra-academic competition, and the fate of colleagues becomes bound up with the fate of an idea. This has always been the case with social movements; it has not heretofore been the case, to quite the same degree, with social research. It is with almost a nostalgic feeling that I recently went back to the volume *Eleven Twenty-six: A Decade of Social Research,* published on the occasion of the tenth anniversary of this building. The "Young Turks" who summed up there the results of ten years of eager and brilliantly exploratory work could only see more of the same ahead; they were full of hope. Were a new building and money to be given to a comparable social science group today, it could hardly escape moments of doubt about the ever growing claims that are made on all sides for the social sciences; as one cadre of scholars said to me when I visited them in their new gleaming tower several years ago, where they had "everything," "Now they have taken away all our alibis!"

Social scientists, in my judgment, will never be able to cope with the hazardous intellectual problems I discussed at the beginning of my remarks—the problems of merging the concepts of a variety of fields or deciding where and when they should be merged—so long as we can so ill afford failures and mistakes, both psychologically and in terms of public relations. We know intellectually, but we do not fully believe, that there is risk and uncertainty, as well as profit, in any intellectual endeavor which is worthwhile. So much is this so that, drawing on Malinowski's theory of magic, we can view the boundaries of the disciplines and the terminological and methodological schemes of the various schools as so many scaffoldings to shore up our morale. Anybody who has really struggled, as, for example, Parsons has, at the boundary between economics and sociology knows how well-nigh intractable the real problems are—apart from all the more or less factitious and time-bound obstacles presented by current intellectual conventions which mark off the newer from the older fields (and have indeed only separated economics from sociology in the last several generations). It is hard not to rely on some wooden semantics, which will give one the courage to walk into these difficulties. But let him who is without fear pull the first nail in the scaffolding. What is often, in the view of the older sciences, called "jargon" in the newer ones has this morale-sustaining function, whereas the surviving scaffoldings of the older disciplines are no longer thought of as jargon but as part of the structure.

Pending the social security of social scientists, then, we must look forward to an era of jargon, of schemes and counterschemes. And it makes sense to try to reduce the fanaticism, the deadly seriousness, of the proponents and opponents of each scheme, including one's own. It also makes sense to train ourselves and our students in the art of translation, so that we can shift easily from one set of metaphors to another, one set of models to another, without losing the morale that comes from holding on to a metaphor or a model.

But translators and diplomats, while necessary, are of course not a substitute for programs, for common tasks. Despite the proliferation of models, however, it is striking how few new fields have developed since the *Eleven Twenty-six* volume was written. There are, of course, areas of fabulous growth, such as small-group research or, as Bernard Berelson pointed out earlier today, public opinion research. Compared, however, to the new specialties that have emerged at the juncture of physics and chemistry, or of physics and biology, the social sciences have been curiously static in the relations they have engendered among each other. The original hopes were a bit extravagant. With hopes, possibly, as with social theories, it may be best to be a Mertonian, a man working in the middle range, to talk less of "breakthrough" or of "basic" research and to make fewer claims all round.

Yet it is all too easy to preach an end to innocence. There is innocence in the hope expressed in *Eleven Twenty-six* (or 1313) that because people are housed in the same building and walk the same corridors they will talk to each other; the lingua franca of social science, based either on common topics or common terms, seems further away than ever, nor will the semantic shift from the term "social sciences" to the term "behavioral sciences" make any difference. But this development should hardly be a cause for comfort to those skeptics who have always pooh-poohed any experimental approach to questions of academic boundaries. While I think there is every justification for individual scholars pursuing traditional, if less glamorous, paths, without feeling under pressure to be fashionably interdisciplinary, I also think that *Schadenfreude* in the fact of the actual pitfalls of experiment is not becoming to a scholar. In intellectual as in other activities, it is worthwhile occasionally attempting to bridge impossible barriers among the disciplines and beyond them, because in the process, though it be by its nature unending and often self-defeating, our understanding grows.

The Changing Times

It is an honor, and I certainly regard it as a great privilege, to have been invited to take part in this celebration and to speak at this Convocation.

I might begin by telling you that when I was collecting my thoughts before writing this address, I studied the program to see what subjects were going to be discussed and who would be discussing them. It was only too plain that this is a company of scholars among whom a few stray tycoons and a journalist have—on the presumption that they can read and write—been allowed to infiltrate.

As one of these outsiders, I do, however, have a pleasant advantage. I can say freely what I have long believed. It is that in the social sciences the University of Chicago has achieved an eminence which is second to none in the Western world. During this most difficult and dangerous quarter of a century, Chicago has been an example of the freedom of the mind—of originality in the pursuit of knowledge and of faithfulness to the great tradition of wisdom.

Chicago has been a reminder that free men must love the truth and be unafraid, and that when their heads are bloody—as now and then Chicago's head has been—their heads must always be unbowed.

This is the kind of occasion when the speaker who occupies my place on the program has no choice about the subject of his talk. He is not free to take a definite subject about which he might conceivably have acquired some learning. Those subjects are reserved for the round tables.

An anniversary speaker has but one possible subject: he must look back upon the past and he must look forward into the future.

This is, as it happens, a moment in the history of the modern world when this, the perennial subject of an anniversary speaker, is also the living subject of our most serious practical concern. We have arrived at a turning point in the history of our time. We have arrived at a great divide between two eras, and what for most of our lives we have thought of as the present and the contemporary is now the recent past and behind us. We have come into a future which even ten years ago few could, and almost no one did, imagine.

There has been a revolution of the most radical kind in the technology of war, and this revolution is having enormous consequences upon the balance and the structure of power throughout the world. This technological revolution is not completed. It is proceeding far more rapidly than our ability to assess its political consequences. But we have reached the point—we reached that point in the past year— when all the great powers have realized, and have publicly recognized, that none of them can face the risk of a modern nuclear war. There exists, as a result, a military stalemate which compels the great powers to avoid war even at the expense of their objectives, even though the issues of the struggle between them remain unsettled and unresolved.

No man can be sure he is reading correctly the history of his own time. But as I read our recent history, this fundamental change of view has meant that there is a devaluation and downgrading of the political issues, that there is an upgrading of the necessity of avoiding war.

This fundamental change began in 1949 when the Soviet government showed that it had developed nuclear weapons. The change came to a climax in 1954 when the hydrogen bomb had been tested and its awful consequences had been realized in London, in Washington, and in Moscow.

The famous meeting at the summit last July in Geneva was the direct result of the fact that the big governments and informed opinion throughout the world had realized the enormous and revolutionary character of the modern weapons. The so-called spirit of Geneva was essentially a public acknowledgment that it had become impossible to contemplate a resort to nuclear warfare. There was no agreement at Geneva that we were all going to think alike, and none that our interests had suddenly become compatible. But there was an agreement that for the time being it was impossible to contemplate a war among the great powers.

No one knows how long this military stalemate will last. But while the stalemate does last, we find ourselves living in a time when war and the threat of war have become unusable instruments for the promotion of the national purposes of the great powers. There has been, as we know, no disarmament. But the armaments of the great powers are, for the time being, neutralized.

The Soviet Union cannot use its military forces to support a Communist uprising inside the lands protected by the Western powers. For the risk of war is too incalculably great to justify an attempt to expand the Communist orbit by military action. The Western powers cannot use their military power to roll back the frontiers of the Communist orbit. For the risks of war are too incalculably great. The struggle between the two great systems goes on. It will go on. But we now have reason to think—indeed we know when we look, for example, at Egypt—that this struggle is going to be waged with measures and with instruments which do not provoke or challenge a total war.

The first statesman in a high place who realized that the modern weapons had made war an intolerable and unusable instrument of national policy was Sir Winston Churchill. Not long thereafter—about one year ago last June—Churchill came to Washington, where, it is fairly plain, he talked to President Eisenhower about the revolutionary character of the new weapons. Shortly after that—in October, 1954—the President made the historic declaration—the most significant declaration of the new era—that "there is no alternative to peace."

Soon after that the Soviet government came to the same conclusion. The Soviet General Staff and the Soviet rulers had, so it appears, been effectively briefed by the Soviet scientists on the effects of the hydrogen bomb. It was then there took place an alteration in the Soviet attitude. I am not saying that there were not other reasons for this alteration. But it is clear, I think, that the determining cause of the change was the danger of nuclear war. The Soviet rulers began to talk peace in the manner of men who have realized that a war now would be radically unlike the two world wars of this century—and that for them, as well as for their adversaries, the war would be incalculable, irrational, and unpredictably destructive.

This marks a new era. But we must realize that we are entering this new era with our minds conditioned by our experiences in the old era. Our minds are conditioned by the great depression, by the rise of Hitler, by the aggression of Japan, by the failure to organize and to arm the allied resistance, by Munich, by Hitler's defeat and conquest of Europe, by the fact that the liberation of Europe could not be achieved without the Red Army, and that this led to the communist occupation of the eastern half of Europe. Our minds are conditioned by the Cold War among the victors, by the Chinese Revolution, by the Greek Civil War, and by the Korean War.

How have these experiences conditioned our minds? In many different ways, of course. But in one general way which I would like to mention. Our minds have, if I may say so, been conditioned to assume that the challenges to which we must respond are primarily foreign, alien, and external. Since the first World War, when we were drawn into war against our will, we have felt ourselves threatened by events for which not we, but others, were responsible. Our greatest decisions have, in fact, been reactions forced upon us by challenges from the outside. We were attacked at Pearl Harbor. Then we began to prepare for war. We saw western Europe bankrupt and prostrate and on the verge of anarchy. Then we produced the Marshall Plan. We saw western Europe, which is our own strategic frontier, defenseless and threatened with conquest. Then we rearmed ourselves and organized NATO.

And so we have acquired the habit of reacting rather than acting, of making great and necessary decisions only after, only when, we have been pushed, prodded, and provoked by events beyond our own immediate control.

Each spring in Washington, for example, the battle has to be fought in Congress to obtain appropriations for foreign aid, that is to say, for the means to deal with the new responsibilities which the world wars have brought to this country. Congress has never liked spending American money abroad. In the old days the Administration used to wait for good Old Joe to help it out by doing something outrageous enough to provoke Congress into voting the appropriations. And as we know, year after year, good Old Joe would play his part and would commit some kind of infuriating outrage.

Now good Old Joe has gone to what we all hope is his just reward.

And since then it has been harder for the President to get Congress to underwrite our foreign policy. For without the spurs and the whip to which it used to react, the old nag rather likes just to amble along.

I would suggest that in the time ahead of us the big challenges will probably not look as if they came, and may not in fact come, from the outside. They will appear as internal issues of our own democratic society. Yet the world will not be at peace. It is only too plain, is it not, that while we are not now faced with a third world war, we are not in sight of a peace of collaboration with the Soviet Union, and much less with China. Vast areas of the globe—much of Asia, most of Africa, some of Latin America, the core of Europe, will not be in a settled order. The great ideological struggle will be going on.

In all the vast unsettled areas of the world we must expect to be the rivals, not the partners, of the great Communist powers. We shall be competing with them for the friendship and for the confidence of the emerging peoples, for influence and for power and for profit. These areas were once—as recently as the first World War—under the hegemony of the Atlantic powers in western Europe and in North America. China, southern Asia, the whole South Pacific, the Middle East, eastern Europe, all of Africa, and the whole Western Hemisphere were within the cultural and political orbit of the Western liberal democratic society.

We can be certain, I think, that in the time to come we shall be the rivals of the Soviets and of the Chinese in all the lands where the Atlantic nations were, until recently, the leaders and so often the masters.

I do not know how to predict the outcome of that rivalry. But I shall dwell on one aspect of it which concerns especially this company who are here today, this company of men who work in the problems of human society. I said a few minutes ago that a characteristic of the era of the world wars was that our democratic societies were presented with a series of external challenges. If we are now, as I believe, entering a period when war and the threat of war cannot be used by the great powers, then the rivalry for power and influence will be diffused. It will not be concentrated; it will not be brought to a head in some capital issue of peace or war.

If this is the kind of time we are entering, we shall find it harder than it has been to agree on what needs to be done, harder, that is to say, to form national policies. During the period of the world wars the imperatives of policy were not obscure. In the thirties there was no real doubt about the intentions of Hitler, and of the Japanese war lords, or that they would dominate the world if the Western democracies did not rearm, unite, and resist. Nor was there any real doubt of Stalin's intentions in the postwar period—no real doubt that he in his turn meant to expand and to dominate unless and until he was resisted and checked.

The Western democracies did not always obey these imperatives as soon as they appeared. They were often too late with too little. But the crucial problems of that era were not what *ought* to be done. They were problems of the will to do what ought to be done, problems of the willingness to see what was dangerous and disagreeable, of the willingness to do what was dangerous and painful.

In the era we are now entering the imperatives of policy are likely to be much less clear and much less compelling. The President will not be able to go confidently to the people or to the Congress, saying that this is what we must do to be saved, saying that this is what we must do to defend the country and to insure its survival. Our rivalry with the Soviet Union and with China will be made up of myriads of little issues, enormously important in the aggregate, none of them in itself quite obviously vitally important.

We must take it as not unlikely, indeed as probable, that this will reduce big national policies to a collection of items that are treated by Congress as domestic and as local questions. We have, I believe, a good preview of what is coming in the way Congress has been disintegrating and devaluing the foreign economic policies of the Administration. This has happened because, unlike the great policy of Lend-Lease during the war and of the Marshall Plan after the war, the measures to promote the development of backward countries do not appear as imperatives of national survival. Honest men can differ about their wisdom or their practicality. Nothing spectacular happens immediately if such measures are postponed.

The sovereign question in the time to come may, I submit to you, be this: When the democracies are not challenged and compelled from the outside, are they able to form and to carry out national policies which their vital interests in the long run, but not in the short run, require? For when war is not the issue, the objectives of public policy are not regarded as imperatives. They are unclear and they are controversial. Our public purposes and our policies will now have to be hammered out on the anvil of public debate.

In those debates this company of scholars will be deeply involved. May I be so bold as to say how scholars are involved in the great and crucial debates which will shape our future?

The inner principle of a free and democratic society is that the decisions of government are made with the consent of the governed and that this consent is not to be manufactured but is to be reached by a continuing rational debate. Within a free and democratic society it is necessary to agree to act on the assumption that the members of the community are living in a rational order. This means that they have all agreed to believe that by sincere inquiry and rational debate they will be able to hammer out a common understanding of what is true for their democracy and what is right.

The scholar is a guardian of the assumptions of this continuing debate. He is the originator of the terms in which the debate is carried on. He is the critic of the evidence put out by the debaters, and of their logic.

The scholar, whose work in life it is to inquire and to submit his findings to his peers, can by his exertions and by his example promote, defend, purify, and enrich this debate and dialectic. For the sovereign principle of the scholar's calling is the active principle of a free society.

I am talking about dialectic and debate among scholars themselves, among men of equal learning and of equal obligation to seek the truth disinterestedly. It is here primarily, rather than in the newspapers and on the lecture platform and before the television, that the public issues can best be defined, can best be analyzed, elucidated, civilized, and put into conceptual terms that will help to make the hurly-burly of popular debate orderly and productive.

I do not mean to say, please note, that scholars, should not, as citizens, participate in the public debate. I think they should. But this is not their true vocation. Their true vocation is to give their first interest and their prime energy to their own inquiries and to the debates with their own peers. I would not shrink from the notion that the debates of the scholars are above the battle. It is good for, I would say it is necessary to, the outcome of the battle that there should always be men who have earned the right to be listened to, and who are above the battle where they can see the whole field and both sides.

We shall in the days to come need such men to give definition, to give shape, and to give direction to the countless issues which public opinion will be called upon to decide. So I urge you to think of yourselves not only as teachers, and not only as men who are inquiring into the unknown, but also to think of yourselves as the makers of the concepts, as the shapers of the terms and the patterns of the discourse, as the guardians of the rules of the argument, with which the debates by which freedom lives are carried on.

The Social Sciences Today

It is fitting that we should honor the Social Science Research Building upon its twenty-fifth year. Great men and women have paced its
halls, written in its offices, and lectured in its classrooms. I think of
Robert Park, William Ogburn, Henry Schultz, Charles Merriam,
Jacob Viner, Frank Knight, Fay-Cooper Cole, William Dodd,
Andrew McLaughlin, and a host of other who have been part of it
during this quarter of a century. It could even be said that a good
deal of what we call "social science" was invented within that building.

Indeed, some unkind people suggest that those walls echoed with
more stimulating teaching and housed more novel ideas a quarter of
a century ago than they do today. I have heard this same comment
about most buildings that house social scientists today on any campus, and it may mean only that the beginning of a science is more
exciting than its later and more mature development. We need to
remember that Albion Small was the first real professor of sociology
in the United States and that Charles Merriam was one of the origi-
nators of the science of politics and administration. These pioneering
leaders painted with a broad brush and inevitably it is less exciting
to fill in the detail of a large canvas.

There are, however, some winds of controversy that have pene-
trated even so remote and sheltered a place as a chancellor's office,
and I have begun to wonder whether the social scientists have not
reached a crisis in their affairs. With a surprising uniformity, every
department of sociology in the country agrees that all its senior
members very definitely belong in the department, but there is a
remarkable lack of uniformity on who should be added to the group.
Perhaps there can be a legitimate controversy over who is a *good*
sociologist, but I have heard some bickering even on the question of
who *is* a sociologist. Locally, in our psychology department we have
agreed that there is biopsychology and social psychology, but nobody can describe to my satisfaction the difference between a bio-

psychologist and a biologist or can tell me what social psychology is. Harvard solemnly adopts and publishes a report on how a department of psychology ought to be organized and no less solemnly proceeds to do the exact opposite. At the meetings of the trade association of university presidents, called the Association of American Universities, where we talk in hushed tones about what we all know and publicly deny, I find a similar confusion. It gives us some comfort, however, to hear that a large foundation which chose to end all this confusion by changing the name to "behavioral sciences" is having difficulty in its new training center in discovering who are competent to train whom and in what. We are careful in universities to dignify the process of fragmenting by the euphonious title of interdisciplinary research, but it is alarming to note that history moves into the humanities, that economics becomes mathematics, that anthropology and psychology ally themselves with biology, and that geography is at home with the physical sciences. It is fashionable these days to deplore specialization and to urge cross-fertilization, but this can be carried to the point where there is nothing in which to specialize and no parent stock with which to cross-fertilize. There certainly is some confusion here, and these are the reasons why I said that the social sciences are currently facing a crisis in their affairs.

We need to remind ourselves again that social science as science is very young. I was sharply reminded of this the other day in reading a Harvard report to discover that their Department of Sociology—since abandoned for another and larger configuration—was not established until 1929. And, after all, the first building on any campus to house social scientists is only twenty-five years old. It is a very young science indeed, and the youth of all sciences has been plagued with difficulties. The problem in the social sciences is rendered even more acute by their enormous importance in the field of action. It just happens to be the case that a Supreme Court decision on desegregation has more immediate importance than any amount of sound theory or empirical fact on the whole problem of race relations. And, as the Marxists smilingly await the inevitable economic collapse of the West, economics cannot be a cloistered science, dealing, as the astronomers and physicists do, with matters which are uncharged with fearful emotions. There is almost no one these days so illiterate and uninformed that he does not believe himself to be an informed psychologist, economist, political scientist, and sociologist. And as Chancellor I have had ample opportunity to observe that hell hath no fury like a layman scorned. It is not easy to make a sober and deliberate science within this highly emotional context.

There is another problem of which most of us are painfully aware. The essence of science is regularity, and regularity involves the rigid techniques and controls of the laboratory. The atom is complicated, goodness knows, and it takes all sorts of expensive and complicated machinery to force it to divulge its composition; but the atom is simplicity itself as compared with man or society or man's functioning in society. It is hard to get controls so that experiments can be repeated by other competent experts. The factors that enter a human or social situation are so enormously complex that our mathematics cannot encompass the variables. It is precisely this problem of methodology, in my judgment, which has brought the social sciences to the crisis in their affairs.

I read the other day a biography of Paracelsus, a doctor of medicine in the early sixteenth century. His real and more picturesque name was Dr. Theophrastus Bombastus ab Hohenheim, and he stood on the border between magic and science, with a foot in both. He prided himself, on the one hand, in "Godlike knowledge of the occult," and yet he praised reason and experiment as the only true sources of knowledge. He opened the path to biochemistry, he began chemical medicine, he formulated the first theory of metabolism, and he shook the foundations of the ancient four-humor doctrine of Galen to which most doctors then subscribed. At the same time he was mixing up hell-brews of viper fat and unicorn horn while he pondered the oneness of man and the universe. He was a child of two different worlds, but, in announcing his course of lectures at the University of Basle, he said, "If I want to prove anything I shall not do so by quoting authorities but by experiment and by reasoning thereupon." He saw clearly the necessary relationship between theory and experiment, and, to paraphrase the later words of Immanuel Kant, he saw that theory without fact was empty and that empirical investigation without theory was blind. This insight was the basis of scientific medicine, and much of the enormous progress made in the science over the last four hundred years is due to a clear recognition of this methodological truth.

Perhaps the social sciences stand today somewhere near the position that Paracelsus occupied. If so, the problem is one, I suggest, of methodology, and, specifically, the correct and appropriate relationship between theory and experience.

It is too easy today in the social sciences, in my judgment, to confuse theory and thesis. There are too many people who enter the field with a ready-made conclusion, obtained from their local household gods rather than their laboratories, and proceed to gather facts and footnotes to substantiate it. They want to get something done, and I admire their motives but not their science. There is the sociologist who wants a better society of a certain kind, the economist who selects a certain way to eliminate the trough of the business cycle, the political scientist who wants peace in his time and at his price, the psychologist who is struggling with the problem of his own adjustment. It is from this background that we so often find a social scientist of a minority group who gathers data about the difficulties of other minority groups, the young liberal who chooses to make a study of a Communist group in Canada, the second-generation immigrant historian who writes of the woes of the immigrant in America, the conservative political theorist who sees in Burke an excuse for pleading the cause for a new elite, the outraged political scientist who suddenly discovers the recent doings of congressional investigating committees worthy of serious scientific study. Now the problems that underlie these concerns are important; but I suggest that too often a valued thesis becomes confused with sound theory, and there is a resulting selection and emphasis. The trace of a tear is there; a cause lurks in the background.

There has developed another school among the social scientists, and they gather facts with a vengeance. They count things and correlate things and obtain medians and means and standard deviations. This school flourishes most among, though it is not limited to, the educationalists; and, though Johnny may not be able to read, he has been well counted and correlated. The psychologists and sociologists gather vast quantities of data which fail somehow to add up to an important conclusion or a conclusion of any kind. Even historians confuse themselves and their readers on the meaning of the historical process by endless undigested statistics of a significant period. Now I may seem to speak of all this more scornfully than I intend to. The gathering of facts is at the heart of scientific research; but, if it is unrelated to interpretation and theory, it is trivial and confusing.

The fact-gathering becomes so elaborate and monumental that the problem which initiated it disappears along with any possible conclusion.

The social sciences are very young, and confusion is typical of adolescence and upon the whole a very good thing. Perhaps it is not enough to say that the fundamental problem is one of methodology. If I were to hazard one jaundiced diagnosis upon this happy occasion, I would suggest that the largest single problem in the social sciences comes from the fact that the field is overpopulated with propounders of partisan theses disguised as theories, collectors of inadequate tested statistics presented, presumably, as significant facts, and elaborators of methodologies designed to cure bias and secure significance. This is the reason, I believe, why it is so hard for administrators and perhaps even for experts to identify the sound workers.

Yet if methodology is thought of as the way appropriately to relate theory and fact, it is precisely the problem of methodology in this sense that has created the difficulty in the beginnings of all the sciences. Galileo, for example, laid the foundation of mechanics by solving a problem of methodology. Having set forth a mathematical solution of the problem of uniformly accelerated motion in *Two New Sciences,* he has speakers discuss his solution. The first, after stating his enthusiastic agreement with the solution, actually misinterprets it and falls into one of the traditional errors. A second speaker, who represents Galileo, instead of expressing dismay at this result, remarks that he discovered the true solution by initially falling into and then correcting this same error. Here at the beginning of mechanics a true theory can be confused with an enthusiastically held thesis, and accurately observed facts can be arranged to support an erroneous theory.

It is not easy to relate properly theory and fact when the issues dealt with are of enormous importance and emotionally charged. And it is not easy to put them together when the material studied is of great complexity and the controls hard to establish. But it remains the case that a field of study becomes a science when theory is formulated upon the basis of fact and facts are sought and interpreted upon the basis of theory. It is my hope that this building we honor today will still be standing when this problem has been solved.

The Role of Government in Promoting Economic Stability

In all or virtually all countries, whether raw-material-producing, rapidly developing, or maturely industrialized, governmental action is required for the achievement and maintenance of economic stability. The kinds of action appropriate for use in a country depend on many factors, including, for example, the attitudes and aspirations of its people; its political, economic, and social institutions; the degree of dependence of its economy on international markets and sources of supply; and the extent and rate of its industrial development. The role of government in promoting economic stability at any particular time and place may vary widely, depending on the prevailing combination of these and other factors.

To formulate and demonstrate a universally applicable pattern that would show the varying roles of government appropriate to different combinations of factors would be indeed an achievement. In this paper I have not undertaken that broad task. Rather, I have directed my attention to the more manageable problem of the promotion of economic stability in the United States at the present time. I am hopeful, however, that much of the discussion which follows may be found relevant also to the stability problems of other countries.

The subject of economic stability is a highly appropriate one for this occasion. Economic stability in both theory and practice highlights the interrelations of economics and political science. It is in matters relating to economic stability, moreover, that the discipline of economics has made perhaps its largest and certainly its most spectacular advances in the quarter-century since this Social Science Research Building was dedicated. It would be hard to find a more striking contrast than that between the methods proposed today by economists for dealing with depression and those proposed in 1930.

The hard years of the 1930's accelerated the advance of economic analysis in this area and led to its aceptance by economists and policy-makers. The fear that the depression of the 1930's might return and the belief that government could prevent this from happening led to the passage of the Employment Act of 1946, in which the federal government officially recognized its responsibility for promoting economic stability. The Act did not, however, spell out government's role in meeting the responsibility it had accepted. It is with the role, not the question of responsibility, that this paper is concerned.

I

On its face the matter seems simple enough. The usual statement of the argument runs something like the following. The economic stability of the country requires a uniform flow of total spending on consumption and capital formation. Too slow a flow means depression, too fast a flow, inflation. To maintain a uniform flow of spending, a diminution in any segment of the flow must be offset by an increase in the flow elsewhere. Individuals and businesses, and for that matter states and local governments, often react to a diminished total flow of spending by reducing their own spending, and to an increased total flow by enlarging their own spending, thus accentuating both downward and upward movements of economic activity. Only through collective action, that is, through government, can there be any certainty of a compensatory increase or decrease of spending. Government can and should achieve compensatory changes to maintain uniform total spending. It should do this through fiscal policy, that is, by altering the volume of its revenues and expenditures, and through monetary policy, that is, by encouraging or discouraging private spending through control of credit. Once government has demonstrated that it can and will take the action necessary to achieve a stable economy, individuals and businesses will no longer feel the need to protect themselves by changes in their spending that accentuate economic fluctuations. The task of government then will be a relatively easy one—just a touch now and then to the accelerator or the brake, and the machine will run smoothly. Perhaps I exaggerate, but I think not.

The argument I have just stated goes to the heart of the stability problem and specifies the chief aspects of the role of government in meeting it. The statement is, however, a tremendous oversimplification both of the problem and of the difficulties in meeting it.

To begin with, it is significant that the original Full Employment Bill of 1945 and the Employment Act of 1946 as it finally emerged were both concerned more with high-level employment than they were with "economic stability" as that term would be defined on the basis of the dictionary meanings of the words. The "declaration of policy" of the Employment Act refers neither to the term "economic stability" nor to the concept, being devoted to spelling out various more or less consistent objectives culminating in "maximum employment, production, and purchasing power." It is not until the section dealing with the duties and functions of the Council of Economic Advisers is reached that reference is made to the development and recommendation of "national economic policies . . . to avoid economic fluctuations or to diminish the effects thereof," and this is only one among several policy objectives that are referred to.

As the language of the Employment Act indicates, economic stability is socially and politically acceptable only if the level of business activity is sufficiently high that the amount of unemployment is low. Moreover, since the population and productivity are increasing, the level of activity also must grow, otherwise unemployment will rise to an unacceptable level. "Economic stability and growth" thus connotes a high and growing level of business activity, as well as price stability and the avoidance of large fluctuations in economic magnitudes generally.

The growth element in this hybrid of economic stability and growth has increased in importance with the passing years, perhaps because unemployment has not proved thus far to be the threat it had been feared to be. Growth sufficient to hold unemployment to an acceptably low level is no longer deemed sufficient; competition is keen in setting higher and higher "practical targets" for the national product of future years and decades. There are, however, at least two reasons for minimizing in this paper the emphasis on economic growth. One is that another topic of this conference is devoted to that subject. The second is that stability and growth not only are distinguishable goals of policy but in some respects are conflicting goals. To be sure, a substantial degree of economic stability is a requirement for economic growth, and economic growth eases the adjustments that must be made even in a stable economy. On the other hand, the process of achieving a high degree of stability may tend to stifle economic growth while the process of achieving very rapid growth may have a disturbing effect. "Economic stability" as a goal of national policy is thus not only somewhat more than the words connote but also somewhat less, since complete stability is not part of the objective.

The possible conflict among the three goals which in combination are often referred to as economic stability may be seen in questions that are often raised. How small a volume of unemployment is consistent with a stable price level? If high employment and stable prices prove to be inconsistent, which is more important? May rapid technological change, such as automation, bring about rapid growth of national product at the expense of employment? If so, which is more important, growth or full employment? These questions suggest that adding the objectives of full employment and economic growth to economic stability may considerably complicate the role of government.

Thus far we have been talking about the stabilization of national aggregates. These aggregates, of course, are only statistical totals of numerous pieces or sectors both on the production side of the national accounts and on the income side. Various kinds of sectors may be noted, such as regions and localities, industries, business enterprises, even families and individuals. Each of us is likely to be more keenly interested in the sectors of which he is a part or which directly affect him than in the national aggregate, of which we may not even be aware. The sectors are more subject to instability than are the national aggregates, since the aggregates average out divergent changes of the sectors. In any but a stagnant society the fortunes of some sectors are rising while those of others are falling. A policy of promoting "free competitive enterprise" puts the stamp of approval on this process, and growth through technological change makes it inevitable. Presumably it is not part of economic stabilization policy to prevent these changes from taking place. In any event, the inexorable procession from the cradle to the grave, the growth of population, the depletion of natural resources, and the depreciation of capital goods make some of the changes inevitable.

If the national aggregates can be kept stable, the problem of making adjustments to such changes in the sectors is greatly facilitated. On the other hand, instability in the national aggregate often originates in the instability of an important sector. Moreover, if within acceptable national aggregates there are too many adversely affected regions, localities, industries, business enterprises, or even families and individuals, there may be a good deal of human misery and economic waste, as well as important political repercussions.

Thus, the scope of governmental responsibility for promoting economic stability may turn out to be considerably broader than our earlier description would indicate. It may include, for example, the stimulation of employment in a temporarily depressed city or industry, or the rehabilitation of a declining region. In such cases measures other than fiscal and monetary policy will probably have to be employed, since even a general inflationary movement might not be sufficient to restore prosperity to the distressed sector. Among the methods used might be the allocation of government contracts, government loans to finance new industries or the modernization of old ones, construction of power plants, government research to find new uses for old products, technical assistance to local or industrial groups, changes in tariff rates, changes in transportation rates, elimination of unfair competitive practices if these have been a factor, and assistance in moving people out of dying areas and helping them to find jobs elsewhere. There might be some temptation to attempt to slow up industrial shifts that affected a sector unfavorably, even though the change would promote economic progress for the country as a whole. In such cases the problem of harmonizing the goals of economic stability and economic growth would become even more difficult.

Turning to another aspect, it is a safe generalization that, the more violent the economic disturbance, the larger the role that government will be called upon to play in promoting economic stability. Fiscal and monetary policies, broadly conceived, may well be adequate to deal with instabilities that are generated by the operation of the economy itself. Severe shocks that come to the economy from the outside, however, may require other and more drastic measures to maintain stability. For the United States economy, such shocks have been largely in connection with the mobilization and demobilization associated with war and the threat of war. A major objective of war mobilization is to expand greatly the volume of productive effort, to divert a large proportion of that effort from civilian to military production, to do this in a tremendous hurry, and to do it with a minimum of disturbing effects on the economy, since such effects would undermine civilian morale and the war effort. A major problem is to avoid or minimize price inflation. The tax increases and credit controls of fiscal policy and monetary policy are, of course, crucial in this effort. They are not likely to be sufficient, however, partly because rate increases are held down by political factors, but also because taxes are unsuited to get at some sources of purchasing power, notably accumulated wealth. The effects of high rates on incentives to produce efficiently are also a limiting factor. In this situation it is necessary to resort to price controls, rationing, and perhaps other types of direct controls.

Another development to be avoided in time of war is the destruction of viable relationships within the economy. One of the major foundations of wartime morale is the belief that, when the war is over, economic relations between various groups can be restored to their prewar pattern. Complete reliance on the market to allocate resources, goods, and services might destroy all semblance of prewar relationships. The allocation of scarce items, such as food, clothing, and housing, through the price system at a time of national crisis could result in social upheaval. A major purpose of economic stabilization is to avoid social upheaval, and it is accordingly necessary to turn at such a time to direct controls. The economic sectors require stabilizing action in time of war more than in time of peace, since the disruption is so much greater. Moreover, it may be some years after the war has ended before the recovery and redirection of production will permit an end to direct controls. Since postwar patterns of relationship are always somewhat different from prewar, the aim should be to reach as soon as possible a viable and stable pattern for the future rather than to attempt the restoration of the past. A consideration in the design of wartime controls should be that they not set up such strong vested interests that the later shift to less drastic measures would be unduly delayed and would itself be seriously disturbing when it did take place.

Countries for which foreign trade is an important fraction of total trade face an additional stabilization problem, namely, the possibility of a balance-of-payments deficit culminating in a foreign-exchange crisis. This problem has not been adequately appreciated in the United States because it has been largely outside our direct experience. Foreign trade, while large in total, is relatively only a small fraction of the national product of the United States. For a variety of reasons this country also has long had a so-called favorable balance of trade and has accumulated very large monetary reserves. For perhaps most other countries, however, foreign trade is of critical importance. Many of them, especially during and since the war, have had an unfavorable trade balance, particularly in relation to the United States, and continue to have inadequate monetary and foreign-exchange reserves. For such countries foreign-exchange crises are urgent signals for action.

A government has open to it several courses of action in meeting balance-of-payments difficulties. Internal demand may be held down indirectly through the imposition of credit restraints and higher taxes and directly through rationing and other direct controls. Imports may be restricted either by quantitative limitations on less necessary imports or by limiting the use of foreign exchange. Finally, the currency may be devalued in international exchange, but this step is likely to be viewed as a last resort to be used only when other methods have failed to restore a workable equilibrium.

The kinds of governmental action that are appropriate in meeting balance-of-payments difficulties depend at least in part on the reasons for those difficulties. In some situations the underlying causes of a dangerous loss of foreign exchange are within the country itself. For example, an expansion of domestic purchasing power may enlarge the demand for imported goods, at the same time absorbing in domestic consumption goods needed for export. Domestic price increases that result from the expanded demand may lead to rising wages and other costs, thus reducing the ability of the country's export industries to sell goods abroad in competition with other producers. In essence, this is an inflationary movement that is reflected in foreign-exchange difficulties. An approaching foreign-exchange crisis, indeed, is likely to exert a much more powerful stimulus to anti-inflationary action than would otherwise be exerted by the creeping upward movement of domestic prices and wages.

Vigorously applied anti-inflationary fiscal and monetary measures may solve the balance-of-payments problem without resort to direct controls over imports or foreign exchange.

In other cases, however, the causes of the balance-of-payments difficulty may lie outside the country. Thus countries that are heavily dependent on the sale of raw materials abroad find themselves large-ly at the mercy of world demand and world prices. A drop in demand and prices for their export commodities may drastically reduce their supply of foreign exchange. In such a situation, internal deflationary measures may or may not be called for, depending on the internal economic situation, but they are not likely to be adequate in meeting the problem. Direct limits on the use of foreign exchange or quanti-tative restrictions on imports also are likely to be required.

The foregoing comments are not intended to imply that the raw-material-producing, economically underdeveloped countries are never responsible for their foreign-exchange difficulties. Frequently the cause is to be found directly in their own unsound practices. It is not easy to see, however, that even with the best of practices they could have protected themselves adequately against the wide fluctuations that have occurred in their raw-material markets. It is accordingly not surprising that, in addition to taking such immediate steps as were open to them to meet their balance-of-payments diffi-culties, these countries have also reacted in ways that have some-times irked the more highly industrialized countries. One such reac-tion is a drive to achieve greater internal diversity and balance through promoting the industrialization of their economies along lines that would undoubtedly involve an uneconomic use of resources if the world were an economically stable one. A second reaction is to press for international measures designed to stabilize the demand for and prices of raw materials. If such stability could be secured and assured, the drive for industrialization might be placed on a sounder basis with benefit to all countries. Thus far, however, there has been neither the wit nor, I fear, the will on the part of the in-dustrialized countries to design measures for meeting through inter-national action the problem of stabilizing raw-material prices and markets.

While rarely troubled by the destabilizing influence of foreign-exchange problems, the United States does not thereby escape concern for international economic relations in its promotion of economic stability. The tremendous impact of United States economic activities on other countries and the large stake of this country in the economic strength of the whole free world make the stability of other countries part of our responsibility. When aggregate demand in this country decreases, there is a temptation to support demand for domestic production by cutting off imports, either through direct limitations or through higher tariffs. With respect to some commodities this is the United States policy at the present time. The stabilization of our own economy is important in maintaining the economic stability of the other countries of the world, but obviously such methods undermine rather than support their stability.

Much of the record of the United States in meeting its international economic responsibilities seems admirable, for example, in the case of the Marshall Plan. We should not be too self-congratulatory, however, since in that case our motivation may have been more a matter of fear of the political and security consequences of an economic collapse in Europe than of concern for its economic stability as such. We have no reason for pride in connection with the wide fluctuations in demand for and prices of raw materials which resulted from the Korean fighting and the rearmament boom that accomapnied it. The wide swings upward and later downward had highly distressing economic effects on many countries. Little concern seems to have been shown over this development either in Washington or in the country at large, except regarding those manifestations that directly threatened United States stability. Our restrictions on the export of scarce commodities during the same period seem also to have been imposed with little regard for their impact on the economies of other countries.

The promotion of economic stability is thus by no means a simple problem. In considering the role of government, there is at least one other complication. Economic stability, even when combined with employment and growth, is not the only goal of governmental policy. The declaration of policy of the Employment Act speaks not only of "maximum employment, production, and purchasing power" but also of "free competitive enterprise and the general welfare." There are other objectives of government not stated in the Employment Act except as the "general welfare" may include all "good" things that government can do. Economic freedom and economic security are examples of important objectives. Promoting the objective of freedom of the individual may require avoidance of an action by government that would promote stability. Promoting the objective of economic security of the individual may require action by government that would interfere with growth. And so on. It is a task of the economist to discover ways and means of harmonizing apparently conflicting objectives, but, when they cannot be harmonized, the policy-makers—in the last analysis the public—must choose among them and determine the priorities.

The discussion thus far has related to the role of the federal government, which is the only government in the United States capable of taking collective action for the country as a whole. States and localities should also do what they can. The possibilities of compensatory fiscal action by states and localities are limited. States and localities are fiscally weaker than the federal government. Local financial powers derive from the state, while state taxing powers and accordingly borrowing powers are restricted by the competitive position of each state in the national economy. States have no monetary powers. Moreover, the beneficial effects of compensatory action taken in any one state tend to be diffused throughout the national economy. A state cannot expect to achieve large results from compensatory fiscal action unless its neighbors and trading partners are also carrying on similar action. In the absence of federal assistance, a neutral impact on economic stability is perhaps as much as can be hoped for from state fiscal action. States should, however, be able to avoid adding to economic instability by perverse fiscal action. The possibility of developing a type of federal-state fiscal relationship that would permit compensatory fiscal action by states may merit further examination.

II

Let us turn now from the factors which complicate the role of government in promoting economic stability to the question of whether government is able to perform that role and thus discharge the responsibility it has accepted. This question may be approached by considering the conditions that must be met if the government's performance is to be adequate to the task. The first condition is that maintenance of economic stability must not require action that would undermine and eventually destroy the kind of political and economic system that we are prepared to live with. It is less than twenty years ago—only day before yesterday in the life of the nation—that we were in the grip of a seemingly endless period of depression, discouragement, and stagnation so serious that it might not be tolerated if it were to occur again. Books were written to show that stagnation was the normal state of our mature economy. Today, employment is at a high, although not full, level, the economy is dynamic, and the prevailing attitude is one of enthusiastic expectation of a glorious future. Undoubtedly, many elements have figured in this striking transformation. Among the elements it is clear that the massive governmental spending of the wartime period was a major force. It is not certain that deficits, as well as spending, were necessary to achieve the transformation, since we have had no experience with massive government spending without large deficits. Likewise, it is not clear whether or to what extent inflation was a positive influence.

What will the next twenty years bring forth? Are we sure we have found the secret of a dynamic economy? Will our economy, having been raised to its present position, avoid serious depression and continue to function indefinitely at a high and rising level? Or are we still getting adjusted to the impact of the war, and do we face a new major downward movement in the not-so-distant future? Shall we face again the necessity of resorting to massive government spending, large government deficits, or substantial further inflation? These are not trivial questions. The necessity for repeated resort to such measures—and I am not talking, of course, about the ordinary workings of fiscal policy—would pose a very serious threat to our economic, social, and political system. I believe the probability is high that economic stability can be maintained on a long-term basis without resort to large-scale spending, deficits, or inflation. I can see no excuse for a depression like that of the thirties. I would suggest, however, that we do not have enough proof to be entirely certain about the matter.

Another condition that needs to be met is that the government have the economic intelligence to recognize what the appropriate course of action is at any particular time and when the course should be changed. The general level of ability of economists in the federal government is impressively high. It appears that all the techniques currently available to economists are being used by the government economists. Are these techniques enough? Despite the great strides that have been made in economic understanding, we still seem to lack adequate methods of forecasting and perhaps even of assuredly recognizing the major turns in business activity, and our knowledge of the strength of the effects of various stabilizing measures and of the lags in their action leaves much to be desired. Doubts continue to be expressed by some economists whether economic knowledge has reached the point that measures can be so designed and so timed as to promote stability consistently instead of often being neutral or positively perverse. Personally, I have no doubt that government economists will reach correct conclusions a very large part of the time. I hasten to say that my faith in what is said publicly is of a considerably lower order, but that is a different matter. I suppose that blunders, perhaps serious blunders, will be made by government economists in the future as they have been in the past. Nevertheless, if we had no more serious worries than the ability of professional economists to advise regarding the state of the economy and the appropriate course of action, I for one would feel reasonably satisfied that the chances of maintaining a stable economy were very good.

Another condition for the success of government as an economic stabilizer concerns the quality of the officials. Government officials—and not only government economists—must have the education, experience, and integrity required, first, to formulate imaginatively the stabilization measures for presentation to policy-makers for decision, and, second, after the decision is made, to administer such measures effectively and expeditiously. Government officials over the world differ widely in their ability to meet these tests. Some, it may be feared, are so deficient in the necessary qualities that governmental efforts to promote economic stability could scarcely be other than self-defeating. The United States government is among the comparatively well-administered governments of the world. Officials in the federal service are relatively well educated and experienced. The standard of integrity is relatively high. Unfortunately, career service continues to be politically vulnerable at the higher levels, as many able former bureaucrats are painfully aware, and many of the more capable people tend to leave the service when attractive outside opportunities are presented. Despite this weakness, I believe United States government officials have shown that they can devise and administer effectively the stabilization measures decided upon. All in all, the federal official deserves far better of public opinion that he receives. Nevertheless, officials are human and should not be subjected to unnecessary strains. The administration of taxes and government contracts, along with other functions requiring unusual integrity and judgment, imposes a sufficient strain on ability and integrity without the adoption of other measures requiring officials to grant or withhold valuable privileges or to apply intricate rules to a very large number of people. I have in mind price control and rationing among other measures. Such measures, of course, may be clearly necessary in some situations. With the understanding and support of the public they may be successfully administered for a considerable period of time. But they impose a strain on good government that should be avoided whenever possible.

Another requirement for successful promotion of economic stability is a government so organized that it can integrate policies with divergent objectives into a consistent, unified stabilization-promoting policy and can make quick changes in the direction and magnitude of stabilization measures. As I have pointed out elsewhere,[1] the United States government leaves much to be desired in these respects. The separation of legislative and executive branches of the government affords checks and balances. However desirable these may be in other respects, they interfere with achieving flexibility and integrated policy. Moreover, neither Congress nor the Executive Branch is satisfactorily organized from the viewpoint of promoting economic stability. Congressional action is fragmented under the committee system. An election every two years keeps short-run rather than long-run considerations in the foreground of attention in the Congress. The Executive Branch is divided into numerous departments and agencies that have different and sometimes divergent objectives. Departmental officials acting under congressional directives are prone to consider these objectives to be more important for

1. "Political and Administrative Requisites for Achieving Economic Stability," *Papers and Proceedings, American Economic Review*, XL, No. 2 (May, 1950), 166–69.

their operations than economic stability. Some steps toward integrated policy formulation have, of course, been taken. The Budget Bureau and Council of Economic Advisers—notably the chairman of the Council under the revised legislation—in the Executive Branch, and the Joint Committee on the Economic Report in the Legislative Branch, serve as co-ordinating and integrating elements. Their influence seems to be growing, but there is no evidence that integration of policy for the promotion of economic stability has been achieved in either branch.

I do not wish to paint too dark a picture. Certainly the government often has risen to high standards of unity and speed of action in critical situations. Moreover, monetary policy has proved in recent years to be a flexible instrument, although it is subject to strong political pressures when the business situation seems to be sagging. The "built-in stabilizers," those revenue and expenditure measures that automatically compensate in part for changes in national income and business activity, require no congressional and little administrative action. But, aside from these, the application of fiscal policy as well as the imposition or granting of power to impose specific credit controls, tax incentives, price controls, wage controls, and rationing might be difficult or impossible to achieve and would be time-consuming at best.

For governmental stabilizing measures to be fully effective, the public must have faith in their efficacy. Otherwise the magnitude of upward or downward movements in the economy growing out of every man's effort to defend his own situation might be so great that government action would find it difficult, perhaps impossible, to offset. In the United States, faith in the ability and intention of the government to prevent serious depressions and to promote economic growth has developed to a very considerable degree in the period since the adoption of the Employment Act. How long this faith would endure in the presence of a long slide in business activity is, of course, another question. The changeableness of opinion in the business world has often been noted.

Be that as it may, there has been a growth of such faith; it seems to be accounted for by several reasons. Economic conditions have been far more satisfactory to most people than was anticipated when the Employment Act was passed. The two recessions that have occurred have proved short lived and have been followed by periods of high prosperity and substantial economic growth. Both major political parties have demonstrated that they accept the responsibilities assumed in the Employment Act and have taken action to end recessions and promote full employment and economic growth. The long-announced postwar depression has not appeared, and decreasing attention is paid to cries of "Wolf! Wolf!"

There is no comparably widespread faith in the ability and intention of the government to prevent at least creeping inflation. The wartime experience has made many people very sensitive to inflation, and they have sought to protect themselves against it. Such action psychologically reinforces their expectation of further inflation. Economists have pointed out only too clearly the inflationary combination of cost escalation that runs through business, labor, and agriculture; a decided stickiness of prices on the downward side; and a monetary and fiscal policy that tends to validate price rises in order to avoid unemployment. Certain economists with a political turn of mind have accepted inflation as being not particularly harmful and much more palatable politically than any real effort to harmonize high employment and stable prices would be. A few economists have gone even so far as to say, to my consternation, that some continued inflation would be desirable for the economy.

Moreover, the postwar experience has not been encouraging for the development of faith in the power and will of government to maintain stable prices. When price controls and rationing were removed under strong political pressure shortly after the war, certain trusted political and business leaders said that prices would not rise and, indeed, would fall. Instead, prices jumped upward and continued to rise for many months. Prices went up sharply during the Korean crisis until they were brought to rein by price controls, reinforced by changes in monetary action, tax increases, and other developments. Fortunately, the price controls of this period were not removed until the upward movement had spent its force. In the light of the experience and of the discussions it is not surprising that if you ask a businessman today whether, assuming the continuation of the present Administration, he expects further price inflation, the chances are substantial that he will say that he does—at least if your experience resembles mine.

The increasing faith in a tremendous future for the economy and in the efficacy of government action to avoid depressions represents a great advance in promoting the stability and growth of the economy. It is an advance, however, that presents us with danger as well as benefit. The benefit is that businesses and consumers, acting on their new belief, will not run for cover when a downturn occurs, reducing their spending and thus aggravating the problem of stopping the downturn. This permits a little governmental action to be successful and avoids the need for more drastic measures when downward movements occur. The danger is that businesses and consumers, confident in the protecting arm of government action, will engage in unjustified expansion. Consumers may expand purchases through reducing their rate of savings and through credit expansion, to a degree that cannot be maintained. Business may expand productive capacity in some industries beyond the realities of near-future demand. Moreover, confidence that recessions and depressions are a thing of the past, together with expectations of price rises in the future, encourages the process of pushing up prices on the cost side and pulling them up on the demand side.

I do not consider these to be imaginary bugaboos. In the past our depressions have followed, and at least to some extent have been caused by, excessive booms. I wonder if we have lived long enough in the atmosphere of faith in the efficacy of governmental stabilizing measures to avoid being overstimulated by it. For example, how much of the capital expansion program of business in which we now rejoice will prove to be well planned and soundly geared to future growth, how much is planned but based on illusion, and how much is not based on anything except the urge to get on the band wagon and not be left behind by the "wave of the future"? That all three elements are present today seems clear, although I am in no position to judge whether the elements of illusion and band wagon–jumping are as yet important enough to be dangerous. Optimism engendered by faith in a new era of government-underwritten prosperity could give rise to indiscriminate expansion programs. If this were to occur, the result might well be a distortion of productive capacity that would soon have the appearance and much of the effect of general overcapacity or underconsumption and could lead to the very depression that is no longer feared.

I suggest these as possible dangers, not as certainties. If they are recognized, they can be met. However, there are biases that work against efforts to meet them. Both economic and political considerations emphasize the need to keep business levels high and rising. Policy-makers no doubt would avoid taking action to support today's economy if the consequences were clearly trouble for tomorrow's, but, when the consequences are not clear, the temptation is very great to go ahead despite the possible danger.

The last and perhaps most basic condition for government success in promoting economic stability is that people shall really want it. Placing responsibility for economic stability on government will not produce the required action in a democracy unless the people want the result badly enough to support the governmental action that is necessary. The people have made up their minds that they will not tolerate any more depressions. As a result the government is able to take action that helps prevent depressions. To be sure, there is an important contributing factor. Such action does not run afoul of the interests of large groups. Reduction of taxes and liberalization of credit are popular with almost everyone, and even increased government spending for useful projects can usually command large political support.

On the other hand, the people have not clearly decided that they will not tolerate any more inflation. There are many people in the country who suffer much more than they benefit from rising prices. However, they have created no "countervailing power" either in the economic field or in the political field. It may be possible to develop a politically powerful organization of consumers, insurance policy-holders, teachers, government employees, and others who are particularly harmed by inflation. The difficulty is that for most people their interests as producers are more real to them and seem more important than their interests as consumers. They do not want higher prices on what they buy, but they press for higher prices for what they have to sell. The machinery of escalation is built into the definition of farm parity price and into collective-bargaining agreements. It has become a matter for special note and commendation when a business does not follow an increase in wages by an increase in prices. Moreover, the kind of actions that government must take to stop inflation are politically unpopular. To stop inflation, it is necessary to cut down buying, and this annoys the buyer as well as the seller. Tightening credit brings cries of anguish, for example, from real estate interests. Raising taxes brings cries of anguish from everyone. As far as I know, there is no example in our history when taxes have been increased as an anti-inflationary measure when the Treasury already anticipated a surplus. Imposing price controls, wage controls, or rationing is politically unthinkable in the absence of an emergency such as that of war. Until the public is clearer in its mind about the harm done by inflation, rising prices constitute a lesser political risk than firm action to halt them and hold them stable for the long run.

III

In conclusion, let me summarize briefly and make a few final comments. The federal government has assumed responsibility for promoting economic stability and at least sufficient economic growth to keep unemployment at a tolerably low level. There is not likely to be any turning back from this responsibility.

The problem of maintaining economic stability is a broad one which involves both national economic aggregates and various sectors of the economy. The government's role requires it to deal with both. Moreover, its preparations must include consideration of great as well as minor disturbances. The methods used and policies followed should be consistent with our foreign economic policy, which should not be sacrificed to secure minor benefits for particular sectors. Our immediate problems on the sectoral side appear to be low and falling agricultural prices, pockets of local depression and deterioration, and transitional employment problems that may grow out of applications of the newer technology commonly popularized as automation. On the side of over-all aggregates, our immediate problem is the danger of overexpansion of production and productive capacity in some industries based on excessive faith in the new era of government-underwritten prosperity. A second problem is creeping inflation, which cannot be expected always merely to creep.

Although the government is better prepared than at some times past to deal with the stabilization problem, it needs further instruments and needs to use in a better way the instruments it already has. Major expansion and improvement is needed in the statistical materials compiled and supplied by the federal government for its own use and to permit individuals and businesses, labor unions, and agricultural organizations to adapt their operations to the needs of a stabilized economy. Automatic stabilizers should be studied and improved and allowed to work without political interference. The Federal Reserve System should have the powers to impose price controls and rationing in case of great disturbances to the economy. In dealing with sectoral problems, it will be necessary to tailor the methods to the particular need, and this may require operations of government along many lines. More knowledge continues to be needed about the way the economy works.

The machinery of government is inadequate both in its provision for policy integration and in the flexibility of administrative action. Serious consideration needs to be given to how the government can be improved in these respects.

There is need to build up a political force against inflation. In this connection it should be observed that little attention has been given to adapting the basic institutional structure of United States industry, labor, and agriculture to the objective of economic stability.

Much more public understanding of the way the economy works and of the problems of economic stabilization is required. It is difficult to achieve this education when elections can be won more readily by distorting the problems and sometimes even by giving misinformation.

Finally, it must be recognized that government acting without the understanding and co-operation of the public can scarcely be strong enough to maintain economic stability. There is need to bring our personal actions into consistent relationship with the requirements of stabilization. This is part of our public duty as citizens. No individual can do much. Many individuals working together can do a great deal. Large businesses, labor organizations, agricultural organizations, state and local governments, if they act concurrently, can help avoid the necessity for stronger collective action on the part of government.

The Role of Government in Promoting
Economic Growth

As a people we value highly both prosperity and progress. The civic art on which we are dependent in achieving these is now better at promoting economic stability than it is in its understanding of economic growth, although our particular economic organization is such that, when the level of production is high, the rate of growth is rapid. We, however, do not as yet have the understanding and skill required to promote an optimum rate of economic growth, and we do quite badly when it comes to advising other countries on how best to proceed.

I shall restrict my remarks, in the main, to poor countries,[1] and my thesis is that in most poor countries there is not much economic growth to be had by merely taking up whatever slack may exist in the way the available resources are being utilized. To achieve economic growth of major importance in such countries, it is necessary to allocate effort and capital to do three things: increase the *quantity* of reproducible goods; improve the *quality* of people as productive agents; and raise the *level* of the productive arts. The first of these represents additions to the stock of particular tangible resources and the second and third as adding to the stock of particular intangible resources. Some economic growth, also, may be had from enlarging the scope of the market. In the opposite direction, a part of the gain from these several sources, varying from country to country, is canceled by diminishing returns against such non-reproducible factors as exist.

What, then, is the role of government in promoting economic growth? It depends not only upon how one envisages the process of

1. This paper is being restricted to "poor" countries and, in the main, to countries that have as yet achieved little or no economic growth, although most of the second and positive part of my thesis is equally applicable to "rich" countries.

economic growth but also upon one's conception of what are the best ways of acquiring and allocating the effort and capital to increase the stock of these recources and of achieving a larger market. All too much attention is being directed to taking up the existing slack in countries that now have a poor collection of resources on the assumption that there are many underemployed resources readily available for economic growth. Moreover, there has been all too much emphasis on particular tangible resources relative to the stock of intangible resources to achieve an optimum rate of economic growth from some given expenditure of effort and capital. The redirection of both private and public efforts here implied will be the burden of a later part of this paper.

One needs to take cognizance of the great differences in beliefs that are now held about the role of government in promoting economic growth. The issues are most unsettled. Nor is it any wonder, given the state of affairs in the world, that there should have arisen such widespread differences about the relevant facts and the standards or values by which they should be rated. Economic development has become a major objective in many countries where our concept of a good society is suspect. Received Western values are on the defensive, as are its forms of social and political organization. For one, a new vigorous nationalism has taken root in soil just freed from colonialism. It is striving for internal unification and control, and it views with fear the entry of foreign capital, economic aid, and assistance. Some of the basic ideas of mercantilism come closer to explaining the economic policies of this new nationalism than do the prevailing notions among us about economic development. The vast struggle for political power among nations that is now under way cannot help but leave its scars. At the level of propaganda it is obvious that the respective economic systems are pitted one against the other. But what is not so obvious is the relevance of the economic experiences of Russia and China, on the one hand, and of the recent upsurge in production and income, especially in western Europe, on the other, to the role of government in bringing about economic growth. One needs to recognize, however, that the climate of opinion has become charged by ideological conflicts, and as a consequence it is increasingly difficult to discuss and communicate and not be misunderstood. Moreover, politics and economics are being fused once again under the white heat of the international struggle for power. It is hard to believe that these issues have not and will not seriously impair our perspective on the role of government.

One notes, also, that governments are not entirely neutral in selecting advice as they bestir themselves. Most of them preside over poor countries. At best, they want to undertake measures which will increase the production, income, and wealth of their countries. The compulsion is to do it rapidly; the operating horizons are almost always exceedingly short. As governments, they turn for advice to those few countries that have become rich or to those that are now making impressive progress although still quite poor. Nor should one be surprised to find that the advice they want and usually receive is mostly governmental advice featuring the role of government. This note is sounded here not to condemn the process or the advice but to characterize it.

A comment on the meaning of economic growth will be necessary. It is here taken to mean a rising stream of output where the rate of increase in output exceeds that of population. Economic growth, as I shall use the term, accordingly means a rise in per capita output. There are several reasons for taking this as my definition. A rate of increase in output which is somewhat greater than that of population is the goal of most countries now entering upon programs to promote their economic development. Then, too, the data on which I want to draw are cast in these terms. Nor do I want to become enmeshed in the age-old problem, still present in all too many countries, of population growth absorbing all the additional output, so that no rise in per capita output occurs. The many conceptual and measurement difficulties that arise in determining output are acknowledged, but I shall not enter into them here. Nor shall I consider the personal distribution of income except as it is affected by measures to improve the quality of people as productive agents.[2]

I shall now elaborate somewhat on the proposition that most countries cannot achieve economic growth simply by putting so-called underemployed resources to more productive work. A con-

2. The definition of economic growth which I have offered is closely parallel to that employed by Professor W. Arthur Lewis in his recent book, *The Theory of Economic Growth* (London: George Allen & Unwin, 1955), chap. i.

trary belief about the facts is widely held. A large literature has appeared in recent years based on the belief that countries, however poor the collection of resources at their disposal, can do wonders by recombining the resources already at hand. The mainspring of this view has been the notion that in agriculture one finds many workers whose marginal productivity is not only far below that in other sectors but that it is zero,[3] and, of course, the agricultural sector bulks large in nearly all poor countries. One suspects that this view of an abundance of underemployed resources is a piece of the aftermath of the mass unemployment of the thirties.

I know of no evidence for any poor country anywhere that would even suggest that a transfer of some small fraction, say, 5 per cent, of the existing labor force out of agriculture, with other things equal, could be made without reducing its production. I am, of course, ruling out putting new and additional non-labor resources into farming, the substitution of capital for the labor withdrawn, or the introduction of a better technology. Given the wide range for substitution among factors so characteristic of agriculture, it is all but impossible to construct even a theoretical model which would permit the possibility of a zero marginal product for any appreciable part of the labor supply.

In Peru a modest road was recently built down the east slopes of the Andes to Tingo Maria, using some labor from farms along the way mostly within walking distances; agricultural production in the area dropped promptly because of the withdrawal of this labor from agriculture. In Belo Horizonte, Brazil, an upsurge in construction in the city drew workers to it from the nearby countryside, and this curtailed agricultural production.

The marginal productivity of labor in agriculture in poor countries is very low because of the poor collection of resources, but it is not zero. Moreover, in such a country it is very low for labor generally. And in situations, and there are many, where for many years, often for decades, agriculture has approximated a kind of stationary state, one is likely to find the average and the marginal values of labor more nearly the same than would be the case in a rapidly

3. See P. N. Rosenstein-Rodan, "Problems of Industrialization of Eastern and South-eastern Europe," *Economic Journal*, LIII (June–September, 1943), 202.

developing economy like that of the United States. The more sophisticated presentation of this underemployment notion by Eckaus[4] which appeared recently, based on a "technological restraints hypothesis," falls not on its logic as a bit of theory but on its relevance.

The record, as I see it, is as follows: A poor country which has been virtually stationary for a long period is not likely to reveal any appreciable malallocation of factors, say, as between agriculture and the rest of the economy or within agriculture, whereas a country undergoing rapid economic growth, more likely than not, will have in it areas that have been bypassed and others that have become depressed as a consequence of its economic development. There is more malallocation of resources of this kind in western Europe, the United Kingdom, Canada, and the United States, for example, than in poor countries that have as yet achieved little or no economic growth.[5]

There are, however, a few countries where exceptional circumstances exist which led me at the outset to qualify this part of my thesis. These exceptional countries can achieve considerable increases in output by taking up the existing slack. I would place the Argentine and Chile and, perhaps, also Paraguay in his exceptional class. The case of the Argentine, which is not so poor, is clear enough. A study[6] of the earlier growth and recent decline of the agricultural sector of that country indicates that agricultural production currently is fully one-third less than one would have predicted from the characteristic of these agricultural resources, the value of the products, and the progress that was under way up to the early forties and from the growth of agriculture in other countries with comparable resources. The Argentine, however, has been engaged in a very special kind of economic folly for which it has paid a high price. And the Argentine could, if it would, produce much more

4. R. S. Eckaus, "Factor Proportions in Underdeveloped Areas," *American Economic Review,* XLV (September, 1955), 539.

5. But even in these Western countries these depressed pockets and by-passed communities do not provide enough resource slack on which to base an appreciable economic growth.

6. I refer here to a study made by Marto Ballesteros at the University of Chicago.

than it has by simply utilizing more efficiently the fine set of resources at its disposal.

Chile, also far from poor, is operating a long way below its optimum, given the collection of resources that it has at hand, mainly because of what it has done in living with its inflation. I would venture the guess from observations and such data as are available that Chile is foregoing between a fifth to a fourth of its normal output in order to indulge itself in a vast, chronic imbalance in governmental receipts and payments. Inflation itself need not give rise to serious resource malallocations. With flexible product and factor prices and flexible foreign-exchange rates and with interest rates attuned to the declining value of money, what would remain may be represented as a special tax on money and near-money. The rub, however, is that where there is inflation the government, as a rule, feels compelled to act and by all manner of devices impairs the flexibility of prices and places restrictions on foreign exchange and trade. Moreover, many administrative and even entrepreneurial talents, always scarce especially in poor countries, are employed to administer these controls. As controlled prices and rates diverge increasingly from the underlying structure of "real" values, the incentives for corruption mount, and, although such corruption acts as a partial corrective of some extreme distortions, it is a high price to pay in terms of public and private integrity.[7]

Suffice it then to say, on the first part of my thesis, that not much economic growth is to be had from efforts to put existing underemployed resources to work because they are relatively unimportant, except in a few countries like the Argentine and Chile. The widely held notion that a substantial fraction of the labor in agriculture in poor countries has a marginal productivity of zero is an illusion. On the contrary, it is very doubtful that any appreciable part of the labor in agriculture in such poor countries is far below the average in its productivity. In general, it appears to be true that such factor disproportionality as does exist does not provide a firm foundation from which to launch a government program of economic growth.

7. Paraguay is a special case where an exceedingly rough-and-ready policy of reaching for public revenue by "taxing" foreign-trade transactions has greatly impaired the output of its principal industry, the raising of cattle.

Therefore, to place a government into this position and role is a mistake.

Let me now take an affirmative tack and explore that part of my thesis which says that economic growth of major importance is dependent upon increasing the stock of particular intangible resources, represented by the *level* of the productive arts and by the *quality* of human agents, and by adding to the stock of conventional reproducible goods. Both sets require effort and capital; both need to be augmented at the same time; and it is a mistake to concentrate solely on the tangible set as is the case where industrialization is viewed as the way of achieving the optimum rate of economic growth.

In my remaining remarks I can give only the bare bones of an approach. Most theorizing about economic growth is based on the belief (assumption) that capital narrowly conceived, namely, where it is restricted to the stock of reproducible goods, is the fundamental variable. To the best of my knowledge, no evidence has been produced to support this particular belief on the all-important role that additional reproducible capital goods play in economic growth as herein defined.

The economic history of the United States as interpreted by Fabricant, drawing upon the research riches of the National Bureau of Economic Research, certainly does not support this belief on the contribution and role of capital when it is restricted to reproducible goods.[8] During the last eight decades (1869–73 to 1949–53) the per capita output of the United States rose at a rate of 1.9 per cent per year (compounded). In exploring where this remarkable economic growth (i.e., output per capita) came from, Fabricant ascribed only about one-tenth of it to the rise in the stock of tangible capital consisting of structures, including housing, equipment, inventories, and net foreign assets (but excluding consumers' equipment, military assets, and land and subsoil assets).[9]

8. Solomon Fabricant, *Economic Progress and Economic Change,* a part of the *34th Annual Report of the National Bureau of Economic Research* (New York, May, 1954).

9. It, of course, took a large amount of additional capital of this type simply to stay abreast of the growth in population. This particular achievement in output and the contribution that such capital has made to it we are leaving aside, for we are here concentrating on the rise in output which is in excess of the growth in population.

Fabricant puts it thus, "With a given 'dose' of labor and tangible capital we have learned to produce a larger and larger volume of goods for consumption and investment: output per unit of input has risen somewhat under fourfold, or about 1.7 per cent a year on the average. . . . [This] Improvement in national efficiency has been a remarkable persistent process." He also points out that this upward trend in *national efficiency* occurred in each of the several major parts of the eight decades and in all corners of the economy. Thus, according to Fabricant, about nine-tenths of the remarkable economic growth of the United States (the rise in output per capita) since about the Civil War has come from sources other than increases in labor and in the stock of tangible capital. One need not indorse these precise results, nor would Fabricant, I am sure, contend that they will not have to be revised substantially as the underlying researches proceed. But the direction and the magnitudes of these estimates, even allowing for the many conceptual and measurement difficulties to be resolved, are so decisive that they cannot be put aside in theorizing about economic growth.

One, of course, would prefer to have comparable estimates for one or more poor countries in process of achieving economic growth, for instance, for Mexico and Brazil and for Japan with its development of longer standing. But, unfortunately, no such estimates are at hand; nor can they be had without undertaking years of difficult and often very tedious research. We must build, therefore, with the straw and clay we have.[10]

How, then, is economic growth to be represented? The economic experiences of the United States since the Civil War—and these are not inconsistent with one's observations of the process of economic development in poor countries—do not support the view that economic growth (rising per capita output) is wholly or even primarily dependent upon increases in the stock of reproducible goods. The major key to this rise in output per capita Fabricant has called the "improvement in national efficiency," namely, the observed increases in the ratio of output to inputs of labor and of reproducible goods. This means that economic growth is determined in part by

10. There are some sector data; for example, those growing out of the work of Clarence Moore, while at the University of Chicago, to determine the changes in outputs and inputs on agriculture in Mexico and Brazil.

adding to the stock of reproducible goods and in part, and probably much the larger part, by factors which give rise to the improvements in national efficiency.

Economic growth, therefore, is here represented as some function of three basic variables, each determined (presumably in large part) by the amount of effort and capital allocated to its development, that is, to increasing its magnitude; these variables are, as stated at the outset of this paper: (1) the quantity of reproducible goods; (2) the quality of people as productive agents; and (3) the level of the productive arts. In addition, a larger market improves the national efficiency and becomes a special factor in this process. These variables must then be cast into a framework which takes account of whatever diminishing returns occur as a consequence of the non-reproducible factors and the drag that these place on economic growth.

In advancing this formulation, I take it to be meaningful to approach the quality of human agents and, also, the level of the productive arts as economic variables, that is, as variables which are at least in substantial part determined by resource allocations, namely, largely determined by the effort and other inputs that are committed to their development. It might be argued that this approach is simply an extension of the theorizing about economic growth which is based on increasing the existing stock of capital. I would not disagree with such an interpretation; however, if viewed as an extension, it drastically redefines the role of capital and related effort on which economic growth is dependent.

My closing remarks will be addressed to some of the implications of this approach to the role of government. I enter upon these with some misgivings for reasons already touched upon.

Let me first restate two major inferences which emerged from the first part of this paper.

1. Quite aside from whether it is a proper role of government, it is a mistake for governments of poor countries to undertake programs of economic development based on so-called underemployed resources.

2. It is also a mistake for governments in poor countries to key all programs of economic development to industrialization. To do so creates "factor disproportionality" where none had existed before.

I consider the rest of these observations as tentative and exploratory.

1. The growth in output to be had in most poor countries from additional effort and capital allocated to improving the quality of its people as productive agents is, so it would appear, substantially higher than that from equivalent inputs to increase the stock of many forms of reproducible goods, although these goods usually are given top priority in programs of economic development. This statement implies that relatively more resources should be allocated, for example, for health services, for extending knowledge about nutrition, and for education, both the most elementary and in depth. Of the resources devoted to measures which improve the quality of people as productive agents, the health services appear to fare relatively better than does education.

What is the role of government in this exceedingly important area? Surely it cannot be rated as minor. I would cite Puerto Rico as the outstanding example of what can and should be done in improving the quality of its people preparatory to entering upon rapid economic development. Mexico, also, has been doing unusually well in broadening its educational base and in acquiring depth in terms of trained personnel. Puerto Rico and Mexico may well be exceptions to the rule that most poor countries allocate all too few of the resources at their disposal to these services. In both of these countries the respective governments have performed a distinctly positive role in this area.

2. Efforts and capital expended to raise the level of the productive arts—scientific work, technological research, development of new techniques of production and their dissemination—by universities, research institutes, agricultural experiment stations, and extension services and in other ways indicate a rate of return, measured in economic growth, that is undoubtedly very high. Poor countries presumably may draw upon the technology of rich countries where the level of the productive arts is much higher. The possibilities of doing so, however, are more restricted than is commonly believed. Rich countries have evolved a technology that is appropriate to an economy where labor is dear relative to capital. The basic scientific and technological knowledge can be drawn upon, but the gap be-

tween this knowledge and useful techniques of production applicable to a poor country is usually very considerable.

The excellent joint work on corn of the Rockefeller Foundation and of the government of Mexico demonstrates that it is no easy matter to take the scientific knowledge on corn hybrids and on corn-breeding already established in the United States and develop useful corn varieties for Mexico. Experiment stations that do well are hard to come by. In the United States there are still all too many states that have not established satisfactory conditions for such agricultural research. Extension services organized to disseminate useful knowledge to farmers are a fairly recent innovation and as yet not well understood.

The role of government in this area is most complex. It is all too easy for governments to underrate the contributions of business, foreign and domestic, as effective carriers of new technology. It appears that more useful techniques are being transferred from the United States to Latin America by business firms than through any other single channel, although very important contributions are being made by foundations, universities, Point Four, and by United States–supported religious activities in agriculture, education, and health. Governments, nevertheless, can and, virtually of necessity, must play an important role not only in creating conditions that facilitate the functioning of business as a carrier of technology but also in institutionalizing scientific work, technological research, experiment stations, and extension services.

3. In the area where effort and capital is allocated to increase the stock of reproducible goods there is, as I have already stressed, in many poor countries, all too much emphasis on industrialization relative to that placed on improving the quality of people as productive agents and on raising the level of the productive arts. Also, other sectors, that is, agriculture, mining, transportation and communication, financial institutions, distribution, and the service industries, usually receive too little attention in programs of economic development. Here, again, let me call attention to the achievements of Puerto Rico and Mexico with the inference that they have come closer than have most countries in finding the optimum combinations of effort and capital in promoting economic growth in this complex area.

4. Let me also restate a truth, long accepted as a truism, namely, that the instability of government which is all too characteristic of many poor countries hangs like the sword of Damocles over all effort and capital devoted to economic growth.

We shall continue, as a people, to value prosperity and progress highly. We want these for ourselves, and we are prepared to help many other countries achieve them. But our understanding of economic growth is far from satisfactory, and we do quite badly in our endeavors to help poor countries and their governments in achieving this important national objective. It has been the burden of this paper that we could and should do much better in this particular civic art.

New Bridges between Theory and Practice

It is exhilarating to have one's calling elevated by the choice of a graceful and respectful nomenclature. The practice of the administrative art is an occupation which is charged with special hazards and which has a high degree of vulnerability to attack. The weapons used are semantic ones rather than atomic ones. The very words used to describe the calling, even when printable, tend to be charged with hostility. In the code duello of our frontier days there were certain epithets that could be used only when accompanied by a smile. I still insist that people smile when they use the word "bureaucrat" as a synonym for a public official. It is an invigorating shot in the ego for administrators, therefore, to have the program for this session refer to their calling as "administrative art" and as a part of the "civic arts." I remember once that Franklin D. Roosevelt, just after a visit to the White House by Congressman Hamilton Fish, received a group from the Executive Branch and was in high good humor. He opened the meeting by saying, "It certainly does make a fellow feel awfully important to have his Congressman call upon him." It certainly makes administrators feel a new respect for their vocation when social scientists refer to it in these flattering terms. It creates a good-feeling tone for the subject of my short discourse on the problem of building new bridges between the worlds of theory and practice in the general area of public administration.

There is a special need at this juncture for a new rapprochement between the areas of theory and practice, between the universities and the bureaus, between the scholar and the official, and, one might say, between gown and town. Increasingly, the daily burdens on the scientist and the official are growing, and increasingly, I fear, the gaps between theory and practice are widening. The administrator senses, in approaching his daily tasks, a lack of certainty in the way in which he manages men, money, and materials in the accomplishment of a program. He is finding that many assumed doctrines which he has inherited, and many unspoken assumptions which have become the use and wont of his departmental behavior, are not entirely applicable to the complex problems which beset him. Daily pressures under which he labors prevent him from exploring and re-examining these doctrines and assumptions. Indeed, he is only vaguely conscious of their inadequacy and is not able entirely alone to identify and define what these problems are. But he is compelled, in spite of these vague misgivings, to go along on the basis of old premises, from day to day, as best he can.

The social scientists are in a strategic position to make basic contributions with regard to a thoroughgoing re-examination of these inherited and often unspoken assumptions and doctrines. Indeed, they are doing so daily in a number of areas, but I believe their work can be more focused on the problems to which I refer and can become much more illuminating than they have been to date.

In the structure of intellectual organization, public administration has come to have a strong affinity with political science, even though in some institutions it is allied with studies of law and with studies of business administration. I see no objection to these varieties of structure. I believe that increasingly we are correcting some earlier errors which were based on a premise that there could be a complete insulation of politics and policy from administration. We have come to perceive that this is a sterile and misleading approach. For the administrator works in an environment created by political forces. His highest function is in the field of policy formation or of decision-making and of securing consent for policy. His performance and success depend on political sanctions, and, whereas his function is not entirely that of the politician, there are large elements of politics in the broader sense of the word involved in the administrative role. This is particularly true at the higher echelons where administrators must gain consent for their programs and budgets and cannot ignore political forces, both formal and informal, which are the road to gaining political consent and authorization. I am not contending that politics and administration are one and the same but that they are so closely related that the attempt to isolate the fields can be as misleading as is the newer tendency to equate them.

But having identified this special dependency of administration on the political environment in which it works and its close affinity to political science, it is even more important to point out that public administration needs *all* the social sciences to illuminate its work, and not just one. Nor would any of the social sciences be happy to be excluded from fields infringing on administration, and I doubt that we could keep them out of the act even if we wanted to. The general proposition that all the social sciences might well devote more attention to throwing more light on the problems which beset public officials is almost too obvious to be elaborated or defended. Just to cite one field, with the enormous increase in government intervention at all levels, in services, in expenditure, in taxation, and in regulation, the relation between economics and administration becomes increasingly important. Much more work in public finance is required in the universities, in the field of taxation, in the field of expenditure, and the effect of government regulation, taxation, and expenditure on the rest of the economy. There have been a few distinguished combined chairs in political science and economics occupied by specialists in public finance, but they have been declining in number just at a time when government fiscal officers at all levels need to look more and more to research for deeper analysis and for advanced ideas in the whole area of public fiscal policy and practice.

At this point, I feel obliged to pause and put in the record the disturbing decline in interest among political students in the entire field of state and local government which is particularly marked east of the Mississippi and north of the Potomac.

One can go through the whole category of the social sciences and find an opportunity for contributions in every field. Indeed, it is a normal phenomenon in the history of American government almost from its inception to call in scientists. The geographers have much to contribute in the field of regional physical planning and in the field of conservation. Their growing concern with metropolitan areas is welcome. The statisticians and sociologists have insights and techniques which public administrators can and do use. The various varieties of psychologists are in demand in governmental programs and could be used even more. Chester Barnard points out that the insights of the anthropologists might throw light on the caste and status systems prevailing in governmental agencies. If time permitted, I could give them numerous examples of contrasts between informal organizations and the formal chart. In this company it is unnecessary to expand this list. The point to be stressed here is that the modern administrator needs the help of all the social sciences and, I might add, of all the arts and sciences, both hard and soft.

Let me come now to a number of problems on which officials need enlightening and in which a tactful, even though critical, social investigative technique would be productive. The elements of hierarchy and how they relate to many of the elements of communication and consultation in a large government agency are fruitful areas for social research. Every large agency is bothered by the problem of "layering," a term which gained currency by the colorful edicts of the late General Brehon Somervell during World War II. By layering is meant the moving of papers and services through formal channels, up and down the hierarchy, and the suppression of lateral communications among the various specialists whose views must be sought for a finished piece of staff work. Americans are very proficient on the mechanical side of the handling of paper, and very profligate in their use of paper, but the ideas and policies expressed in the papers are of far greater importance than the mechanization of their handling. Much government work at the level of policy formation consists of the reviewing of papers by experts in various fields, and still we have had no important scientific study of this process which is basic in the whole field of decision-making. The British have made a small beginning in the study of handling of government papers.

As head of a federal agency, I learned to scrutinize most carefully the document which revealed the greatest number of initials of various experts, an exhibit purporting to show a perfect chain of scrutiny and approval. These often were the least adequately prepared, because everyone in the chain of reference depended on his predecessor's scrutiny of the paper and therefore tended to give the document the most imperfect and perfunctory consideration. What is the optimum number of surnames to induce responsible visas? How does a top administrator circumvent the perverse specific gravity of public business by which vexatious details, because of their lightness, I presume, float up to his desk, while major and heavy controversial problems are politely concealed at lower echelons?

These may seem like small subjects for social research, but they can have important consequences when they result in a major decision emanating from a department which proves to be completely ridiculous, and unfortunately too many examples of this kind of thing can be found. Under what conditions should a problem be treated by endless routing of papers, and when should an administrator call a conference of his chief experts to thrash out basic problems implied in the papers?

This naturally leads into a series of questions involved in the use of the conference method and of committees. Hours are spent on conferring in agency after agency. I know a classic example of a government office in which committee conferences succeeded in holding up program after program, without resolution. Some interesting preliminary studies on committee behavior have been made by social scientists, but in public administration we need very much more definitive research to guide the administrator as to when to use this device and how to use it. The increasing use of committees by business organizations makes one conclude that the value of such research would not be confined entirely to government agencies, and one might even venture the thought that the investigation of the problem of the use of committees might be useful on university campuses.

The factors contributing to the prestige and morale of a career corps and its responsibility to the party in power need re-examination. Personnel tenure and status present a dilemma which every administrator faces. It is particularly acute today in the government service in which new standards of loyalty and security have been imposed. It is the dilemma of a decent balance between oversecurity of tenure and undersecurity of tenure—of giving an administrator some ability to reward talent and penalize inefficiency and neglect without placing a permanent government staff at the mercy of a sluggish officialdom or at the whims of inexperienced and partisan executives. A common impression among laymen is that government civil service offers too much protection, but the recent abuses of loyalty and security measures have led certain scholars to the conclusion that the government official has too little rather than too much security of tenure and that the penalties of this calling and its insecurities are so great that young people are being discouraged from entering public life.

The distinguished personnel task force of the second Hoover Commission bravely attacked the really intricate question of the role of the permanent career man versus the role of the political policy officer, a subject on which relatively little hard thinking had been done. Our literature has been proceeding too long on certain unjustified assumptions concerning practices in the British civil service which were inappropriately translated and applied to American practice and which were entirely unsuited to our government structure and traditions. Parenthetically, this raises questions of the soundness of our previous work in comparative government and administration. Learned papers have appeared recently on the theory of advice and the place of the temporary expert consultant and his relation to the career man and the political policy official, but much more precise doctrine based on factual research and creative experimentation is required before we can use much of this material in practice.

Another area of work in which scholars can assist is in the development of ethical concepts in public service. At first glance this field may seem to belong more to the humanities and to the philosophers than to the social researcher, but social research could help to identify the causes of low standards of ethics in a department, the structural and environmental conditions which lead to corrupt practices, and indeed suggest a means for their avoidance and correction.

One of the increasingly baffling problems of modern administrators is the administration of a function for which no one department has the exclusive competence. In the fields of national defense and foreign relations, we have tried various devices of cabinet councils and interdepartmental committees with formal secretariats, and at the top level the National Security Council has been designed toward this end. The unification of the armed services by the creation of a Department of Defense is another illustration of a way in which this problem has been approached. But at the local and municipal level the problems of traffic and metropolitan planning, of urban renewal and urban redevelopment, are not soluble by any one existing department and require co-ordinated efforts of numerous agencies and often involve the active support of citizen groups. At the state

level the co-ordination of policy in the conservation of natural resources transcends the jurisdiction of any one department and requires new machinery for a concerted approach. The interdepartmental committees with formal secretariats have now been in use
for some time for these multipurpose programs, but we have great
need of basic investigation and evaluation of the various devices that
have been used and which are applicable in fields which cannot be
organized entirely by means of administrative hierarchies.

The whole problem of delegation, the psychological barriers to
delegation of authority, and how delegation can be accomplished
without abdication by those responsible would be rewarding subjects of study in this country as well as in other lands. I am convinced that in underdeveloped countries one of the prime obstacles
to action is the fantastic degree of overcentralization which prevails
in their capitals. New techniques of social science in comparative
government and administration are being advocated and promise to
throw great light on practices at home and abroad, particularly at a
time when Americans are undertaking to advise everybody in the
world on practically everything.

Public administrators will not do the basic research involved in
these basic problems themselves. They must look to the trained social scientist in the various disciplines to help identify, investigate,
and synthesize in the solution of these problems. The public administrator and his agency can provide the social laboratory for the investigator, can assist him in stating the problem, and can make available the tools for research and exercise a critical judgment with
regard to findings and conclusions. Because the public official is subject to strict accountability by the necessary but frequently irrational
forces of politics and the press, the social scientist must bear in mind
that he must use a conservative and tactful type of investigation in
a governmental milieu.

Before I conclude, I feel compelled to cast out a number of cave-
ats in the manner in which scholars approach the field of public administration. First, I would hope they would approach tax-supported
agencies with a special degree of the objectivity which the social
sciences justly pride themselves on. They should put themselves in
the proper frame of mind. They must correct for their initial antipa-
thies to administration which are prevalent in a scholarly atmos-

phere and must divest themselves of hostilities which I suppose they sometimes feel in the administration of their own universities. I am not contending that the social researcher should lose his critical faculty or should refrain from informing the administrator of any shortcomings that his investigations might reveal, but a co-operative effort in social research in the administrative field requires an initial rapport and special identification with the problems and pressures of a government-agency environment. In fact, such an approach will be more effective. The persons interviewed will talk more freely under these conditions, and the agency will be more apt to "come clean" and present its problems and furnish data and co-operation. Empathy should begin at home and not be confined to inquiries in Samoa or Kamchatka.

Second, I wish to point out that it is particularly important in social research in government departments that people be not asked too many questions beyond their competence to answer and that their feelings of inferiority not be magnified by consultation on problems over which they have no jurisdiction and to which they have little, if anything, to contribute. In the preparation for the interview and in the questionnaire this sensitivity is frequently lacking and results in resistances to social research which are unnecessary and could be avoided. A file clerk in the Government Printing Office has little to say about executive-legislative relations.

Third, it is necessary to face the fact that the new methodologies and vocabularies of the social scientist are frequently not only incomprehensible to the practitioner but infuriating to him. The newer methods probably present a much more precise technique of research under which sharper studies are undertaken and more accurate even if sometimes more limited conclusions can be drawn. The social science of today has at once more abstraction in it and more quantification, and both of these are difficult for the layman to follow. It is indispensable, therefore, in conducting social research in bureaus and departments of government that as much attention be given to translation and interpretation of findings and of methods as is given to the rigorous accuracy and objectivity of the survey.

Working in the government is like working in an illuminated fishbowl. Innovation in public agencies is frequently subjected to deliberate distortion and abuse as a result of ignorance and of political

maneuver. If new insights and new procedures are to gain acceptance in that environment, they must be stated in terms that are both
understandable and usable by the practitioner and explainable to
his political mentors.

Fourth and finally, it seems to me that a basic tenet of the ethics
of social research in a democracy is that human beings, unlike
guinea pigs and atoms, should not be experimented upon without
their knowledge and consent.

The gap between theory and practice has grown too wide in social
research in the governmental sector. It is in the interests of bridging
this gap that I have suggested these self-denying ordinances. Their
observance will contribute greatly to keeping open the doors to the
trained and mature social scientist of the city halls, state capitals,
and federal bureaus of the nation which so greatly need his continued researches and insights.

GORDON R. CLAPP

The Social Scientist and the Administrative Art

A scholar of the law and a devotee of the art of energizing its processes, after observing the inner workings of the Tennessee Valley Authority in its brighter days, asked some of us to put to paper the secret of that organization's apparent ability to integrate the ideas and actions of its noticeably strong-willed staff. He observed, he said, a subtle influence that seemed to moderate differences without smothering the clarity or the variety and distinction of the individual administrative and professional judgments.

We declined his invitation to try to describe the processes by which this result was achieved, if indeed it was. We thought we were too involved with our work to become clinical reporters. But our reason for declining went deeper than that. As we thought about the request, we decided that the subject was so elusive that available vocabularies would carry us willy-nilly into what would be interpreted not as an "art" of administration but as an exposition of the process of manipulation of human minds. The distinction between these two methods in our view was real and important. We were quite sure we were engaged in the pursuit of the administrative art; we were trying hard to avoid the practice of trying to manipulate. We were not sure we could describe the difference. Perhaps we should have admitted that we were not sure we knew how the result our scholarly friend believed he observed was really obtained.

Today's assignment has similar pitfalls.

Our subject has slippery surfaces, and its center is elusive. Even basic definitions are difficult. I shall not attempt to define the boundaries or the center of the social scientist's role. Nor shall I try to put into capsule form the content of the administrative art. The program-makers must have had ideas on both subjects, and I leave the problem of definitions to them. In this brief paper I shall make a few observations, a series of allusions to the nature of the administrative art, and some of the types of problems in which some administrators might welcome the contribution of the social scientist.

What is the relationship of anthropology, sociology, political science, psychology—social and otherwise—to the art of management? I suggest a common denominator of focal interest to which all social scientists subscribe—or so I understand—and of which all administrators worthy of the name are presumably aware, namely, the human being. To the administrator human beings abound in three categories: those to whose interests the purpose of his administrative performance is aimed—always referred to as "the general public," whether general or very special in fact; those who are working members of the organization over which he has responsible charge; and those who comprise the upper reaches of the hierarchy and its dangling participants of which he is a part—"the team" of which he is a member, as the revised edition of the administrative dictionary now so happily phrases it.

These categories are by no means complete. There is virgin soil here for the anthropologist and others to analyze if they would help the administrator understand more cogently the propulsive, compulsive, impulsive, and expulsive forces which play around and within him as he pursues his art.

Discussion of the administrator's pursuit of his art with the hierarchy above and around him is better left to one's memoirs; it is essentially personal and subjective and at times can become so absorbing a preoccupation as to crowd out any time for reflection upon one's relationship to his physician or to his God. Perhaps this suggests an unusually fruitful field for research for the social scientist— possibly a group of mature scholars and researchers including a political scientist, sensitive to the structure of government and the theory and practice of executive responsibility, and an anthropologist whose familiarity with the phenomena of taboos, cultural inhibitions, and the origins of witchcraft might help him to pierce the formalisms of structural organization and legal concepts. Certainly the group should include someone at least familiar with and, preferably, professionally competent in psychiatry. Their objective would be to discover, describe, and analyze the factors that operate upon human beings and the problems of responsible humans in the upper power levels of our executive circles in government. It would be interesting and, I believe, relevant to discover, for example, what produces the statement attributed to a ranking member of the White House staff and directed to the head of an agency who proposed to take a certain position on a public question, "To hell with the merits; you're supposed to be a member of the team"—or words to that effect.

I am quite in earnest when I suggest that it would be worthwhile to appraise the "team" concept as a device in the art of administration. The hypothesis to be examined, revised, discarded, or confirmed might be something like this: The "team" concept is a useful device for rallying forces when the participants are tired of trying to be profound or discerning or when they are incapable of imaginative executive leadership; it can be useful when the objective of the game is so unclear that the players find small intrinsic incentive, generated by their depth of understanding or conviction, to pursue the goal. It is not a concept that brings out the best human talent or the best-informed inner will to act. At its worst, the "team" concept is usually a device to divorce the intellects of lower rank, distinguished from the lower-grade intellects, from the processes of executive decision. Loyalty to the chief becomes the highest value; quality of judgment, even integrity, becomes the sand of subversion in the well-oiled human cogs and gears. At its best, the "team" plea can be useful in encouraging the participants to search for a common goal or to join in discovering one through the responsible and free play of participating minds in a process built upon respect for the integrity, dignity, and talent of the participants. Examination of best and worst cases could get beneath the labels applied as symbols to denote different systems. The essence or substance of differing systems of executive method is what we need to know how to recognize in order to nurture the best.

For example, given two agencies with reasonable similarity in respect to the competence of its individual members, what makes one lethargic, apathetic, and erratic in its course and performance and the other purposive, energetic, and reasonably creative in its performance? I suspect that at the root of the causes may be found a fundamental difference in at least two respects—the presence or absence of a deep faith within the key administrators in the latent intellectual and emotional reasonableness of human beings and rejection or acceptance of the desire to reform people as contrasted with the willingness to let them reform themselves. I believe that one's beliefs and convictions about these two variables lie close to the heart of whatever may be the administrative art. If social scientists are equipped to probe the administrative environment without disrupting it, they should be able to discover and judge these variables and possibly evaluate them.

We do not need proof or provable theses so much as we need questions and hypotheses which will stimulate insights among practitioners. The methodology of social science research can encourage administrators to be more self-consciously analytical and reflective about whatever art they believe they practice.

A more limited and suggestive hypothesis might be something like this: The key to the performance of an organization is the positive willingness of individuals to spend and apply their energies, singly and in groups, to the tasks committed to their hands. How to elicit within and among the farthest reaches of an organization the positive self-induced desire, intent, and energy to decide to act is the central problem of administrative leadership.

If the validity of this hypothesis can be demonstrated, and I believe it can—in fact, it has been demonstrated—then maybe a penetrating commentary on Tolstoi's "The Second Epilogue" is relevant to those who are concerned about the improvement and the purpose of the administrative art. The comment follows: "If any organizations are good, those are best which have as their aim not to reform men but to enable them to reform themselves, and which remain continuously aware that, insofar as their purpose is to change material conditions, their work is itself merely conditional—a means, and at best a doubtful means, never an end, and, therefore, carrying within it no kind of justification of fanaticism or coercion or violence —or, even, of collective self-righteousness."[1]

When viewed in the context of these ideas, the "security" blight visited upon our public services borders on tragedy. It demonstrates

1. Charles Morgan, *Reflections in a Mirror* (New York: Macmillan Co., 1945), p. 214.

that we have not yet learned how to treat a cancerous skin disease in the public service body without endangering its vital organs—the source of energy and the will to perform the public's business. Surely the administrative art merits a better test than its ability to conduct a "numbers game" and get away with it.

The administrative art will improve if it is pursued as a search for the processes by which human differences become occasions for creative and forward resolution and action. It will become an object of shame if destruction of human values is the by-product of its practice. Here is an area of inquiry which begs eloquently for calm, courageous analysis by social scientists and for the ways and means made available to them by those who control the purse strings of research.

The highest service of administration is achieved in the realm of ideas, the products of the human mind. The will to think and think on purpose is the greatest asset a competent organization can possess. The creation of processes by which the will to think becomes the will to act with a sense of responsibility that attempts to assess the human consequences of its alternatives of decision is the object of the art and science of administration. It deals with the most valuable resource of the globe—the human personality. This resource, I believe, is the central subject for the social scientist and the administrator.

You may detect in these observations two basic implications or assumptions: perfection in administrative science, process, and art assumes the intelligent application of mature social science methods of inquiry and analysis; and means or methods in administration are more important than ends. The highest purpose of administration is to build processes which encourage and promote the growth of human talents, especially the talent to select progressively richer ends or goals and more effective means to achieve them. Behind these assumptions, there is another: an abiding faith, as it were, in the power of the human race through its individual members, and its ever changing social units and systems, to reach an ever higher level of self-disciplined rationality and culture—regenerate in the means it evolves to live creatively and peacefully.

American Diplomatic Negotiation, Postwar

I am not intimately familiar with or competent to discuss American diplomacy prior to World War II, as to either its purposes or its effectiveness. I am only concerning myself with our international problems and their treatment since the end of the war, for I believe there is good reason for making this division.

During our entire diplomatic history up to World War II, the United States has been on the sidelines in world affairs. Our diplomats have been in effect experienced correspondents reporting the plays in the great game of world affairs, in which Great Britain and occasionally a lesser European country was carrying the ball. We suddenly awoke at the end of the war to find ourselves out on the field, calling the signals, and having to carry the ball. It seems superfluous to suggest that we were unprepared for this role and that the first task we should have undertaken was to equip and train ourselves for our new responsibility.

As far as the State Department is concerned, there has been only minor and ineffective reorganization, no real reappraisal of the suitability of its personnel for their new role, and almost no change in their policies of operation.

If one is as frankly critical as I, he may properly be asked what should be done, and I am prepared to suggest some answers. The first fact that we must recognize is that there is a world struggle to the death between communism and democracy, between slavery and freedom. Second, we must recognize that we are the leader of the free nations in their attempt to survive.

If we are to give the leadership that will enable the free world to survive without a war, it will be through diplomatic negotiation. However, diplomatic negotiation cannot very well be separated from the personalities which undertake it, nor can it be successful unless we have a definite end that we wish to achieve, nor will we likely achieve our goal unless we have the drive of righteous moral purpose to carry us through and are guided by realistic policies administered by courageous and able leaders supported by the force of public opinion.

Let us discuss the personalities first. If the United States is to provide leadership to the other nations of the world, it will be exercised through the men who represent us in those countries. Our ambassadors and ministers not only must be *simpático*, as the Spanish say, but must be leaders.

There is an alarming tendency in many places to think that the secret to better personnel in the State Department is the establishment of a foreign-service curriculum, school, or institute, and the hope has even been expressed that eventually all members of the foreign service would be graduates of this school, the same as our military leaders are graduates of West Point and Annapolis. I believe this is an unfortunate parallel. The problems encompassed in our international relations deal with almost every area of human experience, and it is a mistake to think that competent leaders will emerge solely from one source. Men of outstanding ability develop in all areas of activity and all disciplines, and their recruitment for tasks in world leadership can both broaden and introduce new vigor into a foreign service that otherwise can too easily become ingrown.

Men with practical experience in politics have frequently demonstrated a greater capacity for dealing with the political leaders of other countries than those who know only the theory. Likewise, economic problems which plague almost every nation are likely to be attacked more realistically by men with practical business experience than those who have had none.

If I may offer an example to support my point, in the last eight years we have sent five ambassadors to India; three of them, including my colleague in Greece, had served as Assistant Secretaries of State and might be presumed therefore to be our top-level diplomats. Chester Bowles, whose background was business and politics, captured the respect and affection of the Indian people way over and beyond the career officials. If Mr. Bowles's appraisal of the present ambassador, former Senator John Sherman Cooper, is correct, he would have to be rated also as superior to the career men.

It is unfortunate at the present time that most of our ambassadorial appointments are made on the basis of finding a job for a career diplomat rather than the selection of the man best qualified to deal with the problems of a particular country.

The emphasis on a career service is to some extent justified as being the alternative to the past practice of appointing generous contributors to the party coffers or exiling political misfits or trouble-makers without regard to their qualifications for diplomatic negotiation. Ambassadors are our generals in the cold war, and it should be as unthinkable that they, any more than military generals, should be appointed for political considerations alone. I predict that the first party to place an appropriate plank in their platform on this matter will gain many supporters.

The personnel administration of our foreign service can never be put on a sound basis until many of the present legislative provisions are repealed and sound procedures are set up which will enable those responsible for our foreign policy to select the best available men, wherever they may be found. Morale will be improved when promotions are made on the basis of accomplishment rather than on the basis of time served and the avoidance of initiative.

Given adequate leaders, however, we still will not have successful diplomatic negotiation unless we know what we want to accomplish. The tragedy of the last ten years is that in no country, to my knowledge, have we had a detailed plan and timetable for reaching a definite goal. A major problem for our foreign policy to deal with today is that of the underdeveloped areas of the world, which include over a billion people, have a substantial proportion of the most strategic raw materials, and are of vital concern to the United States in the struggle with Russia for world power. The economic development of these areas in a manner that will align them with the free nations and save them from communism is just as important to the interest of our country as was the economic recovery of Europe in the immediate postwar period in order to save it from communism.

The Marshall Plan faced the comparatively simple problem of restoring a highly developed economy in a mature industrial society with social and political institutions similar to ours. The development of underdeveloped areas is incomparably more complex and difficult. It involves creating something that has not previously existed. It involves dealing with people whose traditions are dissimilar to ours and whose emotions we frequently find difficult to understand. Furthermore, such development involves to a large degree changing social and political institutions which are resistant to change. A successful effort to raise the economic level of a whole nation without toppling it in the process can be achieved only by a carefully co-ordinated and comprehensive plan. The main responsibility for this planning must rest on the shoulders of the men representing us in a particular country who will have the responsibility for carrying it through.

When our forefathers declared their independence, they did so with the confidence that the "Laws of Nature and of Nature's God" entitled them to do so. They further decreed "that all men . . . are endowed by the Creator with certain inalienable Rights," and, finally, they pledged to each other their lives, fortunes, and sacred honor "with a firm reliance on the protection of Divine Providence."

Only as we depend on spiritual laws for the power to support our diplomatic negotiations, as we depend on physical laws to give force to our military weapons, can we hope to succeed. But the record of the last ten years does not reveal any such moral stature or constancy. If, as our forefathers declared, "Wherever any Form of Government becomes destructive of these ends [life, liberty, and the pursuit of happiness], it is the Right of the People to alter or to abolish it," why have we supported the French in their suppression of the people of Indochina and of Morocco to exercise that right?

On a tablet at the main entrance of the Statue of Liberty is inscribed, "Give me your tired, your poor, your huddled masses yearning to breathe free." But our Congress long refused to admit the displaced persons of Europe, and the legislation now on the books has defeated its purpose by its own restrictions.

If we recognize the inalienable rights of men, why did we lend our support to dispossessing a million Palestinian Arabs of their land and property to provide a home for the Jewish refugees whom we refused to admit to our land? If we believe in the freedoms and the defense of minorities, why did not we raise our voice in protest at the recent rape, rioting, and destruction by the Turks against the Greeks, Jews, and Armenians? If America cannot resume the moral stature which it once held in the eyes of the world, its diplomats will become as sounding brass or tinkling cymbals.

Once our country resumes its moral position, accepts the responsibility for leadership to support that position, develops plans to that end, and has the leaders to carry them through, I am confident that the outdated and unrealistic policies which still hamper us in an effective program of diplomatic negotiation would be quickly changed or discarded, but these policies reflect to some extent a public opinion that needs to be enlightened. An Assistant Secretary of State at a meeting in Chicago a few years ago was asked why we could not adopt some of the policies which Russia was using with such devastating effect in Asia. He replied that there were three reasons: we could not back a revolution, we had to deal with the constituted authorities, and it is not our policy to interfere in the internal affairs of other countries. To the extent that we have criticized Russia for these actions, it would seem consistent for us to abstain from them ourselves, but in reality we are then abandoning to Russia the weapons by which one can fight effectively in the cold war.

The idea that we cannot back a revolution is, of course, inconsistent with our own history. What would Lafayette, Von Steuben, Kosciuszko, and Rochambeau, with his six thousand French troops who supported us in our Revolution, say to this policy of disinterest in the desire of others to achieve the same freedom they helped us to achieve? Actually we are denying, on the one hand, today, while stating, on the other, that we must deal with the constituted authorities, for we are refusing to do just that in Red China.

The idea that we should not interfere in the internal affairs of other countries was realistic when we played no part in world leadership, but there is no effective way that a country can give leadership if it does not interfere. Furthermore, there is no way that we can give aid to another country without interfering, for if such aid is channeled through the constituted authorities it acts as an indorsement and in support of them, and this is an interference in their affairs. We must recognize that, whereas in years past there was little more than friendship and social obligation that could be used as a leverage in diplomatic negotiation, today practically every country in the world wants something that we have, whether it be our aid, our know-how, trade, etc., and this gives us the leverage and the power to support changes within other countries which may not be to the interests of the politicians in power but to the benefit of the great majority of people.

In another area it is quite obvious that the State Department policy of shifting personnel every two or three years in order to insure objective reporting is totally unsuited to our present task of giving real leadership throughout the world and bringing things to pass. Unless the chief of mission and his principal assistants can remain at one post long enough to obtain a knowledge of the local situation that is comparable to that of the local political leaders, they cannot command their respect or have the knowledge and influence to carry out an effective policy. A tour of longer than five years rather than less would be desirable. The effective, if somewhat limited, accomplishments of our Christian missions in establishing colleges, hospitals, and agricultural programs over the past one hundred and fifty years was not accomplished by men who were shifted every two years to a different part of the world but rather by those who dedicated themselves to a particular area and people.

More than anything else, the present policy of centralizing all power in Washington must be changed. Competent leaders will not accept responsibility unless it is accompanied by appropriate authority. We should choose able men as our ambassadors, give them a major voice in the drawing-up of the plans and wide latitude in effecting these plans, and hold them responsible for results.

I am afraid some will think I have strayed from my subject, but what I have tried to say is that diplomatic negotiation is the focus of our moral purpose, our world responsibility, and the practical embodiment of the organization, personnel policies, planning, and administrative leadership of our government. Unless all these things are in tune, our diplomatic negotiation cannot serve our present needs.

Our greatest need today is for the understanding and support of public opinion for sound foreign policies. It is significant that 84 per cent of our present national budget is to pay for past, present, and future wars. Since war represents the failure of our foreign policy, we can get a sense of proportion of the importance of this subject to our generation. A proportionate emphasis on the study of foreign policy should be given in our schools and colleges at the same time we are trying through the processes of adult education to equip our nation in a short period of time for the responsibilities of world leadership which are necessary to its survival.

The Art of Diplomatic Negotiation

I

The traditional methods of diplomacy have been under continuous attack since World War I and have to a considerable extent been discarded in practice since the end of World War II. Three main arguments have been directed against them. First, they have been held responsible for the political catastrophes which have befallen mankind in the last four decades or so; methods which appear to have been so unsuccessful must be replaced by better ones. Second, traditional diplomacy has been held to run counter to the principles of democracy, and from the assumption that democracy makes for peace and autocracy, for war, it has been concluded that diplomacy must be "open," that is, exposed to public scrutiny in all its processes. Finally the traditional diplomatic practices, with their seemingly useless and wasteful formalities, horse-trading, and compromises, have seemed to violate moral principles with which democratic nations have felt themselves identified; in other words, the age-old conflict between political realism and idealism has been transferred to the sphere of diplomacy.

These arguments against traditional diplomacy arise from the basic philosophic position, prevalent in our time, that political practices are the result of subjective preferences, to be changed at will. In truth, however, the traditional methods of diplomacy have not been invented by stupid and evil or, for that matter, wise and good men—even though they have certainly been used and abused by such men—but have grown ineluctably from the objective nature of things political. In their essence they are the reflections of that objective nature, to be disregarded only at the risk of political failure. Whenever two autonomous social entities, anxious to maintain their autonomy, engage in political relations with each other,

404

they cannot but help resort to what we call the traditional methods of diplomacy. And it does not matter in this respect whether these diplomatic relations are carried on between two members of a family, two businessmen, two baseball clubs, two political parties, or two sovereign nations. On all levels of such relations, secrecy of negotiation—to mention only their most prominent and controversial aspect —is not an arbitrary procedural device to be used or dispensed with at will but grows from the objective nature of negotiations. No negotiations of any kind—be they for the contraction of a marriage, the sale of a piece of property, a deal for baseball players, or an international treaty—can be carried out in public without defeating their very purpose: the transformation of conflicting or inchoate interests into a common purpose of the contracting parties.

The specific arguments against the traditional methods of diplomacy are as untenable as is the basic philosophic position from which they stem. If it be true that the traditional practices of diplomacy constitute the method by which the business of foreign policy must be transacted, the failure of a particular foreign policy or of a whole era to bring peace and order to the world cannot be attributed to these practices per se but, at worst, to their incorrect use. This logical deduction is borne out by the experiences of recent history, for the disorganization of international society since World War I has indeed been concomitant with the neglect, misunderstanding, and abuse of the traditional practices of diplomacy. While it would be far-fetched to suggest that the decline of diplomacy is responsible for the catastrophes which have befallen the world in recent times, it cannot be doubted that that decline has contributed to international disorder, itself being an outgrowth of a deep-seated disorder in the intellectual sphere.

Both the arguments that democracy means peace and that diplomacy is immoral and therefore undemocratic have grown from an intellectual attitude which is hostile to the very idea of foreign policy as an independent sphere of thought and action. They assume that the kind of foreign policy which a nation pursues is determined by the kind of domestic institutions it possesses and the kind of political philosophy to which it adheres. All recorded history militates against that assumption. The national interest of great powers and, in good measure, the methods by which it is to be secured are impervious to ideological or institutional changes. As far back as April 30, 1823, Canning warned that "the general acquisition of free institutions is not necessarily a security for general peace." Our experience of total wars, waged by democracies for democratic tenets, gives substance to that warning.

The argument that diplomacy is particularly immoral and, hence, incompatible with democratic government similarly assumes that one can escape from the moral dilemmas of foreign policy by foreswearing foreign policy itself. At the bottom of this argument there is a dual illusion: the illusion of the moral superiority of domestic politics over foreign policy and the illusion of the possibility of escaping foreign policy altogether. Both philosophic analysis and historic experience shows that the moral problems which foreign policy raises are but a peculiar—and particularly drastic—manifestation of the moral problem of politics as such. Taking a wider view, one can even say that the moral problem of politics is but a peculiar instance of the moral problem which man encounters whenever he acts with reference to his fellow men. What distinguishes in this respect foreign policy from domestic politics and from the human situation in general is not the substance of the problem, which is identical on all levels of human interaction, but the social conditions under which the problem arises on the international plane.

There is, then, no road by which one could escape the moral problem of politics, domestic or international; we can only endeavor to smoothen its sharp edges and to mitigate its practical consequences by changing not its substance but the social environment within which it is bound to arise in one form or another. It is not by accident that those who have tried to do more have taken a negative attitude toward foreign policy; for in the traditional methods of diplomacy they could not help but see the outward manifestations of the political risks and moral liabilities of foreign policy itself. Opposition to the traditional methods of diplomacy is everywhere intimately connected with either an isolationist or a universalistic attitude toward international relations. Both consider the traditional methods of diplomacy at best superfluous and at worst pernicious, for they so regard foreign policy itself. In the isolationist view, a country can afford to dispense with an active foreign policy and, hence, also with diplomacy. In the universalistic view, foreign policy, carried on through diplomatic methods by sovereign nations, belongs to a dying age and is a stumbling block to the establishment of a more peaceful and orderly organization of the world.

This thought reveals itself in the recent attempts to set up the procedures of the United Nations as an alternative to the traditional methods of diplomacy. Here, again, we are in the presence of the assumption that nations have a choice between the traditional methods of diplomacy and some other way of dealing with each other—a way which somehow leads to freedom from the risks and liabilities of foreign policy. In truth, of course, the procedures of the United Nations, as they have emerged in the practice of the organization, do not differ in substance from the traditional practices of diplomacy. What distinguishes the former from the latter is nothing but the social setting and the legal requirements which influence the way in which the traditional business of diplomacy is carried on within the agencies of the United Nations. The United Nations and traditional diplomacy are not mutually exclusive alternatives between which nations must choose. Rather, they supplement each other, serving identical purposes and partaking of the same qualities and characteristics. The Secretary-General of the United Nations, in his *Annual Report on the Work of the Organization for July 1, 1954 through June 15, 1955,* has called attention to this relationship in these words:

We have only begun to make use of the real possibilities of the United Nations as the most representative instrument for the relaxation of tensions, for the lessening of distrust and misunderstanding, and for the discovery and delineation of new areas of common ground and interest. . . . Conference diplomacy may usefully be supplemented by more quiet diplomacy within the United Nations, whether directly between representatives of Member Governments or in contacts between the Secretary-General and Member Governments. The obligations of the Charter, the environment of institutions dedicated to seeking out the common ground among the national interests of Member States, the wide representation from all continents and cultures, the presence of the Secretariat established as a principal organ of the United Nations for the purpose of upholding and serving the international interest—all these can provide help not to be found elsewhere, if they are rightly applied and used.

Within the framework of the Charter there are many possibilities, as yet largely unexplored, for variation of practices. . . . It is my hope that solid progress can be made in the coming years in developing new forms of contact, new methods of deliberation and new techniques of reconciliation.

With only slight adjustments, discussions of major issues of a kind that have occurred outside the United Nations could often be fitted into its framework, thus at the same time adding to the strength of the world organization and drawing strength from it.

II

With these considerations we are entering into the positive task of ascertaining what the functions of traditional diplomacy are and in what its permanent value consists. A nation, existing as it does as an equal among other nations, can deal with the outside world in one of three different ways. It can deny the importance of the other nations for itself and its own importance for them and retreat into the impotence of isolation. Or it can deny the equality of the other nations and try to impose its own will upon them by force of arms. In either case, at least in its pure, extreme realization, a nation can afford to dispense with diplomacy. Or a nation can want to pursue its interests in active contact and on the basis of equality with other nations, assuming the universality of that desire. In that case it cannot do without the constant redefinition and adjustment of its interests for the purpose of accommodating the interests of other nations.

Conflict of interests—actual, seeming, or potential—is the overriding fact of international society, as it is one of the overriding facts of all societies, even those most highly integrated and centralized. Diplomacy in all its diverse historic and social manifestations is the technique of accommodating such conflicting interests. That technique proceeds in two stages: the ascertainment of the facts of conflict and the formulation of the terms of settlement.

Nation A pursues certain interests, and so does nation B, and the interests of A and B are on the face of them in conflict. Both nations want to settle this conflict peacefully. How can they go about it? They have to define their respective interests and ascertain the point of conflict. That investigation may lead them to one of three possible conclusions.

If what A wants, being vital to itself, B cannot cede without endangering its vital interests, if not its very existence, because of the intrinsic importance of the territory, frontier, port, or air base at issue, diplomatic accommodation is impossible. When Francis I of France was asked why he always made war against Charles V of Austria, he is reported to have answered: "Because we both want the same thing: Italy." As long as both kings wanted Italy badly enough, they could either go to war over it or else leave the issue unsettled, hoping for future developments to deflect the energies of both sides toward less contentious objectives. Often in history nations have indeed avoided war over their vital interests by allowing time to take the sting out of their conflicts. Yet in such cases it is to the restraint of warlike passions and the renunciation of quick and radical solutions rather than to the practices of diplomacy that the credit for the preservation of peace must go.

Nation A may again pursue an objective vital to itself, which nation B could cede only at the price of a vital interest of its own. Yet in contrast to the type of conflict just discussed, the importance of the objective to both sides is here not intrinsic to the objective itself but rather the result of a peculiar configuration of interests which are subject to manipulation. For instance, the Soviet Union has a vital interest in preventing a united Germany from joining the Western alliance, and the United States has a similarly vital interest in preventing such a Germany from being absorbed by the Soviet bloc. Taken by themselves, these positions are obviously incompatible and, as the history of East-West negotiations has thus far shown, not subject to diplomatic accommodation. Yet one can well imagine, without committing one's self to its practical feasibility in the immediate future, an over-all European or world-wide settlement of which a German settlement would form an organic part, satisfactory to the interests of both sides which could not be reconciled to the unification of Germany considered in isolation. In situations such as this, it is the task of diplomacy to redefine the seemingly incompatible vital interests of the nations concerned in order to make them compatible.

This task of diplomacy is, as it were, strategic in nature and truly creative, not often attempted and rarely successful. It yields in practical importance to that function with which diplomacy is typically associated in the popular mind: the function of bargaining issuing in a compromise. In conflicts to which this function applies, nation A seeks an objective which nation B either is willing to grant only in part or refuses to grant at all without compensation. Conflicts of this kind concern non-vital interests of which nations are willing to dispose by way of negotiations. The technique of diplomacy consists here in ascertaining the interests of both sides and in allocating the objective at issue in view of these interests and of the power available for their support.

The same diplomatic technique serves not only the peaceful settlement of conflicts among nations but also the delineation and codification of common interests. In this respect it performs its classic function for the negotiation of treaties serving a common purpose of the contracting parties. Called upon to settle a conflict between two nations, diplomacy must create out of the conflicting interests a community of interests, a compromise which cannot satisfy all parties completely, but with which no party will be completely dissatisfied. When the representatives of two nations meet to negotiate a treaty, say, of commerce or alliance, they must discover and make precise an already existing community of interests. This community of interests, before it is crystallized in legal stipulations, is amorphous and inchoate, obscured and distorted by seeming and real conflicts. It is the task of diplomacy to define the area of that pre-existing community of interests and to express it in terms sufficiently precise to serve as a reliable foundation for future action. It need only be mentioned in passing that this function of diplomacy is identical with that of contractual negotiations on all levels of social interaction.

III

It must be obvious from what has been said thus far that the traditional methods of diplomacy are of vital importance to a nation which seeks to pursue its interests successfully and peaceably. A nation which is unwilling or unable to use diplomacy for that end is of necessity compelled either to forsake its interests or to pursue them by war. As pointed out before, nations have always had a choice among three alternatives: diplomacy, war, and renunciation. Which one of these alternatives a nation would choose in a concrete situation was a matter of rational calculation; none of them was a priori excluded on rational grounds.

Modern technology, especially in the form of all-out atomic war, has destroyed this rational equality among diplomacy, war, and renunciation and has greatly enhanced the importance of diplomacy. In view of that technology, there is no longer safety in renunciation or victory in war. From the beginning of history to World War II the risks inherent in these three choices were commensurate with the advantages to be expected. Nations would miscalculate and suffer unexpected losses; but it was never rationally foreordained that they could not win. War, in particular, was a rational means to a rational end; victory would justify the risks and losses incurred, and the consequences of defeat were not from the outset out of all proportion to the gains to be expected from victory.

The possibility of all-out atomic war has destroyed these rational relationships. When universal destruction is the result of victory and defeat alike, war itself is no longer a matter of rational choice but becomes an instrument of suicidal despair. The pursuit of a nation's interests short of all-out atomic war, then, becomes a matter of self-preservation. Even on the assumption—at present a moot one—that limited wars can and will still be safely waged, the risk of such a limited war developing into an all-out atomic one will always be present. Hence, the imperative of the avoidance of all-out atomic war at the very least gives unprecedented urgency to the pursuit of a nation's interests by peaceful means. Such peaceful pursuit, as we know, spells diplomacy. Neither diplomacy nor all-out atomic war is today one among several rational choices available to a nation. As all-out atomic war is tantamount to suicide, so successful diplomacy provides the only certain chance for survival. A nation which under present conditions is either unwilling or unable to take full advantage of the traditional methods of diplomacy condemns itself either to the slow death of attrition or the sudden death of atomic destruction.

IV

The vital importance which the traditional methods of diplomacy receive from the possibility of all-out atomic war is underlined by the more specific political developments which may well mark the year 1955 as the beginning of a new era in international relations. The first decade following World War II has been characterized on the international scene by three basic political phenomena: the bipolarity of international politics, the tendency of this bipolar political system to transform itself into a two-bloc system, and the policy of containment. These three basic facts have combined in minimizing the traditional methods of diplomacy, both as a matter of fact and in terms of the objective opportunities available.

During that decade effective power for purposes of foreign policy was concentrated in Washington and Moscow, and these two power poles tended to attract like magnets most of the other centers of power. Whatever they might have preferred had they been free to choose, Great Britain and France, Poland and China, had to lean upon one or the other of the superpowers for political, military, and economic support. Such countries could not have remained neutral, let alone changed sides, in the East-West conflict, short of a domestic revolution of radical dimensions. In such a situation, rigid in its alignments and inflexible in either side's conception of the interests involved, the main task of both sides is not to make and receive concessions but, at the very least, to hold the line and, at the very best, to advance it unilaterally. Since the balance of power made the latter alternative unfeasible short of a general war, both sides were of necessity reduced to a policy of containment which for all practical purposes forsook advancement at the expense of the other side while at the same time preventing the other side from advancing.

Such a situation of cold war offered little opportunity for the use of diplomatic methods either within the two-power blocs or between them. The inner coherence of the two blocs resulted primarily from the ineluctable necessity which made their members seek shelter under the roof of one or the other of the superpowers. During that period the discrepancy of strength between the two superpowers and their respective allies was so obviously extreme, and the consequences for those who would dare step out of line so obviously dire, that there was very little need for diplomacy to crystallize so obvious a community of interests.

The relations between the two blocs were no less clearly defined by the objective situation. The essence of the policy of containment was military rather than political. It consisted in the main in the warning, supported by actual preparedness, that a step taken by the other side beyond the line of military demarcation of 1945 would of necessity lead to a general war.

The services which diplomacy was able to perform for this policy of containment were hardly different from those diplomacy has traditionally performed for the conduct of real war. It could announce the conditions for the settlement of the cold war and use such and similar announcements for purposes of psychological warfare. The very modalities of the cold war, then, inevitably transformed diplomacy into a mere auxiliary of a war waged against the enemy not for the purpose of accommodating conflicting interests but for the triumph, however verbal, of one nation over the other. Thus it is not by accident that during the first decade following World War II the traditional methods of diplomacy virtually ceased to operate in the relations between East and West and that the moves which were carried on under the labels and with the personnel of diplomacy at the many East-West conferences and within the United Nations served purposes not only far removed from, but often diametrically opposed to, those of traditional diplomacy.

If indications do not deceive, this period of postwar history has come to a close. It is being replaced by an era which is marked by greater flexibility within the two power blocs, tending toward a loosening of their inner coherence, if not their dissolution, and, consequently, by greater flexibility between the two power blocs as well. To meet the problems of this new era, the methods of the cold war will prove to be inadequate. As the conditions of the cold war led necessarily to the disuse and misuse of the practices of diplomacy, so the new era of international relations with equal necessity calls for the restoration of these practices.

Four facts are in the main responsible for this fundamental change in international relations: the decrease in the dependence of the great powers of second rank upon the superpowers; the impending rise of Germany and Japan to great second-power status; the impending dispersion of atomic power among a multitude of nations, some of which, by virtue of their possession of atomic power, will gain or regain the status of great powers; and, finally, the spread and sharpening of the colonial revolutions in Asia, Africa, and Latin America.

Viewed from the vantage point of the United States, each of these new facts requires the vigorous application of the traditional practices of diplomacy. Since neither the American atomic monopoly nor extreme dependence upon American support can any longer be relied upon to secure the coherence of the Western alliance, the United States must again resort to the time-honored diplomatic method of fashioning a legally and politically viable community of interests out of the one that objectively exists in an inchoate and ill-defined form. Germany and Japan, no longer being the object of the victors' dispositions, must be persuaded by the same methods to see in association with the West the best chance for pursuing their interests. It is hardly necessary to emphasize that a similar approach to the colonial revolutions has been long overdue.

Thus the situation which confronts the United States at the moment of this writing poses the perennial problem of diplomacy with renewed urgency. The objections to its use are without merit. Its indispensability for a successful and peaceful foreign policy grows from the very nature of things political. The possibility of all-out atomic war has made its successful use the condition of survival. The apparent end of the cold war has made its restoration of vital concern for the foreign policy of the United States.

Social Science and Humanism

We have been assigned the task of discussing humanism and the social sciences. As appears from our program, humanism is understood in contradistinction to science, on the one hand, and to the civic art, on the other. It is thus suggested to us that the social sciences are shaped by science, the civic art, and humanism or that the social sciences dwell in the region where science, the civic art, and humanism meet and perhaps toward which they converge. Let us consider how this meeting might be understood.

Of the three elements mentioned, only science and humanism can be said to be at home in academic life. They certainly exhibit one characteristic of academic life. According to an old adage, man is a wolf to man, woman is more wolfish to woman, but a scholar in his relations to scholars is the most wolfish of all. Science and humanism are then not always on friendly terms. We all know the scientist who despises or ignores humanism, and the humanist who despises or ignores science. To understand this conflict, tension, or distinction between science and humanism, we do well to turn for a moment to the seventeenth century, to the age in which modern science constituted itself. At that time Pascal contrasted the spirit of geometry (i.e., the scientific spirit) with the spirit of finesse. We may circumscribe the meaning of the French term by referring to terms such as these: subtlety, refinement, tact, delicacy, perceptivity. The scientific spirit is characterized by detachment and by the forcefulness which stems from simplicity or simplification. The spirit of finesse is characterized by attachment or love and by breadth. The principles to which the scientific spirit defers are alien to common sense. The principles with which the spirit of finesse has to do are within common sense, yet they are barely visible; they are felt rather than seen. They are not available in such a way that we could make them the premises of our reasoning. The spirit of finesse is active not in reasoning but rather in grasping in one view unanalyzed wholes in their distinctive characters. What is meant today by the contrast between science and humanism represents a more or less profound modification of Pascal's contrast between the spirit of geometry and the spirit of finesse. In both cases the contrast implies that, in regard to the understanding of human things, the spirit of science has severe limitations—limitations which are overcome by a decidedly non-scientific approach.

What are these limitations as we observe them today within the social sciences? Social science consists of a number of disciplines which are specialized and which are becoming ever more specialized. There is certainly no social science in existence which could claim that it studies society as a whole, social man as a whole, or such wholes as we have in mind when we speak, for example, of this country, the United States of America. De Tocqueville and Lord Bryce are not representative of present-day social science. From time to time one or the other special and specialized science (e.g., psychology or sociology) raises the claim to be comprehensive or fundamental; but these claims always meet strong and justified resistance. Co-operation of the various disciplines may enlarge the horizon of the co-operating individuals; it cannot unify the disciplines themselves; it cannot bring about a true, hierarchic order.

Specialization may be said to originate ultimately in this premise: In order to understand a whole, one must analyze or resolve it into its elements, one must study the elements by themselves, and then one must reconstruct the whole or recompose it by starting from the elements. Reconstruction requires that the whole be sufficiently grasped in advance, prior to the analysis. If the primary grasp lacks definiteness and breadth, both the analysis and the synthesis will be guided by a distorted view of the whole, by a figment of a poor imagination rather than by the thing in its fulness. And the elements at which the analysis arrives will at best be only some of the elements. The sovereign rule of specialization means that the reconstruction cannot even be attempted. The reason for the impossibility of reconstruction can be stated as follows: The whole as primarily known is an object of common sense; but it is of the essence of the scientific spirit, at least as this spirit shows itself within the social sciences, to be distrustful of common sense or even to discard it altogether. The common-sense understanding expresses itself in common language; the scientific social scientist creates or fabricates a special scientific terminology. Thus scientific social science acquires a specific abstractness. There is nothing wrong with abstraction, but there is very much wrong with abstracting from essentials. Social science, to the extent to which it is emphatically scientific, abstracts from essential elements of social reality. I quote from a private communication by a philosophically sophisticated sociologist who is very favorably disposed toward the scientific approach in the social sciences: "What the sociologist calls 'system,' 'role,' 'status,' 'role expectation,' 'situation,' and 'institutionalization' is experienced by the individual actor on the social scene in entirely different terms." This is not merely to say that the citizen and the social scientist mean the same things but express them in different terms. For "the social scientist qua theoretician has to follow a system of relevances entirely different from that of the actor on the social scene. . . . His problems originate in his theoretical interest, and many elements of the social world that are scientifically relevant are irrelevant from the point of view of the actor on the social scene, and vice versa." The scientific social scientist is concerned with regularities of behavior; the citizen is concerned with good government. The relevances for the citizen are "values," "values" believed in and cherished, nay, "values" which are experienced as real qualities of real things: of man, of actions and thought, of institutions, of measures. But the scientistic social scientist draws a sharp line between values and facts: he regards himself as unable to pass any value judgments.

To counteract the dangers inherent in specialization as far as these dangers can be counteracted within the social sciences, a conscious return to common-sense thinking is needed—a return to the perspective of the citizen. We must identify the whole in reference to which we should select themes of research and integrate results of research, with the over-all objectives of whole societies. By doing this, we will understand social reality as it is understood in social life by thoughtful and broad-minded men. In other words, the true matrix of social science is the Civic Art and not a general notion of science or scientific method. Social science must either be a mere handmaid of the Civic Art—in this case no great harm is done if it forgets the wood for the trees—or, if it does not want to become or to remain oblivious of the noble tradition from which it sprang, if it believes that it might be able to enlighten the Civic Art, it must indeed look farther afield than the Civic Art, but it must look in the same direction as the Civic Art. Its relevances must become identical, at least at the outset, with those of the citizen or statesman; and therefore it must speak, or learn to speak, the language of the citizen and of the statesman.

From this point of view, the guiding theme of social science in this age and in this country will be democracy, or, more precisely, liberal democracy, especially in its American form. Liberal democracy will be studied with constant regard to the co-actual or co-potential alternatives and therefore especially to communism. The issue posed by communism will be faced by a conscientious, serious, and relentless critique of communism. At the same time, the dangers inherent in liberal democracy will be set forth squarely; for the friend of liberal democracy is not its flatterer. The sensitivity to these dangers will be sharpened and, if need be, awakened. From the scientistic point of view, the politically neutral—that which is common to all societies—must be looked upon as the clue to the politically relevant—that which is distinctive of the various regimes. But from the opposite point of view which I am trying to adumbrate, the emphasis is put on the politically relevant: the burning issues.

Social science cannot then rest satisfied with the over-all objectives of whole societies as they are for the most part understood in social life. Social science must clarify those objectives, ferret out their self-contradictions and halfheartednesses, and strive for knowledge of the true over-all objectives of whole societies. That is to say, the only alternative to an ever more specialized, an ever more aimless, social science is a social science ruled by the legitimate queen of the social sciences—the pursuit traditionally known by the name of ethics. Even today it is difficult, in dealing with social matters, consistently to avoid terms like "a man of character," "honesty," "loyalty," "citizenship education," etc.

This, or something like this, is, I believe, what many people have in mind when speaking of a humanistic approach, as distinguished from the scientistic approach, to social phenomena. We must still account for the term "humanism." The social scientist is a student of human societies, of societies of humans. If he wishes to be loyal to his task, he must never forget that he is dealing with human things, with human beings. He must reflect on the human as human. And he must pay due attention to the fact that he himself is a human being and that social science is always a kind of self-knowledge. Social science, being the pursuit of human knowledge of human things, includes as its foundation the human knowledge of what constitutes humanity or, rather, of what makes man complete or whole, so that he is truly human. Aristotle calls his equivalent of what now would be called social science the liberal inquiry regarding the human things, and his *Ethics* is the first, the fundamental, and the directive part of that inquiry.

But, if we understand by social science the knowledge of human things, are we not driven to the conclusion that the time-honored distinction between social science and the humanities must be abandoned? Perhaps we must follow Aristotle a step further and make a distinction between the life of society and the life of the mind, and hence assign the study of the former to social science and the study of the latter, or a certain kind of study of the latter, to the humanities.

I do not have to go into another implication of the term "humanism"—viz., the contradistinction of human studies to divinity, since our program is silent about divinity. I may limit myself to the remark that humanism may be said to imply that the moral principles are more knowable to man, or less controversial among earnest men, than theological principles.

By reflecting on what it means to be a human being, one sharpens his awareness of what is common to all human beings, if in different degrees, and of the goals toward which all human beings are directed by the fact that they are human beings. One transcends the horizon of the mere citizen—of every kind of sectionalism—and becomes a citizen of the world. Humanism as awareness of man's distinctive character as well as of man's distinctive completion, purpose, or duty issues in humaneness: in the earnest concern for both human kindness and the betterment and opening of one's mind—a blend of firm delicacy and hard-won serenity—a last and not merely last freedom from the degradation or hardening effected especially by conceit or pretense. One is tempted to say that to be inhuman is the same as to be unteachable, to be unable or unwilling to listen to other human beings.

Yet, even if all were said that could be said and that cannot be said, humanism is not enough. Man, while being at least potentially a whole, is only a part of a larger whole. While forming a kind of world and even being a kind of world, man is only a little world, a microcosm. The macrocosm, the whole to which man belongs, is not human. That whole, or its origin, is either subhuman or superhuman. Man cannot be understood in his own light but only in the light of either the subhuman or the superhuman. Either man is an accidental product of a blind evolution or else the process leading to man, culminating in man, is directed toward man. Mere humanism avoids this ultimate issue. The human meaning of what we have come to call "Science" consists precisely in this—that the human or the higher is understood in the light of the subhuman or the lower. Mere humanism is powerless to withstand the onslaught of modern science. It is from this point that we can begin to understand again the original meaning of science, of which the contemporary meaning is only a modification: science as man's attempt to understand the whole to which he belongs. Social science, as the study of things human, cannot be based on modern science, although it may judiciously use, in a strictly subordinate fashion, both methods and results of modern science. Social science must rather be taken to contribute to the true universal science into which modern science will have to be integrated eventually.

To summarize, to treat social science in a humanistic spirit means to return from the abstractions or constructs of scientistic social science to social reality, to look at social phenomena primarily in the perspective of the citizen and the statesman, and then in the perspective of the citizen of the world, in the twofold meaning of "world": the whole human race and the all-embracing whole.

Humanism, as I have tried to present it, is in itself a moderate approach. But, looking around me, I find that it is here and now an extreme version of humanism. Some of you might think that it would be more proper on the present occasion to present the median or average opinion of present-day humanistic social scientists rather than an eccentric one. I feel this obligation, but I cannot comply with it because of the elusive character of that median opinion. I shall therefore describe the extreme opposite of the view which appeals to me, or, rather, one particular expression, which is as good as any other, of that opposite extreme. Median social science humanism can be defined sufficiently for our purpose by the remark that it is located somewhere between these two extremes.

The kind of humanism to which I now turn designates itself as relativistic. It may be called a humanism for two reasons. First it holds that the social sciences cannot be modeled on the natural sciences, because the social sciences deal with man. Second, it is animated, as it were, by nothing except openness for everything that is human. According to this view, the methods of science, of natural science, are adequate to the study of phenomena to which we have access only by observing them from without and in detachment. But the social sciences deal with phenomena whose core is indeed inaccessible to detached observation but discloses itself, at least to some extent, to the scholar who relives or re-enacts the life of the human beings whom he studies or who enters into the perspective of the actors and understands the life of the actors from their own point of view as distinguished from both his point of view and the point of view of the outside observer. Every perspective of active man is constituted by evaluation or is at any rate inseparable from it. Therefore, understanding from within means sharing in the acceptance of the values which are accepted by the societies or the individuals whom one studies, or accepting these values "histrionically" as the true values, or recognizing the position taken by the human beings under consideration as true. If one practices such understanding often and intensively enough, one realizes that perspectives or points of view cannot be criticized. All positions of this kind are equally true or untrue: true from within, untrue from without. Yet, while they cannot be criticized, they can be understood. However, I have as much right to my perspective as anyone else has to his or any society to its. And every perspective being inseparable from evaluation, I, as an acting man and not as a mere social scientist, am compelled to criticize other perspectives and the values on which they are based or which they posit. We do not end then in moral nihilism, for our belief in our values gives us strength and direction. Nor do we end in a state of perpetual war of everybody against everybody, for we are permitted to "trust to reason and the council table for a peaceful coexistence."

Let us briefly examine this position which at first glance recommends itself because of its apparent generosity and unbounded sympathy for every human position. Against a perhaps outdated version of relativism one might have argued as follows. Let us popularly define nihilism as the inability to take a stand for civilization against cannibalism. The relativist asserts that objectively civilization is not superior to cannibalism, for the case in favor of civilizaton can be matched by an equally strong or an equally weak case in favor of cannibalism. The fact that we are opposed to cannibalism is due entirely to our historical situation. But historical situations change necessarily into other historical situations. A historical situation productive of the belief in civilization may give way to a historical situation productive of belief in cannibalism. Since the relativist holds that civilization is not intrinsically superior to cannibalism, he will placidly accept the change of civilized society into cannibal society. Yet the relativism which I am now discussing denies that our values are simply determined by our historical situation: we can transcend our historical situation and enter into entirely different perspectives. In other words, there is no reason why, say, an Englishman should not become, in the decisive respect, a Japanese. Therefore, our believing in certain values cannot be traced beyond our decision or commitment. One might even say that, to the extent to which we are still able to reflect on the relation of our values to our situation, we are still trying to shirk the responsibility for our choice. Now, if we commit ourselves to the values of civilization, our very commitment enables and compels us to take a vigorous stand against cannibalism and prevents us from placidly accepting a change of our society in the direction of cannibalism.

To stand up for one's commitment means among other things to defend it against its opponents not only by deed but by speech as well. Speech is required especially for fortifying those who waver in their commitments to the values we cherish. The waverers are not yet decided to which cause they should commit themselves, or they do not know whether they should commit themselves to civilization or to cannibalism. In speaking to them, we cannot assume the validity of the values of civilization. And, according to the premise, there is no way to convince them of the truth of those values. Hence the speech employed for buttressing the cause of civilization will be not rational discourse but mere "propaganda," a "propaganda" confronted by the equally legitimate and perhaps more effective "propaganda" in favor of cannibalism.

This notion of the human situation is said to be arrived at through the practice of sympathetic understanding. Only sympathetic understanding is said to make possible valid criticism of other points of view—a criticism which is based on nothing but our commitment and which therefore does not deny the right of our opponents to their commitments. Only sympathetic understanding, in other words, makes us truly understand the character of values and the manner in which they are legitimately adopted. But what is sympathetic understanding? Is it dependent on our own commitment, or is it independent of it? If it is independent, I am committed as an acting man, and I am uncommitted in another compartment of myself, in my capacity as a social scientist. In that latter capacity I am, so to speak, completely empty and therefore completely open to the perception and appreciation of all commitments or value systems. I go through the process of sympathetic understanding in order to reach clarity about my commitment, and this process in no way endangers my commitment, for only a part of my self is engaged in my sympathetic understanding. This means, however, that such sympathetic understanding is not serious or genuine and is, indeed, as it calls itself, "histrionic." For genuinely to understand the value system, say, of a given society, means being deeply moved and indeed gripped by the values to which the society in question is committed and to expose one's self in earnest, with a view to one's own whole life, to the claim of those values to be the true values. Genuine understanding of other commitments is then not necessarily conducive to the reassertion of one's own initial commitment. Apart from this, it follows from the inevitable distinction between serious understanding and histrionic understanding that only my own commitment, my own "depth," can possibly disclose to me the commitment, the "depth," of other human beings. Hence my perceptivity is necessarily limited by my commitment. Universal sympathetic understanding is impossible. To speak crudely, one cannot have the cake and eat it; one cannot enjoy both the advantages of universal understanding and those of existentialism.

But perhaps it is wrong to assume that all positions ultimately rest on commitments, or at any rate on commitments to specific points of view. We all remember the time when most men believed explicitly or implicitly that there is one and only one true value system of universal validity, and there are still societies and individuals who cling to this view. They too must be understood sympathetically. Would it not be harsh and even inconsistent to deprive the Bible and Plato of a privilege which is generously accorded to every savage tribe? And will sympathetic understanding of Plato not lead us to admit that absolutism is as true as relativism or that Plato was as justified in simply condemning other value positions as the relativist is in never simply condemning any value position? To this our relativist will reply that, while Plato's value system is as defensible as any other, provided it is taken to have no other support than Plato's commitment, Plato's absolutist interpretation of his value system, as well as any other absolutism, has been refuted unqualifiedly, with finality, absolutely. This means however that Plato's view as he understood it, as it reveals itself to us if we enter sympathetically into his perspective, has been refuted: it has been seen to rest on untrue theoretical premises. So-called sympathetic understanding necessarily and legitimately ends when rational criticism reveals the untruth of the position which we are attempting to understand sympathetically; and the possibility of such rational criticism is necessarily admitted by relativism, since it claims to reject absolutism on rational grounds. The example of Plato is not an isolated one. Where in fact do we find, outside certain circles of present-day Western society, any value position which does not rest on theoretical premises of one kind or another—premises which claim to be simply, absolutely, universally true, and which as such are legitimately exposed to rational criticism? I fear that the field within which relativists can practice sympathetic understanding is restricted to the community of relativists who understand each other with great sympathy because they are united by identically the same fundamental commitment or rather by identically the same rational insight into the truth of relativism. What claims to be the final triumph over provincialism reveals itself as the most amazing manifestation of provincialism.

There is a remarkable contrast between the apparent humility and the hidden arrogance of relativism. The relativist rejects the absolutism inherent in our great Western tradition—in its belief in the possibility of a rational and universal ethics or of natural right—with indignation or contempt; and he accuses that tradition of provincialism. His heart goes out to the simple preliterate people who cherish their values without raising exorbitant claims on their behalf. But these simple people do not practice histrionic or sympathetic understanding. Lacking such understanding, they do not adopt their values in the only legitimate manner, that is, as supported by nothing except their commitment. They sometimes reject Western values. Therewith they engage in invalid criticism, for valid criticism presupposes histrionic understanding. They are then provincial and narrow, as provincial and narrow as Plato and the Bible. The only people who are not provincial and narrow are the Western relativists and their Westernized followers in other cultures. They alone are right.

It almost goes without saying that relativism, if it were acted upon, would lead to complete chaos. For to say in the same breath that our sole protection against war between societies and within society is reason, and that according to reason "those individuals and societies who find it congenial to their systems of values to oppress and subjugate others" are as right as those who love peace and justice, means to appeal to reason in the very act of destroying reason.

Many humanistic social scientists are aware of the inadequacy of relativism, but they hesitate to turn to what is called "absolutism." They may be said to adhere to a qualified relativism. Whether this qualified relativism has a solid basis appears to me to be the most pressing question for social science today.

Humanism and the Social Sciences: But What about John de Neushom?

We are met here today, somewhat belatedly, to celebrate with appropriate discourse the Twenty-fifth Anniversary of the Social Sciences Research Building. This is not the first such occasion. There were speeches, of hope and promise, at the dedication of the building in December, 1929, and more speeches, of hope and appraisal, at the Tenth Anniversary in December, 1939. Indeed, an outsider might wonder at the number of celebrations, to say nothing of the amount of oratory, lavished upon so young a building. But this is wholly within our Chicago tradition. The University was born late but matured rapidly, and, thanks to President Harper's foresight and his quarter system, we have already celebrated our Two Hundred and Sixty-seventh Convocation.

Were we dedicating the hall initially instead of re-rededicating it, 1126 East Fifty-ninth Street most probably would have been christened the Behavioral Sciences Research Building, in token of the friendly spirit of co-operation we have ever borne toward the foundations. But architectural sketches made soon after Harper's death in 1906 show at the same address a Gothic structure labeled "Building of the Historical Group,"[1] and this bit of University lore has encouraged me to discuss the broad topic assigned today in terms of the discipline I profess, with some passing reference to the edifice we are commemorating. Fortunately, Mr. Strauss's treatment has been at once so broad and so lucid that my own parochial view may be condoned, particularly since the historian's craft, in greater degree than the other disciplines here represented, is commonly said to bridge over the no man's land between the humanities and the

1. Photographs of sketches made in 1902 (calling the building simply "History") and in 1906 are reproduced in Haynes McMullen, "The Administration of the University of Chicago Libraries, 1892–1928" (unpublished Ph.D. dissertation, University of Chicago, 1949), pp. 91 and 99.

social sciences. Though neither a purely creative artist nor what it seems now the fashion to call a "hard scientist," the successful historian must combine in some measure the spirit of each.

This ambivalence is illustrated in its shallowest manifestation in the internal organization of our faculties. When the divisions were established at Chicago in 1931, the history department was assigned budgetarily to the social sciences, but individual historians elected as they pleased membership in that faculty or the humanities. That the majority should enter the social science division was perhaps inevitable. James Harvey Robinson's *New History* had lessened the suspicions with which historians had viewed their parvenu colleagues, who had gained first respectability, then an enviable and waxing prestige. And there were more tangible inducements at hand: a brand-new office, an automatic elevator which then worked, and the expectation of munificent grants for research. Within so large a department there were of course divergent views as to the nature of history, and some talked more confidently than others about scientific history; but, as I came to know those men, as a graduate student and as a very junior colleague, it did not seem that their differences were fundamental. A Pulitzer prize winner in United States constitutional history became a social scientist; a world authority on the Athenian constitution, a humanist—but in either case the aim and the method were essentially similar.

In 1929 planning for the exterior decoration of the new building had evoked one mild controversy. The iconography was to be chaste and simple: four abstract plaques representing techniques, six medallions with portraits of eminent scholars, and a single inscription to go over the large bay window facing the Midway. For the last, the Committee on Symbolism submitted a quotation from Lord Kelvin, somewhat mutilated by four sets of ellipses: "When you cannot measure . . . your knowledge is . . . meager . . . and . . . unsatisfactory."[2] That a physicist should be chosen to speak for the social sciences seemed inappropriate to some, though apparently not to the majority of the faculty, and you may read the legend there today, with the ellipses innocently disguised as rosettes. The historians could find some consolation in the profile of Gibbon

2. "Report of Committee on Symbolism, January 31, 1929," and covering letter, April 6, 1929, in files of Department of Buildings and Grounds.

which was carved in one of the medallions gracing the back porch, but, if the Kelvin motto had been taken literally, their claim to office space would have been tenuous.

The dilemma was, as historians measure time, of recent origin. From the time of Herodotus, history had been accounted a form of belles-lettres, not without utility to the civic and administrative arts —to borrow the categories of our printed program—but literary rather than scientific in nature. Such instruction in history as was given in the medieval university—and it was as feeble as that in an American high school—was in the study of grammar, the very foundation of the humanistic trivium. Even later when proper chairs of history were established, the alignment remained the same. Thus at the University of Leiden the rivalry between the humanities, including history, and scientific and professional studies can be seen in the valedictory address of the *rector magnificus* in 1720, which bears in English translation the formidable title: *AN ORATION BY MR. PETER BURMAN AGAINST THE STUDIES OF HUMANITY. SHEWING That the Learned Languages, History, Eloquence and Critick, are not only Useless, but also Dangerous to the Studies of Law, Physick, Philosophy, and above all of Divinity; to which last Poetry is a special help* (London, 1721). In defense of my own calling, I hasten to add that Mr. Peter Burman was himself Professor of History and Eloquence and that his title and oration, with its frightening conclusion that all "Professors of antiquated Humanity" should be exiled to Russia, were written in ironic vein. But irony or no irony, the dual nature of his chair showed where history belonged in the academic scheme of things.

But increasingly in Burman's century and the next the idea gained currency that, however questionable had been its past, history could and should be made a science. This belief grew out of the popular enthusiasm for the vast achievements of the natural sciences but was influenced by two divergent forces: the grand projects of the philosophers who turned to universal history, and the refinement of historical methodology, particularly in the critical handling of sources, within the German seminars. The new critical techniques, which had got their start in studies normally considered humanistic, were propagated in Europe and America through the influence of Ranke and his disciples until they were accepted by all serious historians. The idea of history as a body of universal laws discoverable by the inductive method gained acceptance more slowly. Indeed, the new critical standards tended to encourage minuscule studies until the monograph became the favorite medium of the academic historian, and it was left to outsiders to develop the new concept. This was the situation when Henry Thomas Buckle published in 1857 the first volume of his *History of Civilization in England,* and even after a century what he has to say about method and his application of his methodological principles to the data of intellectual history are of interest in the context of today's discussion.

Buckle begins with praise for the amount of information about the past that men had gathered and an indictment of the use made thereof by his predecessors, a form of critique popular among historians since the time of Thucydides and Polybius. "I hope," he wrote, "to accomplish for the history of man something equivalent, or at any rate analogous, to what has been effected for the different branches of natural science. In regard to nature, events apparently the most irregular and capricious have been shown to be in accordance with certain fixed and universal laws."[3] That such had not been accomplished for history was partly because of the greater complexity of social phenomena, partly because historians had been "of inferior ability to the investigators of nature."[4] Buckle's confidence that he might prove an exception to this harsh judgment was not wholly unfounded. A man of brilliant mind and real if not profound speculative powers, he aimed at the sort of universality of knowledge we commonly associate with the Renaissance. He had a remarkable memory, great linguistic facility, and enough means to indulge uninterruptedly his passion for reading. In spite of delicate health, his regular habits of work gave him in time a vast and curious erudition, the results of which may be seen in the citations in his history or, more intimately, in his *Commonplace Book,*[5] published posthumously, which has more of the flavor of Frazer's *Golden Bough* or Sumner's *Folkways* than of the working notes of the conventional historian.

3. *History of Civilization in England* (2 vols.; New York, 1934), I, 5.

4. *Ibid.*

5. *Miscellaneous and Posthumous Works of Henry Thomas Buckle* (3 vols.; London, 1872), Vols. II and III.

So spacious was the scope of his plan that the two stout volumes he published before his early death in 1862 constitute no more than an introduction. Having thrown out the ideas of free will and pre-destination as superstitions, Buckle proposed to look at history as a process of modification of man by nature and of nature by man; the historian's task was to determine whether it was mind or nature that had exerted the greater influence on human actions. Such a judgment could be made because of the great regularity of human behavior: "The actions of man, being determined solely by their antecedents, must have a character of uniformity, that is to say, must, under precisely the same circumstances, always issue in the same results."[6] In an oft-quoted passage, Buckle advances as proofs of this regularity some statistics on crime as interpreted by the Belgian mathematician, Quételet. Murder, the most arbitrary and ir-rational of crimes, he says, "is committed with as much regularity, and bears as uniform a relation to certain known circumstances, as do the movements of the tides, and the rotations of the seasons."[7] Thus for any time period the number of murders, or even the type of weapon used, can be predicted with great precision; in any sui-cide, "the individual felon only carries into effect what is a neces-sary consequence of preceding circumstances."[8]

The recognition of regular patterns in demographic phenomena was not original with Quételet. John Graunt, a London haberdasher, had won membership in the Royal Society as early as 1662 with his *Natural and Political Observations Made upon the Bills of Mortal-ity*,[9] in which he pointed out the constant proportion, in deaths officially reported in England, of certain chronic diseases, of certain types of accidents, and of suicides. But Graunt's interest was in the application of these data to the civic and administrative arts; Buckle's, in their use for a method based on analogies with the nat-ural sciences. The latter's emphasis on regularity in human affairs

6. *History of Civilization*, I, 14–15.

7. *Ibid.*, citing L. A. Quételet, *Sur l'homme et le développement de ses facultés* (2 vols.; Paris, 1835), I, 7, and II, 164, 247.

8. *History of Civilization*, I, 20.

9. John Graunt, *Natural and Political Observations Mentioned in a Following Index, and Made upon the Bills of Mortality* (London, 1662). I have used the edition of Walter F. Willcox (Baltimore, 1939).

and in quantitative judgments based thereon is wholly within the spirit of the Lord Kelvin quotation, and that emphasis seems to me to mark a fundamental difference between the historian as social scientist and the historian as humanist.

May I illustrate my point by reference to a body of data precisely of the sort Buckle referred to? If my analysis has for emphasis something of the exaggeration of a caricature, it is only in the belief that a caricature by its very exaggeration can sometimes show truths missed by a Leica camera.

Those of us who work in the more remote periods of history have a peculiarly sensitive skin in this matter of quantitative measurements, since the records left by early folk are seldom full enough or precise enough or continuous enough to warrant the use of an elaborate statistical method. This lack is felt for much of the history of the Middle Ages, but one happy exception of sorts may be found in the official rolls of Norman and Plantagenet England, where our relative wealth of information is the result of voluminous recording by the Anglo-Norman bureaucrats and the quiet internal history of England that has made for a high survival rate of early muniments. Among the various courts of record whose reports have come down to us in considerable part is that of the coroner. The true purpose of that officer, as the name indicates, was to look after the interests of the crown, but his inquests served pretty much the same purpose as a coroner's inquest today: to examine, through a sworn jury, the circumstances in each death by other than natural causes and to establish in preliminary fashion responsibility for the death. Thus the coroner's rolls contain for an earlier age the same type of information used by Quételet.

In the year our university was founded J. E. Thorold Rogers published three such rolls for the city of Oxford during the reigns of the first two Edwards.[10] That Thorold Rogers was a pioneer in the statistical approach to medieval England is immaterial here, for his interest was in the early history of his own university, not in economics. The rolls were incomplete, having been mutilated, he thought, by generations of attorneys, and, though other fragments

10. In *Oxford City Documents, Financial and Judicial, 1288–1665* ("Oxford Historical Documents," Vol. XVIII [Oxford, 1891]), pp. 145–74.

were subsequently added by H. E. Salter,[11] the record is still not a full one. But this is so normal a circumstance for the medievalist, whose data are provided by chance survival rather than by a planned economy, that we may examine with some gratitude the twenty-eight cases which appeared in 1891.

So meticulous is the reporting that we can find for most cases the sort of details Buckle cited: the status of the victim and assailant; the place and time of the crime and of the death; the length, breadth, and depth of the wound, measured in inches rather than in Bertillon's centimeters; and the value of the criminal's personal property. One might make, if he cared, tables to show the high proportion of crimes committed after curfew, or the preference for knives over swords, poleaxes, and clubs as weapons, or the relatively high ratio of the Irishmen involved to the estimated population of Oxford. It would be, of course, a travesty on Buckle's intent to project so small and haphazard a sampling into laws, but my point is that it is this type of information that is often both the most adaptable to exact measurement and the most inconsequential for the historian.

At the same time the documents give inadvertently a great deal of casual information about the topography and customs of Oxford and its university at a time when the collegiate system was only beginning, and some of this lends itself to the less universal forms of generalization common among even the most cautious historians. So stereotyped is the process described in these cases that even without further substantiating evidence we could say with some confidence how a coroner's inquest was conducted. From the surnames of the several hundred persons mentioned as participants, jurors, or pledges, one could gain a fair idea of the trades and professions practiced in Oxford. But the most useful purpose of these documents has been to illustrate in gory detail what Huizinga has called "the violent tenor of life"[12] in the later Middle Ages, and particularly as that was manifested in academic circles.

Thus one might show that, of five accidental deaths, three were of scholars and a fourth occurred at the graduation feast of a young

11. *Records of Medieval Oxford: Coroners Inquests, the Walls of Oxford, etc.* (Oxford, 1912), pp. 1–55.

12. Johan Huizinga, *The Waning of the Middle Ages* (London, 1924), chap. i.

clerk, where a pregnant woman was so crushed in the throng as to lose a son by abortion. The one suicide was a scholar. In thirteen of the twenty-three homicides, the murderer was a scholar, and in ten cases the victim, not always guiltless himself, was of similar status. A clue to the uninhibited conduct of these academic folk may be seen in the fact that only one was arrested, and he faced no graver threat than trial in an ecclesiastical court whose punishments were notoriously light. Few if any of the murders seems to have been premeditated, and the trivial nature of the motives especially shows a society with little self-restraint: a quarrel with a town harlot over her price, a shouted insult, or the perpetual gang fights between the North and South nations, as violent as, if of lesser scope than, our own North-South conflict. The total picture helps explain the constant friction between town and gown and makes more plausible the accounts of those great riots by which Oxford, like other medieval universities, won its most valued privileges.

But beyond his interest in the documents as they elucidate legal institutions or academic customs, the historian as humanist may harbor some legitimate curiosity about these folk as individuals. About John Potus, stabbed to death in Blake Hall, who left in chattels a tapestry of Rheims, a linen garment, a sword, a chest, and a plate, total value 2s. 6d., and a *librum codicem*, value unknown, in pawn in the university loan chest. Or about Robert de Honiton, who, going up into the bell tower of St. Michael's to help ring in the New Year of 1301, fell through a trap door and died later from gangrene. Or about Gilbert de Foxlee, a cantankerous scholar who died from wounds received when he tried persistently to crash the party of the Oxford guild of tailors reveling on Midsummer Eve. Or about John de Neushom, "clericus et doctor puerorum," whose body was found on the banks of the Cherwell: he had gone after dinner to hunt switches for castigating his pupils and, climbing into a willow tree to cut some switches, had fallen into the millpond called Temple Mile and had drowned.

The historian, as social scientist, seeks such regularities as his sources will allow; because of the inadequate nature of his data and perhaps because of his temperament, his generalizations are rarely stated as the sort of laws Buckle wanted. The most fruitful are frequently no more than suggested explanations of broad movements in history—a Turner frontier thesis, a Pirenne burg-mercantile theory —without universal applicability. The historian, as humanist, cannot be content to essay a sort of Gallup poll of the past. The evidence of common sense, if not of the calculus, warns him that the contingent may be as decisive as the regular. Few bodies of statistical data have been subjected to a closer scrutiny than the reports of the New York Stock Exchange, and some informed persons are said to have found in them a high degree of predictability. In the early autumn there were those who believed some adjustment in stock prices was due, but no one could predict that a clot of blood in a robust man vacationing in Colorado would set in train on September 26 the wildest selling since that Black Friday in October, 1929.

Beyond his conservative views about predictability, the historian as humanist has more positive reason for including in his interests the unique as well as the regular. History is still a form of literature, and its whole cloth must contain the warp of individual experience as well as the woof of abstraction. The expression "human interest" has taken on a degraded connotation as being journalistic rather than scholarly; but the historian, if he is not to be a Dr. Dryasdust, must have some of the journalist's concern for the who, where, when, and what. This is not to agree with Aristotle's dictum that history gives no general truths but only particular facts. It is rather to accept the distinction William James makes in "The One and the Many" between your humanist and your scientist or philosopher, ending so: "What our intellect really aims at is neither variety nor unity taken singly, but *totality*. In this, acquaintance with realities is as important as understanding their connexion. Curiosity goes *pari passu* with the systematizing passion."[13]

Henry of Huntingdon, a twelfth-century English chronicler, summed up quaintly the dual nature of history, that "most delightful of studies and the one which is invested with the noblest and brightest prerogatives."[14] "History," he wrote—and here he is as interested as was Buckle in applying the data of experience to the problems of behavior—"brings the past to view, as if it were the present, and

13. In *Pragmatism* (New York, 1916), p. 130.

14. *The Chronicle of Henry of Huntingdon*, trans. Thomas Forester (London, 1853), pp. xxv–xxvii.

enables us to judge of the future by picturing to ourselves the past."
But he goes on to expound a view that is thoroughly humanistic:

Besides, the knowledge of former events has this further pre-eminence,
that it forms a main distinction between brutes and rational creatures. For
brutes, whether they be men or beasts, neither know, nor wish to know,
whence they come, nor their own origin, nor the annals and revolutions of
the country they inhabit. Of the two, I consider men in this brutal state
to be the worst, because what is natural in the case of beasts, is the lot of
men from their own want of sense; and what beasts could not acquire if
they would, such men will not though they could.

For totality, then, the historian must be interested in human
beings as well as in humanity, in men as well as in man, in persons
as well as in peoples. Without apology, he may accept Buckle's vital
statistics and still ask, "But what about John de Neushom?"

The Historian's Use of Generalization

Fifteen years ago, when the Social Science Building of the University of Chicago celebrated its tenth anniversary, I was one of a panel that discussed the question of generalization in the social sciences.[1] Having been requested to address myself to the subject of the historian's use of generalization, I made some obvious remarks to the effect that the historian uses generalizations at times with explicit purpose, but uses them often, whether explicitly or implicitly. That point of view, by no means original then, has since become shopworn, largely because, in the United States at least, it has been familiarized by the bulletins (Nos. 54 and 64) prepared for the Social Science Research Council by two separate committees on historiography.[2] No informed person, so far as I know, ever denied that historians study and should study the unique; and nowadays few (probably none of whom sits among you) question that historians should also study the general.

If, today, like the minister who complains to those who have taken extra pains to come to church that church attendance has fallen off, I seem to scold you, if I now crave your indulgence for a further elaboration of what probably is obvious to all of you, my excuse is that the obvious is not always familiar, and the familiar is not always contemptible. In its present rudimentary state, social science is to a large degree an effort to make the obvious familiar and respectable. And I should like this afternoon to engage in some such effort with regard to certain kinds of generalization actually employed by historians.

I shall arrange these generalizations in three categories, without

1. Louis Wirth (ed.), *Eleven Twenty-six: A Decade of Social Science Research* (Chicago, 1940), pp. 259–62.

2. Merle Curti *et al.*, *Theory and Practice in Historical Study* (New York, 1946), and Thomas C. Cochran *et al.*, *The Social Sciences in Historical Study* (New York, 1954).

pretending that this arrangement is the best or that these three categories are exhaustive. Of each category I shall give concrete illustrations selected from some recent writings by historians. In the first category are generalizations which, if made at all, are usually made *explicitly*. In the second are generalizations which are made *implicitly* by nearly all historians and frequently with awareness. In the third are the *"hidden"* generalizations, made implicitly and usually without awareness by historians among others.

The term "generalization," for my purposes, can be defined simply. It is a proposition that describes some attribute common to two or more objects. For the historian the objects would most probably be human beings in the past, their institutions, or their actions. Of course, a generalization is not much of a generalization if it applies to only two objects, but it certainly is not a statement about the unique. I wish to underline that, although I shall occasionally speak of what I think historians *should* do in the nature of generalization, I mean primarily to deal here with generalizations that they in fact *do* use.

Not all historians try to propound generalizations explicitly. Some hold that the historian's task is to be purely descriptive or at the most interpretative, being persuaded that appropriate descriptions and interpretations are inherent in the events themselves and will emerge clearly if the events are properly arranged. Historians of this school look askance at colleagues who believe that there are lessons to be learned from history—that man's past experience has some didactic value for today and tomorrow. Such historians are frequently to be found in the fields of history where the sources are rarest, where a high degree of consensus on the particulars is possible among the experts, and where the discovery of any new particular is unusual and therefore important. Because these historians are more or less able to master their sources, they feel comparatively certain of the validity of their descriptive and interpretative efforts, and they are likely to confuse a subjective certitude with an objective certainty.

The bold historians, the ones who do not confuse certitude and certainty and who dare to risk both in a quest for a broad approach to the experience of mankind, are concerned with the perennial human problems and therefore with the familiar problems of their own day. Naturally they have to run the risk of widespread criticism. Nevertheless, such a concern has characterized the work of the famous authors of universal histories—for example, Herodotus, St. Augustine, Bossuet, Voltaire, Condorcet, H. G. Wells, Spengler, and Toynbee—even if some of them may now seem to have had a rather narrow concept of the universe. For Toynbee, whose concept of the universe is the most inclusive of all these, the boldness of the quest for the lessons of history is such that he transcends the usual concept of historical sources and gives greater weight than I believe most historians would give to mythology, biblical lore, poetry, and fiction as evidence—or, perhaps more accurately stated, as illustration of conclusions already reached. These renowned authors made explicit generalizations—general with regard to either the happenings of the past or the trends of history and their possible direction in the future.

You may object that these writers, even when they called themselves "historians" and their writings "studies of history," were not historians in fact but philosophers using history as a tool or a source. I am not disposed to quarrel with you, nor do I think the historians named would do so either, for the difference sometimes seems to be academic. Instead I would ask you to name your own historians. Name the "purest" historians you can think of who dealt with a subject of more than particular and provincial dimensions—Thucydides, Polybius, the Venerable Bede, Froissart, Winckelmann, Ranke, Guizot, Parkman, Maitland, Mommsen. All of them must have made some sort of explicit generalization, even though it might be only to posit that no philosophy of history can hold true generally.

An important recent attack of this sort upon explicit generalization by historians comes from the pen of one of the world's most reputed historians, Pieter Geyl. Geyl has been fighting a running battle with Arnold Toynbee over a period of years. He doubts that Toynbee's generalizations in *The Study of History* are "laws of mankind's historic life" derived as "reliable conclusions" from "empirical investigation."[3] For, says Geyl, "the study of history cannot supply us with forecasts having universal validity."[4] And when, in criticism of Toynbee, he proclaims his own "dominant conviction" that "Western civilization will prove to have sufficient moral and intel-

3. "Toynbee the Prophet," *Journal of the History of Ideas*, XVI (1955), 264.
4. *Ibid.*, p. 265.

lectual reserves to continue the struggle for existence and will survive," he apologizes for taking this glimpse into the "large possibilities hidden in the impenetrable future" by stating that he is "not now speaking as a historian."[5]

In the running fight between Toynbee and Geyl, I find myself more on Geyl's side than on Toynbee's. This declaration of partisanship I do not mean to be taken as implying any lack of admiration for the learning, courage, and insight of Mr. Toynbee's *Study*. I mean only that I have grave doubts about Toynbee's methods of proof and the logical consequence of his conclusion from his data. But I also consider Geyl mistaken when he suggests that as a historian he has no right to look for "reliable conclusions about the laws of mankind's historic life." In fact, two of the passages I have already quoted from Geyl are themselves conclusions about the laws of mankind's historic life. Is the statement to the effect that the study of history cannot supply forecasts of universal validity anything but a statement assumed to have universal validity as a forecast? Is the conviction that Western civilization will prove strong enough morally and intellectually to survive in the struggle for existence anything but another such forecast?

Geyl's apology for the latter statement on the grounds that in making it he is temporarily stepping out of his role as a historian does not appear acceptable to me. I know him as a historian, a very good historian indeed. I also am convinced that he is not schizophrenic. I do not believe that he can step out of his role as a historian if he thinks about history even when his thinking may not be at the level of objectivity he himself sets for historians. What his apology in fact does is to betray a prejudice that he shares with a great number of "pure" historians—to wit, that when a historian makes a forecast about historical developments, even if it comes (to use Geyl's phrase) out of his "reading of history," he does so not as historian but in some other capacity such as citizen, philosopher, or Christian. What would one think of a mathematician or a physicist who, when he thought about the trends, the nature, or the theory of mathematics or of physics, claimed that in so doing he was not acting as a mathematician or a physicist? Yet a comparable claim is common among historians. Depart from your sources, the "pure" historians believe,

5. *Ibid.*, p. 263.

and you cease to be a historian. As if the sources had any validity as history unless checked against the timeless realities of human experience!

Sometimes even the "purest" historians are willing to make at least one concession in the direction of the timeless realities of human experience. They are usually ready to draw general conclusions about the past. They are well disposed toward typologies like ancient cults, medieval towns, or the American frontier and hence toward corollaries about typical attributes, causes, or effects. But they deny themselves all right to claim that such generalizations have any validity for the future. They might not quarrel with a general statement like this: Up to a certain point in the past "the really great discoveries which had ultimately proved to be beneficial to mankind had been made by men and women who were driven, not by the desire to be useful, but merely by the desire to satisfy their curiosity."[6] At least, they might not quarrel with this statement because it is a generalization, though they might (for such is the nature and function of historians) insist that they knew of instances that made them doubt its validity. If they thought it valid, they would not object to its claim to general applicability so long as it referred only to the past and was couched in the past tense. But put it in the present tense or, more emphatically, in the future tense, and they would say that, even if they were to read the history of science that way, they would have no business as historians to make such statements. So when Abraham Flexner, the author of the generalization under consideration, goes on to say, "It is almost certain that efforts aiming at the immediately practical will fail unless they are based upon a long succession of experiments and endeavors that have no such practical use in mind," they will wash their hands of his forecast. It may be all right for Flexner, using the history of science as his source, to forecast; but a "pure" historian, they would contend, may not do so, or must do so only apologetically. For the pure historian, not only is all history past but also the historian qua historian has no future.

This kind of historian, if he consistently applied his definition of a historian as one who deals only with the past and avoids contempla-

6. Abraham Flexner, "The Usefulness of Useless Knowledge," reprinted in the *Journal of Chronic Diseases*, II (1955), 243.

tion of the future, would automatically cut himself off from the necessity of examining the validity of such forecasts by others. Fortunately, historians sometimes are not consistent, and so they are among the foremost to pounce upon the facile generalization claiming universal validity. In that way they make what is perhaps the historian's best contribution to the social sciences next to furnishing narratives and descriptions of the recorded experience of mankind— that is, they check the looseness of others' generalizations about human experience.

Although providing generalizations may perhaps be less important than some of the historian's other functions, it nevertheless is a function that he cannot avoid. Why not? Assuredly he can avoid, if that is his purpose, making the two kinds of explicit generalizations of which I have already spoken—the generalization about types of human affairs of the past and the generalization assumed to have universal validity for past, present, and future. But certain other kinds of generalizations, even when explicit, are harder to avoid.

In fact, as all of us know, some explicit generalizations are *faits accomplis* for the historian. For example, no matter how averse to generalization a historian may be, he has to use ready-made names or explain why he does not use them. He has to be quite firm in the intention to stick to the particular if he declines to say something in the nature of comparison when he deals with such things as the Third Punic War, "the Second Hundred Years' War," the fifth partition of Poland, the second World War, or the Fourth French Republic. This pitfall for the die-hard particularist who claims that history does not repeat itself probably yawns still wider for historians who organize their work topically and deal with commonly accepted categories such as "nations," "wars," "universities," or "revolutions" (usually all already so designated) rather than with events organized on a geographical-chronological basis. But, if consistent, the particularist would rarely employ a topical arrangement of his data.

The snare that, for the particularist, lies hidden in ready-made terms is perhaps greater yet when he deals with periodization in history. When we historians use phrases—and we use them all the time—like "the river cultures," "the Hellenistic Age," "the Age of Reason," and "the Age of Materialism," we are saying something general about a given period of history. We may believe it to be an untrue generalization or we may believe that, while true enough, it is not the only correct way or the best way to characterize the period, but we are generalizing nonetheless; and, if we attempt to modify the commonly accepted names for historical periods or movements, we run the risk of generalizing along different lines.

The historian is faced by yet another kind of explicit generalization that is imposed upon him as a sort of *fait accompli*. This one results from the application of his unavoidably comparative method. It is summed up in Vico's comment on the Latin words *verum* and *factum*.[7] *Verum* means literally *something that is true* and commonly is translated *truth*. *Factum* means literally *that which has been done* and commonly is translated *fact*. Hence, Vico's comment (*verum et factum . . . convertuntur*) seems to mean that a deed that some men actually have done is easily converted by other men into a concept of a truth. That perhaps too complicated idea may be simplified to mean that what man can do man can understand. In fact, R. G. Collingwood considers Vico's work just as crucial in the history of the historian's method as Bacon's in the history of the scientist's; it marks the point in modern historiography at which a student of the historical method first openly declared that the historian must begin with his own understanding derived from his own experience and place in history and then apply that understanding to his sources.[8]

Some historians find Collingwood—or Vico—confusing. They believe that understanding by the subject is inferior to observation of the object as an avenue toward historical truth, and they think that the two avenues are independent and can be traveled in turn. They use at least two arguments to justify their view. One is that, if there is no one objective synthesis in the records themselves, then any interpretation is as good as any other. This conclusion seems to me to be a nonsequitur. The history that is contained in the raw records is a far remove from what actually happened. Although the raw

7. *De antiquissima Italorum sapientia ex linquae Latinae originibus eruenda,* chap. i, par. 1, in *Opere di Giambattista Vico* (Naples, 1858), I, 71. The Italian version (*ibid.*) reads: "Presso i Latini *vero* e *fatto* si adoperano promiscuamente o . . . sono convertibili." The Latin is: "Latinis *verum* et *factum* reciprocantur seu . . . convertuntur." See also Arthur Child, *Making and Knowing in Hobbes, Vico, and Dewey* (Berkeley and Los Angeles, 1953), pp. 283–94.

8. *The Idea of History* (Oxford, 1946), pp. 63–65.

records may provide our best means of discovering what actually happened if we ever can, the data derived from an analysis of the historical records have to be assayed against an imaginative re-creation, a re-enactment in the mind, of the historical reality. Because not the least of the prerequisites for a historian's imaginative re-creation of a historical reality is his own appreciation of recent and present reality, and because different historians qualify in this regard to differing degrees, some historians' ability to reconstruct past reality is superior to others'.

What, then, about the claim that history is itself a means of understanding the present? This claim is the second argument of those who question the validity of the view that the historian understands history only in the light of the present, that history is present thought about the past. I do not deny that one's unconscious place in the historical process and a fortiori one's conscious knowledge of history condition thinking about the present; I would not remain a historian if I did not think so. But this is no chicken-egg riddle. No possible doubt arises as to which came first. The historian starts and has no choice but to start as the child who knows only the world he has experienced; and, no matter if his learning about the past becomes as prodigious as Toynbee's or his specialization as minute as the narrowest museum antiquarian's, his experience of the present is bound to continue to be quantitatively greater than his knowledge of the past unless he leads the life of a recluse (and thus *ipso facto* cuts himself off from reality and so from a proper understanding of all human behavior).

The historian who says he lives in the past rather than in his own time is using a figure of speech that does him credit only if it is at least partly untrue. His claim probably means merely that he makes a noble effort to understand the persons, events, and conditions of his period of study in their own setting. But he can understand them only by their resemblance or lack of resemblance to the real persons, events, and conditions he knows, which, as he matures, naturally become more intelligible to him by comparison with the persons, events, and conditions of the earlier period, and vice versa. If his figure of speech, then, is true at all, it is true only in so far as he may have a more systematic and better co-ordinated understanding of his specialized field of history than of the present; finished persons, events, and conditions are more readily pigeonholed inside neater frames of reference than unfinished ones. And if the pigeonholing is in any way correct, to that extent it may be of some service in a correct pigeonholing and systematizing of the present.

Just as the trends of the past are frequently connected with the trends of the present and may conceivably be extrapolated into the future, so parallels, more or less perfect, sometimes may be drawn between similar developments at various times. Hence, if historians will not, other social scientists or politicians and journalists using history will try to anticipate certain things that may happen in the future under certain conditions because they happened under similar conditions in the past, unless they can be controlled by changing the conditions. Is a man excusable for deliberately refraining from trying to predict or control the future merely because he is a historian and so must not forecast? Suppose he is a historian of World War I and World War II, is not his obligation greater than that of others to apply his knowledge to the effort, even if perhaps foredoomed to futility, to predict or to control (i.e., avert or shape the course of) World War III? Suppose he is a historian of the League of Nations, is not his obligation greater than that of others to apply his knowledge to the effort to predict or to control the future of the United Nations?

The didactic obligation of the historian seems to derive directly from the interchangeability of *verum* and *factum:* not only can man understand better that which he can do but he can do better that which he can understand. Does not the historian have at least the obligation to question the superficial forecasts of others, thus venturing after a fashion some negative speculation about the future?

I have placed the several classes of generalizations which I have so far described in the category of *explicit generalizations* on the ground that a practiced historian ought to be able to recognize them and hence to use or to avoid them as he pleases. I come now to the categories of generalizations that a historian has to use, whether he intends to or not, unless he deliberately chooses not to engage in certain kinds of historical writing. These generalizations are implicit; they are inherent in the historian's method or in his medium of expression.

For one class of implicit generalization Vico's dictum is likewise appropriate. The interchangeability of *factum* and *verum* works both ways. It seems to justify not only drawing lessons from man's experience to apply in the future but also applying the present accumulation of human experience to an understanding of man's past. The whole of the historian's method of analyzing evidence rests upon a sweeping generalization similar to that upon which all generalizations regarding human behavior rest: Today's student can understand the behavior of mankind in the past because human beings are not so different at different times and in different places as to make their testimony and artifacts mutually unintelligible even if at times astounding. Any historian who analyzes a surviving record or who accepts the conclusions based upon the anthropologist's or archeologist's interpretation of artifacts is applying this generalization, even if he may be unaware that he is doing so.

Another class of implied generalization that the historian often uses, though he may not necessarily be aware of using it, is the causal generalization. Seldom does the historian these days avoid probing into the motives of the actors or into the economic, cultural, or social forces and influences in the events he deals with. Yet an explanation of *why* a man or a group of men behave as they do requires some application of the general rules of logic as well as of psychology; and an explanation of the process, the *how*, by which events came to be requires some application of general principles borrowed from philosophy or some social science or possibly from natural science, even if such general principles are truisms and have been in the public domain since the Old Stone Age or have become the claptrap of matrons sporting familiarity with Hegel, Marx, Darwin, Freud, and Einstein. In addition, if, as the historian is regularly called upon to do, he attempts to assess blame for historical disaster, merit for historical achievement, or the value of the work of others in his specialized field, he is obliged to apply standards of judgment that are based not only on generalizations regarding methods within his own field but also on generalizations regarding the good, the true, and the beautiful, and perhaps other criteria derived from, or at any rate belonging equally to, other fields. Such generalizations he must use to perform such assessments whether he uses them knowingly or unknowingly. The historian who studiously avoids such assessments, if he is doing something avowedly other than compilation or the editing of documents, would have to be a narrative or descriptive historian of an exceedingly rare purity.

So far I have discussed two main categories of generalizations commonly used by historians. In the first category, *generalizations probably explicit* (and therefore avoidable, if such is the intention), I have placed four classes: (1) the universal laws, or perpetual trends or cycles, sometimes sought by historians as the lessons of history; (2) generalizations about types of historical persons, institutions, or events (periodization is a special kind of generalization within this class); (3) comparisons of two or more parallel features of the past; and (4) anticipation for the purpose of prediction or control of future eventualities from future conditions if future conditions should resemble those known to have been true in the past. In the second category, *implicit generalizations,* I have mentioned three classes. Two of these are inherent in the historian's method and so are not easily avoidable. They are (1) the underlying assumption about the essential sameness of the human character, an assumption that enables the historian of today to understand the witnesses and vestiges of remoter ages, and (2) the generalizations about human motives and social forces that enable the historian to attempt to explain the *whys* and *hows* of the historical process. Critical standards form a third class of methodological generalization but one that can be avoided if an express effort is made to do so. These two main categories of generalizations, whether avoidable or unavoidable, are usually made knowingly by the historian, who, in fact, can hardly present his findings unless he employs at least some of them.

The third main category of generalization is also implicit but so subtly implicit as to be almost hidden. The historian (along with other scholars whose medium of expression is language) is generally unaware of having used it. I do not mean the kind of loose talk that implies a generalization in such phrases as "Moscow objects" (where what in fact is meant is that "some persons in authority in the Russian government object") or "the American national character" (where what is meant is a stereotype that fits some of the American people some of the time but not all of them at any time). Such phrases have become widely acceptable rhetorical short cuts because they are understood to stand for what they are intended to stand for or would otherwise be patently false. I speak rather of the category of generalization that is implied by certain kinds of words that for lack of a better name I call *singularizing words* and *generalizing words.* Singularizing words comprise not only adjectives in the superlative degree, like *best, most,* and *first,* but also emphatic adverbs like *even* and *especially,* verbal phrases like *single out,* and phrases like *par excellence.* Generalizing words comprise adjectives like *every* and *all,* adverbs like *naturally,* and phrases like *as usual.* I can perhaps make my point clearer by examples.

The examples that I am about to give (like some I have already given) are random in the sense that they come from history books and articles that were brought to my attention by chance while I was preparing the first draft of this paper. They are quotations taken from authors who I hope will not mind my quoting them anonymously in order to make a point that has at best only indirect relevance to the problems with which they were concerned and carries no intrinsic criticism of their findings. This chance collection of historical literature provided a workable sample of the things historians are continually writing in the nature of hidden generalizations. I take from one article the declaration: "The term 'conflict' in the context of the document [under discussion] did not necessarily mean war." This is a careful statement by a careful historian in an article dealing with a particular episode and is, so far as I know, beyond dispute as a historical fact. But behind it lies a generalization, apparently derived from a knowledge of diplomatic discourse, that "the term *conflict* when used in a diplomatic document is likely to mean *war.*" Without this generalization in the background of the reader's consciousness the sentence would be meaningless or at least might have a meaning the writer did not intend. In another article I found the statement: "Malthus . . . was execrated by even so staunch a Francophobe as Coleridge." The generalization that gives meaning to this sentence, an affirmation of a particular fact about two specific persons, is something to the common-sense effect that "if a writer says harsh things about France, Francophobes may be expected to approve of what he says." In a book that I consider a highly respectable example of biography, the kind of history that is most likely to deal with unique events, I read: "Trotsky was possessed of a sixth sense, as it were, an intuitive sense of history, which singled him out among the political thinkers of his generation." The generalization on which the meaning of this passage rests runs to this effect: "The political thinkers of Trotsky's generation (with the exception of Trotsky himself) did not have an intuitive sense of history." Another author wrote: "The Chinese predilection for ancient authorities . . . helped to preserve their oldest medical classics as the bases of all subsequent medical thinking." This sentence contains several hidden generalizations, although they are probably not all unwittingly applied: (1) that the Chinese have a predilection for ancient authorities; (2) that a predilection for ancient authorities helps to preserve classical texts; and (3) that classical texts may become the basis of subsequent thinking. The generalizing word that called my attention to this sentence was the adjective *all*. Finally, no word implies exclusiveness more than *unique*. The sentiment that "history deals with the unique" is, to begin with, itself a generalization, and, in addition, it raises the query: How is one to recognize the unique without first having become familiar with the general?

In thus classifying the historian's generalizations, I may have given certain impressions that I did not intend. Let no one assume that I am opposed to the historian's dealing with the unique and individual. Such an opposition would be in excessively bad taste from a biographer who has split the life of one man into so many small segments for special study that he spends more time studying some segments than the subject spent living them. I mean only to indicate that the historian as a rule makes generalizations, whether simple or esoteric, and can only with deliberate effort and probably doubtful success avoid making them. In fact, for evaluating either historical evidence or what Charles Beard has taught us to call "history-as-actuality," the once living reality toward which historical evidence is a means of approach, I can perceive of no way that is divorced from generalizations drawn from one's own experience of reality and from other disciplines that deal with human behavior.

Let no one suppose, either, that I believe that, because generalizations need not and often will not come from a careful analysis of the historical sources and may arise full grown from some subcortical portion of the brain, one generalization is as good as another. Let me repeat, for the sake of emphasis, a point I have already made—that an important service the historian can render to social science is to test and to check the relative merit of the generalizations of others in the light of his own knowledge of human experience. All I am trying to say in these remarks is that, when the historian does think in general terms, which I hold will probably be oftener than he suspects, he try to do so knowingly so that his effort may be directed not toward avoiding generalizations altogether but toward avoiding untenable ones.

Nor is anything I have said to be taken as an indication that I disapprove of either the study of remote periods of history or the kind of study that deals with man's achievements in letters and the other arts—the sort of historical enterprise that is carried on by humanistic faculties. The contrary is true. One of my principal criticisms of the social sciences as pursued in the United States and elsewhere today is that they sometimes lack depth. They are devoted all too often to merely journalistic inquiries into local affairs and current events rather than to the lessons derivable from the record of human behavior over the centuries.

A quotation from Thomas Arnold of Rugby that I have used before seems to me worthy of recall on this occasion: "The largest part of that history which we commonly call ancient is practically modern, as it describes society in a stage analogous to that in which it now is, while on the other hand most of what is called modern history is practically ancient, as it relates to a state of things that has passed away."[9] When I last quoted Arnold's provocative observation,[10] I was addressing historians who might so intently fix their gaze upon the near as to lose historical perspective. Today, a score and five years after an enlightened effort brought forth on this campus a new building dedicated to the proposition that the social sciences are a dignified and independent field of study, it is altogether fitting and proper that we social scientists here highly resolve to study not alone the ephemeral problems of human behavior that clamor for attention but also those which have endured over the ages and are still alive and modern.

Whether we study the old or the new, somewhere in the reports

9. Vol. I, Appendix I, p. 636, of his translation of Thucydides (Oxford, 1820–35).

10. *Understanding History: A Primer of Historical Method* (New York, 1950), pp. 203–4.

of our findings generalizations will crop out. For such is the nature of man, his thought processes, and his language. No honest scholar need feel ashamed because his generalizations are not golden or may not even glitter. Even a common-sense truth or a "law" so modified and conditional as to be a truism is better than an untruth or an un-examined platitude. Since, however, we must have generalizations, conscious or unconscious, explicit or implicit, overt or hidden, we should bend our efforts toward safeguarding their clear intelligence and their enduring validity. The path of the detail-monger would perhaps be easier, and it has, and deserves to have, its own rewards. But who can say that it comes from or leads to a higher sense of responsibility to that Truth to which we all owe our allegiance?

Guilt by Association: The Game of Presumptions

It is clear that our elaborate program against communism and subversion has had an important impact on American civil liberties. A substantial part of that impact stems from the fact that what the program tries to do is to *identify* those who are Communists, subversive, or disloyal as well as those who are "security risks" by reason of doubt as to their loyalty or reliability. A wide range of governmental agencies—federal, state, and local—plus various private groups, have felt impelled to "get into the act" and help hunt down these undesirable or dubious characters. Public opinion, frightened by the cold war and the danger of internal treachery, has approved having as many Communist-hunters as possible.

The "exposure" of Communists, subversives, and security risks in this climate of opinion has become in *fact*, though not in *law*, a *punitive* process. The mere setting in motion of an inquiry into a man's loyalty instantly creates an almost overwhelming presumption of his guilt and puts on him a stigma which will remain even if he is cleared. In many cases simple accusation inflicts punishment in the form of loss of job and of reputation. The inquiries have many of the aspects of criminal trials without the relevant legal safeguards, and the damage done to the man involved may be more brutal and lasting than a criminal penalty. The Supreme Court, referring to one phase of the program, said, "There can be no dispute about the consequences visited upon a person excluded from public employment on disloyalty grounds. In the view of the community the stain is a deep one; indeed it has become a badge of infamy" (*Wieman* v. *Updegraff* [1952]). While this result may not be intended by loyalty and security boards, there is no doubt that legislative committees are complacently aware that, while they have no power to impose criminal penalties, they may nevertheless

451

punish a man by branding him as disloyal and thus bring about his ruin.

It is the purpose of this paper to analyze the use we have made of the doctrine of "guilt by association" in our drive against communism and subversion, in an effort to determine whether in doing so we have violated our American tradition of justice and fair play.

I shall begin by reviewing some well-established principles of American law, for guilt by association is but a striking label for a presumption or inference drawn from the fact of man's associations. Presumptions of guilt have long existed in criminal law, and the rules of circumstantial evidence in a criminal trial are rules for weighing the inferences which may properly be drawn from facts and circumstances other than the defendant's own proved conduct. The courts, in fact, are very familiar with a good deal of what lies behind the phrase "guilt by association." As I read the cases, there are three principles which American courts have established in this field in an effort to secure substantial justice.

The first principle is that guilt is personal. The law does not punish a man for the criminal acts of another, for opinions or intentions unaccompanied by any overt acts, or for the simple act of associating with guilty persons.

The principle that guilt is personal has never been seriously challenged. When Mr. Charles Evans Hughes went to Albany in 1920 to protest against the notorious action of the New York Assembly in expelling the five Socialists, he declared: "It is of the essence of the institutions of liberty that it be recognized that guilt is personal and cannot be attributed to the holding of opinion or of mere intent in the absence of overt acts." From that doctrine there has been no dissent.

The doctrine of the courts that guilt is personal does not, of course, undermine the well-established law of criminal conspiracy. The government may make it a crime for persons to conspire together to do an unlawful act, or to do a lawful act in an unlawful manner. It may make it a crime for persons to conspire together to do an act which any one of them singly might lawfully do. It follows that a man who knowingly joins a group which is engaged in a criminal conspiracy becomes himself a criminal, even though he may engage in no overt acts in violation of law.

The courts follow a second cardinal principle in dealing with presumptions of guilt. This is that any presumption of guilt must be fairly rebuttable and that, if it is not rebuttable, it denies due process of law. In other words, a man may not be presumed to be guilty of crime and then be denied the opportunity to prove, if he can, that the presumption is false. He may not succeed in doing this, but it is his constitutional right to be allowed to try to do so. This is such a basic rule of justice and fair play that breaches of it have been rare. Some southern states attempted to set up a form of peonage among Negro laborers by creating an irrebuttable presumption of fraud, punishable as a crime, against the laborer who received an advance of wages and then quit his job before he had paid the money back. The Supreme Court has held these statutes invalid.

The Court adhered to this basic principle in dealing with the Los Angeles and Oklahoma loyalty-oath legislation. Los Angeles barred from public employment anyone who within the previous five years had belonged to designated subversive organizations. The Supreme Court held the provision valid, but only on the explicit assumption that it would be so administered as to permit public employees to rebut the presumption of disloyalty by showing that their membership in such organizations had, in fact, been innocent because of their ignorance of the nature of the group or for other reasons. The Oklahoma statute also barred from public service persons who had belonged to such subversive organizations, but made it impossible for any such employee to rebut the presumption of disloyalty or unfitness thus established. A unanimous Court held that the statute denied due process of law by creating a conclusive presumption of guilt.

A third judicial principle governing presumptions of guilt is that there must be a rational connection between a fact and any inference or presumption of guilt drawn from it. There must be something more than mere coincidence. The fact that a man is found standing near a burning building will not rationally support a presumption that he set fire to it. There may be countless innocent reasons for his being there. This rule was clearly stated by Justice Holmes back in 1916. He said: "As to presumptions, of course the legislature may go a good way in raising one or in changing the burden of proof, but there are limits. It is essential that there be some rational connection between the fact proved and the ultimate fact presumed, and that the inference of one fact from proof of another shall not be so unreasonable as to be a purely arbitrary mandate."

In 1943 the Supreme Court held void on this ground a section of the National Firearms Act of 1938, which created the presumption that the possession of firearms by a person who has been convicted of a crime of violence, or is a fugitive from justice, shall be presumptive evidence that such firearms were received or transported by such person through interstate commerce in violation of federal law. The Court sternly rejected this presumption as an irrational one and held that the section denied due process of law.

We have, then, three principles for dealing with presumptions of guilt. Guilt is personal; a presumption of guilt must always be rebuttable; and there must be a rational relationship between facts and the presumptions of guilt derived from them. These principles embody what we may call our American tradition of justice and fairness in this complicated area. In carrying on our program against communism and subversion, we have violated certainly the last two of these principles.

In the first place, in the operation of our program against subversion there can be no doubt that punishments and disabilities are inflicted upon many persons as the result of presumptions of disloyalty which are in fact irrebuttable. They are irrebuttable for several reasons.

The first reason is that the procedures of both loyalty and security boards, and of legislative investigating committees, do not provide an assured opportunity to rebut. Security boards are obliged to operate under such rigid security restraints upon disclosing the "confidential" sources and nature of accusations against an employee that in many cases he does not know who is accusing him or the precise charge against him. How can a man rebut the presumption of disloyalty created by the statement of an anonymous accuser that he is "an ideological Communist" or a "Communist sympathizer"? Without a bill of particulars he is helpless, and this the security board declares it cannot give him.

When legislative committees began investigating subversion, their rules of procedure (if they could be said to have any) usually afforded no opportunity for a person against whom a presumption of disloyalty had arisen to appear and rebut it. This was intentional, not inadvertent. In 1943 a special committee of the House of Representatives was set up to consider the charges of disloyalty made by Mr. Dies against Messrs. Lovett, Watson, and Dodd (whose dismissal was later held by the Supreme Court to be a bill of attainder). This committee refused to hear any witness in defense of the three men. Even the agencies which employed the men were not allowed to appear. As one of the committee members remarked, "What could have been accomplished by bringing in every Tom, Dick, and Harry and letting him testify?" This arbitrary attitude no longer prevails, and most committees will try to give a person some chance to rebut accusations or presumptions of disloyalty which have grown out of the committee hearings. But here, as before the security boards, the right to rebut is whittled down by the committee's refusal, in many cases, to disclose the sources of its information or the details of the accusation.

Some investigating committees have indulged in the practice of "citing" the names of long lists of persons as members of suspect or subversive organizations. The Tenney Committee in California did this repeatedly. These persons were not declared to be disloyal; just the fact of membership was noted, and from such "citation" a presumption of disloyalty arose, and was intended to arise. What the citation did not note was the time and circumstances of such membership, which, if known, would in many cases have completely rebutted the presumption. There is a clear example of this: The National Council for American-Soviet Friendship was organized early in World War II to publicize in this country the war effort of our then valued ally, the Soviet Union. It commanded nation-wide support and approval. It held a dinner in New York in 1944 to mark the anniversary of the founding of the Red Army, and Generals Marshall, MacArthur, Pershing, Clark, and Eisenhower all sent messages of congratulation. Later the Attorney-General, believing that the Council had become infiltrated by Communists, listed it as a subversive organization. It is clear that the bald statement by a legislative committee than A. was a member of the National Council for American-Soviet Friendship now creates a presumption of A.'s disloyalty but one which he might easily rebut by showing that his membership did not extend beyond the time when all our best generals were praising it. But he gets no opportunity to do this.

Public opinion is heavily responsible for the injustices which arise in cases like this. The public mind has been conditioned to view any accusation of disloyalty as a conclusive finding that a man is disloyal. We are being taught to reason that, if a man is accused, he is guilty. His denial will not convince the casual newspaper reader or radio listener that he is free from taint. There must be something wrong with him, or no accusation would have arisen. "Cited by the House Committee on Un-American Activities" is a brand he will always carry, whether justly or not.

In the second place, we are using the doctrine of "guilt by association" in such a way as to create presumptions of disloyalty which have no logical connection with the fact from which the presumption arises. "Guilt by coincidence" is a better term. The prevalence and wide popular acceptance of this type of loose reasoning warrants a close look at it.

Anyone familiar with elementary logic is acquainted with the "fallacy of the undistributed middle" and will readily see that the following syllogism is a perfect example of it:

> *Major premise:* Communists condemn Negro discrimination.
> *Minor premise:* Jones condemns Negro discrimination.
> *Conclusion:* Jones is a Communist.

When thus nakedly exposed, the absurdity of this form of reasoning is clear. It has, however, become the stock in trade of many loyalty and security boards, almost all legislative investigating committees, and all private and commercial Communist-hunters. The illustrations of its use are countless. The Tenney Committee in California branded a theater as Communist-controlled on the ground that some Communists attended it and thereby became "audience sponsors" of it. When Walter Gellhorn's book, *Security, Loyalty and Science*, was published in 1950, it was widely and favorably reviewed. Senator McCarthy, in a speech read into the *Congressional Record*, remarked ominously that "it is significant to note that this book has been favorably reviewed by the same two New York newspapers (the *Times* and the *Herald-Tribune*) that favorably reviewed Owen Lattimore's book." An American Legion chapter protests against the use in the public schools of "records produced by a corporation one of whose directors was affiliated with Communist-front organizations." A national patriotic magazine announces: "If Communists and left-wingers are against such a bill [the McCarran Immigration and Nationality Bill], then it is safe to say that loyal Americans should be for it." The same magazine announced that it could identify Communists and left-wingers among schoolteachers by the very simple process of sending them free sample copies of the magazine, and then keeping a list of those who did not sub-scribe to it.

The use of this fallacy of "guilt by coincidence" has brought about a number of results which I believe are both unjust and dan-gerous, and I shall comment on some of these briefly.

In the first place, it has resulted in putting the brand of disloyalty or unreliability upon many wholly loyal Americans. It is a well-known fact that Communists, as a matter of party policy, have sup-ported a great many worthy causes in this country. Loyal Americans have supported the same causes. But, in doing so, they risk con-tamination through the doctrine of guilt by coincidence. Walter Gellhorn quotes the chairman of a departmental loyalty board, un-der the Truman Loyalty Program, as follows: "Of course, the fact that a person believes in racial equality doesn't *prove* that he's a Communist, but it certainly makes you look twice, doesn't it? You can't get away from the fact that racial equality is part of the Com-munist line." One may well wonder whether if we had had a Com-munist party in this country before the Civil War, and if that party had come out in opposition to slavery, patriotic and decent Ameri-cans could also have opposed slavery without being branded as Communists.

The second result of guilt by coincidence flows logically from the first. This result is to increase the timidity of people of good will who cannot afford to run the risk of being entrapped in an associa-tion which may prove dangerous and possibly disastrous. It is a lot easier and safer not to join anything or sign anything. By stifling your humanitarian impulses, and resisting the temptation to lend your name to a reform movement or to a petition to correct what you believe to be an injustice, you run no risk of possible contami-nation. Thus we place a premium upon caution and rigid conformity; we place the most serious pitfalls in the path of the social crusader, for there are so many chances for him to wind up in bad company. The point I am making was effectively dramatized by the experience of Judy Holliday, the motion-picture and television actress. She had apparently lent support to a number of "causes" in Hollywood which were alleged to be Communist fronts. She appeared before the House Committee on Un-American Activities, and, being more fortunate (and a great deal better-looking) than many others similarly situated, she convinced the Committee that these associations had been innocently and naïvely entered into. But is there not an element of tragedy in her somewhat rueful comment to the press after the ordeal was over: "I don't say 'Yes' to anything now except cancer, polio, and cerebral palsy and things like that." She had burned her fingers once; she would play safe in the future. It is depressing to see generous human impulses ruthlessly stifled through the fear of such accusations.

A third result of the fallacy which we are discussing seems to me to be peculiarly vicious and dangerous. This is the widespread belief, systematically nurtured, that anyone who criticizes the personnel, the procedures, or the policies by which we are dealing with communism and subversion must be Communistic or disloyal, since Communists also indulge in such criticism. This has proved a powerful weapon in the hands of public officials who use ruthless and unjust methods in the game of "punitive exposure" of subversives. Congressman J. Parnell Thomas, in the early days of the Dies Committee, bluntly stated that those who criticized the Committee were "un-American," while the Tenney Committee in California asserted that "the minions of Hitler and Stalin are the ones who want our committee killed."

In 1952 Senator Mundt read into the *Congressional Record* a long speech entitled, "What Is a Communist?" In it Senator Mundt lists twenty characteristics by which one may tell a Communist from one who is not. Five of these ways in which to identify a Communist are: criticism of the Federal Bureau of Investigation, criticism of the House Committee on Un-American Activities, criticism of the Mundt antisubversion bills, criticism of the McCarran Act, criticism of the loyalty program. Senator Mundt does not say that criticism of these five measures would be conclusive evidence of Communist sympathies, but it is clear that such criticism would certainly raise in the Senator's mind very grave suspicion of the loyalty of such a critic.

In the spring of 1954, Edward R. Murrow ran a televised program in which he documented various criticisms against the methods employed by Senator McCarthy in the course of his previous activities. Senator McCarthy was given free time by the Columbia Broadcasting Corporation for a program in which to reply to Mr. Murrow's criticisms. He did not reply to them. He spent his time presenting earlier associations of Mr. Murrow which he stated indicated Murrow's affiliation with and sympathy for, if not communism, at least groups and organizations favorable thereto. The inference was perfectly plain: only men of doubtful loyalty criticize the Senator.

The debates in the Senate on the resolution to censure Senator McCarthy brought out sharply this doctrine of the disloyalty of criticism. The Senate and the American people were told by Senator McCarthy and his friends, and they were told very little else, that the move to censure him actively aided the Communist conspiracy in the United States. His colleagues in the Senate were not actually called Communists; they were merely handmaidens of communism. The entire defense strategy was to create as strongly as possible an implication, if not of disloyalty, at least of co-operation with communism, upon the part of those who had ventured to criticize the senator from Wisconsin.

This doctrine of the disloyalty of criticism was not, of course, invented in the twentieth century. Those who have read Marian Starkey's admirable book, *The Devil in Massachusetts*, will recall that, during the days of the Salem witchcraft trials, the easiest and quickest way to get one's self accused of being a witch was to cast doubt upon the reliability of two neurotic girls who started the whole macabre enterprise or to criticize the way in which the trials were being conducted. The present-day use of the doctrine is not made more attractive by reminding ourselves of the gruesome effectiveness with which it was applied in old Salem.

I have no doubt that there are vigorous critics of the House Committee on Un-American Activities or of Senator McCarthy or of the present security program who are themselves disloyal and subversive. Certainly, however, American public opinion should be trained to draw the distinction between these disloyal persons and those who-criticize the measures and the men involved in our fight against subversion in the hope that we may achieve a wiser management and administration of this important enterprise.

In the fourth place the fallacious doctrine of guilt by coincidence is having a frightening impact upon the administration of justice, although happily this is not yet widespread. "Softness" toward communism is evidence of sympathy for the Communist cause, and it is but a short and easy step from this to the view that rigidly impartial and impersonal administration of justice in dealing with Communists adds up to "softness." There has been increasing evidence of the growth of this unhealthy doctrine. When the first trial of Alger Hiss resulted in a hung jury, the trial judge was bitterly attacked on the floor of Congress for judicial conduct stigmatized as "soft" toward Hiss. When Justice Douglas granted a last-minute stay to the Rosenbergs to permit the consideration of a point of law, a member of the House of Representatives introduced a resolution to impeach him. In 1951 Senator Bricker proposed that the Senate Judiciary Committee should investigate federal judges, particularly their actions on Communists or alleged Communists. He said he was referring particularly to cases involving the eleven convicted Communist leaders, Harry Bridges, Frederick Vanderbilt Field, and Earl Browder. In May of this year Senator Eastland introduced a resolution proposing that the Senate Judiciary Committee should investigate "the extent and degree of participation by individuals and groups identified with the Communist conspiracy, Communist-front organizations, and alien ideologies, in the formation of the 'modern scientific authority' upon which the Supreme Court relied in the school integration cases."

As a result of this same doctrine it is becoming increasingly hard to get non-Communist lawyers to defend a Communist or a person charged with crimes of subversion, since there is a growing popular feeling that, if you are his lawyer, you must share his political views and his disloyalty. This of course is a serious defeat of justice and a break with one of the fine traditions of the American bar. In 1770 John Adams and Josiah Quincy defended in court in Massachusetts the British officers who were being tried for the Boston Massacre. John W. Davis tells us that, when John Randolph Tucker was chided by some of his friends for serving as defense attorney for the Chicago anarchists in 1887, he replied, "I don't defend anarchy; I defend the Constitution." In 1920 Charles Evans Hughes went to Albany as a representative of the bar of the city of New York to protest to the New York Assembly against its expulsion of five Socialist members. Wendell Willkie defended the Communist William Schneiderman in the Supreme Court against deportation proceedings. When the Nazi saboteurs were captured in the summer of 1942, President Roosevelt assigned Kenneth Royall, later Secretary of the Army, to defend them. All this spells out the American tradition of justice and fair play. We seem to be turning our backs upon all this and creating a climate of opinion which holds that Communists and other subversives are not really entitled to complete criminal justice and that only those lawyers and judges who are themselves disloyal will undertake to see that they get it.

I conclude by pointing out that there are plenty of situations in which full knowledge and careful appraisal of a man's associations are wholly justifiable in making certain decisions about him. Such associations are evidence, and it is entirely proper to examine that evidence carefully in an effort to determine what inferences, if any, may properly be drawn from it. The demands of national security justify in some cases the setting-up of presumptions of unfitness or even of disloyalty arising from certain types of association. But our American tradition, firmly imbedded in long-established principles of law, condemns the setting-up of presumptions of guilt which are irrebuttable or of presumptions which have no rational connection with the facts or situations from which they are drawn. Such deviations from sound principles not only subject innocent people to cruelty and injustice but undermine some of the basic principles of our democracy.

The Dilemma of Specialization

We have been commemorating the foundation of a research center within our University, and our thoughts have inevitably often touched upon the problems of the relation between research and education and of education for research. It may therefore be fitting if this last evening is devoted to a problem in this field which must give concern to many of us. Research, of necessity, requires specialization, often in a very minute field. It is probably also true that those exacting standards which fruitful scientific work demands can be acquired only through the complete mastery of at least one field, which today means that it must be a narrow field and, also, that it ought to be one which has its own firmly established standards. Thus a progressive tendency toward specialization seems to be inevitable, bound to continue and to grow, both in research and in university education.

This applies, of course, to all scientific branches and is not peculiar to the study of society, which is our particular concern. It is so conspicuous a fact that the sad joke about the scientific specialist who knows more and more about less and less has become about the one thing which everybody believes to know about science. There seem to me to exist, however, in this respect important differences among the various fields, special circumstances which ought to warn us not to accept in the social sciences too readily a tendency which natural scientists can treat as a regrettable necessity to which they may submit with impunity. It may well be that the chemist or physiologist is right when he decides that he will become a better chemist or physiologist if he concentrates on his subject at the expense of his general education. But in the study of society exclusive concentration on a specialty has a peculiarly baneful effect: it will not merely prevent us from being attractive company or good citizens but may impair our competence in our

462

proper field—or at least for some of the most important tasks we have to perform. The physicist who is only a physicist can still be a first-class physicist and a most valuable member of society. But nobody can be a great economist who is only an economist—and I am even tempted to add that the economist who is only an economist is likely to become a nuisance if not a positive danger.

I do not wish to exaggerate a difference which in the last resort of course is one of degree; but it still seems to me so great that what in one field is a venal offense is a cardinal sin in the other. What we face is a true dilemma imposed upon us by the nature of our subject or, perhaps I should say, by the different significance we must attach to the concrete and particular as against the general and theoretical. Although the logical relation between theory and its application, of course, is the same in all sciences and although theory in our field is quite as indispensable as anywhere, there is no denying that the interest of the natural scientist is concentrated on the general laws, while our interest in the end is mainly in the particular, individual, and unique event, and that in a sense our theories are more remote from reality—requiring much more additional knowledge before they can be applied to particular instances.

One result of this is that in the natural sciences specialization is predominantly what might be called systematic specialization—specialization in a theoretical discipline—while at least in the research in the social sciences topical specialization is more common. Of course this contrast is again not absolute. The expert in the topography of Mars, in the ecology of Nyasaland, or in the fauna of the Triassic is as much a topical specialist as anyone in the social sciences; yet even there the share of general knowledge which qualifies the specialist is probably much greater in the natural sciences than in the social. The ecologist will need to learn less when he shifts from Nyasaland to Alaska than the archeologist when he shifts from Crete to Peru. The former is readily done, while the latter requires almost a new training.

A further consequence is that the disparity between the age at which the human mind works at its best and the age at which one can have accumulated the knowledge demanded from the competent specialist becomes greater and greater as we move from the purely theoretical subjects to those in which the concern with the concrete is the main part. Every one of us probably lives for most of his life on the original ideas which he conceived when very young. But while this means for the mathematician or logician that he may do his most brilliant work at eighteen, the historian, to go to the other extreme, may do his best work at eighty.

I trust I will not be misunderstood as identifying the difference between the natural and the social sciences with that between the theoretical and the historical. This is certainly not my view. I am not defending what I regard as the erroneous view that the study of society is nothing but history, but I merely want to stress that the need for understanding history arises in every application of our knowledge. The degree of abstraction which the theoretical disciplines in our field requires makes them at least as theoretical, if not more so, than any in the natural sciences. This, however, is precisely the source of our difficulty. Not only is the individual concrete instance much more important to us than it is in the natural sciences, but the way from the theoretical construction to the explanation of the particular is also much longer.

For almost any application of our knowledge to concrete instances, the knowledge of one discipline, and even of all the scientific knowledge we can bring to bear on the topic, will be only a small part of the foundations of our opinions. Let me first speak of the need of using the results of scientific disciplines other than our own, though this is far from all that is required. That concrete reality is not divisible into distinct objects corresponding to the various scientific disciplines is a commonplace, yet a commonplace which severely limits our competence to pronounce as scientists on any particular event. There is scarcely an individual phenomenon or event in society with which we can deal adequately without knowing a great deal of several disciplines, not to speak of the knowledge of particular facts that will be required. None of us can feel but very humble when he reflects what he really ought to know in order to account for even the simplest social process or to be able to give sensible advice on almost any political issue. We are probably so used to this impossibility of knowing what we ideally ought to know that we are rarely fully aware of the magnitude of our shortcomings. In an ideal world an economist who knows no law, an anthropologist who knows no economics, a psychologist who knows no philosophy, or a historian who does not know almost every subject should be inconceivable; yet the fact is, of course, that the limitations of our capacities make such deficiencies the rule. We can do no better than be guided by the particular topic which we take up for research and gradually acquire whatever special technical equipment is demanded by it. Indeed, most successful research work will require a very particular combination of diverse kinds of knowledge and accomplishments, and it may take half a lifetime until we are better than amateurs in three-quarters of the knowledge demanded by the task we have set ourselves. In this sense, fruitful research undoubtedly demands the most intense specialization—so intense, indeed, that those who practice it may soon cease to be of much use in teaching the whole of any one of the conventional subjects. That such specialists are badly needed, that today the advance of knowledge depends largely on them, and that a great university cannot have enough of them is as true in our fields as it is in the natural sciences.

Yet professors, curiously enough, want students, and preferably students all of whose work they direct. Thus the multiplicity of research specializations tends to produce a proliferation of teaching departments. It is here where the educational problem begins, because not every legitimate research specialty is equally suitable as a scientific education. Even if we look at it entirely as education for research, it must be doubtful whether the composite knowledge demanded by a particular empirical object ought to be taught as a whole in those decisive years during which a student must learn what real competence is, during which his standards are set and the conscience of a scholar formed. It seems to me that at this stage the complete mastery of one clearly circumscribed field, of the whole of a systematically coherent subject, should be acquired. It cannot always be, as I am a little inclined to wish, a theoretical field, because some of the descriptive and historical disciplines have, of course, their own highly developed techniques which it takes years to master. But it ought to be a field that has its own firmly established standards and where it is not true that most workers, except those who have already spent a lifetime in it, are inevitably more or less amateurs in much of the field.

Let me illustrate what I mean from a subject which, for my present purpose, has the advantage of not being represented in this University, so that I shall not offend any susceptibilities. It is ancient economic history, which to me has always seemed not only a particularly fascinating subject but also one of the greatest importance for the understanding of our own civilization. I ardently wish it were represented and taught here. But by this I do not mean that there ought to exist a separate department of ancient economic history in which students should from the beginning of their graduate career divide their energies among the variety of disciplines and accomplishments which a competent ancient economic historian must command. I believe, rather, that the men who will do good work in such a field will do much better if, in the first instance, they get a thorough training in the classics, or in ancient history, or in archeology, or in economics; and, only when they are really competent in that one field and start to work largely on their own, will they begin to work seriously on the other subjects.

When I stress here the need of intense systematic specialization during a certain phase of education, I do not, of course, approve of the system of prescribed courses or lectures which leaves the student no time for exploring anything else and which often prevents him from following that intellectual curiosity which ought to gain him more education than anything which is formally offered. If there is anything I somewhat miss in the great American universities, it is that attitude of intellectual adventure among the students, an attitude which leads them, concurrently with their specialized work, to range over wide fields, to sample a great variety of courses, and to make them feel that the university and not their department is their intellectual home. I do not believe that this is so much the fault of the students as of university organization, which keeps the students largely ignorant of what happens outside their departments, in the form of extra fees or rigid departmental schedules, and tends even to put obstacles in the way of their inclinations. It is only by the greatest freedom in this respect that the student will discover his true vocation.

What I do mean is that there must be a period or phase in his education when the chief object is to acquire complete mastery of one well-defined subject and when he will learn to distrust superficial knowledge and facile generalizations. But I am, of course, speaking only of a necessary phase in the process of education for research. My chief point is, rather, that different things are true of different phases. If it seems to me to be untrue that all the recognized research specialties are equally suitable as a basic training, it seems to be no less untrue that the advanced work usually leading to a Ph.D. thesis must fit into any one of the already established research specialties. What I am arguing is that only certain kinds of specializations deserve the name of "disciplines" in the original sense of a discipline of the mind and even that it is not so important which discipline of this kind a mind has undergone as that he has experienced all the rigor and strictness of such a schooling. I can even see some merit in the belief on which English higher education used to be based that a man who has thoroughly studied either mathematics or the classics can be presumed to be capable of learning on his own almost any other subject. The number of true disciplines which achieve this object may today be much larger, but I do not think that it has become coextensive with the number of research specialties.

There is another side to this which I can best explain with reference to my own field. I happen to believe that economic theory is one of those true disciplines of the mind, but I regret that most of those whose basic training is mainly in pure economic theory tend to remain specialists in this field. What I have said implies that those of us who teach such subjects ought do so in the awareness and the hope, and even with the deliberate aim, that those whom we train as specialists ought not to remain specialists in this field but should use their competence for some other, realistic or topical specialization. I would be happier to see even the majority of economic theorists we turn out become economic historians, or specialists in labor economics, or agricultural economics—though I must admit to some doubts about the suitability of these topics as basic training.

Please note that what I have said about such composite subjects is said in no slighting spirit but rather from an appreciation of the very high demands which they put on our mental equipment. It is based on the recognition that for most worthwhile research subjects we ought to be masters of more than one systematic subject and on the belief that we are more likely to achieve this if we use the short period during which we work under close guidance to become real masters of one. I am also pleading for such a period of intense specialization only on the assumption that it is preceded by a good general education which, I am afraid, American schools hardly provide and which our College so manfully struggles to supply. But my main emphasis, of course, is on how far we still are, at the end of such an indispensable period of specialization, from being competent to deal with most of the problems human civilization offers. Until now I have spoken only of the limited and modest tasks which most of us can reasonably set ourselves and where still the ideal after which we must strive far exceeds our powers. I have not spoken of the need for synthesis, of efforts to understand our civilization, or any other civilization, as a whole, and still less of the even more ambitious conception of a comparative study of civilizations. I will not comment on such efforts beyond saying that it is fortunate that there do still occasionally arise exceptional men who have the power and the courage to make the human universe their province. You will have the privilege, later this evening, to listen to a great scholar who has probably come nearer than any other living man to achieve the seemingly impossible in this field.

We certainly ought to feel nothing but admiration for the mature scholar who is willing to run the serious risk of disregarding all the boundaries of specialization to venture on tasks for which perhaps no man can claim full competence. While I sympathize with the healthy prejudice which brings it about that the scholar who produces a best seller thereby rather lowers himself in the estimation of his peers—and sometimes even wish that there were more of it in this country—the suspicion of boundary violations as such must not go so far as to discourage attempts which are beyond the scope of any specialist. And I would go even further, although the economist suffers perhaps more from—and tends, therefore, also to be more intolerant of—intrusions into his preserve than other social scientists. It is perhaps not unjust to suggest that in other subjects, too, there is a little too much of a clannish spirit among the representatives of the recognized specialties, which makes them almost resent an attempt at a serious contribution even from a man in a neighboring field—although the basic kinship of all our disciplines makes it more than likely that ideas conceived in one field may prove fertile in another.

The grand efforts toward a comprehension of civilization as a whole, of which I have just spoken, are specially significant in our context in one respect: they raise particularly clearly one difficulty which to a lesser degree affects all our efforts. I have so far spoken only of the constant need to draw on knowledge belonging to specializations other than our own. But, though the need to know many disciplines presents a formidable difficulty, it is only part of our problem. Even where we study only some part or aspect of a civilization of which we and our whole way of thinking are a part, this means, of course, that we cannot take for granted much that in the normal course of life we must unquestioningly accept if we are to get our work done, or even if we are to remain sane; it means that we must question systematically all the presuppositions which in acting we unreflectedly accept; it means, in short, that in order to be strictly scientific we ought to see, as it were, from the outside what we never can see as a whole in such a manner; and, in practice, it means that we have constantly to deal with many important questions to which we have no scientific answer, where the knowledge on which we must draw is either that knowledge of men and the world which only rich and varied experience can give or the accumulated wisdom of the past, the inherited cultural treasures of our civilization which to us must thus at the same time be tools which we use in orienting ourselves in our world and objects of critical study. This means that in most of our tasks we need not only be competent scientists and scholars but ought also to be experienced men of the world and, in some measure, philosophers.

Before I develop these points, let me briefly remind you of one respect where with us specialization goes less far than in the natural sciences: we do not know as sharp a division between the theoretician and the practitioner as there exists between the physicist and the engineer or between the physiologist and the doctor. This is not an accident or merely an earlier stage of development but a necessary consequence of the nature of our subject. It is due to the fact that the task of recognizing the presence in the real world of the conditions corresponding to the various assumptions of our theoretical schemes is often more difficult than the theory itself, an art which only those will acquire to whom the theoretical schemes have become second nature. We cannot state simple, almost mechanical criteria by which a certain type of theoretical situation can be identified, but we have to develop something like a sense for the physiognomy of events. We can, therefore, only rarely delegate the application of our knowledge but must be our own practitioners, doctors as well as physiologists.

The factual knowledge, the familiarity with particular circumstances, which we cannot leave to our engineers but must ourselves acquire, is, moreover, only in part of the kind which can be ascertained by established techniques. Although we endeavor to add by systematic effort to the knowledge of the world and of man, this effort can neither displace nor make unnecessary that knowledge of the world which is acquired only by extensive experience and a steepening in the wisdom contained in the great literature and our whole cultural tradition.

I need not say more about the necessity of a knowledge of the world in the usual sense, of the variety of human situations and characters with which we ought to be familiar. But I must say a word about what seems to me the unfortunate effect of the separation of what we now call the social *sciences* from the other human studies. By this I do not mean merely such paradoxical results as that as scientific a discipline as linguistics, from whose method and approach the other social sciences might well profit, should, for purely historical reasons, be counted among the humanities. What I have in mind is mainly the climate in which our work will prosper; the question whether the atmosphere produced by the pursuit of the humanities proper, of literature and the arts, is not so important to us as the austerity of the scientific one. I am not sure that the results of the ambition to share in the prestige and the funds available for scientific research were always fortunate and that the separation of the social sciences from the humanities, of which this building is a symbol, was altogether a gain. I do not wish to overstress this point, and I will readily admit that, if I were speaking to a European rather than to an American audience, I might well stress the opposite view. But that here the separation of the humanities from what we mean to dignify by the name of social sciences may have gone too far ought not to be concealed when we are looking back at twenty-five years of existence in a separate home.

We must admit, however, that there is one respect in which our attitude indeed differs from that of the humanities and in which we may even be disturbing and unwelcome in their circle. It is that our approach to the traditions which they cultivate must in some measure always be a critical and dissecting one; that there is no value which we must not on occasion question and analyze, though we can, of course, never do so for all values at the same time. Since our aim must be to discover what role particular institutions and traditions play in the functioning of society, we must constantly put the dissolving acid of reason to values and customs which not only are dear to others but are also so largely the cement which keeps society together. Especially in the study of that experience of the human race which is not preserved as explicit human knowledge but rather implicit in habits and institutions, in morals and mores— in short, in the study of those adaptations of the human kind which act as non-conscious factors and of whose significance we are not normally aware and which we may never fully understand, we are bound all the time to question fundamentals. This, I need hardly add, is, of course, the opposite to following intellectual fashions. While it must be our privilege to be radical, this ought not to mean "advanced" in the sense that we claim to know which is the only forward direction.

Such constant practice is a heady wine which, if not paired with modesty, may make us little better than a nuisance. If we are not to become a mainly destructive element, we must also be wise enough to understand that we cannot do without beliefs and institutions whose significance we do not understand and which, therefore, may seem meaningless to us. If life is to proceed, we must, in practice, accept much which we cannot justify, and even that reason cannot always be the ultimate judge in human affairs. This is, though not the only, yet perhaps the main, point where, whether we want it or not, we must in some measure be philosophers. By philosophy I mean here, in the first instance, not so much those problems which, like those of logic, have themselves already become the subjects of highly specialized and technical disciplines, but rather that remaining body of inchoate knowledge from which the distinct disciplines only gradually detach themselves and which has always been the province of philosophers. But there are, of course, also two highly developed branches of philosophy to which we cannot afford to be total strangers. The problems of ethics are constantly with us, and questions of scientific method are bound to be more troublesome for us than in most other fields. What Einstein once said about science, "Without epistemology—insofar as it is thinkable at all—it is primitive and muddled," applies even more to our subjects.

Rather than be slightly ashamed of this connection, I feel we ought to be proud of the intimate relation which for centuries has existed between the social sciences and philosophy. It is certainly no accident that, so far as economics is concerned, in England, the country which has so long been leading in the subject, a list of her great economists, if we leave out only two major figures, might readily be taken for a list of her great philosophers: Locke, Hume, Adam Smith, Bentham, James and John Stuart Mill, Samuel Bailey, W. S. Jevons, Henry Sidgwick, down to John Neville and John Maynard Keynes—all occupy equally honored places in the history of economics as in that of philosophy or of scientific method. I see little reason to doubt that other social sciences would equally profit if they could attract a similar array of philosophic talent.

I have said enough, however, to describe our dilemma and must hasten to my conclusion. A true dilemma, of course, has no perfect solution, and my main point has been that we *are* faced by a true dilemma—that our task puts conflicting demands upon us which we cannot all satisfy. The choice imposed upon us by our imperfections remains a choice between evils. The main conclusion must thus probably be that there is no single best way and that our main hope is to preserve room for that multiplicity of efforts which true academic freedom makes possible.

But as a norm for academic education certain general ideas seem to emerge. We probably all agree that the main need for students who enter upon their graduate careers is a good general education. I have been arguing for the need for a following period of intense specialization in one of a somewhat limited number of subjects. But this, I feel, ought not regularly to continue to the end of the graduate work—and, if my contention is accepted that not all topical specializations are equally suitable as basic training, cannot always mean the end. Many students will of course continue to do their specialized research in the field of their basic training. But they should not have to or regularly do so. At least for those who are willing to shoulder the extra burden, there ought to be opportunities to work, wherever possible under the guidance of competent specialists, on any suitable combination of knowledge. There ought to be opportunities for men who want to strike out in their own new field on some new combination of specialism or some other border-line problem. There is clearly an urgent need for a place in the University where the specialisms again meet, which provides the facilities and the climate for work which is not on well-established lines, and where requirements are flexible enough to be adapted to the individual tasks. The whole position in the field which I have been surveying seems to me to call for a sort of College of Advanced Human Studies as a recognized part of the organization of the social sciences and the humanities, some such institution as our chairman has so devotedly and judiciously striven to provide with his pathbreaking conception of the Committee on Social Thought.

Program of Meetings on the Occasion of the Twenty-fifth Anniversary of the Dedication of the Social Science Research Building

Thursday, November 10, 1955
OPENING SESSION

"Address of Welcome," CHAUNCY D. HARRIS, Dean of the Division of the Social Sciences, University of Chicago

"Science, Society, and the Modes of Law," FRANK H. KNIGHT, Morton D. Hull Distinguished Service Professor Emeritus of the Social Sciences, University of Chicago

Friday, November 11, 1955
SOCIAL SCIENCE AS SCIENCE
(A Series of Concurrent Round Tables)

1. *Models in the Social Sciences: Their Uses and Limitations*

   Chairman: RALPH W. GERARD, Professor of Neurophysiology, Mental Health Research Institute, University of Michigan

   Speakers: DR. JAMES G. MILLER, Professor of Psychiatry and Chief, Mental Health Research Institute, University of Michigan; HERBERT A. SIMON, Professor of Administration, Carnegie Institute of Technology

   Commentators: HAROLD HOTELLING, Professor of Statistics, University of North Carolina; LEO GOODMAN, Professor of Sociology, University of Chicago

2. *Psychoanalytic Thought and the Social Sciences*

   Chairman: DAVID RIESMAN, Professor of the Social Sciences, University of Chicago

   Speaker: HAROLD D. LASSWELL, Professor of Law and Political Science, Yale University

   Commentators: BRUNO BETTELHEIM, Professor of Educational Psychology and Principal of the Sonia Shankman Orthogenic School, University of Chicago; WALTER A. WEISSKOPF, Professor of Economics, Roosevelt University

475

3. *The Comparative Approach to the Study of Culture*

Chairman: SOL TAX, Professor of Anthropology, University of Chicago

Speaker: CLYDE K. M. KLUCKHOHN, Professor of Anthropology, Harvard University

Commentators: MELVILLE HERSKOVITS, Professor of Anthropology, Northwestern University; MILTON SINGER, Paul Klapper Professor of Social Sciences (College) and Anthropology, University of Chicago; JULIAN STEWARD, Graduate Research Professor of Anthropology, University of Illinois

4. *Analysis of Social Structure*

Chairman: FRED EGGAN, Professor of Anthropology, University of Chicago

Speaker: GEORGE P. MURDOCK, Professor of Anthropology, Yale University

Commentators: TALCOTT PARSONS, Chairman of the Department of Social Relations, Harvard University; W. LLOYD WARNER, Professor of Anthropology and Sociology, University of Chicago

5. *The Study of Small Groups*

Chairman: FRED L. STRODTBECK, Associate Professor of Sociology, University of Chicago

Speakers: ROBERT F. BALES, Associate Professor of Social Relations, Harvard University; MURRAY HORWITZ, Associate Professor of Education, University of Illinois; HERBERT A. THELEN, Professor of Education, University of Chicago

6. *Culture and Personality in Relation to Human Development*

Chairman: FRANCIS S. CHASE, Professor of Educational Administration and Chairman of the Department of Education, University of Chicago

Speakers: WILLARD C. OLSON, Dean of the School of Education, University of Michigan; ALLISON DAVIS, Professor of Education, University of Chicago

Commentators: E. T. McSWAIN, Dean of the School of Education, Northwestern University; WILLIAM E. HENRY, Associate Professor of Psychology and Chairman of the Committee on Human Development, University of Chicago

7. *Ecological and Cultural Aspects of Urban Research*

Chairman: EDWARD L. ULLMAN, Professor of Geography, University of Washington

Speakers: PHILIP M. HAUSER, Professor of Sociology, University of Chicago; EVERETT C. HUGHES, Professor of Sociology and Chairman of the Department, University of Chicago

Commentators: AMOS H. HAWLEY, Professor of Sociology, University of Michigan; DONALD J. BOGUE, Associate Professor of Sociology, University of Chicago; HAROLD M. MAYER, Assistant Professor of Geography, University of Chicago

8. *Industrial Organization and Economic Growth*

Chairman: EARL J. HAMILTON, Professor of Economics, University of Chicago

Speaker: GEORGE STIGLER, Professor of Economics, Columbia University

Commentators: W. F. OGBURN, Sewell L. Avery Distinguished Service Professor Emeritus of Sociology, University of Chicago; CORWIN D. EDWARDS, Professor of Government and Business, University of Chicago

9. *International Aspects of Economic Stability*

Chairman: GARFIELD V. COX, Robert Law Professor of Finance, formerly Dean of the School of Business, University of Chicago

Speaker: JACOB VINER, Professor of Economics, Princeton University

Commentators: D. GALE JOHNSON, Professor of Economics, University of Chicago; ARNOLD C. HARBERGER, Associate Professor of Economics, University of Chicago

10. *The Study of Public Opinion*

Chairman: CLYDE W. HART, Director of the National Opinion Research Center and Research Associate (Professor) in Sociology, University of Chicago

Speaker: BERNARD R. BERELSON, Director of the Behavioral Sciences Program, Ford Foundation

Commentators: GABRIEL ALMOND, Professor of Public and International Affairs, Princeton University; LEO ROSTEN, Special Editorial Adviser, *Look* Magazine; DOUGLAS WAPLES, Professor of International Communication and Chairman of the Committee on Communication, University of Chicago

LUNCHEON

Presiding: MORTON GRODZINS, Professor of Political Science, Chairman of the Department, Formerly Dean of the Division of the Social Sciences, University of Chicago

Speaker: DAVID RIESMAN, Professor of the Social Sciences, University of Chicago: "Some Observations on the Older and Newer Social Sciences"

CONVOCATION

Speaker: WALTER LIPPMANN: "The Changing Times"

Conferring of Honorary Degrees

RECEPTION

Honoring Recipients of Honorary Degrees

DINNER

Presiding: LEONARD D. WHITE, Ernest De Witt Burton Distinguished Service Professor of Public Administration

Speaker: LAWRENCE A. KIMPTON, Chancellor of the University of Chicago: "The Social Sciences Today"

Saturday, November 12, 1955
THE ROLE OF THE SOCIAL SCIENTIST

CONFERENCE I. THE SOCIAL SCIENTIST AND THE CIVIC ART: ECONOMIC POLICY

Topic 1. The Role of Government in Promoting Economic Stability

Chairman: EDWARD H. LEVI, Dean of the Law School, University of Chicago

Speaker: ROY BLOUGH, Professor of International Business, Graduate School of Business, Columbia University

Commentators: SUNE CARLSON, Director of the Bureau of Economic Affairs, United Nations; MEYER KESTNBAUM, Chairman of the Commission on Intergovernmental Relations and President of Hart, Schaffner and Marx

Topic 2. The Role of Government in Promoting Economic Growth and Development

Chairman: REXFORD G. TUGWELL, Professor of Political Science, University of Chicago

Speaker: T. W. SCHULTZ, Charles L. Hutchinson Distinguished Service Professor of Economics and Chairman of the Department, University of Chicago

Commentators: GOTTFRIED HABERLER, Paul M. Warburg Professor of Economics, Harvard University; HARVEY S. PERLOFF, Resources for the Future, Inc.

CONFEENCE II. THE SOCIAL SCIENTIST AND THE
CIVIC ART: POLITICS

Topic 1. The Social Scientist and the Administrative Art

Chairman: HERMAN FINER, Professor of Political Science, University of Chicago

Speakers: HERBERT EMMERICH, Director of the Public Administration Clearing House; GORDON CLAPP, President of the Research and Development Corporation

Commentators: SIMEON E. LELAND, Dean of the College of Liberal Arts, Northwestern University; CHARLES S. HYNEMAN, Professor of Political Science, Northwestern University; ROGER GRÉGOIRE, Director of the European Productivity Agency

Topic 2. The Art of Diplomatic Negotiation

Chairman: QUINCY WRIGHT, Professor of International Law, University of Chicago

Speakers: JOHN NUVEEN, John Nuveen & Company; HANS J. MORGENTHAU, Professor of Political Science, University of Chicago

Commentators: WALTER JOHNSON, Professor of American History and Chairman of the Department, University of Chicago; J. H. A. WATSON, British Embassy

CONFERENCE III. HUMANISM AND THE SOCIAL SCIENCES

Chairman: JOHN A. WILSON, Andrew MacLeish Distinguished Service Professor of Egyptology, University of Chicago

Speakers: LEO STRAUSS, Professor of Political Philosophy, University of Chicago; JAMES CATE, Professor of Medieval History, University of Chicago

Commentators: STANLEY PARGELLIS, Librarian of the Newberry Library; ANDRÉ SIEGFRIED, Member of the French Academy, Professor Emeritus of the Collège de France

LUNCHEON

Presiding: RALPH W. TYLER, Director of the Center for Advanced Study in the Behavioral Sciences, Formerly Dean of the Division of the Social Sciences, University of Chicago

Speaker: LOUIS GOTTSCHALK, Professor of Modern History, University of Chicago: "The Use of Generalization by the Historian"

CONFERENCE IV. CIVIL LIBERTY

Chairman: C. HERMAN PRITCHETT, Professor of Political Science, University of Chicago

Speaker: ROBERT E. CUSHMAN, Professor of Government, Cornell University

Commentators: SAMUEL A. STOUFFER, Professor of Sociology, Harvard University; MORTON GRODZINS, Professor of Political Science and Chairman of the Department, University of Chicago; HARRY KALVEN, Professor of Law, University of Chicago; ARTHUR C. McGIFFERT, JR., Professor of American Religious Thought, University of Chicago, President of the Chicago Theological Seminary

CONFERENCE V. THE DILEMMA OF SPECIALIZATION

Chairman: JOHN U. NEF, Professor of Economic History and Chairman of the Committee on Social Thought, University of Chicago

Speaker: FRIEDRICH A. HAYEK, Professor, Committee on Social Thought, University of Chicago

Commentators: ARNOLD J. TOYNBEE, Director of Studies of the Royal Institute of International Affairs and Research Professor of International History, University of London; HERRLEE G. CREEL, Professor of Early Chinese Literature and Institutions and Chairman of the Department of Oriental Languages and Literatures, University of Chicago; GUSTAVE E. VON GRUNEBAUM, Professor of Arabic, University of Chicago

COMMITTEE ON THE TWENTY-FIFTH
ANNIVERSARY CELEBRATION

LEONARD D. WHITE, *Chairman*	WALTER JOHNSON
FRED EGGAN	JEROME G. KERWIN
MILTON FRIEDMAN	EDWARD SHILS
NORTON GINSBURG	HERBERT A. THELEN
PHILIP M. HAUSER	WILLIAM B. CANNON, *Secretary*

Ability, in tasks; *see* Task ability

Abramovitz, Moses, 275

Absolutism, in Western tradition, 425

Abstraction, degrees of, 464

Academic freedom, as freedom for intellectual adventure, 466

Academy of Arts and Sciences, Conference on Totalitarianism, 329

Acceptance: cultural, 215; of scientific ideas, 89

Acceptant/Active; *see* Value-emphases

Accomplishment, as basis of government appointment, 400

Achievements, postulate of, 204

Acting-out, expressions of, 191–95, 196–200 *passim*

Action: and impulses, 186; inhibition of, 171–73

Active/Acceptant; *see* Value-emphases

Activity: as factor in Bales' study, 155; as framework for personality traits, 151; gross, 155; measurement of amount of, 154; metabolic and motor, 63; relationship of, to task ability and liking, 156

Acts, overt, and law, 452

Adams, John, 460

Adams, Robert M., 6

Adaptation, of group culture, 195–98

"Address of Welcome," Chauncy D. Harris, 1–8

Administration: art of (*see* Administrative art); dependency of, 386; public (*see* Public administration)

Administrative Art: and loyalty, 395; and methodology, 396; methods for improving, 397; nature of, 394; practice of, 384; relationship of, to hierarchy, 394

Administrator: factors for success of, 385; function of, 385

Adolescent: Freud as an, 220–24; "Mac" (case study), 224–25; parent-child system attacked by, 214

Advertising, criticisms of, 273

Affect, expressions of, 193

Africa, 263

Age: importance of, in grasping knowledge, 463–64; social aspects of, 203

Age-status: acceptance of, 214; attainment of, 227; male and female, 215; social reality of, 226

Agency, of government, 387

Aggregation, level of, 74

Aggression: chronic, toward parents, 213; conditions generating, 168; as need, 165–70

Agricultural economics, seminar on, 4

Agriculture: in stationary state, 375; transfer of labor force from, 375

Agriculture, Department of, 311

Aichhorn, August, 99

Alihan, 234, 248

Alternatives, in foreign policy, 410

Altruism, emphasis on, 122

American Association for Public Opinion Research, presidency of, 310

American Civilization, field of, 320

"American Diplomatic Negotiation, Postwar," John Nuveen, 398–403

American Psychologist, 29 n.

American Sociological Society, 231, 247

American-Soviet Friendship, National Council for, 455

Amplifiers, 62

Analogies, in theory, 70

Analogues: electromechanical, 74; information, 39

Analogy: critique of, 46–50; and disanalogy, 41, 46; errors in, 74; reasoning by, in economics, 289; of society and biological evolution, 47; in systems, 58; as theory, 73–83

Analysis, of value elements, 128 n.

Ancient history, economic, 466

Angell, James R., 1

Anthropologist: access of, to big powers, 329; common culture of, 330; ideal type of, 325; image of historian of, 328; non-urban, 258; vulnerability of, 330–31

Anthropology: American cultural, 327; British social, 327; comparative method in, 116; current trends in,

331; model-building in, 44; as "newer" social science, 319
Anti-Semitism, 221–22
Anxiety: role of, 101; of status, 212; of upwardly mobile, 218; *see also* Status-anxiety
Approach, humanistic, 418
Arbitrariness, frustration and, 167
Areas, underdeveloped; *see* Underdeveloped areas
Argentina, economic analysis of, 376
Argonne National Laboratory, 336
Aristotle, 75, 419
Armaments race, 73
Arnold, Thomas, 449
Arousal, of psychological needs, 165–70
Art, administrative; *see* Administrative art
"Art of Diplomatic Negotiation, The," Hans J. Morgenthau, 404–14
Artis, Jay W., 243 n.
Asch, Solomon E., 172
Ashby, W. Ross, 43, 55, 59, 68 n.; *Design for a Brain*, 78
Aspiration, level of, 60
Association: free (*see* Free association); guilt by (*see* Guilt by association); restraints of human, 93
Assumptions: in model-building, 49; underlying theory-building, 31
Attainder, bill of, 455
Attitudes: negative, 152; versus objective conditions, 181
Austerity, of scientific atmosphere, 470
Authoritarian Personality, The, 314
Authority: delegation of, 390; origins of, in parent-child relationship, 227
Automation, effect of, 356
Autonomy/Dependence; *see* Value-emphases

Bacon, Francis, 12, 442
Bailey, Samuel, 472
Balance of payments: causes of difficulty in, 359–60; deficit in, 359–60; disequilibrium of, 286, 293–94; equilibrium of, 285, 287, 289, 296; and industrialization, 279–82; stability of equilibrium of, 283
Balance of power, 146; *see also* Moiety
Balandier, G., 264, 265
Bales, Robert F., 151 n., 154 n.; "Task Status and Likeability as a Function of Talking and Listening in Decision-making Groups," 148–61
Ballesteros, Marto, 376 n.
Bargaining, function of, in diplomacy, 409
Barnard, Chester, 386
Barriers, between disciplines, 321
Basic Initiating Rank, of participation, 158
Basle, University of, 350
Bauer, Wilhelm, 300
Beard, Charles, 448
Becker, Howard S., 337
Bede, 438
Behavior: on binary basis, 118; coded and uncoded, 50; of committees, 388; as event, 188; imitation of, by computers, 50; influence of, on power, 175; of mankind, sameness of, 445–46 *passim*; political as "new" field of study, 313 (*see also* Political behavior); as purposive, 185 n.
Behavioral sciences: definition of, 29–30; as new term, 349; relationship of, to public opinion study, 312; "theory group," 30
Behaviorism, absurdity of, 14
"Behaviorist," as opposed to "subjectivist," 309
Bell, Wendell, 237
Benedict, Ruth, 227, 326
Benney, Mark, 261
Bentham, Jeremy, 472
Ben-Zeev, Saul, 193–94
Berbers: attitude of, toward city men, 262; community structure of, 140–43; *see also* Political moiety
Berelson, Bernard, 4, 339, "The Study of Public Opinion," 299–318
Berkeley, E. C., 42 n.
Bernard, L. L., 232 n., 301
Bernet, Eleanor, 243 n.
Bertalanffy, L. von, 40
Bertillon, Jacques, 230 n.
Best sellers, prejudice against, 468
Bews, J. W., 246
Biological evolution, used as analogy, 47
Biological sciences, problem of information transfer in, 36
Bion, W. R., 185–200 *passim*

"Biosocial Theory in Human Development," Olson, Willard C., 201–11
Bipolarity, of international politics, 411
Birdseye, Clarence, 273
Blake, R. R., 164 n.
Blizzard, Samuel W., 238
Blough, Roy, "The Role of Government in Promoting Economic Stability," 353–71
Blumer, Herbert, 303, 314
Boas, Frank, 331
Bogue, Donald J., 236–54 *passim*
Booth, Charles, 230 n.
Borgatta, Edgar F., 151 n.
Boring, Edwin G., 80 n.
Bossuet, J. R., 438
Boundaries: academic, experimental approach to, 339; of political science, 333; of social science, 322; of system, 61–62
Bowen, Elenore Smith, 330
Bowles, Chester, 399
Braidwood, Robert J., 6
Brain, as computing device, 74
Brazil, example of labor transfer in, 375
Breese, Gerald, 238
Bricker, Senator John, 460
Bridenbaugh, Carl, 267
Bridges, Harry, 460
Briggs, Asa, 267
British Commonwealth, compared to Creek Confederacy, 144; *see also* Political moiety
Browder, Earl, 460
Brues, Austin, 336
Bryce, James, 303, 306, 416
Buckle, Henry Thomas, 429–32 *passim*
Budget Bureau, 366
Buffer-stock proposals, 284–87 *passim*; critique of, 287–88
Bureau of Applied Social Research, 311
Burgess, E. W., 106, 231–52 *passim*, 256
Burman, Peter, 428
Burns, Arthur E., 275
Bury, J. B., 24
Bush, Robert R., 70 n.
Bush, Vannevar, 42
Business: as carrier of technology, 382; and sample survey, 311

Business activity, level of, 355
Businessmen, in United States foreign service, 399

Calhoun, John C., 145
Canada, 295
Cancer Research, Association for, 336
Cannon, J. S., 61
Cantril, Hadley, 312
Capital: expansion, dangers of, 368, 370; foreign, entry of, 373
Capitalism, appraisal of, 270–72
Caplow, Theodore, 238
Career diplomat: role of, 388–89; in United States foreign service, 400; *see also* Diplomacy
Carper, James, 337
Carter, Launor F., 150 n.
Carthaginians, and Berbers, 143–44; *see also* Political moiety
Cartography, in ecological research, 243–46
Cate, James L., "Humanism and the Social Sciences: But What about John de Neushom?" 426–35
Categories: all-or-none, 117; bipolar, 117; defined functionally, 108; as operational indexes, 96; use of, 107; of value, 108
Catharsis: as inhibiting action, 171; prevention of, 153
Causality, as prejudice, 16
Cell, as system, 54
Cells, theory of, 76
Census, Bureau of the, 237, 241–43, 311; tract concept of, development of, 241
Center for Counseling, 8
Center for Family Study, 8
Center of Midwest Administration, 8
Center for the Study of American Foreign Policy, 8
Center for the Study of Human Evolution, 8
Center for the Study of Leisure, 8, 261
Central Intelligence Agency, 330
Central nervous system, 77
Centralization, of government power, 403
Change, of opinion; *see* Opinion change
"Changing Times, The," Walter Lippmann, 340–47
Charles R. Walgreen Foundation, 8

Chicago: An Experiment in Social Science Research, 2

Chicago: growth of, 255; as social laboratory, 2

Chicago, University of, 311, 340

Chicago Community Inventory Reports, 8, 238, 238–39 n.

Child: ego attacks on, 213; hostility of, to parent, 213

Chile, economic analysis of, 377

Churchill, Winston, 342

Citing, practice of, 455

Citizen: perspective of, 417; values for, 417

City, the: academic interest in, 255; study of, 258, 261

City, Region and Regionalism, 240

City man: concept of, 261; image of, 265; and popular culture, 261

Civic Art, matrix of social science, 417

Civil liberties: and antisubversion program, 451; and Communists, 451

Civilization: difficulty of comprehending, 469; need for understanding, 468; as surviving system, 61; values of, 422

Civilizations, Comparative Study of, 468

Clapp, Gordon R., "The Social Scientist and the Administrative Art," 393–97

Clark, R. A., 150 n.

Classes, organization of, 133

Classics, training in, importance of, 466–67

Classification: Census Bureau, 240–43; of phenomena, 42

Clusters, of value-emphases, 120–24 *passim*

Code linkages, 38

Coding: arbitrary nature of, 38; development of, 63; as linkage within systems, 32; in models, 35–37 *passim; see also* Systems

Cohen, A. R., 167 n.

Cincidence, guilt by, 453–57 *passim*

Cole, Fay-Cooper, 348

College of the University of Chicago, 468

Collingwood, R. G., 325, 442

Collusion, in social life, 16

Colonialism, freedom from, 373

Columbia University, 311

Commitment: basis for point of view on, 424; to values, 422

Committee on Behavioral Sciences, 7

Committee on Communication, 7

Committee on Divisional Master's Degree, 7

Committee on Far Eastern Civilizations, 7

Committee on Home Economics, 7

Committee on Human Development, 7, 332

Committee on International Relations, 7

Committee on Race Relations, 7

Committee on Social Thought, 7, 473

Committee on Statistics, 7

Commodities: price of, 290–91; speculation in, 291–93

Commonplace Book, Henry Thomas Buckle, 429

Communality, perceptual, 199

Communication: and distortion, 56; in government agency, 387; inhibition of, 171–73; mass (*see* Mass communication); process of, 153; among social sciences, 321; system of, 37; in therapy, 95

Communism versus democracy, 398

Communists, and civil liberties, 451

Community: delineation of, in ecological research, 236; as focus of ecology, 249; of interests, 410, 414; and society, 256–57

Competition: definition of, 272–73; Marshall's view of, 270–71; versus monopoly, 269–82 *passim;* perfect, conditions of, 270; Schumpeter's view of, 271–72; theory of, 271

Computer: central nervous system as, 77; electronic (*see* Electronic computer)

Concepts, ethical: of public service, 389; interdisciplinary merging of, 338

Conditioning, 35; analogues to, 70

Condorcet, Marquis de, 438

Conduct, among non-conformists, 101

Conflict: in group participation, 194; and motivation, 163; between needs and demands, 184; psychological induction and solution of, 166–70; range of psychological, 170–73; between valences, 170–73

Congressional Record, 456

Congruence, of activity factor and task ability factor, 161

Connection, rational, principle of law, 453

Conscious, the, strength of, 92

Consciousness: inexplicability of, 20

Consensus: among historians, 437; required for action, 26

Consultant, government, role of, 389

Consumer: demands of, and perfect competition, 270; and public interest as, 369

Consumption theory, 69–71

Containment: military aspect of, 412; policy of, 411–13

Contemporary Cultures, Research on, Columbia University, 329

Content, of theory, 67–69

"Content analysis," origin of, 96

Context: interpersonal, focus of attention, 95; impact of, 93; social, emphasis upon, 107; sociopsychosomatic, significance of, 107

Continuity, of society, 227

"Contrariety," hypothesis of, 160

Contrast, of rural-urban differences, 263

Controls: cultural, for maintenance of status groups, 227; democratic, 17; difficulty in obtaining, 350

Controversy, between "behaviorists" and "subjectivists," 309

Conventions, intellectual, between "older" and "newer" social sciences, 338

Convergence, of disciplines, 267

Cooley, Charles H., 230 n.

Cooper, John Sherman, 399

Co-operation, in group participation, 194

Corn, hybridization of, 382

Corrective problem, definition of, 105

Couch, Arthur S., 148 n., 150 n., 151 n.

Coules, J., 152

Council of Economic Advisers, 355, 366

Countertransference, 50, 100

Countervailing power, 369

Countries, "poor," 372–83 *passim;* economic mistakes of, 380; government instability in, 380; *see also* Underdeveloped areas

Couvreur, L., 240

Cowhig, James, 237

Credit control, 354

Creek Confederacy, 137–39; *see also* Political moiety

Criminal conspiracy, law of, 452

Critical study, requirements for, 469

Criticism, disloyalty of, 459

"Cultural Aspect of Urban Research, The," Everett C. Hughes, 255–68

Culture: common, of anthropologists, 330; as "covert," 94; definition of, 117; development of common, 196; identification with, 226; interplay of personality with, 86; popular (*see* Popular culture); separation of natural and artificial, 25

Culture contact, consequences of study of, 331

Culture and personality, school of, 331

Currency, exchange value of, 296

Current Sociology, 240

Cushman, Robert E., "Guilt by Association: The Game of Presumptions," 451–61

Cybernetics, analogy of, 165

Darwin, Charles, 246–47

Data: amount of, in public opinion study, 315; in ecological research, 241–43; relationship of, to conclusions, 351; subjective, relationship of, to sample interview, 310

Davie, M. R., 234

Davis, Allison, "The Ego and Status-Anxiety," 212–28

Davis, Beverly; *see* Duncan, Beverly Davis

Davis, John W., 460

Debate, of public policy, 346–47

Debt fund, Canadian operations of, 295

Decentralization, 62

Decision-making: and conflict behavior, 170; field of, in government work, 387

Decision theory, 40, 80

Defense, Department of, 389

Defense mechanism, conflict and, 171–73

Defenses, against stress, 59–60

Deficiencies, environmental, 165, 175

Deficit spending, 363

Deflation: anticipation of, 292; of wages, 285

Delegation, problem of, 390

Della Piana, G. M., 174 n.

Demerath, N. S., 237, 252

Democracy: versus communism, 398; and freedom to change laws, 24; origins of, 23; as theme of social sciences, 418

Democratic process, in economic stabilization, 369

Demography, and ecology, 230; *see also* Ecology

Denial, as inhibition of perception, 171

Denney, Reuel, 26

Departmentalism, problem of, 324

Dependence/Autonomy; *see* Value-emphases

Dependency: of administration, 386; needs for psychological, 186

Depression: current danger of, 368–69; measures to avoid, 354

Design for a Brain, W. R. Ashby, 78

Dession, George H., 105

Deutsch, M., 182

Development, economic, 373; individual differences in, 202–4

Development of a science: attention to method of, 308–9; construction of interrelated propositions in, 314; emergence of new problems in, 305–6; influences on, 312–14; institutional recognition of, 310; intensified collection of empirical data in, 307–8; period of theoretical speculation in, 306–7

"Deviant," types of, 156

Deviation: problem of, in city, 266; social, study of, 267

Devil in Massachusetts, The, Marian Starkey, 459

Dewey, John, 1

Dialectic, of traditions, 262

Dichotomies: as designed by Parsons, 129; as found in all cultures, 118

Dickinson, Robert E., 240

Dies, Martin, 455

Dies Committee, 458

Differences: in public opinion study, 1930–55, 299–316 *passim;* urban-rural, 263

Diffusion, 45; lack of, 265

"Dilemma of Specialization, The," F. A. Hayek, 462–73

Diplomacy: as alternative to war, 410; current changes in, 414; functions of, 409–10; influence of technology on, 410; as "open," 404; traditional methods of, 404–14 *passim;* transformation of, 413

Diplomat, career, 400

Diplomatic negotiation: as focus of United States moral purpose, 403; relationship of, to United States leadership, 398

Discipline, importance of, in scholarship, 467

Discipline/Fulfilment; *see* Value-emphases

Disciplines: and American environment, 86; barriers between, 321; discontinuity between, 318; unification of, 416

Discontinuity, and public opinion study, 317–18

Displacement: collection of affect by, 152; of older social sciences, 335

Disproportionality factor: in economic growth, 377; in poor countries, 380

Distortion, in systems, 56–57

Division of the Social Sciences, 253, 322

Documents, government, disposition of, 387

Dodd, Stuart, 455

Dodd, William, 348

Dollard, John, 169 n.

"Dominant" modality in culture, 120 n.

Doob, L. W., 169 n.

Dornbush, Sanford M., 239 n.

Douglas, William O., 460

Drives: biological, 168–69; categories of, 198; primitive, impetus of, 92

Duality, in non-literate culture, 118 n.

Duncan, Beverly Davis, 236–54 *passim*

Duncan, Otis Dudley, 236–54 *passim*

Eastland, John, 460

Eckhaus, R. S., 376

"Ecological Aspects of Urban Research," Philip M. Hauser, 229–54

Ecological research: classification of, 236–40; data in, 241–43; development of, 232–40; effect of, on political science, 234; European, 239–40; foundations of, 229–40; methods in, 243–46; prospects for, 251; schematic presentations in, 249; shifting interest of, 236; theory in, 246–51

Ecology: Critique of, 234–35; current hypothesis in, 250; definitions of, 229–30; human, comparison of, with plant ecology, 249–50; role of, in social science, 234

Economic concentration, as measure of monopoly, 276–77

Economic Development and Cultural Change, Research Center in, 8

Economic difficulties, from Korean War, 361

Economic equilibrium, in growth conditions, 272; *see also* Equilibrium

Economic freedom versus security, 362

Economic growth: definition of, 374; function of, 380; and industrial structure, 276; limitations of, 372, 383; relations of, to goods and labor, 378; sources of, 379–80; and underemployed resources, 374; and use of technology, 381

Economic progress: and industrial organization, 269–82 *passim;* Marshall's views of, 270–71; Schumpeter's views of, 271–72

Economic Progress and Economic Change, Solomon Fabricant, 378 n.

Economic risks, as obstacles, 275; *see also* Risks

Economic stability: concern with, 355; government's role in, 353–71; versus growth, 355–57; maintenance of, 363

Economic stabilization, international aspects of, 283–99

Economics: advances in, 371; fusion of, with politics, 373–74; as "older" social science, 319; relation of, to administration, 386; techniques of, 364

Economists: current functions of, 335; theoretical, 320

Economy: of learning, 77; theories of, 75

Education: for research, 462; task of, 26

Efficiency: and competition, 271; national, improvement in, 380; as social problem, 27; in systems, 60–61

Eggan, Fred, 7

Ego, 74; involvement of, 165; self-defense of, 225; threatened by status-anxiety, 220

Ego-identity: concept of, 212; of status, 213

Ego psychology, 89; *see also* Freud, Anna

"Ego and Status-Anxiety, The," Allison Davis, 212–28

Egoism, emphasis on, 122

Einstein, Albert, 37

Eisenhower, Dwight D., 342

Elasticity, in foreign exchange, 297–98

Electromechanical laws, 74

Electronic computer: as analogue, 40, 79–83; problem-solving in, 82; programming in, 38, 71, 80–81; used as theory, 81

Eleven Twenty-six: A Decade of Social Research, 3, 337

Emmerich, Herbert, "New Bridges between Theory and Practice," 384–92

Emotion: integration of work and, 197; tendency to express, 198

Emotionality, modalities of, 191

"Emotionality and Work in Groups," Herbert Thelen, 184–200

Emphases, of value, in culture, 120; *see also* Value-emphases

Empirical generalizations, in human development, list of, 210–11

Empirical propositions, 68

Employment: concern for high-level, 355; full (*see* Full employment); level, stability of, 283, 285; stimulation of, 357

Employment Act of 1946, 353, 355, 361, 366, 367

Encylopaedia of the Social Sciences, 3, 300–301

Energy: distortion of, 56–57; exchange, 32, 35; input of, 41, 51; relation of, to entropy, 36–37; required for crossing systems, 55; required for equilibrium, 62; spread of, in systems, 55–56; and stimulus response, 57; in systems, 63; transfer of, 36, 54; transmission of, and information, 50

Engels, Friedrich, 230 n.
Entities, of disease, 101
Entrepreneur, as innovator, 269–82
Entropy, as related to energy, 36–37, 40
Environment: political, relationship of, to administration, 386; as related to psychological needs, 163–83 *passim*
Epidemics, spread of, 56
Equifinality, 40–41
Equilibrium: strains toward, 41; of variables, 62
Equilibrium displacement, assumption of, 184
Equilibrium systems, 32, 57–58; *see also* Systems
Era, new, in world affairs, 343
Eriksen, C. W., 176 n.
Erikson, Erik H., 212, 214, 223, 323
Errors: in analogies, 74; of commission, 68–69, 74–75; of omission, 68–69, 74; in prediction, 48
Essentials, abstraction of, 417
Ethics, relevance of, to social science, 418
Ethnocentrism, comparison of, to systems of cultural values, 116
Ethnography, resources of, 134
Ethnologist, sources of material for, 257
Euclidean geometry, 71
Evans-Pritchard, E. E., 136, 323
Evidence, circumstantial, 452
Evil, concept of, 121; *see also* Value-emphases
Exchange Fund Account, Canadian, 295
Exchange market, peculiarities in, 290
Exchange rate: characteristics of, 289–91; flexibility, critique of, 289–97 *passim;* manipulation of, 292–94
Existentialism, 424
Exline, R. V., 182 n.
Exogamy, of the moiety, 135; *see also* Moiety; Political moiety
Expansion, unjustified, danger of, 368
Experiment, relationship of, to theory, 350
Exponential growth, 53

Fabricant, Solomon, 276, 378–79
Factor analysis, 39, 195

Factor prices: deflation of, 287; flexibility of, 285
Factorial designs, in ecological research, 245
Facts, gathering of, 351
Fallacy, of undistributed middle, 456
Far East, 263
Fashion, intellectual, 471
"Feed back," inability to, 152
Feedback: in electronic devices, 52; mechanisms of, 32; negative, as condition for survival, 61–62; ratio, 159–60
Fenichel, Otto, 219 n.
Fertile Crescent, 6
Festinger, L., 73 n., 177
Fez, land of, 263
Field, Frederick Vanderbilt, 460
"Field work," among anthropologists, 330
Fight, need to, 186
Fight situation, anxiety in, 194–95
Finesse, spirit of, 415–16; *see also* Pascal, Blaise
Firey, Walter, 234–35, 237
Fiscal policy, application of, 366
Fish, Congressman Hamilton, 384
Fisher's log, series distribution, 78
Flexibility, of the University of Chicago, 323
Flexner, Abraham, 440
Flight: acting-out in, 191–93; assumption of, 191–92; and dependency, 193; measurements of, 192–200 *passim;* needs for, 186
Flow, in therapy, 96
Folklore, uses of, 257
Forecasts, by historians, 439–41 *passim*
Foreign currency, speculations in, 290
Foreign policy: hostility to, 405–6; major problem of, 400; moral problems of, 406; study of, 403; tenets of, 402
Foreign trade, United States concern with, 359–61
Form, W. H., 237
Form, and matter, 36–37
Foxlee, Gilbert de, 433
France, 267
Frank, Jerome, 104
Frazer, Sir James, *The Golden Bough*, 429

Free dissociation, Freudian technique of, 89, 96
Freedman, Ronald, 238
Freedom, and order, 11
Freiberg, Moravia, 216, 220
French Sociological Society, 267
Frequency distributions, 78
Freshmen, at Harvard, 153
Freud: His Life and His Mind, Helen Walker Puner, 220–23
Freud, Anna, 107, 219 n.
Freud, Sigmund: and anti-Semitism, 221–23; and anxiety of social dangers, 216–17; on countertransference, 50; definitions of anxiety by, 218; and dreams of status, 220; and early experience, 91; on ethnic identity, 220–24 *passim;* and ideas and methods, 88; relationship of, to father, 222; as theorist, 43–44
Freudian theory of unconscious, 74
Friedman, Milton, 4
Froissart, Jean, 438
Fromm, Erich, 101, 104, 123
Frustration-aggression theory, 167, 206
Fulbright, Senator J. W., 29
Fulfilment/Discipline; *see* Value-emphases
Full employment, effect of, 335
Full Employment Bill, of 1945, 355
Function: mathematical, 49; teleological, 16
Functional equivalents, in need reduction, 170
Functional relationships: ecological concern with, 236; in systems, 31, 34
Furez, Margaret, 243 n.
Future, The, and historians, 440–41

Galen, 350
Galileo, Galilei, 352
Gallup, George, 309
Gallup-AIPO poll, establishment of, 300
Galpin, Charles J., 230 n.
Games, theory and practice of, 80
Gaps, cultural, rural-urban, 264–65
Gardner, Mrs. Burleigh, 216
Gelhorn, Walter, 456
General, the, study of, 436
"General Education," 323
General education: importance of,

468, 472; misuses of, 323; *see also* "General Education"
General/Unique; *see* Value-emphases
Generalization: among anthropologists, 329; historical (*see* Historical generalization); in social science, 43
Generalizing words, category of, 447–48; *see also* Historical generalization
Genetics: broadened thinking in, 209; and information theory, 80
Geneva, "spirit of," 341
Gennep, Arnold van, 257
Genotype, of culture, 125
Geographers, development of, 322
Geometrical theories, 70–71
Geometry, as the scientific spirit, 415–16; *see also* Pascal, Blaise
Gestalt, in relation to system, 34
Gettys, W. E., 234
Geyl, Pieter, 438–39
Gibbs, J. Willard, 66
Gini index, 244
Glidewell, John C., 192, 197, 199
Goal-blocking, 168
Goal-seeking, and problem-solving, 165
Goal-striving, as teleological, 40
Goals: as internal strains, 41; of perception, 164; value consequences of, 102
Gold: accumulation of, 286; as international standard, 284
Goldman, M., 166–82 *passim*
Good, concept of, 121; *see also* Value-emphases
Goods: reproducible, quantity of, 380; reproducible capital, role of, 378
Gorer, Geoffrey, 329
Gosnell, H. F., 307
Gottschalk, Louis, 5; "The Historian's Use of Generalization," 436–50
Government: American, comparison of, with Berbers', 144 (*see also* Political moiety); awarding of contracts by, 365; and compensatory spending, 354; local and state, field of, 386; officials, quality of, 364–65; responsibility of, increasing scope of, 357; roles of, 372–73, 382; and sample surveys, 311
Gown versus town, 433
Gras, N. S. B., 231 n.

Graunt, John, 430
"Great man," type of, 155
Green, Howard Whipple, 243 n.
Group, adaptation to, 190; conceptual approach to, 187–90; decision-making, 148; dynamic of, 199; part-whole relationships in, 187; phases in life of, 194–95; purposes of, 186; "simply organized," 151; survival of, conditions for, 191; as system, 54, 185 n.; as therapeutic unit, 98
Group culture: adaptive balance in, 195–98; organization of, 191
Group/Individual; *see* Value-emphasis
Group interaction, natural units of, 194
Group participation, predispositions in, 194
Group therapy, readjustment of, to psychoanalytic theory, 99
Groupings, of disciplines, 323
Growth, in economic life; *see* Economic growth
Growth motivation, in social environment, 175
Growth rates, 53–54; economic study of, 275
Grunebaum, Gustave von, 4, 261
Guetzkow, Harold, 73 n.
Guilt: by association, doctrine of, 452; legal, as personal, 452–54 *passim;* presumptions of, 452–54 *passim*
"Guilt by Association: The Game of Presumptions," Robert E. Cushman, 451–61
Guizot, François, 438
Guthrie, E. R., 70
Guttman, Louis, 309

Haas, M. R., 140
Haeckel, Ernst, 229
Handbook of Social Psychology, contribution of public opinion studies to, 302
Hannibal, 221, 222
Hansen, Marcus, 309, 331
Haret, Spiru C., 47
Harlow, H. F., 165, 177
Harper, William Rainey, 2
Harris, Chauncy D., 237; "Address of Welcome," 1–8
Harris, Dorothy L., 245 n.
Harrison, Shelby M., 231 n.

Harvard University, 319, 349
Harvard Values Project, 126
Hatt, Paul, 234
Hauser, Philip, 4; bibliography on cities, 255; "Ecological Aspects of Urban Research," 229–54; on sampling, 4
Hawley, Amos H., 234–49 *passim*
Hayek, F. A., "The Dilemma of Specialization," 462–73
Health, conceptions of, 102
Henry, Jules, 333 n.
Henry, William E., 217 n., 266, 314
Henry of Huntingdon, 434
Herodotus, 438
Herskovits, Melville, 130, 323
Hess, Robert D., 212
Hierarchy: as area for social research, 387; relationship of, to administration, 393
Higher education, English, 467
Hilgard, E. R., 164
Hill, William F., 199
Hiss, Alger, 460
Historian: contribution of, to social science, 441; hostility to, 327; as humanist, 334; ideal type of, 325; as member of research team, 268; as particularist, 441; "pure," 438–39 *passim;* successful elements of, 427; task of, 437, 444; and typologies, 440; universalist, 438
"Historian's Use of Generalization, The," Louis Gottschalk, 436–50
Historical generalization, categories of, 436–50 *passim*
Historical reality, re-enactment of, 443
Historical situation, values determined by, 422
Historiography, landmark in, 442
History: department of, 427; diplomatic, of United States, 398; idea of, as body of laws, 429; study of, as a science, 18–19, 319, 428–35 *passim,* 464; universalist, 438
History of Civilization in England, Henry Thomas Buckle, 429
History of Freedom and Thought, The, J. B. Bury, 24
Hollerith machine, invention and spread of, 306
Holliday, Judy, 458
Hollingshead, A. B., 234–49 *passim*
Holmes, Oliver Wendell, 29, 453

Holst, Herman von, 1
Homans, George C., 70, 73 n., 78
Homesteader, culture of, 126–28, *passim*
Honiton, Robert de, 433
Hoover, Edgar M., 252
Hoover Commission, 389
Horney, Karen, 103
Horwitz, Murray, "Psychological Needs as a Function of Social Environments," 162–83
Hostility: experimentally induced, 175; within family, 213; as need, 165–70; phenomenal, 166–68, 175
Howell, F. Clark, 6
Hughes, Charles Evans, 452
Hughes, Everett C., 4, 332–33; "The Cultural Aspect of Urban Research," 255–68
Huizinga, Johan, 432
Human behavior, theory of, 163, 184–87
Human development: list of empirical generalizations in, 210–11; models of, 203–9; theory in, 201–11
Human Dynamics Laboratory, 184
Human ecology; *see* Ecology
Human mind, development of, 463–64
Humanism: and moral principles, 419; relativistic, 421–25 (*see also* Relativism); versus science, 415
"Humanism and the Social Sciences: But What about John de Neushom?" James L. Cate, 426–35
Humanities, barrier against, 322
Hume, David, 472
Huntington, Ellsworth, 335
Hurwicz, Leonid, 309
Hutchinson, W. T., 5
Huxley, Julian, 246 n.
Hydraulic mechanisms, 70
Hydrogen bomb, consequences of, 341
Hyman, Herbert, 309

Id, as noun, 74
Idea of Progress, The, J. B. Bury, 24
Ideal, of a society, 28
Ideal man, image of, 261
Identification: with age-status, 213; "with aggressor," 226; with culture of higher status group, 226; with persons of higher status, 225
Identities, formal, 41–46

Identity: of boundary functions, 45; of ego (*see* Ego-identity); of status (*see* Status-identity)
Iklé, Fred, 237
Illinois, University of, 337
Image, of self-system, 111
"Impact of Psychoanalytic Thinking on the Social Sciences, The," Harold D. Lasswell, 84–115
Imperatives, of national policy, 345
Impulses: acting-out of, 186; and action, 186; potency of biological, 106; thwarting of, 186
Income, and consumption, 69–71
Incorporation, of values of higher status group, 226
Indecision, resulting from conflict, 178–80
Indeterminacy, in human development theory, 205
Indexes, use of, in psychoanalytic theory, 96
India, 399
Individual, as system, 54
Individual differences, as neglected theoretical area, 202
Individual/Group; *see* Value-emphases
Individual predictions versus explanatory principles, 208–9
Individualism, and psychoanalysis, 86
"Industrial Organization and Economic Progress," George J. Stigler, 269–82
Industrial research, concentration of, 279–82
Industrialization: and balance of payment, 279–82; in poor countries, 380; overemphasis on, 382
Inferiority, feelings of, 224–25; *see also* "Mac" (case study)
Inflation: measures to avoid, 354, 370; as negative influence, 363, 369–71; as neglected problem, 367
Information: distortion of, 56–57; exchange, rate of, 35; input of, 41, 51; and mass, 37; negative, 37; processing of, 63, 75–76, 83; spread of, 55–56; in systems, 32; theory, and coding, 80; theory, role of, 38; transfer, 36, 54; transmission of, and energy, 50
In-groups, of anthropologists, 326
Inhibition, conditions of, 171–73

Initiation, of interaction, 153
Initiative, among scholars, 336
Inkeles, Alex, 314
Innovation, economic conditions for, 273–82 *passim*
Input: dimensions of, 62; of labor, 379; to increase goods, 381
Input-output: relations of, 35; in systems, 32
Insight, place and efficacy of, 114
Instinct, 35
Intelligence theories, and model of human development, 206–7
Interaction: amount of, 153; chain of, 108; differences in, 161; between great and little traditions, 261
Interaction Process Analysis, Robert F. Bales, 154 n.
Interaction variables, in categories of stress, 188
Interests: conflict of, 408; community of, 410, 414
International aspects of economic stabilization; *see* Economic stabilization.
International equilibrium, problems of, 285
International relations: changes in, 413; new era in, 411–13
Interpretation, as Freudian method, 89, 96
Interrupted tasks, recall of, 176
Intervening variables, in small-group research, 191
Interview, effect of, on public opinion study, 310
Interviewing, method of, in public opinion study, 309
Introduction to the Science of Sociology, R. E. Park and E. W. Burgess, 248
Introspection, computers helpful in, 82
Isard, Walter, 236, 245
Islam, description of, 262
Isolationist attitude, toward foreign policy, 406
Issues, political, status of, 341

James, William, 434
"Jargon," function of, 338
Jeffress, Lloyd A., 79 n.
Jesus Christ, birth of, 69
Jevons, W. S., 472
Jews, Viennese, 221–23

Joint Committee on the Economic Report, 366
Jones, Ernest, 99 n., 221–22
Judson, Harry Pratt, 1
Julien, C. A., 262

Kansas City (Mo.), 268
Kant, Immanuel, 75, 350
Karesh, Robert, 236, 245
Karsten, A., 182 n.
Kelvin, William Thomson, 427
Kendrick, John, 276
Keyfitz, Nathan, 245 n.
Keynes, John Maynard, 472
Kimpton, Lawrence A, "The Social Sciences Today," 348–52
Kish, Leslie, 237
Kitagawa, Evelyn M., 237–54 *passim*
Kluckhohn, Clyde, 94; Russian Research Center, 329; "Toward a Comparison of Value-Emphases in Different Cultures," 116–32
Kluckhohn, Florence, 121 n.
Knight, Frank, 270, 348; "Science, Society, and the Modes of Law," 9–28
Kornhauser, A. W.: opinion data and class, 307; questionnaire instruction, 309
Kroeber, Alfred L., 87, 328

La Barre, Weston, 186 n., 326
La Blacke, P. G. Vidal de, 230 n.
Labor: division of, 149; marginal productivity of, 375; marginal value of, 375
Labor requirements: decline in, 278; per unit output, 276
Lacrosse, 139; *see also* Political moiety
Lag, in response to stress, 58–59
Laidlow, Walter, 241
Lamb, Robert K., 268
Language: ambiguity of, 11; analogical, 67–68; of the citizen, 418; and cultural independence of biology, 20; and ideas, 66–67; mathematical, 67–68; phonemic systems found in, 118; in therapy, 95; verbal, 67–68
Lasswell, Harold D.: analysis by, of newspapers and leaflets, 307; "departure" of, from public opinion study, 312; "Impact of Psychoanalytic Thinking on the Social Sciences," 84–115; introduction by, of

Freudianism into public opinion study, 314; "partial incorporation" of, 333

Lattimore, Owen, 456

Laughlin, J. Laurence, 1

Lauwe, P. Chombart de, 240

Law: as condition for social life; due process of, 453; historical, 17–18; jural, 22; prescriptive, 21; for primitive man, 21; responsibility in, 64; revolution in, 23–24; sanctity of, 25

Laws, universal, of history, 429, 439, 446

Lawyer, attitudes toward, 460

"Layering," definition of, 387

Lazarsfeld, Paul F., 309, 312

Le Tourneau, Roger, 263

Leaders, United States ambassadors as, 399

Learning, 35; as drive reduction, 41; economy of, 77; and needs, 176–83 *passim;* of a new culture, 226; theories of, 75; theory, and model of human development, 208

Leavitt, H. J., 152–53

Lee, F. J., 166 n., 167–74 *passim*

Legislation, loyalty-oath, 453

Legitimation, in small-group experiment, 166

Leiden, University of, 428

Lerner, Abba, 70

Level: of productive arts, 372, 378, 380; rate of return in economic growth, 381

Levy, D. M., 168

Lewin, Kurt: on environment, 164; on regression, 172; theory of conflict of, 170; on valence and need, 162; on Zeigarnik effect, 176

Lewis, W. Arthur, 374 n.

Lieberman, S., 192

Life, reaction to stress in, 185

Likeability: area of, 154; as factor in Bales's study, 155; as framework for personality traits, 151

Likert, Rensis, 309, 311

Liking, experimentally induced, 175; relationship of, to task ability and activity, 156

Limitations: of computers, 80; of systems, 54

Lindzey, Gardner, 73 n.

Link, cultural, lack of, 264

Lippmann, Walter, 303, 307; "The Changing Times," 340–47

Literature, methodological, in public opinion study, 309

Llewellyn, Karl, 323

Local Community Research Committee, 2, 234

Local moiety, definition of, 135; *see also* Moiety

Locke, John, 472

Log-normal distribution, 78

Lorenz curve, applied to ecology, 244

Los Angeles, 453

Lotka, Alfred, 73, 230 n.

Lovett, Robert M., 455

Lowden, Frank O., 5

Lowell, James A., 303, 307–8

Loyalty, as value in administration, 395

"Mac" (case study), 224–25

MacCannell, E. H., 246 n.

McCarran Immigration and Nationality Bill, 457

McCarthy, Joseph, 456–57

McDougall, William, 180

McKenzie, R. D., 231–49 *passim*

McNeill, William H., 5

McNemar, Q., 303

McPhee, William N., 309

McQuown, Norman A., 6

Macroeconomics, 69–71

Maitland, Frederic W., 438

Malallocation, of economic factors, 376

Malinowski, Bronislaw, 87, 338

Malthus, Thomas, 247

Man: behavior of, sameness in, 445–46 *passim* (*see also* Behavior); pluralistic interpretation of, 20; as romantic animal, 12; *see also* Clusters; Human behavior; Ideal man

Management, art of, and social sciences, 394

Manipulation, of human minds, 393

Market, enlargement of, 372, 380

Market research, relationship of, to university, 311

Marshall, Alfred, 270

Marshall Plan, 361, 400

Martin, Walter T., 238

Marxist attitude, toward psychoanalysis, 112–13

Maslow, A., 175

Mass, and information, 37

Mass communication, development of, 311

Mass society, emergence of, 306

Massachusetts Institute of Technology, 42

Masséna, 222

Mathematical statements, 67

Mathematical theories, 70; compared to verbal, 71–73, 74–83 *passim*

Mathematics, as model, 44

Mathis, Andrew, 197

Matri-clans, and matri-sibs, 137

Matter, and form, 36–37

Mayhew, Henry, 230 n.

Mead, Margaret, 314, 326

Meaning, of theory, 75

Measurement: of data, 308; quantitative, in study of history, 431

Mechanism, 120; *see also* Value-emphases

Meerdink, J., 240 n.

Meetings, of groups, 153

Memory: in computers, 80; effect of need in, 177–78; and motivation, 177

Menninger, William, 92

Mental/Physical; *see* Value-emphases

Mercantilism, ideas of, 373

Merriam, Charles E., 87, 234, 334, 348

Metabolism, 61

Method: comparative, in history, 442; of cross-cultural comparison, 117; dominance of, 313; inductive, in study of history, 429; of kinship analysis, 133

Methodology: historical, 428; preoccupation with, 331; problem of, 350; relationship of, to administration, 396

Metropolitan areas, prospective research in, 251

Metropolitan community, internal composition of, 237

Mexico: development of corn varieties in, 382; personnel training in, 381

Meyersohn, Rolf B., 261

Michigan, University of, 311

Microscopic level, laws at, 74

Middle Ages, later, 432

Middle East (Arab), 263

Mill, J. S., 41–42, 472

Miller, James G., 76 n., 77–79 *passim*;

"Toward a General Theory for the Behavioral Sciences," 29–65

Miller, Neale E., 169 n., 170

Misconceptions, about computers, 79

Mobility, in academic life, 336

Modalities, in culture, 120 n.

Model of human development: and Frustration-Aggression theory, 206; and intelligence theories, 206–7; predictions made from, 203–9; and psychoanalytic theory, 205–6

Models: adaptive balance as, 200; in anthropology, 44; assumptions in, 49; critiques of, 47, 49; definition of, 43, 66–68; in ecological research, 245; for economic stabilization, 285; electronic, 50–52; of individual differences in development, 202–4; in mathematics, 44; in natural sciences, 39; predictions from, 48; *see also* Systems

"Models: Their Uses and Limitations," Herbert A. Simon and Allen Newell, 66–83

Modifiability, of the adult, 90

Moiety: as "balance of power," 146; definition of, 134; extension of, 146; principle of, 145; types of, 135

Mommsen, Theodor, 438

Monetary policy, 366

"Moniac," the, 70, 75

Monopoly: versus competition, 269–82 *passim;* as condition for innovation, 273–79; as departure from perfect competition, 272; Marshall's view of, 270–71; Schumpeter's view of, 271–72

Montaigne, 12, 140

Morgan, Charles, 396

Morgenthau, Hans J., "The Art of Diplomatic Negotiation," 404–14

Mormons, culture of, 126–28 *passim*

Morris, Charles, 129 n., 131

Moslems, 262

Mosteller, Frederick, 70 n.

Motivation: critique of, work on, 162; need aspects of, 163

Motives, psychological, 174; *see also* Psychological motives

Movements, nativistic, 265

Mowrer, O. H., 169 n.

Mueller, R. A. H., 152

Multiplier theory, economic, 297

Multivariate analysis, in ecological research, 245
Mundt, Karl, 458
Murdock, George Peter, "Political Moieties," 133–47
Murray, Henry A., 180
Murrow, Edward R., 459
Myth, place of, in history of man, 12

National aggregates, stabilization of, 355–56
National Firearms Act, 454
National Opinion Research Center, 311
National Resources Board, Urbanism Committee, 234
National Science Foundation, 29
National Security Council, 389
Nationalism, 373
Nature-nurture, problem of, 201
Navaho, culture of, 126–28 *passim*
Need; *see* Psychological needs
Nef, John U., 4
Negotiation: diplomatic (*see* Diplomatic negotiation); secret, 405
Network, of affective relations, 148
Neumann, John von, 79 n.
Neushom, John de, 426, 433, 435; *see also* Cate, James L.
Neville, John, 472
"New Bridges between Theory and Practice," Herbert Emmerich, 384–92
New History, James Harvey Robinson, 427
New York Stock Exchange, 434
Newcomer, reception of, 327
Newell, Allen, "Models: Their Uses and Limitations," 66–83
Nissen, H. W., 164, 177
Noise, as negative information, 37
Non-random relationships, 38
Norman Wait Harris Foundation, 8
Norms: agreement on, 28; of the analyst, 101; cultural, deviation from, 102; opportunity for creation of, 153
Northrop, F. S. C., 120, 124
Northwestern University, 319
Nouns, preference of, over verbs, 74
Novelty, recurring emergence of, 20
Now/Then; *see* Value-emphases
Numbers, cardinal and ordinal, 47

Nutter, G. W., 278
Nuveen, John, "American Diplomatic Negotiation, Postwar," 398–403

Objective reference, in veridicality, 173–75
Objectives, of public policy, 346
Odum, H. T., 61
Office of Naval Research, 184
Official political policy, role of, 389
Ogburn, William F., 87, 236, 348
Oklahoma, 453
Olson, Willard C., "Biosocial Theory in Human Development," 201–11
Ontology, as error in verbal theory, 75
Opinion: change, limitations on, 315; climate of, 451; public (*see* Public opinion)
Opposition, rural-urban, 265
Order, and freedom, 12
Orderliness, priority given in culture, 120
Organ, as system, 54
Organism: as analogue, 76–79; as system, 33
Organization: economic, structure of, 372; theory of, 77
Orientations, of value, 108
Orthogonal relationship of activity and sociability, 159
Other/Self; *see* Value-emphases
Output: dimensions of, 62; and economic growth, 374; growth in, for personal welfare, 381; ratio to input of labor, 379
Overcentralization, in underdeveloped countries, 390
Overlapping, of areas of competence, 389
Overstimulation, and government, 368
Overtalking, dangers of, 152
Ownership, intellectual, of public opinion study, 313
Oxford, England, 431–32

Pair, as therapeutic unit, 98
Pairing, needs for, 186
Pappenfort, Donnell, M., 239 n.
Paracelsus, 350
Paraguay, economic analysis of, 377 n.
Parallels, historical, 444, 446
Parameters, choice of, 47–48
Parent: and child's hostility, 213; cultural identity of, 214

Pareto income distribution, 78
Park, Robert E., 231–52 *passim;* 255, 259, 348
Parkman, Francis, 438
Parsons, Talcott, 129, 133, 320, 338
Participation, amount of, 158
Particularist, as historian, 441
Particularity, as against universalism, 125
Pascal, Blaise, 415–16
Past, the: and historians, 440–41; intellectual, discontinuity with, 317
Pastore, N., 167 n.
Patient, modifiable by knowledge, 114
Peace, of collaboration, 344
Pearson, Karl, 120
Peer group, of anthropologist, 326
People: in Puerto Rico and Mexico, 381; quality of, as productive agents, 372, 374, 378, 380; *see also* Human development; Man
Perception: functional theorists of, 164; inhibition of, 171–73; and veridicality, 173
Perfect competition; *see* Competition, perfect
Performance, quality of, in large and small research laboratories, 281
Periodization, 441; *see also* Historical generalization
Permeability, of system's boundaries, 61
Personality: definition of, 185 n.; human, as resources, 397; interplay with culture, 86; as involvement in events, 188
Personnel, of United States Department of State, 399
Perspectives: anthropological, 133; historical, 449
Peru: example of labor transfer in, 375; flexible exchange rate in, 295
Phenomenology, 75
Philosophy, as necessary part of social science, 469, 471
Phoneme, definition of, 117; *see also* Language
Photosynthesis, 61
Physical/Mental; *see* Value-emphases
Pinkerton, R. C., 61
Pirenne, Henri, 434
Pitts, Walter, 81
Planning, program of education and research in, 7

Plato, 36, 92, 404
Platt, John R., 62
Polanyi, Michael, 336
Policy: foreign (*see* Foreign policy); of government, 346
Political behavior, field of, 313, 333–34
Political Behavior, Committee on, of the Social Science Research Council, 314
"Political Moieties," George Peter Murdock, 133–47
Political moiety: basis of, 136; of Berber people, 140–43 *passim;* of Creek Confederacy, 137–39 *passim;* dichotomous basis of, 136; efficacy of, 146; lacrosse as mechanism in, 139; role of, 144–45
Political science: Affinity of, to public administration, 385; changes in, 333–34; influence of ecological research on, 234; as "older" social science, 319
Politics: fusion of, with economics, 373–74; international, bipolarity of, 411; moral problems of, 406; origin of, 21
Polling, earlier name of, 301
Polls; *see* Public opinion polls
Polybius, 429, 438
Popular culture, and city man, 261
Population, and economic growth, 374
Population Research and Training, Center for, 8, 252, 254
Potus, John, 433
Power: countervailing, absence of, 369; expectation of, induced, 175; in group, as controlled by organization, 166
Practice, relationship of, to theory, 384
Practices, of child-rearing, 94
Precipitation, rate of, 40
Precision, in models, 51
Predictability, historian's attitude toward, 434
Prediction: of conduct, 108; by general theory, 46; among historians, 444, 446; limitations of, 9, 15; through models, 48
Predispositions, persistence of childhood, 90
Premises, of value position, 424

Pressure, systems in, 59
Price, instability of, as external phenomenon, 288
Price control, 365, 367, 370
Price-fixing, power of, in large companies, 274
Price level: national, 284–94 *passim;* world, 288
Primitive, in Redfield, 260
Princeton University, 311
Principles, of law, 452–54 *passim; see also* Guilt
Priorities, system of, 125
Private enterprise versus state enterprise, 269
Probability mechanisms, generative distributions in, 78–79
Problem-solving: in man and machines, 81–82, 165; and needs, 164
Process: psychosomatic, 93; punitive, and subversion, 457; sociopersonal, 108
Producers, public's interests as, 369
Production: costs of, 289; level of, 372
Productivity, marginal, of labor, 375
Profile, of cultures, 126, 127; *see also* Homesteader; Mormon; Navaho; Spanish-American; Zuni
Profits, as reward for innovation, 273
Program: antisubversion, 451; necessity for, 339
Propaganda: effective techniques of, 14; substitution of, for truth, 423
Propositions: empirical, 68; in social science, 45; about systems, 52–64 *passim; see also* Models; Systems
Prosperity, in social sciences, 336
Provincialism, 425; *see also* Relativism
Psephology, 303
Psychoanalysis: as changing discipline, 89; effects of, in social sciences, 89, 94, 104–15 *passim;* reception of, in social sciences, 84–115 *passim*
Psychoanalysts, selection of, 104 n.
Psychoanalytic theory, and human development model, 205–6
Psychological environment, assumptions about, 180
Psychological motives, and situational relativity, 174
Psychological needs: arousal of, 165–70; change in conditions of, 180–83; complications in study of, 182, 182 n.; concepts of, conditions of use,

163; conflict range of, 170–73; and deficiency states, 175; derived from environmental conditions, 164–65; determinants of, 164; generative circumstances, 165–83 *passim;* identified by small-group research, 180–83; and learning, 176–83; listing of, 185–86; and memory, 177–78; reduction of, 168, 170, 176; satisfaction of, 167, 170; systems of, analysis of, 170–73 (*see also* Models; Systems); and valence, 162, 168, 173, 176, 183; veridicality of, responses related to, 173–75
"Psychological Needs as a Function of Social Environment," Murray Horwitz, 162–83
Psychophysiology, field of, 322
Public administration: affinity of to political science, 385; area of, 384; needs of, 386–90 *passim;* and problem of overlapping, 389; relation of, to economics, 386
Public opinion: definition of, 299; history of, 299–305; as a science (*see* Development of a sceince); as scientific research, 4; and subversion, 451; support of, 403; types of, 300; in Western history (*see* Bauer, Wilhelm)
Public opinion polls: availability of data in, 308; of George Gallup, 311; of Elmo Roper, 311; uses and abuses of, 301
Public Opinion Quarterly, 300, 311
Public opinion research: academic attitude toward, 312; conditions for vitality of, 316–17; criticism of, 303; data and methods of, 309–10, 315; differences between 1930 and 1955, 299–316 *passim;* growth of, 302, 313, 339; intellectual shift of, 312; theory in, 315
Public Opinion Research, American Association for; *see* American Association for Public Opinion Research
Public Opinion Research, Office of, 311
Public opinion study; *see* Public opinion research
Puerto Rico, 381
Puner, Helen Walker, *Freud: His Life and His Mind,* 220–23 n.

Purchasing power, parity theory of, 284
Pythagorean theorem, 69

Q-sorts, self-perceptual, 195, 199
Quantification, of data, 308
Quantity, of reproducible goods, 372, 378, 380
Quantity/Quality; *see* Value-emphases
Questionnaires, construction of, 309; *see also* Public opinion research
Quételet, Lambert, 430–31 *passim*
Quincy, Josiah, 460
Quinn, James A., 232–33, 249

Radio, invention and spread of, 306
Radio Research, Office of, 311
Ramsey, G. V., 164 n.
Random impulse, 37
Rank: of individual within group, 158; socially defined, 212; system of, 212; *see also* Basic Initiating Rank
Ranke, Leopold von, 428, 438
Raphael, Edna, 239 n.
Raphelson, Alfred C., 162 n.
Rapoport, Anatole, 56
Rashevsky, Nicolas, 78
Rates: of precipitation, 40; similarities in, 49
Ratio, of feedback, 159; *see also* Feedback
Rationalization, 60
Ratzel, Friedrich, 230 n.
Reacting, habit of, 343
Reaction, third-generation; *see* Third-generation reaction
Real income, national, index of, 287
Reality: denial of, as defense, 60; historical (*see* Historical reality)
Rebut, principle of law, 453–54 *passim; see also* Law
Receiving, of interaction, 153
Recession, current dangers of, 368–69
Reciprocal demands, economic, 285, 287
Reckless, Walter C., 231
Reconciliation, psychological: definition of, 213; to female status, 215; to objective social sanctions, 228; to parent of same sex, 228
Reconstruction, of the whole, 416
Recruitment, for United States foreign service, 399; *see also* Career diplomat
Redfield, Robert, 7, 259–61, 322
Redick, Richard, 240
Reduction: of dimensions, 38; of social power, 167; of systems, 40
Regression, increasing range of, 172
Regularities, in history, 435
Reinforcement theory: applied to hostility, 168; assertions about responses, 176; and drives, 162
Reiss, Albert J., Jr., 235–36, 238, 243 n.
Rejection, of scientific ideas, 89
Relationships: in social service systems, 45; of status (*see* Status-relationships)
Relativism: cultural, assumptions of, 330; ethical, early simplicity of, 329; place in social science, 425
Relativity theory, 37
Relaxed/Tense; *see* Value-emphases
Religion, origins of, 21
Renunciation, as alternative of foreign policy, 410; *see also* Diplomacy; War
Representatives, House of, 455
Repression: as defense, 60; as inhibition of function, 171; and veridicality, 174
Research: "basic," 339; education for, 462, 465; interdisciplinary, as process of fragmenting, 349; market (*see* Market research); small-group, 148; *see also* Small-group research
Research laboratories, large versus small, 281
"Residual member," type of, 156
Resources: abundance of, 375; allocation of, 381; as basis of economic development, 374, 380; collection of, 373; fixed flow of, 270
Response tendencies, strength and direction of, 163
Responses: of systems, 58–59; veridicality of, 173–75
Responsibility, in law, 64
Return to Laughter, Elenore Smith Bowen, 330
Revolution, in technology, 341
Rhodes, Albert L., 243 n.
Richardson, Lewis F., 73, 78
Riecken, Henry W., 73 n.

Riesman, David, 122; Center for Study of Leisure, 261; paradox of shift from inner- to other-directed, 149; and psychoanalysis, 101; "Some Observations on the 'Older' and the 'Newer' Social Sciences," 319–39

Ritual, place in history of man, 12

Rivalry, between nations, 344

Robinson, Claude, 301

Robinson, James Harvey, 427

Robinson, W. S., 244 n.

Rockefeller Foundation, 311

Rockefeller Memorial, 1

Rogers, Carl, 303

Rogers, J. E. Thorold, 431

Roget, Peter Mark, 66–67

Role: of career diplomat, 389; concept of, 34; of government (*see* Government); of political policy official, 389

"Role of Government in Promoting Economic Growth, The," Theodore W. Schultz, 372–83

"Role of Government in Promoting Economic Stability, The," Roy Blough, 353–71

Role theory: applied to hostility, 168; and valence, 162

Romney, Kimball, 7

Roosevelt, Franklin D., 384, 461

Roosevelt College, 70

Roper-*Fortune* poll, establishment of, 300

Rorschach card, 56

Rosenberg, Ethel, 460

Rosenberg, Julius, 460

Rosenwald, Julius, 274

Rosenzweig, Saul, 176 n.

Ross, Frank A., 244 n.

Royall, Kenneth, 461

Ruml, Beardsley, 2

Rural versus urban, 255–68 *passim*

Russian Research Center, 329

Rustics, 264; *see also* City

St. Augustine, 438

Sakoda, J. M., 150 n.

Salter, H. E., 432

Sample: effect of, on public opinion study, 310 (*see also* Public opinion research); Random, of Harvard Freshmen, 153

Sample interview: effect of, on subjective data, 310; method of, in public opinion study, 310; *see also* Public opinion research

Sample survey: early development of, 311; "invention" of, 309; *see also* Public opinion research

Sampling, as method of public opinion study, 309; *see also* Public opinion research

Sanctions, political, relationship of, to administrator, 385; *see also* Administrative art; Administrator

Sapir, Edward, 87, 123

Satisfaction, questionnaires on, 161

Scale, for intensity rating, addenda, 130

Scaling: method of, in public opinion study, 309 (*see also* Public opinion research); of value-emphases, 128

Schmid, Calvin, 246

Schneiderman, William, 461

Schnore, Leo, 238

Scholar, as critic of public policy, 346

Scholarly synthesis, need for, 468

School, of foreign service, 399; *see also* Career diplomat

Schultz, Henry, 348

Schultz, Theodore W., 4; "The Role of Government in Promoting Economic Growth," 372–83

Schumpeter, Joseph, 271–72, 275

Science: code of, 17; conditions for vitality of a, 316–17; in contradistinction to humanism, 415; development of a, 305–15; history of a, 305–15; influence of, on democracy, 24; in the study of man, 13–15

"Science, Society, and the Modes of Law," Frank H. Knight, 9–28

Sciences, behavioral; *see* Behavioral sciences

Scientific atmosphere, and social scientists, 470

Scientific disciplines, breadth of, 464

Scientific knowledge, increasing, as detriment to small business, 279–82

Scientific method: on "collusion," 17; critique of, 9

Scientism, menace of, 28

Scripps Foundation for Research in Population Problems, 252 n.

Sears, Richard, 274

Sears, Robert R., 169 n.

Secrecy, of political negotiation, 405; *see also* Diplomacy

Security, national, 461

"Security risks," 451

Self-disclosure, by analyst, 101

Self/Other; *see* Value-emphases

Selye, H., 58–59

Senate Judiciary Committee, 460

Seulowitz, Warren, 131–32

Seventeenth century, science and humanism in, 415

Shannon, C. E., 70, 80

Sheldon, W. H., 123

Shevsky, Eshref, 237

Shils, Edward, 247

Shiman, Ruth, 326

Sidgwick, Henry, 472

Similarities: of functions, 49; perception of, 42

Simon, Herbert A., "Models: Their Uses and Limitations," 66–83

Singer, Milton, 7, 259–61

Slack, and resources, 372–73

Slater, Philip E., 148 n., 151 n.

Small, Albion W., 1–2, 84, 255, 348

Small business, specialized facilities for, 281

Small-group research: growth of, 339; role of, 164, 180–83

Small groups, voting experiments in, 58

Smith, Adam, 269–70, 472

Smith, Joel, 237

Smith-Lasswell-Casey bibliography, 300, 302

Social approaches, limitations of, 201

Social environment: experimental manipulation of, 182; influence exerted by, 178–79

Social moiety, definition of, 135; *see also* Moiety

Social power, as condition for need satisfaction, 167

Social processes, accounting for, difficulty of, 464

Social psychology as "newer" social science, 319

Social reality, abstraction from, 417

Social Relations, Department of (Harvard), 332

Social relations, field of, 319

"Social Science and Humanism," Leo Strauss, 415–25

Social Science Research Council, Committee on Political Behavior, 314

Social sciences: boundaries of, 322; at Chicago, 332; contributions of historians to, 441; definitions of, 319; eminence of, 340; and ethics, 418, 472; versus human studies, 420, 470; interdisciplinary courses in, 319; limitations of, 416; lingua franca of, 339; and physical science, differences between, 462–64; problems of information transfer in, 36; and public administration, 390–92; relationship of, to democracy, 418; relationship of, to management, 394; relationship between "older" and "newer," 325; relevances of, 418; as static, 339; in the twenties, 87; uses of, by psychoanalysts, 103; worldly success of, 337

"Social Sciences Today, The," Lawrence A. Kimpton, 348–52

"Social Scientist and the Administrative Art, The," Gordon R. Clapp, 393–97

Social scientists: approach of, to the humanities, 470–71; contribution of, to public administration, 385–92 *passim;* historian's image of, 325; models for, 322; relationship of, to norms of disease, 106; separation of fact and value by, 417; as students of cities, 268

"Social specialist," type of, 156

Social structure: described by models, 48; objectives of study of, 133

Social system, the group as, 185 n.; *see also* Models; Systems

Socialism versus capitalism, 269

Socialization, in the United States, 227

Socializing, as experience of child, 92

Society: Collected Papers of Robert E. Park, 255

Society: and community, 256–57; development of, as analogies, 47; as "discontinuous," 227; ecological aspect of, 255; institutional practices of, 108; moral aspect of, 255; need for knowledge of, 11; problem of free, 11; as system, 54; theory of, 77; Western democratic, 344

Sociologists, and cities, 258

Sociology: distribution curves in, 79; as "newer" social science, 319

Sociometric choice, rejection of, 199

"Sociopsychoanalysis," early stages of, 111; *see also* Lasswell, Harold D.

"Sociopsychosomatic," the prefix as relevant context, 95; *see also* Lasswell, Harold D.

"Softness," toward Communists, 460

Soma, interaction with symbols, 93

"Some International Aspects of Economic Stabilization," Jacob Viner, 283–99

"Some Observations on the 'Older' and the 'Newer' Social Sciences," David Riesman, 319–39

Somervell, Brehon, 387

Soviets, government of the, 342

Spanish-Americans, culture of, 126–28 *passim*

Spatial distribution, studies of, 232

Specialization: attitudes toward, 349; need for, 463; sovereign rule of, 416; tendency toward, 462

Speculation in foreign currency, 290

Spencer, Herbert, 74, 76

Spengler, Oswald, 438

Spoehr, Alexander, 140

Sportsmanship, in free society, 27

Spykman, Nicholas, 266

Stability, and environment, 163

Stabilization: of national aggregates, 355–56; programs of, national, 283–99; regional, 356–57

Stabilizers, automatic, 371

Stable prices, maintenance of, 367

Stalemate, of military, 341–42

Standards, firmly established, need for, in studying, 465

Starkey, Marian, 459

State, in system, spatial spread of, 41

State Department, United States, 330, 398–99, 403

Status: of age (*see* Age-status); and culture, 212; definition of, 212; as group-sanctions, 212; involvement of, with both gains and deprivations, 213

Status-anxiety, 217–25 *passim*

Status-identity, 212–15, 225–26

Status-relationships, 212

Status-subordination, 219–20

Status systems, 227

Step functions, in communication transmission, 41

Stephan, Frederick F., 244 n., 309

Steward, J. H., 134

Stewart, John Q., 236–45

Stigler, George J., "Industrial Organization and Economic Progress," 269–82

Stimulus-response, as input-output, 33, 57

Stock, Dorothy, 184–200 *passim*

Stone, Gregory P., 237

Storage, of data, 62

Stouffer, Samuel: *Communism, Conformity, and Civil Liberties,* 263; "departure" of, from public opinion study, 312; origins of public opinion study of, 314; sample design of, 309

Strain reduction, 56–57; as drive satisfaction, 33; rate of, 62

Strains: internal, and goals, 41; on officials, types of, 365

Strauss, Leo, 4; "Social Science and Humanism," 415–25

Straw polls, 301

Stress: capability, for meeting, 185–189; in groups, 190; in systems, 59–60

Stress reaction: consequences of, 186; life as, 184–85

Stress situations, mobilization of energy in, 185

Strotz, Robert, 71

Structure, of United States, unadapted to economic stability, 370

Structures: "primary group," 148; versus process, in ecological research, 236

Study of History, The, Arnold Toynbee, 439

"Study of Public Opinion, The," Bernard Berelson, 299–318

Subgroups, breakdown of, 160

"Subjectivist," as opposed to "behaviorist," 309

Subjectivity, in social science, 64–65

Subordination, in status; *see* Status-subordination

Substance, defined by technique, 309

Subversion, threat of, 451

Sullenger, T. Earl, 238

Sullivan, Harry Stack, 87

Sumner, William, *Folkways,* 429

Sundkler, Bengt, 265

Superego, as noun, 74
Supply and demand, predictions of, 273
Suppression, as inhibiting action and communication, 171
Supreme Court, 451–53 *passim*
Survey, sample; *see* Sample survey
Survey analysis, method of, in public opinion study, 309
Survival: of species, 63; in terms of system equilibrium, 61
Swanton, J. R., 140
Symbol: as event of reference, 97; interaction with soma, 93
Symbolism, Committee on, 427
Systems: boundaries of, 34 ff.; chemical, 40; constituents of, 41; cost of defenses in, 59–60; of cultural values, 116, definition of, 33, 43; distortion of energy in, 56–57; in ecological research of metropolitan areas, 251; energy in movements within, 55; growth rate of, 53–54; inhibitory energy in, 171–73; input and output of, 62; levels of, 45, 54; limits of, 54; living things as, 32; and man's information-processing, 83; men as, 69; open, 40; organization of, 64; of phonemes, 119 (*see also* Language); political, cross-cultural approach to, 133; power output of, 60–61; pressures on, 59; psychological need for, 170–73; in psychology, 33; range of, 62; relationships in, 45; of social ranking, 216; spread of energy in, 55–56; stability range of, 32; of status (*see* Status-systems); and stress, 58–59; termination of, 61–62; two-party (*see* Two-party system); variables in, 57–58
Systems theory: general, 76–79; proponents of, 76

Talamanca, D. M. F., 240
Task involvement, conditions of, 165
"Task specialist," type of, 155
"Task Status and Likeability as a Function of Talking and Listening in Decision-making Groups," Robert F. Bales, 148–61
Taskability: area of, 154; as factor in Bales's study, 155; as framework for personality traits, 151; relationship of, to liking and activity, 156

Tautology, reasoning as, 69
Tax, Sol, 7
Taxes, administration of, 365
Taylor, W. P., 246
Teacher Education, Center for, 8
"Team," concept of, 394–95
Techniques: of ethnographic structural analysis, 133; importance of, 313; and substance, 309; of technology, 382; *see also* Underdeveloped areas
Technology: influence of, on diplomacy, 410; revolution in, 341; in underdeveloped areas, 375
Teleology, 40–41
Tennessee Valley Authority, 393
Tenney Committee, 455
Tense/Relaxed; *see* Value-emphases
Tension, definition of, 185 n.; mobilization of, 189; sexual, as factor in American response to psychoanalysis, 86
Tension reduction: acting-out as, 189; conditions of, 177
Terms, ready-made, 441
Tests, of personality, 153
Thelen, Herbert A., "Emotionality and Work in Groups," 184–200
Then/Now; *see* Value-emphases
Theoretician, and practitioner, in natural and social sciences, 469
Theories: analogical, 73–83; economic, 75; geometrical, 70–71; inadequacies of, 68; mathematical and verbal, 69–73, 74–83 *passim*
Theory: of cells, 76; confusion of, with thesis, 351; content of, 67–68; of culture's social values, 107; definition of, 75; in ecological research, 246–51; of games, 80; of general systems, 76–79; of groups, 76; logical properties of, 68; meaning of, 75; as model, 66; nature of, 67; of organizations, 77; paucity of, in public opinion study, 315; probability, inapplicability of, 15; relationship of, to experiment, 350; relationship of, to practice, 384; role of, 202–4; of society, 77; of value, 128
Theory construction: general, 73; use of computers for, 71
Therapist, as noncommittal, 99
Therapy: complexities of communica-

tion in, 97; goal values of, 108; group, 99 (*see also* Group therapy)

Thesis, confusion of, with theory, 351

Thibaut, J. W., 152

Thinking, inhibition of, 171–73

Third-generation reaction: among anthropologists, 331; definition of, 331; among students, 332

Thomas, J. Parnell, 458

Thomas, W. I., 267

Thompson, Warren S., 238, 242

Threat, goal-directed activity and, 168

Threshold phenomena, 55

Thrupp, Sylvia L., 4, 261, 267

Thucydides, 429, 438

Thunen, Johann H. von, 230 n.

Thurstone, L. L., 309

Tocqueville, Alexis de, 303, 306, 416

Tolstoi, Leo, 396

Tonnies, Ferdinand, 256–57, 303, 307

Totality, historian's aim of, 434–35

"Toward a Comparison of Value-Emphases in Different Cultures," Clyde Kluckhohn, 116–32

"Toward a General Theory for the Behavioral Sciences," James G. Miller, 29–65

Town versus gown, 433

Toynbee, Arnold, 438

Traditional diplomacy: attack on, 404; effect on, by atomic war, 411; functions of, 408–10; postwar fate of, 413; uses and abuses of, 405; value of, 408

Traditions, in Redfield, 259–60

Traits, of personality, 150

Transfer: of attitudes, 152; of training, 77

Transmission, in systems, 55

Trends: effect of, on scholars, 336; of the past, 444

Truman Loyalty Program, 457

Tucker, John Randolph, 460

Tugwell, Rexford G., 4

Turing machine, 77, 80

Turner, Frederick Jackson, 434

Tustin, Arnold, 71

Two-bloc system, in international relations, 411

Two-party system: function of, 144; stability of, 145

Typologies, uses of, by historians, 440, 446

Un-American Activities, House Committee on, 458

Unconscious, the impact of, 92

Underdeveloped areas, 284, 288; and foreign policy, 400; overcentralization in, 390

Undergraduates, interdisciplinary courses for, 319

Understanding, of value system, 423

Unemployment: chronic, 287; prevention of, 289, 294; *see also* Employment

Unique, the, study of, 436

Unique/General; *see* Value-emphases

United Nations, 407

United States, economic stability in, 353–71 *passim*

Universalism, as against particularity, 125

Universalist, attitude of, toward foreign policy, 406

Universities, Association of American, 349

Urban: in Redfield, 260; research, ecological aspects of, 229–54; versus rural, 255–68 *passim*; sociology, foundations of, 229–40; structure and function, temporal and mobility aspects of, 238–39

Urban Community, The, 231, 247

Urbanism Committee; *see* National Resources Board

Urbanization, interdisciplinary seminar on, 4

Utility, of equilibrium state, 62

Valence: distinguished from value, 170; and need, 162, 168, 173, 176, 183; as overemphasized topic, 162

Valence concepts, motivation related to, 163

Valency, maintenance of group culture's assumptions as, 193

Validity, of values, 422

Value: as genetic and environmental input, 33; of traditional diplomacy, 408; valence and, 170

Value-emphases: Active/Acceptant, 123; Autonomy/Dependence, 122; definition of, 116; Determinant/Indeterminate, 120; Discipline/Fulfilment, 123; Evil/Good, 121; Individual/Group, 122; Mechanism/Voluntarism, 120; Now/Then, 124;

"Physical"/"Mental," 123; Quality/Quantity, 124; Self/Other, 122; Tense/Relaxed, 124; Unique/General, 124; Unitary/Pluralistic, 121

Values: awareness of, 103; for the citizen, 417; determination of, 422; list of: respect, rectitude, wealth, skill, enlightenment, power, 109–10; marginal, of labor, 375; operational definitions of, 112; sharing in acceptance of, 421; Western, 373

Vance, R. B., 236, 252

Variables: as magnitudes and functions, 32; related to economic growth, 380; in research, 102; in system, 57–58

Variant, modality in culture, 120 n.

Verbal theories, compared to mathematical, 71–73, 74–83 *passim*

Veridicality, of responses, 173–75 *passim*

Vico, 442

Vienna, 220; University of, 84

Viner, Jacob, 348; "Some International Aspects of Economic Stabilization," 283–99

Vining, Rutledge, 252

Violation, of principles of law, 454

Vitality, conditions for, in science, 316–17

Voltaire, 438

Volterra, E., 73

Voluntarism, 120; *see also* Value-emphases

Wallis, W. Allen, 4

Walter, W. Grey, 70

Waples, Douglas, 307

War: as alternative of foreign policy, 410 (*see also* Diplomacy; Renunciation); atomic, effect of, on diplomacy, 411; Department of, 311; modern nuclear, 341; technology of, 341

Ward, Aaron Montgomery, 274

Warner, W. Lloyd, 7, 133, 216, 314, 326

Washburn, Sherwood L., 5

Watershed, in development of public opinion, 300; *see also* Berelson, Bernard; Public opinion research

Weber, Adna F., 230 n.

Wells, G. P., 246 n.

Wells, H. G., 246, 438

Wherry, R. J., 150 n.

White, Elijah L., 239 n.

White, Leonard, 2, 255

White, William A., 86

Whitehead, Alfred North, 64

Williams, Marilyn, 237

Willkie, Wendell, 461

Winckelmann, Johann, 438

Wirth, Louis, on ecology, 231–49 *passim*

Wispé, Lauren G., 149

Wittfogel, Karl, 134

Wohl, R. Richard, 266

Wolff, Philippe, 267

Wolff, Pietor de, 240

Words: generalizing (*see* Generalizing words); history of, 13; *see also* Language

Work: concepts of, 187; integration of emotion and, 197

World War II, 398

Young, P. T., 173

Youth, of social sciences, 349

Yule, G. Udney, 78

Zeigarnik effect, 176, 179

Zero-feature, 125

Zipf, George K., 245

Zonal hypothesis, ecological, 247

Zorbaugh, Harvey W., 231 n.

Zuni, culture of, 126–28 *passim*

PRINTED IN U.S.A.